Personality
DISORDERS
Toward the DSM-V

*In memory of David Thoreson Lykken (1928–2006),
valued mentor, brilliant thinker, courageous scholar,
and pioneer in the study of personality disorders.*

Personality DISORDERS

Toward the DSM-V

William O'Donohue
University of Nevada, Reno

Katherine A. Fowler
Emory University

Scott O. Lilienfeld
Emory University

SAGE Publications
Los Angeles • London • New Delhi • Singapore

For information:

Sage Publications, Inc.
2455 Teller Road
Thousand Oaks, California 91320
E-mail: order@sagepub.com

Sage Publications India Pvt. Ltd.
B 1/I 1 Mohan Cooperative
    Industrial Area
Mathura Road, New Delhi 110 044
India

Sage Publications Ltd.
1 Oliver's Yard
55 City Road
London, EC1Y 1SP
United Kingdom

Sage Publications Asia-Pacific Pte. Ltd.
33 Pekin Street #02-01
Far East Square
Singapore 048763

Printed in the United States of America

Library of Congress Cataloging-in-Publication Data

Personality disorders: Toward the DSM-V/[edited by] William O'Donohue, Katherine A. Fowler, Scott O. Lilienfeld.
    p. cm.
Includes bibliographical references and index.
ISBN 978-1-4129-0422-3 (pbk. : alk. paper)
    1. Personality disorders. 2. Psychotherapy. I. O'Donohue, William T.
II. Fowler, Katherine A. III. Lilienfeld, Scott O., 1960-
[DNLM: 1. Diagnostic and statistical manual of mental disorders.
2. Personality Disorders. 3. Personality Disorders—classification.
WM 190 P4676 2007]

RC554.P4777 2007
616.85'81—dc22   2007000009

This book is printed on acid-free paper.

                    10   11   10   9   8   7   6   5   4   3   2

Acquisitions Editor:	Kassie Graves
Editorial Assistant:	Veronica Novak
Production Editor:	Libby Larson
Copy Editor:	Rachel Keith
Typesetter:	C&M Digitals (P) Ltd.
Proofreader:	Caryne Brown
Indexer:	Michael Ferreira
Cover Designer:	Janet Foulger
Marketing Manager:	Thomas Mankowski

Contents

Foreword _____

C. Robert Cloninger
Washington University

The study of personality disorders is at a critical point in its development. Human beings are naturally curious about their inner nature and what motivates their feelings, thoughts, and behavior. The study of human personality has an ancient and rich history that has led to many insightful theories and approaches to both well-being and personality disorder. In the mid 20th century, personality theory and research flourished with the genius of many diverse thinkers, such as Freud, Allport, and Eysenck (Hall & Lindzey, 1970). Subsequently, work on personality was mostly stagnant, with little empirical research on personality and a clinical shift to categorical, behavioral, and biological approaches to mental disorders until the publication of the third edition of the *Diagnostic and Statistical Manual of Mental Disorders* (DSM-III; American Psychiatric Association, 1980). DSM-III was both atheoretical and poorly grounded empirically, and most DSM categories had little construct validation. These limitations may have led psychiatry unwittingly toward the field's current state of diagnostic dysfunction (Cloninger, Svrakic, & Przybeck, 2006).

Nevertheless, DSM-III placed personality disorders on a separate axis, which called attention to the importance of diagnosing personality disorders. There was a rapid increase in research and publications about personality and its disorders. Reliable methods for the assessment of personality and its disorders were developed, including both categorical and dimensional approaches (Cloninger, 1999b). Work on the etiology, development, and treatment of personality disorders began with renewed enthusiasm. New organizations for the study of personality disorders and the *Journal of Personality Disorders* were

Author's note: Correspondence concerning this paper should be addressed to C. Robert Cloninger, M.D., Wallace Renard Professor of Psychiatry, Genetics, & Psychology, Washington University, St. Louis, Missouri 63131. E-mail: clon@tci.wustl.edu

founded to bring together clinicians and researchers from psychology, psychiatry, and related areas. However, during the past decade the field has once again become stagnant. Publications and research continue, but the field is not really moving forward.

Progress in understanding personality disorders is currently paralyzed by a pervasive reluctance or resistance to face fundamental questions about human nature. Most work either is atheoretical, such as that based on DSM categories or descriptive personality tests derived by factor analysis, or is designed to confirm preexisting theories, such as behaviorism or psychoanalysis. There is no progressive program of hypothesis testing and refinement to answer the basic questions about human nature that have always inspired passionate interest in personality. Researchers with different assumptions about human nature collect themselves into narrow social networks that are self-affirming but blind or aggressive toward the assumptions and work of others. In compliance with tradition and funding pressures, research is mostly focused on evidence for the validity of discrete categories. The most important work on personality is now being done outside the field of personality disorders, mostly by neuroscientists using functional brain imaging and developmental biologists studying gene-environment interactions (Kaasinen, Aalto, Nagren, & Rinne, 2004; Keltikangas-Jaervinen, Raeikkoenen, Ekelund, & Peltonen, 2004; Pezawas et al., 2005). There is so much conflict about the content of the dimensions of personality among clinicians investigating personality disorder that some clinicians seriously advocate describing personality using checklists of the symptoms of the current committee-defined categories (Skodol et al., 2005) rather than resolving the number and content of personality dimensions scientifically. There is so much overlap among putative categories of personality disorder that the most common diagnosis is personality disorder not otherwise specified (Verheul & Widiger, 2004). Yet little work is done to apply and further evaluate evidence that the presence of any personality disorder can be reliably made by evaluating core features common to all personality disorders, such as self-directedness and cooperativeness (Cloninger, 2000).

Research on dimensional approaches is also not progressing because advocates of particular models are strongly resistant to communication and fundamental change. When alternative three- and five-factor models were found not to explain some aspects of human personality (Zuckerman & Cloninger, 1996), advocates of alternative models continued to debate the advantages of one incomplete model over another incomplete model (Widiger, Simonsen, Sirovatka, & Regier, 2006). For example, models of personality based on lexical traditions in English and other languages initially suggested that there were only five factors of personality. More thorough studies found evidence for seven dimensions of personality, showing that the evidence for only five was based on incomplete lists of descriptors that neglected words for positive and negative valence (Waller, 1999; Waller & Zavala, 1993). Even when their own data show that positive and negative valence adds to the prediction of personality pathology beyond markers of the Big Five, proponents of the Big Five have continued to argue that five factors are comprehensive (Simms, 2007). When five-factor models were unable to explain most of the variance in a specific sixth dimension, such as spirituality or self-transcendence as measured by the Temperament and Character Inventory (Cloninger, 2006a; Zuckerman & Cloninger, 1996), they tried to ignore this by saying that spirituality was not something they wanted to measure, despite its importance for psychopathology and well-being (Cloninger, 2004). Like the absentminded White Queen in *Alice in Wonderland*, something is not real unless you want it to be. But facts do not change just because we want to ignore them.

Psychosocial and neurobiological research has also revealed that human personality is an expression of nonlinear dynamic systems involving many genetic and environmental variables that influence development (Cloninger, Svrakic, & Svrakic, 1997). Yet personality researchers continue to depend on categorical systems or factor-analytic methods that ignore nonlinear dynamics. The result is that descriptions of personality disorders and of personality factors provide a view of differences between people that does not correspond well to the internal dynamics or motivation relevant to personality development or treatment (Cervone, 2004). Social-cognitive psychologists generally ignore the work of personality researchers because DSM and factor-analytic models do not provide a model of the within-person structure of personality. It is possible to model the within-person structure of personality, as I do in my seven-factor psychobiological model, but the result is not what is given by the linearity assumptions made by factor analysis (Cloninger, Svrakic, & Przybeck, 1993). For example, neuroticism is a factor in most factor-analytic models of personality, but a person can be high in neuroticism if he or she has an anxiety disorder without personality disorder or if he or she has a personality disorder without prominent anxiety. In fact, neuroticism is a composite of two traits regulated by different genetic determinants and different brain networks, which I have called harm avoidance and self-directedness (Cloninger, 2006a). Harm avoidance (but not self-directedness) is strongly related to individual differences in anxiety regulation mediated by limbic structures such as the connectivity of the amygdala and the subgenual anterior cingulate cortex (Pezawas et al., 2005). In contrast, self-directedness (but not harm avoidance) is related to individual differences in executive cognitive processes mediated by the prefrontal cortex (Cloninger, 2004). Yet people trained in personality psychology and factor analysis often ignore the extensive and important work being done regarding the psychosocial and neurobiological bases of personality development (Kaasinen et al., 2004; Kaasinen, Maguire, Kurki, Bruck, & Rinne, 2005; Keltikangas et al., 2004), thereby treating each human being as a black box devoid of inner experience and emitting only self-reports or externally observable behaviors. Don't we need to focus on inner experience if the distress and behaviors associated with personality disorders are the expression of maladaptive regulation of inner experiences?

Much current psychotherapy research about personality disorders is consumed by an effort to demonstrate efficacy and effectiveness so that they can be considered evidence-based therapies, like the drugs that meet FDA standards (Westen & Morrison, 2001). Advocates of different forms of treatment, such as dialectical behavior therapy or transference-based psychotherapy, compare one treatment to another but seem reluctant to report that outcomes are largely explained by aspects of treatment common to all effective therapies, such as a helping therapeutic alliance (Gerstley et al., 1989; Lambert, 2004). There is little evidence of the importance of specific procedures for specific diagnoses, and yet the number of different evidence-based psychotherapies is growing like the number of newly patented medicines. Unfortunately, there is no corresponding increase in the average levels of happiness and mental health in the general population as a result of either the new medications or the new psychotherapies (Cloninger, 2004). Where has the field gone wrong?

Can a field of research be described as having a malaise or stagnation akin to a personality disorder? Such a statement would mean that the field is making untested and maladaptive assumptions about inner experience and behavior that are pervasive and inflexible and that impair scientific progress. The field of research on personality disorder seems to be infected with such a malaise, which I hope is curable. Committee-defined criteria and factor-analytically derived tests are no substitute for a coherent and testable theory of personality and its disorders.

In their insightful introduction, Fowler, O'Donohue, and Lilienfeld describe 13 serious problems that plague the field. These are the unanswered fundamental issues that I have suggested are the cause of a serious malaise and stagnation of the field. They include the basic questions about whether personality disorders really exist as categories and about the number and content of the dimensions of personality. Until these questions are answered, it is difficult or impossible to make progress on derivative issues of construct validity, such as the etiology, course, and treatment of personality disorders. How do you describe the causes and course of something that doesn't exist as a taxon or discrete category (Meehl, 1995)? If you could, why would you want to when you could obtain more complete information by characterizing continuous dimensions of clinical variability and their configural interactions? Perhaps unique configurations of traits do have distinct developmental trajectories and require specific treatment procedures (Cloninger & Svrakic, 1997). Even if that is the case, as I think it may be, then we need to know precisely how to specify those configurations in a highly reliable fashion before progress can be made (Kendell, 1982). In my opinion, an integrative approach is also needed that considers the path to well-being (Cloninger, 2006b) and not just particular states of disability (Skodol et al., 2005).

The contributors to this important book have done an excellent job on their assignments to deal with individual putative categories of personality disorder. There is impressive individual and group talent at work in the field of personality disorders. The diversity of their perspectives and recommendations illustrates, nevertheless, the serious problems that beset the field as a whole. The differences in perspective across chapters reveal much about the controversies within the field. Most chapters do focus on one putative category of personality disorder, and the majority of these relate one category of personality disorder on Axis II of DSM to one category of mental disorder on Axis I of DSM. For example, there are several pairs of Axis I–Axis II relationships discussed as parts of a continuous spectrum or frequently comorbid conditions: paranoid personality disorder with delusional disorder, schizotypal personality disorder with schizophrenia, avoidant personality disorder with social anxiety disorder, obsessive-compulsive personality disorder with obsessive-compulsive disorder, and depressive personality disorder with major depressive disorder. Of course, there are serious questions about the categorical nature of both Axis I and Axis II conditions (Kendell, 1982), so such pairings really tell us little about the fundamental question regarding categories and dimensions. The categories of Axis I provide little validity for personality categories because the Axis I conditions also have serious problems with uncertain boundaries, extensive comorbidity, and nonspecific response to treatment. Counterbalancing the chapters emphasizing spectra bridging Axis I and Axis I, Widiger notes the incomplete coverage of personality disorder by existing categories, and Morey and Hopwood emphasize the high prevalence of personality disorder not otherwise specified. But does it make sense to try to correct this problem by fewer dimensions than are known to exist or by putative categories with little construct validity?

The current criteria for most putative categories are criticized, except for obsessive-compulsive personality disorder, which is regarded as part of a spectrum with obsessive-compulsive disorder, body dysmorphic disorder, and pathological gambling. Such spectra are also controversial, however, with body dysmorphic disorder more closely resembling social anxiety disorder and pathological gambling overlapping with impulse control disorders like antisocial personality. So should we make body dysmorphic disorder part of the avoidant–social anxiety spectrum, or avoidant personality disorder part of the obsessive spectrum?

More generally, how do the various spectra overlap? Do they overlap as extensively as the clusters of personality disorders do? Disease spectra and the personality clusters to which they are related can be specified by their deviation on specific temperaments: Cluster A and related Axis I disorders with low reward dependence (i.e., aloof and cold), Cluster B and related Axis I disorders with high novelty seeking (i.e., impulsive and quick-tempered), and Cluster C and related Axis I disorders with high harm avoidance (i.e., anxious and pessimistic; Battaglia, Przybeck, Bellodi, & Cloninger, 1996; Cloninger, 2000; Goldman, Skodol, McGrath, & Oldham, 1994; Mulder & Joyce, 1997). As a result, clusters and the spectra related to them exist in all possible combinations rather than being mutually exclusive. The various clusters and syndromes within clusters show complex patterns of overlap and differentiation that can be better represented as a multidimensional configuration than by a unidimensional spectrum or set of independent spectra (Svrakic, Whitehead, Przybeck, & Cloninger, 1993).

For example, Patrick questions the adequacy of the behavioral criteria for antisocial personality disorder, preferring the concept of psychopathy as described by Cleckley and later Hare. The criteria for antisocial personality disorder are specified as reliably rated behaviors based on the classical work of Lee Robins (1966), so it is comparable to Axis I syndromes such as social anxiety rather than disorders specified in terms of inner experience and motivation, as personality traits are usually defined. When antisocial syndromes are assessed in terms of personality and inner experience, at least two configurations of personality traits are identified: both groups are immature in character traits such as self-directedness and cooperativeness, high in novelty seeking, and low in reward dependence, but primary psychopaths ("antisocial personality disorder") are low in harm avoidance, and secondary psychopaths ("borderline personality disorder") are high in harm avoidance (Cloninger, 2005). Some suggest that primary psychopathy is a taxon with poor response to treatment, but it can also be well described as an extreme configuration of traits normally distributed in the general population (Cloninger, 2005).

Likewise, some evidence for the categorical nature of schizophrenia (Cloninger, Martin, Guze, & Clayton, 1985; Lenzenweger, McLachlan, & Rubin, 2007) and schizotypy (Lenzenweger & Korfine, 1992) has also been presented, but the separation of even these putative categories from neighboring conditions is at best incomplete and weak. Early concepts of etiology that motivated categorical models, such as single genes or single traumatic events, have been found to oversimplify the complex adaptive systems underlying the development of psychopathology. Current research indicates that configurations of multiple sets of genetic and environmental variables influence the development of psychopathology, thereby motivating the search for the best ways to deconstruct the complex determinants of mental disorders in terms of either symptoms or the causes of symptoms (Cloninger, 2004). In fact, all the personality disorders, including schizotypal personality, can be defined as extreme configurations of normal personality traits (Cloninger, 1999a). Categorical thinking is now more of a hindrance to understanding personality disorders and psychopathology than it is a benefit.

None of these controversies would matter much except that people with personality disorders frequently have short and miserable lives, as well as a serious and costly impact on society through their maladaptive behaviors. Therefore, the stagnation of the field in not being able to face and answer the fundamental questions about the nature of personality and its disorders is unsatisfactory and harmful. It is remarkable that so many obviously bright people cannot find a way to communicate with one another in an open-minded way so that they can make progress beyond what was known two decades ago when the same questions were being asked and tentatively answered (Cloninger, 1987; Cloninger et al., 1993; Svrakic et al., 1993). Personality and its disorders are too important to be treated like a private cottage industry in which no one is permitted to question the local authority's basic assumptions.

Personality disorders are too important for us to rely on poorly grounded dimensional representations of unvalidated categories without resolving the number and content of the underlying dimensions, even if they are not currently familiar to clinicians. The field needs to move forward, not wallow in stagnant pools of ignorance and illusion.

At least for the personality disorders, DSM is really only a system of classification for cataloguing and billing purposes and does not even begin to be an adequately validated scientific basis for research and treatment. As long as research classification and case descriptions are based on such an antiquated categorical system, little or no progress in understanding disorders of personality is likely, as evidenced by the current impasses stalemating the field.

Personality Disorders is an important book because it clearly exposes the major controversies facing the field. Each chapter is an erudite contribution that stands on its own quality. In addition, the insightful reader will be able to compare the divergent, and sometimes contradictory, perspectives and conclusions of different chapters. Consideration of the contradictions and unanswered questions throughout the book reveals the harsh consequences of blind reliance on false assumptions about how nature can be carved at its joints, when there are actually no such joints.

References

American Psychiatric Association. (1980). *Diagnostic and statistical manual of mental disorders* (3rd ed.). Washington, DC: Author.

Battaglia, M., Przybeck, T. R., Bellodi, L., & Cloninger, C. R. (1996). Temperament dimensions explain the comorbidity of psychiatric disorders. *Comprehensive Psychiatry, 37,* 292–298.

Cervone, D. (2004). The architecture of personality. *Psychological Review, 111*(1), 183–204.

Cloninger, C. R. (1987). A systematic method for clinical description and classification of personality variants: A proposal. *Archives of General Psychiatry, 44,* 573–587.

Cloninger, C. R. (1999a). Measurement of psychopathology as variants of personality. In C. R. Cloninger (Ed.), *Personality and psychopathology* (pp. 33–66). Washington, DC: American Psychiatric Press.

Cloninger, C. R. (Ed.). (1999b). *Personality and psychopathology*. Washington, DC: American Psychiatric Press.

Cloninger, C. R. (2000). A practical way to diagnose personality disorder: A proposal. *Journal of Personality Disorders, 14*(2), 99–108.

Cloninger, C. R. (2004). *Feeling good: The science of well-being*. New York: Oxford University Press.

Cloninger, C. R. (2005). Antisocial personality disorder: A Review. In World Psychiatric Association (Series Ed.) & M. Maj (Vol. Ed.), *Evidence and experience in psychiatry: Vol. 8. Personality disorders* (pp. 125–129). London: Wiley.

Cloninger, C. R. (2006a). Personality as a dynamic psychobiological system. In T. A. Widiger, E. Simonsen, P. Sirovatka, & D. A. Regier (Eds.), *Dimensional models of personality disorders: Refining the research agenda for DSM-V*. Washington, DC: American Psychiatric Association.

Cloninger, C. R. (2006b). The science of well-being: An integrated approach to mental health and its disorders. *World Psychiatry, 5,* 71–76.

Cloninger, C. R., Martin, R. L., Guze, S. B., & Clayton, P. J. (1985). Diagnosis and prognosis in schizophrenia. *Archives of General Psychiatry, 42,* 12–25.

Cloninger, C. R., & Svrakic, D. M. (1997). Integrative psychobiological approach to psychiatric assessment and treatment. *Psychiatry, 60,* 120–141.

Cloninger, C. R., Svrakic, D. M., & Przybeck, T. R. (1993). A psychobiological model of temperament and character. *Archives of General Psychiatry, 50,* 975–990.

Cloninger, C. R., Svrakic, D. M., & Przybeck, T. R. (2006). Can personality assessment predict future depression? A twelve-month follow-up of 631 subjects. *Journal of Affective Disorders, 92*(1), 35–44.

Cloninger, C. R., Svrakic, N. M., & Svrakic, D. M. (1997). Role of personality self-organization in development of mental order and disorder. *Development and Psychopathology, 9,* 881–906.

Gerstley, L., McLellan, A. T., Alterman, A. I., Woody, G. E., Luborsky, L., & Prout, M. (1989). Ability to form an alliance with the therapist: A possible marker of prognosis for patients with antisocial personality. *American Journal of Psychiatry, 146*(4), 508–512.

Goldman, R. G., Skodol, A. E., McGrath, P. J., & Oldham, J. M. (1994). Relationship between the Tridimensional Personality Questionnaire and DSM-III-R personality traits. *American Journal of Psychiatry, 151,* 274–276.

Hall, C. S., & Lindzey, G. (1970). *Theories of personality*. New York: Wiley.

Kaasinen, V., Aalto, S., Nagren, K., & Rinne, J. O. (2004). Insular dopamine D2 receptors and novelty seeking personality in Parkinson's disease. *Movement Disorders, 19*(11), 1348–1351.

Kaasinen, V., Maguire, E. A., Kurki, T., Bruck, A., & Rinne, J. O. (2005). Mapping brain structure and personality in late adulthood. *NeuroImage, 24,* 315–322.

Keltikangas-Jaervinen, L., Raeikkoenen, K., Ekelund, J., & Peltonen, L. (2004). Nature and nurture in novelty seeking. *Molecular Psychiatry, 9*(3), 308–311.

Kendell, R. E. (1982). The choice of diagnostic criteria for biological research. *Archives of General Psychiatry, 39,* 1334–1339.

Lambert, M. J. (Ed.). (2004). *Bergin and Garfield's handbook of psychotherapy*. New York: Wiley.

Lenzenweger, M. F., & Korfine, L. (1992). Confirming the latent structure and base rate of schizotypy: A taxometric analysis. *Journal of Abnormal Psychology, 101*(3), 567–571.

Lenzenweger, M. F., McLachlan, G., & Rubin, D. B. (2007). Resolving the latent structure of schizophrenia endophenotypes using expectation-maximization–based finite mixture modeling. *Journal of Abnormal Psychology, 116*(1), 16–29.

Meehl, P. E. (1995). Bootstraps taxometrics: Solving the classification problem in psychopathology. *American Psychologist, 50*(4), 266–275.

Mulder, R. T., & Joyce, P. R. (1997). Temperament and the structure of personality disorder symptoms. *Psychological Medicine, 27*, 99–106.

Pezawas, L., Meyer-Lindenberg, A., Drabant, E. M., Verchinski, B. A., Munoz, K. E., Kolachana, B. S., et al. (2005). 5-HTTLPR polymorphism impacts human cingulate-amygdala interactions: A genetic susceptibility mechanism for depression. *Nature Neuroscience, 8*(6), 838–834.

Robins, L. N. (1966). *Deviant children grown up: A sociological and psychiatric study of sociopathic personality.* Baltimore: Williams & Wilkins.

Simms, L. J. (2007). The Big Seven model of personality and its relevance to personality pathology. *Journal of Personality, 75*(1), 65–94.

Skodol, A. E., Oldham, J. M., Bender, D. S., Dyck, I. R., Stout, R. L., Morey, L. C., et al. (2005). Dimensional representations of DSM-IV personality disorders: Relationships to functional impairment. *American Journal of Psychiatry, 162*(10), 1919–1925.

Svrakic, D. M., Whitehead, C., Przybeck, T. R., & Cloninger, C. R. (1993). Differential diagnosis of personality disorders by the seven-factor model of temperament and character. *Archives of General Psychiatry, 50*, 991–999.

Verheul, R., & Widiger, T. A. (2004). A meta-analysis of the prevalence and usage of the personality disorder not otherwise specified (PDNOS) diagnosis. *Journal of Personality Disorders, 18*, 309–319.

Waller, N. G. (1999). Evaluating the structure of personality. In C. R. Cloninger (Ed.), *Personality and psychopathology* (pp. 155–197). Washington, DC: American Psychiatric Press.

Waller, N. G., & Zavala, J. (1993). Evaluating the Big Five. *Psychological Inquiry, 4*, 131–134.

Westen, D., & Morrison, K. (2001). A multidimensional meta-analysis of treatments for depression, panic, and generalized anxiety disorder: An empirical examination of the status of empirically supported therapies. *Journal of Consulting and Clinical Psychology, 69*(6), 875–899.

Widiger, T. A., Simonsen, E., Sirovatka, P. J., & Regier, D. A. (Eds.). (2006). *Dimensional models of personality disorders: Refining the research agenda for DSM-V.* Washington, DC: American Psychiatric Association.

Zuckerman, M., & Cloninger, C. R. (1996). Relationships between Cloninger's, Zuckerman's, and Eysenck's dimensions of personality. *Personality and Individual Differences, 21*, 283–285.

Acknowledgments_____

First of all, we would like to acknowledge our chapter contributors. We know that it can be a challenge for busy and productive individuals to take time out of their professional and personal lives to write a book chapter. We very much appreciate their time, dedication, and excellent work. Second, we'd like to thank our editor at Sage, Veronica Novak, whose patience, support, and astute judgment were invaluable in completing this project. We extend our thanks to Kassie Graves and the art department personnel at Sage, who were also very helpful. Without their support and professionalism this book would not have been possible. Third, we'd like to thank Rachel Keith for her perspicacious and astute editing and proofing. She made this often arduous process a pleasure. Fourth, we'd like to thank the wonderful individuals who helped us finish this book, especially Crissa Draper, Amy Harper, and Lauren Tolle. Finally, we'd like to thank our families, Jane, Katie, Anna, and Sahil, for being there.

1

Introduction

Personality Disorders in Perspective

Katherine A. Fowler
Emory University

William O'Donohue
University of Nevada, Reno

Scott O. Lilienfeld
Emory University

The personality disorders are a complex, controversial, and fascinating class of diagnoses. Decades of clinical observations of developmentally fixated "character types" (Freud, 1916/1991), "neurotic styles" (Shapiro, 1965), and "character disorders" (e.g., Horney, 1939) preceded the formal classification "personality disorders," which first emerged in 1980 in the third edition of the *Diagnostic and Statistical Manual of Mental Disorders* (DSM-III; American Psychiatric Association [APA], 1980). Most of the newly termed personality disorders were not new; indeed, some (e.g., schizoid personality, paranoid personality) had been included in prior editions of the DSM. In preparing the third edition, however, the DSM committee arrived at the consensus that personality disorders are a different "kind" of diagnostic category from the vast majority of disorders listed in the DSM. Thus, DSM-III was the first edition to adopt a multiaxial approach, assigning personality disorders to a separate axis (Axis II) from "clinical conditions" (Axis I). The most recent edition, DSM-IV-TR (APA, 2000), briefly states the rationale for this decision:

The listing of Personality Disorders and Mental Retardation on a separate axis ensures that consideration will be given to the possible presence of Personality Disorders and Mental Retardation that might otherwise be overlooked when attention is directed to the usually more florid Axis I disorders. (p. 28)

The above seems to imply that a diagnosis of personality disorder may provide the context for, or be overshadowed by, more "florid" Axis I diagnoses (such as depression or schizophrenia). It is interesting to speculate why personality disorders share this axis with mental retardation. Both are fairly pervasive across many situations, and both certainly bear implications for the diagnosis and treatment of Axis I disorders (e.g., cognitive therapy for depression might be contraindicated or implemented quite differently in either context); perhaps these similarities justify their placement on Axis II and explain in part why DSM-IV relegates personality disorders to a different diagnostic class from the other mental disorders. Moreover, it has been suggested that most personality disorders tend to be ego-syntonic (i.e., consistent with self-concept), whereas most Axis I disorders are ego-dystonic (i.e., inconsistent with self-concept; Grove & Tellegen, 1991).

DSM-IV-TR (APA, 2000) provides a broad definition of personality disorder:

A Personality Disorder is an enduring pattern of inner experience and behavior that deviates markedly from the expectations of the individual's culture, is pervasive and inflexible, has an onset in adolescence or early adulthood, is stable over time, and leads to distress or impairment. (p. 629)

This seemingly simple summary actually alludes to a complex set of properties, requiring exegesis of its key phrases. Without some clarification, we cannot make reliable and valid diagnoses and come to a shared understanding of personality disorders. For example, the following terms and phrases raise important questions:

1. *Enduring:* How long must an individual exhibit features of a personality disorder before a diagnosis is applicable?

2. *Pattern:* How consistently over time must an individual exhibit the characteristics in question? If there are periods of time when the individual does not exhibit these characteristics, how long can these time periods be?

3. *Inner experience:* Clearly, this term potentially comprises an extremely broad range of mental processes, including emotions, thoughts, impulses, fantasies, schemas, and memories. Which of these are considered most central to the conceptualization of personality disorders?

4. *Deviates markedly:* Whether a deviation is "marked" is clearly subjective. DSM-IV-TR encourages one to consider the individual's context (e.g., family, culture) in making this determination. This is a step in the right direction, as it emphasizes that norms are not universal. However, it leads to the next point of inquiry:

5. *Individual's culture:* Culture has many facets, including ethnicity, sexual orientation, socioeconomic status, geographic region, and gender. To which of these do we look to determine cultural norms, and what are the limits? How do we avoid confounding "cultural norms" with stereotypical perceptions?

6. *Pervasive:* How cross-situationally consistent must personality disorder features be for an individual to meet criteria? For example, can a person meet criteria for a personality disorder if he or she exhibits marked features in personal life but less marked features at work?

7. *Inflexible:* How much flexibility is allowed, and in which domains (e.g., work, school, relationships), and how pervasive must this inflexibility be?

8. *Onset in adolescence or early adulthood:* How does one discern "onset"? Must the person fully meet criteria by a certain age, or do some prodromal symptoms count? Particularly in the case of late adolescence and early adulthood, determining developmental norms is a difficult task. How do we find a balance between overpathologizing normal-range teenage behavior and overlooking true pathology? Furthermore, the age limits constituting adolescence and early adulthood are not specified.

9. *Leads to distress and impairment:* How does one establish the causal link between the symptoms and distress/impairment? What kinds of and how much distress/impairment are required?

Three levels of general questions surround personality disorders. First, there are *semantic questions*, such as those raised above. Second, there are *operational questions*: Once the semantics are clarified, what is the best way to gather the information we need? For example, say "enduring" is taken to mean "for at least 3 years." Should we ask the client to self-report start dates and end dates of symptoms? Should we review records that cover this period, if available, to see if there are any corroborating or contradictory indicators? Should we use information provided by other informants who know the client well? The third problem is the *measurement question*: How does one begin to construct measures with adequate content- and criterion-related validity? This is no easy task, especially as many of these measures aim to assess complex constructs such as "impairment," which requires historical or normative information often accessible only to the affected individual ("inner experience"). Part of the controversy regarding personality disorders can be tied to this complexity and to what some understandably perceive to be a lack of progress on these questions.

The DSM-IV Personality Disorders

DSM-IV-TR officially recognizes 10 personality disorders (PDs) and includes three others for further study (depressive personality disorder, passive-aggressive personality disorder, and sadistic personality disorder). A brief description of each of the 10 recognized PDs follows:

> *Paranoid Personality Disorder* is a pattern of distrust and suspiciousness such that others' motives are interpreted as malevolent;
>
> *Schizoid Personality Disorder* is a pattern of detachment from social relationships and a restricted range of emotional expression;
>
> *Schizotypal Personality Disorder* is a pattern of acute discomfort in close relationships, cognitive or perceptual distortions, and eccentricities of behavior;
>
> *Antisocial Personality Disorder* is a pattern of disregard for, and violation of, the rights of others;
>
> *Borderline Personality Disorder* is a pattern of instability in interpersonal relationships, self-image, and affects, and marked impulsivity;
>
> *Histrionic Personality Disorder* is a pattern of excessive emotionality and attention seeking;
>
> *Narcissistic Personality Disorder* is a pattern of grandiosity, need for admiration, and lack of empathy;
>
> *Avoidant Personality Disorder* is a pattern of social inhibition, feelings of inadequacy, and hypersensitivity to negative evaluation;
>
> *Dependent Personality Disorder* is a pattern of submissive and clinging behavior related to an excessive need to be taken care of;
>
> *Obsessive-Compulsive Personality Disorder* is a pattern of preoccupation with orderliness, perfectionism, and control. (APA, 2000, p. 685)

The same three levels of questions noted in our discussion of PD conceptualization in general can be asked regarding individual diagnoses. Take paranoid PD, for example: there are semantic questions (e.g., what is meant by "suspiciousness"?), operational questions (how do we go about capturing this meaning?), and measurement questions (how do we develop a test that provides a valid measure of "suspiciousness"?). When these questions are multiplied across all the criteria for all of the diagnoses, we can again see both the potential for controversy and the large amount of work that lies ahead.

The individual diagnoses are organized into three broad clusters representing presumed superordinate features that characterize each group:

Cluster A (odd/eccentric disorders):

Paranoid personality disorder

Schizoid personality disorder

Schizotypal personality disorder

Cluster B (dramatic, emotional, or erratic disorders):

Antisocial personality disorder

Borderline personality disorder

Histrionic personality disorder

Narcissistic personality disorder

Cluster C (anxious/fearful disorders):

Avoidant personality disorder

Dependent personality disorder

Obsessive-compulsive personality disorder

These clusters presumably "carve nature at its joints" better than the individual diagnoses. There are consistent findings of high co-occurrence of diagnoses within each cluster but less co-occurrence of diagnoses in different clusters (Morey, 1988; see below).

Major Questions and Controversies in Personality Disorder Research

One consistent finding is that the prevalence of personality disorders in the general population is fairly high. For example, Mattia and Zimmerman (2001) averaged data across a number of epidemiological studies and found that in community samples, 13% of individuals had at least one personality disorder.

Moreover, the prevalence of many of the individual diagnoses was relatively high; for example, obsessive-compulsive personality disorder was present in 4% of the population, while histrionic, schizotypal, and dependent personality disorders were each present in 2% of the population. This high prevalence is one reason that personality disorders remain an area of lively debate.

It is beyond the scope of this chapter to settle these contentions, as many of the issues remain unresolved in the literature. Furthermore, we do not mean to imply that these controversies are unique to personality disorders. Nevertheless, to provide a context for the remaining chapters, we give you their general flavor:

1. **The predictive utility and perhaps even the existence of personality itself have been called into question.** For several decades, psychologists actively debated whether personality is a valid construct rather than merely a convenient summary label that we invoke to describe behaviors that happen to covary (Mischel, 1968). Personality, particularly for radical behaviorists, was a controversial construct. Skinner (1957) argued that "personality is nothing but the locus of behavior" (p. 182). He thought of personality as an "explanatory fiction" (p. 182) that often seems to involve circular reasoning. For example, imagine that someone observes Jane acting in a consistently outgoing and friendly fashion and asks, "Why does Jane behave this way?" If the answer is that she has an "extraverted personality" and if one concludes that she has an extraverted personality by observing that she is generally outgoing and friendly, this is a tautological, pseudo-explanation. Radical behaviorists would be more comfortable using personality traits as descriptive rather than explanatory concepts.

   Personality researchers responded to these criticisms. In particular, they demonstrated that many personality trait measures predict laboratory and biological indices that cannot merely be derived from the behaviors subsumed by the trait labels themselves (Kenrick & Funder, 1988). Nevertheless, some critics justifiably continue to argue that some personality disorders (e.g., dependent personality disorder) are little more than summary labels for behaviors that merit clinical attention.

   Mischel re-ignited this controversy in the late 1960s in his book *Personality and Assessment* (1968), in which he pointed to the cross-situational inconsistency of personality traits and thereby called into question the traditional assumption of traits as pervasive behavioral dispositions. Once again, researchers responded to this criticism in a variety of ways. Some suggested that the sample of studies Mischel used to bolster his claim was unrepresentative and demonstrated how a review of different studies did not support his claim (e.g., Block, 1977), while others suggested that examination of moderator variables, such as tendency to "self-monitor" (Snyder, 1974) and prediction of aggregated behaviors (i.e., trends) rather than single behaviors, yield considerably higher estimates of cross-situational consistency (Bem & Allen, 1974; Epstein, 1979).

Although many consider these controversies resolved when it comes to personality in general, they bear repeating with respect to personality disorders. Personality disorder researchers should meet these challenges as personality researchers did by demonstrating that these conditions predict important external criteria (e.g., natural history, laboratory findings).

2. **It is not clear whether personality disorders are underpinned by categories or by dimensions.** The DSM-IV-TR adopts a categorical system for the diagnosis of personality disorders, as it does with all other disorders. Some have argued (e.g., Trull, 2005) that a dimensional system is better suited to the diagnosis of personality disorders. Categorical discriminations are made when constructs have or are thought to have clear boundaries in nature (tall or short, for example). Dimensional ratings, in contrast, simply provide a value on a continuum (such as 5' 10"). In general, categorical approaches presume that natural discontinuities exist, whereas dimensional approaches presume the existence of natural continua. Although dimensional systems seem to have the advantage of precision, they raise questions about which dimensions of personality and/or psychopathology ought to be used in conceptualizing personality disorders. Is the use of cutoffs on dimensions for a particular disorder ever justified for pragmatic or social purposes? And, finally, can we measure a dimension accurately? For example, we can measure height, but can we measure extraversion with the same reliability and validity?

3. **If personality disorders are better conceptualized dimensionally, it is not clear which system (e.g., Big Five, Big Three) is the most useful for doing so.** Several dimensional models have been investigated as alternatives to the current DSM categorical conceptualization of personality disorders. Of these, the model necessitating the least departure from the current system adopts the approach of rating match to a prototypical description of each disorder. Although some have found that this approach may increase reliability (e.g., Heumann & Morey, 1990), others have noted that it does not necessarily increase validity for two reasons: (1) the validity of the prototypes is still dependent on the validity of the conceptualizations found in the DSM, and (2) this approach does not address the problem of symptom heterogeneity found within most personality disorders (Clark, 1999).

A different dimensional approach examines the possibility that personality disorders are best expressed as constellations of normal-range personality traits. Of these alternative conceptualizations, the five-factor model of personality (FFM) has received the most research attention. The FFM was derived from lexical studies of the English language, in which an overinclusive list of colloquial trait adjectives was factor-analyzed, yielding five separable dimensions: (1) extraversion (social potency, positive affectivity); (2) agreeableness (desire to get along with others); (3) conscientiousness (constraint, self-discipline); (4) neuroticism (anxiety, irritability); and (5) openness (intellect, unconventionality). Widiger, Trull, Clarkin, Sanderson, and Costa (1994) give an example of the characterization of a personality disorder within this framework:

> From the perspective of the FFM avoidant personality disorder involves: a) introversion, particularly the facets of low gregariousness (no close friends, avoids significant interpersonal contact, and unwilling to get involved with others; APA, 1987); low excitement-seeking (exaggerates potential dangers, difficulties, or risks in doing anything outside of normal routine); and low activity (avoidance of social and occupational activities, and canceling of social plans) . . . and b) neuroticism, particularly the facets of vulnerability, self-consciousness, and anxiety (e.g., easily hurt by criticism and disapproval, reticent in social situations because of fear of saying something foolish, fears being embarrassed, and afraid of being disliked). (p. 49)

They further raise the still unresolved question of whether using this model to describe personality disorders is superior to the current DSM system. Part of the argument for doing so is that the FFM may provide an overarching and parsimonious model that accommodates all of the personality disorders on Axis II. Moreover, such a model could underscore trait commonalities that both underlie these disorders and account for their extensive covariation (see #4 below). Currently, several research groups are examining these questions (e.g., Bagby, Costa, Widiger, Ryder, & Marshall, 2005; Miller, Bagby, Pilkonis, Reynolds, & Lynam, 2005). Alternative dimensional models to the FFM, such as three-factor models (e.g., Clark, 1999; Cloninger, 1987), have been proposed and continue to be an active source of investigation.

4. **The rampant comorbidity among many personality disorders calls into question their validity and/or existence as independent syndromes.** Fiester, Ellison, Docherty, and Shea (1990) reported two kinds of comorbidity among PDs. First, they found that individuals diagnosed with one personality disorder are likely to be diagnosed with at least one other. In four samples of individuals diagnosed with a personality disorder, Widiger and Rogers (1989) found that the average proportion of patients who met criteria for at least one additional personality disorder was 85%, with a range of 76% for dependent personality disorder to 100% for paranoid personality disorder. Second, they found that many persons diagnosed with a personality disorder are also diagnosed with a mood disorder, anxiety disorder, or schizophrenia.

They concluded that "the fundamental relationships of these disorders to one another remains a puzzle" (p. 111). Moreover, they proposed some potential explanations for this second type of comorbidity, such as: (1) one personality disorder causes another disorder; (2) the other disorder causes the personality disorder; (3) the personality disorder and the other disorder influence and affect each other; and (4) the personality disorder and the other disorder are etiologically separable and unrelated coeffects of some other disturbance. More research is needed to investigate these possibilities.

5. **There are serious problems with the reliability of personality disorders.** The DSM personality disorders suffer from problems of internal consistency, test-retest reliability, and interrater reliability. Morey (1988) found that the internal consistency among diagnostic features for the DSM-III personality disorders as revealed by the median correlation among the criteria within each disorder ranged from $r = .10$ to $r = .34$. Loranger et al. (1988) studied the test-retest reliability of personality disorder diagnoses over a 1-week to 6-month interval. The median kappa for the presence or absence of the disorder on both occasions ranged between .52 and .57, except in the case of compulsive personality disorder (now called obsessive-compulsive personality disorder), in which it was only .26. Overall, there was a trend toward fewer observed diagnoses and traits over time. With regard to interrater reliability, in the DSM-III field trials the kappa coefficient for the presence or absence of any personality disorder was .61 based on a joint-interview design. The interrater reliability evidence for later versions of the DSM is scarcely more promising (see Zimmerman, 1994, for a review).

6. **There is a paucity of evidence for the construct validity of most personality disorders, including their natural history and laboratory correlates.** The chapters that follow will reveal that much information about the course, family history, and laboratory and physiological correlates of personality disorders is lacking. Of course, this criticism must be tempered by the fact that many other groups of disorders in the DSM-IV also lack this sort of information (e.g., sexual dysfunctions and paraphilias). This paucity of evidence leaves the DSM vulnerable to the radical behaviorists' criticism that these disorders are little more than tautological summary labels for covarying thoughts, emotions, and behaviors.

7. **The best means of assessing personality disorders is unclear.** Currently, there are a number of omnibus instruments for the assessment of personality disorders, such as the Personality Disorders Examination (Loranger, 1988), the Structured Clinical Interview for DSM-III-R Personality Disorders (SCID-II; Spitzer, Williams, & Gibbon, 1987), and the Personality Disorders Questionnaire–4+ (PDQ-4+; Hyler & Rieder,

1994). In a thorough review of the extant measures, Perry (1992) found that although several instruments showed moderate to high levels of interrater and test-retest reliability for some diagnoses, many showed poor levels. Perry also found little agreement among the measures (median kappa = .25), calling into question the convergent validity of commonly used personality disorder measures.

Moreover, Zimmerman (1994) has suggested that most of the following fundamental questions regarding personality disorder assessment remain unresolved: (1) Who should provide information (e.g., client, relatives, both)? (2) What instruments should be used? and (3) When should the assessment be conducted (e.g., when the patient is free of Axis I symptoms, or when he or she is experiencing them)?

8. **The distinction between Axis I and Axis II psychopathology is frequently unclear and seemingly arbitrary.** The rationale for these two axes has never been entirely clear or grounded in solid evidence (Harkness & Lilienfeld, 1997). For example, some Axis I problems, such as schizophrenia and cyclothymic disorder, can last at least as long as Axis II disorders, particularly if they are left untreated. In addition, the DSM's placement of Axis II disorders has often been inconsistent. For example, cyclothymic disorder appears to be a subsyndromal form of bipolar disorder and is located on Axis I, whereas schizotypal personality disorder appears to be a subsyndromal form of schizophrenia and is located on Axis II. Additionally, as mentioned previously, the way in which Axis I and Axis II pathology interact remains unclear. Thus one can raise potentially interesting questions, such as, does dysphoria set the stage for the perhaps more florid histrionic personality disorder, or is it the other way around? That is, although the DSM seems to view personality disorders as a distinct class of disorders, it has not clearly elucidated the distinctive properties of this class.

9. **The diagnosis of certain personality disorders may be compromised by gender bias.** According to DSM-IV-TR (APA, 2000), some personality disorders are diagnosed more frequently in men (e.g., antisocial personality disorder, narcissistic personality disorder, obsessive-compulsive personality disorder, and the Cluster A disorders), whereas others are diagnosed more frequently in women (e.g., borderline personality disorder, histrionic personality disorder, and dependent personality disorder). However, there have been inconsistent findings: for example, Golomb, Fava, Abraham, and Rosenbaum (1995) found no significant gender differences for borderline, histrionic, and dependent personality disorders.

Some have argued that the DSM unfairly pathologizes individuals who are extreme examples of stereotypical sex roles (both male and female), and that the conformity of many healthy individuals to these roles accounts for the observed pattern of sex differences in personality disorder diagnosis (e.g., Caplan, 1987; Landrine, 1989). Moreover, a widely cited study by Warner (1978) reported that clinicians tended to diagnose males with antisocial personality disorder and females with histrionic personality disorder when they were given identical patient profiles that were supposed to describe a patient with histrionic personality disorder. Taken together, these points raise questions of sex bias in both the diagnostic decision-making process and in the criteria themselves.

In a 1991 review, Widiger and Spitzer examined several potential sources of sex bias in PD diagnosis: (1) social-cultural sex bias (in which differences result from differences in child rearing, social opportunities, etc.), (2) sampling sex bias (in which sex differences are caused by data collection at sites where one sex with a disorder happens to be more represented than the other), and (3) diagnostic sex bias (in which either the assessment instruments or the diagnostic criteria cause false positives or false negatives that misrepresent true prevalence for one sex). They concluded that for questions of gender bias to be properly examined, the DSM must first clarify the threshold at which behaviors become maladaptive (to protect against false positives). They further emphasized that differential prevalence rates do not necessarily indicate bias and may instead reflect appropriate attention to the base rates of disorders in the real world.

10. **There is a marked paucity of well-conducted research examining effective treatments for most personality disorders.** As the chapters that follow will underscore, beyond a few treatments for borderline personality disorder that have promising empirical support, there are few documented effective interventions for personality disorders. Furthermore, clinical lore regarding the intractability of some personality disorders (e.g., antisocial personality disorder; see Fowler & Lilienfeld, 2006) has led to marked pessimism surrounding therapeutic intervention, possibly further contributing to this inertia. These observations highlight the importance of further well-conducted treatment outcome studies for personality disorders.

11. **There is disagreement regarding specific diagnostic criteria for most personality disorders.** As will be discussed in greater detail within several chapters, there have been numerous changes in personality disorder diagnostic criteria across the DSM revisions. These changes reflect a lack of consensus in the field surrounding these criteria. For example, there has been particular controversy surrounding antisocial personality disorder. Some argue that this diagnosis should be modified to include dispositional criteria (e.g., lack of empathy, superficial charm), which were largely eliminated in DSM-III (APA, 1980) in an attempt to increase reliability, but which may have decreased validity (Lykken, 1995).

12. **There is marked symptom heterogeneity within diagnoses.** Since its third edition (DSM-III; APA, 1980), the DSM has employed a largely polythetic classification system—that is, one that lists a number of characteristics, of which the individual is required to possess only a subset to meet the diagnosis. As a result, it is possible for there to be little to no overlap in symptoms among patients with the same diagnosis. This problem is not limited to personality disorders but is a consequence of the DSM's classification method, which some criticize as a "Chinese menu" approach.

13. **Many personality disorders appear to be heterogeneous in etiology.** Recent findings suggest that some personality disorders (e.g., antisocial personality disorder, borderline personality disorder) subsume distinct variants that differ in etiology, course, and treatment response (Bradley, Conklin, & Westen, 2005; Skeem, Poythress, Edens, Lilienfeld, & Cale, 2003). These results raise concerns regarding the construct validity of some current personality disorder conceptualizations, because such diagnoses may comprise multiple syndromes.

Despite myriad surrounding controversies, personality disorder diagnoses are frequently associated with important social and clinical outcomes. For example, individuals with paranoid personality disorder are disproportionately likely to become involved in litigation (see Chapter 3), and individuals with borderline personality disorder have a high rate of suicide attempts (see Chapter 7).

Findings such as these bring us full circle in our delineation of current controversies surrounding personality disorders as we return to questions of predictive validity. Because many personality disorders show associations with important real-world outcomes, the controversies outlined in this chapter are more than discouraging theoretical musings or armchair debates. Instead, they should be considered potentially fruitful and interesting lines of inquiry that may improve our understanding of important clinical phenomena.

Purpose and Outline of This Volume

We intend this handbook to be a widely used resource that will appeal to a broad audience, including researchers, beginning and advanced graduate students, and practitioners in a variety of mental health settings. We asked that our contributors minimize the use of technical terms, supplying a user-friendly summary and integration of major trends, findings, and future directions.

The book is organized by two broad sections: (1) an opening section (including this chapter) that reviews basic theoretical and methodological controversies in personality disorder research and practice and highlights proposed alternatives to DSM-IV Axis II conceptualizations, and (2) a section in which the DSM-IV personality disorders, organized by cluster, as well as the three personality disorders designated for further research, are discussed and critically evaluated. Each of these chapters includes a summary and thoughtful integration of the best available scientific evidence bearing on the etiology, assessment, diagnosis, and (where relevant) treatment of the disorder. Further, chapters include discussion of any relevant psychobiological models and correlates. Wherever possible, case examples are offered as illustrations of each disorder's clinical presentation. Finally, each chapter includes explicit recommendations for further research, with a focus on unresolved conceptual and methodological issues. This includes a thoughtful review and evaluation of alternative conceptualizations (e.g., dimensional, interpersonal, behavior analytic) of each disorder, with an eye toward the publication of DSM-V. You will notice that the controversies outlined in the previous section provide the scaffolding for the chapters that follow.

By now, you have read most of Chapter 1, which is framed on the current state of personality disorder research and practice issues. In Chapter 2, Widiger further discusses problems with current Axis II conceptualizations, such as pejorative connotations of its nomenclature, seemingly arbitrary diagnostic boundaries, and inadequate coverage of clinical phenomena. He then provides a thorough review of proposed alternative models, including dimensional models, prototype matching approaches, and possible reconfigurations of the Axis I/Axis II distinction.

In Chapter 3, Bernstein and Useda present and discuss paranoid personality disorder (PPD). They highlight important differential diagnostic challenges, such as distinguishing between the extreme suspiciousness that characterizes PPD and the paranoid delusions that characterize paranoid schizophrenia. They present the history of paranoia in the psychiatric literature and critique the current DSM conceptualization, which they argue may overrepresent cognitive features of the condition. Further, they note potentially important social consequences for individuals affected by PPD, such as relationship difficulties and involvement in unnecessary litigation, as they underscore the need for effective treatments for PPD. As of now, they add, the treatment literature is unfortunately composed solely of case studies. Although some of these have shown promising results, they point to the need for larger-scale treatment studies as well as further construct validation efforts as an important future direction for PPD research.

In Chapter 4, Mittal, Kalus, Bernstein, and Siever present and discuss schizoid personality disorder (SCD). They outline the historical conceptualization of "schizoid character" as first described by Bleuler, its subsequent revisions, and the present DSM conceptualization, in which it mirrors a subsyndromal variant of the "negative" symptoms associated with schizophrenia. They discuss the extremely low prevalence of SCD in clinical settings, describe psychometric problems regarding low internal consistency of the diagnosis, and critically evaluate the sensitivity and specificity of the individual criteria. Additionally, they discuss differential diagnostic challenges in distinguishing SCD from avoidant personality disorder and Asperger's syndrome. Last, they discuss the difficulties inherent in drawing individuals with SCD into treatment, due to their characteristic social isolation, and the resulting lack of treatment outcome studies. They conclude with recommendations regarding potential treatment strategies as well as recommended changes for DSM-V.

In Chapter 5, Bollini and Walker present and discuss schizotypal personality disorder (SPD). From the outset, they emphasize SPD as an Axis II condition for which there is a good deal of empirical support. They address the history of SPD as a condition conceptualized as a reflection of biological liability for schizophrenia rooted in Meehl's (1962) concept of "schizotaxia." They discuss the extension of this conceptualization into the diathesis-stress model of schizophrenia spectrum disorders, which for decades has been the dominant etiologic model of schizophrenia. They present evidence establishing genetic links between SPD (the criteria for which describe positive and negative subsyndromal features of schizophrenia) and schizophrenia. Further, they discuss the evidence for environmental factors (e.g., obstetrical complications) that may be important in the etiology of SPD. Additionally, they discuss brain and psychophysiological abnormalities common to both SPD and schizophrenia. They conclude by noting the lack of controlled treatment studies of SPD, a target for future research.

In Chapter 6, Patrick presents and discusses antisocial personality disorder (APD) and a related syndrome, psychopathy. He first describes the history of psychopathy as a construct that evolved into the more behavior-based APD diagnosis now found in the DSM. He then presents recent empirical findings regarding APD, with an emphasis on APD's place in a broader context of impulse control disorders. This is followed by a discussion of contemporary conceptualizations of psychopathy, a construct that many agree provides a richer picture of personality features often associated with chronic criminal behaviors, and that possesses a somewhat paradoxical mix of behavioral and personality pathology and adaptive personality features. Finally, Patrick discusses the lack of well-controlled APD treatment studies and offers suggestions for future treatment efforts based on work with other externalizing conditions.

In Chapter 7, Bradley, Conklin, and Westen present and discuss borderline personality disorder (BPD). They first examine the history of the borderline construct, from its roots in Kernberg's assertion that these patients' personality organization lies on the borderline between neurosis and psychosis to more contemporary views of BPD as a disorder of emotion dysregulation. They then introduce contemporary biological findings, including behavior genetics support for subsyndromal markers (i.e., endophenotypes) of BPD and neuroimaging studies. Further, they discuss literature regarding life events potentially etiologically relevant to BPD, such as separation from caretakers and childhood abuse. Additionally, they review findings related to the course and outcome of BPD, including high suicide rates and symptom reduction in middle age. They present findings regarding the most widely discussed contemporary therapy for BPD, which has shown promising empirical support: dialectical behavior therapy (DBT; Linehan, 1993). They discuss other interventions for which there are encouraging preliminary findings. They conclude with a discussion of future directions for BPD research, including improvement of diagnostic criteria and procedures and further examination of recent findings of subtypes of BPD.

In Chapter 8, Blagov, Fowler, and Lilienfeld present and discuss histrionic personality disorder (HPD). First they trace its historical roots, from ancient concepts of "wandering womb," through its early psychiatric examination by Charcot, and finally to the present, where it has been separated from somatization symptoms and now describes a personality pattern of excessive attention seeking. They then discuss the considerable overlap between HPD and other Cluster B disorders, as well as findings related to associations between HPD and Axis I conditions. This is followed by a discussion of the impact of gender and culture on HPD diagnosis and prognosis and a review of theories that posit antisocial personality disorder and HPD as gender-typed manifestations of the same underlying construct. They then present the extant treatment literature for HPD, which consists primarily of treatments under development, awaiting empirical support. They conclude with a discussion of future directions for HPD research, including elucidating its real-world impact, identifying endophenotypic markers that might differentiate it from other Cluster B disorders, and conducting controlled treatment studies.

In Chapter 9, Levy, Reynoso, Wasserman, and Clarkin present and discuss narcissistic personality disorder (NPD). First, they present the history of narcissism, from its roots in Greek mythology and Freudian theory to current DSM conceptualizations. They follow with a discussion of the extensive literature on subtypes of NPD and the disorder's co-occurrence with a number of Axis I and Axis II conditions, including its frequent comorbidity with substance abuse. Although there are no controlled treatment studies of NPD, they briefly discuss findings from case studies. They then present the extant data regarding its course and outcome, including reports of symptom remittance over time and some evidence of increased suicide risk in NPD patients. Additionally, they discuss the relation between features of NPD and contemporary Western culture. They conclude with recommendations for future research, including more research on course and outcome and well-done treatment studies.

In Chapter 10, Herbert presents and discusses avoidant personality disorder (APD). He begins by reviewing the extensive literature examining the extent to which APD can be considered a distinct syndrome above and beyond the sum of its clinical features (shyness, social anxiety, and interpersonal avoidance). In his discussion of overlap between APD and Axis I and II pathology, he particularly highlights findings pertaining to the overlap between APD and the condition that presents the greatest differential diagnostic challenge: social anxiety disorder (SAD). Due to their high degree of overlap and the greater body of research on SAD, Herbert then reviews literature on the etiology, cognitive and social skills deficits, and assessment of APD and SAD together. He adds that there is little literature regarding interventions specifically for APD, whereas there is a large literature supporting interventions for SAD, particularly social skills training and pharmacotherapy. He concludes with recommendations for future research, such as clarifying whether APD should be considered a subtype of SAD rather than a personality disorder and carrying out further treatment research.

In Chapter 11, Bornstein presents and discusses dependent personality disorder (DPD). He traces its history from early diagnosticians' mentions of exaggerated dependency needs to current DSM conceptualizations of DPD. He then reviews findings from behavior genetics studies and studies of parenting styles as they relate to DPD. Adding to his discussion of possible etiologic factors, Bornstein reviews cultural factors that may influence the perception of dependency as pathological. He then discusses epidemiological findings, which indicate that DPD is one of the most prevalent personality disorders in clinical settings and has a higher prevalence in women. Further, he discusses controversies over potential gender bias of DPD criteria and diagnosis. Bornstein then reviews the sparse treatment literature regarding DPD symptom reduction (for which there are conflicting results) and the impact of DPD on treatment outcome. He concludes with recommendations for future research, including criteria revision, careful evaluation of the temporal stability of DPD, and testing of different conceptual frameworks, such as those that incorporate symptom intensity and adaptiveness (as dependence on others can at times be an adaptive strategy).

In Chapter 12, Bartz, Kaplan, and Hollander present and discuss obsessive-compulsive personality disorder (OCPD). They first review the history of OCPD as one of the few personality disorders that have appeared in some form in every edition of the DSM, with few changes to its criteria over time. They then present a major diagnostic controversy surrounding OCPD: its relation to obsessive-compulsive disorder (OCD). They discuss psychoanalytic, cognitive, and interpersonal conceptualizations of OCPD. Following this, they review recent proposals of an obsessive-compulsive spectrum, which some have argued may be mediated by biological mechanisms (e.g., serotonergic dysfunction) that result in varied but related clinical manifestations (e.g., OCD, OCPD, body dysmorphic disorder). Further, they present etiologic theories of OCPD as an adaptation to Axis I pathology such as anxiety disorders, with which it demonstrates a high degree of overlap. The literature regarding treatment of OCPD lacks well-controlled studies, but Bartz and her colleagues present and discuss different treatment models (psychodynamic, cognitive, pharmacotherapeutic) and present case study results when available. Last, they highlight more rigorous treatment studies and more research on the possible conceptualization of OCPD as an obsessive-compulsive spectrum disorder as key areas for future research.

Finally, in Chapter 13, Morey, Hopwood, and Klein present and discuss the three personality disorders designated for further research: depressive personality disorder (DPD), passive-aggressive personality disorder (PAPD), and sadistic personality disorder (SPD). They cite the high prevalence of PDNOS (personality disorder not otherwise specified) diagnoses in clinical settings as a rationale for examining other potential personality disorders that have been identified in prior clinical and research literature but excluded from the current DSM. They first discuss PAPD (also called negativistic personality disorder) and review theories regarding its etiology, such as dramatic shifts in parenting style in childhood and cognitive mechanisms such as overfocus on authority and power. Next, they discuss historical and current conceptualizations of SPD, including its differentiation from sexual sadism. They underscore the potential importance of SPD if it accompanies a diagnosis of antisocial personality disorder (APD), as it adds information not found in the criteria for APD and would uniquely characterize those predisposed to cruelty and violence as well as criminality. Last, they discuss DPD and its roots in German phenomenological literature on "depressive temperament." They review long-standing controversies regarding the relationship of DPD with Axis I mood disorders (particularly cyclothymia) as well as behavior genetics studies that have indicated higher rates of mood disorders in relatives of probands with DPD. Morey, Hopwood, and Klein offer suggestions for future research on each of the three disorders.

We hope you will find that the 13 issues raised within this chapter come into sharper focus as you read through the volume. In many cases, however, there are a number of unanswered questions pertaining to these controversies, and we therefore further hope that these chapters will help stimulate your thought and interest and raise new questions toward the future of personality disorder research.

References

American Psychiatric Association. (1980). *Diagnostic and statistical manual of mental disorders* (3rd ed.). Washington, DC: Author.

American Psychiatric Association. (2000). *Diagnostic and statistical manual of mental disorders* (4th ed., text revision). Washington, DC: Author.

Bagby, R. M., Costa, P. T., Jr., Widiger, T. A., Ryder, A. G., & Marshall, M. (2005). DSM-IV personality disorders and the five-factor model of personality: A multimethod examination of domain- and facet-level predictions. *European Journal of Personality, 19,* 307–324.

Bem, D. J., & Allen, A. (1974). On predicting some of the people some of the time: The search for cross-situational consistencies in behavior. *Psychological Review, 81,* 506–520.

Block, J. (1977). Advancing the science of psychology: Paradigmatic shift or improving the quality of research? In D. Magnusson & N. S. Endler (Eds.), *Personality at the crossroads: Current issues in interactional psychology* (pp. 37–64). Hillsdale, NJ: Erlbaum.

Bradley, R., Conklin, C. Z., & Westen, D. (2005). The borderline personality diagnosis in adolescents: Gender differences and subtypes. *Journal of Child Psychology and Psychiatry, 46,* 1006–1019.

Caplan, P. (1987). The psychiatric association's failure to meet its own standards: The dangers of self-defeating personality disorder as a category. *Journal of Personality Disorders, 1,* 178–182.

Clark, L. A. (1999). Dimensional approaches to personality disorder assessment and diagnosis. In C. R. Cloninger (Ed.), *Personality and psychopathology* (pp. 219–244). Washington, DC: American Psychiatric Press.

Cloninger, C. R. (1987). A systematic method for clinical description and classification of personality variants: A proposal. *Archives of General Psychiatry, 44,* 573–588.

Epstein, S. (1979). The stability of behavior: I. On predicting most of the people much of the time. *Journal of Personality and Social Psychology, 37,* 1097–1126.

Fiester, S. J., Ellison, J. M., Docherty, J. P., & Shea, T. (1990). Comorbidity of personality disorders: Two for the price of three. *New Directions for Mental Health Services, 47,* 103–114.

Fowler, K. A., & Lilienfeld, S. O. (2006). Antisocial personality disorder. In J. E. Fisher & W. O'Donohue (Eds.), *Practice guidelines for evidence-based psychotherapy.* New York: Springer.

Freud, S. (1916/1991). Some character-types met with in psycho-analytic work. In M. F. R. Kets de Vries & S. M. Perzow (Eds.), *Handbook of character studies: Psychoanalytic explorations* (pp. 27–50). Madison, CT: International Universities Press.

Golomb, M., Fava, M., Abraham, M., & Rosenbaum, J. F. (1995). Gender differences in personality disorders. *American Journal of Psychiatry, 152,* 579–582.

Grove, W. M., & Tellegen, A. (1991). Problems in the classification of personality disorders. *Journal of Personality Disorders, 5*(1), 31–41.

Harkness, A. R., & Lilienfeld, S. O. (1997). Individual differences science for treatment planning: Personality traits. *Psychological Assessment, 9,* 349–360.

Heumann, K. A., & Morey, L. C. (1990). Reliability of categorical and dimensional judgments of personality disorders. *American Journal of Psychiatry, 147,* 498–500.

Horney, K. (1939). What is a neurosis? *American Journal of Sociology, 45,* 426–432.

Hyler, S. E., & Rieder, R. O. (1994). *Personality diagnostic questionnaire–4+.* New York: Authors.

Kenrick, D. T., & Funder, D.C. (1988). Profiting from controversy: Lessons from the person-situation debate. *American Psychologist, 43,* 23–34.

Landrine, H. (1989). The politics of personality disorder. *Psychology of Women Quarterly, 13,* 325–339.

Linehan, M. M. (1993). *Cognitive-behavioral treatment of borderline personality disorder.* New York: Guilford Press.

Loranger, A.W. (1988). *Personality disorders examination (PDE) manual.* Yonkers, NY: DV Communications.

Lykken, D. T. (1995). *The antisocial personalities.* Hillsdale, NJ: Erlbaum.

Mattia, J. I., & Zimmerman, M. (2001). Epidemiology. In W. J. Livesley (Ed.), *Handbook of personality disorders: Theory, research and treatment* (pp. 107–123). New York: Guilford Press.

Meehl, P. (1962). Schizotaxia, schizotypy, schizophrenia. *American Psychologist, 17,* 827–838.

Miller, J. D., Bagby, R. M., Pilkonis, P. A., Reynolds, S. K., & Lynam, D. R. (2005). A simplified technique for scoring DSM-IV personality disorders with the five-factor model. *Assessment, 12,* 404–415.

Mischel, W. (1968). *Personality and assessment*. New York: Wiley.

Morey, L. C. (1988). The categorical representation of personality disorder: A cluster analysis of DSM-III-R personality features. *Journal of Abnormal Psychology, 97*, 314–321.

Perry, J. C. (1992). Problems and considerations in the valid assessment of personality disorders. *American Journal of Psychiatry, 149*, 1645–1653.

Shapiro, D. (1965). *Neurotic styles*. Oxford, UK: Basic Books.

Skeem, J. L., Poythress, N., Edens, J. F., Lilienfeld, S. O., & Cale, E. (2003). Psychopathic personality or personalities? Exploring potential variants of psychopathy and their implications for risk assessment. *Aggression and Violent Behavior, 8*, 513–546.

Skinner, B. F. (1957). *Verbal behavior*. New York: Appleton-Century-Crofts.

Snyder, M. (1974). Self-monitoring of expressive behavior. *Journal of Personality and Social Psychology, 30*, 526–537.

Spitzer, R. L., Williams, J. B. W., & Gibbon, M. (1987). *Structured clinical interview for DSM-III-R personality disorders (SCID-II)*. New York: New York State Psychiatric Institute.

Trull, T. J. (2005). Dimensional models of personality disorder: Coverage and cutoffs. *Journal of Personality Disorders, 19*, 262–282.

Warner, R. (1978). The diagnosis of antisocial and hysterical personality disorders: An example of sex bias. *Journal of Nervous and Mental Disease, 166*, 839–845.

Widiger, T. A., & Rogers, J. H. (1989). Prevalence and comorbidity of personality disorders. *Psychiatric Annals, 19*, 132–136.

Widiger, T. A., & Spitzer, R. L. (1991). Sex bias in the diagnosis of personality disorders: Conceptual and methodological issues. *Clinical Psychology Review, 11*, 1–22.

Widiger, T. A., Trull, T. J., Clarkin, J. F., Sanderson, C., & Costa, P. T., Jr. (1994). A description of the DSM-III-R and DSM-IV personality disorders with the five-factor model of personality. In P. T. Costa, Jr., & T. A. Widiger (Eds.), *Personality disorders and the five-factor model of personality* (pp. 41–56). Washington, DC: American Psychological Association.

Zimmerman, M. (1994). Diagnosing personality disorders. *Archives of General Psychiatry, 51*, 225–249.

2 Alternatives to DSM-IV

Axis II

Thomas A. Widiger
University of Kentucky

Personality disorders could be among the more important diagnoses within the American Psychiatric Association's (APA) *Diagnostic and Statistical Manual of Mental Disorders* (APA, 2000). They have the unique distinction of being placed on a separate diagnostic axis, thereby drawing the attention of many clinicians who may otherwise not have considered them. They were placed on a separate axis in DSM-III (APA, 1980) to encourage clinicians to recognize the presence of maladaptive personality traits even when their attention is understandably drawn to a disorder of more pressing concern (Frances, 1980; Spitzer, Williams, & Skodol, 1980). The reason that the authors of the multiaxial system of DSM-III wanted to draw attention to personality disorders was the "accumulating evidence that the quality and quantity of preexisting personality disturbance may . . . influence the predisposition, manifestation, course, and response to treatment of various Axis I conditions" (Frances, 1980, p. 1050).

Personality disorders, however, are among the more controversial and problematic within the diagnostic manual. Maser, Kaelber, and Weise (1991) surveyed clinicians from 42 countries with respect to DSM-III-R (APA, 1987): "The personality disorders led the list of diagnostic categories

Author's note: Correspondence concerning this chapter should be addressed to Thomas A. Widiger, Ph.D., 115 Kastle Hall, Department of Psychology, University of Kentucky, Lexington, Kentucky 40506–0044. E-mail: widiger@uky.edu

with which respondents were dissatisfied" (p. 275). There are many reasons for this dissatisfaction, and there are a number of proposed alternatives. This chapter will begin with a brief description of some of the more fundamental and pressing concerns, followed by a discussion of proposals that have been made for the next edition of the diagnostic manual.

Problems With Axis II of DSM-IV

A number of significant problems and concerns have been raised with respect to the personality disorder diagnoses. Seven briefly outlined here are unreliability of diagnoses in general clinical practice, pejorative connotations, heterogeneity within diagnoses, excessive diagnostic co-occurrence, inconsistent and unstable diagnostic boundaries, inadequate coverage, and inadequate scientific base.

Diagnostic Unreliability

One of the major innovations of DSM-III (APA, 1980) was the provision of behaviorally specific diagnostic criterion sets (Spitzer et al., 1980). "The order of inference is relatively low, and the characteristic features consist of easily identifiable behavioral signs or symptoms" (APA, 1980, p. 7). These behaviorally specific diagnostic criteria substantially improved the ability of clinicians to obtain reliable diagnoses (Nathan & Langenbucher, 1999). However, the development of behaviorally specific diagnostic criterion sets has been problematic for the personality disorders. As acknowledged in DSM-III-R, "for some disorders . . . , particularly the personality disorders, the criteria require much more inference on the part of the observer" (APA, 1987, p. xxiii). Narcissistic lack of empathy and borderline identity disturbance, for example, are abstract clinical constructs that can be interpreted in a variety of ways by different clinicians and can be inferred on the basis of a variety of behaviors. As a result, personality disorders continue to be diagnosed unreliably in general clinical practice (Mellsop, Varghese, Joshua, & Hicks, 1982; Nazikian, Rudd, Edwards, & Jackson, 1990; Spitzer, Forman, & Nee, 1979).

Studies have also indicated that, in the absence of a structured interview, clinicians routinely fail to identify all of the clinically significant maladaptive personality functioning that is present (Blashfield & Herkov, 1996; Wood, Garb, Lilienfeld, & Nezworski, 2002; Zimmerman & Mattia, 1999a, 1999b). Illustrating the general phenomenon of diagnostic overshadowing (i.e., once a diagnosis has been made, there is a tendency to attribute all other problems to that disorder, leaving coexisting conditions unrecognized), clinicians tend to diagnose personality disorders hierarchically, failing to conduct additional assessments once a particular construct has been identified (Blashfield & Flanagan, 1998; Herkov & Blashfield, 1995). The personality disorder that is provided preferential attention may even be idiosyncratic to the clinician (Gunderson, 1992; Mellsop et al., 1982).

Pejorative Connotations

The Assembly of the American Psychiatric Association has passed a number of resolutions to explore proposals to change the name of borderline personality disorder and to move the personality disorders to Axis I. The motivation for these resolutions has been in large part the frustration many clinicians reportedly experience in obtaining insurance coverage. There is an unfortunate perception that Axis II is for disorders for which there is currently no effective treatment (Frances et al., 1991). There is compelling empirical research indicating that at least some personality disorders are in fact treatable (Leichsenring & Leibing, 2003; Perry, Banon, & Ianni, 1999). Nevertheless, the perception that they are untreatable has fueled arguments for their reformulation as Axis I disorders. For example, Liebowitz et al. (1998) argued during the development of DSM-IV that most instances of avoidant personality disorder should be diagnosed on Axis I as a generalized social phobia because there are more effective treatments available: "We believe that the more extensive evidence for syndromal validity of social phobia, including pharmacological and cognitive-behavioral treatment efficacy, make it the more useful designation in cases of overlap with avoidant personality" (p. 1060).

Heterogeneity Within Diagnoses

Most of the personality disorder diagnostic criterion sets in DSM-III (APA, 1980) were monothetic, in that all of the criteria were required in order to provide a diagnosis. However, it soon became apparent that persons with the same diagnosis rarely had all of the same personality features. Therefore, the authors of DSM-III-R switched to polythetic criterion sets in which only a subset of diagnostic criteria are required (Widiger, Frances, Spitzer, & Williams, 1988). For example, in DSM-IV, any four of eight optional criteria are required for the diagnosis of obsessive-compulsive personality disorder (APA, 2000).

Polythetic criterions sets, however, do not actually resolve the problems associated with the heterogeneity among persons sharing the same diagnosis. Polythetic criterion sets are simply an acknowledgment or acceptance of the problematic heterogeneity. For example, it is now possible for two patients to meet the DSM-IV criteria for obsessive-compulsive personality disorder yet not have any diagnostic features in common!

The differences among patients sharing the same diagnosis are not trivial. For example, only a subset of persons who meet the DSM-IV criteria for antisocial personality disorder will have the prototypical features of the callous, ruthless, arrogant, charming, and scheming psychopath (Hare, 2003), and there are even important differences among persons who would be diagnosed as psychopathic (Brinkley, Newman, Widiger, & Lynam, 2004; Skeem, Poythress, Edens, Lilienfeld, & Cale, 2003).

Excessive Diagnostic Co-occurrence

DSM-IV provides diagnostic criterion sets to help guide the clinician toward the correct diagnosis and a section devoted to differential diagnosis that indicates "how to differentiate [the] disorder from other disorders that have similar presenting characteristics" (APA, 2000, p. 10). The intention of this information is to help the clinician determine which particular disorder is present, the selection of which will indicate the presence of a specific pathology that will explain the occurrence of the symptoms and suggest a specific treatment that will ameliorate the patient's suffering (Frances, First, & Pincus, 1995).

It is evident, however, that DSM-IV routinely fails in the goal of guiding the clinician to the presence of one specific personality disorder. Studies have consistently indicated that many patients meet diagnostic criteria for an excessive number of personality disorder diagnoses (Bornstein, 1998; Lilienfeld, Waldman, & Israel, 1994; Livesley, 2003; Widiger & Trull, 1998). The maladaptive personality functioning of patients does not appear to be adequately described by a single diagnostic category.

Inconsistent, Unstable, and Arbitrary Diagnostic Boundaries

An additional problem has been establishing a consistent, nonarbitrary boundary with normal personality functioning. The existing diagnostic thresholds lack a compelling rationale (Tyrer & Johnson, 1996). In fact, no explanation or justification has ever been provided for most of them (Samuel & Widiger, 2006). The thresholds for the DSM-III schizotypal and borderline diagnoses are the only two for which a published rationale has ever been provided. The DSM-III requirements that the patient have four of eight features for the schizotypal diagnosis and five of eight for borderline (APA, 1980) were determined on the basis of maximizing agreement with similar diagnoses provided by clinicians (Spitzer, Endicott, & Gibbon, 1979). However, the current diagnostic thresholds for these personality disorders bear little relationship with the original thresholds established for DSM-III. Blashfield, Blum, and Pfohl (1992) reported a kappa of only -.025 for the DSM-III and DSM-III-R schizotypal personality disorders, with a reduction in prevalence from 11% to 1%. Seemingly minor changes to diagnostic criterion sets have resulted in unexpected and substantial shifts in prevalence rates that profoundly complicate scientific theory and public health decisions (Blashfield et al., 1992; Narrow, Rae, Robins, & Regier, 2002).

Inadequate Coverage

Clinicians provide a diagnosis of personality disorder not otherwise specified (PDNOS) when they determine that a person has a personality disorder not adequately represented by any one of the 10 officially recognized diagnoses (APA, 2000). PDNOS is often the single most frequently used diagnosis in clinical practice, one explanation being that the existing categories are not providing adequate coverage (Verheul & Widiger, 2004). Westen and Arkowitz-Westen (1998) surveyed 238 psychiatrists and psychologists with respect to their clinical practice and reported that "the majority of patients with personality pathology significant enough to warrant clinical psychotherapeutic attention (60.6%) are currently undiagnosable on Axis II" (p. 1769). The clinicians reported the treatment of commitment difficulties, intimacy problems, shyness, work inhibition, perfectionism, and devaluation of others, issues not well described by any of the existing diagnoses. One approach to this problem is to add more diagnostic categories, but there is considerable reluctance to do so, in part because this would further increase the difficulties of excessive diagnostic co-occurrence and differential diagnosis (Pincus, McQueen, & Elinson, 2003).

Inadequate Scientific Base

Blashfield and Intoccia (2000) conducted a computer search and concluded that there were "five disorders (dependent, narcissistic, obsessive-compulsive, paranoid, and passive-aggressive) that had very small literatures, averaging fewer than 10 articles per year" (p. 473). "The only personality disorder whose literature is clearly alive and growing is that of borderline personality disorder" (p. 473). They characterized the literature concerning the dependent, narcissistic, obsessive-compulsive, paranoid, passive-aggressive, schizoid, and histrionic personality disorders as "dead" or "dying" (p. 473).

The conclusions of Blashfield and Intoccia (2000) may have been overly negative. Their search appears to have missed (for example) the considerable research literature concerning psychopathy (Hare, 2003), the many studies on sociotropy, dependency, and attachment (Bornstein, 1992), and the many studies concerning narcissism and conflicted self-esteem published in the general personality literature (Ronningstam, 2005). Nevertheless, their warning is well taken: "Disorders with literature growth that is dead or dying are not succeeding at accumulating new empirical knowledge, nor are they likely to be stimulating substantial clinical interest" (Blashfield & Intoccia, 2000, p. 473). DSM-III provided specific and explicit criterion sets, in part to facilitate the development of systematic empirical studies that would provide the Robins and Guze (1970) follow-up, family history, and laboratory construct validation studies that would document their validity as distinct diagnostic entities (Spitzer et al., 1980). Yet it is challenging to even find a systematic study devoted to an understanding of the etiology, pathology, family history, or treatment of the histrionic, schizoid, paranoid, obsessive-compulsive, and other personality disorders despite the provision over 20 years ago of research diagnostic criteria within DSM-III.

Proposals for DSM-V

Quite a few proposals will be considered by the authors of DSM-V to address the above problems. These proposals will run the gamut from tinkering with criterion sets to improve their specificity to deleting the more problematic or weakly validated diagnoses. Described below are proposals that involve fundamental alterations.

Abandonment of the Concept of Personality Disorder

One proposal for DSM-V is to abandon the concept of a personality disorder. Proposals have been made to redefine personality disorders as early-onset, chronic variants of existing Axis I disorders (First et al., 2002; Siever & Davis, 1991). A strong precedent for such a shift in conceptualization and classification is schizotypal personality disorder. Schizotypal personality disorder is genetically related to schizophrenia, most of its neurobiological risk factors and psychophysiological correlates are shared with schizophrenia (e.g., eye tracking, orienting, startle blink, and neurodevelopmental abnormalities), and the treatments that are effective in ameliorating schizotypal symptoms overlap with treatments used for persons with schizophrenia (Raine, 2006). In fact, the World Health Organization's (WHO) International Classification of Diseases (ICD; WHO, 1992), the parent classification to the APA diagnostic manual, does not recognize the existence of schizotypal personality disorder, instead including a diagnosis of schizotypal disorder within its manual's section on disorders of schizophrenia. It is quite possible that a DSM-V personality disorders work group will follow the lead of the WHO and transfer schizotypal personality disorder out of the personality disorders section and into the section of the manual dealing with schizophrenia-related disorders (First et al., 2002).

A similar fate could befall other personality disorders. Just as schizotypal personality disorder could be readily subsumed within an existing section of Axis I, avoidant personality disorder could be reclassified as a generalized social phobia (Liebowitz et al., 1998); depressive personality disorder (currently in an appendix to DSM-IV; APA, 2000) as an early-onset dysthymia; borderline personality disorder as an affective dysregulation and/or impulse dyscontrol disorder; schizoid as an early-onset and chronic variant of the negative (anhedonic) symptoms of schizophrenic pathology (although empirical support for a genetic relationship with schizophrenia is equivocal [Miller, Useda, Trull, Burrs, & Minks-Brown, 2001]); paranoid personality disorder as an early-onset, chronic, and milder variant of a delusional disorder; obsessive-compulsive personality disorder as a generalized and chronic variant of obsessive-compulsive anxiety disorder (although there is in fact only weak evidence to support a close relationship between the obsessive-compulsive anxiety and personality disorders [Costa, Samuels, Bagby, Daffin, & Norton, 2005]); antisocial personality disorder as an adult variant of conduct disorder; and passive-aggressive personality disorder (currently in an appendix to DSM-IV [APA, 2000]) as an adult variant of oppositional defiant disorder (with which it was explicitly affiliated in DSM-III [APA, 1980]). Three personality disorders would be left behind in such a move as they have no apparent location within Axis I: histrionic, narcissistic, and dependent. For some, however, these diagnoses would not be greatly missed, as they have a strong psychodynamic heritage (Millon et al., 1996), and the trend in psychiatry appears to be toward disorders in which neurobiological etiology is better established (Charney et al., 2002; Hyman, 2002).

A concern with reformulating personality disorders as early-onset and chronic variants of Axis I disorders, beyond the fundamental consideration that the diagnostic manual would no longer recognize the existence of maladaptive personality functioning, is that it might create more problems than it solves (Widiger, 2003). It appears that persons have constellations of maladaptive personality traits not well described by just one or even multiple personality disorder diagnoses (Bornstein, 1998; Livesley, 2003; Trull & Durrett, 2005; Widiger & Sanderson, 1995), but these constellations of maladaptive personality traits would be even less well described by multiple diagnoses across the broad classes of mood, anxiety, impulse dyscontrol, delusional, and disruptive behavior disorders. In addition, the existing problem of lack of coverage would be further worsened by the deletion of personality disorder diagnoses that could not be subsumed within an existing Axis I diagnosis.

Prototype Matching

A much less radical proposal for DSM-V is to provide a dimensional profile of the existing (or somewhat revised) diagnostic categories (Oldham & Skodol, 2000; Tyrer & Johnson, 1996; Widiger & Sanderson, 1995). A personality disorder could be characterized as prototypical if all of the diagnostic criteria are met, moderately present if one or two criteria beyond the threshold for a categorical diagnosis are present, threshold if the patient just barely meets diagnostic threshold, subthreshold if symptoms are present but just below diagnostic threshold, traits if no more than one to three symptoms are present, and absent if no diagnostic criteria are present (Oldham & Skodol, 2000). Oldham and Skodol propose further that, if a patient meets diagnostic criteria for three or more personality disorders, a diagnosis of "extensive personality disorder" be provided, along with an indication of the extent to which each personality disorder is present.

This proposed revision would be beneficial in shifting clinicians somewhat toward a more dimensional model of classification. It would encourage them to provide a more comprehensive and precise description of a patient's profile of maladaptive personality functioning and would discourage fruitless differential diagnoses of overlapping constructs. In addition, reliability of diagnoses do generally improve when a more quantitative, dimensional classification is used (Widiger & Sanderson, 1995).

Another version of the prototype matching proposal is provided by Westen and Shedler (2000). This proposal is similar to Oldham and Skodol's (2000) in that it largely retains the existing diagnostic categories, each of which would be rated on a five-point scale. However, an important difference is that Westen and Shedler's five-point rating is not based on the number of diagnostic criteria. They propose instead that the diagnostic manual provide a narrative description of a prototypical case of each personality disorder (half to full page, containing 18 to 20 features), and that the clinician indicate on a five-point scale the extent to which a patient matches this description (i.e., 1 = little to no match; 2 = slight match, only minor features; 3 = significant match; 4 = good match, patient has the disorder; and 5 = very good match, prototypical case). "To make a diagnosis, diagnosticians rate the overall similarity or 'match' between a patient and the prototype using a 5-point rating scale, considering the prototype as a whole rather than counting individual symptoms" (Westen, Shedler, & Bradley, 2006, p. 847).

A limitation of the prototype matching proposal of Oldham and Skodol (2000) is that clinicians would continue to describe patients in terms of markedly heterogeneous and overlapping constructs. A profile description of a patient in terms of the antisocial, borderline, dependent, histrionic, and other DSM-IV constructs would essentially just reify the excessive diagnostic co-occurrence that is currently being obtained (Bornstein, 1998; Lilienfeld et al., 1994). The problem of excessive diagnostic co-occurrence would be "solved" by simply accepting it. This is comparable to the decision made by the authors of DSM-III-R (APA, 1987) to address the problematic heterogeneity of the diagnostic categories by abandoning monothetic criterion sets that required homogeneity and converting to polythetic criterion sets that accepted the existence of the problematic heterogeneity (Widiger et al., 1988).

Westen et al. (2006) suggest that their version of the prototype matching procedure does actually address the problem of diagnostic co-occurrence. They empirically compared the extent of diagnostic co-occurrence obtained with their prototype matching with the extent of diagnostic co-occurrence obtained when the same clinicians systematically consider each DSM-IV diagnostic criterion. They reported considerably less diagnostic co-occurrence with their prototype matching. However, their findings could in fact indicate that their prototype matching procedure is now "solving" the problem of diagnostic co-occurrence by simply neglecting to provide an adequate recognition of its existence. The fact that diagnostic co-occurrence increased when the clinicians were encouraged to consider specific features of other personality disorders suggests that the co-occurrence is actually present but is not being recognized when clinicians are allowed to base their diagnoses on whatever feature or features they wish to consider. Prior studies have shown that clinicians who do not systematically use diagnostic criterion sets grossly underestimate the extent of maladaptive personality functioning actually present (Blashfield & Herkov, 1996; Wood et al., 2002; Zimmerman & Mattia, 1999a, 1999b).

A concern regarding the narrative prototype matching procedure is that it is essentially a return to the method used for DSM-II (APA, 1968), in which only a narrative description of each disorder was provided. Clinical diagnoses were grossly unreliable prior to DSM-III because no specific or explicit guidelines were provided regarding which features should be used to determine whether or not a person was close enough to a prototypical case to warrant a diagnosis (Spitzer et al., 1980). One had no way of knowing which features, or even how many, were being used to make a diagnosis. Westen et al. (2006), however, suggest that reliable and valid diagnoses can be obtained in the absence of specific and explicit criterion sets. Rather than spending 2 hours systematically assessing each diagnostic criterion, "clinicians could make a complete Axis II diagnosis in 1 or 2 minutes" (Westen et al., 2006, p. 855). They reported in their study good validity for their prototype matching approach. However, it should perhaps be noted that the validity data were in all cases provided by the same clinicians who conducted the prototype matching. Validation was confined simply to the internal consistency of each clinician's description (Smith, 2005).

One of the more telling findings of Westen et al. (2006) was their comparison of prototype matching based on their rich narrative descriptions (consisting of 18 to 20 features) with matching based on a grossly simplified description consisting of just one sentence (i.e., the single essential feature of each respective personality disorder described in DSM-IV [APA, 2000]). They compared the validity of the richer narrative prototype matching with the validity of the grossly simplified version to determine if the prototype match procedure outperformed the specific and explicit criterion sets simply because it provided more information. They discovered that "the data were strikingly similar" (p. 852) even when the clinicians based the matching on just one sentence. "The rate of comorbidity was [again] substantially lower than with the DSM-IV dimensional diagnoses . . . and the pattern of external correlates was equivalent" (p. 852). In other words, the rich depth and breadth of information provided within the narrative descriptions wasn't actually necessary, perhaps because the clinicians had already reached their conclusions months before the study was conducted (average length of treatment prior to onset of study was over 1 year).

Specific and explicit criterion sets may not be useful or necessary for reaching a diagnosis once a clinician is well familiar with the patient (e.g., after 1 year of treatment). A diagnostic manual is generally used during an intake for treatment or research. At this time, the clinician can be very unfamiliar with the patient's symptomatology, and specific and explicit criterion sets can be very useful, if not necessary, for obtaining reliable and valid diagnosis. They compel the clinician to assess for the presence of a given mental disorder in a systematic, comprehensive, consistent, and replicable manner (Rogers, 2003; Spitzer et al., 1980; Zimmerman, 2003).

The prototype matching of Westen and Shedler (2000) can be supported by the Shedler-Westen Assessment Procedure–200 (SWAP-200), a clinician's ranking form of 200 items drawn from the psychoanalytic and personality disorder literature (Shedler, 2002; Westen & Shedler, 1999a). The SWAP-200 is "a method for studying personality and personality pathology that strives to capture the richness and complexity of psychoanalytic constructs and formulations" (Shedler, 2002, p. 429). Comparable to the descriptions of the narrative prototype matching procedure, SWAP-200 items are not ranked on the basis of a systematic administration of a series of questions; instead, the SWAP-200 relies on "the empathically attuned and dynamically sophisticated clinician given free rein to practice his or her craft" (Shedler, 2002, p. 433). Nevertheless, the requirement that clinicians consider each of the 200 SWAP-200 items does at least ensure that they do not simply ignore many of the sentences within the narrative descriptions.

Initial research with the SWAP-200 has reported good to excellent convergent and discriminant validity (e.g., Westen & Shedler, 1999b; Westen, Shedler, Durrett, Glass, & Martens, 2003). However, the positive results obtained with the SWAP-200 should be tempered by methodological limitations of the initial research (Widiger & Samuel, 2005b). For example, clinicians who provided the personality disorder criterion rankings were again the same persons who provided the SWAP-200 rankings (e.g., Conklin & Westen, 2005; Shedler & Westen, 2004; Westen & Shedler, 1999a, 1999b; Westen et al., 2003). This is comparable to having conductors of semistructured interviews provide their own criterion diagnoses in a study testing the validity of their semistructured interview assessments. Determining whether the results of the interview are in agreement with the impressions of the person conducting the interview is not a compelling test of the validity of the interview (Smith, 2005). An additional methodological concern is that the clinicians in each study have been provided with guidelines for the distribution of their rankings. For example, in the typical SWAP-200 administration, clinicians are required to identify half of the items as absent and also required to identify an increasingly restrictive distribution of more highly ranked items. Only eight SWAP-200 items can be given the highest rankings (e.g., Westen & Shedler, 1999b), no matter the opinions of the raters or the symptoms present; potentially, this could force clinicians to overcorrect and generate more discriminant validity than they actually see. (For a different view, see Chapter 7.) If a clinician has provided a patient with the highest rating of 7 for 12 SWAP-200 items, he or she is presented with a list of these 12 items and told to shift four to a lower rating. It is perhaps not surprising that clinicians often shift out of this list those items that are least convergent with the other items. Convergent and discriminant validity of a semistructured interview would also be improved dramatically if interviewers were instructed to code half of the diagnostic criteria as absent and identify only a few of the diagnostic criteria as present.

Dimensional Model of Classification

Categorical classifications of psychopathology have become so problematic that an APA Research Planning Work Group for DSM-V concluded that it will be "important that consideration be given to advantages and disadvantages of basing part or all of DSM-V on dimensions rather than categories" (Rounsaville et al., 2002, p. 12). They suggested in particular that the first section of the diagnostic manual to be converted to a dimensional classification might be the personality disorders section. "If a dimensional system of personality performs well and is acceptable to clinicians, it might then be appropriate to explore dimensional approaches in other domains" (Rounsaville et al., 2002, p. 13). The APA subsequently cosponsored a series of international conferences devoted to further enriching the empirical database in preparation for the eventual development of DSM-V. The first conference was devoted to reviewing the research and setting a research agenda that would be most useful and effective in leading the field toward a dimensional classification of personality disorder (Widiger & Simonsen, 2005b; Widiger, Simonsen, Krueger, Livesley, & Verheul, 2005).

By one count, there are at least 18 alternative proposals for a dimensional model of personality disorder (Widiger & Simonsen, 2005a). Even if one confines the list to dimensional models of general personality structure that have been applied to the DSM-IV personality disorders, the list remains extensive, including, for example, Eysenck's (1987) three dimensions of neuroticism, extraversion, and psychoticism; Harkness and McNulty's five factors of positive emotionality/extraversion, aggressiveness, constraint, negative emotionality/neuroticism, and psychoticism (Harkness, McNulty, & Ben-Porath, 1995); Tellegen's (1982) three dimensions of negative affectivity (emotionality), positive affectivity (emotionality), and constraint; the interpersonal circumplex dimensions of agency and communion (Pincus & Gurtman, 2006); Millon's six polarities of self, other, active, passive, pleasure, and pain (Millon et al., 1996); Zuckerman's (2002) five dimensions of sociability, activity, aggression-hostility, impulsive sensation seeking, and neuroticism-anxiety; Cloninger's (2006) seven factors of novelty seeking, harm avoidance, reward dependence, persistence, self-directedness, cooperativeness, and self-transcendence; and the five-factor model dimensions of neuroticism, extraversion, openness, conscientiousness, and agreeableness (Widiger, Costa, & McCrae, 2002).

The existence of so many alternatives could suggest that the proposals are so disparate that no consensus is likely to emerge (Millon et al., 1996). However, it is apparent that most, perhaps all, of these alternative models can be integrated within a common hierarchical structure (Bouchard & Loehlin, 2001; John & Srivastava, 1999; Larstone, Jang, Livesley, Vernon, & Wolf, 2002; Markon, Krueger, & Watson, 2005; Trull & Durrett, 2005; Widiger & Mullins-Sweatt, 2005; Zuckerman, 2002). This should not be surprising, as most of them are attempting to do largely the same thing (i.e., identify the fundamental dimensions of maladaptive personality functioning that underlie and cut across the existing diagnostic categories).

Widiger and Simonsen (2005a) provide a potential integration. At one level would be four to five broad domains of general personality functioning: emotional instability, antagonism versus compliance, extraversion versus introversion, constraint versus impulsivity, and (perhaps) unconventionality. These broad domains could be confined largely to a description of normal personality structure. Based on the elevations obtained within each domain, one would proceed to assess for maladaptive variants (approximately two to four within each domain) that would consist of more specific facet scales. For example, persons who evidence a high level of constraint could be assessed for the maladaptive variant of compulsivity, whereas persons who evidence a low level of constraint could be assessed for the maladaptive variant of impulsivity.

A dimensional classification of personality disorder would address many of the limitations inherent in a categorical classification of personality disorder. Heterogeneity among persons is addressed through the provision of multifactorial descriptions of an individual's personality profile. Any reasonably comprehensive dimensional model would also be able to cover a greater range of maladaptive personality functioning than the existing diagnostic categories in a number of ways: by avoiding the inclusion of redundant, overlapping constructs; by organizing the traits within a hierarchical structure; by representing a broader range of maladaptive personality functioning along a single dimension (e.g., antagonism versus compliance); by including aspects of normal and abnormal personality functioning not currently represented within DSM-IV (e.g., alexithymia and closed-mindedness); and by allowing for the representation of relatively unique or atypical personality profiles (Widiger & Samuel, 2005a). The need for the frequently used wastebasket NOS diagnosis would decrease substantially.

An additional advantage of this approach is the integration of the classification of abnormal personality traits with the existing research on general personality structure (Widiger, Simonsen, Krueger, et al., 2005). For example, there is considerable cross-cultural support for the five-factor model of general personality structure in terms of both emic (Ashton & Lee, 2001) and etic (Allik, 2005) research. Emic studies use constructs or measures that are indigenous to a particular culture. The extensive lexical research on the structure of trait terms within different languages would be considered emic research (Church, 2001). Etic studies use constructs or measures imported from one culture into another. McCrae and his colleagues' cross-cultural study of the five-factor personality structure using observer ratings by 11,985 persons sampled from 51 different cultures would be considered an etic study

(McCrae, Terracciano, & 78 Members of the Personality Profiles of Cultures Project, 2005). Roberts and DelVecchio (2000) documented temporal stability for the five-factor domains across the life span in their integrative meta-analysis of 152 longitudinal studies. Mervielde, De Clercq, De Fruyt, and Van Leeuwen (2005) and Shiner and Caspi (2003) indicated how the fundamental childhood temperaments are well integrated within the five-factor personality structure. The search for the specific genes of personality has produced quite mixed results, but it is encouraging that two meta-analytic reviews of the molecular genetics research has provided support for the five-factor domain of neuroticism (Schinka, Busch, & Robichaux-Keene, 2004; Sen, Burmeister, & Ghosh, 2004). Behavior genetics research has supported the heritability of most personality traits. Yamagata et al. (2006) went further with a multivariate behavioral genetics study (using twin samples from three different countries) to provide genetic support for the specific five-factor personality structure. In sum, this is a scientific foundation for construct validity that is not even remotely evident for the personality disorder diagnostic categories (Blashfield & Intoccia, 2000).

A further advantage of integrating the classification of personality disorder with general personality structure is the ability to provide a more comprehensive description of each individual's personality, including traits that might facilitate treatment responsivity (Widiger & Simonsen, 2005a). For example, moderate elevations within the domain of conscientiousness (or constraint) are likely to predict willingness and ability to maintain the rigors of a demanding clinical regimen, moderate levels of agreeableness (compliance) can suggest an increased likelihood of establishing therapeutic rapport and engagement within interpersonal models of therapy, and moderate levels of openness (unconventionality) would likely suggest interest and motivation for questioning existing cognitive schemas or engaging in a dynamic exploration of unconscious conflicts (Sanderson & Clarkin, 2002).

An integration of the classification of personality disorder with general personality structure might even help with the stigmatization of a mental disorder diagnosis, as no longer would a personality disorder be conceptualized as something qualitatively distinct from general personality. All persons vary in the extent to which they are agreeable versus antagonistic or constraining versus impulsive. Persons with personality disorders would no longer be said to have disorders that are qualitatively distinct from normal psychological functioning but would instead simply be persons who have maladaptive variants of the personality traits that are evident within all persons.

A limitation of this proposal is the absence of established cutoff points for clinical decisions. Inherent in a dimensional model of classification is the absence of qualitative distinctions, yet clinicians do have to make a number of specific decisions (e.g., whether to treat a patient, whether to provide a particular medication, whether to provide disability coverage, and whether to hospitalize a patient). However, the absence of illusory qualitative distinctions within a dimensional model does not imply that no useful clinical distinctions could be made. In fact, a dimensional classification could be better suited to these myriad clinical decisions than the existing diagnostic categories, as it can provide different cutoff points for different clinical decisions (Trull, 2005; Widiger & Samuel, 2005a).

Widiger et al. (2002) recommended that the cutoff point for diagnosis be based on the Global Assessment of Functioning (GAF) scale provided on Axis V of DSM-IV (APA, 2000). A score of 71 or above on the GAF indicates a normal range of functioning (e.g., problems are transient and expectable reactions to stressors); a score of 60 or below represents a clinically significant level of impairment (moderate difficulty in social or occupational functioning, such as having few friends or significant conflicts with co-workers; APA, 2000). Further explication of this scale is provided by the Global Assessment of Relational Functioning (GARF) and the Social and Occupational Functioning (SOF) scales (APA, 2000). There is no empirical support for using this cutoff point to provide a diagnosis of personality disorder (First, 2005), but it is at least an explicit rationale that is consistent with the definition of mental disorder provided in DSM-IV and that can be applied uniformly across different variants of maladaptive personality functioning, in contrast to the inconsistent and unexplained diagnostic thresholds that are currently provided (Samuel & Widiger, 2006).

An additional concern is clinical utility (First, 2005; Verheul, 2005). A significant limitation of the five-factor model of general personality structure as a classification of personality disorder is that current versions of this model focus primarily on the normal variants of personality functioning (e.g., altruism, openness to aesthetics, straightforwardness) that are unlikely to be the focus of clinical interventions. However, an integrative model (Widiger & Simonsen, 2005a) would have as its facets scales from such instruments as the Dimensional Assessment of Personality Pathology (DAPP; Livesley, 2003) and the Schedule for Nonadaptive and Adaptive Personality (SNAP; Clark, Simms, Wu, & Casillas, in press) that would describe precisely the behaviors and traits that are of direct clinical interest and attention (e.g., mistrust, manipulativeness, insecure attachment, identity problems, affective lability, & self-harm; Clark et al., in press; Livesley, 2003).

Conclusions

The problems that bedevil the personality disorder diagnoses are not theirs alone. Excessive diagnostic co-occurrence, lack of treatment specificity, and inadequate boundaries with normal psychological functioning are fundamental problems endemic to the diagnostic manual (Rounsaville et al., 2002; Watson, 2005; Widiger & Clark, 2000). Nevertheless, these problems do appear to be particularly problematic for the personality disorders (First et al., 2002), perhaps contributing to the lack of interest among researchers in empirically studying the etiology, pathology, treatment, or course of individual personality disorders. It might be premature for the next edition of the diagnostic manual to abandon the personality disorder diagnostic categories, replacing them with early onset and chronic variants of Axis I disorders or with a dimensional model of general personality structure. However, any such revision could also represent a bold and innovative paradigmatic shift that could help advance and reinvigorate a seriously troubled field. In any case, researchers should continue to work toward the further development of these proposed alternatives.

References

Allik, J. (2005). Personality dimensions across cultures. *Journal of Personality Disorders, 19,* 212–232.

American Psychiatric Association. (1968). *Diagnostic and statistical manual of mental disorders* (2nd ed.). Washington, DC: Author.

American Psychiatric Association. (1980). *Diagnostic and statistical manual of mental disorders* (3rd ed.). Washington, DC: Author.

American Psychiatric Association. (1987). *Diagnostic and statistical manual of mental disorders* (3rd ed., revised). Washington, DC: Author.

American Psychiatric Association. (2000). *Diagnostic and statistical manual of mental disorders* (4th ed., text revision). Washington, DC: Author.

Ashton, M. C., & Lee, K. (2001). A theoretical basis for the major dimensions of personality. *European Journal of Personality, 15,* 327–353.

Blashfield, R. K., Blum, N., & Pfohl, B. (1992). The effects of changing Axis II diagnostic criteria. *Comprehensive Psychiatry, 33,* 245–252.

Blashfield, R. K., & Flanagan, E. (1998). A prototypic nonprototype of a personality disorder. *Journal of Nervous and Mental Disease, 186,* 244–246.

Blashfield, R. K., & Herkov, M. J. (1996). Investigating clinician adherence to diagnosis by criteria: A replication of Morey and Ochoa (1989). *Journal of Personality Disorders, 10,* 219–228.

Blashfield, R. K, & Intoccia, V. (2000). Growth of the literature on the topic of personality disorders. *American Journal of Psychiatry, 157,* 472–473.

Bornstein, R. F. (1992). The dependent personality: Developmental, social, and clinical perspectives. *Psychological Bulletin, 112,* 3–23.

Bornstein, R. F. (1998). Reconceptualizing personality disorder diagnosis in the DSM-V: The discriminant validity challenge. *Clinical Psychology: Science and Practice, 5,* 333–343.

Bouchard, T. J., & Loehlin, J. C. (2001). Genes, evolution, and personality. *Behavior Genetics, 31,* 243–273.

Brinkley, C. A., Newman, J. P., Widiger, T. A., & Lynam, D. R. (1994). Two approaches to parsing the heterogeneity of psychopathy. *Clinical Psychology: Science and Practice, 11,* 69–94.

Charney, D. S., Barlow, D. H., Botteron, K., Cohen, J. D., Goldman, D., Gur, R. E., et al. (2002). Neuroscience research agenda to guide development of a pathophysiologically based classification system. In D. J. Kupfer, M. B. First, & D. A. Regier (Eds.), *A research agenda for DSM-V* (pp. 31–83). Washington, DC: American Psychiatric Association.

Church, A. T. (2001). Personality measurement in cross-cultural perspective. *Journal of Personality, 69,* 979–1006.

Clark, L. A., Simms, L. J., Wu, K. D., & Casillas, A. (in press). *Manual for the schedule for nonadaptive and adaptive personality (SNAP-2).* Minneapolis: University of Minnesota Press.

Cloninger, C. R. (2006). Differentiating personality deviance, normality, and well-being by the seven-factor psychobiological model. In S. Strack (Ed.), *Differentiating normal and abnormal personality* (2nd ed., pp. 65–81). New York: Springer.

Conklin, C. Z., & Westen, D. (2005). Borderline personality disorder in clinical practice. *American Journal of Psychiatry, 162,* 867–875.

Costa, P. T., Jr., Samuels, J., Bagby, M., Daffin, L., & Norton, H. (2005). Obsessive-compulsive personality disorder: A review. In M. Maj, H. S. Akiskal, J. E. Mezzich, & A. Okasha (Eds.), *Personality disorders* (pp. 405–439). New York: Wiley.

Eysenck, H. J. (1987). The definition of personality disorders and the criteria appropriate for their description. *Journal of Personality Disorders, 1,* 211–219.

First, M. B. (2005). Clinical utility: A prerequisite for the adoption of a dimensional approach in DSM. *Journal of Abnormal Psychology, 114,* 560–564.

First, M. B., Bell, C. B., Cuthbert, B., Krystal, J. H., Malison, R., Offord, D. R., et al. (2002). Personality disorders and relational disorders: A research agenda for addressing crucial gaps in DSM. In D. J. Kupfer, M. B. First, & D. A. Regier (Eds.), *A research agenda for DSM-V* (pp. 123–199). Washington, DC: American Psychiatric Association.

Frances, A. J. (1980). The DSM-III personality disorders section: A commentary. *American Journal of Psychiatry, 137,* 1050–1054.

Frances, A. J., First, M. B., & Pincus, H. A. (1995). *DSM-IV guidebook.* Washington, DC: American Psychiatric Press.

Frances, A. J., First, M. B., Widiger, T. A., Miele, G., Tilly, S. M., Davis, W. W., et al. (1991). An A to Z guide to DSM-IV conundrums. *Journal of Abnormal Psychology, 100,* 407–412.

Gunderson, J. G. (1992). Diagnostic controversies. In A. Tasman & M. B. Riba (Eds.), *Review of psychiatry* (Vol. 11, pp. 9–24). Washington, DC: American Psychiatric Press.

Hare, R. D. (2003). *Hare Psychopathy Checklist—Revised (PCL-R) technical manual.* North Tonawanda, NY: Multi-Health Systems.

Harkness, A. R., McNulty, J. L., & Ben-Porath, Y. S. (1995). The Personality Psychopathology Five (PSY-5): Constructs and MMPI-2 scales. *Psychological Assessment, 7,* 104–114.

Herkov, M. J., & Blashfield, R. K. (1995). Clinicians' diagnoses of personality disorder: Evidence of a hierarchical structure. *Journal of Personality Assessment, 65,* 313–321.

Hyman, S. (2002). Neuroscience, genetics, and the future of psychiatric diagnosis. *Psychopathology, 35,* 139–144.

John, O. P., & Srivastava, S. (1999). The Big Five trait taxonomy: History, measurement, and theoretical perspectives. In L. A. Pervin & O. P. John (Eds.), *Handbook of personality: Theory and research* (2nd ed., pp. 102–138). New York: Guilford Press.

Larstone, R. M., Jang, K. L., Livesley, W. J., Vernon, P. A., & Wolf, H. (2002). The relationship between Eysenck's P-E-N model of personality, the five-factor model of personality, and traits delineating personality dysfunction. *Personality and Individual Differences, 33,* 25–37.

Leichsenring, F., & Leibing, E. (2003). The effectiveness of psychodynamic therapy and cognitive behavior therapy in the treatment of personality disorders: A meta-analysis. *American Journal of Psychiatry, 160,* 1223–1232.

Liebowitz, M. R., Barlow, D. H., Ballenger, J. C., Davidson, J., Foa, E. B., Fyer, A. J., et al. (1998). DSM-IV anxiety disorders: Final overview. In T. A. Widiger, A. J. Frances, H. A. Pincus, R. Ross, M. B. First, W. Davis, et al. (Eds.), *DSM-IV sourcebook* (Vol. 4, pp. 1047–1076). Washington, DC: American Psychiatric Association.

Lilienfeld, S. O., Waldman, I. D., & Israel, A. C. (1994). A critical examination of the use of the term "comorbidity" in psychopathology research. *Clinical Psychology: Science and Practice, 1,* 71–83.

Livesley, W. J. (2003). Diagnostic dilemmas in classifying personality disorder. In K. A. Phillips, M. B. First, & H. A. Pincus (Eds.), *Advancing DSM: Dilemmas in psychiatric diagnosis* (pp. 153–190). Washington, DC: American Psychiatric Association.

Markon, K.E., Krueger, R. F., & Watson, D. (2005). Delineating the structure of normal and abnormal personality: An integrative hierarchical approach. *Journal of Personality and Social Psychology, 88,* 139–157.

Maser, J. D., Kaelber, C., & Weise, R. F. (1991). International use and attitudes toward DSM-III and DSM-III-R: Growing consensus in psychiatric classification. *Journal of Abnormal Psychology, 100,* 271–279.

McCrae, R. R., Terracciano, A., & 78 Members of the Personality Profiles of Cultures Project. (2005). Universal features of personality traits from the observer's perspective: Data from 50 cultures. *Journal of Personality and Social Psychology, 88,* 547–561.

Mellsop, G., Varghese, F., Joshua, S., & Hicks, A. (1982). Reliability of Axis II of DSM-III. *American Journal of Psychiatry, 139,* 1360–1361.

Mervielde, I., De Clercq, B., De Fruyt, F., & Van Leeuwen, K. (2005). Temperament, personality, and developmental psychopathology as childhood antecedents of personality disorders. *Journal of Personality Disorders, 19,* 171–201.

Miller, M. B., Useda, J. D., Trull, T. J., Burr, R. M., & Minks-Brown, C. (2001). Paranoid, schizoid, and schizotypal personality disorders. In P. B. Sutker & H. E. Adams (Eds.), *Comprehensive handbook of psychopathology* (3rd ed., pp. 535–558). New York: Plenum.

Millon, T., Davis, R. D., Millon, C. M., Wenger, A. W., Van Zuilen, M. H., Fuchs, M., et al. (1996). *Disorders of personality: DSM-IV and beyond.* New York: Wiley.

Narrow, W. E., Rae, D. S., Robins, L. N., & Regier, D. A. (2002). Revised prevalence estimates of mental disorders in the United States: Using a clinical significance criterion to reconcile 2 surveys' estimates. *Archives of General Psychiatry, 59,* 115–123.

Nathan, P. E., & Langenbucher, J. W. (1999). Psychopathology: Description and classification. *Annual Review of Psychology, 50,* 79–107.

Nazikian, H., Rudd, R. P., Edwards, J., & Jackson, H. J. (1990). Personality disorder assessments for psychiatric inpatients. *Australian and New Zealand Journal of Psychiatry, 24,* 37–46.

Oldham, J. M., & Skodol, A. E. (2000). Charting the future of Axis II. *Journal of Personality Disorders, 14,* 17–29.

Perry, J. C., Banon, E., & Ianni, F. (1999). Effectiveness of psychotherapy for personality disorders. *American Journal of Psychiatry, 156,* 1312–1321.

Pincus, A. L., & Gurtman, M. B. (2006). Interpersonal theory and the interpersonal circumplex: Evolving perspectives on normal and abnormal personality. In S. Strack (Ed.), *Differentiating normal and abnormal personality* (2nd ed., pp. 83–111). New York: Springer.

Pincus, H. A., McQueen, L. E., & Elinson, L. (2003). Subthreshold mental disorders: Nosological and research recommendations. In K. A. Phillips, M. B. First, & H. A. Pincus (Eds.), *Advancing DSM: Dilemmas in psychiatric diagnosis* (pp. 129–144). Washington, DC: American Psychiatric Association.

Raine, A. (2006). Schizotypal personality: Neurodevelopmental and psychosocial trajectories. *Annual Review of Clinical Psychology, 2,* 291–326.

Roberts, B. W., & DelVecchio, W. F. (2000). The rank-order consistency of personality traits from childhood to old age: A quantitative review of longitudinal studies. *Psychological Bulletin, 126,* 3–25.

Robins, E., & Guze, S. B. (1970). Establishment of diagnostic validity in psychiatric illness: Its application to schizophrenia. *American Journal of Psychiatry, 126,* 107–111.

Rogers, R. (2003). Standardizing DSM-IV diagnoses: The clinical applications of structured interviews. *Journal of Personality Assessment, 81,* 220–225.

Ronningstam, E. (2005). Narcissistic personality disorder: A review. In M. Maj, H. S. Akiskal, J. E. Mezzich, & A. Okasha (Eds.), *Personality disorders* (pp. 277–327). New York: Wiley.

Rounsaville, B. J., Alarcon, R. D., Andrews, G., Jackson, J. S., Kendell, R. E., & Kendler, K. (2002). Basic nomenclature issues for DSM-V. In D. J. Kupfer, M. B. First, & D. E. Regier (Eds.), *A research agenda for DSM-V* (pp. 1–29). Washington, DC: American Psychiatric Association.

Samuel, D. B., & Widiger, T. A. (2006). Differentiating normal and abnormal personality from the perspective of the DSM. In S. Strack (Ed.), *Differentiating normal and abnormal personality* (2nd ed., pp. 165–183). New York: Springer.

Sanderson, C., & Clarkin, J. F. (2002). Further use of the NEO-PI-R personality dimensions in differential treatment planning. In P. T. Costa, Jr., & T. A. Widiger (Eds.), *Personality disorders and the five-factor model of personality* (2nd ed., pp. 351–375). Washington, DC: American Psychological Association.

Schinka, J. A, Busch, R. M., & Robichaux-Keene, N. (2004). A meta-analysis of the association between the serotonin transporter gene polymorphism (5-HTTLPR) and trait anxiety. *Molecular Psychiatry, 9,* 197–202.

Sen, S., Burmeister, M., & Ghosh, D. (2004). Meta-analysis of the association between a serotonin transporter polymorphism (5-HTTLPR) and anxiety-related personality traits. *American Journal of Medical Genetics: Part B, 127B,* 85–89.

Shedler, J. (2002). A new language for psychoanalytic diagnosis. *Journal of the American Psychoanalytic Association, 50,* 429–456.

Shedler, J., & Westen, D. (2004). Dimensions of personality pathology: An alternative to the five-factor model. *American Journal of Psychiatry, 161,* 1743–1754.

Shiner, R. L., & Caspi, A. (2003). Personality differences in childhood and adolescence: Measurement, development, and consequences. *Journal of Child Psychology and Psychiatry, 44,* 2–32.

Siever, L. J., & Davis, K. L. (1991). A psychobiological perspective on the personality disorders. *American Journal of Psychiatry, 148,* 1647–1658.

Skeem, J. L., Poythress, N., Edens, J. F., Lilienfeld, S. O., & Cale, E. M. (2003). Psychopathic personality or personalities? Exploring potential variants of psychopathy and their implications for risk assessment. *Aggression and Violent Behavior, 8,* 513–546.

Smith, G. T. (2005). On the complexity of quantifying construct validity. *Psychological Assessment, 17,* 413–414.

Spitzer, R., Endicott, J., & Gibbon, M. (1979). Crossing the border into borderline personality and borderline schizophrenia. *Archives of General Psychiatry, 36,* 17–24.

Spitzer, R. L., Forman, J. B. W., & Nee, J. (1979). DSM-III field trials: I. Initial inter-rater diagnostic reliability. *American Journal of Psychiatry, 136,* 815–817.

Spitzer, R. L., Williams, J. B. W., & Skodol, A. E. (1980). DSM-III: The major achievements and an overview. *American Journal of Psychiatry, 137,* 151–164.

Tellegen, A. (1982). *Brief manual for the Multidimensional Personality Questionnaire.* Unpublished manuscript, University of Minnesota, Minneapolis.

Trull, T. J. (2005). Dimensional models of personality disorder: Coverage and cut-offs. *Journal of Personality Disorders, 19,* 262–282.

Trull, T. J., & Durrett, C. A. (2005). Categorical and dimensional models of personality disorder. *Annual Review of Clinical Psychology, 1,* 355–380.

Tyrer, P., & Johnson, T. (1996). Establishing the severity of personality disorder. *American Journal of Psychiatry, 153,* 1593–1597.

Verheul, R. (2005). Clinical utility for dimensional models of personality pathology. *Journal of Personality Disorders, 19,* 283–302. .

Verheul, R., & Widiger, T. A. (2004). A meta-analysis of the prevalence and usage of the personality disorder not otherwise specified (PDNOS) diagnosis. *Journal of Personality Disorders, 18,* 309–319.

Watson, D. (2005). Rethinking the mood and anxiety disorders: A quantitative hier-archical model for DSM-V. *Journal of Abnormal Psychology, 114,* 522–536.

Westen, D., & Arkowitz-Westen, L. (1998). Limitations of Axis II in diagnosing personality pathology in clinical practice. *American Journal of Psychiatry, 155,* 1767–1771.

Westen, D., & Shedler, J. (1999a). Revising and assessing Axis II, Part I: Developing a clinically and empirically valid assessment method. *American Journal of Psychiatry, 156,* 258–272.

Westen, D., & Shedler, J. (1999b). Revising and assessing Axis II, Part II: Toward an empirically based and clinically useful classification of personality disorders. *American Journal of Psychiatry, 156,* 273–285.

Westen, D., & Shedler, J. (2000). A prototype matching approach to diagnosing personality disorders: Toward DSM-V. *Journal of Personality Disorders, 14,* 109–126.

Westen, D., Shedler, J., & Bradley, R. (2006). A prototype approach to personality disorder diagnosis. *American Journal of Psychiatry, 163,* 846–856.

Westen, D., Shedler, J., Durrett, C., Glass, S., & Martens, A. (2003). Personality diagnoses in adolescence: DSM-IV Axis II diagnoses and an empirically derived alternative. *American Journal of Psychiatry, 160,* 952–966.

Widiger, T. A. (2003). Personality disorder and Axis I psychopathology: The problematic boundary of Axis I and Axis II. *Journal of Personality Disorders, 17,* 90–108.

Widiger, T. A., & Clark, L. A. (2000). Toward DSM-V and the classification of psychopathology. *Psychological Bulletin, 126,* 946–963.

Widiger, T. A., Costa, P. T., Jr., & McCrae, R. R. (2002). A proposal for Axis II: Diagnosing personality disorders using the five-factor model. In P. T. Costa, Jr., & T. A. Widiger (Eds.), *Personality disorders and the five-factor model of personality* (2nd ed., pp. 431–456). Washington, DC: American Psychological Association.

Widiger, T., Frances, A., Spitzer, R., & Williams, J. (1988). The DSM-III-R personality disorders: An overview. *American Journal of Psychiatry, 145,* 786–795.

Widiger, T. A., & Mullins-Sweatt, S. (2005). Categorical and dimensional models of personality disorder. In J. Oldham, A. Skodol, & D. Bender (Eds.), *Textbook of personality disorders* (pp. 35–53). Washington, DC: American Psychiatric Press.

Widiger, T. A., & Samuel, D. B. (2005a). Diagnostic categories or dimensions: A question for DSM-V. *Journal of Abnormal Psychology, 114,* 494–504.

Widiger, T. A., & Samuel, D. B. (2005b). Evidence-based assessment of personality disorders. *Psychological Assessment, 17,* 278–287.

Widiger, T. A., & Sanderson, C. J. (1995). Toward a dimensional model of personality disorders in DSM-IV and DSM-V. In W. J. Livesley (Ed.), *The DSM-IV personality disorders* (pp. 433–458). New York: Guilford Press.

Widiger, T. A., & Simonsen, E. (2005a). Alternative dimensional models of personality disorder: Finding a common ground. *Journal of Personality Disorders, 19,* 110–130.

Widiger, T. A., & Simonsen, E. (2005b). The American Psychiatric Association's research agenda for the DSM-V. *Journal of Personality Disorders, 19,* 103–109.

Widiger, T. A., Simonsen, E., Krueger, R., Livesley, J., & Verheul, R. (2005). Personality disorder research agenda for the DSM-V. *Journal of Personality Disorders, 19,* 317–340.

Widiger, T. A., & Trull, T. J. (1998). Performance characteristics of the DSM-III-R personality disorder criteria sets. In T. A. Widiger, A. J. Frances, H. A. Pincus, R. Ross, M. B. First, W. W. Davis, et al. (Eds.), *DSM-IV sourcebook* (Vol. 4., pp. 357–373). Washington, DC: American Psychiatric Association.

Wood, J. M., Garb, H. N., Lilienfeld, S. O., & Nezworski, M. T. (2002). Clinical assessment. *Annual Review of Psychology, 53,* 519–543.

World Health Organization. (1992). *The ICD-10 classification of mental and behavioural disorders: Clinical descriptions and diagnostic guidelines.* Geneva, Switzerland: Author.

Yamagata, S., Suzuki, A., Ando, J., One, Y., Kijimi, N., Yoshimura, K., et al. (2006). Is the genetic structure of human personality universal? A cross-cultural twin study from North America, Europe, and Asia. *Journal of Personality and Social Psychology, 90,* 987–998.

Zimmerman, M. (2003). What should the standard of care for psychiatric diagnostic evaluations be? *Journal of Nervous and Mental Disease, 191,* 281–286.

Zimmerman, M., & Mattia, J. I. (1999a). Differences between clinical and research practices in diagnosing borderline personality disorder. *American Journal of Psychiatry, 156,* 1570–1574.

Zimmerman, M., & Mattia, J. I. (1999b). Psychiatric diagnosis in clinical practice: Is comorbidity being missed? *Comprehensive Psychiatry, 40,* 182–191.

Zuckerman, M. (2002). Zuckerman-Kuhlman Personality Questionnaire (ZKPQ): An alternative five-factorial model. In B. de Raad & M. Perugini (Eds.), *Big Five assessment* (pp. 377–397). Kirkland, WA: Hogrefe & Huber.

3

Paranoid Personality Disorder

David P. Bernstein

Maastricht University

J. David Useda

University of Rochester School of Medicine

Description of the Disorder

Paranoid personality disorder (PPD) is characterized by a pervasive mistrust of other people (American Psychiatric Association [APA], 1994; Bernstein, Useda, & Siever, 1995; Miller, Useda, Trull, Burr, & Minks-Brown, 2001). Other common features of the disorder include quarrelsomeness, hostility, emotional coldness, hypersensitivity to slights or criticism, stubbornness, and rigidly held maladaptive beliefs of others' intents (APA, 1994; Bernstein et al., 1995; Miller et al., 2001). The prototypical picture is of someone who is preoccupied with real or imagined slights or threats, mistrusts the intentions or motives of others, and rarely trusts the seemingly benign appearance of things. The guiding underlying assumption is that others are malevolent—they can betray, hurt, take advantage, or humiliate. Thus, measures must be taken to protect oneself—by keeping one's distance from other people, not appearing weak or vulnerable, searching for signs of threat even in seemingly innocuous situations, preemptively attacking others who are viewed as threatening, and vigorously counterattacking when threatened or provoked. People with paranoid personality disorder tend to hold grudges, have "enemies," are often litigious, and can be pathologically jealous, preoccupied with their partner's supposed sexual infidelities. Thus, in many respects, their antagonistic behavior exemplifies one extreme pole of the agreeableness-antagonism dimension of the five-factor model of personality (Widiger, Trull, Clarkin, Sanderson, & Costa, 2002).

41

Not surprisingly, this pattern of antagonistic behavior often causes difficulties in interpersonal relationships, including provocation of the very kinds of attacks these individuals fear. For example, people with paranoid personality disorder may correctly deduce that others are speaking ill of them or plotting against them behind their backs, but they do not recognize that this may be a consequence of their own antagonistic behavior. It is important to note, however, that people with paranoid personality disorder are usually not frankly psychotic, although they may experience transient psychotic-like symptoms under conditions of extreme stress (Miller et al., 2001). Unlike the symptoms of psychotic disorders such as paranoid schizophrenia and delusional disorder, in which a frank break with reality has occurred, the unfounded beliefs in paranoid personality disorder are rarely of psychotic proportions. Thus someone with paranoid personality disorder may believe without cause that coworkers are harassing him, for example, when he receives a call with no one responding on the other end. However, he is not likely to believe that the CIA is plotting against him. Thus his beliefs are plausible but often unfounded.

CASE EXAMPLE

A woman believed, without cause, that her neighbors were harassing her by allowing their young children to make loud noise outside her apartment door. Rather than asking the neighbors to be more considerate, she stopped speaking to them and began a campaign of unceasingly antagonistic behavior: giving them "dirty looks," pushing past them aggressively in the hallway, slamming doors, and behaving rudely toward their visitors. After over a year had passed, when the neighbors finally confronted her about her obnoxious behavior, she accused them of purposely harassing her. "Everyone knows that these doors are paper thin," she said, "and that I can hear everything that goes on in the hallway. You are doing it deliberately." Nothing that the neighbors said could convince her otherwise. Despite their attempts to be more considerate about the noise outside her apartment, she continued to behave in a rude and aggressive manner toward them.

Neighbors and visitors commented that the woman appeared tense and angry. Her face looked like a hard mask. She was rarely seen smiling. She walked around the neighborhood wearing dark sunglasses, even on cloudy days. She was often seen yelling at her children, behavior that had earned her the nickname "the screamer" among the parents at her children's school. She had forced her children to change schools several times within the same district because she was dissatisfied with the education they were receiving. An unstated reason, perhaps, was that she had alienated so many other parents. She worked at home during the day at a job that required her to have little contact with other people. She had few social contacts, and in conversation was often perceived to be sarcastic and hypercritical.

This case illustrates some of the central features of PPD according to the DSM-IV (APA, 1994), including the paranoid person's unwavering belief that others are out to harm her (PPD criterion 1), tendency to read malevolent intentions into otherwise benign events (PPD criterion 4), and persistence in holding grudges (PPD criterion 5). Many of the associated features of the disorder are also evident, including the paranoid person's tension and hostility, aloofness, hypercriticalness, and tendency to provoke reactions in other people that confirm her conviction that others can't be trusted.

Differential Diagnosis

PPD must be distinguished from other disorders involving paranoia, particularly paranoid schizophrenia and delusional disorder (APA, 1994). Unlike PPD, paranoid schizophrenia and delusional disorder involve frank delusions—that is, false beliefs of psychotic proportions. However, the presence of such beliefs is not always evident, as paranoid persons may take pains to hide such "crazy" beliefs from others. Moreover, the unwarranted beliefs of someone with PPD are not always so easy to distinguish from true delusions. In the above case, for example, the differential diagnosis would become easier if the woman began to accuse her neighbors of bugging her telephone, intercepting and opening her mail, surreptitiously breaking into her apartment, and so forth. Although such suspicions are not bizarre, they are of such an extreme nature that they suggest a delusional process may be present.

Finally, people with PPD sometimes develop transient delusions when under extreme stress (Miller et al., 2001). For example, a man with longstanding PPD developed lung cancer. Shortly after receiving the diagnosis, he developed the unfounded belief that his brothers, with whom he worked in a family business, were trying to swindle him, and cut off relations with them. His delusions did not appear to have a neurological basis: they occurred in the absence of delirium and other neurological complications due to the illness, and prior to his beginning medical treatment with radiation and chemotherapy. After his medical condition stabilized and he began taking antidepressant medication, this belief eventually disappeared and was never spoken about again.

PPD must also be distinguished from other personality disorders that share overlapping diagnostic features, particularly the other Cluster A personality disorders: schizotypal personality disorder, which can also be characterized by suspiciousness or paranoid ideation (schizotypal criterion 5), and schizoid personality disorder, which can also be characterized by aloofness (schizoid criteria 2 and 5) and emotional coldness (schizoid criterion 7; APA, 1994; Bernstein et al., 1995; Miller et al., 2001). However, schizotypal individuals display odd or eccentric ideas, peculiar thinking or speech, unusual perceptual experiences, and other "schizophrenia-like" features that are not seen in PPD. Schizoid individuals, on the other hand, are socially withdrawn because of a preference for being alone rather than a desire to protect themselves from imagined threats.

PPD also shows a high degree of content overlap with personality disorders outside of Cluster A, particularly borderline (e.g., criterion 8, "inappropriate, intense anger," and criterion 9, "transient, stress-related paranoid ideation"), narcissistic (e.g., criterion 9, "arrogant and haughty"), and avoidant (e.g., criterion 1, "avoids occupational activities involving significant interpersonal contact," criterion 3, "shows restraint within interpersonal relationships because of fear of being shamed or ridiculed," and criterion 4, "is preoccupied with being criticized or rejected") personality disorders (APA, 1994; Bernstein et al., 1995; Miller et al., 2001).

Outstanding Issues

There is a paucity of empirical literature on PPD, despite the fact that this disorder is easily recognized and has long been described in the clinical and theoretical literature (Millon & Davis, 1996). Ten years ago, when we first reviewed the literature on paranoid personality disorder, we noted a similar state of affairs (Bernstein, Useda, & Siever, 1993; Bernstein et al., 1995). Over the past 10 years, the most notable developments have been a promising new questionnaire for PPD (Useda, 2002) and some interesting but inconclusive research findings on the question of whether PPD is a schizophrenia spectrum disorder (Asarnow et al., 2001; Nicolson et al., 2003). Otherwise, the literature on PPD during this period has consisted mostly of single-case studies and some theoretical articles written from a psychoanalytic object relations perspective. This is a pity, because PPD deserves greater attention.

The costs of PPD include disruptive behavior in the workplace, unnecessary litigation, relationship problems (e.g., pathological jealousy), violence (e.g., stalking), and increased psychiatric comorbidities (Miller et al., 2001). PPD patients are seen in a variety of clinical populations, and they can pose special problems for treatment when their mistrust affects the therapeutic relationship (Miller et al., 2001). Nevertheless, in our own experience, some PPD patients can achieve good therapeutic outcomes when they are given treatments appropriate to their problems (see "What Kinds of Treatments Are Likely to Be Most Effective for People With PPD?" below). Thus, there is a need for more research on PPD, including both fundamental studies (e.g., phenomenological, epidemiological, longitudinal, and laboratorial) and studies of promising assessment and treatment approaches. We hope that this chapter will stimulate more researchers to study this important but still poorly understood personality disorder.

This chapter is organized around the following unanswered questions about PPD:

Are the DSM-IV criteria for PPD valid descriptors of the disorder?

What theoretical models might explain the features of PPD?

Is PPD a true category or a dimension that cuts across categories?

Is PPD a schizophrenia-spectrum or delusional-spectrum disorder?

Which environmental factors might contribute to the development of PPD?

What is the most accurate means of assessing PPD?

What kinds of treatments are likely to be most effective for people with PPD?

Descriptive and Theoretical Issues

Are the DSM-IV Criteria for PPD Valid Descriptors of the Disorder?

Paranoid phenomena have long been described in the clinical and theoretical literature (Millon & Davis, 1996). By the end of the 19th century, clinicians recognized that paranoid phenomena could manifest themselves in a variety of forms and psychiatric contexts, from the frank persecutory beliefs and delusions systems often seen in schizophrenia to more subtle and circumscribed forms of paranoia (Millon & Davis, 1996). Kraepelin's (1921) seminal nosology of psychiatric disorders described three types of paranoid conditions resembling today's conceptualizations of paranoid schizophrenia, delusional disorder, and paranoid personality disorder, respectively. Most relevant to the present discussion, Kraepelin recognized that some individuals displayed milder paranoid phenomena characterized by fixed delusions but without the hallucinations and chronic deterioration of personality seen in dementia praecox (i.e., schizophrenia). A long-standing debate, which continues to this day, centers on the question of whether less severe paranoid disorders, such as PPD and delusional disorder, lie on a genetic continuum with schizophrenia, or whether they form a paranoid spectrum distinct from that of schizophrenia (Asarnow et al., 2001; Coryell & Zimmerman, 1989; Kendler & Gruenberg, 1982; Kendler, Masterson, & Davis, 1985; Maier, Lichtermann, Minges, & Heun, 1994; Nicolson et al., 2003).

A diagnostic term for paranoid personality disorder has existed in the psychiatric nomenclature of the United States since 1952 (APA, 1952) and has been included in every edition of the DSM. DSM-III (APA, 1980) and subsequent editions of the DSM recognized three personality disorders characterized by oddness and eccentricity: paranoid, schizoid, and schizotypal personality disorders. The description of schizotypal personality was based largely on features—such as suspiciousness, peculiar ideation, and peculiar interpersonal behavior—seen in the biological relatives of schizophrenics in the Danish Adoption Study of the 1960s (Kety, Rosenthal, Wender, & Schulsinger, 1968). Thus from its inception, schizotypal personality disorder was conceptualized as a schizophrenia spectrum disorder. Although individuals with PPD are sometimes seen among the relatives of schizophrenic probands, the genetic connection between PPD and schizophrenia remains an open question (see below).

The six main traits associated with PPD, as described in the extensive clinical and theoretical literature on PPD (Cameron, 1943, 1963; Kraepelin, 1921; Kretschmer, 1925; Millon, 1969, 1981; Shapiro, 1965; Sheldon, 1940; Sheldon & Stevens, 1942; Turkat, 1985) and by the DSM-IV's Associated Features section (APA, 1994), are mistrust/suspiciousness, antagonism/aggressiveness, introversion/excessive autonomy, hypersensitivity, hypervigilance, and rigidity. Mistrust/suspiciousness is a lack of trust in others. PPD individuals question the loyalty or truthfulness of other people and are prone to think that others are "out to get them" and to respond defensively. Hypersensitivity is one's tendency to perceive others' remarks or comments as attacks or criticisms directed against oneself, one's beliefs, or one's performance of a task. PPD individuals tend to believe that others are judging them negatively, and, in response, they tend to experience anger and anxiety. Antagonism/aggressiveness is a tendency to feel angry, to be combative toward others, and to view others and the world as hostile. Introversion/excessive autonomy is a tendency to distance oneself from others, remain aloof, and feel tense around others. Hypervigilance is a tendency to continually scan the environment in an attempt to confirm hypotheses about the malevolent intentions or motives of others. Rigidity is a personality trait in which an individual's beliefs, behavior, and affective style are not readily open to questioning or change.

The DSM-IV criteria for PPD, however, appear to overrepresent the cognitive PPD trait mistrust/suspiciousness and to underrepresent the prototypical behavioral, affective, and interpersonal expressions of paranoid personality traits (Table 3.1). As is evident from Table 3.1, nearly all of the DSM-IV PPD criteria (six of seven) reflect the cognitive trait of mistrust/suspiciousness. Three of the seven DSM-IV criteria reflect the affective/interpersonal trait of hypersensitivity; two reflect the affective/interpersonal trait of antagonism; two reflect the cognitive trait of hypervigilance; one reflects the interpersonal trait of introversion; and one reflects the cognitive trait of rigidity. Thus the DSM-IV criteria mainly reflect the cognitive features of PPD, especially mistrust/suspiciousness, and poorly represent the other primary traits that have long been thought to underlie the disorder. Ironically, a sample selected on the basis of DSM-IV criteria without additional assessment would not be representative of PPD as it is represented in the DSM-IV's own description (i.e., in the Associated Features section for PPD) or in the clinical literature specific to PPD. For this reason, the diagnostic criteria for PPD appear to be greatly in need of revision.

Table 3.1   Correspondence of DSM-IV PPD diagnostic criteria to the primary traits of PPD

Individuals Exhibit the DSM-IV Diagnostic Criteria for PPD When They . . .	Does This Behavior Correspond to the Six Main Traits Associated With PPD?					
	Mistrust/ Suspiciousness	Antagonism/ Aggressiveness	Introversion/ Excessive Autonomy	Hyper- sensitivity	Hyper- vigilance	Rigidity
1. Suspect that others exploit, harm, or deceive	Yes	No	No	No	No	No
2. Doubt others' loyalty or trustworthiness	Yes	No	No	No	No	No
3. Are reluctant to confide in others for fear that information will be used against them	Yes	No	Yes	No	No	No
4. Read hidden or demeaning meanings into benign remarks or events	Yes	No	No	Yes	Yes	No
5. Bear grudges (i.e., are unforgiving of insults, injuries, or slights)	No	Yes	No	Yes	No	Yes
6. Perceive attacks on their character or reputation and are quick to react with anger or counterattack	Yes	Yes	No	Yes	Yes	No
7. Have recurrent suspicions of their partner's sexual infidelity	Yes	No	No	Yes	No	No

SOURCE: Reprinted with permission from the *Diagnostic and Statistical Manual of Mental Disorders,* Fourth Edition, Text Revision, (Copyright 2000). American Psychiatric Association.

For the DSM-V, we recommend that the PPD criteria be substantially revised to reflect the primary traits underlying the disorder in a more balanced and proportionate manner. Such a revision should result in greater diagnostic validity for PPD and may reduce the now considerable diagnostic overlap between PPD and other Axis II disorders that share some paranoid features (e.g., borderline, schizotypal, narcissistic, and avoidant personality disorders). An improved PPD criteria set would have important ramifications for this underresearched and often clinically neglected personality disorder. For one thing, it would lead to more accurate selection of PPD cases for research purposes. For example, diagnostic criteria that more accurately reflect the phenotype of PPD would be of considerable benefit for future family/genetics studies, including studies that seek to identify a schizophrenia-spectrum or delusional-spectrum genotype. From a clinical perspective, criteria that better reflect the underlying traits of PPD should lead to better assessment and, as everyone hopes, better treatment of PPD. A self-report questionnaire assessing these revised criteria, the Paranoid Personality Disorder Features Questionnaire (Useda, 2002), has recently been developed and has shown promising initial evidence of reliability and validity (see below).

What Theoretical Models Might Explain the Features of PPD?

Traditional psychoanalytic models of PPD have focused on the defense mechanism of projection: that is, the disavowing of one's own aggressive feelings and thoughts by projecting them onto another person (e.g., "I'm not feeling hostile toward you; you are feeling hostile toward me!" Vaillant, 1994). Despite controversy over the validity of the concept of projection (Holmes, 1978), there is considerable empirical support for the notion that patients with severe personality disorders employ projection and other maladaptive defenses. For example, studies using both self-rated and clinician-rated measures of defensive style have found that the use of projection as a defense is highly associated with severe personality disorders, including paranoid, borderline, and antisocial personality disorders (Drake & Vaillant, 1985; Koenigsberg et al., 2001; Lingiardi et al., 1999; Paris, Zweig-Frank, Bond, & Guzder, 1996). Moreover, improvements in maladaptive defenses such as projection predict the outcome of psychodynamic psychotherapy over and above other predictors, including the severity of pretreatment psychopathology (Bond & Perry, 2004).

However, paranoid phenomena may also be explained using more contemporary cognitive processing models (Williams, Watts, MacLeod, & Mathews, 1997). For example, the misattributions of people with PPD (e.g., reading malevolent intentions into benign remarks or events) may be understood in terms of characteristic cognitive biases (Williams et al., 1997), including attentional biases (e.g., overfocusing on possible signs of threat), interpretative biases (e.g., misinterpreting innocuous comments or behavior as malevolent), and memory biases (e.g., dwelling on past slights or insults). Such cognitive processing models have the advantage of being amenable to empirical testing using standardized laboratory procedures. Moreover, the development of cognitive models has led to more effective forms of cognitive therapy for disorders, such as social phobia, that, like PPD, are characterized by misinterpretation of social cues (Bögels & Mansell, 2004). Because cognitive schemas, such as the conviction that others are not trustworthy, appear to be so central to PPD pathology (Beck, Freeman, & Associates, 1990), cognitive information processing models may prove to be highly fruitful in terms of our understanding and treating this difficult disorder.

Beck and his colleagues (1990) have argued that the core cognitive schemas in PPD concern feelings of inadequacy. These feelings of inadequacy, in combination with poor social skills and the external attribution of blame as a means of reducing anxiety, account for the features of PPD. In some respects, the cognitive biases in PPD described by Beck and his colleagues (1990) resemble those in social phobia, which is also characterized by feelings of inadequacy and the overfocusing on and misinterpretation of social cues (Bögels & Mansell, 2004). Unlike social phobics, however, who are painfully aware of their feelings of adequacy and dwell on their past social blunders, people with PPD attribute the *cause* of their feelings of inadequacy to others ("I am not inferior; you are trying to make me feel inferior!"). Thus, the central interpretative bias in PPD appears to be a causal misattribution or externalization of blame onto other people (Beck et al., 1990). Rather than dwelling on their past social mistakes, as in social phobia, people with PPD ruminate on the injuries and injustices others have caused them. Beck and his colleagues' cognitive model of PPD appears to be a useful one that warrants empirical investigation.

Another potentially useful model is the integrative cognitive model of Jeffrey Young (Bernstein, 2005; Young, Klosko, & Weishaar, 2003). Young has posited that early maladaptive schemas (i.e., chronic, repetitive self-defeating themes or patterns originating in adverse childhood experiences and early temperament), schema modes (i.e., transient state–related patterns of schematic activation), and maladaptive coping mechanisms (i.e., maladaptive ways of coping with schematic activation) are the conceptual core of personality disorders. Young has identified 18 specific early maladaptive schemas (e.g., defectiveness, abandonment, emotional deprivation) as well as a variety of schema modes and three broad forms of maladaptive coping (i.e., schema surrender, schema avoidance, and schema overcompensation). Young and his colleagues have developed an integrative psychotherapy for personality disorders, schema therapy, which targets these maladaptive beliefs and coping mechanisms (Young et al., 2003). In a recent 3-year randomized clinical trial in the Netherlands, schema therapy produced substantial reductions in the features of borderline personality disorder, including improvements in the core personality characteristics (e.g., identity disturbance, unstable relationships) and behavioral features of the disorder (e.g., suicidal and parasuicidal behavior; Giesen-Bloo, Arntz, van Dyck, Spinhoven, & van Tilburg, 2004). A randomized clinical trial of the efficacy of schema therapy for PPD and other personality disorders (e.g., narcissistic, obsessive-compulsive, avoidant) is currently under way in the Netherlands (A. Arntz, personal communication, November 10, 2005).

Factor-analytic studies of the Young Schema Questionnaire, a self-report measure of early maladaptive schemas, have supported the validity of nearly all of the 18 early maladaptive schemas proposed by Young (Schmidt, Joiner, Young, & Telch, 1995; Waller, Meyer, & Ohanian, 2001). Retrospective studies have also found that early maladaptive schemas are associated with etiologic factors hypothesized by Young, such as childhood trauma and insecure attachment, in both clinical and nonclinical samples (Cecero, Nelson, & Gillie, 2004; Leung, Thomas, & Waller, 2000; Waller, Meyer, Ohanian, Elliott, et al., 2001). Thus empirical research on the schema therapy model, though still in its early stages, supports the construct validity of early maladaptive schemas and related concepts.

Young has not applied his model specifically to PPD. However, the early maladaptive schemas that appear most relevant to PPD are defectiveness/ shame, abuse/mistrust, and vulnerability to harm. Thus the person with PPD has deep feelings of inferiority and inadequacy (i.e., defectiveness); anticipates that others are out to harm, exploit, or humiliate him (i.e., abuse/ mistrust); and feels fundamentally unsafe in the world (i.e., vulnerability to harm). As a result, he adopts a belligerent, overcompensating form of coping: he presents a hostile, aggressive face toward others, remains vigilant to possible attacks, and preemptively attacks or counterattacks in situations where he feels that he will be, or has been, harmed. Young's model would also posit that these early maladaptive schemas, schema modes, and maladaptive coping responses have their origins in childhood experiences, such as early experiences of abuse or neglect. Like Beck and his colleagues' (1990) model, Young's model (Young et al., 2003) appears to hold considerable promise for aiding our understanding of the cognitive mechanisms in PPD and is worthy of empirical investigation.

Empirical Issues

Although PPD has a long history in the clinical and theoretical literature (Cameron, 1943, 1963; Kraepelin, 1921; Kretschmer, 1925; Millon, 1969, 1981; Shapiro, 1965; Sheldon, 1940; Sheldon & Stevens, 1942; Turkat, 1985), research to date has provided only limited information about the course, family history, and treatment of this severe personality disorder.

Prevalence. The prevalence of PPD appears to range from about 0.5% to 2.5% in the general population, from about 2% to 10% in psychiatric outpatient settings, and from about 10% to 30% in psychiatric inpatient settings (APA, 1994; Bernstein, Useda, et al., 1993; Bernstein et al., 1995; Miller et al., 2001). However, these epidemiological data were based on DSM-III or DSM-III-R criteria for PPD; no more recent data on the population prevalence of PPD based on DSM-IV criteria are available. PPD has been found to be more prevalent among males than among females in clinical samples (APA, 1994; Bernstein, Useda, et al., 1993; Bernstein et al., 1995; Miller et al., 2001).

Longitudinal Course. There is scant evidence regarding the longitudinal course of PPD (Bernstein, Cohen, et al., 1993). However, recent evidence suggests that personality disorders in general exhibit a more fluctuating course than was previously believed possible (Grilo et al., 2004; Warner et al.,

2004). Thus even people with severe personality disorders, such as borderline personality disorder, may live for months or years without presenting serious manifestations of the disorder. Thus, it appears that the phenotypic manifestations of personality disorders exhibit a variable course over the life span, probably due to factors such as life stress and adaptation to changing life circumstances, while the underlying trait vulnerability for personality disorders appears to remain intact (Warner et al., 2004). On the other hand, it seems possible that some individuals "grow out of" their personality disorders, either because they obtain professional help or, more typical, due to ameliorative life experiences. There is no obvious reason that these considerations would not apply equally to PPD as they would to other severe personality disorders.

CASE EXAMPLE

A divorced man with long-standing PPD became noticeably warmer, less critical, more trusting, and more open to other people after he happily remarried and experienced the birth of his second child, a beloved daughter. Although he remained emotionally aloof compared to the average person and at times could still be sarcastic, belittling, and combative, these traits had considerably diminished—a noticeable and welcome change for friends, coworkers, and family members.

Is PPD a True Category or a Dimension That Cuts Across Categories?

Diagnostic Comorbidity. Patients with PPD often exhibit features of other personality disorders, especially the other Cluster A personality disorders (i.e., schizoid and schizotypal), but also the Cluster B personality disorders (i.e., borderline, narcissistic, and antisocial) and avoidant personality disorder (APA, 1994; Bernstein et al., 1995; Miller et al., 2001). In fact, one rarely finds a case of PPD that is not accompanied by one or more other comorbid personality disorders (Widiger & Rogers, 1989; Zimmerman, 1994). Studies of inpatient samples indicate that three fourths of those diagnosed with PPD receive additional personality disorder diagnoses (Widiger & Trull, 1998; Zimmerman, 1994). In studying an outpatient sample, Morey (1988) reported that those diagnosed with PPD most frequently received additional diagnoses of borderline (48%), narcissistic (35.9%), and avoidant (48.4%) personality disorders. In their review of the performance of the DSM-III-R criteria based on published and unpublished data sets, Widiger and Trull (1998) reported a high degree of overlap (i.e., > 38%) between PPD and borderline, avoidant, schizoid, schizotypal, and narcissistic personality disorders.

There are several potential explanations for the high degree of comorbidity between PPD and other personality disorders, including phenomenological

similarity between the personality disorders, artifactual overlap due to impre-
cision in the DSM diagnostic criteria, and the presence of shared or related
underlying pathological processes. For example, both PPD and narcissistic
personality disorder may share an underlying pathological process, namely,
overcompensation for underlying feelings of inferiority and inadequacy. Thus,
both paranoid and narcissistic individuals may be hypersensitive to slights or
potential humiliations, but they cope with them in different ways: the paranoid person through aggression, and the narcissistic person through grandiosity. Clinical observation suggests that some individuals develop both paranoid
and narcissistic forms of adaptation and therefore exhibit a comorbidity
between the personality disorders based on a shared underlying etiology. Such
individuals may be observed to fluctuate between paranoid and narcissistic
modes of adaptation (Young, 2003), depending on situational factors, such as
triggering life events.

CASE EXAMPLE

A successful businessman usually acted as if he were "on top of the world"—
dressing impeccably, making sure that he was seen in the company of famous
people and in all the "right places," and trumpeting his accomplishments to
anyone who would listen. However, when his business began to crumble, he
blamed members of his management team, whom he accused of conspiring
against him, smeared their reputations, and forced some of them to resign from
the company. Thus when his usual narcissistic, grandiose mode of compensa-
tion failed and his inadequacies were publicly exposed, he resorted to an attack
on his "enemies," whom he perceived to be the source of his humiliation.

Categories Versus Dimensions. The high rates of comorbidity between
PPD and other personality disorders, especially across clusters, raises the
question of whether PPD is truly a discrete disorder or is more accurately
described as a dimension that cuts across diagnostic categories. These issues
touch on a major debate regarding personality disorder measurement: the
dimensional versus categorical approach to personality disorder classification (Widiger & Frances, 2002). The dimensional approach focuses on the
degree to which one exhibits a syndrome or construct. Although a variety of
dimensional systems for personality disorders have been proposed, there
appear to be two major variants of the dimensional approach. In the first
approach, personality disorders are conceptualized as the extreme ends of
dimensions that are shared with normal personality (Widiger & Frances,
2002). Most of the research based on this "normative" approach to personality disorders has utilized the five-factor model of personality as a theoretical framework (Widiger & Frances, 2002). In the alternative approach,
personality disorders are conceptualized as spectrum variants of mental

illness, with Axis I disorders forming the extreme ends of the continuum (Siever & Davis, 1991).

When viewed from the perspective of the five-factor model of personality, there is consistent empirical evidence that PPD is negatively related to the personality dimension of agreeableness and positively related to the dimension of neuroticism (Costa & McCrae, 1990; Saulsman & Page, 2004; Trull, 1992; Wiggins & Pincus, 1989). These associations are moderate in magnitude. In addition, there is less consistent evidence that PPD shows weak, negative relationships to the personality dimensions of extraversion and conscientiousness (Saulsman & Page, 2004). Thus there is some empirical support for the notion that PPD lies on a continuum with normal personality. However, the hypothesized inverse relationship between PPD and extraversion—that is, the excessive need for autonomy often described in the clinical and theoretical literature on PPD—has received somewhat weaker empirical support. Evidence bearing on the question of whether PPD lies on a continuum with more extreme paranoid conditions—namely, schizophrenia and delusional disorder—is discussed below.

Is PPD a Schizophrenia-Spectrum or Delusional-Spectrum Disorder?

Family/Genetics Studies. It has long been noted that characteristics such as suspiciousness, referential thinking, and peculiar ideas are prevalent among relatives of schizophrenics (Bleuler, 1922; Kretschmer, 1925; Ray, 1863/1968). The famous Danish Adoption Study of the 1960s (Kety et al., 1968) was the first methodologically sophisticated attempt to study the prevalence of subsyndromal schizophrenialike traits in the adopted biological offspring of schizophrenic probands. The findings of this study supported the existence of a "schizophrenia spectrum"—a continuum of schizophrenialike characteristics in the nonpsychotic relatives of schizophrenic individuals. The description of these nonpsychotic but peculiar relatives of schizophrenics became the basis for the DSM-III/DSM-IV criteria for schizotypal personality disorder and, to a lesser degree, the other Cluster A personality disorders, PPD and schizoid personality disorder (Spitzer, Endicott, & Gibbon, 1979). Considerable subsequent evidence has been found to support the notion that schizotypal personality disorder falls on the schizophrenia spectrum (Siever & Davis, 2004). However, the evidence for PPD and schizoid personality disorder is less conclusive (Asarnow et al., 2001, Nicolson et al., 2003).

Another possibility is that PPD is a delusional spectrum disorder, on a genetic continuum with delusional disorder. The differential diagnosis between PPD and delusional disorder is based on the presence of frank delusions in the latter. However, in practice, this distinction is sometimes difficult to make (see "Differential Diagnosis" above). In fact, individuals with delusional disorder often have features that are quite similar to those of PPD (e.g., pathological jealousy). Moreover, when under stress, people with PPD can sometimes develop transient delusions (Miller et al., 2001). These considerations suggest the possibility that PPD and delusional disorder share a common genetic diathesis that is different from the genetic diathesis of schizophrenia.

Two recent well-designed studies have addressed the question of whether PPD and other putative schizophrenia spectrum disorders are overrepresented among the relatives of schizophrenic probands. Asarnow and his colleagues (2001) found only slightly and nonsignificantly elevated morbid risks of PPD in the relatives of probands with childhood-onset schizophrenia compared to ADHD and community control groups. In contrast, Nicolson and his colleagues (2003) found large and statistically significant morbid risks of PPD in both child- and adult-onset schizophrenic probands compared to community controls. Both studies supported the hypothesized genetic linkages between schizotypal PD and schizophrenia but found no evidence of a genetic relationship between schizoid PD and schizophrenia. Interestingly, Asarnow and his colleagues (2001) also found elevated rates of avoidant personality disorder in the relatives of probands with childhood-onset schizophrenia compared to community controls. Thus the findings of the above studies offer contradictory support for the notion that PPD is a schizophrenia spectrum disorder.

The hypothesis that PPD is a delusional spectrum disorder has also received some empirical support (Baron et al., 1985; Erlenmeyer-Kimling et al., 1995; Kendler, Gruenberg, & Strauss, 1981; Kendler & Hays, 1981; Kendler, Masterson, et al., 1985; Winokur, 1985). However, many of these studies were hampered by small samples of probands with delusional disorder, and no recent replication of these findings using larger samples has been attempted. Thus the idea that PPD shares genetic linkages with delusional disorder remains an intriguing possibility.

However, a major shortcoming of all of these studies has been the uncertain diagnostic validity of PPD. Because the DSM-IV criteria may not fully represent the PPD phenotype, the ability to determine whether genetic linkages for PPD exist may have been hampered.

Which Environmental Factors Might Contribute to the Development of PPD?

There is relatively little research on environmental factors in the etiology of PPD. However, evidence from one longitudinal study suggests that traumatic childhood events, such as childhood abuse and neglect, may play a role in the development of PPD (Johnson, Cohen, Brown, Smailes, & Bernstein, 1999; Johnson, Smailes, Cohen, Brown, & Bernstein, 2000). Johnson and colleagues (Johnson et al., 1999, 2000) found that children with substantiated histories of child abuse or neglect were at significantly greater risk for Cluster A personality disorders, including PPD, in young adulthood, even when other risk factors were taken into account. There is a considerable body of literature suggesting that childhood physical abuse is associated with anger and aggression in children and adolescents (Kolko, 2002)—features that are similar to those seen in PPD. Childhood physical abuse may therefore prove to play a specific etiologic role in the development of PPD. However, this hypothesis remains to be tested empirically.

In general, research suggests that both genetic and environmental factors play significant roles in the development of the traits that make up personality disorders (Livesley, Jang, & Vernon, 1998). There is little reason to suspect that PPD would be an exception. For example, an analysis of twin study data revealed that the types of traits that appear to characterize PPD, such as suspiciousness, hostility, oppositionality, and restricted expression of affect, have both strong heritable and environmental components (Livesley et al., 1998).

What Is the Most Accurate Means of Assessing PPD?

Accurate and efficient assessment of PPD is essential in treatment. Without an initial understanding of the client's paranoid perception of the world, a clinician who approaches a PPD client in a manner that may threaten her excessive need for autonomy and privacy may never see her after the first session. The therapeutic environment itself, with its emphasis on trust and disclosure, may be overwhelming to the PPD client. Furthermore, it would not be typical of a PPD client to present with complaints of paranoia (Turkat, Keane, & Thompson-Pope, 1990). Some (or perhaps many) PPD individuals may be falling through the cracks of the mental health system because they do not readily disclose problems with "paranoia" and may initially fail to be identified as possessing significant PPD traits. In addition, PPD individuals who are not delusional may draw less clinical attention than paranoid psychotic individuals who require more frequent and longer hospitalizations, antipsychotic medication, and more consistent follow-up. Furthermore, PPD individuals often drop out of therapy early or do not follow through with treatment plans (Turkat, 1985; Oldham & Skodol, 1994). Therefore, accurate and efficient assessment of significant and relevant PPD features is essential in diagnosis and selection of a treatment modality that takes into account the great difficulty a PPD client may have with disclosure as well as with the therapeutic relationship.

The Paranoid Personality Disorder Features Questionnaire (PPDFQ). The PPDFQ (Useda, 2002) is a dimensional measure that assesses the six main traits associated with PPD as described by the clinical and theoretical literature on PPD (Cameron, 1943, 1963; Kraepelin, 1921; Kretschmer, 1925; Millon, 1969, 1981; Shapiro, 1965; Sheldon, 1940; Sheldon & Stevens, 1942; Turkat, 1985) as well as the DSM-IV's (APA, 1994)

Associated Features section on PPD: Mistrust/suspiciousness, antagonism, introversion, hypersensitivity, hypervigilance, and rigidity. Thus the PPDFQ appears to assess the fundamental traits underlying PPD in a more balanced and proportionate manner than do the DSM-IV's own PPD diagnostic criteria, which, as has already been noted, overemphasize the cognitive features of PPD. The PPDFQ provides additional diagnostic information (i.e., the presence *and* degree of impairment associated with specific maladaptive variants of the core personality traits of PPD) compared to other self-report questionnaires of PPD currently in use (e.g., MMPI PPD profiles [Merritt, Balogh, & Kok, 1998]).

PPDFQ items for each of these six traits were originally written to represent three modes of expression (i.e., cognitive, affective, and interpersonal/behavioral) of an underlying trait. Many items focused on the participant's assessment of his or her interpersonal relationships and interpersonal situations as well as on his or her interpretations of others' behaviors. For example, the item "I think most other people are hostile" was developed to represent the cognitive mode of antagonism. The item "I make an effort to pick up on every detail of another person's behavior" was written to reflect the behavioral mode of hypervigilance. The item response format was a five-point Likert scale assessing level of agreement (0 = strongly disagree; 1 = disagree; 2 = neutral, neither disagree nor agree; 3 = agree; 4 = strongly agree). The measure was designed to assess functioning over the previous 2 years.

Initial findings on the reliability and validity of the PPDFQ in a normative college student sample ($N = 106$) are encouraging (Useda, 2002). The test-retest reliability of the six PPDFQ scores over a 6-week interval was good, and the hypothesized relationships between the PPDFQ subscales and the five-factor model of personality as well as Livesley's dimensional model of personality pathology were supported. Further validation of the PPDFQ in clinical samples is clearly indicated. It is hoped that the PPDFQ will prove a useful tool that will improve the validity of dimensional assessments of PPD in future studies.

What Kinds of Treatments Are Likely to Be Most Effective for People With PPD?

The treatment literature on PPD is limited to single-case studies. We could locate no report in the literature of a clinical trial of any treatment for PPD—psychotherapeutic or psychopharmacological. Perhaps one reason for this is that PPD patients are perceived by some clinicians to be untreatable. Clearly, their mistrust, antagonism, introversion, rigidity, and other features present challenges for psychotherapists, given that therapy is usually predicated on one's ability to form a trusting relationship with the therapist and to examine one's own assumptions about oneself, others, and the world.

A thorough discussion of possible treatment approaches to use with PPD patients is beyond the scope of this chapter. However, a few general guidelines can be suggested. First, the goal of therapy with PPD patients is to help them recognize and accept their own feelings of vulnerability; heighten their feelings of self-worth and reduce their feelings of shame; help them develop a more balanced, trusting view of others; and reduce their reliance on counterproductive self-protective strategies, such as bullying, threatening, and intimidating others and keeping others at a distance. A variety of therapeutic approaches could be employed to accomplish these goals (e.g., cognitive-behavioral, psychodynamic). However, regardless of theoretical orientation, it is essential that the patient's mistrust and self-protective mechanisms be confronted directly in an empathic but clear and straightforward manner.

It is an old adage that you cannot "talk a paranoid person out of his paranoia." However, many individuals with PPD have some capacity to take perspective on their own suspicious cognitions. An approach of "collaborative empiricism" can be very helpful in this regard, in which the therapist invites the patient to join in a process of examining his or her beliefs in the light of objective evidence. Thought records can be used to help the patient identify and modify his or her maladaptive cognitions by weighing the evidence supporting them and contradicting them. In conducting this sort of inquiry, it is important to acknowledge that the patient's suspicions about others often contain a kernel of truth.

For example, one of us (D. P. B.) treated a PPD patient for 3 years using schema therapy (Bernstein, 2005; Young et al., 2003), an integrative form of psychotherapy that combines cognitive, behavioral, psychodynamic object relations, and existential/humanistic approaches. The patient had largely unfounded fears that his coworkers didn't respect him and that his boss was looking for an excuse to fire him. While there was little objective evidence to support his belief that others disrespected him or that his own job was in jeopardy, his workplace environment did appear to be a ruthless one in which senior staff deliberately fostered competition among coworkers, and many of his colleagues worried about their job security. The patient appeared to be relieved that his therapist validated the realistic aspects of his perceptions, rather than treating his beliefs as "crazy." Moreover, recognizing that many of his coworkers might also be feeling insecure about their jobs helped the patient to accept his own feelings of vulnerability. The patient was then able to engage in a process of collaborative empiricism with his therapist, in which they weighed the evidence supporting and contradicting his beliefs. The patient's "evidence" that others disrespected him was based mainly on ambiguous social interactions in which colleagues had appeared unfriendly or hadn't solicited his opinion during meetings. After examining the evidence critically, the patient was able to recognize that his colleagues' behavior could be open to a variety of alternative explanations. Moreover, the patient came to see that his own self-protective tendency to keep others at a distance was probably responsible for some of the unfriendliness he was experiencing. Similarly, his own tendency to keep quiet during meetings for fear of appearing stupid was probably responsible for the fact that others didn't solicit his opinions.

As a behavioral intervention, the therapist recommended that the patient take some of his colleagues out to lunch. After doing so, the patient noticed that his colleagues were more friendly and relaxed around him, contradicting his view that they didn't like him. Shortly thereafter, he received a glowing evaluation from his supervisor. Rather than being relieved, the patient reacted to this good news with mistrust: he couldn't believe that his supervisor could actually hold him in such high regard, and insisted that the supervisor must be secretly criticizing him behind his back! After some discussion, the patient was able to recognize that his reaction was based on a core defectiveness schema—the belief that he was irrevocably flawed, unlikable and unlovable. It was this core belief that was responsible for his frequent perception that others disrespected him. It was also responsible for his conviction that his wife was planning to leave him, despite the abundant evidence that she cared deeply for him and was satisfied with their relationship. Thus, the empathic but persistent confrontation of the patient's mistrustful beliefs and self-defeating coping mechanisms led over time to greater feelings of self-worth and self-acceptance, less mistrustful attitudes, greater ability to "reality test" his own suspicious beliefs, and more effective ways of relating to others.

Summary

PPD is a severe personality disorder that has received far less empirical attention than it deserves, given its prevalence in clinical populations and its negative consequences, such as disruptive behavior and interpersonal distress, unnecessary litigation, psychiatric comorbidity, and violence. In this chapter, we have recommended that the DSM-IV criteria for PPD be substantially revised to increase their validity and have discussed new directions for PPD research and treatment. We hope that this chapter will stimulate researchers and clinicians to pursue these new avenues with the goal of improving understanding and treatment of this difficult disorder.

References

American Psychiatric Association. (1952). *Diagnostic and statistical manual of mental disorders*. Washington, DC: Author.

American Psychiatric Association. (1980). *Diagnostic and statistical manual of mental disorders* (3rd ed.). Washington, DC: Author.

American Psychiatric Association. (1994). *Diagnostic and statistical manual of mental disorders* (4th ed.). Washington, DC: Author.

Asarnow, R., Nuechterlein, K., Fogelson, D., Subotnik, K., Payne, D., Russell, A., et al. (2001). Schizophrenia and schizophrenia-spectrum personality disorders in the first-degree relatives of children with schizophrenia: The UCLA Family Study. *Archives of General Psychiatry, 58*, 581–588.

Baron, M., Gruen, R., Rainer, J. D., Kane, J., Asnis, L., & Lord, S. (1985). A family study of schizophrenic and normal control probands: Implications for the spectrum concept of schizophrenia. *American Journal of Psychiatry, 142,* 147–454.

Beck, A. T., Freeman, A. T., & Associates (1990). *Cognitive therapy of personality disorders.* New York: Guilford Press.

Bernstein, D. P. (2005). Schema therapy for personality disorders. In S. Strack (Ed.), *Handbook of personology and psychopathology* (pp. 462–477). Hoboken, NJ: Wiley.

Bernstein, D. P., Cohen, P., Velez, C. N., Schwab-Stone, M., Siever, L., & Shinsato, L. (1993). Prevalence and stability of the DSM-III-R personality disorders in a community-based survey of adolescents. *American Journal of Psychiatry, 150,* 1237–1243.

Bernstein, D. P., Useda, J. D., & Siever, L. J. (1993). Paranoid personality disorder: Review of the literature and recommendations for DSM-IV. *Journal of Personality Disorders, 7,* 53–62.

Bernstein, D. P., Useda, J. D., & Siever, L. J. (1995). Paranoid personality disorder. In W. J. Livesley (Ed.), *The DSM-IV personality disorders* (pp. 45–57). New York: Guilford Press.

Bleuler, E. (1922). Die Probleme der Schizoidie und der Syntonie [The problem of schizoidness and syntony]. *Zeitschrift fur die Gesamte Neurolagie und Psychiatrie, 78,* 373–388.

Bögels, S. M., & Mansell, W. (2004). Attention processes in the maintenance and treatment of social phobia: Hypervigilance, avoidance, and self-focused attention. *Clinical Psychology Review, 24,* 827–856.

Bond, M., & Perry, C. (2004). Long-term changes in defense styles with psychodynamic psychotherapy for depressive, anxiety, and personality disorders. *American Journal of Psychiatry, 161,* 1665–1671.

Cameron, N. (1943). The paranoid pseudo-community. *American Journal of Sociology, 49,* 32–38.

Cameron, N. (1963). *Personality development and psychopathology.* Boston: Houghton Mifflin.

Cecero, J., Nelson, J., & Gillie, J. (2004). Tools and tenets of schema therapy: Toward the construct validity of the Early Maladaptive Schema Questionnaire—Research Version (EMSQ-R). *Clinical Psychology and Psychotherapy, 11,* 344–357.

Coryell, W. H., & Zimmerman, M. (1989). Personality disorder in the families of depressed, schizophrenic, and never-ill probands. *American Journal of Psychiatry, 146,* 496–502.

Costa, P. T., Jr., & McCrae, R. R. (1990). Personality disorders and the five-factor model of personality. *Journal of Personality Disorders, 4,* 362–371.

Drake, R. E., & Vaillant, G. E. (1985). A validity study of Axis II of DSM-III. *American Journal of Psychiatry, 142,* 553–558.

Erlenmeyer-Kimling, L., Squires-Wheeler, E., Adamo, U. H., Basset, A. S., Cornblatt, B. A., Kestenbaum, C. J., et al. (1995). The New York High-Risk Project: Psychoses and Cluster A personality disorders in offspring of schizophrenic parents at 23 years of follow-up. *Archives of General Psychiatry, 52,* 857–865.

Giesen-Bloo, J., Arntz, A., van Dyck, R., Spinhoven, P. & van Tilburg, W. (2004, November). *Schema focused vs. transference focused psychotherapy for borderline personality disorder: Results of a multicenter trial.* Paper presented at the 2nd European Congress for Psychotherapy, Amsterdam, Netherlands.

Grilo, C., Sanislow, C., Gunderson, J., Pagano, M., Yen, S., Zanarini, M., et al. (2004). Two-year stability and change of schizotypal, borderline, avoidant, and obsessive-compulsive personality disorders. *Journal of Consulting and Clinical Psychology, 72,* 767–775.

Holmes, D. (1978). Projection as a defense mechanism. *Psychological Bulletin, 85,* 677–688.

Johnson, J., Cohen, P., Brown, J., Smailes, E., & Bernstein, D. (1999). Childhood maltreatment increases risk for personality disorders during early adulthood. *Archives of General Psychiatry, 56,* 600–606.

Johnson, J., Smailes, E., Cohen, P., Brown, J., & Bernstein, D. (2000). Associations between four types of childhood neglect and personality disorder symptoms during adolescence and early adulthood: Findings of a community-based longitudinal study. *Journal of Personality Disorders, 14,* 171–187.

Kendler, K. S., & Gruenberg, A. M. (1982). Genetic relationship between paranoid personality disorder and the "schizophrenic spectrum" disorders. *American Journal of Psychiatry, 139,* 1185–1186.

Kendler, K., Gruenberg, A., & Strauss, J. (1982). An independent analysis of the Copenhagen sample of the Danish adoption study of schizophrenia: V. The relationship between childhood social withdrawal and adult schizophrenia. *Archives of General Psychiatry, 39,* 1257–1261.

Kendler, K., & Hays, P. (1981). Paranoid psychosis (delusional disorder) and schizophrenia: A family history study. *Archives of General Psychiatry, 38,* 547–551.

Kendler, K. S., Masterson, C. C., & Davis, K. (1985). Psychiatric illness in first-degree relatives of patients with paranoid psychosis, schizophrenia and medical illness. *British Journal of Psychiatry, 147,* 524–531.

Kety, S. S., Rosenthal, D., Wender, P. H., & Schulsinger, F. (1968). The types and prevalence of mental illness in the biological and adoptive families of adopted schizophrenics. In D. Rosenthal & S. S. Kety (Eds.), *The transmission of schizophrenia* (pp. 345–362). Oxford, UK: Pergamon Press.

Koenigsberg, H., Harvey, P., Mitropoulou, V., New, A., Goodman, M., Silverman, J., et al. (2001). Are the interpersonal and identity disturbances in the borderline personality disorder criteria linked to the traits of affectivity and impulsivity? *Journal of Personality Disorders, 15,* 358–370.

Kolko, D. (2002). Child physical abuse. In L. Berliner & J. Myers (Eds.), *The APSAC handbook on child maltreatment* (2nd ed., pp. 21–54). Thousand Oaks, CA: Sage.

Kraepelin, E. (1921). *Manic-depressive insanity and paranoia.* Edinburgh, UK: Livingstone.

Kretschmer, E. (1925). *Physique and character.* London: Kegan Paul.

Leung, N., Thomas, G., & Waller, G. (2000). The relationship between parental bonding and core beliefs in anorexic and bulimic women. *British Journal of Clinical Psychology, 39,* 205–213.

Lingiardi, V., Lonati, C., Delucchi, F., Fossati, A., Vanzulli, L., & Maffei, C. (1999). Defense mechanisms and personality disorders. *Journal of Nervous and Mental Disease, 187,* 224–228.

Livesley, W. J., Jang, K. L., & Vernon, P. A. (1998). Phenotypic and genetic structure of traits delineating personality disorders. *Archives of General Psychiatry, 55,* 941–948.

Maier, W., Lichterman, D., Minges, J., & Heun, R. (1994). Personality disorders among the relatives of schizophrenic patients. *Schizophrenia Bulletin, 20,* 481–493.

Merritt, R., Balogh, D., & Kok, C. (1998). DSM-IV Cluster A personality disorder diagnoses among young adults with a 2-7-8 MMPI profile. *Assessment, 5,* 273–285.

Miller, M. B., Useda, J. D., Trull, T. J., Burr, R. M., & Minks-Brown, C. (2001). Paranoid, schizoid and schizotypal personality disorders. In H. E. Adams & P. B. Sutker (Eds.), *The comprehensive handbook of psychopathology* (3rd ed., pp. 535–559). New York: Plenum.

Millon, T. (1969). *Modern psychopathology: A biosocial approach to maladaptive learning and functioning.* Philadelphia: Saunders.

Millon, T. (1981). *Disorders of personality: DSM-III Axis II.* New York: Wiley.

Millon, T., & Davis, R. (1996). *Disorders of personality: DSM-IV and beyond.* New York: Wiley.

Morey, L. C. (1988). Personality disorders in DSM-III and DSM-III-R: Convergence, coverage, and internal consistency. *American Journal of Psychiatry, 145,* 573–577.

Nicolson, R., Brookner, F., Lenane, M., Gochman, P., Ingraham, L., Egan, M., et al. (2003). Parental schizophrenia spectrum disorders in childhood-onset and adult-onset schizophrenia. *American Journal of Psychiatry, 160,* 490–495.

Oldham, J. M., & Skodol, A. E. (1994). Do patients with paranoid personality disorder seek psychoanalysis? In J. M. Oldham & S. Bone (Eds.), *Paranoid: New psychoanalytic perspectives* (pp. 151–166). Madison, CT: International Universities Press.

Paris, J., Zweig-Frank, H., Bond, M., & Guzder, J. (1996). Defense styles, hostility, and psychological risk factors in male patients with personality disorders. *Journal of Nervous and Mental Disease, 184,* 153–158.

Ray, I. (1863/1968). *Mental hygiene.* New York: Hafner.

Saulsman, L., & Page, A. (2004). The five-factor model and personality disorder empirical literature: A meta-analytic review. *Clinical Psychology Review, 23,* 1055–1085.

Schmidt, N., Joiner, T., Young, J., & Telch, M. (1995). The Schema Questionnaire: Investigation of psychometric properties and the hierarchical structure of a measure of maladaptive schemas. *Cognitive Therapy and Research, 19,* 295–321.

Shapiro, D. (1965). *Neurotic styles.* New York: Basic Books.

Sheldon, W. H. (1940). *The varieties of human physique: An introduction to constitutional psychology.* New York: Harper.

Sheldon, W. H., & Stevens, S. S. (1942). *The varieties of temperament: A psychology of individual differences.* New York: Harper.

Siever, L., & Davis, K. (1991). A psychobiological perspective on the personality disorders. *American Journal of Psychiatry, 148,* 1647–1658.

Siever, L., & Davis, K. (2004). The pathophysiology of schizophrenia disorders: Perspectives from the spectrum. *American Journal of Psychiatry, 161,* 398–413.

Spitzer, R. L., Endicott, J., & Gibbon, M. (1979). Crossing the border into borderline personality and borderline schizophrenia: The development of criteria. *Archives of General Psychiatry, 36,* 17–24.

Trull, T. J. (1992). DSM-II-R personality disorders and the five-factor model of personality: An empirical comparison. *Journal of Abnormal Psychology, 101,* 553–560.

Turkat, I. D. (1985). Paranoid personality disorder. In I. D. Turkat (Ed.), *Behavioral case formulation* (pp. 155–198). New York: Plenum.

Turkat, I. D., Keane, S. P., & Thompson-Pope, S. K. (1990). Social processing errors among paranoid personalities. *Journal of Psychopathology and Behavioral Assessment, 12,* 263–269.

Useda, J. D. (2002, April). The construct validity of the Paranoid Personality Disorder Features Questionnaire (PPDFQ): A dimensional assessment of paranoid personality disorder. *Dissertation Abstracts International, 62,* 9B. (UMI No. 4240)

Vaillant, G. E. (1994). Ego mechanisms of defense and personality psychopathology. *Journal of Abnormal Psychology, 103,* 44–50.

Waller, G., Meyer, C., & Ohanian, V. (2001). Psychometric properties of the long and short version of the Young Schema Questionnaire: Core beliefs among bulimic and comparison women. *Cognitive Therapy and Research, 25,* 137–147.

Waller, G., Meyer, C., Ohanian, V., Elliott, P., Dickson, C., & Sellings, J. (2001). The psychopathology of bulimic women who report childhood sexual abuse: The mediating role of core beliefs. *Journal of Nervous and Mental Disease, 189,* 700–708.

Warner, M., Morey, L., Finch, J., Gunderson, J., Skodol, A., Sanislow, C., et al. (2004). The longitudinal relationship of personality traits and disorders. *Journal of Abnormal Psychology, 113,* 217–227.

Widiger, T. A., & Frances, A. (2002). Toward a dimensional model for the personality disorders. In P. T. Costa, Jr., & T. A. Widiger (Eds.), *Personality disorders and the five-factor model of personality* (2nd ed., pp. 23–44). Washington, DC: American Psychological Association.

Widiger, T. A., & Rogers, J. H. (1989) Prevalence and comorbidity of personality disorders. *Psychiatric Annals, 19,* 132–136.

Widiger, T. A., & Trull, T. J. (1998). Performance characteristics of the DSM-III-R personality disorder criteria sets. In T. A. Widiger, A. J. Frances, H. A. Pincus, R. Ross, M. B. First, W. W. Davis, et al. (Eds.), *DSM-IV sourcebook* (Vol. 4, pp. 357–373). Washington, DC: American Psychological Association.

Widiger, T. A., Trull, T. J., Clarkin, J. F., Sanderson, C., & Costa, P. T., Jr. (2002). A description of the DSM-IV personality disorders with the five-factor model of personality. In P. T. Costa, Jr., & T. A. Widiger (Eds.), *Personality disorders and the five-factor model of personality* (2nd ed., pp. 89–99). Washington, DC: American Psychological Association.

Wiggins, J. S., & Pincus, A. L. (1989). Conceptions of personality disorders and dimensions of personality. *Psychological Assessment, 1,* 305–316.

Williams, J. M. G., Watts, F. N., MacLeod, C., & Mathews, A. (1997). *Cognitive psychology and emotional disorders.* Chichester, UK: Wiley.

Winokur, G. (1985). Familial psychopathology in delusional disorder. *Comprehensive Psychiatry, 26,* 241–248.

Young, J., Klosko, J., & Weishaar, M. (2003). *Schema therapy: A practitioner's guide.* New York: Guilford Press.

Zimmerman, M. (1994). Diagnosing personality disorders: A review of issues and research methods. *Archives of General Psychiatry, 51,* 225–245.

4

Schizoid Personality Disorder

Vijay A. Mittal
Emory University

Oren Kalus
Ulster County Mental Health

David P. Bernstein
Maastricht University

Larry J. Siever
Mount Sinai School of Medicine

Introduction

Schizoid personality disorder (SCD) is one of the DSM's (American Psychiatric Association [APA], 2000) three "odd/eccentric" cluster personality disorders (along with schizotypal and paranoid personality disorders), which are characterized by phenomenological similarities to schizophrenia. SCD is distinguished from the other two personality disorders in this cluster by the prominence of social, interpersonal, and affective deficits (i.e., negative symptoms) in the absence of psychotic-like cognitive/perceptual distortions (i.e., positive symptoms).

Despite a rich and extensive clinical tradition regarding the schizoid character, its pre-DSM-III (APA, 1980) status was handicapped by considerable heterogeneity and lack of clearly operationalized diagnostic criteria. The architects of DSM-III attempted to subdivide and sharpen the boundaries of this heterogeneous diagnosis by adding schizotypal and paranoid personality disorders to the "odd" cluster and moving avoidant personality disorder to the "anxious" cluster. The narrowing of the schizoid personality disorder diagnosis that resulted from these changes raised further questions, however, about its diagnostic boundaries and about whether the diagnosis is a valid separate entity. Evidence of extensive criterion overlap as well as comorbidity with other personality disorders (particularly schizotypal and avoidant) has been of particular concern in this regard. The low prevalence rates of DSM-IV-TR (APA, 2000) schizoid personality disorder have further complicated attempts to address these issues empirically. The scarcity of data on DSM-IV-TR schizoid personality disorder has remained a significantly limiting factor in resolving these concerns and in considering the status of SCD as we approach DSM-V.

Historical Background

Bleuler (1924) used the term "schizoid" to describe a tendency to turn inward and away from the external world, the absence of emotional expressiveness, simultaneous contradictory dullness and sensitivity, and pursuit of vague interests. From the 1950s until the mid 1970s, the term was used to describe schizophrenia-like spectrum disorders (Miller, Useda, Trull, Burr, & Minks-Brown, 2001) and encompassed the conceptions that are now delineated into separate Cluster A personality disorders (Wolff, 1998).

Although most historical clinical descriptions of schizoid personality disorder are consistent with DSM-IV-TR criteria, there appear to be some discrepancies. In addition to describing the familiar negative symptoms of schizoid personality disorder outlined in the DSM, many clinicians described the presence of contradictory affective and cognitive states in schizoid personality disorder that were not recognized in DSM-III (some of these features may have been absorbed into other personality disorders, such as schizotypal and avoidant). Kretschmer (1925), for example, differentiated two types of schizoid characteristics—the hyperaesthetic and the anaesthetic—that contrasted inner sensitivity with overt insensitivity. Rather than separating these contrasting behavioral tendencies into two distinct diagnostic groups, as DSM-III did with the schizoid and avoidant categories, Kretschmer suggested that these characteristics may coexist in the same person. Several clinicians have suggested that the schizoid individual's apparent outward insensitivity and indifference often belie marked inner sensitivity. This association highlights a problem with one of the DSM-III-R's (APA, 1987) schizoid personality disorder criteria, which is based on an inferred inner state–subjective indifference to rejection or criticism. In an effort to eliminate this ambiguity, this criterion was revised in DSM-IV to emphasize a more objective behavioral description and to increase specificity for the context in which the relative lack of emotional expression takes place (APA, 1994).

Another area in which the traditional literature differs from DSM-IV-TR concerns the schizoid's sexuality. Observations by Terry and Rennie (1938) of compulsive masturbation in SCD individuals are consistent with the DSM criterion of absent sexual relationships but not with the absence of sexual desire. Other clinical features either not reported or deemphasized in DSM-IV-TR include autistic thinking, fragmented self-identity, and symptoms of derealization/depersonalization. Numerous clinicians (particularly psychodynamically oriented ones) have stressed the fragmented personality structure and the use of such primitive defensive mechanisms as splitting. Guntrip (1969) and other clinicians reported the frequent presence of depersonalization, derealization, absence of feeling, and disembodiment in SCD individuals. The psychoanalytic literature also makes extensive references to the "primitive character structure" of the schizoid and in particular to an identity disturbance that may contrast with the more dramatic and affectively charged identity disturbance reported in borderline personality disorder patients. Bleuler (1954) and other clinicians also emphasized the phenomenological similarities between schizoid personality and schizophrenia, which anticipated current questions concerning the relationship of all three Cluster A diagnoses to schizophrenia.

The Diagnosis of Schizoid
Personality Disorder

Daryl is a 28-year-old male who lives in an apartment above his parents' garage. Because he tends to avoid interacting with his family, his parents felt that he would feel happy about the move to his own space. He appeared indifferent to the change. Daryl works as a computer programmer in a small firm and is in danger of losing his job. His supervisor is becoming frustrated because Daryl seems indifferent to feedback or criticism. His coworkers describe him as a "loner" and report being disconcerted by his apparent lack of emotion. Daryl's mother complains that he never smiles or frowns at anything. When she tries to include him in family activities, he appears cold and detached. Daryl has little interest in making friends and has never been in a romantic relationship. He has never been excited by the prospect of sexual intercourse. Although he spends most of his free time building models of airplanes, he does not overtly enjoy this activity. When complimented about his airplanes, Daryl appears not to notice or to care.

Prevalence

It has been noted that schizoid personality is among the least frequently observed of the personality disorders (Miller et al., 2001). This low prevalence has likely contributed to the dearth of information surrounding the demographic characteristics of the disorder. DSM-IV-TR notes that SCD may be first apparent in late childhood. Because this is a period in which cooperative play is in ascendance, the social isolation associated with SCD becomes more salient. In addition, the disorder is also more common in men than in women (APA, 2000). See Table 4.1 for the DSM-IV-TR criteria for SCD.

The DSM-IV-TR does not provide data regarding SCD prevalence. This omission may be due to the uncommon appearance of schizoid individuals in clinical settings, or to the fact that current conceptions of SCD identify only the most severe cases of the disorder (Wolff, 1998). Considerable variation in the prevalence rates is apparent across clinical settings. Estimates of the prevalence of SCD in the general population based on community surveys (Reich, Yates, & Nduaguba, 1989), nonpsychiatric controls (Drake & Vaillant, 1985), and relatives of psychiatric patients (Zimmerman & Coryell, 1990) have ranged from 0.5% to 7%.

Prevalence rates vary considerably depending on the DSM version. Studies using DSM-III-R criteria generally report higher prevalence rates than those using DSM-III criteria. For example, Morey and Heumann

Table 4.1   DSM-IV-TR criteria for diagnosing schizoid personality disorder

Criteria	Description
A.	A pervasive pattern of detachment from social relationships and a restricted range of expression of emotions in interpersonal settings, beginning by early adulthood and present in a variety of contexts, as indicated by four (or more) of the following.
(1)	Neither desires nor enjoys close relationships, including being part of a family
(2)	Almost always chooses solitary activities
(3)	Has little, if any, interest in having sexual experiences with another person
(4)	Takes pleasure in few, if any, activities
(5)	Lacks close friends or confidants other than first-degree relatives
(6)	Appears indifferent to the praise or criticism of others
(7)	Behavior or appearance that is odd, eccentric, or peculiar
B.	Does not occur exclusively during the course of Schizophrenia, a Mood Disorder With Psychotic Features, another Psychotic Disorder, or a Pervasive Developmental Disorder and is not due to the direct physiological effects of a general medical condition.

SOURCE: Reprinted with permission from the *Diagnostic and Statistical Manual of Mental Disorders,* Fourth Edition, Text Revision, (Copyright 2000). American Psychiatric Association.

Note. If criteria are met prior to the onset of Schizophrenia, add "Premorbid," e.g., "Schizoid Personality Disorder (Premorbid)."

(1988) compared DSM-III with DSM-III-R SCD diagnoses in the same group of 291 personality-disordered patients, reporting a substantially higher prevalence using DSM-III-R criteria (1.4% versus 11.0%). These differences reflect changes incorporated into DSM-III-R that provided a richer and potentially more sensitive description and attempted to reduce the risk of oversimplification (Akhtar, 1987). For example, the use of a polythetic system that does not require any single feature added further flexibility and may have increased the sensitivity of the diagnosis.

Based on DSM-IV criteria, results from an epidemiological catchment area study found prevalence rates between 0.7% and 0.9% (Samuels et al., 2002). Prevalence rates are also dependent on classification systems. For example, a Swedish community sample study utilizing the International Classification of Diseases (ICD-10; World Health Organization, 1992) system found SCD prevalence to be as high as 4.5% (Ekselius, Tillfors, Furmark, & Fredrikson, 2001).

Psychometric Properties

The internal consistency of measures of schizoid personality disorder is poor; a recent study using the Diagnostic Interview for DSM-IV Personality Disorders (DIPD-IV) reported a Cronbach's alpha coefficient of .47 and mean intercriterion correlation of .11 (Grilo et al., 2001). By a large margin (histrionic PD being the next lowest, alpha = .64), this is the poorest internal consistency of any personality disorder (Grilo et al., 2001). Other studies have reported slightly higher levels of internal consistency, with alpha ranging between .63 (Farmer & Chapman, 2002) and .68 (Ottosson, Ekselius, Grann, & Kullgren, 2002). Nevertheless, schizoid personality disorder had the lowest consistency of any of the personality disorders in each of these studies.

Because of the low base rate of SCD, studies aiming to determine sensitivity, specificity, and predictive power of individual criteria have been marked by an insufficient sample size for conducting appropriate analyses (Farmer & Chapman, 2002). Some past research has examined criterion performance for the DSM-III-R conceptualization of SCD. (Due to criterion changes in the DSM-IV-TR, these data will be reported only for those items which have remained constant throughout subsequent revisions.) The results of three studies examining the performance of the DSM-III-R criteria (Millon & Tringone, 1989 [N = 26]; Morey & Heumann, 1988 [N = 32]; Freiman & Widiger, 1989 [N = 8]) were divergent, although some trends were apparent. Of the criteria reflecting impaired capacity for interpersonal relationships, only "neither desires nor enjoys close relationships . . ." demonstrated high sensitivity (.62–.87) and specificity (.86–.93) and was considered prototypical (78/100) by clinicians. The criterion "almost always chooses solitary activities" showed high sensitivity

(.73–.88) and was judged prototypical (76/100) but had moderate specificity (.78–.88). The criterion "lacks close friends or confidants . . ." also demonstrated high sensitivity (.69–.72), but it had the lowest specificity (.55–.68) of all the schizoid criteria. The low specificity of criteria indicates that these features are shared with other personality disorders.

In contrast to the criteria referring to interpersonal relationships, the criteria "has little, if any, desire to have sexual experiences . . ." and "appears indifferent to the praise and criticism of others" demonstrated low sensitivity (.62–.75; .00–.34), mid to low prototypicality (71/100; 55/100), but high specificity (.78–1; .93–.95). These criteria may define a subgroup of patients dominated by deficits in both affective responsivity and capacity for pleasure. It was concluded that retaining these criteria in subsequent versions of the DSM, despite their low sensitivity, might be justified by their possible ability to identify a subset of atypical cases. There are currently no data concerning the DSM-IV-TR criteria "takes pleasure in few, if any, activities" and "behavior or appearance that is odd, eccentric, or peculiar."

Compatibility of DSM and ICD-10 Criteria

The revisions to SCD introduced in DSM-III-R and further modified in DSM-IV have not produced satisfactory levels of agreement between DSM and ICD-10. A study examining prevalence rates in a Swedish community sample and comparing these rates between ICD-10 and DSM-IV found that differences were most striking for the classification of SCD (ICD-10 = 4.5%; DSM-IV = 0.9%; Ekselius et al., 2001). The kappa was .32, which is a low level of agreement in view of the fact that the next lowest value was .50 for antisocial/dyssocial personality (Ekselius et al., 2001). This conclusion is further supported by a study examining the concordance of personality disorders between DSM-IV and ICD-10, which found schizoid to exhibit the poorest agreement between systems (kappa = .37; Ottosson et al., 2002). This discordance is attributable to arbitrary thresholds (Ottosson et al., 2002) and additional ICD-10 criteria that do not have corresponding DSM-IV items (e.g. ., "marked difficulty in recognizing and adhering to social convention, resulting in eccentricity of behavior" [World Health Organization, 1992, p. F60.1]).

Comorbidity

Rates of comorbidity of SCD with other personality disorders are listed in Table 4.2. The highest co-occurrence is with schizotypal personality disorder, perhaps because of the high overlap between the two criteria sets

Table 4.2 Comorbidity of schizoid personality disorder with other Axis II disorders

	PRN	SZT	ATS	BDL	HST	NAR	AVD	DPD	OCP
	Percentage of criterion group receiving schizoid diagnosis								
Dahl (1986)	0	80	40	20	20	0	60	0	0
Morey (1988)	47	38	3	19	9	28	53	19	16
Freiman & Widiger (1989)	62	62	25	38	0	38	88	0	0
Skodol et al. (1988)	40	60	0	60	0	20	80	20	20
Millon & Tringone (1989)	4	27	0	0	0	8	23	15	8
Farmer & Chapman (2002)	5	27	0	8	0	0	10	–	3

Note. Key to personality disorder abbreviations: PRN, paranoid; SZT, schizotypal; ATS, antisocial; BDL, borderline; HST, histrionic; NAR, narcissistic; AVD, avoidant; DPD, dependent; OCP, obsessive compulsive. The blank for DPD on the Farmer and Chapman (2002) study is due to an insufficient sample size.

(e.g., social isolation, restricted affect). Avoidant personality disorder also demonstrated high comorbidity with SCD. Lesser degrees of comorbidity were demonstrated with paranoid, antisocial, and borderline personality disorders. Although SCD is sometimes considered a member of the schizophrenia spectrum, sharing some overlap with other Cluster A disorders, it has also been evaluated in the context of Asperger's syndrome (Wolff, 1998). The sections that follow will discuss SCD's overlap with avoidant personality disorder, its relationship with Asperger's disorder, and the role of SCD in the schizophrenia spectrum.

Schizoid and Avoidant Personality Disorders

Kretschmer (1925) distinguished between two disorders: anaesthetic (withdrawn due to indifference) and hyperaesthetic (withdrawn due to an overstimulation of outside influences). This distinction, which parallels the DSM-IV-TR distinction between schizoid and avoidant personality types, has engendered numerous controversies (Miller et al., 2001). Despite their phenotypic similarities, avoidant personality is listed as a Cluster C anxious disorder, whereas schizoid is in Cluster A, the odd and eccentric group.

Some studies suggest that SCD can be distinguished from avoidant personality disorder (Trull, Widiger, & Frances, 1987) on the basis of intimacy needs and sensitivity to rejection. However, contrasting historical descriptions suggesting that sensitivity and insensitivity coexist in schizoid personality disorder and more recent studies suggesting that anxiety and other clinical symptoms occur in both disorders (Overholser, 1989) call for additional investigation.

Although some researchers have argued that the etiology of the social withdrawal symptom presentation is sufficient to draw a line between SCD and avoidant personality disorder (see Chapter 10), the research literature has demonstrated poor discriminant validity between the two disorders. A recent study revealed that of those persons given a diagnosis of SCD, 40% met criteria for avoidant personality disorder (Farmer & Chapman, 2002). Another study examining comorbidity of personality disorders found that schizoid and avoidant personality disorders were correlated at a significant rate ($r = .51$; Solano & De Chavez, 2000). In addition, personality measures have demonstrated difficulty in distinguishing between the two disorders. An analysis of discriminant validity utilizing three measures, the International Personality Disorder Examination (Loranger, Susman, Oldham, & Russakoff, 1987), the Personality Diagnostic Questionnaire (Hyler & Rieder, 1994), and the Millon Clinical Multiaxial Inventory (Millon, Millon, & Davis, 1994), found that avoidant and schizoid personality disorders were not clearly distinguishable from each other due to high intercorrelations (Blackburn, Donnelly, Logan, & Renwick, 2004).

Schizoid and Asperger's Syndrome

A recent body of literature points to a possible link between SCD and Asperger's syndrome. There is significant overlap in the phenomenological criteria for both disorders: solitary activity, lack of empathy, emotional detachment, increased sensitivity, paranoid ideation, unusual styles of communication, and rigidity of mental set (Wolff, 1998). In a study of parents of autistic children, Wolff (1998) found a heightened level of schizoid personality traits in the parents compared with matched control pairs. Both disorders additionally share nonverbal behavior deficits that often interfere with interpersonal relationships.

Despite these similarities, researchers have noted differences between the two disorders. Wolff (1998) asked, "If there is an overlap between Asperger's and SCD, how is it possible that autism and schizophrenia rarely aggregate in the same families, or occur so rarely in the same person?" (p. 124). The clinical presentation of the two disorders is quite different. Asperger's disorder, or autism, becomes evident between 2 and 3 years of age when imaginative play is in ascendance. In contrast, schizoid children do not appear to be lacking in fantasy proneness; to the contrary, schizoids sometimes appear to have trouble distinguishing make-believe from reality (Wolff, 1998).

Whereas autism is usually apparent in early childhood, schizoid traits are usually first apparent in middle childhood, when the development of social skills and such activities as team sports are more common. Although the disorders share similar symptoms, it is likely that they stem from separate etiologies.

Dimensions and Boundaries
in the Schizophrenia Spectrum

There is considerable item overlap and comorbidity between SCD and schizotypal personality disorder. SCD shares deficit symptoms with schizotypal personality disorder, specifically those contributing to an asociality due to deficits in interpersonal skills and affect expression (Siever, Kalus, & Keefe, 1993). One group of researchers reported that schizoid personality correlated highly ($r = .65$) with schizotypal personality (Solano & De Chavez, 2000). Other researchers found that of those persons given a diagnosis of SCD, 80% met criteria for schizotypal personality disorder (Farmer & Chapman, 2002). A longitudinal study following 141 schizoid adolescents discovered that three fourths of this sample met DSM-III criteria for schizotypal personality disorder (Wolff, 1991). Although SCD shares several social deficit symptoms with schizotypal personality disorder, the two disorders can be distinguished by the absence of positive symptoms (e.g., magical thinking) in schizoid personality disorder.

Because elevated rates of all three disorders in Cluster A are found in the families of schizophrenic patients relative to the general population, all three disorders may reflect a shared genetic predisposition (Miller et al., 2001). One line of studies, examining the history of mental illness in the relatives of schizophrenic individuals, suggests that the boundaries of schizophrenia-related disorders may extend beyond schizotypal personality disorder to include schizoid and paranoid personality disorders (Baron et al., 1985; Gunderson, Siever, & Spaulding, 1983). Cluster A disorders are often seen in the biological relatives of patients with schizophrenia. In a controlled family study of inpatients with schizophrenia, it was found that Cluster A personality disorders occurred at a rate of 2.1% in probands in comparison to a rate of 0.3% in matched control families (Maier, Lichtermann, Minges, & Heun, 1994). In addition, the premorbid histories of individuals with schizophrenia often include paranoid, schizoid, and schizotypal personality disorder diagnoses. Furthermore, the high-risk offspring of schizophrenic patients followed longitudinally are later distinguishable from normal controls only by the prevalence of all Cluster A disorders, not by each separately (Erlenmeyer-Kimling et al., 1995). A retrospective study in which family members of schizophrenic patients were interviewed using the Structured

Clinical Interview for DSM-IV Axis II Personality Disorders (SCID-II; First, Gibbon, Spitzer, Williams, & Benjamin, 1997) found that 27.5% of the sample met criteria for premorbid SCD (Solano & De Chavez, 2000). Nevertheless, retrospective designs are vulnerable to hindsight bias, which may adversely affect the validity of reports. A prospective study is necessary to replicate and extend these findings.

In contrast, other studies suggest that a relationship with schizophrenia extends to schizotypal personality disorder but not to SCD (Baron et al., 1985). For example, Maier, Lichtermann, Minges, and Heun (1994) examined psychiatric illnesses in the relatives of schizophrenic patients. They found that of the Cluster A disorders, SCD occurred the least frequently in probands (between 0.3% and 0.7%). Given that schizotypal personality disorder, another Cluster A disorder believed to overlap etiologically with schizophrenia, occurred in 2.1% of relatives, it seems likely that the relationship between SCD and schizophrenia is tenuous at best.

As noted, the historical definition of SCD may add to the confusion surrounding the methodology of studies aimed at determining the boundaries of SCD. Some studies examining the genetic boundaries of the schizophrenia spectrum may also have been confounded by a failure to distinguish between SCD and schizotypal personality disorder. Evidence that negative rather than positive symptoms are associated with increased heritability in schizophrenia (Dworkin & Lenzenweger, 1984) would theoretically support a familial/genetic link between schizophrenia and SCD, because the latter is largely expressed through mild negative symptoms.

Assessment

Although there are no measures designed to explicitly assess SCD, a number of comprehensive structured interviews include scales assessing the disorder. For example, the SCID-II (First et al., 1997) is a widely used instrument in the assessment of personality disorders. Interrater reliability estimates for SCD using this measure (kappa = .90 for categorical assessments and intraclass correlation = .93 for dimensional assessments) have been formed (Maffei et al., 1997). A similar interview, the Structured Interview for DSM-IV Personality Disorders (SIDP-IV; Pfohl, Blum, & Zimmerman, 2001), also demonstrated good psychometric properties for SCD. For example, a recent study revealed that the SIDP-IV found higher levels of SCD in familial-high-risk siblings of schizophrenia patients versus normal controls (Auther, 2003).

In addition, there are several self-report questionnaires that assess SCD. The DSM-IV and ICD-10 Personality Questionnaire (DIP-Q) is a self-report measure designed to measure DSM-IV and ICD-10 personality disorders using 140 true/false questions (Ottosson, Grann, & Kullgren, 2000). Although this measure is useful because it offers diagnoses based on both diagnostic systems, a study examining the test-retest reliability reported a kappa value of only .42 for SCD (Ottosson, Grann, & Kullgren, 2000). In terms of internal consistency, the study reported Cronbach's alpha statistics of .68 and .69 for the DSM-IV and ICD-10, respectively. More research is necessary to evaluate the validity of this instrument for assessing SCD.

Another potentially useful assessment tool focuses on a specific symptom dimension of SCD. Chapman, Chapman, and Raulin (1976) developed the Social Anhedonia Scale (SocAnh), a 40-item self-report measure that gauges level of indifference to other people. A high score on the scale, which has an internal consistency between .80 and .90 (Chapman et al., 1976), has been found to correlate with schizophrenia spectrum disorders (Kwapil, 1998). Nevertheless, there are no known data concerning this scale's ability to differentiate among Cluster A disorders.

Treatment

There are few reported treatments of SCD, partly because such patients are theoretically unlikely to request treatment; aloof and "loner" behavior tendencies that characterize the disorder also would probably make the seeking of treatment unlikely (Stone, 1993). In addition, clinical reports indicate that few schizoid individuals see indifference to interpersonal contact and avoidance of others as problematic (Miller et al., 2001). When schizoid persons do seek help, it is rarely for prolonged periods of time (Stone, 1993). In fact, it is often a comorbid Axis I disorder (Miller et al., 2001), an acute stress, familial pressure, or a shift in life circumstances (Siever & Kendler, 1987) that leads the schizoid individual to appear in mental health settings.

There are no well-controlled studies of treatment efficacy for SCD. However, a few researchers have suggested target areas for treatment pending further research. For example, Beck and his colleagues (1990) suggest increasing social contact, learning skills useful for identifying emotions in the self as well as others, and using group therapy as a tool for practicing role playing and modeling appropriate behavior. Major changes and modifications of character structure are considered unlikely, probably because of theorized constitutionally determined limitations in affective response and expression (Millon, 1981). Therapy should probably be aimed at achieving modest reductions in social isolation and at promoting more effective adjustment to new circumstances. It is important to note that these therapeutic techniques have not been tested in controlled trials. The role of drug therapy for SCD remains an open question.

SCD seems to persist across the lifetime. A longitudinal study following a sample of schizoid children and comparing them with demographically matched normal controls demonstrated an increase in treatment for psychiatric disorders and a decrease in occupational functioning and rate of involvement in intimate relationships (Wolff, 1991). However, the course of illness is not entirely bleak; rates of independent living and employment for these individuals were not different from those of control subjects (Wolff, 1991).

Toward DSM-V

The current DSM classification system relies on an approach in which criteria are counted and then held in comparison to a cutoff value. For such personality disorders as SCD, in which the signs and symptoms appear to be highly subjective, this approach may be particularly problematic. Because a number of symptoms are vague and subjective, the threshold for a criterion is inevitably somewhat arbitrary. For example, the wording of criterion 2 ("almost always . . .") and criterion 4 ("takes pleasure in few . . .") leaves considerable room for clinical interpretation. In addition, a number of the criteria for SCD, such as criterion 6 ("appears indifferent . . .), rely heavily on behavioral observations (see Table 4.1). These criteria leave room for errors based on the context of assessment and biases resulting from the rater's experience.

Future research using taxometric methods (Meehl, 1995) should determine whether SCD is qualitatively or quantitatively different from normality. These methods estimate accurate base rates, locate optimal cuts on indicators, and provide a classification of individuals as accurate as indicators will permit. They also help determine whether a disorder, such as SCD, is underpinned by a taxon (category in nature) rather than a dimension. If taxometric methods prove SCD to be qualitatively distinct, then future conceptions of the disorder should focus on identifying a discrete biological etiology, such as a dominant gene, a configural set of genes, or prenatal or perinatal insult. Such a finding could also imply that SCD is a member of the schizophrenia spectrum, which appears to be qualitatively distinct from normality. This state of affairs may seem paradoxical, given that the schizophrenia spectrum is marked by dimensional variation. Nevertheless, it's useful to recall that within a taxon one can find dimensional variation attributable to polygenic factors, environmental influences, and the like. Taxometric methods could also help to establish whether SCD differs in kind or degree from avoidant personality disorder, a condition with which it overlaps substantially.

Alternatively, taxometric methods could suggest that SCD is underpinned by a latent dimension rather than a taxon. A dimensional approach to conceptualizing SCD has been gaining increased support (Matthews, Saklofske, Costa, Deary, & Zeidner, 1998). Dimensional models treat personality as a multivariate space and view personality dysfunction as extreme constellations of this space. One example is offered by researchers working to translate personality disorders into a five-factor model (FFM; Widiger, Trull, Clarkin, Sanderson, & Costa, 1994). Widiger and his colleagues (1994) presented promising data for the use of the FFM in conceptualizing SCD. They found that low levels of extraversion, low levels of neuroticism, especially on facets such as self-consciousness, and low levels of openness to experience best characterized SCD. A follow-up study (Trull & Widiger, 1997) provided further validity for this conceptualization by demonstrating that SCD was negatively correlated with measures of extraversion. A recent study determined that once comorbid symptomatology is removed from Cluster A disorders, SCD is characterized by low levels of such extraversion facets as positive emotions, warmth, and gregariousness (Trull, Widiger, & Burr, 2001).

A number of other dimensional models show promise for further conceptions of SCD. One criticism that surrounds the five-factor model is that it is based on personality constructs described by laypersons and omits complex personality features seen in clinical settings (Shedler & Westen, 2004). One alternative dimensional model has been derived from a card-sorting method: the Shedler-Westen Assessment Procedure-200 (SWAP-200). Researchers interviewed a large sample of psychiatrists and clinical psychologists who characterized specific personality disorders seen in their clinical work using a set of 200 personality-descriptive statements (Shedler & Westen, 2004). A Q (within-subject) factor analysis of these data yielded 12 dimensions: schizoid orientation, psychological health, psychopathy, hostility, narcissism, emotion dysregulation, dysphoria, obsessionality, thought disorder, oedipal conflict, dissociation, and sexual conflict statements (Shedler & Westen, 2004). The schizoid orientation dimension (Shedler & Westen, 2004) may be particularly suitable for describing and classifying SCD. For example, the highest factor loading (.58)—"appears to have little need for human contact; is genuinely indifferent to the presence of others" (p. 1749)—bears some similarities to several DSM-IV-TR criteria for SCD, but the next-highest loading (.57)—"tends to think in concrete terms and interpret things in overly literal ways; has limited ability to appreciate metaphor, analogy, or nuance" (p. 1749)—offers a new clinical perspective on SCD. By highlighting clinically relevant facets of the disorder, the SWAP-200 offers to enrich clinical description and potentially add criteria that differentiate SCD from schizotypal and avoidant personality disorders.

Conclusions

Given the dearth of empirical information, many aspects of SPD remain poorly understood. Despite a rich clinical history, appropriate DSM placement of the diagnosis remains unclear. Information on prevalence is inconsistent at best, and more discriminating diagnostic features are sorely needed. Most DSM-IV-TR SCD criteria with high specificity demonstrate unsatisfactory sensitivity, and those with high sensitivity generally have low specificity. There are no good treatment outcome data, and information on the course of illness is limited. Distinguishing SCD from other phenomeno-logically similar personality disorders in Cluster A and from avoidant per-sonality disorder remains a key concern. The question of whether SCD is part of the schizophrenia spectrum disorders requires additional investiga-tion. Future research should incorporate biological markers (e.g., deviant smooth eye tracking, attentional deficits) that have been observed in schizo-typal personality disorder and schizophrenia (Siever et al., 1993). In addi-tion, family history studies and designs including less seriously affected individuals are necessary to determine the extent of genetic overlap between SCD and both Asperger's disorder and schizophrenia (Wolff, 1998).

References

Akhtar, S. (1987). Schizoid personality disorder: A synthesis of developmental, dynamic, and descriptive features. *American Journal of Psychotherapy, 41,* 499–518.

American Psychiatric Association. (1980). *Diagnostic and statistical manual of men-tal disorders* (3rd ed.). Washington, DC: Author.

American Psychiatric Association. (1987). *Diagnostic and statistical manual of men-tal disorders* (3rd ed., revised.). Washington, DC: Author.

American Psychiatric Association. (1994). *Diagnostic and statistical manual of men-tal disorders* (4th ed.). Washington, DC: Author.

American Psychiatric Association. (2000). *Diagnostic and statistical manual of men-tal disorders* (4th ed., text revision). Washington, DC: Author.

Auther, A. M. (2003). Social anhedonia and schizophrenia-spectrum personality traits in genetic high-risk adolescents and young adults. *Dissertation Abstracts International, 63,* 7B. (UMI No. 3464)

Baron, M., Gruen, R., Rainer, J. D., Kane, J., Asnis, L., & Lord, S. (1985). A family study of schizophrenic and normal control probands: Implications for the spec-trum concept of schizophrenia. *American Journal of Psychiatry, 142,* 447–454.

Beck, A. T., Freeman, A. T., Pretzer, J., Davis, D. D., Fleming, B., Ottaviani, R., et al. (1990). *Cognitive therapy of personality disorders.* New York: Guilford Press.

Blackburn, R., Donnelly, J. P., Logan, C., & Renwick, S. J. D. (2004). Convergent and discriminative validity of interview and questionnaire measures of personality dis-order in mentally disordered offenders: A multitrait-multimethod analysis using confirmatory factor analysis. *Journal of Personality Disorders, 18*(2), 129–150.

Bleuler, E. (1924). *Textbook of psychiatry* (A. A. Brill, Trans.). New York: Macmillan.

Bleuler, M. (1954). The concept of schizophrenia [Letter to the editor]. *American Journal of Psychiatry, 111,* 382–383.

Chapman, L. J., Chapman, J. P., & Raulin, M. L. (1976). Scales for physical and social anhedonia. *Journal of Abnormal Psychology, 85,* 374–382.

Dahl, A. (1986). Some aspects of the DSM-III personality disorders illustrated by a consecutive sample of hospitalized patients. *Acta Psychiatrica Scandinavica, 73*(Suppl. 228), 61–66.

Drake, R., & Vaillant, G. (1985). A validity study of Axis II of DSM-III. *American Journal of Psychiatry, 142,* 553–558.

Dworkin, R., & Lenzenweger, M. (1984). Symptoms and the genetics of schizophrenia: Implications for diagnosis. *American Journal of Psychiatry, 141,* 1541–1546.

Ekselius, L., Tillfors, M., Furmark, T., & Fredrikson, M. (2001). Personality disorders in the general population: DSM-IV and ICD-10 defined prevalence as related to sociodemographic profile. *Personality and Individual Differences, 30,* 311–320.

Erlenmeyer-Kimling, L., Squire-Wheeler, E., Hildoff, U., Bassett, A. S., Cornblatt, B. A., Kestenbaum, C. J., et al. (1995). The New York High-Risk Project: Psychoses and Cluster A personality disorders in offspring of schizophrenic patients at 23 years of follow-up. *Archives of General Psychiatry, 52,* 827–865.

Farmer, R. F., & Chapman, A. L. (2002). Evaluation of DSM-IV personality disorder criteria as assessed by the Structured Clinical Interview for DSM-IV Personality Disorders. *Comprehensive Psychiatry, 43,* 285–300.

First, M. B., Gibbon, M., Spitzer, R. L., Williams, J. B. W., & Benjamin, L. S. (1997). *Structured clinical interview for DSM-IV Axis II personality disorders.* Washington, DC: American Psychiatric Press.

Freiman, K., & Widiger, T. A. (1989). [Co-occurrence and diagnostic efficiency statistics]. Unpublished raw data.

Grilo, C. M., McGlashan, T. H., Morey, L. C., Gunderson, J. G., Skodol, A.E., Tracie, S. M., et al. (2001). Internal consistency, intercriterion overlap and diagnostic efficiency of criteria sets for DSM-IV schizotypal, borderline, avoidant and obsessive-compulsive personality disorders. *Acta Psychiatrica Scandinavica, 104,* 264–272.

Gunderson, J. G., Siever, I. J., & Spaulding, F. (1983). The search for a schizotype: Crossing the border again. *Archives of General Psychiatry, 40,* 15–22.

Guntrip, H. (1969). *Schizoid phenomena, object relations, and the self.* New York: International Universities Press.

Hyler, S. E., & Rieder, R. O. (1994). *Personality diagnostic questionnaire–4+.* New York: Authors.

Kretschmer, E. (1925). *Physique and character.* London: Kegan Paul.

Kwapil, T. R. (1998). Social anhedonia as a predictor of the development of schizophrenia-spectrum disorders. *Journal of Abnormal Psychology, 107,* 558–565.

Loranger, A. W., Susman, V. L., Oldham, J. M., & Russakoff, L. M. (1987). Personality Disorder Examination: A preliminary report. *Journal of Personality Disorders, 1,* 1–13.

Maffei, C., Fossati, A., Agostoni, I., Barrao, A., Bagnato, M., Deborah, D., et al. (1997). Interrater reliability and internal consistency of the Structured Clinical Interview for DSM-IV Axis II Personality Disorders (SCID-II), Version 2.0. *Journal of Personality Disorders, 11*(3), 279–284.

Maier, W., Lichtermann, D., Minges, J., & Heun, R. (1994). Personality disorders among the relatives of schizophrenia patients. *Schizophrenia Bulletin, 20*(3), 481–493.

Matthews, G., Saklofske, D., Costa, P. T., Jr., Deary, I. J., & Zeidner, M. (1998). Dimensional models of personality: A framework for systematic clinical assessment. *European Journal of Psychological Assessment, 14*(1), 36–49.

Meehl, P. E. (1995). Bootstraps and taxometrics. *American Psychologist, 50*(4), 266–275.

Miller, M. B., Useda, D., Trull, T. J., Burr, M., & Minks-Brown, C. (2001). Paranoid, schizoid, and schizotypal personality disorder. In H. E. Adams & P. B. Sutker (Eds.), *Comprehensive handbook of psychopathology* (3rd ed.). New York: Kluwer Academic/Plenum.

Millon, T. (1981). *Disorders of personality: DSM-III, Axis II.* New York: Wiley Interscience.

Millon, T., Millon, C., & Davis, R. (1994). *MCMI-III manual.* Minneapolis, MN: National Computer Systems.

Millon, T., & Tringone, R. (1989). [Co-occurrence and diagnostic efficiency statistics]. Unpublished raw data.

Morey, L. (1988). Personality disorders in DSM-III and DSM-IIIR: Convergence, age, and internal consistency. *American Journal of Psychiatry, 145,* 573–577.

Morey, L., & Heumann, K. (1988). [Co-occurrence and diagnostic efficiency statistics]. Unpublished raw data.

Ottosson, H., Ekselius, L., Grann, M., & Kullgren, G. (2002). Cross-system concordance of personality disorder diagnosis of DSM-IV and diagnostic criteria for research of ICD-10. *Journal of Personality Disorders, 16*(3), 283–292.

Ottosson, H., Grann, M., & Kullgren, G. (2000). Test-retest reliability of a self-report questionnaire for DSM-IV and ICD-10 personality disorder. *European Journal of Psychological Assessment, 16,* 53–58.

Overholser, J. C. (1989). Differentiation between schizoid and avoidant personalities: An empirical test. *Canadian Journal of Psychiatry, 34*(8), 785–790.

Pfohl, B., Blum, N., & Zimmerman, M. (2001). *Structured interview for DSM–IV personality (SIDP-IV).* Washington, DC: American Psychiatric Press.

Reich, J., Yates, W., & Nduaguba, M. (1989). Prevalence of DSM-III personality disorders in the community. *Social Psychiatry and Psychiatric Epidemiology, 24,* 12–16.

Samuels, J., Eaton, W. W., Bienvenu, J., III, Brown, C. H., Costa, P. T., Jr., & Nestadt, G. (2002). Prevalence and correlates of personality disorders in a community sample. *British Journal of Psychiatry, 180,* 536–542.

Shedler, J., & Westen, D. (2004). Dimensions of personality pathology: An alternative to the five-factor model. *American Journal of Psychiatry, 161,* 1743–1754.

Siever, L. J., Kalus, O. F., & Keefe, R. S. E. (1993). The boundaries of schizophrenia. *Psychiatric Clinics of North America, 16*(2), 217–244.

Siever, L. J., & Kendler, K. S. (1987). Schizoid/schizotypal/paranoid personality disorders. In J. O. Cavenar (Ed.), *Psychiatry.* New York: Basic Books.

Skodol, A. F., Rosnick, L., Kellman, D., Oldham, J., & Hyler, S. (1988). Validating structured DSM-III-R personality disorder assessments with longitudinal data. *American Journal of Psychiatry, 145,* 1297–1299.

Solano, J. J. R., & De Chavez, M. G. (2000). Premorbid personality disorders in schizophrenia. *Schizophrenia Research, 44,* 137–144.

Stone, M. H. (1993). Long-term outcome in personality disorders. *British Journal of Psychiatry, 162,* 299–313.

Terry, G. C., & Rennie, T. (1938). Analysis of paraergesia. *American Journal of Orthopsychiatry, 9,* 817–918.

Trull, T. J., & Widiger, T. A. (1997). *Structured interview for the five-factor model of personality (SIFFM): Professional manual.* Odessa, FL: Psychological Assessment Resources.

Trull, T. J., Widiger, T. A., & Burr, R. (2001). A structured interview for the assessment of the five-factor model of personality: Facet-level relations to the Axis II personality disorders. *Journal of Personality, 69*(2), 175–198.

Trull, T. J., Widiger, T. A., & Frances, A. (1987). Covariation of criteria sets for avoidant, schizoid, and dependent personality disorders. *American Journal of Psychiatry, 144*(6), 767–771.

Widiger, T. A., Trull, T. J., Clarkin, J. F., Sanderson, C., & Costa, P. T., Jr. (1994). A description of the DSM-III-R and DSM-IV personality criteria sets. In P. T. Costa, Jr., & T. A. Widiger (Eds.), *Personality disorders and the five-factor model of personality* (pp. 41–56). Washington, DC: American Psychological Association.

Wolff, S. (1991). "Schizoid" personality in childhood and adult life: III. The childhood picture. *British Journal of Psychiatry, 159,* 629–635.

Wolff, S. (1998). Schizoid personality in childhood: The links with Asperger syndrome, schizophrenia spectrum disorders, and elective mutism. In E. Schopler & Z. B. Gary (Eds.), *Asperger syndrome or high-functioning autism? Current issues in autism* (pp. 123–138). New York: Plenum.

World Health Organization. (1992). *International classification of diseases* (10th revision). Geneva, Switzerland: Author.

Zimmerman, M., & Coryell, W. H. (1990). Diagnosing personality disorders in the community: A comparison of self-report and interview measures. *Archives of General Psychiatry, 47,* 527–531.

5 Schizotypal Personality Disorder

Annie M. Bollini
Emory University

Elaine F. Walker
Emory University

Introduction

Many of the diagnostic entities in the *Diagnostic and Statistical Manual of Mental Disorders* (DSM; American Psychiatric Association [APA], 2000) are derived from a combination of clinical experience, untested theoretical assumptions, and consensus. This is especially true of the Axis II disorders. But the diagnostic entity of schizotypal personality disorder (SPD) is largely grounded in empirical research. It is the product of research findings accumulated from behavior genetics and longitudinal studies conducted over several decades.

In this chapter, we begin by briefly reviewing the historical origins of SPD and presenting a typical case of an adolescent who meets criteria for SPD. Next, we discuss recent approaches to the assessment of schizotypal signs and syndromes, and then we turn to the accumulating empirical literature on the course and correlates of SPD. Finally, we draw on these findings to speculate on the validity and reliability of the SPD construct as it is currently conceptualized and offer directions for future research.

Historical Background

Although it is true that research (Kety, Rosenthal, Wender, & Schulsinger, 1968; Meehl, 1962, 1973a, 1973b) guided the conceptualization of SPD as a diagnostic entity, clinical observations served as the initial impetus for that research. These observations were largely drawn from the literature on schizophrenia. In fact, even the earliest descriptive writings on dementia praecox, and subsequently those on schizophrenia, contained comments on behavioral abnormalities observed in some biological relatives of patients. Bleuler (1924, 1969) and Kraepelin (1919/1971) noted that some first-degree relatives of probands, though not psychotic, had odd behavioral propensities that were enduring and similar to the symptoms of schizophrenia.

Concomitant with these trends in the psychiatric literature, research psychologists were advancing new ideas about the origins of vulnerability for schizophrenia, and this work also contributed to conceptualizations of SPD. In a seminal article, Meehl (1962) coined the term "schizotaxia" to refer to a constitutionally based behavioral syndrome that reflects the genetic liability for schizophrenia. On the biological level, Meehl described this vulnerability as a syndrome involving a subtle "neurointegrative" defect (i.e., problems with associated neural systems) with genetic origins. Meehl proposed that schizotaxia did not always progress to clinical schizophrenia. He hypothesized that, depending on environmental circumstances, some schizotaxic individuals remain stable over time, whereas others progress to either "schizotypy" or schizophrenia. Stressful social environments were presumed to be capable of triggering the transition to schizophrenia. This notion parallels the diathesis-stress model of schizophrenia spectrum disorders that has dominated the field over the past several decades (Gottesman, 1991; Meehl, 1973a, 1973b; Walker & Diforio, 1997).

With the publication of Meehl's paper in 1962, the terms *schizotaxia* and *schizotypy* entered the literature on schizophrenia and set the stage for systemic investigations of the presence of subclinical psychotic signs in nonclinical populations. Loren and Jean Chapman have been at the forefront of this field of research. These investigators and their colleagues began by obtaining retrospective self-reports of premorbid signs from schizophrenia patients (Freedman & Chapman, 1973). Patients reported that prior to the clinical onset of their illness, they experienced increased thought blocking, mental fatigue, inability to focus attention, visual illusions, misidentification of people, acute auditory perceptual abnormalities (i.e., heightened sensitivity to noises/sounds), and impaired perception of speech. The Chapmans subsequently coined the term "psychosis proneness" to refer to a predisposition, or diathesis, for psychosis, similar to the concept of schizotaxia. Drawing on the diathesis-stress model, the Chapmans assumed that psychoses, both schizophrenia and affective, arise from the interaction between environmental stress and a predisposition, or proneness, to psychotic thinking. Along with their colleagues, the Chapmans developed paper-and-pencil screening inventories to measure several key dimensions of psychosis proneness: the Physical Anhedonia Scale, the Perceptual Aberration Scale, the Magical Ideation Scale, the Impulsive Nonconformity Scale, and the Social Anhedonia Scale (Chapman & Chapman, 1980; Chapman, Chapman,

& Miller, 1982; Chapman, Chapman, & Raulin, 1976). They sought to test their assumptions about psychosis proneness by administering these scales to large numbers of college students who would be followed longitudinally. When subjects were followed 10 years after completing the scales, the authors found a significantly elevated rate of psychotic disorders in those designated as psychosis prone based on their scores obtained while they were in college (Chapman, Chapman, Kwapil, Eckblad, & Zinser, 1994).

Meehl's (1962) assumptions about the behavioral manifestations of vulnerability to schizophrenia were also reflected in research on the genetic origins of schizophrenia. The early behavior genetics studies of schizophrenia, primarily using family history and adoption methods, established that a behavioral syndrome, which included oddities in social behavior, perceptions, and ideation, was more common in the relatives of patients than in the general population (for a review, see Gottesman, 1991). As described in greater detail later, one of the earliest and most seminal studies was conducted by Kety and his colleagues (1968; Kety, Rosenthal, Wender, Schulsinger, & Jacobsen, 1976), who used reviews of hospital records and interviews with biological and adoptive relatives of schizophrenia patients. The investigators discovered an elevated rate of what they labeled "borderline" or "possible schizophrenia" (i.e., the presence of some clinically meaningful symptoms of schizophrenia, but too few to qualify for an Axis I diagnosis) in the biological relatives of patients.

Case Study

The following case study is a description of a young man who meets criteria for SPD. It depicts some of the symptoms, behaviors, and cognitive deficits that are characteristic of an individual with SPD.

Martin is a 17-year-old male high school student. His mother brought him to a university psychological center to participate in a research study about adolescent development because she was motivated to obtain the incentive: a free psychological assessment. She told the interviewer that she has been concerned about Martin's emotional and social functioning over the last 2 to 3 years and offered that his behavior reminded her of her eldest brother, who had a schizophrenia diagnosis when he was a youth.

As part of the study, Martin participated in a structured clinical interview. He was distant and reserved and made little eye contact with the interviewer. When asked a question, he frequently asked the interviewer to repeat or rephrase it, and he seemed to have difficulty providing examples to supplement his experiences. When answering a question, he was often vague or went off on tangents. He described feeling nervous around people, especially new people, and he frequently found himself preoccupied with questioning their

(Continued)

(Continued)

> intentions. He said he had no friends and preferred to do activities alone; he spent most of his time playing video games. In addition, he talked about his experiences with telepathy. He believed he was able to read some people's thoughts, especially those of his family. On several occasions, he had felt as if one of his parents had stolen thoughts from his head, but he explained to the interviewer that he had learned to deal with this problem by avoiding his parents. On occasion, he noticed objects and flashes of light out of the corner of his eye, but then he realized there was nothing there and told the interviewer it was probably in his head. During the interview, he seemed completely unconcerned about any aspects of his life other than his parents' reluctance to buy him a newer version of his current gaming system.

Martin's story is typical of a person who meets criteria for SPD. He is experiencing perceptual abnormalities, has unusual beliefs, and is socially isolated. The next sections describe the diagnostic system used to identify people with SPD and detail the genetic, developmental, and behavioral aspects of the disorder and its relation to schizophrenia.

The Diagnosis of SPD

In the late 1970s, the accumulating body of evidence gave rise to the syndrome labeled "schizotypal personality disorder," which entered the psychiatric nomenclature. Spitzer and his collaborators (Spitzer, Endicott, & Gibbon, 1979) proposed formal criteria for the new diagnostic category for the DSM-III (APA, 1980), and these were included in all subsequent revisions of the DSM. It is classified as an Axis II personality disorder, and thus is assumed to reflect an enduring set of behavioral propensities. Despite revisions of the DSM (i.e., DSM-III-R [APA, 1987], DSM-IV [APA, 1994], and DSM-IV-TR [APA, 2000]), the diagnostic criteria for SPD have remained relatively constant. At this point, there is not sufficient research on the longitudinal course of symptoms and functioning in people who meet current DSM criteria for SPD to warrant making modifications to these criteria in the next DSM revision. Once sufficient data are available, however, there may be a reasonable basis for revision. As it is currently defined, SPD involves both behavioral deficits, or negative signs, and behavioral abnormalities, or positive signs.

The DSM-IV diagnostic criteria for SPD include attenuated versions of the defining features of schizophrenia. Thus, for example, individuals with SPD report unusual sensory experiences that may be troubling, but the experiences do not qualify as hallucinations because their validity is questioned by the individual. Likewise, although unusual ideas may be present, they are not delusional in nature.

Schizotaxia did not become part of the nomenclature. Instead, this concept has been used by researchers to refer to the constitutional liability to schizophrenia. The results of nearly four decades of research, however, suggest that schizotaxia, too, may reflect a meaningful clinical condition, as well as an underlying liability for more severe schizophrenia-related conditions. Faraone, Green, Seidman, and Tsuang (2001) have recently reformulated the concept of schizotaxia, and their conceptualization differs from Meehl's (1962, 1973) in three ways. They assume that (1) the etiology of schizotaxia derives from both genetic factors and biological consequences of adverse environmental factors (e.g., pregnancy or delivery complications), whereas Meehl assumed the etiology was solely genetic; (2) schizotaxia reflects a multifactorial polygenic etiology, while Meehl proposed a single, major gene; and (3) schizotaxia is a stable condition in most cases, so neither schizotypy nor schizophrenia is the only, or most likely, outcome. These investigators are now beginning to conduct research aimed at identifying the components of schizotaxia based on studies of first-degree relatives of schizophrenia and SPD patients.

Exploring the Dimensions and Boundaries of SPD

As discussed in other chapters, there has been an ongoing debate about the relative merits of categorical versus dimensional approaches to personality. Both of these perspectives are reflected in the literature on SPD. The categorical approach is used in clinical practice, as well as in some clinical research studies in which SPD is conceptualized as a diagnostic entity with multiple indicators. In both realms, the DSM criteria are applied for diagnosis. For clinical research on SPD, structured interviews are typically employed so that information is obtained in a consistent manner. There are several structured clinical interviews for the personality disorders, such as the Structured Clinical Interview for DSM-IV Axis II Personality Disorders (SCID-II; First, Gibbon, Spitzer, Williams, & Benjamin, 1997) and the Structured Interview for DSM-IV Personality (SIDP-IV; Pfohl, Blum, & Zimmerman, 1994). There is one clinical interview specifically designed to assess SPD: the Structured Interview for Schizotypy (SIS; Kendler & Lister-Sharp, 1989).

The dimensional approach to schizotypy is reflected in a rapidly accumulating body of literature. As the phenomenology of SPD became more widely recognized in the clinical and research communities, investigators began to explore the measurement of the key features presumed to define the syndrome. Assuming that these features reflect relatively enduring behavioral and psychological dimensions and thus vary along a continuum, several self-report scales (e.g., the Schizotypal Personality Questionnaire) were developed to index schizotypal traits. A pivotal assumption guiding this work is that schizotypal signs are a manifestation of the genetic liability to schizophrenia and will occur at a higher frequency and intensity in the biological relatives of schizophrenia patients. Research findings consistent with this assumption have been obtained for some of the presumed signs of schizotypy (Kendler, Gruenberg, & Strauss, 1981).

The published measures of schizotypy vary in the extent to which they rely on the individual's self-report and in the emphasis they place on various features of SPD. The SIS was originally developed for behavior genetics research (Kendler & Lister-Sharp, 1989). It relies on both self-report and examiner observations. The SIS contains two sections and distinguishes between symptoms and signs. The first part is a structured interview with questions intended to yield information about schizotypal *symptoms* and social relationships. Based on the results, the examiner rates the subject, using seven-point scales, on 19 dimensions, including childhood social isolation, ideas of reference, magical thinking, and impulsivity. The second part of the SIS contains 16 scales and involves ratings of schizotypal *signs* based on the interviewer's observations of the individual's behavior. Examples of these scales are rapport, attention seeking, grooming, and enjoyment of the interview. Average intraclass correlations in the original studies were of the order of .8 for symptoms and .7 for signs. Advantageous features of the SIS are (1) questions that aid the interviewer in making contextual assessments of the pathological nature of certain symptoms (e.g., suspiciousness, ideas of reference) and (2) symptom probes designed to make responding in the affirmative appear nondeviant.

The SIS was revised by Vollema and Ormel (2000), primarily to standardize the rating procedures. In this revision (SIS-R), a four-point scale was introduced to provide more explicit criteria (i.e., frequency, duration, and level of conviction) for rating symptoms and signs. The SIS-R was administered to a sample of psychiatric patients with personality disorders, and the results showed that most schizotypal symptoms can be assessed reliably with the SIS-R, but only four of the nine individual schizotypal signs (e.g., goal-directed behavior, loosening of associations, amount of speech, and oddness) can be reliably assessed (Vollema & Ormel, 2000).

As described previously, the Chapman scales for measuring psychosis proneness represented the first systematic attempt to index subclinical signs of risk for psychotic disorders. This line of research has been extended in subsequent measures designed to index the DSM criteria for SPD. Notable among these is the Schizotypal Personality Questionnaire (SPQ), which is a relatively brief self-report instrument that provides subscale scores for each of the nine DSM schizotypal personality disorder criteria (Raine, 1991). The SPQ taps both positive tendencies (i.e., distortions of normal functioning, such as hallucinations, bizarre delusions, and disorganized thoughts) and negative tendencies (i.e., diminution of normal functioning, such as restricted range of emotion, social withdrawal, decreased goal-directed behavior) and includes items pertaining to ideas of reference, suspiciousness, magical thinking, and unusual perceptual experiences. The SPQ was developed for the study of schizotypy in the general population and as a screening device for SPD. This instrument has high test-retest reliability (.82) over a 2-month period and high convergent validity ($r = .65$–$.81$), but low, though significant, discriminant validity ($r = .19$–$.37$). Factor analysis of the SPQ yields three factors: cognitive-perceptual, interpersonal, and disorganized. This factor structure has been documented in both nonpatient and patient samples (Raine et al., 1994; Vollema & Hoijtink, 2000).

Another example of a self-report measure is the Kings Schizotypy Questionnaire (KSQ). The KSQ is a forced-choice (yes/no) self-report measure of schizotypy developed by Williams (1993). The KSQ contains items based on the DSM-III criteria for SPD as well as on self-reported subjective experiences described by psychiatrically well relatives of schizophrenia patients. In the development of the questionnaire, high internal consistency and test-retest reliability were established (Williams, 1993), and this instrument was found to differentiate schizophrenia from nonschizophrenia individuals at a high rate (Jones et al., 2000). Factor analysis confirmed that the KSQ tapped the major dimensions of schizotypy, including both positive and negative signs (Claridge et al., 1996; Williams, 1993).

Prevalence of SPD

Specifying base rates for personality disorders has proven difficult. Diagnosing any personality disorder can take several hours of interviewing. Moreover, people who meet criteria for these disorders are likely to be disinclined to initiate evaluation, treatment, or research participation. This may be especially true of individuals who meet criteria for SPD, as they manifest signs of social withdrawal. Because their social interactions are reduced, they are less likely to be clinically detected. For these reasons, estimates of the base rate of SPD are probably conservative.

The DSM-IV reports that the prevalence of SPD in the general population is 3% (APA, 1994). This figure is based on studies of SPD yielding estimates between 1% and 3%. In first-degree relatives of *normal* controls, the SPD prevalence rate was found to be 1% (Maier, Lichtermann, Klingler, Heun, & Hallmayer, 1992). This figure is presumed to be an underestimate of the population rate due to the fact that the probands were screened for psychiatric disorder. A large-scale study of consecutive psychiatric admissions to a community hospital found that 2% met criteria for SPD (Loranger, 1990). Finally, based on phone interviews, another study found that 3% of the respondents met criteria for SPD (Zimmerman & Coryell, 1990). Because the 3% rate obtained via phone interview is based on the most representative sample, it is probably the most valid estimate of the population rate. However, this 3% figure should be considered conservative, as this estimate is based on a random sample of individuals who were willing and able to respond to a telephone survey about their mental health. Some with SPD would not agree to such an interview or have a telephone. Nonetheless, at 3%, SPD would be one of the more common personality disorders, because the prevalence of all personality disorders combined is estimated to be about 11% (Lenzenweger, 1999).

The estimated prevalence of SPD is much higher, possibly three to four times higher, than the prevalence of schizophrenia. As described in the following sections, the majority of those who meet criteria for SPD do not develop any psychotic disorder, although the risk for schizophrenia is significantly elevated in individuals with SPD (Miller, Byrne, et al., 2002; Yung et al., 1998).

The Genetic Link Between Schizotypal Personality Disorder and Schizophrenia

The genetic relation between schizophrenia and SPD has been the subject of investigation for several decades. The concept of SPD hinges on its genetic link with schizophrenia, and as currently defined, SPD and schizophrenia share common features such as odd beliefs, social impairment, and abnormalities in perceptual experiences and emotional expression. However, SPD criteria specify an attenuated version of the psychotic symptoms necessary for a schizophrenia diagnosis. How strong is the genetic link between the two disorders?

To address this question, researchers have conducted family, twin, and adoption studies. Most examine the rate of schizophrenia or SPD in first- and second-degree family members of probands (i.e., index individuals with SPD or schizophrenia). Findings from these diverse approaches converge to lend substantial support to the notion that SPD and schizophrenia share a genetic liability.

As noted earlier, Kety and his colleagues (1968) published a landmark report from the Danish Adoption Study that fueled interest in schizotypy. They conducted assessments of the biological relatives of adoptees (probands) who were diagnosed with schizophrenia in young adulthood. The study also included the biological relatives of a group of normal adoptees. In most cases, the adoptees who were the subject of this research had been placed in their adoptive homes in infancy. The investigators found a significantly higher rate of schizophrenia in the biological relatives of the probands with schizophrenia (5.3%) than in the relatives of those probands without the illness (1.8%), confirming a genetic contribution to the etiology of schizophrenia. In addition, they observed an elevated rate (15.9%) of milder psychiatric syndromes in the biological relatives of the adopted schizophrenia patients compared to relatives of nonschizophrenia probands (4.9%). These syndromes were characterized by subclinical versions of some of the defining symptoms of schizophrenia. Thus a subgroup of the relatives of probands manifested interpersonal deficits, odd ideas, unusual perceptual experiences, and behavioral abnormalities.

The findings from the Danish Adoption Study not only provided further evidence for the genetic etiology of schizophrenia but also suggested the existence of less severe behavioral manifestations of the genetic vulnerability.

This and subsequent reports led to the notion of "schizophrenia spectrum disorders" and set the stage for the development of diagnostic criteria for SPD, which were published in 1979 (Spitzer, Endicott, & Gibbon, 1979).

In an effort to validate the diagnostic criteria proposed for SPD, Kendler and his colleagues (1981) used the SIS to rediagnose a subset of the biological relatives from the Kety et al. (1968) investigation. Consistent with predictions, they found a higher rate of SPD (10.5%) in biological relatives of schizophrenic adoptees than in controls (1.5%). In contrast, the rates of SPD in the *adoptive* relatives of both the schizophrenia and control adoptees were very low (2%–3%) and strikingly similar. This report yielded the first empirical support for the validity of the newly developed criteria for SPD.

The majority of the investigations aimed at understanding the genetic relation between SPD and schizophrenia have used the family method. Studies of the family members of SPD probands have revealed significantly elevated rates of schizophrenia (2%–4%) and other schizophrenia spectrum disorders (14–15%) when compared to the relatives of individuals with other personality disorders (Battaglia, Bernardeschi, Franchini, Bellodi, & Smeraldi, 1995; Siever et al., 1990). Similarly, studies of the biological relatives of schizophrenia patients replicate the findings from the Danish Adoption Study. The rate of SPD is significantly higher in family members of schizophrenia patients than in relatives of normal controls (Gershon, DeLisi, Hamovit, & Nurnberger, 1988; Kendler & Gruenberg, 1984). Along the same lines, a meta-analysis using data from three large-scale family studies revealed that when data on relatives were aggregated, the odds ratios (OR) for schizophrenia (OR = 16.2), SPD (OR = 5.0), and nonaffective psychosis (OR = 4.0) were higher for relatives of schizophrenia probands than for normal control probands (Kendler & Gardner, 1997).

Adoption and family studies have established a genetic link between schizophrenia and SPD. The mode of transmission of the genetic vulnerability, however, has not yet been established, although the prevailing assumption is that it is polygenic (Gottesman, 1991). Thus, it is assumed that multiple, additive, and/or interactive genes, rather than a single major genetic locus, confer the risk for schizophrenia. This raises the question of whether SPD and schizophrenia are behavioral expressions of the same or different polygenotypes. Perhaps the SPD relatives of schizophrenia probands possess only a subset of the genes required for the schizophrenia phenotype. The full complement of "risk genes" (i.e., complete polygenotype) may be required for schizophrenia. A related question concerns the heritability of the polygenotype. Does its presence always lead to schizophrenia, or, as implied by the prevailing diathesis-stress model, do environmental factors interact to determine the nature of the phenotypic expression? It is possible that the polygenotype can be expressed as either SPD or schizophrenia, depending on environmental factors. Research on twins has the potential to shed light on this issue.

Twin studies are a powerful methodological tool for exploring the genetic contribution to psychiatric syndromes. The results of twin studies provide support for the notion that the phenotypic expression of the genetic vulnerability to schizophrenia can vary, with SPD being one of the variants (Torgersen, 1994). Several studies have shown that SPD occurs more frequently in the monozygotic (MZ) co-twins of schizophrenia patients than in the dizygotic (DZ) co-twins of patients. For example, Farmer, McGuffin, and Gottesman (1987) examined the Maudsley twin sample and obtained the maximum MZ/DZ concordance ratio (7.68) when diagnostic criteria were broadened to include "spectrum disorders," namely, SPD, affective disorder with mood-incongruent delusions, and atypical psychosis, in addition to schizophrenia. In contrast, adding paranoid disorder (paranoia) and all other affective disorder categories reduced the ratio. Similarly, Torgersen and Kringlen (1991) interviewed MZ and DZ twin pairs with schizophrenia probands and found a significantly elevated rate of SPD in the co-twins. But the concordance rates were elevated for both MZ and DZ pairs, and the MZ/DZ concordance ratio was not large, indicating that shared environmental factors, including the prenatal environment, also play a role in the development of SPD. Further, when Torgersen (1984) examined co-twins of probands with SPD, he found that no MZ co-twins met diagnostic criteria for schizophrenia. This finding is consistent with data on the base rates of SPD and schizophrenia, as well as the assumption that shared environmental factors play a role in the expression of both SPD and schizophrenia.

Taken together, the findings on MZ twins indicate that the same polygenotype can result in schizophrenia or SPD. Consistent with this notion, Risch and Baron's (1984) quantitative genetic modeling analysis of data on twin pairs with one schizophrenia proband revealed that the best fit was obtained with broader diagnostic criteria that included both schizophrenia and SPD, rather than schizophrenia alone. When the broad phenotype was used, all single-locus models without polygenic background were excluded, but the results were consistent with polygenic inheritance. Further, the polygenic model was a better fit for the data when SPD was included in the phenotype, again suggesting that SPD is an alternative manifestation of the liability to schizophrenia.

Of course, schizophrenia and SPD vary in their symptom expression. It is of interest to know whether the risk rate for either disorder in relatives varies as a function of the proband's symptom profile. Some findings indicate that the negative signs of schizophrenia and schizotypy are more heritable than the positive signs. Dworkin and Lenzenweger (1984) studied twin pairs with schizophrenia probands and found that concordance rates in the MZ pairs were higher when probands had a greater number of negative symptoms, but there was no evidence of a similar relationship for positive symptoms. The authors concluded that negative symptoms may be indicative of a more heritable genotype. Similarly, when Torgersen (1984) examined the MZ and DZ concordance rates for DSM Cluster A disorders, SPD showed significant heritability, higher than that of borderline personality disorder. But the genetic influences on SPD were significantly more pronounced for the social withdrawal and paranoid/suspicious features than they were for the "psychotic-like" ideational and perceptual anomalies. Along these lines, a recent report by MacDonald and colleagues (MacDonald, Pogue-Geile, Debski, & Manuck, 2001) examined the occurrence of schizotypal signs in MZ and DZ twins using the Chapman scales. The findings indicated that social anhedonia (negative sign) and perceptual aberration (positive sign) were more strongly influenced by genes than were indices of ideational abnormality (positive sign). Finally, when the KSQ was administered to large samples of schizophrenia patients, their healthy first-degree relatives, and unrelated controls, it did not distinguish the relatives from controls, although schizophrenia patients scored higher on the KSQ (Jones et al., 2000). The authors conjectured that their results might be due to defensive responding and/or self-selection bias among relatives, or the fact that the KSQ does not assess negative signs. Taken together, these studies indicate that the negative signs of SPD may be under greater genetic control than the positive signs (Faraone et al., 2001).

In contrast, other findings suggest that positive signs evidence greater heritability. Baron, Gruen, and Romo-Gruen (1992) found that the risk for both schizophrenia and SPD was higher in first-degree relatives of schizophrenia patients with predominantly positive symptoms than it was in relatives of patients with mainly negative symptoms. Kremen et al. (1998) compared SPQ scores of normal controls to the scores of the biological relatives of schizophrenia patients. Relatives scored higher on positive schizotypy, particularly the cognitive-perceptual factor of the SPQ, when compared to controls. No differences were found for the negative and disorganization schizotypy dimensions. Yaralian et al. (2000) also found that the relatives of schizophrenia patients had elevated scores on the cognitive-perceptual factor of the SPQ, particularly for the "unusual perceptual experiences" and "ideas of reference" subscales.

These results suggest that previous failures to demonstrate elevated scores on positive symptoms of schizotypy may be a function of the measure. The earlier studies used measures other than the SPQ, such as the Perceptual Aberration Scale, which may not be as sensitive as the SPQ to individual differences in the positive signs of schizotypy. As mentioned, the SPQ assesses four positive features of SPD: ideas of reference, magical thinking, unusual perceptual experiences, and suspiciousness, and these items contributed to the differentiation of biological relatives from controls in both the Yaralian et al. (2000) and Kremen et al. (1998) studies. Some of these items are not assessed by the Perceptual Aberration Scale, which may account for the discrepancy between studies that do and do not find group differences for positive schizotypy. Clearly, more research is needed to identify the key dimensions of schizotypy that are genetically influenced and linked to schizophrenia.

In summary, there is substantial support from family, adoption, and twin studies that schizophrenia and SPD share a common genetic liability. But the MZ concordance rates for both schizophrenia and SPD indicate that environmental factors also play a key role (Gottesman, 1991).

Obstetrical complications (OCs) are considered to be one such environmental factor. OCs occur at higher rates in the medical histories of schizophrenia patients than in nonpsychiatric samples (Cannon, Barr, & Mednick, 1991; Schulsinger, Parnas, Mednick, Teasdale, & Schulsinger, 1987). Bakan and Peterson (1994) found that college undergraduates with SPD traits experienced substantially more OCs during their births. Artificial labor induction and birth defects were the most commonly reported OCs in the high SPD trait group.

Environment may also play a key role in the expression of a vulnerability to SPD. Although there are no reports on the role of psychosocial factors in the expression of SPD, there is a large body of literature documenting that psychosocial stressors influence the onset and course of schizophrenia. In particular, stress (Ventura, Neuchterlein, Hardesty, & Gitlin, 1992) and other environmental factors, such as the amount of expressed emotion (i.e., critical comments, negative emotional overinvolvement) in families, have been found to exacerbate symptoms and precipitate relapse (Butzlaff & Hooley, 1998). More recent research suggests that characteristics of the patient's illness, such as symptom severity and presence of negative symptoms, elicit more critical comments and greater emotional overinvolvement in mothers (King, 2000). Thus the relationship between negative expressed emotion in family members and poor outcome in patients appears to be bidirectional.

The Developmental Link Between SPD and Schizophrenia

SPD and schizophrenia also share a developmental link. Specifically, SPD signs, and even the full SPD syndrome, often predate the onset of schizophrenia. Retrospective and follow-back studies have demonstrated that most people who develop schizophrenia as adults experience social problems, such as having fewer friends and poor social adjustment (Done, Crow, Johnstone, & Sacker, 1994) well before manifesting the illness (Walker, Grimes, Davis, & Smith, 1993; Walker & Lewine, 1990). Further, prospective research has shown that the transition rate to schizophrenia is much higher in SPD individuals than in mentally healthy controls and those with other psychological disorders.

Follow-back studies have revealed that, even in childhood, preschizophrenia children, especially adolescents, are rated by their teachers as showing more social maladjustment (Done et al., 1994), less responsiveness in social situations, and fewer instances of positive emotion (Walker et al., 1993; Walker & Lewine, 1990). In adolescence, there is typically a gradual increase in adjustment problems, including social withdrawal, irritability, negative affect, and noncompliance (Walker, Baum, & Diforio, 1998). These behaviors are part of the criteria for SPD and suggest the presence of subthreshold as well as clinically significant SPD prior to the development of schizophrenia.

Evidence of a developmental progression from SPD to schizophrenia is also provided by prospective studies. There has been a resurgence of interest in the clinical progression of SPD, with the goal of identifying more sensitive and specific predictors of schizophrenia. This renewed emphasis on prediction stems, in part, from evidence that a longer duration of untreated psychosis leads to worse disease prognosis and course (McGlashan, 1999). Thus targeting vulnerable individuals for intervention prior to the clinical manifestation of schizophrenia may prevent illness onset or reduce severity. A substantial proportion of young adults who meet DSM criteria for SPD subsequently develop schizophrenia. Several recent short-term longitudinal studies have found that about 20% to 40% of young adults with SPD develop schizophrenia within 1 to 5 years (Miller, Byrne, et al., 2002; Yung et al., 1998). Thus the proportion of schizotypals who develop schizophrenia is high in light of the population base rate of schizophrenia, which is 1% to 2% (Gottesman, 1991).

In a study using the SIS, biological relatives of schizophrenia patients were assessed at 16 to 25 years of age, then followed over time to monitor their psychiatric status (Miller, McGlashan, et al., 2002). The goal was to determine which symptom dimension ratings from the SIS best predicted clinical course. Within 3 years, 7/78 (9%) of the participants who had no Axis I disorder at entry into the study developed a psychotic disorder. The best predictor from the SIS was social withdrawal, such that 5/12 (42%) scoring above the cutoff on this scale developed a psychiatric illness and 64/66 (97%) of those below the cutoff remained healthy. Thus, social withdrawal showed reasonably high sensitivity and specificity for predicting psychotic outcome over a short period of time; these findings are particularly noteworthy because schizophrenia has a heterogeneous clinical picture that does not always include social withdrawal. In contrast, for odd behavior, there was high sensitivity but low specificity; 6/7 (86%) of the onset cases scored high, as did 28/71 (39%) of those who remained healthy. A combination of four factors—social withdrawal, psychotic-like symptoms, socioemotional dysfunction, and odd behavior—was the best predictor, with 6/9 (67%) of the participants who scored above the cutoff point falling ill and 68/69 (99%) of those scoring below it remaining well. This combination of signs and symptoms is consistent with a diagnosis of SPD.

Functional and Biological Parallels Between SPD and Schizophrenia

There is a vast literature documenting various cognitive and physical abnormalities in patients with schizophrenia. To explore the validity of the SPD criteria and shed light on etiologic mechanisms, investigators have sought to determine whether similar abnormalities are present in SPD. The results of this research generally indicate that those who meet criteria for SPD show functional deficits and physical abnormalities that parallel those observed in schizophrenia, although the magnitude of the deficits typically is less severe in SPD.

Cognitive Functioning

Cognitive impairment is well established in schizophrenia and involves generalized deficits, especially pronounced deficiencies in verbal memory, attention, and executive functions, such as vigilance, working memory, and planning (Cornblatt, Green, & Walker, 1999; Heinrichs & Zakzanis, 1998). Individuals who meet criteria for SPD show a similar pattern (Voglmaier, Seidman, Salisbury, & McCarley, 1997). For example, Voglmaier et al. (1997, 2000) found that unmedicated SPD patients manifested general cognitive impairment, including more pronounced deficits in verbal fluency, learning, and retention. Along the same lines, other investigators have shown that SPD is associated with poorer verbal and spatial working memory (Farmer et al., 2000; Harvey, Powchick, Mohs, & Davidson, 1995; Keefe et al., 1995; Park & McTigue, 1997; Park, Pueschel, Sauter, Rentsch, & Hell, 1999; Saykin et al., 1991).

In addition to impairments in verbal functions, adults who meet criteria for SPD show deficits in sustained attention (Condray & Steinhauer, 1992; Nuechterlein et al., 2002). Attentional deficits have also been found in college students who score high on schizotypal traits (Lenzenweger, Cornblatt, & Putnick, 1991).

Findings have been mixed with respect to executive functioning. Some researchers have reported that individuals with SPD manifest deficits in aspects of executive functioning related to concept formation, abstract reasoning, and perseverative errors when compared to normal controls (Diforio, Walker & Kestler, 2000; Lyons, Merla, Young, & Kremen, 1991; Spaulding, Garbin, & Dras, 1989). In contrast, others have found that individuals with subthreshold and clinical SPD perform similarly to normal controls on measures of executive functions that tap vigilance (Condray & Steinhauer, 1992; Raine et al., 1992). Executive functioning comprises several cognitive abilities (e.g., planning, sequencing, monitoring), and the discrepancy among these studies may be due to the use of different measures.

Motor and Physical Correlates of SPD

Consistent with the assumption that schizophrenia has neurodevelopmental origins, investigators have found physical correlates of the illness, including motor and dermatoglyphic abnormalities (i.e., abnormal patterns on the top layer of skin on the hands) and minor physical anomalies. Like schizophrenia patients (Cornblatt et al., 1999), individuals with SPD manifest abnormalities in motor functions. They show more abnormal spontaneous movements (Walker,

Lewis, Loewy, & Palvo, 1999) and less motor proficiency (Neumann & Walker, 1999) than non-SPD individuals. Recent investigations of SPD have also revealed an elevated rate of minor physical anomalies and dermatoglyphic abnormalities, namely, asymmetries in finger ridge counts (Weinstein, Diforio, Schiffman, Walker, & Bonsall, 1999). These results are consistent with the assumption that SPD and schizophrenia share an underlying neural substrate.

Psychophysiology

There is a substantial literature documenting abnormal psychophysiological responses in both schizophrenia and SPD. Parallel abnormalities have been found in prepulse inhibition, heart rate, electrodermal activity, and other autonomic nervous system–controlled responses.

Prepulse inhibition (PPI) of the startle response refers to the decrease in the startle response (measured with eye blink or skin conductance) to the onset of the startling stimulus (e.g., air puff, aversive noise) when it is preceded by the presentation of a "warning," or prestimulus. PPI is presumed to be a measure of sensorimotor gating—the ability to suppress, or gate, sensory, motor, or cognitive stimuli. Compared to normal and psychiatric controls, schizophrenia patients display less PPI of the startle response, suggesting they are hyperresponsive (Kumari, Soni, & Sharma, 1999; Weike, Bauer, & Hamm, 2000). Consistent with this pattern, schizotypal individuals show deficits in PPI when compared to healthy controls (Cadenhead, Geyer, & Braff, 1993). Along the same lines, P50 suppression paradigms assess the effectiveness of inhibition of the brain electrical response to the second of two auditory stimuli presented in rapid succession. The suppression of the second click is reduced in both schizophrenia (Clementz, Geyer, & Braff, 1997; Freedman et al., 1997) and SPD patients (Cadenhead, Light, Geyer, & Braff, 2000).

Reflexive eye movement responses are also aberrant in both schizophrenia and SPD. Saccadic eye movement inhibition is measured with an antisaccade task, in which the participant is asked to make a saccade in the opposite direction of a target. Investigations of this ability reveal that patients with schizophrenia (Fukushima, Fukushima, Morita, & Yamashita, 1990) and SPD (Ross et al., 1998) show a higher proportion of antisaccade errors (i.e., saccade toward the target rather than in the opposite direction as instructed) than normals. These findings suggest abnormal eye movement responses in these groups.

On measures of electrodermal activity, specifically skin conductance (SC), schizophrenia patients show a pattern characterized by extremes of either nonresponding or hyperresponding, with a significantly larger proportion of patients than normals being nonresponders (Bernstein et al., 1982; Dawson & Neuchterlein, 1987; Gruzelier & Raine, 1994). About 40% of schizophrenic participants show electrodermal nonresponding (Ohman, 1981), and this pattern has been linked to the presence of more negative symptoms

(Alm, Lindstrom, Ost, & Ohman, 1984; Bernstein et al., 1981). Results of SC investigations in SPD have been mixed, although most show differences between schizotypal and normal participants (Gruzelier & Raine, 1994; for a review, see Raine, Lencz, & Benishay, 1995). Most studies show a pattern marked by inconsistency of SC responding across trials in SPD participants, such that they show less SC responsivity on some trials and greater responsivity on others compared to normal controls (Wilkins, 1988).

In general, it appears that SPD is associated with abnormalities in PPI, P50, saccadic eye movements, and SC responding similar to those observed in schizophrenia. These findings provide additional support for the etiologic relation between the two disorders and indicate that central nervous system regulation is disrupted in both.

Structural Brain Abnormalities

Investigations of brain morphology in schizophrenia have revealed that patients show volumetric reductions in multiple brain regions, including the frontal and temporal lobes and hippocampus, as well as enlargement of the ventricles (Gur et al., 2000; Kumra et al., 2000; Lawrie & Abukmeil, 1998; Mitelman, Shihabuddin, Brickman, Hazlett, & Buchsbaum, 2003). There is support for similar, though less pronounced, structural abnormalities in schizotypal individuals.

For example, SPD patients have larger ventricular (i.e., cerebrospinal fluid) volumes, reduced cortical gray matter volumes (Dickey et al., 2000), and smaller temporal lobes compared to normal controls (Downhill et al., 2001), especially in superior temporal gyrus gray matter volume (Dickey et al., 1999). Other investigations of temporal lobe volume indicate that medial and inferior temporal gyrus volumes are reduced in SPD, as in schizophrenia (Siever et al., 2000). However, schizophrenia patients show more severe medial temporal lobe abnormalities than SPD individuals (Pearlson et al., 1997). One study showed that SPD individuals demonstrated reduced gray matter volume in the prefrontal cortex compared to both psychiatric and normal control groups (Raine et al., 2002), although some have not replicated this finding (Siever et al., 2002).

In an investigation of ventricular volume in schizophrenia and SPD, schizophrenia patients had the largest left anterior and temporal horns, followed by SPD patients, and then normal controls (Buchsbaum, Yang, et al., 1997). Thalamic volumes also are abnormal in schizophrenia and SPD. Decreased thalamic volumes in the pulvinar region have been reported in both groups (Byne et al., 2001). Additional reductions in the mediodorsal nucleus have been observed in schizophrenia patients, but not in SPD individuals (Siever et al., 2000). These results suggest that the severity of morphological brain abnormalities found in SPD falls between schizophrenia and normality.

Overall, these findings indicate that structural brain abnormalities are a feature associated with SPD. Morphological abnormalities are found in the frontal and temporal regions as well as in the thalamus and ventricles.

Abnormalities in brain morphology may have functional consequences. For example, there is substantial support for the idea that decreased hippocampal volume is related to poorer memory functioning (Walder, Walker, & Bollini, in press). Thus, brain morphological abnormalities linked with SPD may contribute to functional deficits. Furthermore, some studies indicate that SPD brain abnormalities are less pronounced than those observed in schizophrenia. These findings lend further support to the notion that SPD is related to schizophrenia, but the degree of neuropathology appears to be attenuated.

Functional Brain Abnormalities

In addition to structural abnormalities, schizotypal individuals manifest functional brain abnormalities. However, these abnormalities do not consistently parallel those documented in schizophrenia. For example, in a positron-emission tomography (PET) study of SPD in which schizophrenia and normal groups performed a list-learning task, the SPD patients showed higher metabolic rates in the medial frontal and medial temporal areas than normals (Buchsbaum et al., 2002). They also manifested higher metabolic rates in Brodmann area 10 than both normals and unmedicated schizophrenia patients. While performing this same task, SPD individuals displayed increased glucose metabolic rates in the ventral putamen, which suggests decreased dopaminergic activity in this area. However, schizophrenia patients displayed the opposite pattern—namely, decreased glucose metabolic rates—in this area compared to normal controls. This finding was interpreted as support for the notion of anomalous prefrontal cortex activity in schizophrenia and SPD, which is diminished in schizophrenia and compensated for in SPD (Shihabuddin et al., 2001). In contrast to these findings, SPD and normal participants showed similar activation of the thalamic nuclei while performing an auditory learning task (Hazlett et al., 1999).

Studies of resting brain activity also suggest a distinction between SPD and schizophrenia. In an electroencephalogram (EEG) study of frontal activity in unmedicated schizophrenia, SPD, and depression patients, those with schizophrenia showed an increase in delta activity throughout the cortex, with greatest activity in the anterior cingulate gyrus and temporal lobes (i.e., the fusiform gyrus; Mientus et al., 2002). SPD and depressed individuals, in contrast, showed significantly fewer delta waves in the anterior cingulate and right temporal lobe. Thus the schizophrenia and SPD groups showed different patterns of activation. In another EEG study, unmedicated schizophrenia patients showed increased delta activity in the frontal lobe while resting, whereas SPD patients did not show this abnormality (Wuebben & Winterer, 2001). Yet there is evidence that SPD and normal subjects differ in frontal activity during executive functioning tasks. In a single-photon emission computed tomography (SPECT) study of regional cerebral blood flow (rCBF), SPD individuals showed greatest activation in the middle frontal gyrus, whereas normal controls displayed mostly precentral gyrus activation (Buchsbaum, Trestman, et al., 1997).

When compared to normals, schizotypal individuals show abnormal brain activation, particularly in the frontal and temporal brain regions, while resting and during some cognitive tasks. Schizophrenia patients show abnormal activation in similar brain regions; however, the nature of their dysfunctional patterns appears qualitatively different. This finding may reflect differences in the neural bases of the disorder, but it also is possible that antipsychotic medication contributes to these differences. Furthermore, it has been found that decreased or atypical activation of brain circuitry during cognitive performance is related to performance deficits (Heckers et al., 1999). Thus abnormal activation patterns may have functional consequences, and these patterns may contribute to the cognitive deficits characteristic of SPD and schizophrenia.

Neurochemistry

Neurochemical abnormalities have been central to hypotheses about the neuropathophysiology of schizophrenia. Among the neurotransmitters, dopamine has received the most attention for its relation to psychotic symptomatology. Researchers have found higher concentrations of dopamine and homovanillic acid (HVA), a dopamine metabolite, in schizophrenia patients' brains (Davis, Kahn, Ko, & Davidson, 1991), and a relation between these higher concentrations and more severe psychotic symptoms (Davis et al., 1985; Davis et al., 1991). Similarly, there is some evidence that SPD individuals show elevated cerebrospinal fluid HVA concentrations compared to individuals with other personality disorders (Siever et al., 1993). Furthermore, Siever and his colleagues (1993) reported a positive relation between these concentrations and psychotic-like schizotypal symptoms. These findings provide evidence of elevated dopamine in SPD that mimics the pattern found in schizophrenia and lends further support to the notion that the two illnesses are neurochemically related.

Given the assumption that stress can exacerbate schizophrenia symptoms, investigators have examined biological indicators of the stress response. Secretion of the neurohormone cortisol increases in response to stress. There is substantial evidence that, compared to healthy controls, schizophrenia patients show increased baseline and post-dexamethasone cortisol release (Altamura, Guercetti, & Percudani, 1989; Copolov et al., 1989; Walker & Diforio, 1997). Along the same lines, there is evidence of heightened cortisol in schizotypal individuals. SPD adolescents manifest elevated salivary cortisol levels compared to normal controls (Walker, Walder, & Reynolds, 2001; Weinstein et al., 1999). Interestingly, higher cortisol levels in SPD individuals have been linked with more motor abnormalities (Neumann & Walker, 1999) and more severe positive symptoms (Diforio, 1999). These findings suggest hyperactivity of the hypothalamic-pituitary-adrenal (HPA) axis, the neural system that governs cortisol release, in both schizophrenia and SPD. This may be the neural mechanism that mediates the heightened sensitivity to stress that is assumed to be linked with risk for schizophrenia (Walker & Diforio, 1997).

Treatment of SPD

There is a dearth of literature on treatments for SPD. Both psychopharmacology and psychotherapy are currently used to treat schizotypal individuals who come into contact with health care professionals and are distressed to the degree that they require intervention. To date, there are no known published reports of controlled studies that have examined the effect of psychotherapy on schizotypal symptoms. In the absence of guiding research, therapeutic approaches focus on providing support, social skills training, and psychoeducation (Stone, 1985). Interestingly, the schizophrenia literature is increasingly showing that cognitive-behavioral therapy (CBT) is relatively efficacious for treating some aspects of schizophrenia, including positive symptoms and depression (Turkington, Dudley, Warman, & Beck, 2004). Given the biological and developmental connection between schizophrenia and SPD and the fact that SPD symptoms appear to be an attenuated version of the Axis I disorder, it is likely that CBT also would be beneficial for treating SPD. Future studies should examine the effects of CBT on SPD symptoms. At this point, however, there are no empirical findings that implicate one therapeutic approach over another for treating SPD.

Similarly, few reports have been published on the efficacy of psychopharmacological treatments for SPD. The pharmacological approach to date has been use of atypical antipsychotic medication, which is the treatment of choice for schizophrenia. In a recent review of psychopharmacological treatments in personality disorders, Markovitz (2004) reported that only a few studies have examined antipsychotic medication effects in a comorbid schizotypal and borderline personality disordered group and have found SPD symptom improvement. Only one known study to date has examined these effects in a predominantly SPD group; the research team found significantly reduced positive and negative symptoms of SPD within the first 2 months of atypical antipsychotic medication treatment (Koenigsberg et al., 2003). Thus there is modest empirical support for the use of atypical antipsychotics for treating SPD.

Summary and Conclusions

Since its formal inception as a diagnostic entity in 1979, SPD has been the subject of extensive research. We now have evidence indicating that it is a valid and reliable syndrome. It is clear that it has genetic links with schizophrenia and is often a precursor of schizophrenia and other psychotic disorders. Findings from twin studies suggest that schizophrenia and SPD can be alternative expressions of the same polygenotype. An important implication of this idea is that environmental factors are likely playing a role in determining the expression of the constitutional vulnerability to schizophrenia.

Consistent with the findings on genetics, SPD is often accompanied by some of the same functional deficits and biological abnormalities observed in schizophrenia patients. Thus, both disorders appear to involve brain morphological abnormalities and dysfunction. Nonetheless, there are some differences between schizophrenia and SPD, especially in the area of brain activation. These differences are important because (1) they may hold clues about the neuropathophysiology of schizophrenia and (2) they may inform us about the nature of the environmental factors capable of influencing the phenotypic expression of the polygenotype(s) associated with risk for schizophrenia.

It is expected that the pace of research on SPD will increase more rapidly in the near future. The chief reason for the expected increase is the evidence that SPD is one of the best known predictors of schizophrenia. Consequently, researchers are initiating longitudinal studies of SPD to identify which clinical features, in combination with other variables, yield the greatest predictive power. Once the sensitivity and specificity of prediction are adequate to justify preventive intervention, it is expected that clinical trials aimed at preventing the transition from SPD to schizophrenia will ensue (McGlashan, 2001). It is most likely that medication will be the chief intervention strategy for SPD, although psychotherapeutic interventions may also be examined. Nevertheless, some have noted that SPD is a clinical condition that should be treated independent of its association with the Axis I disorder. In cases in which the individual is experiencing distress as a consequence of the symptoms of SPD, it is reasonable to argue that treatment is indicated. Thus another noteworthy future trend will be research on the treatment of SPD.

References

Alm, T., Lindstrom, L., Ost, L.-G., & Ohman, A. (1984). Electrodermal nonresponding in schizophrenia: Relationships to attentional, clinical, biochemical, computed tomographical and genetic factors. *International Journal of Psychophysiology, 1,* 195–208.

Altamura, C., Guercetti, G., & Percudani, M. (1989). Dexamethasone suppression test in positive and negative schizophrenia. *Psychiatry Research, 30,* 69–75.

American Psychiatric Association. (1980). *Diagnostic and statistical manual of mental disorders* (3rd ed.). Washington, DC: Author.

American Psychiatric Association. (1987). *Diagnostic and statistical manual of mental disorders* (3rd ed., revised). Washington, DC: Author.

American Psychiatric Association. (1994). *Diagnostic and statistical manual of mental disorders* (4th ed.). Washington, DC: Author.

American Psychiatric Association. (2000). *Diagnostic and statistical manual of mental disorders* (4th ed., text revision). Washington, DC: Author.

Bakan, P., & Peterson, K. (1994). Pregnancy and birth complications: A risk factor for schizotypy. *Journal of Personality Disorders, 8,* 299–306.

Baron, M., Gruen, R. S., & Romo-Gruen, J. M. (1992). Positive and negative symptoms: Relation to familial transmission of schizophrenia. *British Journal of Psychiatry, 161,* 610–614.

Battaglia, M., Bernardeschi, L., Franchini, L., Bellodi, L., & Smeraldi, E. (1995). A family study of schizotypal disorder. *Schizophrenia Bulletin, 21,* 33–45.

Bernstein, A. S., Frith, C. D., Gruzelier, J. H., Patterson, T., Straube, E., Venables, P. H., et al. (1982). An analysis of the skin conductance orienting response in samples of American, British, and German schizophrenics. *Biological Psychiatry, 14,* 155–211.

Bernstein, A. S., Taylor, K. W., Starkey, P., Juni, S., Lubowsky, J., & Paley, H. (1981). Bilateral skin conductance, finger pulse volume, and EEG orienting response to tones of differing intensities in chronic schizophrenics and controls. *Journal of Nervous and Mental Disease, 169,* 513–528.

Bleuler, E. (1924). *Textbook of psychiatry* (A. A. Brill, Trans.). New York: Macmillan.

Bleuler, E. (1969). *Lehrbuch der Psychiatrie, 11 Auflage; umgearbeitet von M Bleuler.* Berlin, Germany: Springer.

Buchsbaum, M. S., Nenadic, I., Hazlett, E. A., Spiegal-Cohen, J., Fleischman, M. B., Akhavan, A., et al. (2002). Differential metabolic rates in prefrontal and temporal Brodmann areas in schizophrenia and schizotypal personality disorder. *Schizophrenia Research, 54,* 141–150.

Buchsbaum, M. S., Trestman, R. L., Hazlett, E., Seigel, B. V., Jr., Schafer, C. H., Luu-Hsia, C., et al. (1997). Regional cerebral blood flow during the Wisconsin Card Sort Test in schizotypal personality disorder. *Schizophrenia Research, 27,* 21–28.

Buchsbaum, M. S., Yang, S., Hazlett, E., Siegel, B. V., Jr., Germans, M., Haznedar, M., et al. (1997). Ventricular volume and asymmetry in schizotypal personality disorder and schizophrenia assessed with magnetic resonance imaging. *Schizophrenia Research, 27,* 45–53.

Butzlaff, R. L., & Hooley, J. M. (1998). Expressed emotion and psychiatric relapse. *Archives of General Psychiatry, 55*(6), 547–552.

Byne, W., Buchsbaum, M. S., Kemether, E., Hazlett, E. A., Shinwari, A., Mitropoulou, V., et al. (2001). Magnetic resonance imaging of the thalamic mediodorsal nucleus and pulvinar in schizophrenia and schizotypal personality disorder. *Archives of General Psychiatry, 58,* 133–140.

Cadenhead, K. S., Geyer, M. A., & Braff, D. (1993). Impaired startle prepulse inhibition and habituation in schizotypal personality disordered patients. *American Journal of Psychiatry, 150,* 1862–1867.

Cadenhead, K. S., Light, G. A., Geyer, M. A., & Braff, D. L. (2000). Sensory gating deficits assessed by the P50 event-related potential in subjects with schizotypal personality disorder. *American Journal of Psychiatry, 157,* 55–59.

Cannon, T. D., Barr, C. E., & Mednick, S. A. (1991). *Genetic and perinatal factors in the etiology of schizophrenia.* In E. F. Walker (Ed.), *Schizophrenia: A life-course developmental perspective* (pp. 9–31). San Diego, CA: Academic Press.

Chapman, L. J., & Chapman, J. P. (1980). Scales for rating psychotic and psychotic-like experiences as continua. *Schizophrenia Bulletin, 6,* 476–489.

Chapman, L. J., Chapman, J. P., Kwapil, T. R., Eckblad, M., & Zinser, M. C. (1994). Putatively psychosis-prone subjects 10 years later. *Journal of Abnormal Psychology, 103,* 171–183.

Chapman, L. J., Chapman, J. P., & Miller, E. N. (1982). Reliabilities and intercorrelations of eight measures of proneness to psychosis. *Journal of Consulting and Clinical Psychology, 50,* 187–195.

Chapman, L. J., Chapman, J. P., & Raulin, M. L. (1976). Scales for physical and social anhedonia. *Journal of Abnormal Psychology, 85,* 374–382.

Claridge, G., McCreery, C., Mason, O., Bentall, R., Boyle, G., & Slade, P. (1996). The factor structure of "schizotypal" traits: A large replication study. *British Journal of Clinical Psychology, 35,* 103–115.

Clementz, B., Geyer, M., & Braff, D. (1997). P50 suppression among schizophrenia patients and normal comparison subjects: A methodological analysis. *Biological Psychiatry, 41,* 1035–1044.

Condray, R., & Steinhauer, S. R. (1992). Schizotypal personality disorder in individuals with and without schizophrenic relatives: Similarities and contrasts in neurocognitive and clinical functioning. *Schizophrenia Research, 7,* 33–41.

Copolov, D. L., Rubin, R. T., Stuart, G. W., Poland, R. E., Mander, A. J., Sashidharan, S. P., et al. (1989). Specificity of the salivary cortisol dexamethasone suppression test across psychiatric diagnoses. *Biological Psychiatry, 25,* 879–893.

Cornblatt, B. A., Green, M. F., & Walker, E. F. (1999). Schizophrenia: Etiology and neurocognition. In T. Millon (Series Ed.) & P. H. Blaney & R. D. Davis (Vol. Eds.), *Oxford textbooks in clinical psychology: Vol. 4. Oxford textbook of psychopathology* (pp. 277–310). London: Oxford University Press.

Davis, K. L., Davidson, M., Mohs, R. C., Kendler, K. S., Davis, B. M., Johns, C. A., et al. (1985). Plasma homovanillic acid concentration and the severity of schizophrenic illness. *Science, 227*(4694), 1601–1602.

Davis, K. L., Kahn, R. S., Ko, G., & Davidson, M. (1991). Dopamine in schizophrenia: A review and reconceptualization. *American Journal of Psychiatry, 148,* 1474–1486.

Dawson, M. E., & Neuchterlein, K. H. (1987). The role of autonomic dysfunctions within a vulnerability-stress model of schizophrenic disorders. In D. Magnusson & A. Ohman (Eds.), *Psychopathology: An interactional perspective* (pp. 41–58). Orlando, FL: Academic Press.

Dickey, C. C., McCarley, R. W., Voglmaier, M. M., Niznikiewicz, M. A., Seidman, L. J., Hirayasu, Y., et al. (1999). Schizotypal personality disorder and MRI abnormalities of temporal lobe gray matter. *Biological Psychiatry, 45,* 1392–1402.

Dickey, C. C., Shenton, M. E., Hirayasu, Y., Fischer, I., Vogimaier, M. M., Niznikiewicz, M. A., et al. (2000). Large CSF volume not attributable to ventricular volume in schizotypal personality disorder. *American Journal of Psychiatry, 157,* 48–54.

Diforio, D. R. (1999). Cortisol secretion and executive functioning as predictors of symptom development in adolescents at-risk for schizophrenia. *Dissertation Abstracts International, 59,* 8B. (UMI No. 4458)

Diforio, D., Walker, E. F., & Kestler, L. P. (2000). Executive functions in adolescents with schizotypal personality disorder. *Schizophrenia Research, 42,* 125–134.

Done, D. J., Crow, T. J., Johnstone, E. C., & Sacker, A. (1994). Childhood antecedents of schizophrenia and affective illness: Social adjustment at ages 7 and 11. *British Medical Journal, 309,* 699–703.

Downhill, J. E., Jr., Buchsbaum, M. S., Hazlett, E. A., Barth, S., Roitman, S. L., Nunn, M., et al. (2001). Temporal lobe volume determined by magnetic resonance imaging in schizotypal personality disorder and schizophrenia. *Schizophrenia Research, 48,* 187–199.

Dworkin, R. H., & Lenzenweger, M. F. (1984). Symptoms and the genetics of schizophrenia: Implications for diagnosis. *American Journal of Psychiatry, 141,* 1541–1546.

Faraone, S. V., Green, A. I., Seidman, L. J., & Tsuang, M. T. (2001). Schizotaxia: Clinical implications and new directions for research. *Schizophrenia Bulletin, 27,* 1–18.

Farmer, A. E., McGuffin, P., & Gottesman, I. I. (1987). Twin concordance for DSM-III schizophrenia: Scrutinizing the validity of the definition. *Archives of General Psychiatry, 44,* 634–641.

Farmer, C. M., O'Donnell, B. F., Niznikiewicz, M. A., Voglmaier, M. M., McCarley, R. W., & Shenton, M. E. (2000). Visual perception and working memory in schizotypal personality disorder. *American Journal of Psychiatry, 157,* 781–786.

First, M. B., Gibbon, M., Spitzer, R. L., Williams, J. B. W., & Benjamin, L. S. (1997). Structured clinical interview for DSM-IV Axis II personality disorders. Washington, DC: American Psychiatric Press.

Freedman, B., & Chapman, L. J. (1973). Early subjective experiences in schizophrenic episodes. *Journal of Abnormal Psychology, 82,* 46–54.

Freedman, R., Coon, H., Myles-Worsley, M., Orr-Urtreger, A., Olincy, A., Davis, A., et al. (1997). Linkage of a neurophysiological deficit in schizophrenia to a chromosome 15 locus. *Proceedings of the National Academy of Science, 94,* 587–592.

Fukushima, J., Fukushima, K., Morita, N., & Yamashita, I. (1990). Further analysis of the control of voluntary saccadic eye movements in schizophrenic patients. *Biological Psychiatry, 28,* 943–958.

Gershon, E. S., DeLisi, L. E., Hamovit, J., & Nurnberger, J. I. (1988). A controlled family study of chronic psychoses: Schizophrenia and schizoaffective disorder. *Archives of General Psychiatry, 45,* 328–336.

Gottesman, I. (1991). *Schizophrenia genesis: The origins of madness.* New York: Freeman.

Gruzelier, J., & Raine, A. (1994). Bilateral electrodermal activity and cerebral mechanisms in syndromes of schizophrenia and the schizotypal personality. *International Journal of Psychophysiology, 16,* 1–16.

Gur, R. E., Cowell, P. E., Latshaw, A., Turetsky, B. I., Grossman, R. I., Arnold, S. E., et al. (2000). Reduced dorsal and orbital prefrontal gray matter volumes in schizophrenia. *Archives of General Psychiatry, 57,* 761–768.

Harvey, P. D., Powchick, P., Mohs, R. C., & Davidson, M. (1995). Memory functions in geriatric chronic schizophrenic patients: A neuropsychological study. *The Journal of Neuropsychiatry and Clinical Neurosciences, 7,* 207–212.

Hazlett, E. A., Buchsbaum, M. S., Byne, W., Wei, T-C., Spiegel-Cohen, J., Geneve, C., et al. (1999). Three-dimensional analysis with MRI and PET of the size, shape, and function of the thalamus in the schizophrenia spectrum. *American Journal of Psychiatry, 156,* 1190–1199.

Heckers, S., Goff, D., Schacter, D. L., Savage, C. R., Fischman, A. J., Alpert, N. M., et al. (1999). Functional imaging of memory retrieval in deficit vs. nondeficit schizophrenia. *Archives of General Psychiatry, 56,* 1117–1123.

Heinrichs, R. W., & Zakzanis, K. K. (1998). Neurocognitive deficit in schizophrenia: A quantitative review of the evidence. *Neuropsychology, 12,* 426–445.

Jones, L. A., Cardno, A. G., Murphy, K. C., Sanders, R. D., Gray, M. Y., McCarthy, G., et al. (2000). The Kings Schizotypy Questionnaire as a quantitative measure of schizophrenia liability. *Schizophrenia Research, 45,* 213–221.

Keefe, R. S. E., Roitman, S. E., Harvey, P. D., Blum, C. S., Dupre, R. L., Davidson, M., et al. (1995). A pen-and-paper human analogue of a monkey prefrontal cortex activation task: Spatial working memory in patients with schizophrenia. *Schizophrenia Research, 17,* 25–35.

Kendler, K. S., & Gardner, C. O. (1997). The risk for psychiatric disorders in relatives of schizophrenic and control probands: A comparison of three independent studies. *Psychological Medicine, 27,* 411–419.

Kendler, K. S., & Gruenberg, A. M. (1984). An independent analysis of the Danish adoption study of schizophrenia: VI. The relationship between psychiatric disorders as defined by DSM-III in relatives and adoptees. *Archives of General Psychiatry, 41, 555–564.*

Kendler, K. S., Gruenberg, A. M., & Strauss, J. S. (1981). An independent analysis of the Copenhagen sample of the Danish Adoption Study of Schizophrenia. *Archives of General Psychiatry, 38, 982–984.*

Kendler, K. S., & Lister-Sharp, D. J. (1989). The Structured Interview for Schizotypy (SIS): A preliminary report. *Schizophrenia Bulletin, 15, 559–571.*

Kety, S. S., Rosenthal, D., Wender, P. H., & Schulsinger, F. (1968). The types and prevalence of mental illness in the biological and adoptive families of adopted schizophrenics. *Journal of Psychiatry Research, 6*(Suppl. 1), 345–362.

Kety, S. S., Rosenthal, D., Wender, P. H., Schulsinger, F., & Jacobsen, B. (1976). Mental illness in the biological and adoptive families of adopted individuals who have become schizophrenic. *Behavior Genetics, 6, 219–225.*

King, S. (2000). Is expressed emotion cause or effect in the mothers of schizophrenic young adults? *Schizophrenia Research, 45*(1–2), 65–78.

Koenigsberg, H. W., Reynolds, D., Goodman, M., New, A. S., Mitropoulou, V., Trestman, R. L., et al. (2003). Risperidone in the treatment of schizotypal personality disorder. *Journal of Clinical Psychiatry, 64*(6), 628–634.

Kraepelin, E. (1919/1971). *Dementia praecox and paraphrenia* (G. M. Robertson, Ed.; R. M. Barclay, Trans.). New York: Krieger.

Kremen, W. S., Buka, S. L., Seidman, L. J., Goldstein, J. M., Koren, D., & Tsuang, M. T. (1998). IQ decline during childhood and adult psychotic symptoms in a community sample: A 19-year longitudinal study. *American Journal of Psychiatry, 155, 672–677.*

Kumari, V., Soni, W., & Sharma, T. (1999). Normalization of information processing deficits in schizophrenia with clozapine. *American Journal of Psychiatry, 156, 1046–1051.*

Kumra, S., Giedd, J. N., Vaituzis, A. C., Jacobsen, L. K., McKenna, K., Bedwell, J., et al. (2000). Childhood-onset psychotic disorders: Magnetic resonance imaging of volumetric differences in brain structure. *American Journal of Psychiatry, 157, 1467–1474.*

Lawrie, S. M., & Abukmeil, S. S. (1998). Brain abnormality in schizophrenia: A systematic and quantitative review of volumetric magnetic resonance imaging studies. *British Journal of Psychiatry, 172, 110–120.*

Lenzenweger, M. F. (1999). Schizotypic psychopathology: Theory, evidence, and future directions. In T. Millon (Series Ed.) & P. H. Blaney & R. D. Davis (Vol. Eds.), *Oxford textbooks in clinical psychology: Vol. 4. Oxford textbook of psychopathology* (pp. 605–627). London: Oxford University Press.

Lenzenweger, M. F., Cornblatt, B. A., & Putnick, M. (1991). Schizotypy and sustained attention. *Journal of Abnormal Psychology, 100, 84–89.*

Loranger, A. (1990). The impact of DSM-III on diagnostic practice in a university hospital: A comparison of DSM-II and DSM-III in 10,914 patients. *Archives of General Psychiatry, 47, 672–675.*

Lyons, M. J., Merla, M. E., Young, L., & Kremen, W. S. (1991). Impaired neuropsychological functioning in symptomatic volunteers with schizotypy: Preliminary findings. *Biological Psychiatry, 30, 424–426.*

MacDonald, A. W., Pogue-Geile, M. F., Debski, T. T., & Manuck, S. (2001). Genetic and environmental influences on schizotypy: A community-based twin study. *Schizophrenia Bulletin, 27, 47–58.*

Maier, W., Lichtermann, D. Klingler, T., Heun, R., & Hallmayer, J. (1992). Prevalences of personality disorders (DSM-III-R) in the community. *Journal of Personality Disorders, 6,* 187–192.

Markovitz, P. J. (2004). Recent trends in the pharmacotherapy of personality disorders. *Journal of Personality Disorders, 18*(1), 90–101.

McGlashan, T. H. (1999). Duration of untreated psychosis in first-episode schizophrenia: Marker or determinant of course? *Biological Psychiatry, 46,* 899–907.

McGlashan, T. H. (2001). Psychosis treatment prior to psychosis onset: Ethical issues. *Schizophrenia Research, 51,* 47–54.

Meehl, P. E. (1962). Schizotaxia, schizotypy, schizophrenia. *American Psychologist, 17,* 827–838.

Meehl, P. E. (1973a). *Psychodiagnosis: Selected papers.* New York: Norton.

Meehl, P. E. (1973b). Some methodological reflections on the difficulties of psychoanalytic research. *Psychological Issues Monographs, 8*(2, Monograph 30), 104–117.

Mientus, S., Gallinat, J., Wuebben, Y., Pascual-Marqui, R. D., Mulert, C., Frick, K., et al. (2002). Cortical hypoactivation during resting EEG in schizophrenics but not in depressives and schizotypal subjects as revealed by low resolution electromagnetic tomography (LORETA). *Psychiatry Research: Neuroimaging, 116,* 95–111.

Miller, P., Byrne, M., Hodges, A., Lawrie, S. M., Owens, D. G. C., & Johnstone, E. C. (2002). Schizotypal components in people at high risk of developing schizophrenia: Early findings from the Edinburgh high-risk study. *British Journal of Psychiatry, 180,* 179–184.

Miller, T. J., McGlashan, T. H., Rosen, J. L., Somjee, L., Markovich, P. J., Stein, K., et al. (2002). Prospective diagnosis of the initial prodrome for schizophrenia based on the Structured Interview for Prodromal Syndromes: Preliminary evidence of interrater reliability and predictive validity. *American Journal of Psychiatry, 159,* 863–865.

Mitelman, S. A., Shihabuddin, L., Brickman, A. M., Hazlett, E. A., & Buchsbaum, M. S. (2003). MRI assessment of gray and white matter distribution in Brodmann's areas of the cortex in patients with schizophrenia with good and poor outcomes. *American Journal of Psychiatry, 160,* 2154–2168.

Neumann, C. S., & Walker, E. F. (1999). Motor dysfunction in schizotypal personality disorder. *Schizophrenia Research, 38,* 159–168.

Nuechterlein, K. H., Asarnow, R. F., Subotnik, K. L., Fogelson, D. L., Payne, D. L., Kendler, K. S., et al. (2002). The structure of schizotypy: Relations between neurocognitive and personality disorder features in relatives of schizophrenic patients in the UCLA Family Study. *Schizophrenia Research, 54,* 121–130.

Ohman, A. (1981). Electrodermal activity and vulnerability to schizophrenia: A review. *Biological Psychology, 12,* 87–145.

Park, S., & McTigue, K. (1997). Working memory and the syndromes of schizotypal personality. *Schizophrenia Research, 26,* 213–220.

Park, S., Pueschel, J., Sauter, B. H., Rentsch, M., & Hell, D. (1999). Spatial working memory deficits and clinical symptoms in schizophrenia: A 4-month follow-up study. *Biological Psychiatry, 46,* 392–400.

Pearlson, G., Barta, P., Powers, R., Memon, R., Richards, S., Aylward, E., et al. (1997). Medial and superior temporal gyral volumes and cerebral asymmetry in schizophrenia versus bipolar disorder. *Biological Psychiatry, 41,* 1–14.

Pfohl, B., Blum, N., & Zimmerman, M. (1994). *Structured interview for DSM–IV personality disorders.* Iowa City: University of Iowa Hospitals and Clinics.

Raine, A. (1991). The SPQ: A scale for the assessment of schizotypal personality based on DSM-III-R criteria. *Schizophrenia Bulletin, 17,* 555–564.

Raine, A., Lencz, T., & Benishay, D. S. (1995). Schizotypal personality and skin conductance orienting. In A. Raine, T. Lencz, & S. A. Mednick (Eds.), *Schizotypal personality* (pp. 219–249). New York: Cambridge University Press.

Raine, A., Lencz, T., Yaralian, P., Bihrle, S., LaCasse, L., Ventura, J., et al. (2002). Prefrontal structural and functional deficits in schizotypal personality disorder. *Schizophrenia Bulletin, 28,* 501–513.

Raine, A., Reynolds, C., Lencz, T., Scerbo, A., Triphon, N., & Kim, D. (1994). Cognitive-perceptual, interpersonal, and disorganized features of schizotypal personality. *Schizophrenia Bulletin, 20,* 191–201.

Raine, A., Triphon, N., Kim, D., Hesler, A., Bird, L., Lencz, T., et al. (1992). *Schizotypal personality: Factor structure, sex differences, psychiatric differences, genetics, psychophysiology, and neuropsychology.* Paper presented at the 1992 Western Psychological Association meeting, Portland, OR.

Risch, N., & Baron, M. (1984). Segregation analysis of schizophrenia and related disorders. *American Journal of Human Genetics, 36,* 1039–1059.

Ross, R. G., Harris, J. G., Olincy, A., Radant, A., Adler, L. E., & Freedman, R. (1998). Familial transmission of two independent saccadic abnormalities in schizophrenia. *Schizophrenia Research, 30,* 59–70.

Saykin, A. J., Gur, R. C., Gur, R. E., Mozley, P. D., Mozley, L. H., Resnick, S. M., et al. (1991). Neuropsychological function in schizophrenia: Selective impairment in memory and learning. *Archives of General Psychiatry, 48,* 618–624.

Schulsinger, F., Parnas, J., Mednick, S., Teasdale, T. W., & Schulsinger, H. (1987). Heredity-environment interaction and schizophrenia. *Journal of Psychiatric Research, 21,* 431–436.

Shihabuddin, L., Buchsbaum, M. S., Hazlett, E. A., Silverman, J., New, A., Brickman, A. M., et al. (2001). Striatal size and glucose metabolic rate in schizotypal personality disorder and schizophrenia. *Archives of General Psychiatry, 58,* 877–884.

Siever, L. J., Amin, F., Coccaro, E. F., Trestman, R., Silverman, J., Horvath, T. B., et al. (1993). CSF homovanillic acid in schizotypal personality disorder. *American Journal of Psychiatry, 150,* 149–151.

Siever, L. J., Buchsbaum, M. S., Shihabuddin, L., Downhill, J., Byne, W. M., & Hazlett, E. A. (2000). Cortical and subcortical volumes in patients with schizotypal personality disorder [Abstract]. *Biological Psychiatry, 47,* 120S.

Siever, L. J., Koenigsberg, H. W., Harvey, P., Mitropoulou, V., Laruelle, M., Abi-Dargham, A., et al. (2002). Cognitive and brain function in schizotypal personality disorder. *Schizophrenia Research, 54,* 157–167.

Siever, L. J., Silverman, J. M., Horvath, T. B., Howard, K., Coccaro, E., Keefe, R. S. E., et al. (1990). Increased morbid risk for schizophrenia-related disorders in relatives of schizotypal personality disordered patients. *Archives of General Psychiatry, 47,* 634–640.

Spaulding, W., Garbin, C. P., & Dras, S. R. (1989). Cognitive abnormalities in schizophrenic patients and schizotypal college students. *Journal of Nervous and Mental Disease, 177,* 717–728.

Spitzer, R. L., Endicott, J., & Gibbon, M. (1979). Crossing the border into borderline personality and borderline schizophrenia: The development of criteria. *Archives of General Psychiatry, 36,* 17–24.

Stone, M. (1985). Schizotypal personality: Psychotherapeutic aspects. *Schizophrenia Bulletin, 11,* 576–589.

Torgersen, S. (1984). Genetic and nosological aspects of schizotypal and borderline personality disorders: A twin study. *Archives of General Psychiatry, 41,* 546–554.

Torgersen, S. (1994). Personality deviations within the schizophrenia spectrum. *Acta Psychiatrica Scandinavica, 384*(Suppl.), 40–44.

Torgersen, S., & Kringlen, E. (1991). Twin concordance for DSM-III-R schizophrenia. *Acta Psychiatrica Scandinavica, 83,* 395–401.

Turkington, D., Dudley, R., Warman, D. M., & Beck, A. T. (2004). Cognitive-behavioral therapy for schizophrenia: A review. *Journal of Psychiatric Practice, 10*(1), 5–16.

Ventura, J., Nuechterlein, K. H., Hardesty, J. P., & Gitlin, M. (1992). Life events and schizophrenic relapse after withdrawal of medication. *British Journal of Psychiatry, 161,* 615–620.

Voglmaier, M. M., Seidman, L. J., Niznikiewicz, M. A., Kickey, C. C., Shenton, M. E., & McCarley, R. W. (2000). Verbal and nonverbal neuropsychological test performance in subjects with schizotypal personality disorder. *American Journal of Psychiatry, 157,* 787–793.

Voglmaier, M. M., Seidman, L. J., Salisbury, D., & McCarley, R. W. (1997). Neuropsychological dysfunction in schizotypal personality disorder: A profile analysis. *Biological Psychiatry, 41,* 530–540.

Vollema, M. G., & Hoijtink, H. (2000). The multidimensionality of self-report schizotypy in a psychiatric population: An analysis using multidimensional Rasch models. *Schizophrenia Bulletin, 26,* 565–575.

Vollema, M. G., & Ormel, J. (2000). The reliability of the Structured Interview for Schizotypy—Revised. *Schizophrenia Bulletin, 26,* 619–629.

Walder, D. J., Walker, E. F., & Bollini, A. M. (in press). The hippocampus, hypothalamic-pituitary-adrenal axis, cognition and symptoms in schizophrenia. In D. Barch (Ed.), *Cognitive and affective neuroscience of psychopathology.* New York: Oxford University Press.

Walker, E., Grimes, K., Davis, D., & Smith, A. (1993). Childhood precursors of schizophrenia: Facial expressions of emotion. *American Journal of Psychiatry, 150,* 1654–1660.

Walker, E., Lewis, N., Loewy, R., & Palvo, S. (1999). Motor dysfunction and risk for schizophrenia. *Development and Psychopathology, 11,* 509–523.

Walker, E. F., Baum, K. M., & Diforio, D. (1998). Developmental changes in the behavioral expression of vulnerability for schizophrenia. In M. F. Lenzenweger & R. H. Dworkin (Eds.), *Origins and development of schizophrenia: Advances in experimental psychopathology* (pp. 469–491). Washington, DC: American Psychological Association.

Walker, E. F., & Diforio, D. (1997). Schizophrenia: A neural diathesis-stress model. *Psychological Review, 104,* 667–685.

Walker, E. F., & Lewine, R. J. (1990). Prediction of adult-onset schizophrenia from childhood home movies of the patients. *American Journal of Psychiatry, 147,* 1052–1056.

Walker, E. F., Walder, D. J., & Reynolds, F. (2001). Developmental changes in cortisol secretion in normal and at-risk youth. *Development and Psychopathology, 13,* 721–732.

Weike, A. I., Bauer, U., & Hamm, A. O. (2000). Effective neuroleptic medication removes prepulse inhibition deficits in schizophrenia patients. *Biological Psychiatry, 47,* 61–70.

Weinstein, D. D., Diforio, D., Schiffman, J., Walker, E., & Bonsall, R. (1999). Minor physical anomalies, dermatoglyphic asymmetries, and cortisol levels in adolescents with schizotypal personality disorder. *American Journal of Psychiatry, 156,* 617–623.

Wilkins, S. (1988). *Behavioral and psychophysiological aspects of information processing in schizotypics.* Unpublished doctoral dissertation, University of York, UK.

Williams, M. (1993). *The psychometric assessment of schizotypal personality.* Unpublished doctoral dissertation, University of London.

Wuebben, Y., & Winterer, G. (2001). Hypofrontality: A risk-marker related to schizophrenia? *Schizophrenia Research, 48,* 207–217.

Yaralian, P. S., Raine, A., Lencz, T., Hooley, J. M., Bihrle, S. E., Mills, S., et al. (2000). Elevated levels of cognitive-perceptual deficits in individuals with a family history of schizophrenia spectrum disorders. *Schizophrenia Research, 46,* 57–63.

Yung, A. R., Phillips, L. J., McGorry, P. D., McFarlane, C. A., Francey, S., Harrigan, S., et al. (1998). Prediction of psychosis: A step towards indicated prevention of schizophrenia. *British Journal of Psychiatry, 172*(Suppl. 33), 14–20.

Zimmermann, M., & Coryell, W. (1990). Diagnosing personality disorders in the community: A comparison of self-report and interview measures. *Archives of General Psychiatry, 47,* 527–531.

6

Antisocial Personality Disorder and Psychopathy

Christopher J. Patrick

University of Minnesota

Among the various disorders of personality, antisocial personality disorder (APD) and the related syndrome of psychopathy stand as unique in terms of the toll they exact on society. As a function of this impact, these syndromes have long held the fascination of the public at large as well as that of investigators in the scientific community. The goal of this chapter is to review, in a relatively brief but at the same time broad and integrative fashion, what is currently known about these disorders. In doing so, I will highlight overlapping elements of these clinical phenomena as well as important elements that differentiate them. In addition, I will endeavor to link these phenomena to broader constructs in the domains of personality and psychopathology, and in turn to underlying psychological processes that may provide the basis for a clearer, mechanistic understanding of the unique and distinctive features of these clinical syndromes.

The chapter begins with a historical overview of the constructs of psychopathy and antisocial personality. Highlighted in this section is the fact that although the APD construct has achieved prominence in the psychiatric literature during the past 25 years, the construct of psychopathy actually preceded it historically and—from the perspective to be advanced here—can be considered an overarching construct that incorporates APD. Following the historical overview, I provide a summary of concepts and recent empirical findings regarding the APD construct. The emphasis is on placing APD into

Author's note: Preparation of this chapter was supported by grants MH52384, MH65137, and MH072850 from the National Institute of Mental Health, grant R01 AA12164 from the National Institute on Alcohol Abuse and Alcoholism, and funds from the Hathaway endowment at the University of Minnesota.

a broader conceptual framework that encompasses other impulse control disorders (e.g., conduct disorder, alcohol dependence, and drug dependence) with which APD is closely associated. Specifically, drawing on recent research findings, I will argue that the adult antisocial deviance embodied in the APD construct represents one manifestation of a broader disposition toward disinhibitory (externalizing) problems that can be viewed as more basic from an etiologic standpoint. The next section of the chapter is devoted to contemporary conceptualizations of psychopathy and relevant empirical findings. Special emphasis is devoted to the idea of psychopathy as a fundamentally variegated construct, encompassing somewhat paradoxical elements of behavioral pathology on one hand and positive psychological adjustment on the other. The last major section of the chapter considers relations between the constructs of psychopathy and APD from the standpoint of a dual-process model of the etiologic mechanisms underlying these disorders. Following this, I include a brief section on the treatment of these disorders.

Historical Overview of the Psychopathy and APD Constructs

Early Conceptualizations of Psychopathy

The earliest accounts of the syndrome that came to be known as psychopathy emphasized extreme behavioral deviance in the context of intact reasoning and communicative abilities. Over 200 years ago, Philippe Pinel (1801/1962) documented examples of patients "who at no period gave evidence of any lesion of understanding, but who were under the dominion of instinctive and abstract fury, as if the faculties of affect alone had sustained injury" (p. 9). Patients of this kind engaged repeatedly in impulsive acts injurious to themselves and others despite recognizing at a verbal/conceptual level the irrationality of such acts. The label Pinel applied to this syndrome was *manie sans delire* ("insanity without delirium"). As indicated in the foregoing quotation, Pinel hypothesized that the underlying impairment in such cases was an inability to control emotion (affect) as opposed to some deficit in reason or understanding.

Around the same time, the American physician Benjamin Rush (1812) made note of similar cases, but postulated moral weakness (i.e., an impairment in the capacity to experience shame or guilt in relation to contemplated actions and their potential consequences) as the root cause. In contrast with Pinel's notion of a defect in affective control, Rush's etiologic perspective carried with it a social-evaluative component (i.e., individuals of this sort do bad things because they are morally deranged). In his account of the syndrome, Rush also highlighted the manipulative, deceitful nature of such individuals. A perspective similar to Rush's was advanced by the British psychiatric expert J. C. Pritchard (1835), who coined the term "moral insanity" in reference to such cases—connoting the idea that the behavioral deviance in such cases stems from a deficit in the intrinsic sense of decency, fairness, and responsibility that normal individuals possess. However, Pritchard departed from Rush (as well as Pinel) by applying the label "moral insanity" so broadly as to encompass most conditions considered mental disorders at this time (e.g., drug or alcohol addiction; sexual deviations of various kinds, including homosexuality; mood disorders) except those classifiable today as mental retardation or schizophrenia. The result was a broadening of the construct that persisted in large part until Cleckley (1941; see below).

The term "psychopathic" was introduced by German psychiatrist J. L. Koch (1891) as an alternative to Pritchard's term "morally insane." Specifically, Koch proposed the label "psychopathic inferiority" to denote conditions of a chronic nature that in his view reflected an underlying organic (physical, brain-based) cause. Like Pritchard, Koch applied this term to a much broader array of clinical conditions than would be encompassed by current conceptualizations of psychopathy and antisocial personality disorder—including neurotic conditions and some forms of mental retardation as well as "character disorders" of various sorts (i.e., conditions that would now be regarded as "personality disorders"). In the seventh edition of his classic volume *Psychiatrie: Ein Lehrbuch* ("Psychiatry: A Textbook"), Koch's contemporary Emil Kraepelin (1904) used the term "psychopathic personalities" for a narrower range of conditions that he characterized as chronic and constitutional in origin. These included impulse control problems, sexual perversions, obsessional syndromes, and other "degenerative" personalities. Included among the last of these conditions were four groups of individuals who would be regarded as antisocial and/or psychopathic according to current definitions: (1) "morbid liars and swindlers" (charming, deceitful, fraudulent, and lacking in loyalty to others); (2) "criminals by impulse" (driven by impulsive urges to commit crimes such as theft, fire setting, and sexual assault); (3) "professional criminals" (deliberately calculating and self-serving); and (4) "morbid vagabonds" (inadequate, aimless, and irresponsible). In the next (eighth) edition of his text, Kraepelin (1915) revised his typology of pathological personalities, dropping the "professional criminal" subgroup and adding four other types: excitable, eccentric, antisocial, and quarrelsome. The latter two of these (marked by callousness-destructiveness and alienation-hostility, respectively) intersect most clearly with modern conceptualizations of antisocial personality.

Adolf Meyer (1904) introduced these German conceptualizations to the American psychiatric community. Following Koch, Meyer used the term "constitutional inferiority" to describe what he regarded as chronic characterological disorders. However, in contrast with Koch (but like Kraepelin), he explicitly excluded neurotic conditions from this class of disorder. The distinction Meyer drew between these chronic syndromes and neurotic conditions persisted in American psychiatric circles, but his descriptive label for the former ("constitutional inferiority") was superseded in time by Kraepelin's more evaluatively neutral term, "psychopathic personality." The term "sociopathic" was introduced by the German psychiatrist Karl Birnbaum (1909) as a challenge to Kraepelin's characterization of these chronic conditions as constitutional in origin. Birnbaum was part of a revisionist movement, persisting through the 1930s, that viewed most forms of mental disorder (including so-called "psychopathic personalities") as arising primarily from social-environmental factors. However, despite reflecting fundamentally different perspectives on etiology, the terms *psychopathic* and *sociopathic* came to be used interchangeably over time (e.g., whereas Cleckley [1941, 1976] preferred the term "psychopathic personality," the first edition of the *Diagnostic and Statistical Manual of Mental Disorders* [DSM], published by the American Psychiatric Association [APA] in 1952, employed the term "sociopathic personality disturbance").[1]

Influential figures in this area during the 1920s and 1930s included Kurt Schneider (in Germany) and Eugen Kahn (in America). Both espoused a decidedly broad perspective on the construct of psychopathy. In the third edition of his volume *Die Psychopathischen Persönlichkeiten* ("The Psychopathic Personalities"; 1934), Schneider identified 10 distinctive subtypes of psychopaths, several of which (e.g., "hyperthymic," "depressive," "insecure," and "asthenic") fall clearly outside modern conceptualizations of psychopathy and antisocial personality. Likewise, Kahn's (1931) list of psychopathic subgroups (16 in all) included several patently neurotic conditions (e.g., "nervous," "anxious," "sensitive," "depressive"), as well as other assorted types that bear minimal resemblance to contemporary notions of psychopathy or APD (e.g., "compulsive," "moody," "sexually perverse," "eccentric").

Cleckley's "Mask of Sanity"

American psychiatrist Hervey Cleckley countered this historical inclination toward diagnostic overinclusiveness with the publication of his seminal volume *The Mask of Sanity,* which appeared in its initial edition in 1941. Drawing on his own clinical experiences with patients at the Veteran's Administration Hospital in Augusta, Georgia—one of the largest psychiatric hospitals in the United States at the time his book was written—Cleckley presented a variety of vivid case examples to illustrate the personality and behavioral characteristics of individuals he viewed as psychopathic. In contrast with prior writers who defined "psychopathic personality" as a term encompassing various forms of delinquency, impulse control problems, addictions, and sexual deviations (as well as, in some cases, neurotic conditions and organic brain syndromes), Cleckley explicitly rejected this broad conceptualization. Instead, he characterized psychopathy as a highly distinctive clinical syndrome with a unique underlying etiology, which he regarded as affective in nature (i.e., a core deficit in emotional reactivity). Based on the material provided in his case descriptions, Cleckley proposed a list of 16 specific criteria he believed could be used to identify psychopathic individuals.

Perhaps the most essential element in Cleckley's conceptualization, embodied in the title of his book, is the idea that psychopathy entails the juxtaposition of severe underlying pathology against the overt appearance of robust mental health. In contrast with other psychiatric patients who present as confused, agitated, dysphoric, withdrawn, or otherwise disturbed, psychopaths appear poised, sociable, and generally well adjusted upon initial contact. It is only through ongoing observation across a range of situations that the psychopath's characteristic deviancy becomes evident. Table 6.1 illustrates this by organizing Cleckley's (1976) 16 diagnostic criteria for psychopathy into three distinctive categories. The first category consists of indicators of positive psychological adjustment (i.e., good intelligence and social charm, absence of delusions/irrationality, absence of nervousness, and suicide rarely carried out). With these indicators, Cleckley was referring not merely to the absence of salient mental disturbance but also to the presence of resiliency and good adjustment:

> The surface of the psychopath . . . shows up as equal to or better than normal and gives no hint at all of a disorder within. Nothing about him suggests oddness, inadequacy, or moral frailty. His mask is that of robust mental health. (p. 383)

Table 6.1 Cleckley's (1976) 16 diagnostic criteria for psychopathy, grouped by conceptual category

Conceptual Category	Criterion Number and Label
Positive adjustment	
	1. Superficial charm and good "intelligence"
	2. Absence of delusions and other signs of irrational thinking
	3. Absence of "nervousness" or psychoneurotic manifestations
	14. Suicide rarely carried out
Chronic behavioral deviance	
	7. Inadequately motivated antisocial behavior
	8. Poor judgment and failure to learn by experience
	4. Unreliability
	13. Fantastic and uninviting behavior with drink and sometimes without
	15. Sex life impersonal, trivial, and poorly integrated
	16. Failure to follow any life plan
Emotional-interpersonal deficits	
	5. Untruthfulness and insincerity
	6. Lack of remorse or shame
	10. General poverty in major affective reactions
	9. Pathologic egocentricity and incapacity for love
	11. Specific loss of insight
	12. Unresponsiveness in general interpersonal relations

However, at odds with this outward appearance of good mental health is the presence of severe behavioral maladjustment: "Yet he has a disorder that often manifests itself in conduct far more seriously abnormal than that of the schizophrenic" (Cleckley, 1976, p. 383).

> The psychopath, however perfectly he mimics man theoretically, that is to say, when he speaks for himself in words, fails altogether when he is put into the practice of actual living. His failure is so complete and so dramatic that it is difficult to see how such a failure could be achieved by anyone less defective than a downright madman. (p. 370)

In Cleckley's diagnostic scheme, this component of the syndrome is captured by indicators of manifest behavioral deviance (see Table 6.1, second section), including impulsive antisocial acts, irresponsibility (unreliability), promiscuity, and an absence of any clear life plan. In addition to items reflecting positive psychological adjustment and overt behavioral deviance, Cleckley's criteria for psychopathy included a third category reflecting the emotional underresponsiveness and absence of genuine social relationships that he viewed as central to the disorder.

Cleckley's conceptualization of psychopathy was influential because he provided a precise definition of the syndrome that had been lacking to that point in history. His vivid case illustrations persuaded even the casual reader that the clinical entity he was describing truly existed; practitioners in psychiatric and forensic settings who routinely encountered individuals of this type could readily identify with his account of the disorder. His conceptualization placed core emphasis on the emotional-interpersonal features that distinguished psychopathic individuals from other criminal and antisocial types. Thus along with descriptions of psychopaths who engaged regularly in antisocial acts and experienced frequent encounters with the law, Cleckley presented examples of "successful psychopaths" who maintained careers as scholars, physicians, and businessmen. Cleckley's view was that the presence of the core underlying emotional-interpersonal deviation was more important in defining the presence of the disorder than marked antisocial deviance.[2]

Moreover, Cleckley's 16 diagnostic criteria for psychopathy (derived directly from his case descriptions) provided an objective means of identifying the disorder that made it amenable to systematic empirical study. David Lykken's (1957) pioneering study of anxiety responses in psychopaths employed Cleckley's criteria as the basis for diagnoses, as did Robert Hare's seminal investigations beginning in the early 1960s. Cleckley's conceptualization remains highly influential to the present day because it served as the foundation for Hare's Psychopathy Checklist—Revised (PCL-R; Hare, 1991, 2003), which has become the dominant assessment instrument for the diagnosis of psychopathy in research studies as well as for clinical assessment. However, it be should be noted that the PCL-R appears to depart importantly from Cleckley's conceptualization, particularly because it omits direct indicators of good mental health. This point is discussed in further detail later.

Emergence of the Concept
of Antisocial Personality Disorder

The roots of the modern psychiatric concept of APD can be traced to the first edition of the DSM (DSM-I; APA, 1952). The formal classification system for psychiatric disorders embodied in the DSM grew out of efforts by the federal government to develop statistics for illness and death among residents of mental hospitals in the United States. DSM-I was modeled loosely after the sixth revision of the International Classification of Diseases (ICD; World Health Organization, 1948), which for the first time included a section devoted to the classification of mental disorders. This initial edition of the DSM contained a category of mental disorders termed "sociopathic personality disturbance"; following earlier conceptualizations of psychopathy, this designation included a broad range of syndromes encompassing sexual deviations of various kinds, addictions, and delinquency. Included among the disorders in this category was a syndrome referred to as "sociopathic personality disturbance: antisocial reaction," intended to capture the aggressive, criminally deviant individual who repeatedly violates the norms and laws of society. (The use of the term "reaction" throughout DSM-I is attributable to the lingering influence of Adolph Meyer, who viewed mental disorders as reactions of the personality to biological, social, and psychological factors.)

The second edition of the DSM (APA, 1968) was developed to align even more closely with the version of the ICD in place at that time, ICD-8. In DSM-II, the term "reaction" was eliminated as a descriptor for disorders. Sexual deviations, addictions, and delinquent personality types were grouped under a category entitled "Personality Disorders and Certain Other Non-Psychotic Mental Disorders." Within this category, the term "antisocial personality" was used for a syndrome corresponding to psychopathy. The diagnostic features of the syndrome closely resembled those proposed by Cleckley and included weak socialization, incapacity for loyalty, selfishness, callousness, irresponsibility, and absence of guilt. A serious limitation of DSM-II (as of DSM-I) was that the basis for diagnostic classifications consisted of prototypical descriptions of each disorder rather than specific, behavior-oriented diagnostic criteria. As a result, the reliability of clinical and research diagnostic classifications using DSM-II was generally poor.

The problem of diagnostic reliability was confronted in the next edition of the DSM, DSM-III (APA, 1980), by the development of more explicit, behavior-oriented criterion sets for disorders patterned after those developed for use in research studies by Feighner et al. (1972) and Spitzer, Endicott, and Robins (1978). The criteria for antisocial personality disorder in the DSM-III were strongly influenced by the work of Lee Robins (1966), who conducted groundbreaking research on the development of "sociopathy" by following up a large sample of individuals ($N = 524$) seen as children in a treatment clinic for juvenile delinquents. Following Cleckley, Robins's initial criteria for sociopathy included items relating to lack of guilt, remorse, and shame, but (due in part to problems in assessing them reliably) these criteria failed to differentiate significantly between sociopaths and nonsociopaths in her study, and thus were discarded as indicators in the criterion sets developed subsequently by Feighner et al. and Spitzer et al. Consequently, the criteria for APD adopted within DSM-III focused exclusively on behavioral indicants of deviance in childhood and adulthood, including such things as truancy, delinquency, stealing, vandalism, irresponsibility, aggressiveness, impulsivity, recklessness, and lying. As a function of this change, the DSM-III diagnosis of antisocial personality proved to be highly reliable. Nevertheless, influential investigators in the area (e.g., Frances, 1980; Hare, 1983; Millon, 1981) were quick to challenge the diagnostic validity of the DSM-III criteria for APD on the grounds that they excluded many of the features Cleckley deemed central to psychopathy, including superficial charm, absence of anxiety, lack of remorse or empathy, and general poverty of affect. Some effort was made to respond to these criticisms in the revised third edition of the DSM (DSM-III-R; APA, 1987) by the addition of lack of remorse (i.e., "feels justified in having hurt, mistreated, or stolen from another," p. 346) as an adult criterion for APD. Some changes were also made in the child criteria for APD (i.e., conduct disorder component) in DSM-III-R, but these changes did not affect the representation of "core features" of psychopathy in the APD criterion set (i.e., in DSM-III-R, as in DSM-III, all of the child criteria remained focused on overt behavioral deviance).

As part of the groundwork for DSM-IV (APA, 1994), specialized field trials were conducted to evaluate proposed revisions to the criterion sets for various disorders. One of these (Widiger et al., 1996) focused on APD. Two proposals were evaluated in the field trial for APD, one entailing increased representation of core affective-interpersonal features of psychopathy (e.g., lack of empathy, inflated self-appraisal, glib/superficial interactive style) in the criteria for APD, and the other involving simplification of the existing criterion set without substantial changes to the diagnosis. Diagnostic data from four major clinical samples (inpatients at a general psychiatric institution; drug treatment and homeless shelter residents; methadone maintenance program outpatients; and incarcerated offenders) were examined, consisting of scores on the existing DSM-III-R criteria along with scores on two alternative criterion sets that provided greater coverage of affective-interpersonal features: a shortened (10-item) version of Hare's (1991) PCL-R, and the research criteria for "dyssocial personality disorder" developed for ICD-10. The field trial data revealed high correspondence among diagnoses based on the three criterion sets for all samples except the prison sample, where the PCL-R criterion set showed some evidence of incremental validity over the other two criterion sets in predicting psychopathy-related variables. However, it was concluded that enhanced validity within this one specific sample was insufficient to warrant a major shift in the criteria for APD, and consequently, changes based on this field trial were limited to simplification of the adult indicators. Specifically, two indicators ("parental irresponsibility" and "failure to sustain a monogamous relationship") were dropped, and two others ("employment-related irresponsibility" and "financial irresponsibility") were combined into a single "irresponsibility" item, resulting in a reduction of the number of adult indicators (from 10 in DSM-III-R to seven in DSM-IV). In addition, some minor changes in the child criteria for APD were instituted based on the results of a separate field trial for conduct disorder (i.e., two items, "staying out at night" and "intimidating others" were added, resulting in 15 indicators in DSM-IV versus 13 in DSM-III-R).

Thus due to the field trial results, no effort was made to increase the representation of core affective-interpersonal features of psychopathy in the criteria for APD in DSM-IV. As a result of this decision, criticisms of the construct validity of the APD criteria by investigators in the psychopathy area have persisted (e.g., Hare & Hart, 1995). The issue of the correspondence between the construct of APD within DSM-IV and the construct of psychopathy embodied in Hare's (1991, 2003) PCL-R is discussed more in subsequent sections.

The DSM Construct of Antisocial Personality Disorder

Clinical Features

Table 6.2 summarizes the diagnostic criteria for APD listed in the text revision of DSM-IV (DSM-IV-TR; APA, 2000), the most recent version of the DSM. Like the criteria for the other disorders in the DSM, the criteria for APD are polythetic—meaning that individuals can achieve a diagnosis of APD in different ways, as long as they meet the criteria for inclusion (i.e., current age at least 18, occurrence of antisocial behavior not limited to episodes of mania or schizophrenic psychosis) and fulfill a sufficient number of the designated child and adult criteria for the disorder (i.e., three or more of 15 possible symptoms of child conduct disorder before age 15, leading to significant social, academic, or occupational impairment, and three or more of seven possible adult features since age 15).

As indicated in Table 6.2, the child criteria for APD include aggressive and destructive behaviors on one hand, and deceitfulness/theft and nonaggressive rule breaking on the other. Formal factor-analytic investigations of the structure of the child APD criteria (e.g., Frick et al., 1991; Tackett, Krueger, Sawyer, & Graetz, 2003) have confirmed that the aggressive and nonaggressive indicators define separate, albeit correlated, factors. Tackett et al. (2003) reported that these two conduct disorder factors showed discriminative associations with

Table 6.2   Diagnostic criteria for DSM-IV-TR antisocial personality disorder

Criterion Category	Summary Description of Criterion
A. Adult antisocial behavior (3 or more of the following since age 15):	1. Repeated participation in illegal acts 2. Deceitfulness 3. Impulsiveness or failure to make plans in advance 4. Hostile-aggressive behavior 5. Engagement in actions that endanger self or others 6. Frequent irresponsible behavior 7. Absence of remorse
B. Age criterion	Current age at least 18
C. Child conduct disorder (3 or more of the following before age 15, resulting in impaired social, academic, or occupational function):	*Aggression toward people or animals:* 1. Frequent bullying, threatening, or intimidation of others 2. Frequent initiation of physical fights 3. Use of dangerous weapons 4. Physical cruelty toward people 5. Physical cruelty toward animals 6. Theft involving victim confrontation 7. Forced sexual contact *Destruction of property:* 8. Deliberate fire setting with intent to cause damage 9. Deliberate destruction of property *Deceptiveness or stealing:* 10. Breaking/entering (house, building, or vehicle) 11. Frequent lying to acquire things or to avoid duties 12. Nontrivial theft without victim confrontation *Serious rule violations:* 13. Frequent violations of parental curfew, starting before age 13 14. Running away from home 15. Frequent truancy, starting before age 13
D. Comorbidity criterion	Antisocial behavior does not occur exclusively during episodes of schizophrenia or mania

SOURCE: Based on information from the American Psychiatric Association, 2000.

aggressive behavior syndrome and delinquent behavior syndrome, respectively, as defined by scores on the Child Behavior Checklist (Achenbach, 1991).

An implication of this work is that there may be distinct variants of child antisocial deviance with different etiologic underpinnings. Along these lines, Moffitt (1993) proposed a distinction between adolescence-limited and life course–persistent subgroups of delinquent individuals. The former was distinguished by a later onset and predominantly nonaggressive forms of deviancy and rule breaking, the latter by early age of onset, aggressive-destructive as well as nonaggressive delinquent behaviors, and continuation of child and adolescent deviancy into adulthood. Moffitt postulated that the early-onset, aggressive subtype of delinquency may have a stronger underlying neurobiological basis (see also Lynam, 1997). Recently, Tackett, Krueger, Iacono, and McGue (2005) reexamined the structure of conduct disorder symptoms in a large sample of male twins recruited from the community, permitting an analysis of differential etiologic contributions to aggressive versus nonaggressive subfactors. The results of this analysis indicated that these two components of conduct disorder have common as well as distinctive etiologic underpinnings. Additive genetic influences and nonshared environment (i.e., experiences unique to the individual) contributed significantly to both components, the proportion of symptom variance attributable to genes being somewhat higher for the aggressive component (35%) than for the nonaggressive component (28%). In addition, a significant contribution of shared environment (i.e., environmental influences common to two siblings growing up in the same household) was found for the nonaggressive component only.

The adult criteria for APD include one specific indicator of aggression (irritability and aggressiveness), three clearly nonaggressive indicators (deceitfulness, impulsivity, and irresponsibility), and three nonspecific indicators (failure to conform to norms with respect to lawful behaviors, reckless disregard for safety of self or others, and lack of remorse). Perhaps because the adult APD criteria do not divide as readily into aggressive and nonaggressive indicators, no parallel factor-analytic work has been done to examine the extent to which distinctive components of this sort underlie adult indicators of APD. Nonetheless, there is evidence in the literature that aggressive forms of adult antisocial behavior have unique neurobiological correlates. For example, a number of published studies have reported evidence of reduced levels of the neurotransmitter serotonin (indexed by concentrations of the serotonin metabolite 5-hydroxyindoleacetic acid [5-HIAA] in cerebrospinal fluid) in antisocial individuals who exhibit severe episodes of impulsive aggressive behavior (e.g., Linnoila et al., 1983; Virkkunen et al., 1994; for a review, see Minzenberg & Siever, 2006). Evidence of reduced brain serotonin has also been reported in antisocial individuals who engage in impulsive suicidal acts (Linnoila & Virkkunen, 1992), which have been conceptualized as an alternative, self-directed expression of impulsive aggressive tendencies (Verona & Patrick, 2000).

The evidence for distinctive correlates of aggressive deviancy suggests that it may be fruitful to examine the structure of adult indicators of antisocial personality, as has been done with indicators of child conduct disorder. To achieve this goal, it would be necessary to partition symptoms of adult antisocial deviance more clearly into aggressive and nonaggressive types and to have multiple indicators of each, which would necessitate some departure from the current DSM-IV-TR criterion set (e.g., failure to abide by laws could be parsed into offenses of a violent versus nonviolent nature; different expressions of irritability/aggressiveness could be scored as separate indicators). If adult antisocial deviance were found to comprise distinctive aggressive and nonaggressive facets, as appears to be the case for child conduct disorder, it would be interesting to explore (particularly in a longitudinal sample) the stability of each of these facets from childhood to adulthood. For example, it might be hypothesized that the aggressive facet would evidence greater stability across time (cf. Moffit, 1993).

Prevalence

The prevalence of APD in the general community is estimated to be about 2%, with rates for men (3%) substantially exceeding those for women (1%; APA, 2000). The gender difference in the prevalence of APD is an intriguing but unresolved issue. One perspective is that gender role stereotypes and socialization pressures account for the difference (i.e., men, by sociohistoric tradition, are expected and encouraged by society to be more aggressive and adventurous, leading to a higher rate of deviance in the form of APD). Another is that the difference in APD prevalence reflects basic biologically rooted differences between women and men in trait dispositions that promote the occurrence of antisocial deviance in people. The ecumenical stance, of course, would be that both factors play a role. Further research, including genetics studies of gender-related differences in traits and affiliated behaviors, may allow us to determine which of these positions, if either, is more substantially correct. Interestingly, despite well-documented differences in arrest rates for individuals from different ethnic groups, robust differences in rates of APD have not been found across ethnic groups in epidemiological studies. For example, the Epidemiological Catchment Area (ECA) study (Robins & Regier, 1991) found no significant differences in the prevalence of APD (diagnosed according to DSM-III criteria) across White, African-American, and Hispanic groups.

The prevalence of APD in clinical settings tends to be substantially higher than in the community at large, particularly within correctional and forensic settings, where estimated base rates run as high as 50% to 80% (Hare, 2003). The very high rate base rate in forensic settings highlights one of the major criticisms that has been leveled against the APD diagnostic criteria, namely, that they are biased so heavily toward criminally deviant behaviors that most individuals who run into serious trouble with the law will be diagnosed with APD, even though such individuals vary widely in the expression of their deviance and in the underlying bases for it. From this perspective, APD is a "wastebasket" category into which various sorts of deviant individuals are placed. However, recent evidence suggests that this position is too extreme. An alternative perspective is that APD reflects in part the influence of a broad trait factor that determines general risk for a variety of impulse control problems, along with other specific etiologic influences that determine the precise expression of risk in particular individuals (Krueger et al., 2002; Krueger, Markon, Patrick, & Iacono, 2005). From this perspective, some individuals will develop APD largely because they have a high general vulnerability to impulse control problems, whereas others will develop APD primarily as a function of unique environmental experiences (e.g., early abuse, deviant peers) that promote the occurrence of antisocial behavior. Individuals of the former sort will tend to show an earlier age of onset of behavioral deviance, greater impulsive aggressive tendencies, and a higher prevalence of comorbid impulse control problems of other types (e.g., alcohol and drug problems).

Comorbidity With Other DSM Disorders

APD shows well-documented patterns of comorbidity with other disorders in the DSM, most notably substance use disorders. In the ECA study (Robins & Regier, 1991), the base rate of substance use disorders (of any type) among individuals diagnosed with APD exceeded 80%. Earlier studies employing DSM-III criteria reported similar high rates of alcohol and drug problems among individuals diagnosed with APD (e.g., Koenigsberg, Kaplan, Gilmore, & Cooper, 1985; Lewis, Rice, & Helzer, 1983). APD has also been shown to be associated with greatly enhanced risk for alcohol and drug use disorders in a number of more recent comorbidity studies (Grant et al., 2004; Kessler & Walters, 2002; Skodol, Oldham, & Gallaher, 1999).

The fact that substance use disorders co-occur with APD to a much greater extent than would be expected if each occurred by chance, given their respective population prevalence rates, implies that something systematic underlies the association between the two. This hypothesis has been confirmed by recent factor-analytic investigations of the diagnostic overlap among common disorders within the DSM. For example, employing diagnostic data from the National Comorbidity Survey (Kessler et al., 1994), Krueger (1999a) reported evidence for two broad factors underlying the most common Axis I disorders: an "externalizing" factor encompassing APD, alcohol dependence, and drug dependence, and an "internalizing" dimension encapsulating the mood and anxiety disorders (see also Krueger, Caspi, Moffitt, & Silva, 1998; Vollebergh, Iedema, Bijl, de Graaf, Smit, & Ormel, 2001). One possible explanation for the systematic association between APD and substance use disorders is that it reflects overlap between the criteria for the two types of disorders. For example, it could be argued that some of the behaviors that define APD (e.g., irresponsibility, recklessness, aggressiveness) are common sequelae of alcohol or drug abuse, so that increased rates of such behaviors would be expected among individuals with substance use problems. However, this seems unlikely to explain the systematic association between APD and substance use disorders. For one thing, the onset of APD typically precedes that of substance use problems in cases where the two are comorbid. In addition, the relationship between APD and substance abuse problems is asymmetric, due to the higher population prevalence of the latter—that is, whereas most individuals diagnosed with APD also show evidence of substance use disorders, the majority of individuals from the general community diagnosed with substance abuse or dependence do not meet criteria for APD.

Another possibility is that APD and substance use problems arise from a common diathesis—i.e., a common underlying trait factor that predisposes individuals toward the development of both types of disorders. Consistent with this possibility, behavior genetics (twin) studies have revealed evidence of shared genetic factors underlying APD and substance use disorders (e.g., Grove et al., 1990; Pickens, Svikis, McGue, & LaBuda, 1995; Slutske et al., 1998). More recent quantitative analyses of etiologic factors contributing to the broad externalizing factor representing the systematic covariance among these disorders have revealed that this factor is substantially heritable (Kendler, Prescott, Myers, & Neale, 2003; Krueger et al., 2002; Young, Stallings, Corley, Krauter, & Hewitt, 2000). This work is described in more detail below.

Personality Correlates

Two personality trait variables in particular, represented in various models of personality, have been shown to be related to APD. One is impulsiveness, represented in the five-factor model (FFM; Digman, 1990) by the conscientiousness factor (reversed) and in Tellegen's (in press) Multidimensional Personality Questionnaire (MPQ) model by the higher-order factor of constraint (reversed). The other is aggressiveness, represented in the FFM by the agreeableness factor (reversed) and in the MPQ by the lower-order trait of aggression. For example, within a sample of adult psychiatric patients ($N = 54$), Trull (1992) reported significant correlations of $-.32$ and $-.36$, respectively, between symptoms of APD assessed by means of clinical interview and scores on the conscientiousness and agreeableness factors of the FFM assessed concurrently by the NEO Personality Inventory (NEO-PI; Costa & McCrae, 1985). Krueger (1999b) reported that, in a community epidemiological sample consisting of young adults ($N = 961$), scores on the MPQ higher-order factors of constraint and negative emotionality (the aggression facet of the latter, in particular) assessed at age 18 predicted diagnoses and symptoms of APD assessed via interview at age 21, even after controlling for the presence of APD at age 18. Notably, these same personality variables (impulsivity and aggression) show reliable associations with substance use disorders (Acton, 2003; Casillas & Clark, 2002; Krueger, 1999b; Lynam, Leukefeld, & Clayton, 2003; Sher, Bartholow, & Wood, 2000; Slutske et al., 2002; Trull & Sher, 1994).

These relations between personality trait variables and psychopathological syndromes have been interpreted in various ways. One perspective is that traits indexed by personality scales reflect basic individual-difference processes from which mental disorder symptoms arise; another is that deviations in personality emerge as a consequence of psychopathology (for a discussion of these perspectives, see Widiger, Verheul, & van den Brink, 1999). A third perspective is that psychopathological symptoms and personality trait variables correlate with one another because they are indicators of a shared underlying (latent) individual differences factor. With regard to APD and substance dependence, this perspective would suggest that these disorders are related to one another and in turn to personality traits of impulsivity and aggression because all of these variables are manifest indicators of a shared underlying externalizing factor. Krueger et al. (2002) evaluated this hypothesis for the broad MPQ factor of constraint by including this personality variable along with child and adult symptoms of APD and alcohol and drug dependence symptoms in a joint-factor analysis. Consistent with the aforementioned hypothesis, the analysis revealed the presence of a single latent factor on which constraint loaded significantly together with all four symptom variables.

Krueger, Markon, Patrick, Benning, and Kramer (in press) extended this work by undertaking a fine-grained analysis of traits and problem behaviors within the domain of externalizing psychopathology to elucidate the scope and structure of this spectrum more fully. They began by identifying various constructs embodied in the DSM definitions of the disorders included in the Krueger et al. (2002) analysis, then developed self-report items to tap these constructs. They also surveyed the literature to identify other behavioral and trait constructs related empirically or conceptually to externalizing psychopathology and developed additional items to index these constructs. Across multiple rounds of data collection and analysis, item response modeling and factor analysis were used to refine the overall item set and thereby clarify the nature of constructs associated with the broad externalizing factor.

Employing this strategy, Krueger et al. (in press) arrived at a final set of 23 constructs, each operationalized by a unique subscale. These constructs included alcohol, drug, and marijuana use and problems; aggression of various sorts; impulsiveness; irresponsibility; rebelliousness; excitement seeking; and blame externalization. Structural analyses of these 23 subscales yielded evidence of one broad superordinate factor ("externalizing") on which all subscales loaded (the strongest indicators being "irresponsibility" and "problematic impulsivity") and two subordinate factors accounting for residual variance in specific subscales—one factor marked by subscales indexing aggression (all forms), callousness, and excitement seeking, and the other marked by subscales indexing substance-related problems. These findings provide support for the idea that problem behaviors and affiliated personality traits within this domain are indicators of a shared underlying factor (externalizing). In addition, consistent with results emerging from structural analyses of the child (conduct disorder) criteria for APD, this more comprehensive analysis of constructs within the externalizing domain revealed evidence of distinctive aggressive and nonaggressive expressions of this general factor.

Neurobiological Correlates

A variety of neurobiological correlates of APD have been identified. For example, as noted earlier, antisocial individuals—in particular, those displaying impulsive aggressive behavior—show evidence of reduced levels of the neuro-transmitter serotonin in the brain. Other research has consistently demonstrated that low resting heart rate is a correlate of antisocial deviance (Ortiz & Raine, 2004; Raine, 1993, 2002). Indeed, prospective studies have reliably found that low resting heart rate in childhood and adolescence predicts antisocial behavior in adulthood (e.g., Maliphant, Hume & Furnham, 1990; Raine & Venables, 1984; Wadsworth, 1976; for a review, see Ortiz & Raine, 2004). This robust association with low resting heart rate has been interpreted as indicating that general physiological hypoarousal represents an underlying risk factor for anti-social behavior (Raine, 1993, 2002)—because it promotes sensation seeking behavior as a means to enhancing arousal (Eysenck, 1967; Zuckerman, 1979).

Neuropsychological studies provide evidence of deficits in frontal brain function in individuals diagnosed as antisocial. Morgan and Lilienfeld (2000) reported meta-analytic evidence for deficits on frontal lobe tasks in individuals exhibiting conduct disorder and adult antisocial behavior. Notably, individuals at risk for alcoholism by virtue of a positive parental history also show evidence of impairment on neuropsychological tests of frontal lobe function (Peterson & Pihl, 1990; Tarter, Alterman, & Edwards, 1985). Iacono, Carlson, and Malone (2000) suggested that impairments in frontal brain function may be generally characteristic of individuals with externalizing problems.

There is also evidence that reduced amplitude of the P300 brain potential response, long known to be an indicator of risk for alcohol problems (Polich, Pollock, & Bloom, 1994), may be a marker of externalizing problems more generally, including APD. A number of studies have reported evidence of reduced P300 brain response amplitude in individuals with APD (Bauer, Hesselbrock, O'Connor, & Roberts, 1994; Bauer, O'Connor, & Hesselbrock, 1994; Costa et al., 2000; Iacono, Carlson, Malone, & McGue, 2002). Reduced P300 response amplitude has also been found in individuals with other impulse control problems, including nicotine dependence (Anokhin et al., 2000; Iacono et al., 2002), child conduct disorder (Bauer & Hesselbrock, 1999a, 1999b, 2002; Kim, Kim, & Kwon, 2001), and atten-tion deficit hyperactivity disorder (Johnstone & Barry, 1996; Klorman, 1991). The implication is that reduced P300 amplitude could be an indica-tor of the general externalizing factor that these disorders share.

Patrick, Bernat, Malone, and their colleagues (2006) evaluated this possibil-ity in a sample of 969 males recruited from the community by examining the association between reduced P300 amplitude and scores on the externalizing factor, defined as the primary component derived from a principal-components analysis of symptoms of various DSM-III-R impulse control disor-ders (i.e., conduct disorder, adult antisocial behavior, and alcohol, drug, and nicotine dependence). These investigators found a highly significant negative association between scores on the externalizing factor and P300 brain response amplitude (i.e., higher externalizing scores, reflecting more severe symptoms of a greater number of impulse problems, were associated with smaller P300 amplitude). Moreover, significant associations between each individual diagnostic variable and P300 amplitude were accounted for entirely by the externalizing factor—that is, after controlling for scores on this common factor, all associations for individual disorders dropped to nonsignificance. These results suggest that the relationship that has been demonstrated between APD and P300 response may reflect the influence of this broad externalizing factor, which accounts for a sizable portion of the variance in APD.

Etiologic Perspectives on Antisocial Personality Disorder

A variety of etiologic models of APD have been proposed, some of them based on the aforementioned neurobiological findings (for reviews, see Raine, 1993; Zuckerman, 1999). Most of these models focus on the underpinnings of APD as a distinctive syndrome, without considering its relations to other forms of psychopathology (e.g., substance use disorders). However, recent efforts have been made to develop integrative etiologic models that accommodate APD's associations with other disorders and distinctive personality traits by conceptualizing APD as one facet of a broader spectrum of traits and problem behaviors. An example of this is the hierarchical spectrum model proposed by Krueger and his colleagues (2002).

The essence of the hierarchical spectrum model is that there is a broad dispositional factor that disorders within a spectrum share, along with unique etiologic influences that determine the unique symptomatic expression of each disorder. The database on which the model was based consisted of symptom scores on four diagnostic variables (child conduct disorder, adult antisocial behavior, alcohol dependence, and drug dependence), along with a trait measure of impulsiveness (the constraint factor of the MPQ) for a sample of male and female twins recruited from the community ($N = 1,048$). A biometric structural analysis revealed a large common factor ("externalizing") on which all of these diagnostic variables loaded substantially (.58–.78); more than 80% of the variance in this common factor was attributable to additive genetic influence (see also Kendler et al., 2003; Young et al., 2000). The remaining variance in each disorder not accounted for by the broad externalizing factor was attributable primarily to nonshared environmental influence—although for conduct disorder there was also a significant contribution of shared environment.

Based on these findings, Krueger et al. (2002) proposed that a general constitutional factor contributes to the development of various disorders in this spectrum, but that the precise expression of this underlying vulnerability (i.e., as antisocial deviance of different kinds, or as alcohol or drug problems) is determined by disorder-specific etiologic influences. Although the analysis pointed to unique environmental experience as the main determinant of diagnostic specificity (with some contribution of family environment for conduct disorder), owing to the somewhat modest sample size and large confidence intervals around parameters in the model reflecting unique etiologic contributions to specific syndromes, the authors allowed for the possibility that specific genetic factors also contribute to the uniqueness of these disorders. Indeed, Kendler et al. (2003) presented evidence for this possibility in a subsequent study. As noted above, Krueger et al. (in press) extended the work of Krueger et al. (2002) by providing a more comprehensive analysis of traits and problem behaviors within the externalizing spectrum. However, an etiologic analysis of this newer, more comprehensive model remains to be undertaken. In particular, it will be important to evaluate differences in etiologic contributions to the two subordinate factors identified by Krueger et al. (in press) in comparison with those for the broad externalizing factor. (For a discussion of possible neurobiological mechanisms, see Patrick & Bernat, 2006.)

Psychopathy: Current Conceptualizations and Empirical Findings

Hare's Psychopathy Checklist—Revised (PCL-R)

Description. The conceptualization that has dominated contemporary experimental research on psychopathy is the construct embodied in Hare's (1991, 2003) Psychopathy Checklist—Revised (PCL-R). The PCL-R was devised to identify incarcerated offenders who exemplify Cleckley's (1976) description of the psychopathic personality. It consists of 20 items (see Table 6.3), each rated on a 0–2 scale (absent, equivocal, or present) on the basis of information obtained from a semistructured interview and prison files.[3] The standard PCL-R interview covers a range of topics, including education/schooling, employment, family background, relationships and children, criminal history, and drug and alcohol use. A number of questions are included to tap features such as grandiosity, lack of remorse, lack of empathy, shallow affectivity, and failure to accept responsibility for actions. The file review is performed to gather additional information as well as to corroborate information collected in the interview. The PCL-R manual (Hare, 2003) provides a narrative description of the sources and types of information to be used in the scoring of each item. Scores on the 20 individual items are summed to yield an overall psychopathy score, and total score cutoffs (Hare, 2003) are applied to designate individuals as psychopathic (total PCL-R score of 30 or higher), nonpsychopathic (total score of 20 or lower), or intermediate (total PCL-R score between 20 and 30). Overall scores on the PCL-R are highly reliable: for example, Hare (2003) reported pooled intraclass correlation coefficients (single rater) of .83 and .86 across seven male prisoner samples and across four male forensic psychiatric samples, respectively.

The original version of this instrument, the PCL (Hare, 1980), evolved out of a global rating system that drew directly on Cleckley's diagnostic criteria.

Table 6.3   Items of the Psychopathy Checklist—Revised (PCL-R; Hare, 2003)

Item Number	Item Label
1.	Glibness/superficial charm[1,a]
2.	Grandiose sense of self-worth[1,a]
3.	Need for stimulation/proneness to boredom[2,c]
4.	Pathological lying[1,a]
5.	Conning/manipulative[1,a]
6.	Lack of remorse or guilt[1,b]
7.	Shallow affect[1,b]
8.	Callous/lack of empathy[1,b]
9.	Parasitic lifestyle[2,c]
10.	Poor behavioral controls[2,d]
11.	Promiscuous sexual behavior
12.	Early behavior problems[2,d]
13.	Lack of realistic, long-term goals[2,c]
14.	Impulsivity[2,c]
15.	Irresponsibility[2,c]
16.	Failure to accept responsibility for own actions[1,b]
17.	Many short-term marital relationships
18.	Juvenile delinquency[2,d]
19.	Revocation of conditional release[2,d]
20.	Criminal versatility[d]

[1]Items comprising Factor 1 in the original two-factor PCL-R model (Harpur, Hakstian, & Hare, 1988). [2]Items comprising Factor 2 in the original two-factor PCL-R model (Harpur, Hakstian, & Hare, 1988).
[a]Items comprising the interpersonal facet in the revised four-factor model (Hare, 2003); these same items comprise the arrogant and deceitful interpersonal style factor in the revised three-factor model (Cooke & Michie, 2001). [b]Items comprising the affective facet in the revised four-factor model (Hare, 2003); these same items comprise the deficient affective experience factor in the three-factor model (Cooke & Michie, 2001). [c]Items comprising the lifestyle facet in the revised four-factor model (Hare, 2003); these same items comprise the impulsive and irresponsible behavioral style factor in the revised three-factor model (Cooke & Michie, 2001). [d]Items comprising the antisocial facet in the revised four-factor model.

This global rating approach, a variant of one employed initially by Lykken (1957), was used for several years in experimental studies of incarcerated male offenders by Hare and his colleagues, beginning in the mid 1960s. Ratings from 1 to 7 were assigned by diagnosticians familiar with the history and behavior of the subject—with 1 signifying that the individual was definitely not a psychopath and 7 signifying that the individual clearly matched the Cleckley prototype description. Scores of 1–2 and 6–7, respectively, were used to assign individuals to nonpsychopathic and psychopathic groups for testing purposes. This global rating system proved to be quite reliable, but the aura of "subjectivity" surrounding it led to calls for a more systematic assessment procedure based on objective behavioral criteria. The strategy Hare took in developing the

PCL was to select items from a large list of candidate indicators that differentiated empirically between individuals assigned low and high scores on the initial global rating system. The original PCL item set comprised 22 items. In the subsequent revised version (Hare, 1991), two of those items ("previous diagnosis as a psychopath or similar" and "antisocial behavior not due to alcohol intoxication") were dropped, and the descriptions of the scoring criteria for the remaining 20 items were revised somewhat. The items and scoring criteria in the most recent (second) edition of the PCL-R (Hare, 2003) remain the same as they were in the first (1991) edition.

It is notable that the behavioral deviance features and emotional-interpersonal features described by Cleckley (Table 6.1, second and third sections) are well represented in the PCL-R. In contrast, the positive adjustment features (Table 6.1, first section) are not. Although it could be argued that the first part of Cleckley's "superficial charm and good 'intelligence'" criterion is captured by item 1 of the PCL-R ("glibness and superficial charm"), a comparison of the wording of Cleckley's criterion with that of PCL-R item 1 reveals a key difference. PCL-R item 1 includes reference to excessive talkativeness, insincerity, slickness, and a lack of believability in the target individual's social presentation. Related to this, the instructions for scoring call for an intermediate rating of 1 in cases where the individual presents with a "macho" or "tough guy" image, whereas a rating of 0 is called for if the individual presents as sincere and straightforward. Thus, the emphasis is on a somewhat deviant ("too good to be true") or hypermasculine self-presentation. The wording of Cleckley's (1976) criterion has a notably different flavor:

> There is nothing at all odd or queer about him, and in every respect he tends to embody the concept of a well-adjusted, happy person. Nor does he, on the other hand, seem to be artificially exerting himself like one who is covering up or who wants to sell you a bill of goods . . . Signs of affectation or excessive affability are not characteristic. He looks like the real thing. (p. 339)

The inclusion of "good 'intelligence'" (reflecting good sense, intact reasoning, and above average or superior intellect) as part of this diagnostic criterion reinforces the impression that Cleckley intended this to be an indicator of positive psychological adjustment.

What might account for the absence of pure indicators of adjustment among the items of the PCL-R? Although information in the PCL-R manual (Hare, 1991, 2003) and in the initial report on the development of the PCL (e.g., Hare, 1980) is somewhat unclear as to what criteria were used to select items, these sources do indicate that indicators were retained if they discriminated low- and high-psychopathy groups defined on the basis of "global ratings" (i.e., degree of match with Cleckley's case examples) and if they showed "good psychometric properties." The latter implies that indicators were chosen that contributed to the reliability (internal consistency) of the overall scale as well as helped to discriminate extreme groups. This item selection strategy, which fits with the aim of indexing a unitary construct, would operate to homogenize the item set: indicators similar to most other indicators in the candidate pool would be retained, while those differing most from the others would be dropped. Because the greater majority of Cleckley's diagnostic criteria (12 of 16) reflect tendencies toward deviance as opposed to adjustment, the initial candidate pool would almost certainly have included more indicators of deviance. Indicators of positive adjustment presumably dropped out because they failed to coalesce with the larger proportion of (pathologic) indicators. This would yield a final item set more uniformly indicative of deviance and maladjustment than Cleckley's original criterion set.

Some of the data contained in the initial report on the development of the PCL (Hare, 1980) appear consistent with this account. Of particular interest are data for a sample of 143 prison inmates who were rated on Cleckley's 16 criteria for psychopathy as well on the 22 items of the original PCL. A principal-components analysis of the Cleckley items in this sample yielded five components, accounting for 64% of the total variance. The largest of these were an emotional-interpersonal component (marked by pathological egocentricity, poverty of affect, unresponsiveness in interpersonal relations, untruthfulness, and lack of remorse), accounting for 29.3% of the variance, and a behavioral deviance component (marked by absence of life plans, unreliability, and failure to learn by experience), accounting for 12.0% of the variance. In addition, a psychological adjustment component clearly emerged (marked by charm and good intelligence, absence of delusions/irrationality, and absence of nervousness), but this accounted for a smaller proportion of the variance (7.1%). A principal-components analysis of the PCL items also yielded five components, accounting for approximately 61% of the overall variance. However, in this case the dominant component, accounting for 27.3% of the total variance, was one reflecting behavioral deviance (proneness to boredom, lack of realistic plans, parasitic lifestyle, and impulsivity). The second component, reflecting the emotional-interpersonal features of psychopathy (lack of remorse, failure to accept responsibility, conning, grandiosity, glibness, and callousness), accounted for only 13% of the variance. These findings are consistent with the idea that the effort to operationalize Cleckley's criteria as a unitary construct in the PCL resulted in an item set generally more reflective of deviance and maladjustment.

The relations that overall scores on the PCL-R show with criterion measures further reinforce the notion that, compared with Cleckley's original conceptualization, the construct underlying the PCL-R as a whole is more purely pathological in nature. For example, overall scores on the PCL-R are highly correlated with overall symptoms of APD (which, as noted earlier, primarily reflect behavioral deviance): the mean correlation across 10 studies reported by Hare (2003) was .67. The personality traits that are correlated most strongly with overall scores on the PCL-R are traits reflecting aggression and impulsivity—that is, agreeableness and conscientiousness from the FFM (significant negative correlations in each case; Lynam & Derefinko, 2006), and lower-order aggression and higher-order constraint from the MPQ (significant positive and negative correlations, respectively; Verona, Patrick, & Joiner, 2001). In addition, overall scores on the PCL-R show robust positive associations with various behavioral indices of aggression (Hare, 2003) as well as with alcohol and drug problems (Reardon, Lang, & Patrick, 2002), and weak positive associations with suicidal behavior (Verona et al., 2001). Also, in contrast with Cleckley's portrayal of psychopaths as low in anxiousness, overall scores on the PCL-R show negligible associations with measures of trait anxiety (Hare, 2003) and weak positive associations with FFM neuroticism (Lynam & Derefinko, 2006). Thus the focus on psychopathy as a unitary construct leads to a picture of the psychopath as more aggressive and psychologically maladjusted than the majority of Cleckley's case examples.

Distinctive Factors of the PCL-R. It is important to note that the PCL/PCL-R, while developed to assess a putatively unitary construct, does include distinctive factors that exhibit discriminant validity in their relations with external criterion variables. Until fairly recently, on the strength of initial factor-analytic work (Hare et al., 1990; Harpur, Hakstian, & Hare, 1988), the PCL-R has been viewed as comprising two correlated dimensions. Within this two-factor model, Factor 1 is marked by items reflecting the emotional and interpersonal features of psychopathy (charm, grandiosity, and deceitfulness/conning; absence of remorse, empathy, and emotional depth; and blame externalization). In contrast, Factor 2 is marked by items describing a chronic antisocial lifestyle, including child behavior problems, impulsiveness, irresponsibility, and absence of long-term goals. Scores on the two PCL-R factors are typically correlated at about .5 (Hare, 1991, 2003). Recently, Cooke and Michie (2001) proposed an alternative three-factor model. In this model, the items of Factor 1 are parsed into two separate (albeit correlated) factors: "arrogant and deceitful personality style," marked by charm, grandiosity, deceitfulness, and manipulation; and "deficient affective experience," encompassing absence of remorse or empathy, shallow affect, and failure to accept responsibility. The third factor in this model ("impulsive-irresponsible behavioral style") consists of a pared-down version of Factor 2, comprising the five indicators deemed to be most traitlike. Even more recently, Hare (2003; see also Hare & Neumann, 2006) proposed a nested four-factor model in which Factor 1 of the original two-factor model was partitioned into "interpersonal" and "affective" facets (mirroring Cooke and Michie's first two factors) and Factor 2 was divided into a "lifestyle" facet (mirroring Cooke and Michie's third factor) and an "antisocial" facet (comprising the remaining antisocial behavior indicators from Factor 2).

Most of the data regarding the distinctive correlates of PCL-R item subsets pertain to the two factors of the original model. These two factors show divergent relations with independent criterion measures of personality and behavior, particularly when their overlap (covariance) is controlled for using partial correlation or hierarchical regression techniques. For example, findings have generally indicated that the unique variance in the emotional-interpersonal component of the PCL-R (Factor 1) is negatively correlated with measures of trait anxiety, whereas the behavioral deviance component (Factor 2) is positively related to trait anxiety (Hicks & Patrick, 2006; Patrick, 1994; Verona et al., 2001).[4] The unique variance in Factor 1 also appears to be positively associated with measures of social dominance (Verona et al., 2001; see also Hare, 1991; Harpur, Hare, & Hakstian, 1989), and in some work, with measures of trait-positive affectivity (Patrick, 1994) and achievement (Verona et al., 2001). These findings indicate that the positive adjustment component of psychopathy contained in Cleckley's conceptualization may be tapped to some extent by the unique variance in Factor 1 (i.e., the part that is unrelated to behavioral deviance). Moreover, recent work by Hall, Benning, and Patrick (2004) examining associations separately for the interpersonal and affective components of Factor 1 (Cooke & Michie, 2001; Hare, 2003) indicates that the interpersonal component in particular accounts for these relations with measures of adjustment/resiliency. In addition, scores on PCL-R Factor 1 show negative associations with measures of empathy (Hare, 2003) and positive associations with constructs reflecting a self-centered interpersonal style, including narcissistic personality and Machiavellianism (Hare, 1991; Harpur et al., 1989; Verona et al., 2001). Factor 1 also shows selective positive associations with indices of instrumental aggression (Patrick, Zempolich, & Levenston, 1997; Woodworth & Porter, 2002).

In contrast, Factor 2 of the PCL-R shows selective positive associations with child symptoms of DSM APD as well as markedly stronger associations than Factor 1 with adult APD symptoms (Hare, 2003; Verona et al., 2001). Factor 2 is associated much more strongly than PCL-R Factor 1 with criminal history variables, such as overall frequency of offending (Hare, 2003). In addition, Smith and Newman (1990) reported that this component of PCL-R psychopathy was positively associated with alcohol and drug dependence, whereas Factor 1 of the PCL-R was unrelated to substance abuse (see also Reardon et al., 2002). Research has demonstrated selective positive associations between PCL-R Factor 2 and various indices of reactive aggression (including child and adult fights, assault charges, and partner abuse; Patrick & Zempolich, 1998; Patrick et al., 1997; see also Woodworth & Porter, 2002). PCL-R Factor 2 is also related positively to suicidal behavior, whereas the unique variance in PCL-R Factor 1 tends to be negatively associated with suicidality (Verona, Hicks, & Patrick, 2005; Verona et al., 2001). In the domain of personality traits, ratings on PCL-R Factor 2 show robust positive correlations with aggression, impulsivity, and overall sensation seeking (Hare, 1991; Harpur et al, 1989).

These divergent associations for PCL-R Factors 1 and 2 are notable for two variables considered to be facets of a single higher-order construct (e.g., Hare, 1991, 2003). Particularly striking are instances in which opposing associations of the two PCL-R factors with criterion measures become stronger once their covariance (overlap) is removed. This phenomenon is known as *cooperative suppression* (Cohen & Cohen, 1975; Frick, Lilienfeld, Ellis, Loney, & Silverthorn, 1999; Paulhus, Robins, Trzesniewski, & Tracy, 2004). In such cases, true associations between the unique part of each predictor variable and external criterion measures are muted or concealed by the variance that the two predictors share. The occurrence of suppressor effects, particularly cooperative suppressor effects, is conceptually important because it signifies the presence of distinctive underlying constructs embedded within a common measurement instrument (Paulhus et al., 2004).

Recently, Hicks and Patrick (2006) applied this formulation to an analysis of relations between the two PCL-R factors and facets of negative emotionality—including distress (or general anxiousness), fearfulness, and anger—as well as depression. For three of these four criterion variables (emotional distress, fear, depression), cooperative suppressor effects were found (i.e., associations for both PCL-R factors increased, in opposing directions, when the two were included concurrently in a prediction model). For the anger variable, a crossover suppression effect was evident (i.e., simultaneous inclusion of the two PCL-R factors in a prediction model resulted in a change in the direction of association for Factor 1—that is, from significantly positive to nonsignificantly negative) and a nonsignificant increase in the positive association for Factor 2). Moreover, for all four criterion variables, prediction using the two PCL-R factors together was superior to that based on PCL-R total scores alone. In particular, for the distress, fear, and depression variables, PCL-R total scores provided negligible predictive power, whereas concurrent use of the two PCL-R factors yielded significant prediction. Hicks and Patrick noted that suppression effects for the two PCL-R factors have previously been reported for other criterion variables, including suicidal behavior (cooperative suppression; Verona et al., 2005) and alcohol/drug problems (crossover suppression; Smith & Newman, 1990).

As noted, the presence of suppressor effects, particularly instances of cooperative suppression, implies that the items of a measurement instrument presumed to index a single broad construct are actually tapping separate, distinctive underlying constructs. In the case of the PCL-R, the occurrence of suppressor effects for its two factors is actually consistent with Cleckley's original idea that the syndrome of psychopathy entails the convergence of paradoxical dispositions toward psychological resiliency and behavioral maladjustment. Although the strategy used to select items for the PCL-R favored the emergence of a unidimensional criterion set, distinctive underlying constructs are nevertheless evident in terms of both internal structure and relations with external criterion measures. As discussed in the final section of this chapter, there is also evidence that these separable components of psychopathy may have distinctive etiologic underpinnings.

Prevalence of PCL-R–Defined Psychopathy. Because the PCL-R was developed for use in male correctional and forensic settings, firm prevalence estimates are available primarily for samples of this kind. Using a total score cutoff of 30, the estimated base rate of PCL-R–defined psychopathy in male correctional and forensic populations is 15% to 25%, versus a base rate of 50% to 80% for DSM-defined APD (Hare, 2003, p. 92). For example, for a sample of 100 male prisoners from a medium-security institution in Canada, the DSM-IV APD field trial report listed base rates of 28% and 70%, respectively, for psychopathy as defined by an abbreviated version of the PCL-R and APD as defined by DSM-III-R criteria. Figure 6.1 depicts this asymmetry in prevalence rates for the two disorders. This difference in prevalence has been attributed to the fact that a PCL-R diagnosis of psychopathy requires the presence of prominent emotional-interpersonal features as well as prominent antisocial deviance (Hare, 2003; Widiger et al., 1996).

As noted earlier, the prevalence of APD among men in the general community is estimated to be about 3% (APA, 2000). Because the PCL-R criteria are tailored to offender samples and limited efforts have been made to assess PCL-R psychopathy in community samples (for a notable exception, see Ishikawa, Raine, Lencz, Bihrle, & Lacasse, 2001), the prevalence of PCL-R–defined psychopathy in the community at large is essentially unknown. Using the median prevalence figures for prison settings (65% for APD and 20% for psychopathy, respectively), and assuming a comparable base rate of criminal psychopathy among APD individuals in the community, the estimated base rate for criminal psychopathy among community males would be approximately 1%. Using an abbreviated, screening version of the PCL-R (the PCL:SV; Hart et al., 1995), Farrington (2006) reported a base rate for psychopathy of approximately 2% (i.e., 8 cases out of 411) in a large sample of community boys followed up to age 48.

However, such estimates do not include individuals who manifest core affective-interpersonal symptoms of psychopathy without meeting criteria for APD. Because the field lacks an agreed-upon set of criteria for diagnosing psychopathy in nonprisoners, population prevalence estimates for noncriminal psychopathy are unknown. Cleckley referred to such cases as "incomplete manifestations" of the syndrome, but he did not speculate about prevalence. Hare (1993) suggested, with dramatic emphasis, that clinically documented cases of psychopathy

> represent only the tip of a very large iceberg . . . The rest of the iceberg is to be found nearly everywhere—in business, the home, the professions, the military, the arts, the entertainment industry, the news media, academe, and the blue-collar world. (p. 115)

However, he did not speculate about prevalence rates.

Women are incarcerated at much lower rates than men, and as noted earlier, the base rate of APD among women is estimated to be only a third of that among men (APA, 2000). In addition, reported base rates of PCL-R–defined psychopathy in female prisoner samples, employing a standard total score cutoff of 30, tend to be lower than for males. Although some studies of incarcerated women have reported base rates within the range that is typical for incarcerated men, others have reported lower base rates (for a review, see Verona & Vitale, 2006). Studies of psychopathy and related constructs in nonincarcerated samples have also yielded reliably lower prevalence figures for women compared to men (Verona & Vitale, 2006). With regard to race/ethnicity, an initial study by Kosson, Smith, and Newman (1990) yielded evidence that overall PCL-R scores were higher among African-American offenders than they were among European-American offenders. A recent meta-analysis of studies of this kind (Skeem, Edens, Camp, & Colwell, 2004) revealed a small but significant effect size for this comparison. With regard to culture, there is evidence that American inmate samples generally score higher on the PCL-R than European inmate samples (Sullivan & Kosson, 2006).

Comorbidity With DSM Disorders. The DSM disorder most frequently associated with PCL-R–defined psychopathy is APD. As noted in the preceding section, the relationship between PCL-R psychopathy and APD is asymmetric. Within offender samples, most individuals who meet criteria for a diagnosis of psychopathy (i.e., PCL-R total score > 30) also meet criteria for a DSM diagnosis of APD; in contrast, the majority of individuals who meet criteria for a diagnosis of APD do not meet PCL-R criteria for psychopathy (see Figure 6.1). Also, as noted earlier, the two PCL-R factors show an asymmetric association with APD: the social deviance (Factor 2) component of the PCL-R is related selectively to the child component of APD, and is also related more substantially to the adult component. This is because the behavioral features embodied in the child and adult criteria for APD overlap substantially with the behavioral features of psychopathy embodied in PCL-R Factor 2. By contrast, only one of the 15 child criteria for APD (lying) and only two of the seven adult criteria (deceitfulness and lack of remorse) intersect with the emotional-interpersonal features of psychopathy embodied in PCL-R Factor 1.

Factor 2 of the PCL-R is also associated selectively with substance use problems (Reardon et al., 2002; Smith & Newman, 1990) and with features of borderline personality disorder (Shine & Hobson, 1997; Warren et al., 2003). In contrast, scores on PCL-R Factor 1 tend to be associated more strongly with diagnostic ratings of narcissistic personality disorder (Harpur et al., 1989; Hart & Hare, 1989, 1998) and histrionic personality disorder (Hart & Hare, 1989; Hildebrand & de Ruiter, 2004). In contrast with Cleckley's description of psychopaths as individuals lacking in anxiousness and "psychoneurotic" features, overall scores on the PCL-R appear to be generally unrelated to depression and symptoms of anxiety disorders (Hare, 2003). However, as noted earlier, the two factors of the PCL-R show opposing, mutually suppressive relations with measures of anxiety and depression—that is, after controlling for the overlapping variance between the two factors, Factor 1 shows negative associations with such measures, whereas Factor 2 shows positive

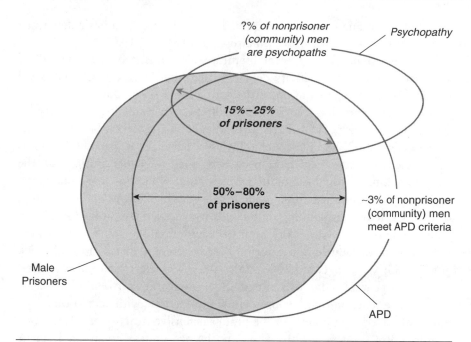

?% of nonprisoner (community) men are psychopaths

Psychopathy

15%–25% of prisoners

50%–80% of prisoners

~3% of nonprisoner (community) men meet APD criteria

Male Prisoners

APD

Figure 6.1   Depiction of prevalence rates and diagnostic overlap for antisocial personality disorder, as defined by DSM-IV criteria (American Psychiatric Association, 2000), and psychopathy, as defined by items of the Psychopathy Checklist—Revised (Hare, 2003), in male prisoner samples (shaded circle) and in the community at large (unshaded portions of circle and ellipse).

associations (Hicks & Patrick, 2006). The fact that the unique variance in Factor 1 is negatively associated with anxiety and depression suggests that this component of the PCL-R (particularly its interpersonal facet [Hall et al., 2004]) captures something of the positive adjustment and resiliency Cleckley described as characteristic of psychopaths. The positive associations for Factor 2, in contrast, are consistent with data indicating that the DSM diagnosis of APD is associated with an increased prevalence of anxiety and mood disorders (APA, 2000, p. 702; see also Krueger, 1999a).

Neurobiological Correlates. Neurobiological correlates of psychopathy have been studied mainly in relation to overall scores on the PCL-R, and in relation to the Cleckley global ratings of psychopathy that served as the referent for the PCL-R. Historically, one of the most consistent findings—beginning with Lykken's (1957) seminal study and continuing with Hare's classic investigations of autonomic reactivity in psychopaths through the 1960s and 1970s—has been that individuals high in overall psychopathy show reduced electrodermal (skin conductance) reactivity to stressors of various kinds, particularly cues signaling an impending noxious event (for reviews, see Arnett, 1997; Hare, 1978; Lorber, 2004; Siddle & Trasler,

1981). This finding has been interpreted as a reflection of a basic deficiency in anxiety or fear (Fowles, 1980; Hare, 1978; Lykken, 1957).

Another reliable finding in the literature, also consistent with the idea of a negative emotional reactivity deficit, is that high PCL-R psychopaths fail to show normal augmentation of the startle blink reflex during viewing of aversive visual stimuli (Herpertz et al., 2001; Levenston, Patrick, Bradley, & Lang, 2000; Patrick, 1994; Patrick, Bradley, & Lang, 1993; Sutton, Vitale, & Newman, 2002; Vanman, Mejia, Dawson, Schell, & Raine, 2003). In this case, reactivity differences have been tied specifically to elevations on the emotional-interpersonal factor of psychopathy. A lack of fear-potentiated startle is evident not just among individuals with high scores on both factors of the PCL-R but also among individuals who score high on Factor 1 only, whereas individuals who score high on Factor 2 alone show normal augmentation of the startle reflex during aversive cuing (Patrick, 1994; Patrick et al., 1993; Vanman et al., 2003). In contrast with electrodermal reactivity, which is a general index of sympathetic arousal, the startle blink reflex is a protective reaction that has been shown to increase with activation of the amygdala, a key component of the brain's defensive (fear) system (see Lang, Bradley, & Cuthbert, 1990). Thus an absence of fear-potentiated startle implies a weakness in reactivity at this basic subcortical level. Consistent with this hypothesis, Blair and his colleagues have reported deficits among psychopathic individuals on behavioral tasks believed to be sensitive to amygdala function (for a review, see Blair, 2006), and recent neuroimaging research has demonstrated reduced amygdala activity during aversive conditioning in high PCL-R scorers (Veit et al., 2002).

A variety of studies employing other methodologies have yielded evidence of differences in brain reactivity or function among individuals high in overall PCL-R psychopathy, including investigations of cerebral asymmetry (for a review, see Hare, 2003, pp. 124–126), brain event-related potential (ERP) studies (e.g., Kiehl, Hare, MacDonald, & Brink, 1999; Williamson, Harpur, & Hare, 1991), and structural and functional neuroimaging studies (for a review, see Raine & Yang, 2006). Nevertheless, studies examining the performance of high-psychopathy individuals on neuropsychological tests of frontal lobe function have not yielded reliable evidence of impairment (e.g., Hare, 1984; Hart, Forth, & Hare, 1990; for a review, see Rogers, 2006), nor have studies examining the P300 component of the event-related potential (for a review of conflicting findings, see Raine, 1993, but see also more recent work by Kiehl, Hare, Liddle, & MacDonald, 1999). This stands in contrast to evidence, cited earlier, that APD is reliably associated with deficits on tests of frontal lobe dysfunction and with reduced amplitude of the P300 brain potential response. Given that Factor 2 of the PCL-R is associated more strongly with APD and that the unique variance in PCL-R Factor 1 (i.e., that unrelated to Factor 2) shows positive associations with some measures of psychological adjustment, it is possible that the two factors of the PCL-R are differentially related to performance on tests of frontal lobe function and to P300 amplitude (i.e., deficits may be evident for Factor 2 only). However, this possibility remains to be examined (Rogers, 2006).

One type of impairment that has been related selectively to PCL-R Factor 2 is reduced autonomic reactivity during mental imagery of emotional situations. Specifically, Patrick, Cuthbert, and Lang (1994) found reduced skin conductance and heart rate reactivity during imagery of fearful text scripts relative to neutral scripts in prisoners who were high on Factor 2 of the PCL-R, regardless of whether they were low or high on Factor 1, compared with prisoners low on Factor 2. The authors' interpretation was that the antisocial deviance component of psychopathy is associated with reduced automatic-elaborative processing of symbolic (in this case, linguistic) affective information (see also Patrick & Lang, 1999). Another neurobiological indicator that appears to be associated preferentially with PCL-R Factor 2 is reduced functioning of the serotonergic neurotransmitter system, which as noted previously is also associated with impulsive aggressive behavior in antisocial individuals (Dolan & Anderson, 2003; Minzenberg & Siever, 2006).

Alternative Self-Report–Based Conceptualizations of Psychopathy

Aside from issues regarding its coverage of the positive adjustment features of psychopathy emphasized by Cleckley, other limitations of the PCL-R include the fact that it is time consuming to administer and that several of its items (those scored on the basis of criminal offense behaviors) are not applicable to individuals outside of forensic and correctional settings. For these reasons, other approaches to the assessment of psychopathy have been sought, many of them self-report based. Because they consist of more general queries about attitudes and behavioral tendencies, standard questionnaire inventories can be used across a range of different participant samples. Self-report questionnaires are also efficient to administer and score and thus are amenable to large-scale screening studies.

Lilienfeld and Fowler (2006) provided an authoritative review of self-report instruments developed to assess psychopathy. As these authors point out, most existing inventories for the assessment of psychopathy correlate much more strongly with the antisocial deviance component of psychopathy embodied in PCL-R Factor 2 than they do with the emotional-interpersonal (Factor 1) component (see also Hare, 1991, 2003). These inventories include the Psychopathic Deviate (Pd) scale of the Minnesota Multiphasic Personality Inventory (MMPI; Hathaway & McKinley, 1943), the Socialization (So) scale of the California Psychological Inventory (Gough, 1960), the Self-Report Psychopathy (SRP) scale (Hare, 1985), and the Primary and Secondary Psychopathy scales developed by Levenson, Kiehl, and Fitzpatrick (1995). However, one self-report inventory that appears to tap the two components of psychopathy more equally is the Psychopathic Personality

Inventory (PPI; Lilienfeld, 1990; Lilienfeld & Andrews, 1996). For example, Poythress, Edens, and Lilienfeld (1998) reported significant correlations of .56 and .44, respectively, between overall scores on the PPI and scores on Factors 1 and 2 of the PCL-R for a sample of 50 youthful offenders. Also, recent factor analyses of the subscales of the PPI (Benning, Patrick, Hicks, Blonigen, & Krueger, 2003; Benning, Patrick, Salekin, & Leistico, 2005) have revealed evidence of two underlying factors with distinctive external correlates. Other research examining the validity of these two PPI factors has yielded findings with interesting conceptual and etiologic implications. For these reasons, we focus the remainder of this section on recent studies that have explored the constructs underlying the two distinctive factors of the PPI.

The Psychopathic Personality Inventory and Its Factors. The PPI was developed using a personality-oriented approach in which the goal was to capture dispositional tendencies or traits considered central to psychopathy (Lilienfeld & Andrews, 1996). This contrasts with inventories such as the So and MMPI-Pd scales, which were developed using an empirical, contrasted-groups strategy. In the development of the PPI, a comprehensive survey of the literature was performed to identify all relevant constructs related to psychopathy, and items were developed to index these constructs. Iterative rounds of data collection and analysis were undertaken to refine the initial item set as well as to clarify the target constructs. The PPI comprises 187 questions, each answered using a four-point scale (false, mostly false, mostly true, true). The inventory yields a total score index of psychopathy, as well as scores on eight subscales reflecting specific elements of the psychopathy construct (see Table 6.4). The eight subscales of the PPI demonstrate good internal consistencies (.70 to .91; Blonigen, Carlson, Krueger, & Patrick, 2003; Lilienfeld & Andrews, 1996), as well as high test-retest reliabilities (.82 to .94 across a mean retest interval of 26 days; Lilienfeld & Andrews, 1996).

As noted, the PPI was developed to comprehensively index personality trait constructs relevant to the domain of psychopathy (Lilienfeld, 1990). Distinctive subscales were developed to index these trait constructs without a priori assumptions about their underlying structure. Recently, Benning et al. (2003) examined the structure of the PPI subscales in a male community sample ($N = 353$) using principal axis factor analysis and found evidence of two dominant factors accounting for a substantial proportion of the covariance (50.9%) among seven of the eight scales. The Social Potency, Stress Immunity, and Fearlessness subscales loaded more predominantly on one factor (PPI-I), and the Impulsive Nonconformity, Blame Externalization, Machiavellian Egocentricity, and Carefree Nonplanfulness subscales loaded more predominantly on the other (PPI-II). In contrast with the two factors of the PCL-R, which are moderately correlated, these two PPI factors were uncorrelated ($r = -.07$). The eighth subscale of the PPI, Coldheartedness, did not load appreciably on either of these factors. This factor structure was replicated by Benning, Patrick, Salekin, et al. (2005) in a sample of male and female college

Table 6.4   Subscales of the Psychopathic Personality Inventory (PPI; Lilienfeld, 1990)

Subscale Label	# of Items	Description of a High Scorer
Social Potency[1]	24	Able to influence and dominate others
Stress Immunity[1]	11	Minimal experience of anxiety
Fearlessness[1]	19	Takes risks; seeks thrills in danger
Impulsive Nonconformity[2]	17	Reckless; rebellious; unconventional
Blame Externalization[2]	18	Blames others; sees self as victim
Machiavellian Egocentricity[2]	30	Aggressive; selfish; exploitative
Carefree Nonplanfulness[2]	20	Present oriented; lacks forethought and planning
Coldheartedness	21	Unsentimental; insensitive; lacks imaginative capacity

[1]Subscales comprising first factor of the PPI (PPI-I; Benning, Patrick, Hicks, Blonigen, & Krueger, 2003).

[2]Subscales comprising the second factor of the PPI (PPI-II; Benning, Patrick, Hicks, Blonigen, & Krueger, 2003). *Note.* The Coldheartedness subscale does not load appreciably on either of the two PPI factors.

students ($N = 326$), and by Ross, Benning, Patrick, Thompson, and Thurston (2005) in a mixed sample comprising male and female college students ($n = 134$) and male and female prisoners ($n = 159$).

Personality and Behavioral Correlates of the PPI Factors. The two distinctive factors of the PPI show conceptually meaningful, and in many cases diverging, patterns of relations with a wide range of criterion measures. Benning et al. (2003) reported that PPI-I and PPI-II showed opposing associations with indices of adjustment, including verbal intelligence, educational attainment, and occupational status and income. Whereas the direction of association in each case was negative for PPI-II, it was positive for PPI-I (i.e., higher PPI-I was associated with better adjustment). In support of the idea that the two PPI factors reflect different facets of an overarching psychopathy construct, PPI-I and PPI-II both showed significant positive correlations with adult symptoms of antisocial personality disorder ($r = .15$ and $.27$, respectively; $p < .01$). However, child symptoms of APD were significantly associated only with PPI-II. PPI-II was uniquely associated with indices of alcohol and drug problems. Likewise, Patrick, Edens, Poythress, Lilienfeld, and Benning (2006) reported positive associations with the Alcohol Problems and Drug Problems scales of the Personality Assessment Inventory (PAI; Morey, 1991) only for PPI-II. PPI-II (but not PPI-I) showed robust correlations (in all cases positive) with the PAI Antisocial Features, Aggression, Borderline Features, and Suicidal Ideation scales. Furthermore, PPI-II showed significant positive correlations with the Anxiety Disorders and Somatization scales of the PAI, whereas correlations for PPI-I with these scales were significantly *negative*. In contrast, PPI-I was associated uniquely (positively) with the PAI Dominance scale. Taken together, these findings indicate that PPI-I taps aspects of social efficacy and adjustment as well as deviancy, whereas PPI-II is associated more uniformly with deviancy and maladjustment (i.e., child and adult antisociality, substance abuse problems, heightened anxiety and somatization, and suicidal ideation).

Ross et al. (2005) examined relations between the two PPI factors and self-report measures of executive functioning along with alternative self-report indices of psychopathy. The measure of executive functioning was the Frontal Systems Behavior Scale (FrSBe; Grace & Malloy, 2001), a 46-item inventory that assesses personality and behavioral characteristics associated with frontal lobe damage. PPI-I showed a modest positive correlation with the Disinhibition subscale of the FrSBe, a *negative* association of comparable magnitude with the Executive Function subscale (reflecting *better* function), and no correlation with the Apathy subscale. In contrast, PPI-II showed robust positive associations with all three subscales of the FrSBe. Ross et al. also examined relations between the two PPI factors and FFM psychopathy prototype scores derived from a revised version of the NEO-PI inventory (NEO-PI-R; Costa & McCrae, 1992). The computation of psychopathy prototype scores was based on the work of Miller, Lynam, Widiger, and Leukefeld (2001), who composed the prototypical personality profile of the psychopath in FFM terms on the basis of input from experts in the field, then devised a methodology for quantifying the resemblance of individual profiles to this expert-generated prototype. Ross et al. found that PPI-I and PPI-II, though uncorrelated, each showed a robust positive association with FFM prototype scores ($r = .61$ and .47, respectively); taken together, the two PPI factors predicted psychopathy prototype scores at a reliability of .76. This pattern of results provides further support for the idea that the two factors of the PPI tap distinctive components of an overarching psychopathy construct.

Some other recent work has examined the correlates of PPI factor scores estimated from scores on a general inventory of personality, the MPQ (Tellegen, in press). Data for both measures were available in the study carried out by Benning et al. (2003), and these authors noted that scores on PPI-I and PPI-II could be predicted with a high degree of accuracy ($r = .70$ and .67, respectively) from the lower-order trait scales of the MPQ. The MPQ trait scales that contributed to the prediction of PPI-I scores were Social Potency (positive), Stress Reaction (negative), and Harm Avoidance (negative); the MPQ trait scales that contributed to the prediction of PPI-II scores were Alienation (positive), Aggression (positive), Control (Negative), Traditionalism (negative), Social Closeness (negative), and Absorption (positive). Benning, Patrick, Blonigen, Hicks, and Iacono (2005) used the regression models from Benning et al. (2003) to estimate PPI factor scores in three study samples for which MPQ data were available as well as scores on a variety of psychopathy-relevant criterion measures.[5] The study samples included a sample of male and female undergraduates recruited from psychology classes ($N = 346$), a large sample of male and female twins recruited from the community ($N = 1,122$), and a sample of male prisoners recruited from a federal correctional facility ($N = 218$).

A variety of interesting findings emerged from analyses of relations between MPQ-estimated PPI scores and available criterion measures in these samples. Within both the undergraduate and prisoner samples, higher scores on PPI-I (estimated by means of the MPQ) were selectively associated with lower temperamental fearfulness and distress and higher activity and sociability; higher scores on the thrill–adventure seeking component of sensation seeking (Zuckerman, 1979); and high narcissism. In contrast, within these samples, higher PPI-II scores were selectively associated with higher temperamental anger and impulsivity; higher scores on the boredom susceptibility component of sensation seeking; and lower socialization as indexed by scores on the So scale. Within both the community and prisoner samples, higher PPI-I scores were associated with lesser symptoms of phobia (particularly social phobia) and lesser symptoms of depression, whereas higher PPI-II scores were associated with greater symptoms of depression and also greater symptoms of alcohol and drug dependence. Interestingly, within the prisoner sample, scores on both PPI factors showed significant negative correlations with a measure of emotional empathy.

Scores on the PCL-R were also available for the prisoner sample in this study, permitting an evaluation of the association between the two factors of the PPI (estimated by means of the MPQ) and those of the PCL-R. Simple correlations revealed a significant correlation between PPI-I and PCL-R Factor 1 only, whereas PPI-II showed significant zero-order associations with both PCL-R factors. When the overlap between the two PCL-R factors was controlled for (using partial correlations), PPI-I showed a significant positive association with PCL-R Factor 1 only ($r = .28$), and PPI-II showed a significant positive association with PCL-R Factor 2 only ($r = .31$). Supplementary analyses of PCL-R scores based on Cooke and Michie's (2001) three-factor model revealed that PPI-I was related most strongly to the interpersonal component of Factor 1 (i.e., compared with the affective component). This finding is interesting because, as noted earlier, the interpersonal component of the PCL-R appears to account largely for associations between Factor 1 and indices of psychological adjustment and resiliency.

The findings from these studies provide strong support for the validity of the two PPI factors as indices of distinctive components of the psychopathy construct. Although parallels are evident between the PPI factors and the PCL-R factors in terms of their relations with external criterion measures (e.g., the first factor of both instruments is selectively related to dominance, narcissism, and low anxiousness; the second factor of both is selectively related to impulsivity, aggression, low socialization, and alcohol and drug problems), the parallels become evident for some measures (e.g., anxiety) only when the overlap between the PCL-R factors is removed using partial correlations. Moreover, correlations between corresponding factors for the two instruments are only modest in magnitude (~.3, based on the findings of Benning, Patrick, Blonigen, et al., 2005), even after controlling for overlap between the PCL-R factors. One variable contributing to this modest correspondence may be the fact that scores on the PCL-R and PPI are derived using different assessment methods (i.e., interview and examination of file records versus self-report). This "method variance" (Campbell & Fiske, 1959) would operate to attenuate relations between the two even if they were indexing the same construct. However, a key divergence between the two that is not easily explained by method variance is the correlated versus uncorrelated nature of their factor structures. What might account for this difference?

One possible explanation concerns the item selection strategies that were used in developing the two instruments. As discussed earlier, candidate items for the PCL-R were retained if they contributed to prediction of global ratings of psychopathy based on Cleckley's criteria and if they showed good psychometric properties (meaning, presumably, positive correlations with other candidate items such that they contributed to internal consistency of the overall inventory). One apparent consequence of this selection strategy is that indicators of positive psychological adjustment included among Cleckley's criteria were omitted from the PCL-R. In contrast, candidate items for the PPI were selected to serve as indicators of target constructs within the broad domain of psychopathy-related personality traits. Although the trait constructs themselves were refined across separate rounds of data collection and items were selected to form internally consistent subscales, there was no a priori requirement that the items as a whole or the subscales be indicators of a single, unitary construct. Thus, the items of the PPI were not constrained to tap one broad, unitary construct. As a result, the two factors of the PPI appear to be indexing components of the psychopathy construct in a more clearly differentiated way. One component (PPI-II) taps impulsive, aggressive (externalizing) tendencies. The other (PPI-I) taps a construct that encompasses aspects of positive adjustment (higher agency, lower anxiety and depression, higher educational and occupational attainment) as well as aspects of deviancy (narcissism, thrill–adventure seeking, low empathy).

Neurobiological Correlates. Although the two distinctive factors of the PPI have become a topic of investigation only recently, findings regarding the neurobiological correlates of these factors have begun to emerge. Benning, Patrick, and Iacono (2005) examined physiological reactivity of groups selected due to their low or high scores on one or the other factor of the PPI as estimated by scores on the MPQ (cf. Benning, Patrick, Blonigen, et al., 2005) in an affective picture viewing paradigm. Participants who scored very high on PPI-I showed a deviant pattern of startle reactivity resembling that of offenders with high scores on PCL-R Factor 1 (i.e., an absence of fear-potentiated startle), whereas participants who scored very high on PPI-II showed no such deviation. This finding suggests that the PPI-I construct taps the diminished emotional reactivity (in particular, reduced defensive reactivity to aversive cues) associated with PCL-R Factor 1. In contrast, participants who scored very high on PPI-II showed *generally* smaller electrodermal responses to picture stimuli (i.e., whether affective or neutral) compared with participants who scored low on PPI-II, suggesting reduced overall arousability for individuals high in the impulsive-antisocial tendencies associated with this PPI factor (cf. Raine, 1997). This finding of reduced electrodermal reactivity in individuals who scored high on PPI-II was also reported in a recent study by Verschuere, Crombez, de Clercq, and Koster (2005).

In another recent investigation, Gordon, Baird, and End (2004) used functional magnetic resonance imaging (fMRI) to examine the brain responses of high and low PPI scorers during performance of a recognition task in which the focus of attention was directed on some trials to the identity of a target face and on other trials to the type of affective expression appearing on the target face. Individuals scoring high on PPI-I showed lesser activation in the right amygdala and affiliated regions of the frontal cortex (i.e., right inferior frontal cortex, medial prefrontal cortex) during emotion processing trials, as well as greater activation in the visual cortex and right dorsolateral prefrontal cortex, compared with individuals scoring low on PPI-I. These groups did not differ in brain activation during identity processing trials. The authors' interpretation was that high PPI-I scorers relied on brain regions associated with cognition and perception to perform the emotion recognition task, whereas low PPI-I scorers relied more on regions known to be involved in affective evaluation and reactivity. Analyses of activation patterns for individuals grouped in terms of PPI-II scores revealed, if anything, evidence of enhanced amygdala activation in high PPI-II scorers compared with low scorers. This finding is consistent with the idea that antisocial individuals lacking the core affective-interpersonal features of psychopathy show normal or enhanced negative emotional reactivity (Patrick, 2007; Patrick & Lang, 1999).

Etiologic Perspectives on Psychopathy

A variety of etiologic models have been advanced to account for the syndrome of psychopathy (for recent reviews, see Blackburn, 2006; Fowles & Dindo, 2006; Hare, 2003; Hiatt & Newman, 2006). These can be grouped into two broad categories. One category consists of theories that propose some underlying emotional deficit or deviation. For example, Cleckley (1976) postulated that psychopaths are generally deficient in their capacity for affective experience:

> Behind the exquisitely deceptive mask of the psychopath the emotional alteration we feel appears to be primarily one of degree, a consistent leveling of response to petty ranges and an incapacity to react with sufficient seriousness to achieve much more than pseudoexperience or quasi-experience. (p. 383)

According to Cleckley, this underlying deficiency (referenced directly in his "poverty in major affective reactions" criterion) accounts for the superficial, manipulative quality of the psychopath's interactions with others as well as the whimsical nature of his or her behavior in other domains. According to this view, the psychopath's "mask of sanity" arises from an adaptive inclination to mimic the affective displays of others so as to "blend in" and achieve basic goals, with no true recognition that these reactions are actually simulated:

> Let us say that, despite his otherwise perfect functioning, the major emotional accompaniments are absent or so attenuated as to count for little. Of course, he is unaware of this, just as everyone is bound, except theoretically, to be unaware of that which is out of his scale or order or mode of experience. (p. 371)

Most other affective models of psychopathy have postulated a more specific impairment in negative emotional reactivity. For example, Lykken (1957) presented experimental evidence that individuals diagnosed as psychopathic according to Cleckley's criteria were deficient in anxiety responses. In his earlier work, Hare (1965, 1978) proposed that psychopathy is marked by an abnormally steep gradient of fear arousal (i.e., punishment cues that are remote in time fail to inhibit the behavior of psychopaths because such cues do not elicit normal anticipatory fear). Fowles (1980), referencing Gray's (1971) neurobiological theory of motivation, postulated that true ("primary") psychopaths have a weak behavioral inhibition (anxiety) system but a normal behavioral activation (appetitive) system. Patrick and his colleagues (Patrick, 1994; Levenston et al., 2000) proposed that psychopathy entails a heightened threshold for activation of the defensive motivational system. Blair (2006) proposed that the core features of psychopathy arise from dysfunction in the subcortical amygdala. In his model, Blair acknowledged the possibility that psychopathy might entail some impairment in positive as well as negative emotional reactivity (cf. Cleckley, 1976). Indeed, some studies have reported evidence of reduced autonomic and electrocortical reactivity to pleasurable stimuli in PCL-R–defined psychopaths (e.g., Verona, Patrick, Curtin, Bradley, & Lang, 2004; Williamson, Harpur, et al., 1991).

The other category of theories consists of those that have postulated some sort of higher cognitive processing deficit or deviation in psychopathy. For example, Newman and his colleagues (Newman, 1998; Patterson & Newman, 1993) have proposed that psychopathy is characterized by a core deficit in response modulation, defined as the ability to switch from an ongoing (dominant) action set to an alternative mode of responding when environmental cues signal the need for a shift. An alternative perspective is that psychopaths are deficient in the ability to process peripheral cues when their attention is prioritized toward specific task-relevant cues in the environment (Jutai & Hare, 1993; Kosson & Newman, 1986). Kosson (1996, 1998), in a refinement of this hypothesis, suggested that psychopaths show impaired processing of secondary stimulus features primarily under task conditions that promote activation of the left hemisphere. Other work has focused on the idea that the dissociation between what psychopaths say and what they actually do reflects some underlying abnormality in language processing. Studies of this kind have focused on deviations in lateralized verbal processing tasks (e.g., Day & Wong, 1996; Hare & McPherson, 1984) and abnormalities in the use of contextual or associative elements of language such as abstraction, connotation, and metaphor (e.g., Brinkley, Bernstein, and Newman, 1999; Brinkley, Newman, Harpur, & Johnson, 1999; Williamson, 1991). It should be noted that work in this area intersects with affective models of psychopathy in that a number of language processing studies have yielded evidence of deviations in the processing of emotional words in psychopaths (e.g., Lorenz & Newman, 2002; Williamson, Harpur, et al., 1991).

   In addition to these affective and cognitive processing models, one other theoretical perspective warrants mention. In contrast with many of the aforementioned models, which emphasize underlying deficits, this perspective views psychopathy as an evolutionary adaptive life strategy that enhances reproductive success (Harris, Skilling, & Rice, 2001; Mealey, 1995). From this perspective, the behavior of psychopaths reflects a cheating strategy that, although socially disruptive, is advantageous from an evolutionary standpoint because it promotes sexual contacts with multiple partners and yields large numbers of offspring. It should be noted that this theoretical position is not necessarily at odds with models that view the affective deviation in psychopathy as a genotypic extreme of normal temperament that favors a goal-oriented approach over avoidance of risk (e.g., Lykken, 1995; Patrick, 2001, 2007).

Integration: A Dual-Process Perspective on the Relation Between Antisocial Personality Disorder and Psychopathy

A theoretical model that provides an integrative perspective on differing facets of the psychopathy construct and on relations between psychopathy and impulse control disorders, including APD and substance abuse and dependence, is the dual-process model of psychopathy. This model was first proposed by Patrick and Lang (1999) to account for diverging relations between components of PCL-R psychopathy and indices of physiological reactivity within different task paradigms. Subsequent elaborations of the model have appeared in publications by Patrick and his colleagues (Patrick, 2001, 2007; Patrick, Hicks, Krueger, & Lang, 2005). A related model that draws on this research base as well as on findings from the developmental literature was proposed recently by Fowles and Dindo (2006).

The dual-process model posits that different etiologic mechanisms underlie distinctive facets of psychopathy. Cleckley characterized psychopathy as a severe behavioral pathology masked by a veneer of normalcy. The "mask" component of the disorder includes aspects of positive psychological functioning and a superficial but engaging affective-interpersonal style. From the dual-process perspective, the mask that Cleckley described reflects an extreme temperament disposition that entails an underlying weakness in emotional reactivity, particularly defensive (fear) reactivity. Neurobiologically, this temperament style is presumed to reflect differences in the functioning of core affect systems (e.g., the amygdala). In terms of personality constructs, this temperament disposition is marked by a blend of traits, including social dominance, low trait anxiousness, and affective fearlessness (i.e., diminished reactivity to threat or danger as opposed to general sensation seeking). In contrast, the behavioral deviance component of psychopathy reflects *externalizing vulnerability*—that is, the broad factor that accounts for the covariance among various impulse control problems, including child and adolescent antisocial behavior and substance use disorders. From a neurobiological standpoint, this vulnerability reflects deviations in the functioning of higher brain systems that operate to regulate emotion and guide decision making and action in situations involving competing cues. In terms of personality traits, high externalizing is marked by traits of impulsiveness (low constraint) and high negative emotionality (particularly aggression and alienation).

Relations between the two factors of the PCL-R and the latent externalizing factor of general psychopathology were examined in a study conducted by Patrick, Hicks, et al. (2005). Scores on the externalizing factor were estimated from child and adult symptoms of APD, measures of alcohol and drug abuse and dependence, and scores on the constraint factor of the MPQ (cf. Krueger et al., 2002). Zero-order correlations between the latent externalizing factor and the two psychopathy factors modeled as latent variables (i.e., using item parcels; cf. Hare & Neumann, 2006) were .44 for Factor 1 and .84 for Factor 2. In addition, a regression-based structural model was used to examine associations between the *unique* variance in each psychopathy factor and the externalizing factor (i.e., the association of each psychopathy factor with externalizing after controlling for the other psychopathy factor). Within this model, the partial association between Factor 2 and the externalizing factor approached unity, whereas the association of the unique variance in Factor 1 with externalizing was nonsignificant. When the model was rerun with Factor 1 parsed into its interpersonal and affective facets, neither facet showed a significant association with externalizing after controlling for Factor 2. The results of this study confirm that the antisocial deviance component of the PCL-R taps the broad externalizing factor, with which APD has also been associated.

As noted in the section on APD, behavior genetics research points to a coherent, genetic basis for the externalizing factor. In addition, neuropsychological and psychophysiological studies indicate that externalizing disorders are associated with alterations in higher brain function, as evidenced by impaired performance on frontal lobe tasks and reduced brain potential response in cognitive processing tasks. The best-established brain response indicator of externalizing psychopathology is the P300 component of the event-related potential (Iacono et al., 2002; Patrick, Bernat, et al., 2006). The close association between PCL-R Factor 2 and externalizing suggests that it would be fruitful to test for an association between P300 response amplitude and this component of the PCL-R specifically, with some consideration of potential moderating effects of age (Hill & Steinhauer, 2001). Research along these lines could help resolve inconsistencies in the literature on psychopathy and brain response (cf. Raine, 1993).

Etiologic models that focus more broadly on cognitive processing deficits may prove to be especially relevant to the antisocial deviance (externalizing) component of psychopathy. For example, Newman's conceptualization of response modulation is reminiscent of processes that have been posited to underlie a brain potential effect known as the error-related negativity (ERN). The ERN is a negative-polarity scalp potential that peaks within approximately 100 milliseconds following an incorrect response in a speeded reaction time task. It is theorized to reflect an error detection (Scheffers, Coles, Bernstein, Gehring, & Donchin, 1996) or conflict monitoring (Carter et al., 1998) process that serves a self-corrective function in the context of performance of an ongoing task. Brain source localization studies have converged on the anterior cingulate cortex as its probable generator (Holroyd, Dien, & Coles, 1998; Luu, Flaisch, & Tucker, 2000; Miltner, Braun, & Coles, 1997). Recent research indicates that individuals high in externalizing tendencies show reduced ERN compared with individuals low in externalizing tendencies (Hall, Bernat, & Patrick, in press). Based on the close association between PCL-R Factor 2 and externalizing, one might predict that this component of the PCL-R would show a selective association with ERN response. Consistent with this hypothesis, Dikman and Allen (2000) reported that individuals who scored low on the So scales, which as noted earlier relate exclusively to Factor 2 of the PCL-R, showed reduced ERN response in a speeded reaction time paradigm.

Based on the external correlates of the second factor of Lilienfeld's (1990) PPI—which include impulsivity and aggression in the domain of personality, and alcohol and drug abuse as well as child and adult antisocial deviance in the realm of problem behaviors—one would also predict a selective association between this component of self-report psychopathy and the broad externalizing factor of DSM psychopathology. Blonigen, Hicks, et al. (2005) recently examined this issue in a large sample of male and female participants recruited from the community. Participants consisted of monozygotic and dizygotic twins, permitting an analysis of both phenotypic and genetic associations between scores on the two PPI factors (estimated using the trait scales of the MPQ) and scores on the externalizing factor, indexed as a composite of symptoms of child and adult antisocial behavior and alcohol, nicotine, and drug dependence (assessed via diagnostic interview). A robust positive phenotypic association between PPI-II and externalizing scores was found for both men and women ($r = .36$ and $.40$, respectively; $p < .001$),[6] whereas corresponding associations between PPI-I and externalizing were low ($r = .15$ and $.04$) and significant for men only ($p < .05$). Significant genetic correlations were also found between PPI-II and externalizing in both gender groups ($r = .45$ and $.52$ for men and women, respectively), indicating significant overlap in genetic contributions to the two variables; corresponding associations for PPI-I were again smaller and significant for men only. These results indicate that PPI-II is selectively associated with externalizing psychopathology in both women and men, and that this association is mediated to a significant extent by common genetic influences.

From the standpoint of the dual-process model, individuals high in externalizing vulnerability only, while impulsive, aggressive, and antisocially deviant, would not exhibit the full psychopathic syndrome described by Cleckley. The other key ingredient in the disorder is an underlying temperamental disposition marked by agency, social dominance, emotional resiliency, and a heightened threshold for defensive (fear) activation. This temperamental style moderates the expression of externalizing to yield the clinical picture of an apparently well-adjusted, likable individual who is nevertheless untrustworthy and self-serving in his or her relations with others and generally capricious in his or her behavior. For ease of reference, and in recognition of prominent theories of psychopathy that have emphasized deficits in defensive (fear) reactivity, I will refer to this temperamental disposition as *low trait fear*. However, it should be borne in mind that this affective disposition might entail some weaknesses in reactivity to positive appetitive stimuli as well as aversive stimuli (cf. Blair, 2006; Verona, Patrick, Curtin, Lang, & Bradley, 2004).

The conceptualization of this underlying temperament disposition emerges from studies of the psychometric and neurobiological correlates of PCL-R Factor 1 (its unique variance, in particular) and of the corresponding factor of Lilienfeld's (1990) PPI. Although these factors are not isomorphic (i.e., PPI-I correlates mainly with the interpersonal component of Factor 1, and only modestly so; Benning, Patrick, Blonigen, et al., 2005), a variety of parallels are evident in their relations with external criterion measures. As described earlier, both are associated positively with personality measures reflecting dominance, agency more broadly (including traits of well-being and achievement in addition to dominance; cf. Patrick, Curtin, & Tellegen, 2002), and narcissism, and negatively with measures of trait anxiousness (stress reactivity) and empathy. Mirroring Cleckley's positive adjustment criteria, both are also associated negatively with anxiety disorder symptoms, depression, and indices of suicidality. Indeed, Blonigen et al. (2005) reported a negative *genetic* association between scores on PPI-I and symptoms of anxiety and depression. With regard to neurobiological correlates, elevations on both PCL-R Factor 1 and PPI-I have been associated with a lack of fear-potentiated startle during exposure to aversive cues and with reduced amygdala reactivity to emotional stimuli in brain imaging studies.

One key question that arises from this dual-process perspective is how to think about individuals who achieve high overall scores on the PCL-R. One possibility is that this group comprises a mixture of individuals who typify one or the other etiologic process (i.e., high externalizing, low trait fear). This possibility was evaluated in a recent study by Hicks, Markon, Patrick, Krueger, and Newman (2004), who tested for the presence of psychopathy subgroups by using a sophisticated (model-based) cluster-analytic technique to categorize MPQ personality profiles of 96 male offenders with high overall PCL-R scores. The analysis yielded evidence of two subgroups: an "aggressive" subgroup characterized by high overall negative emotionality (especially aggression) and low overall constraint, and a "stable" subgroup characterized by high agency (i.e., elevated well-being, social potency, and achievement) and low stress reactivity. The profiles of these two subgroups closely resembled those associated with the externalizing and low trait fear constructs, respectively. Notably, the proportion of aggressive psychopaths (68.8%) was over twice that in the stable group (31.2%), indicating that the PCL-R as a whole is weighted toward the detection of individuals who exhibit extreme externalizing tendencies (particularly high-aggressive externalizers; cf. Krueger et al., in press). Consistent with this finding, in the aforementioned study of relations between PCL-R scores and externalizing (Patrick, Hicks, et al., 2005), the correlation between the PCL-R as a whole and scores on the latent externalizing factor was .7. However, the findings of Hicks et al. (2004) indicate that individuals resembling Cleckley's psychologically well-adjusted prototype are also represented among high PCL-R scorers. It seems reasonable to suppose that individuals who more purely exemplify the low trait fear diathesis (i.e., without accompanying externalizing vulnerability) would be more strongly represented among "successful" psychopathic individuals who achieve positions of stature within the community (e.g., corporate executives, political leaders; see Hall & Benning, 2006; Hare, 1993; Lykken, 1995).

Another key issue is how the affective facet of PCL-R Factor 1 (encompassing absence of remorse, lack of empathy, shallow affect, and failure to accept responsibility for actions) maps onto this dual-process model. The variance in this facet overlaps statistically both with the interpersonal facet and with the behavioral deviance embodied in Factor 2, so one possibility is that deficient affectivity is associated with externalizing vulnerability as well as with low trait fear. In the case of externalizing vulnerability, affective deficits may arise secondarily to impairments in higher brain systems (cf. Davidson, Putnam, & Larson, 2000; Patrick & Lang, 1999). However, the unique variance in the affective facet of the PCL-R must also be considered. This variance relates minimally to personality variables and also shows some association with low social closeness (Hall et al., 2004). The unique variance in the affective facet also shows some relationship to criminal offense behavior, particularly violent types of offenses—suggesting that it taps something of the detached, coldhearted nature of the criminal psychopath. Fowles and Dindo (2006) theorized that this affective component of PCL-R psychopathy arises in part from negative relationship experiences early in life (with parental figures, in particular) that operate separately from the diatheses underlying impulsive-externalizing tendencies and fearless temperament. Further research is needed to establish whether a separate etiologic mechanism underlies this affective facet of PCL-R psychopathy, and the extent to which the unique variance in this facet (which appears to reflect aggressiveness and interpersonal detachment) is part of Cleckley's original conceptualization of the disorder.

Approaches to Treatment of Antisocial Personality Disorder and Psychopathy

Reviews of the literature on the treatment of antisocial and psychopathic individuals have generally emphasized the difficulties inherent in treating such individuals and the ineffectiveness of psychological interventions with these disorders (e.g., Barley, 1986; Blackburn, 1993, chaps. 13–14; Harris & Rice, 2006). For example, Harris and Rice (2006) concluded that standard psychological interventions for offenders, such as individual cognitive-behavioral therapy, group psychotherapy, and therapeutic community programs, are completely ineffective with psychopaths. In fact, these authors cited findings from some outcome studies indicating that psychopathic individuals who participated in psychotherapeutic treatment actually reoffended at *higher* rates after release than psychopathic individuals who did not receive such treatment. As an explanation for this counterintuitive finding, Harris and Rice suggested that participation in psychotherapy led to improvements in the ability of psychopaths to exploit the weaknesses of other people as a function of their increased understanding of others' motives without accompanying increases in emotional sensitivity. However, Rice and Harris did allow that some highly structured forms of behavioral therapy (e.g., behavior modification aimed at specific skills development, multisystemic therapy targeting influences in the family and local community) might prove more effective with this population—while acknowledging that the outcome studies required to evaluate this possibility remain to be done. However, other authors have identified cross-situational generalization and treatment maintenance as problems in highly structured behavioral interventions, particularly when it comes to the treatment of chronic offenders (Barley, 1986; Blackburn, 1993, chap. 13).

The kinds of cognitive and emotional processing impairments that have been posited to underlie psychopathy may pose a basic obstacle to the effectiveness of purely psychological interventions. As has been suggested with attention deficit hyperactivity disorder, induction of changes in the functioning of underlying neural systems—for example, through pharmacological means—may be required first before cognitive and behavioral interventions can have a significant impact on maladaptive behaviors associated with APD and psychopathy. In this regard, evidence has accumulated for the effectiveness of drug treatments for certain impulse control (externalizing) problems, including impulsive aggression (e.g., lithium, selective serotonin reuptake inhibitors; Minzenberg & Siever, 2006), alcoholism (e.g., acamprosate, naltrexone; O'Malley, Croop, Wroblewski, Labriola, & Volpicelli, 1995; Paille et al., 1995), sexual deviancy (e.g., antiandrogens; Briken, Hill, & Berner, 2003), and pathological gambling (e.g., naltrexone; Kim & Grant, 2001). The fact that certain drug treatments (e.g., naltrexone) have proven to be effective with impulse control problems of different kinds fits with the idea that disorders within the externalizing spectrum have shared etiologic underpinnings (Krueger et al., 2002). From the perspective of the hierarchical model of externalizing (Krueger et al., 2002, in press), particular pharmacological treatments may be needed to target neurocognitive impairments associated with general externalizing vulnerability, whereas others may be needed to target distinctive cognitive and affective processing deviations that underlie aggressive and addictive problems within this spectrum.

From the perspective of the dual-process model of psychopathy, an effective intervention strategy would also need to contend separately with the interpersonal and affective elements of psychopathy that are distinguishable from general externalizing vulnerability. As noted in the last part of the preceding section, the affective features of psychopathy (which reflect aggressiveness and social detachment) may intersect with the aggressive subfactor of externalizing. In contrast, the variance in the interpersonal component of PCL-R psychopathy that is distinct from externalizing (and that is tapped by the first factor of the PPI) appears to reflect aspects of positive psychological adjustment (dominance, nonanxiousness, fearlessness) in addition to aspects of deviancy. Precisely because it is associated with resiliency and an absence of distress, this component of psychopathy may pose an important obstacle to therapy that may need to be dealt with in a fundamentally different way from that by which externalizing features of the disorder are dealt with.

In summary, to be maximally effective, therapeutic intervention strategies for APD and psychopathy will need to recognize and contend with the variegated nature of these syndromes. Specifically, multifaceted treatment programs that employ pharmacological as well as psychological-behavioral techniques to target specific processing impairments associated with distinctive symptomatic features—including general impulsiveness, callous aggression, addictive urges, and insouciant narcissism—are likely to offer the best hope for dealing with these challenging and costly disorders (cf. Seto & Quinsey, 2006).

Conclusion

APD and psychopathy are related but distinctive phenomena. APD as defined in the DSM can be seen as one behavioral expression (facet) of a broader underlying vulnerability to problems of impulse control. Among disorders within the externalizing spectrum, APD is characterized particularly by irritability and aggressiveness along with impulsiveness and irresponsibility. Psychopathy as defined by Hare's PCL-R intersects with APD through its social deviance (Factor 2) component, which taps the broad externalizing factor of which APD is an indicator. In addition to externalizing, however, the PCL-R includes items that tap, to some degree, the nexus of positive adjustment and interpersonal-affective deviancy that Cleckley described as the "mask" component of psychopathy. Recent research findings indicate that the first factor of Lilienfeld's (1990) PPI, which comprises elements of dominance, stress immunity, and fearlessness, may tap this mask component in a purer fashion. Other evidence suggests that this component of psychopathy may reflect a different underlying neurobiological mechanism (i.e., individual differences in trait fear) from the externalizing component (i.e., individual differences in anterior brain function). Further systematic research on these two distinctive components of the psychopathy construct, one of which intersects fundamentally with APD, should help to elucidate the essential nature of these high-impact disorders and contribute to improved strategies for dealing with them.

Notes

1. Lykken (1995) proposed that the distinctive use of these two terms be revived. Specifically, he proposed that the term *psychopath* be used for individuals whose pathology is primarily constitutional in origin (i.e., the product of extreme temperament) and that the term *sociopath* be applied to individuals whose pathology is determined more by environmental factors (in particular, by deviant or inadequate parenting).

2. Cleckley's idea that the essence of true psychopathy lies in deficient affectivity and impaired social relations was adopted by other influential writers in the field. Cleckley's contemporary Karpman (1941, 1948) introduced the distinction between primary and secondary psychopathy. Karpman's view, paralleling Cleckley's, was that true ("primary") psychopathy reflects a constitutional deficit in emotional responsiveness, whereas pseudo ("secondary") psychopathy arises from negative socialization experiences that instill hostility, alienation, and rebellious behavior. Johns and Quay (1962) characterized psychopathy as involving a disconnection between affect and cognition (i.e., psychopaths know the "words" of emotion, but not the "music"). McCord and McCord (1964) described "lovelessness" and "guiltlessness" as the essence of the syndrome. This impact of Cleckley on conceptualizations by others in the field helps to explain why experts in psychopathy have been so critical of the DSM's APD construct for its overemphasis on symptoms of behavioral deviance.

3. It should be noted that alternative versions of the PCL-R have been developed for various purposes. A shortened, screening version (PCL:SV; Hart, Cox, & Hare, 1995) was developed for more efficient clinical assessment in forensic populations as well as for use in high-risk community studies. A youth version (PCL:YV; Forth, Kosson, & Hare, 2003) has been developed for use with adolescent offenders. The Antisocial Process Screening Device (APSD; Frick & Hare, 2001), a psychopathy inventory for younger children, was modeled after the PCL-R. In addition, efforts are under way to develop a version of the PCL-R called the Business Scan (B-Scan; Babiak & Hare, 2005) for identifying individuals with psychopathic tendencies in corporate environments.

4. One report, by Schmitt and Newman (1999), failed to detect significant negative relations between PCL-R factor 1 and measures of trait anxiousness. However, the level of interrater reliability for overall PCL-R scores in this study was quite low (only .70) in relation to other published studies, and reliabilities for the two PCL-R factors were not reported. Because factor scores are based on fewer items, reliabilities for these scores would likely have been even lower. The unreliability of PCL-R scores (which would operate to attenuate correlations with criterion measures, including anxiety scales) could account for the discrepancy between the findings of this study and those of other studies that have examined associations between the PCL-R factors and anxiety measures.

5. Other work has shown that the two factors of the PPI can also be effectively estimated using scores from other omnibus inventories of personality. For example, Sellbom, Ben-Porath, Graham, Lilienfeld, and Patrick (2005) reported cross-validated multiple correlations of .62 and .60 for the prediction of PPI-I and PPI-II, respectively, from scores on the restructured clinical scales of the MMPI-2 (Tellegen et al., 2003). Ross et al. (2005) reported average split-half cross-validation reliabilities of .75 and .78 for the prediction of PPI-I and PPI-II, respectively, from scores on the NEO-PI-R. These findings, together with those for the MPQ (Benning et al., 2003), open the door to further investigation of the criterion-related and predictive validity of these distinctive psychopathy constructs in large existing data sets in which scores on one or more of these omnibus inventories of personality are available.

6. The moderate level of association between PPI-II and externalizing in this study probably reflects the fact that the two variables were assessed using different methods (i.e., self-report versus clinical interview). In more recent work (Patrick, 2005), we found a much higher phenotypic association between PPI-II and externalizing ($r = .84$) when both variables were assessed using the same method (i.e., self-report).

References

Achenbach, T. M. (1991). *Manual for the Child Behavior Checklist/4–18 and 1991 profile*. Burlington: University of Vermont.

Acton, G. S. (2003). Measurement of impulsivity in a hierarchical model of personality traits: Implications for substance use. *Substance Use & Misuse, 38,* 67–83.

American Psychiatric Association. (1952). *Diagnostic and statistical manual of mental disorders*. Washington, DC: Author.

American Psychiatric Association. (1968). *Diagnostic and statistical manual of mental disorders* (2nd ed.). Washington, DC: Author.

American Psychiatric Association (1980). *Diagnostic and statistical manual of mental disorders* (3rd ed.). Washington, DC: Author.

American Psychiatric Association. (1987). *Diagnostic and statistical manual of mental disorders* (3rd ed., revised). Washington, DC: Author.

American Psychiatric Association. (1994). *Diagnostic and statistical manual of mental disorders* (4th ed.). Washington, DC: Author.

American Psychiatric Association. (2000). *Diagnostic and statistical manual of mental disorders* (4th ed., text revision). Washington, DC: Author.

Anokhin, A. P., Vedeniapin, A. B., Sirevaag, E. J., Bauer, L. O., O'Connor, S. J., Kuperman, S., et al. (2000). The P300 brain potential is reduced in smokers. *Psychopharmacology, 149,* 409–413.

Arnett, P. A. (1997). Autonomic responsivity in psychopaths: A critical review and theoretical proposal. *Clinical Psychology Review, 17,* 903–936.

Babiak, P., & Hare, R. D. (2005). *The B-Scan 360: Research version.* Toronto, Ontario, Canada: Multi-Health Systems.

Barley, W. D. (1986). Behavioral and cognitive treatment of criminal and delinquent behavior. In W. H. Reid, D. Dorr, J. I. Walker, & J. W. Bonner III (Eds.), *Unmasking the psychopath: Antisocial personality and related syndromes.* New York: W. W. Norton.

Bauer, L. O., & Hesselbrock, V. M. (1999a). P300 decrements in teenagers with conduct problems: Implications for substance abuse risk and brain development. *Biological Psychiatry, 46,* 263–272.

Bauer, L. O., & Hesselbrock, V. M. (1999b). Subtypes of family history and conduct disorder: Effects on P300 during the Stroop test. *Neuropsychopharmacology, 21,* 51–62.

Bauer, L. O., & Hesselbrock, V. M. (2002). Brain maturation and subtypes of conduct disorder: Interactive effects on P300 amplitude and topography in male adolescents. *Journal of the American Academy of Child & Adolescent Psychiatry, 42,*106–115.

Bauer, L. O., Hesselbrock, V. M., O'Connor, S., & Roberts, L. (1994). P300 differences between non-alcoholic young men at average and above-average risk for alcoholism: Effects of distraction and task modality. *Progress in Neuro-Psychopharmacology and Biological Psychiatry, 18,* 263–277.

Bauer, L. O., O'Connor, S., & Hesselbrock, V. M. (1994). Frontal P300 decrements in antisocial personality disorder. *Alcoholism: Clinical and Experimental Research, 18,* 1300–1305.

Benning, S. D., Patrick, C. J., Blonigen, D. M., Hicks, B. M., & Iacono, W. G. (2005). Estimating facets of psychopathy from normal personality traits: A step toward community epidemiological investigations. *Assessment, 12,* 3–18.

Benning, S. D., Patrick, C. J., Hicks, B. M., Blonigen, D. M., & Krueger, R. F. (2003). Factor structure of the Psychopathic Personality Inventory: Validity and implications for clinical assessment. *Psychological Assessment, 15,* 340–350.

Benning, S. D., Patrick, C. J., & Iacono, W. G. (2005). Fearlessness and underarousal in psychopathy: Startle blink modulation and electrodermal reactivity in a young adult male community sample. *Psychophysiology, 42,* 753–762.

Benning, S. D., Patrick, C. J., Salekin, R. T., & Leistico, A. R. (2005). Convergent and discriminant validity of psychopathy factors assessed via self-report: A comparison of three instruments. *Assessment, 12,* 270–289.

Birnbaum, K. (1909). *Die psychopathischen Verbrecher* [The psychopathic criminal]. Leipzig, Germany: Thieme.

Blackburn, R. (1993). *The psychology of criminal conduct.* Chichester, UK: Wiley.

Blackburn, R. (2006). Other theoretical models of psychopathy. In C. J. Patrick (Ed.), *Handbook of psychopathy* (pp. 35–57). New York: Guilford Press.

Blair, R. J. R. (2006). Subcortical brain systems in psychopathy: The amygdala and associated structures. In C. J. Patrick (Ed.), *Handbook of psychopathy* (pp. 296–312). New York: Guilford Press.

Blonigen, D. M., Carlson, S. R., Krueger, R. F., & Patrick, C. J. (2003). A twin study of self-reported psychopathic personality traits. *Personality and Individual Differences, 35,* 179–197.

Blonigen, D. M., Hicks, B. M., Patrick, C. J., Krueger, R. F., Iacono, W. G., & McGue, M. K. (2005). Psychopathic personality traits: Heritability and genetic overlap with internalizing and externalizing psychopathology. *Psychological Medicine, 35,* 1–12.

Briken, P., Hill, A., & Berner, W. (2003). Pharmacotherapy of paraphilias with long-acting agonists of luteinizing hormone-releasing hormone: A systematic review. *Journal of Clinical Psychiatry, 64,* 890–897.

Brinkley, C. A., Bernstein, A., & Newman, J. P. (1999). Coherence in the narratives of psychopathic and nonpsychopathic criminal offenders. *Personality and Individual Differences, 27,* 519–530.

Brinkley, C. A., Newman, J. P., Harpur, T. J., & Johnson, M. M. (1999). Cohesion in texts produced by psychopathic and nonpsychopathic criminal inmates. *Personality and Individual Differences, 26,* 873–885.

Campbell, D. T., & Fiske, D. (1959). Convergent and discriminant validation by the multitrait-multimethod matrix. *Psychological Bulletin, 56,* 81–105.

Carter, C. S., Braver, T. S., Barch, D. M., Botvinick, M. M., Noll, D. N., & Cohen, J. D. (1998). Anterior cingulate cortex, error detection, and the online monitoring of performance. *Science, 280,* 747–749.

Casillas, A., & Clark, L. A. (2002). Dependency, impulsivity, and self-harm: Traits hypothesized to underlie the association between Cluster B personality and substance use disorders. *Journal of Personality Disorders, 16,* 424–436.

Cleckley, H. (1941). *The mask of sanity.* St. Louis, MO: Mosby.

Cleckley, H. (1976). *The mask of sanity* (5th ed.). St. Louis, MO: Mosby.

Cohen, J., & Cohen, P. (1975). *Applied multiple correlation/regression analysis for the social sciences.* New York: Wiley.

Cooke, D. J., & Michie, C. (2001). Refining the construct of psychopathy: Towards a hierarchical model. *Psychological Assessment, 13,* 171–188.

Costa, L., Bauer, L., Kuperman, S., Porjesz, B., O'Connor, S., Hesselbrock, V., et al. (2000). Frontal P300 decrements, alcohol dependence, and antisocial personality disorder. *Biological Psychiatry, 47,* 1064–1071.

Costa, P. T., Jr., & McCrae, R. R. (1985). *The NEO Personality Inventory manual.* Odessa, FL: Psychological Assessment Resources.

Costa, P. T., Jr., & McCrae, R. R. (1992). *NEO PI-R professional manual.* Lutz, FL: Psychological Assessment Resources.

Davidson, R. J., Putnam, K. M., & Larson, C. L. (2000). Dysfunction in the neural circuitry of emotion regulation: A possible prelude to violence. *Science, 289,* 591–594.

Day, R., & Wong, S. (1996). Anomalous perceptual asymmetries for negative emotional stimuli in the psychopath. *Journal of Consulting and Clinical Psychology, 105,* 648–652.

Digman, J. M. (1990). Personality structure: Emergence of the five-factor model. *Annual Review of Psychology, 41,* 417–440.

Dikman, Z. V., & Allen, J. J. (2000). Error monitoring during reward and avoidance learning in high- and low-socialized individuals. *Psychophysiology, 37,* 43–54.

Dolan, M. C., & Anderson, I. M. (2003). The relationship between serotonergic function and the Psychopathy Checklist: Screening Version. *Journal of Psychopharmacology, 17,* 216–222.

Eysenck, H. J. (1967). *The biological basis of personality*. Springfield, IL: Charles C Thomas.

Farrington, D. (2006). Family background and psychopathy. In C. J. Patrick (Ed.), *Handbook of psychopathy* (pp. 229–250). New York: Guilford Press.

Feighner, J. P., Robins, E., Guze, S. B., Woodruff, R. A., Winokur, G., & Munoz, R. (1972). Diagnostic criteria for use in psychiatric research. *Archives of General Psychiatry, 26,* 57–63.

Forth, A. E., Kosson, D. S., & Hare, R. D. (2003). *The Psychopathy Checklist: Youth Version manual*. Toronto, Ontario, Canada: Multi-Health Systems.

Fowles, D.C. (1980). The three arousal model: Implications of Gray's two-factor learning theory for heart rate, electrodermal activity, and psychopathy. *Psychophysiology, 17,* 87–104.

Fowles, D. C., & Dindo, L. (2006). A dual deficit model of psychopathy. In C. J. Patrick (Ed.), *Handbook of psychopathy* (pp. 14–34). New York: Guilford Press.

Frances, A. J. (1980). The DSM-III personality disorders section: A commentary. *American Journal of Psychiatry, 137,* 1050–1054.

Frick, P. J., & Hare, R. D. (2001). *Antisocial process screening device*. Toronto, Ontario, Canada: Multi-Health Systems.

Frick, P. J., Lahey, B. B., Loeber, R., Stouthamer-Loeber, M., Green, S., Hart, E. L., et al. (1991). Oppositional defiant disorder and conduct disorder in boys: Patterns of behavioral covariation. *Journal of Clinical Child Psychology, 20,* 202–208.

Frick, P. J., Lilienfeld, S. O., Ellis, M., Loney, B., & Silverthorn P. (1999). The association between anxiety and psychopathy dimensions in children. *Journal of Abnormal Child Psychology, 27,* 383–392.

Gordon, H. L., Baird, A. A., & End, A. (2004). Functional differences among those high and low on a trait measure of psychopathy. *Biological Psychiatry, 56,* 516–521.

Gough, H. G. (1960). Theory and method of socialization. *Journal of Consulting and Clinical Psychology, 24,* 23–30.

Grace, J., & Malloy, P. F. (2001). *Frontal Systems Behavior Scale: Professional manual*. Lutz, FL: Psychological Assessment Resources.

Grant, B. F., Stinson, F. S., Dawson, D. A., Chou, S. P., Ruan, W. J., & Pickering, R. P. (2004). Co-occurrence of 12-month alcohol and drug use disorders and personality disorders in the United States: Results from the National Epidemiologic Survey on Alcohol and Related Conditions. *Archives of General Psychiatry, 61,* 361–368.

Gray, J. A. (1971). *The psychology of fear and stress*. Cambridge, UK: Cambridge University Press.

Grove, W. M., Eckert, E. D., Heston, L., Bouchard, T. J., Jr., Segal, N., & Lykken, D. T. (1990). Heritability of substance abuse and antisocial behavior: A study of monozygotic twins reared apart. *Biological Psychiatry, 27,* 1293–1304.

Hall, J. R., & Benning, S. D. (2006). The "successful" psychopath: Adaptive and subclinical manifestations of psychopathy in the general population. In C. J. Patrick (Ed.), *Handbook of psychopathy* (pp. 459–478). New York: Guilford Press.

Hall, J. R., Benning, S. D., & Patrick, C. J. (2004). Criterion-related validity of the three-factor model of psychopathy: Personality, behavior, and adaptive functioning. *Assessment, 11,* 4–16.

Hall, J. R., Bernat, E. M., & Patrick, C. J. (in press). Externalizing psychopathology and the error-related negativity. *Psychological Science*.

Hare, R. D. (1965) Temporal gradient of fear arousal in psychopaths. *Journal of Abnormal Psychology, 70,* 442–445.

Hare, R. D. (1978). Electrodermal and cardiovascular correlates of psychopathy. In R. D. Hare & D. Schalling (Eds.), *Psychopathic behavior: Approaches to research* (pp. 107–143). Chichester, UK: Wiley.

Hare, R. D. (1980). A research scale for the assessment of psychopathy in criminal populations. *Personality and Individual Differences, 1,* 111–119.

Hare, R. D. (1983). Diagnosis of antisocial personality disorder in two prison populations. *American Journal of Psychiatry, 140,* 887–890.

Hare, R. D. (1984). Performance of psychopaths on cognitive tasks related to frontal lobe function. *Journal of Abnormal Psychology, 93,* 133–140.

Hare, R. D. (1985). A comparison of procedures for the assessment of psychopathy. *Journal of Consulting and Clinical Psychology, 53,* 7–16.

Hare, R. D. (1991). *The Hare psychopathy checklist—revised.* Toronto, Ontario, Canada: Multi-Health Systems.

Hare, R. D. (1993). *Without conscience: The disturbing world of the psychopaths among us.* New York: Pocket Books.

Hare, R. D. (2003). *The Hare psychopathy checklist—revised* (2nd ed.). Toronto, Ontario, Canada: Multi-Health Systems.

Hare, R. D., Harpur, T. J., Hakstian, A. R., Forth, A. E., Hart, S. D., & Newman, J. P. (1990). The Revised Psychopathy Checklist: Descriptive statistics, reliability, and factor structure. *Psychological Assessment, 2,* 338–341.

Hare, R. D., & Hart, S. D. (1995). A comment on the DSM-IV antisocial personality disorder field trial. In W. J. Livesley (Ed.), *The DSM-IV personality disorders.* New York: Guilford Press.

Hare, R. D., & McPherson, L. M. (1984). Psychopathy and perceptual asymmetry during verbal dichotic listening. *Journal of Abnormal Psychology, 93,* 141–149.

Hare, R. D., & Neumann, C. S. (2006). The PCL-R assessment of psychopathy: Development, structural properties, and new directions. In C. J. Patrick (Ed.), *Handbook of psychopathy* (pp. 58–88). New York: Guilford Press.

Harpur, T. J., Hakstian, A. R., & Hare, R. D. (1988). Factor structure of the psychopathy checklist. *Journal of Consulting and Clinical Psychology, 56,* 741–747.

Harpur, T. J., Hare, R. D., & Hakstian, A.R. (1989). Two-factor conceptualization of psychopathy: Construct validity and assessment implications. *Psychological Assessment, 1,* 6–17.

Harris, G. T., & Rice, M. E. (2006). Treatment of psychopathy: A review of empirical findings. In C. J. Patrick (Ed.), *Handbook of psychopathy* (pp. 555–572). New York: Guilford Press.

Harris, G. T., Skilling, T. A., & Rice, M. E. (2001). The construct of psychopathy. In M. Tonry (Ed.), *Crime and justice: An annual review of research* (pp. 197–264). Chicago: University of Chicago Press.

Hathaway, S. R., & McKinley, J. C. (1943). *The Minnesota Multiphasic Personality Inventory manual.* New York: Psychological Corporation.

Hart, S. D., Cox, D., & Hare, R. D. (1995). *Manual for the Psychopathy Checklist: Screening Version (PCL:SV).* Toronto, Ontario, Canada: Multi-Health Systems.

Hart, S. D., Forth, A. E., & Hare, R. D. (1990). Performance of criminal psychopaths on selected neuropsychological tests. *Journal of Abnormal Psychology, 99,* 374–379.

Hart, S. D., & Hare, R. D. (1989). Discriminant validity of the Psychopathy Checklist in a forensic psychiatric population. *Psychological Assessment, 1,* 211–218.

Hart, S. D., & Hare, R. D. (1998). Association between psychopathy and narcissism: Theoretical reviews and empirical evidence. In E. F. Ronningstam (Ed.),

Disorders of narcissism: Diagnostic, clinical, and empirical implications (pp. 415–436). Washington, DC: American Psychiatric Press.

Herpertz, S. C., Werth, U., Lukas, G., Qunaibi, M., Schuerkens, A., Kunert, H., et al. (2001). Emotion in criminal offenders with psychopathy and borderline personality disorder. *Archives of General Psychiatry, 58,* 737–744.

Hiatt, K. D., & Newman, J. P. (2006). Understanding psychopathy: The cognitive side. In C. J. Patrick (Ed.), *Handbook of psychopathy* (pp. 334–352). New York: Guilford Press.

Hicks, B. M., Markon, K. E., Patrick, C. J., Krueger, R. F., & Newman, J. P. (2004). Identifying psychopathy subtypes on the basis of personality structure. *Psychological Assessment, 16,* 276–288.

Hicks, B. M., & Patrick, C. J. (2006). Psychopathy and negative affectivity: Analyses of suppressor effects reveal distinct relations with trait anxiety, depression, fearfulness, and anger-hostility. *Journal of Abnormal Psychology, 115,* 276–287.

Hildebrand, M., & de Ruiter, C. (2004). PCL-R psychopathy and its relation to DSM-IV Axis I and Axis II disorders in a sample of male forensic psychiatric patients in the Netherlands. *International Journal of Law and Psychiatry, 24,* 233–248.

Hill, S. Y., & Steinhauer, S. R. (2001). Familial/genetic studies of alcohol dependence: Developmental trajectory in P300 amplitude in childhood/adolescence as an endophenotypic marker of risk. *Psychophysiology, 38,* S12.

Holroyd, C. B., Dien, J., & Coles, M. G. H. (1998). Error-related scalp potentials elicited by hand and foot movements: Evidence for an output-independent error-processing system in humans. *Neuroscience Letters, 242,* 65–68.

Iacono, W. G., Carlson, S. R., & Malone, S. M. (2000). Identifying a multivariate endophenotype for substance use disorders using psychophysiological measures. *International Journal of Psychophysiology, 38,* 81–96.

Iacono, W. G., Carlson, S. R., Malone, S. M., & McGue, M. (2002). P3 event-related potential amplitude and risk for disinhibitory disorders in adolescent boys. *Archives of General Psychiatry, 59,* 750–757.

Ishikawa, S. S., Raine, A., Lencz, T., Bihrle, S., & Lacasse, L. (2001). Autonomic stress reactivity and executive functions in successful and unsuccessful criminal psychopaths from the community. *Journal of Abnormal Psychology, 110,* 423–432.

Johns, J. H., & Quay, H. C. (1962). The effect of social reward on verbal conditioning in psychopathic and neurotic military offenders. *Journal of Consulting Psychology, 26,* 217–220.

Johnstone, S. J., & Barry, R. J. (1996). Auditory event-related potentials to a two-tone auditory discrimination paradigm in attention deficit hyperactivity disorder. *Psychiatry Research, 64,* 179–192.

Jutai, J. W., & Hare, R. D. (1983). Psychopathy and selective attention during performance of a complex perceptual motor task. *Psychophysiology, 20,* 146–151.

Kahn, E. (1931). *Psychopathic personalities.* New Haven, CT: Yale University Press.

Karpman, B. (1941). On the need for separating psychopathy into two distinct clinical types: Symptomatic and idiopathic. *Journal of Criminology and Psychopathology, 3,* 112–137.

Karpman, B. (1948). Conscience in the psychopath: Another version. *American Journal of Orthopsychiatry, 18,* 455–491.

Kendler, K. S., Prescott, C. A., Myers, J., & Neale, M. C. (2003). The structure of genetic and environmental risk factors for common psychiatric and substance use disorders in men and women. *Archives of General Psychiatry, 60,* 929–937.

Kessler, R. C., McGonagle, K. A., Zhao, S., Nelson, C. B., Hughes, M., Eshleman, S., et al. (1994). Lifetime and 12-month prevalence of DSM-III-R psychiatric disorders in the United States: Results from the National Comorbidity Survey. *Archives of General Psychiatry, 51,* 8–19.

Kessler, R. C., & Walters, E. E. (2002). The National Comorbidity Survey. In M. T. Tsuang & M. Tohen (Eds.), *Textbook in psychiatric epidemiology* (2nd ed., pp. 343–362). New York: Wiley.

Kiehl, K. A., Hare, R. D., Liddle, P. F., & McDonald, J. J. (1999). Reduced P300 responses in criminal psychopaths during a visual oddball task. *Biological Psychiatry, 45,* 1498–1507.

Kiehl, K. A., Hare, R. D., McDonald, J. J., & Brink, J. (1999). Semantic and affective processing in psychopaths: An event related potential (ERP) study. *Psychophysiology, 36,* 765–774.

Kim, S. W., & Grant, J. E. (2001). An open naltrexone treatment study in pathological gambling disorder. *International Clinical Psychopharmacology, 16,* 285–289.

Kim, M. S., Kim, J. J., & Kwon, J. S. (2001). Frontal P300 decrement and executive dysfunction in adolescents with conduct problems. *Child Psychiatry and Human Development, 32,* 93–106.

Klorman, R. (1991). Cognitive event-related potentials and in attention deficit disorder. *Journal of Learning Disabilities, 24,* 130–140.

Koch, J. L. (1891). *Die psychopathischen Minderwertigkeiten* [The psychopathic inferiority]. Ravensburg, Germany: Maier.

Koenigsberg, H. W., Kaplan, R. D., Gilmore, M. M., & Cooper, A. M. (1985). The relation between syndrome and personality disorder in DSM III: Experience with 2,412 patients. *American Journal of Psychiatry, 142,* 207–212.

Kosson, D. S. (1996). Psychopathy and dual task performance under focusing conditions. *Journal of Abnormal Psychology, 105,* 391–400.

Kosson, D. S. (1998). Divided visual attention in psychopathic and nonpsychopathic offenders. *Personality and Individual Differences, 24,* 373–391.

Kosson, D. S., & Newman, J. P. (1986). Psychopathy and the allocation of attentional capacity in a divided-attention situation. *Journal of Abnormal Psychology, 95,* 257–263.

Kosson, D. S., Smith, S. S. & Newman, J. P. (1990). Evaluating the construct validity of psychopathy in African American and European American male inmates: Three preliminary studies. *Journal of Abnormal Psychology, 99,* 250–259.

Kraepelin, E. (1904). *Psychiatrie: Ein Lehrbuch* [Psychiatry: A textbook] (7th ed.). Leipzig, Germany: Barth.

Kraepelin, E. (1915). *Psychiatrie: Ein Lehrbuch* [Psychiatry: A textbook] (8th ed.). Leipzig, Germany: Barth.

Krueger, R. F. (1999a). The structure of common mental disorders. *Archives of General Psychiatry, 56,* 921–926.

Krueger, R. F. (1999b). Personality traits in late adolescence predict mental disorders in early adulthood: A prospective-epidemiological study. *Journal of Personality, 67,* 39–65.

Krueger, R. F., Caspi, A., Moffitt, T. E., & Silva, P. A. (1998). The structure and stability of common mental disorders (DSM-III-R): A longitudinal-epidemiological study. *Journal of Abnormal Psychology, 107,* 216–227.

Krueger, R. F., Hicks, B., Patrick, C. J., Carlson, S., Iacono, W. G., & McGue, M. (2002). Etiologic connections among substance dependence, antisocial behavior, and personality: Modeling the externalizing spectrum. *Journal of Abnormal Psychology, 111,* 411–424.

Krueger, R. F., Markon, K. E., Patrick, C. J., Benning, S. D., & Kramer, M. (in press). Linking antisocial behavior, substance use, and personality: An integrative quantitative model of the adult externalizing spectrum. *Journal of Abnormal Psychology.*

Krueger, R. F., Markon, K. E., Patrick, C. J., & Iacono, W. G. (2005). Externalizing psychopathology in adulthood: A dimensional-spectrum conceptualization and its implications for DSM-V. *Journal of Abnormal Psychology, 114,* 537–550.

Lang, P. J., Bradley, M. M., & Cuthbert, B. N. (1990). Emotion, attention, and the startle reflex. *Psychological Review, 97,* 377–398.

Levenson, M. R., Kiehl, K. A., & Fitzpatrick, C. M. (1995). Assessing psychopathic attributes in a noninstitutionalized population. *Journal of Personality and Social Psychology, 68,* 151–158.

Levenston, G. K., Patrick, C. J., Bradley, M. M., & Lang, P. J. (2000). The psychopath as observer: Emotion and attention in picture processing. *Journal of Abnormal Psychology, 109,* 373–385.

Lewis, C. E., Rice, J., & Helzer, J. E. (1983). Diagnostic interactions: Alcoholism and antisocial personality. *Journal of Nervous and Mental Disease, 171,* 105–113.

Lilienfeld, S. O. (1990). *Development and preliminary validation of a self-report measure of psychopathic personality.* Unpublished doctoral dissertation, University of Minnesota, Minneapolis.

Lilienfeld, S. O., & Andrews, B. P. (1996). Development and preliminary validation of a self-report measure of psychopathic personality traits in noncriminal populations. *Journal of Personality Assessment, 66,* 488–524.

Lilienfeld, S. O., & Fowler, K. A. (2006). The self-report assessment of psychopathy: Problems, pitfalls, and promises. In C. J. Patrick (Ed.), *Handbook of psychopathy* (pp. 107–132). New York: Guilford Press.

Linnoila, M., & Virkkunen, M. (1992). Aggression, suicidality, and serotonin. *Journal of Clinical Psychiatry, 53,* 46–51.

Linnoila, M., Virkkunen, M., Schwannian, M., Nuutila, A., Rimon, R., & Goodwin, F. K. (1983). Low cerebrospinal fluid 5-hydroxyindoleacetic acid concentration differentiates impulsive from non-impulsive violent behavior. *Life Sciences, 33,* 2609–2614.

Lorber, M. F. (2004). Psychophysiology of aggression, psychopathy, and conduct problems: A meta-analysis. *Psychological Bulletin, 130,* 531–552.

Lorenz, A. R., & Newman, J. P. (2002). Do emotion and information processing deficiencies found in Caucasian psychopaths generalize to African-American psychopaths? *Personality and Individual Differences, 32,* 1077–1086.

Luu, P., Flaisch, T., & Tucker, D. M. (2000). Medial frontal cortex in action monitoring. *Journal of Neuroscience, 20,* 464–469.

Lykken, D. T. (1957). A study of anxiety in the sociopathic personality. *Journal of Abnormal and Social Psychology, 55,* 6–10.

Lykken, D. T. (1995). *The antisocial personalities.* Hillsdale, NJ: Erlbaum.

Lynam, D. R. (1997). Pursuing the psychopath: Capturing the fledgling psychopath in a nomological net. *Journal of Abnormal Psychology, 106,* 425–438.

Lynam, D. R., & Derefinko, K. J. (2006). Psychopathy and personality. In C. J. Patrick (Ed.), *Handbook of psychopathy* (pp. 133–155). New York: Guilford Press.

Lynam, D. R., Leukefeld, C., & Clayton, R. R. (2003). The contribution of personality to the overlap between antisocial behavior and substance use/misuse. *Aggressive Behavior, 29,* 316–331.

Maliphant, R., Hume, F., & Furnham, A. (1990). Autonomic nervous system (ANS) activity, personality characteristics, and disruptive behaviour in girls. *Journal of Child Psychology and Psychiatry and Allied Disciplines, 31,* 619–628.

McCord, W., & McCord, J. (1964). *The psychopath: An essay on the criminal mind.* Princeton, NJ: Van Nostrand.

Mealey, L. (1995). The sociobiology of sociopathy: An integrated evolutionary model. *Behavioral and Brain Sciences, 18,* 523–599.

Meyer, A. (1904). A review of recent problems of psychiatry. In A. Church & F. Peterson (Eds.), *Nervous and mental diseases* (4th ed.). Baltimore: Williams & Wilkins.

Miller, J. D., Lynam, D. R., Widiger, T. A., & Leukefeld, C. (2001). Personality disorders as extreme variants of common personality dimensions: Can the five-factor model adequately represent psychopathy? *Journal of Personality, 69,* 253–276.

Millon, T. (1981). *Disorders of personality: DSM-III: Axis II.* New York: Wiley.

Miltner, W. H. R., Braun, C. H., & Coles, M. G. H. (1997). Event-related brain potentials following incorrect feedback in a time-estimation task: Evidence for a "generic" neural system for error detection. *Journal of Cognitive Neuroscience, 9,* 788–798.

Minzenberg, M. J., & Siever, L. J. (2006). Neurochemistry and pharmacology of psychopathy and related disorders. In C. J. Patrick (Ed.), *Handbook of psychopathy* (pp. 251–277). New York: Guilford Press.

Moffitt, T. E. (1993). Adolescence-limited and life-course-persistent antisocial behavior: A developmental taxonomy. *Psychological Review, 100,* 674–701.

Morey, L. (1991). *The Personality Assessment Inventory professional manual.* Odessa, FL: Psychological Assessment Resources.

Morgan, A. B., & Lilienfeld, S. O. (2000). A meta-analytic review of the relation between antisocial behavior and neuropsychological measures of executive function. *Clinical Psychology Review, 20,* 113–136.

Newman, J. P. (1998). Psychopathic behavior: An information processing perspective. In D. J. Cooke, R. D. Hare, & A. Forth (Eds.), *Psychopathy: Theory, research and implications for society* (pp. 81–104). Dordrecht, Netherlands: Kluwer Academic Publishers.

O'Malley, S. S., Croop, R. S., Wroblewski, J. M., Labriola, D. F., Volpicelli, J. R. (1995). Naltrexone in the treatment of alcohol dependence: A combined analysis of two trials. *Psychiatric Annals, 25,* 681–688.

Ortiz, J., & Raine, A. (2004). Heart rate level and antisocial behavior in children and adolescents: A meta-analysis. *Journal of the American Academy of Child & Adolescent Psychiatry, 43,* 154–162.

Paille, F. M., Guelfi, J. D., Persons, A. C., Royer, R. J., Steru, L., & Parot, P. (1995). Double blind randomized multicentre trial of acamprosate in maintaining abstinence from alcohol. *Alcohol and Alcoholism, 30,* 239–247.

Patrick, C. J. (1994). Emotion and psychopathy: Startling new insights. *Psychophysiology, 31,* 319–330.

Patrick, C. J. (2001). Emotions and psychopathy. In A. Raine & J. Sanmartin (Eds.), *Violence and psychopathy* (pp. 57–77). New York: Kluwer Academic Publishers.

Patrick, C. J. (2005). *What constructs underlie the two factors of the psychopathic personality inventory?* Paper presented at the 1st Annual Meeting of the Society for the Scientific Study of Psychopathy, Vancouver, British Columbia, Canada.

Patrick, C. J. (2006). Getting to the heart of psychopathy. In H. Herve & J. C. Yuille (Eds.), *Psychopathy: Theory, research, and social implications* (pp. 207–252). Hillsdale, NJ: Erlbaum.

Patrick, C. J., & Bernat, E. (2006). The construct of emotion as a bridge between personality and psychopathology. In R. F. Krueger & J. Tackett (Eds.), *Personality and psychopathology* (pp. 174–209). New York: Guilford Press.

Patrick, C. J., Bernat, E., Malone, S. M., Iacono, W. G., Krueger, R. F., & McGue, M. K. (2006). P300 amplitude as an indicator of externalizing in adolescent males. *Psychophysiology, 43,* 84–92.

Patrick, C. J., Bradley, M. M., & Lang, P. J. (1993). Emotion in the criminal psychopath: Startle reflex modulation. *Journal of Abnormal Psychology, 102,* 82–92.

Patrick, C. J., Curtin, J. J., & Tellegen, A. (2002). Development and validation of a brief form of the Multidimensional Personality Questionnaire. *Psychological Assessment, 14,* 150–163.

Patrick, C. J., Cuthbert, B. N., & Lang, P. J. (1994). Emotion in the criminal psychopath: Fear image processing. *Journal of Abnormal Psychology, 103,* 523–534.

Patrick, C. J., Edens, J. F., Poythress, N. G., Lilienfeld, S. O., & Benning, S. D. (2006). Construct validity of the PPI two-factor model with offenders. *Psychological Assessment, 18,* 204–208.

Patrick, C. J., Hicks, B. M., Krueger, R. F., & Lang, A. R. (2005). Relations between psychopathy facets and externalizing in a criminal offender sample. *Journal of Personality Disorders, 19,* 339–356.

Patrick, C. J., & Lang, A. R. (1999). Psychopathic traits and intoxicated states: Affective concomitants and conceptual links. In M. E. Dawson, A. M. Schell, & A. H. Boehmelt (Eds.), *Startle modification: Implications for clinical science, cognitive science, and neuroscience* (pp. 209–230). New York: Cambridge University Press.

Patrick, C. J., & Zempolich, K. A. (1998). Emotion and aggression in the psychopathic personality. *Aggression and Violent Behavior, 3,* 303–338.

Patrick, C. J., Zempolich, K. A., & Levenston, G. K. (1997). Emotionality and violent behavior in psychopaths: A biosocial analysis. In A. Raine, P. A. Brennan, D. P. Farrington, & S. A. Mednick (Eds.), *Biosocial bases of violence* (pp. 145–161). New York: Plenum.

Patterson, C. M., & Newman, J. P. (1993). Reflectivity and learning from aversive events: Toward a psychological mechanism for the syndromes of disinhibition. *Psychological Review, 100,* 716–736.

Paulhus, D. L., Robins, R. W., Trzesniewski, K. H., & Tracy, J. L. (2004). Two replicable suppressor situations in personality research. *Multivariate Behavioral Research, 39,* 303–328.

Peterson, J. B., & Pihl, R. O. (1990). Information processing, neuropsychological function, and the inherited predisposition to alcoholism. *Neuropsychology Review, 1,* 343–369.

Pickens, R. W., Svikis, D. S., McGue, M., & LaBuda, M. C. (1995). Common genetic mechanisms in alcohol, drug, and mental disorder comorbidity. *Drug and Alcohol Dependence, 39,* 129–138.

Pinel, P. (1801/1962). *A treatise on insanity* (D. Davis, Trans.). New York: Hafner.

Polich, J., Pollock, V. E., & Bloom, F. E. (1994). Meta-analysis of P300 amplitude from males at risk for alcoholism. *Psychological Bulletin, 115,* 55–73.

Poythress, N. G., Edens, J. F., & Lilienfeld, S. O. (1998). Criterion-related validity of the Psychopathic Personality Inventory in a prison sample. *Psychological Assessment, 10,* 426–430.

Pritchard, J. C. (1835). *A treatise on insanity and other disorders affecting the mind.* London: Sherwood, Gilbert & Piper.

Raine, A. (1993). *The psychopathology of crime.* San Diego, CA: Academic Press.

Raine, A. (1997). Antisocial behavior and psychophysiology: A biosocial perspective and a prefrontal dysfunction hypothesis. In D. M. Stoff, J. Breiling, & J. D. Maser (Eds.), *Handbook of antisocial behavior* (pp. 289–303). New York: Wiley.

Raine, A. (2002). Biosocial studies of antisocial and violent behavior in children and adults: A review. *Journal of Abnormal Child Psychology, 30,* 311–326.

Raine, A., & Venables, P. H. (1984). Tonic heart rate level, social class, and antisocial behaviour in adolescents. *Biological Psychology, 18,* 123–132.

Raine, A., & Yang, Y. (2006). The neuroanatomical bases of psychopathy: A review of brain imaging findings. In C. J. Patrick (Ed.), *Handbook of psychopathy* (pp. 278–295). New York: Guilford Press.

Reardon, M. L., Lang, A. R., & Patrick, C. J. (2002). Antisociality and alcohol problems: An evaluation of subtypes, drinking motives, and family history in incarcerated men. *Alcoholism: Clinical and Experimental Research, 26,* 1188–1197.

Robins, L. N. (1966). *Deviant children grown up.* Baltimore: Williams & Wilkins.

Robins, L. N., & Regier, D. A. (1991). *Psychiatric disorders in America: The epidemiological catchment area study.* New York: Free Press.

Rogers, R. D. (2006). The functional architecture of the frontal lobes: Implications for research with psychopathic offenders. In C. J. Patrick (Ed.), *Handbook of psychopathy* (pp. 313–333). New York: Guilford Press.

Ross, S. R., Benning, S. D., Patrick, C. J., Thompson, A., & Thurston, A. (2005). *Factors of the Psychopathic Personality Inventory: Criterion-related validity and relationships with the five-factor model of personality.* Manuscript submitted for publication.

Rush, B. (1812). *Medical inquiries and observations upon the diseases of the mind.* Philadelphia: Kimber & Richardson.

Scheffers, M., Coles, M. G. H., Bernstein, P., Gehring, W. J., & Donchin, E. (1996). Event-related potentials and error-related processing: An analysis of incorrect responses to go and no-go stimuli. *Psychophysiology, 33,* 42–53.

Schmitt, W. A., & Newman, J. P. (1999). Are all psychopathic individuals low-anxious? *Journal of Abnormal Psychology, 108,* 353–358.

Schneider, K. (1934). *Die psychopathischen Persönlichkeiten* [The psychopathic personalities] (3rd ed.). Vienna: Deuticke.

Sellbom, M., Ben-Porath, Y., Graham, J. K., Lilienfeld, S. O., & Patrick, C. J. (2005). Assessing psychopathic personality traits with the MMPI-2. *Journal of Personality Assessment, 85,* 334–343.

Seto, M. C., & Quinsey, V. L. (2006). Toward the future: Translating basic research into prevention and treatment strategies. In C. J. Patrick (Ed.), *Handbook of psychopathy* (pp. 589–601). New York: Guilford Press.

Sher, K. J., Bartholow, B. D., & Wood, M. D. (2000). Personality and substance use disorders: A prospective study. *Journal of Consulting and Clinical Psychology, 68,* 818–829.

Shine, J., & Hobson, J. (1997) Construct validity of the Hare Psychopathy Checklist—Revised. *Journal of Forensic Psychiatry, 8,* 546–561.

Siddle, D. A. T., & Trasler, G. B. (1981). The psychophysiology of psychopathic behavior. In M. J. Christie & P. G. Mellett (Eds.), *Foundations of psychosomatics* (pp. 283–303). New York: Wiley.

Skeem, J. L., Edens, J. F., Camp, J., & Colwell, L. H. (2004). Are there racial differences in levels of psychopathy? A meta-analysis. *Law and Human Behavior, 28,* 505–527.

Skodol, A. E., Oldham, J. M., & Gallaher, P. E. (1999). Axis II comorbidity of substance use disorders among patients referred for treatment of personality disorders. *American Journal of Psychiatry, 156,* 733–738.

Slutske, W. S., Heath, A. C., Dinwiddie, S. H., Madden, P. A. F., Bucholz, K. K., Dunne, M. P., et al. (1998). Common genetic risk factors for conduct disorder and alcohol dependence. *Journal of Abnormal Psychology, 107,* 363–374.

Slutske, W. S., Heath, A. C., Madden, P. A. F., Bucholz, K. K., Statham, D. J., & Martin, N. G. (2002). Personality and the genetic risk for alcohol dependence. *Journal of Abnormal Psychology, 111,* 124–133.

Smith, S. S., & Newman, J. P. (1990). Alcohol and drug abuse-dependence disorders in psychopathic and nonpsychopathic criminal offenders. *Journal of Abnormal Psychology, 99,* 430–439.

Spitzer, R. L., Endicott, J., & Robins, E. (1978). Research diagnostic criteria: Rationale and reliability. *Archives of General Psychiatry, 35,* 773–782.

Sullivan, E. A., & Kosson, D. S. (2006). Ethnic and cultural variations in psychopathy. In C. J. Patrick (Ed.), *Handbook of psychopathy* (pp. 437–458). New York: Guilford Press.

Sutton, S. K., Vitale, J. E., & Newman, J. P. (2002). Emotion among females with psychopathy during picture perception. *Journal of Abnormal Psychology, 111,* 610–619.

Tackett, J. L., Krueger, R. F., Iacono, W. G., & McGue, M. (2005). Symptom-based subfactors of DSM-defined conduct disorder: Evidence for etiologic distinctions. *Journal of Abnormal Psychology, 114,* 483–487.

Tackett, J. L., Krueger, R. F., Sawyer, M. G., & Graetz, B. W. (2003). Subfactors of DSM-IV conduct disorder: Evidence and connections with syndromes from the child behavior checklist. *Journal of Abnormal Child Psychology, 31,* 647–654.

Tarter, R. E., Alterman, A. I., & Edwards, K. L., (1985). Vulnerability to alcoholism in men: A behavior-genetic perspective. *Journal of Studies on Alcohol, 46,* 329–356.

Tellegen, A. (in press). *Manual for the Multidimensional Personality Questionnaire.* Minneapolis: University of Minnesota Press.

Tellegen, A., Ben-Porath, Y. S., McNulty, J. L., Arbisi, P. A., Graham, J. R., & Kaemmer, B. (2003). *MMPI-2 Restructured Clinical (RC) scales: Development, validation, and interpretation.* Minneapolis: University of Minnesota Press.

Trull, T. J. (1992). DSM-III-R personality disorders and the five-factor model of personality: An empirical comparison. *Journal of Abnormal Psychology, 101,* 553–560.

Trull, T. J., & Sher, K. J. (1994). Relationship between the five-factor model of personality and Axis I disorders in a nonclinical sample. *Journal of Abnormal Psychology, 103,* 350–360.

Vanman, E. J., Mejia, V. Y., Dawson, M. E., Schell, A. M., & Raine, A. (2003). Modification of the startle reflex in a community sample: Do one or two dimensions of psychopathy underlie emotional processing? *Personality and Individual Differences, 35,* 2007–2021.

Veit, R., Flor, H., Erb, M., Lotze, M., Grodd, W., & Birbaumer, N. (2002). Brain circuits involved in emotional learning in antisocial behavior and social phobia in humans. *Neuroscience Letters, 328,* 233–236.

Verona, E., Hicks, B. M., & Patrick, C. J. (2005). Psychopathy and suicidal behavior in female offenders: Effects of personality and abuse history. *Journal of Consulting and Clinical Psychology, 73,* 1065–1073.

Verona, E., & Patrick, C. J. (2000). Suicide risk in externalizing syndromes: Temperamental and neurobiological underpinnings. In T. E. Joiner (Ed.), *Suicide science: Expanding the boundaries* (pp. 137–173). Boston: Kluwer Academic Publishers.

Verona, E., Patrick, C. J., Curtin, J. J., Lang, P. J., & Bradley, M. M. (2004). Psychopathy and physiological response to emotionally evocative sounds. *Journal of Abnormal Psychology, 113,* 99–108.

Verona, E., Patrick, C. J., & Joiner, T. E. (2001). Psychopathy, antisocial personality, and suicide risk. *Journal of Abnormal Psychology, 110,* 462–470.

Verona, E., & Vitale, J. (2006). Psychopathy in women: Assessment, manifestations, and etiology. In C. J. Patrick (Ed.), *Handbook of psychopathy* (pp. 415–436). New York: Guilford Press.

Verschuere, B., Crombez, G., de Clercq, A., & Koster, E. H. W. (2005). Psychopathic traits and autonomic responding to concealed information in a prison sample. *Psychophysiology, 42,* 239–245.

Virkkunen, M., Rawlings, R., Tokola, R., Poland, R. E., Cuidotti, A., Nemweroff, C., et al. (1994). CSF biochemistries, glucose metabolism, and diurnal activity rhythms in alcoholic, violent offenders, fire setters, and healthy volunteers. *Archives of General Psychiatry, 51,* 20–27.

Vollebergh, W. A. M., Iedema, J., Bijl, R. V., de Graaf, R., Smit, F., & Ormel., J. (2001). The structure and stability of common mental disorders: The NEMESIS study. *Archives of General Psychiatry, 58,* 597–603.

Wadsworth, M. E. J. (1976). Delinquency, pulse rate and early emotional deprivation. *British Journal of Criminology, 16,* 245–256.

Warren, J. I., Burnette, M. L., South, S. C., Preeti, C., Bale, R., Friend, R., et al. (2003). Psychopathy in women: Structural modeling and comorbidity. *International Journal of Law and Psychiatry, 26,* 223–242.

Widiger, T. A., Cadoret, R., Hare, R., Robins, L., Rutherford, M., Zanarini, M., et al. (1996). DSM-IV antisocial personality disorder field trial. *Journal of Abnormal Psychology, 105,* 3–16.

Widiger, T. A., Verheul, R., & van den Brink, W. (1999). Personality and psychopathology. In L. A. Pervin & O. John (Eds.), *Handbook of personality: Theory and research* (2nd ed., pp. 347–366). New York: Guilford Press.

Williamson, S. E. (1991). *Cohesion and coherence in the speech of psychopathic criminals.* Unpublished doctoral dissertation, University of British Columbia, Vancouver, Canada.

Williamson, S. E., Harpur, T. J., & Hare, R. D. (1991). Abnormal processing of affective words by psychopaths. *Psychophysiology, 28,* 260–273.

Woodworth, M., & Porter, S. (2002). In cold blood: Characteristics of criminal homicides as a function of psychopathy. *Journal of Abnormal Psychology, 111,* 436–445.

World Health Organization. (1948). *International statistical classification of diseases, injuries, and causes of death* (6th revision). Geneva, Switzerland: Author.

Young, S. E., Stallings, M. C., Corley, R. P., Krauter, K. S., & Hewitt, J. K. (2000). Genetic and environmental influences on behavioral disinhibition. *American Journal of Medical Genetics, 96,* 684–695.

Zuckerman, M. (1979). *Sensation seeking: Beyond the optimal level of arousal.* Hillsdale, NJ: Erlbaum.

Zuckerman, M. (1999). *Vulnerability to psychopathology: A biosocial model.* Washington, DC: American Psychological Association.

7

Borderline
Personality Disorder

Rebekah Bradley

Emory University

Carolyn Zittel Conklin

Cambridge Health Alliance and Harvard Medical School

Drew Westen

Emory University

Borderline personality disorder (BPD) is one of the most prevalent, most widely studied, and yet most controversial of the personality disorders (PDs) described in the fourth edition of the *Diagnostic and Statistical Manual of Mental Disorders* (DSM-IV; American Psychiatric Association [APA], 1994). Its public health significance arguably rivals that of any other diagnostic syndrome. Patients with BPD constitute 20% of psychiatric

Authors' notes: Preparation of this article was supported in part by National Institute of Mental Health grants MH62377 and MH62378 to the third author. Some of the information presented in this chapter is drawn from an article by the second and third authors: "Conceptual Issues and Research Findings on Borderline Personality Disorder: What Every Clinician Should Know" (Zittel & Westen, 1998). Correspondence concerning this chapter should be addressed to Rebekah Bradley, Ph.D., Director, Trauma Recovery Program, Atlanta VAMC, 1670 Clairmont Road, Atlanta, Georgia 30033. E-mail: rebekah.bradley@emory.edu

inpatients and 10% of patients seen in outpatient mental health clinics (APA, 1994) and are high consumers of emergency room services, crisis lines, and psychiatric consultations requested by other medical services (Ellison, Barsky, & Blum, 1989; Forman, Berk, Henriques, Brown, & Beck, 2004; Gross et al., 2002; Reich, Boerstler, Yates, & Nduaguba, 1989; Zanarini, Frankenburg, Hennen, & Silk, 2004). Between 70% and 75% of BPD patients have a history of at least one self-injurious act (Clarkin, Widiger, Frances, Hurt, & Gilmore, 1983; Cowdry, 1992), and quick calculations with available statistics (APA, 1994; McGlashan, 1986; Samuels et al., 2002; Stone, 1993; Torgersen, Kringlen, & Cramer, 2001) indicate that of the 6 million individuals currently estimated to have BPD in the United States alone, between 180,000 and 540,000 will die by suicide.

In this chapter, we provide a broad overview of the state of knowledge of BPD. We begin by briefly describing the evolution of the diagnosis and contemporary controversies regarding the construct itself and the way it should be defined. We then discuss the assessment of BPD. Next we examine what is known about the development and developmental course of BPD, including its etiology, longitudinal stability, and prognosis. The final section considers treatment approaches, including a number of relatively recent empirical developments in the psychotherapy of BPD.

The Borderline Diagnosis: Evolution and Diagnostic Controversies

The concept of "borderline" has undergone a substantial evolution since its early identification by psychoanalytic clinical theorists, who first identified the construct as "pseudoneurotic schizophrenia," "as-if personality," and eventually "borderline state" (Knight, 1953, 1954). In this section, we briefly describe the evolution of the construct. We then examine contemporary controversies and diagnostic dilemmas in the understanding and diagnosis of the borderline construct.

Evolution of the Borderline Construct

Initially the term *borderline* referred to individuals who seemed neither neurotic nor psychotic but were somewhere in between. This was the conceptualization that Kernberg (1967) later elaborated in his concept of borderline personality organization (BPO). By "personality organization," Kernberg meant enduring ways of feeling, thinking, behaving, experiencing the self and others, and dealing with unpleasant realities. In Kernberg's view, patients with borderline personality organization tend to use drastic, immature ways of dealing with impulses and emotions (e.g., behaviors such as cutting and defensive maneuvers such as denial of obvious realities). They are not psychotic but can become cognitively more disorganized than most people, particularly under stress, and have difficulty maintaining balanced views of the self and significant others ("splitting" their representations into all good and all bad).

Over time, the concept of borderline as a level of disturbance (originally between neurotic and psychotic) shifted from this broader construct to the more specific diagnostic category first defined in the third edition of the DSM (DSM-III; APA, 1980). Kernberg's concept of borderline influenced the description of the disorder in DSM-III, which has remained intact, with small modifications, for the last 20 years. However, his concept of borderline as a form of personality organization is a broader construct that describes a *level* of personality sickness that encompasses many of the DSM-IV PDs, including all the Cluster A (odd, eccentric) PDs; the Cluster B (erratic, dramatic) PDs, with the exception of some higher functioning narcissistic patients; and the more disturbed subset of patients within each of the Cluster C (anxious, fearful) PDs.

Like most diagnoses, the construct of BPD first emerged from the work of prescient clinical observers who attempted to identify patterns of covariation among symptoms not previously understood, followed by research aimed at refining the construct. The initial efforts to establish a more empirically grounded concept of BPD actually began prior to DSM-III with the work of Grinker, Werble, and Drye (1968), who suggested the first empirically derived diagnostic criterion set for the borderline syndrome. This was followed by development of the Diagnostic Interview for Borderline Personality Disorder (DIB; Gunderson & Kolb, 1978; Gunderson, Kolb, & Austin, 1981; Gunderson & Singer, 1975). As editor of DSM-III, Spitzer developed potential diagnostic criteria for BPD by reviewing clinical and research literature and consulting with clinicians expert in treating borderline patients. He then collected data in a national survey of psychiatrists who evaluated the selected criteria. The resulting set of distinguishing borderline characteristics (Spitzer, Endicott, & Gibbon, 1979) became the basis for the BPD criteria in the DSM-III (APA, 1980). This resulted in BPD's becoming an official psychiatric disorder rather than a level of personality structure or disturbance. DSM-IV defines the essential features of BPD as a "pervasive pattern of instability of interpersonal relationships, self-image, and affects, and marked impulsivity that begins by early adulthood and is present in a variety of contexts" (APA, 2000, p. 706).

Current Controversies and Diagnostic Dilemmas

Like the other PDs, the BPD diagnosis in DSM-IV emerged through over half a century of clinical observation, which largely generated the criteria for the disorder in DSM-III (and instruments for assessing it), followed by 25 years of research aimed at refining the diagnosis. The criteria for the disorder clearly capture a group of severely impaired patients frequently seen in mental health settings. However, a number of problems limit the clinical utility and validity of the diagnostic criteria for BPD. We focus here on three: heterogeneity of symptom presentation, categorical diagnosis, and excessive comorbidity with other Axis II disorders as well as Axis I disorders.

With respect to heterogeneity, a patient can receive the BPD diagnosis in over 150 different ways based on varying combinations of the nine criteria for the disorder (Skodol, Gunderson, Pfohl, et al., 2002). Put another way, two patients may both be diagnosed with BPD while sharing only one symptom in common. This fact has important clinical implications because subtypes of BPD seem to exist that do not reflect random variation among criteria but rather meaningful, patterned heterogeneity, such as internalizing and externalizing subtypes of the disorder (Bradley, Zittel, et al., 2005; Conklin & Westen, 2005; Conklin, Bradley, & Westen, 2006; Westen & Shedler, 1999b; Zittel & Westen, 2002).

With respect to categorical diagnosis, the DSM approach to classification assumes that PDs represent categorically distinct classes of psychopathology. However, most research on classification of PDs favors a dimensional rather than a categorical understanding of PD (e.g., Clark, Livesley, & Morey, 1997; Trull, 2001; Widiger, 1995). Consistent with this overall trend in personality research, research on BPD, including research applying taxometric analysis (Meehl, 1995), suggests that the disorder is likely best represented dimensionally and does not represent a distinct taxon (e.g., Rothschild, Cleland, Haslam, & Zimmerman, 2003).

With respect to comorbidity, research using both DSM-III and DSM-IV criteria indicates high levels of comorbidity with other PDs, particularly antisocial PD, avoidant PD, dependent PD, and paranoid PD (Becker, Grilo, Edell, & McGlashan, 2000; Gunderson, Zanarini, & Kisiel, 1991, 1995; Oldham et al., 1992; Stuart et al., 1998). This finding suggests that the diagnostic criteria do not adequately capture a disorder distinct from other disorders or from a general personality pathology dimension. Indeed, many of the DSM-IV PDs—including paranoid, schizoid, schizotypal, antisocial, histrionic, and sometimes dependent—are consistent with borderline personality organization as defined by Kernberg. With the exception of schizoid, all of these PDs show high comorbidity with DSM-defined BPD, tending to cluster together in studies of adaptive functioning, and disorders such as avoidant, narcissistic, and obsessive-compulsive generally showing better adaptive functioning (e.g., Skodol, Gunderson, McGlashan, et al., 2002; Skodol, Gunderson, Pfohl, et al., 2002; Tyrer, 1996). In any case, the comorbidity of BPD with other Cluster B PDs (histrionic, antisocial, and narcissistic; Fyer, Frances, Sullivan, Hurt, & Clarkin, 1988) as well as with disorders such as avoidant and schizotypal PDs (Barasch, Kroll, Carey, & Sines, 1983; Pfohl, Coryell, Zimmerman, & Stangl, 1986), is highly problematic, particularly given that schizotypal and avoidant individuals tend to be socially withdrawn, whereas BPD is associated with fear of aloneness and the trait of extraversion (e.g., Lynam & Widiger, 2001). Borderline PD also shows high comorbidity with most nonpsychotic Axis I disorders, notably mood, anxiety, substance use, and eating disorders (e.g., Zanarini et al., 1998; Zimmerman & Mattia, 1999).

In response to these problems, DSM task forces and PD work groups since DSM-III have attempted to adjust diagnostic criteria with the goal of making BPD less redundant with other diagnoses. For example, the Axis II Work Group for DSM-IV rewrote the DSM-III-R criterion "affective instability: marked shifts from baseline mood to depression, irritability, or anxiety, usually lasting a few hours and only rarely more than a few days." In hopes of better discriminating between major depression and BPD, the word "depression" was replaced with "dysphoria"; in hopes of better differentiating between the mood lability seen in cyclothymic disorder and the unstable affect seen in BPD, the phrase "marked shifts . . . [of] mood" was replaced by "marked reactivity of mood." Such efforts do not appear, however, to have substantially reduced the comorbidity of BPD with other disorders, raising questions about whether the diagnosis remains, in Akiskal's (1996; 2004) words, "an adjective in search of a noun."

In summary, the development of diagnostic criteria for BPD in DSM-III laid the groundwork for a surge of research on the disorder. BPD is now the most highly researched PD and has the strongest empirical evidence regarding its phenomenology, etiology, and treatment. Nevertheless, the research that was in large measure fostered by the presence of DSM criteria since 1980 has resulted in the identification of a number of problems with the diagnosis that remain to be resolved.

Assessment

The Diagnostic Interview for Borderline Personality Disorder (DIB; Gunderson & Kolb, 1978; Gunderson et al., 1981; Gunderson & Singer, 1975) was the gold standard procedure for assessing BPD in the decade following the definition of operational criteria for the disorder in DSM-III. However, what quickly became apparent was that any sample of BPD patients could differ in unknown ways from any other sample, depending on the presence of comorbid PDs. Researchers addressed this problem with the development of structured interviews designed to assess all of the DSM PDs. The advantage of these instruments was that they assessed the range of personality pathology defined by the DSM. The disadvantage was that, in less time than it typically takes to administer the DIB (a semistructured interview for a single disorder), they attempted to assess the roughly 10 PDs defined by the various versions of the DSM since DSM-III. To economize the assessment of these disorders, interviews came to emphasize more the behavioral manifestations of the disorder (e.g., cutting) over the functional or "structural" aspects of personality that originally defined the disorder in the clinical literature. In turn, the diagnostic criteria for the disorder shifted toward readily observable behaviors that could be assessed by structured interview, leading to the possibility of the procedural tail wagging the conceptual dog (Westen, 1997).

Methods for assessing BPD generally rely on patients' self-reported symptoms using either structured interviews or questionnaires. A full review of such measures is beyond the scope of this chapter (see Clark & Harrison, 2001, for a review). However, we briefly present the relative strengths and weaknesses of these approaches.

The currently accepted diagnostic gold standard for the assessment of BPD is a standardized structured interview yoked to DSM criteria (e.g., the Structured Clinical Interview for DSM-IV Personality Disorders [SCID-II; First, Spitzer, Gibbon, & Williams, 1997]; the Structured Interview for DSM-III-R Personality Disorders [SIDP; Pfohl, Blum, Zimmerman, & Stangl, 1989]). A primary advantage of this approach is that it asks questions about each criterion directly, ensuring adequate coverage for a DSM-IV diagnosis. A second advantage is reliability, particularly when this approach is compared with the method more common in clinical practice of conducting unstructured interviews with patients before referring to DSM or International Classification of Diseases (ICD) diagnostic criteria, which yields low interrater reliability (Mellsop, Varghese, Joshua, & Hicks, 1982; Satorius et al., 1993).

However, this approach to PD diagnosis has limitations. First, rates of comorbidity are extremely high, with the average patient receiving any PD diagnosis receiving 4 to 6 of the 10 DSM-IV PDs by structured interview and often even more by questionnaire (see Westen & Shedler, 1999a). Although this problem stems at least in part from the overlap among the DSM-IV disorders themselves, other approaches to diagnosis, such as assessing the patient's match to a prototype of the disorder, show similar external correlates indicative of diagnostic validity while substantially decreasing estimates of comorbidity (Westen, Shedler, & Bradley, 2006). Second, neither structured interviews nor questionnaires correlate strongly with consensus diagnoses made using all available data collected over time by teams of clinicians who not only have access to data from other informants but also know the patients well (e.g., Pilkonis et al., 1995; Pilkonis, Heape, Ruddy, & Serrao, 1991; Skodol, Oldham, Rosnick, Kellman, & Hyler, 1991). The third and most central problem of this approach is reliance on the self-awareness among a group of patients (PD patients) who, almost by definition, are likely to have distorted views of themselves and others. For example, Oltmanns, Turkheimer, and their colleagues have demonstrated across multiple samples that although lay informants converge remarkably well in assessing their peers' personality pathology, aggregated peer assessments tend to correlate only on the order of $r = .20$ to $.30$ with self-reports (Clifton, Turkheimer, & Oltmanns, 2003; Klein, 2003; Oltmanns, Melley, & Turkheimer, 2002; Thomas, Turkheimer, & Oltmanns, 2003). This relatively modest level of self-informant agreement is only slightly lower than meta-analytic estimates, which are in the mid .30s (Klonsky, Oltmanns, & Turkheimer, 2002). For the more overt symptoms of BPD, such as self-mutilation and suicidal ideation, self-report biases are less likely to be problematic. For more subtle personality symptoms, and particularly for externalizing symptoms (see Fiedler, Oltmanns, & Turkheimer, 2004), these biases may be more problematic. Unfortunately, the more subtle personality symptoms appear to be the most stable indicators of the disorder (Grilo et al., 2004; Zanarini, Frankenburg, Vujanovic, et al., 2004).

Another approach to the assessment of personality, including BPD, relies on the use of a systematic clinical interview paired with psychometrically valid instruments for rating data gathered in the interview. Westen and Shedler (1999a; 1999b) developed a Q-sort instrument designed to quantify the judgments of experienced clinical interviewers, combining clinical description with statistical prediction. Clinically experienced observers sort the 200 items of the SWAP-II Q-sort (or its progenitor, the SWAP-200) based either on their observation of a patient over time in treatment or on data ascertained using a systematic clinical interview, the Clinical Diagnostic Interview (CDI; Westen & Muderrisoglu, 2003, 2006; Westen, Muderrisoglu, Fowler, Shedler, & Koren, 1997). The CDI differs from structured PD interviews in that it does not primarily ask patients to describe themselves (although it does not avoid face-valid questions about behaviors, intentions, or phenomenology, such as whether the patient has self-mutilated or thought about suicide). Instead, it asks patients to provide detailed narratives about their symptoms, their school and work history, and their relationship history, focusing on specific examples of emotionally salient experiences. From these data (or from all available clinical data, if the clinician is describing a patient in ongoing treatment), the clinician-informant makes judgments about the ways the patient characteristically thinks, feels, regulates impulses and emotions, views the self and others, and behaves in significant relationships, and these are reflected in the clinician's placement (ranking) of the items.

Several recent studies using the SWAP-200 or the newly developed SWAP-II have focused on BPD (Bradley, Zittel, et al., 2005; Westen, Bradley, & Shedler, 2005; Westen & Shedler, 1999a, 1999b; Zittel & Westen, 2005). These studies indicate that SWAP-based assessment of BPD predicts external correlates, such as adaptive functioning and developmental history, in ways predicted by prior research (Zittel & Westen, 2005). These data also highlight the importance of understanding not only stress-dependent behaviors that are hallmarks of BPD (e.g., self-harming behavior) but also those characteristics (e.g., depressed mood, anxiety, hopelessness) that are characteristic of the everyday experience of BPD patients but not necessarily distinctive to them because they are common in psychiatric samples (Bradley, Zittel, et al., 2005).

In addition, these studies identify aspects of BPD not captured fully by the nine DSM BPD criteria, which are probably better understood as indicators of a latent construct than as the signs and symptoms that exhaustively define the disorder. For example, SWAP-based data provide a more thorough description of affect dysregulation among BPD patients. Specifically, data obtained using the SWAP-200 and SWAP-II reveal that emotion dysregulation in BPD comprises a tendency for emotions to spiral out of control, a tendency to become irrational under stress, and a dependence on others to regulate emotions.

All approaches to assessment have their limitations, and the SWAP is no exception. The most central limitation of most data obtained on BPD so far using the SWAP is that these data rely, like most studies using structured interviews and questionnaires, on the perspective of one informant (in this case, the clinician; in the modal study of BPD, the informant is the patient). Future research using all assessment procedures needs to triangulate data gathered from multiple sources, including self-reports, quantified clinical judgments, informant ratings (e.g., friends and family), and laboratory tasks.

Etiology of BPD

Research on BPD implicates a broad array of factors in the etiology of BPD, including biological/genetic factors, separation and loss, childhood abuse, global family environment, and disrupted attachments. Research on the etiology of BPD has largely addressed each of these domains separately and hence has not yet established models for their combination and interaction, although such work is under way. We will first review research for each of these etiologic factors and then summarize the current status of the field with respect to understanding their interplay.

Biological and Genetic Factors

Clearly, personality traits are heritable (see Plomin, Chipuer, & Loehlin, 1990), although the extent to which genetic transmission contributes to the development of BPD has yet to be fully understood. Nevertheless, a growing number of studies, including two preliminary twin studies (Nigg & Goldsmith, 1994; Torgersen, 1980; Torgersen et al., 2000), suggest the importance of familial aggregation. In a recent review of family studies of BPD, White, Gunderson, Zanarini, and Hudson (2003) found little support for familial links between schizophrenia or bipolar disorders and BPD, some support for familial links with major depression, and stronger support for familial aggregation of impulse spectrum disorders, including BPD itself. As we describe below, research that addresses both main effects and interactive effects in combination with environmental traumas is likely to prove more fruitful (see Nigg & Goldsmith, 1994; Torgersen, 1980; Torgersen et al., 2000; White et al., 2003).

An alternate approach to understanding the heritability of BPD is to look at subsyndromal markers, or endophenotypes, of the BPD construct (e.g., affect dysregulation and relationship instability). A recent study (Zanarini,

Frankenburg, Yong, et al., 2004) found that although the diagnosis of BPD showed familial aggregation, both specific BPD criteria and the broader BPD symptom categories of affect, cognition, impulsivity, and interpersonal relationship disturbance showed even stronger familial aggregation and discriminated better between the relatives of BPD probands and those of comparison subjects. This idea is consistent with theory and research conceptualizing BPD as the extreme presentation of aspects of heritable temperament or traits (e.g., impulsivity, neuroticism, and affective lability; see Paris, 2003; Skodol, Gunderson, Pfohl, et al., 2002, for reviews). Impulsive aggression is a central characteristic of Cluster B Axis II disorders, particularly BPD and APD (Coccaro, Bergeman, & McClearn, 1993; Goodman & Yehuda, 2002; Skodol, Gunderson, Pfohl, et al., 2002), and shows substantial heritability. However, the data on familial aggregation are difficult to interpret because of the complexity in disaggregating heritable temperamental and family environment effects (i.e., having a parent with borderline or related psychopathology increases the likelihood of adverse childhood events).

A burgeoning literature on the neurobiology of BPD focuses primarily on two trait aspects considered central to BPD: affect instability/dysregulation and impulsivity/impulsive aggression (e.g., Siever & Davis, 1991). Most functional neuroimaging research rests on the premise that BPD is associated with hyperreactivity to emotional stimuli, which should be manifest in such neural responses as heightened activation of the amygdala (Donegan et al., 2003; Herpertz et al., 2001). Several studies using functional magnetic resonance imaging (fMRI) do indeed find increased amygdala reactivity when these individuals are exposed to emotion-related stimuli, particularly faces (Donegan et al., 2003; Herpertz et al., 2001). Interestingly, BPD patients appear to show greater amygdala reactivity to neutral faces as well, perhaps supporting prior research linking BPD to a malevolence attribution style (Nigg, Lohr, Westen, Gold, & Silk, 1992; Westen, 1991b). Another study (Schmahl, Vermetten, Elzinga, & Bremner, 2003) identified decreased amygdala volume in BPD subjects (Driessen et al., 2000). Currently, the field is witnessing an explosion of fMRI research with BPD patients that is likely to elucidate the nature of the disorder (e.g., by examining links between amygdala reactivity and hypoactivity of cortical circuits that would normally regulate it, such as the ventromedial prefrontal cortex). At the same time, such research should be treated cautiously from an etiologic standpoint. Finding that BPD patients show greater amygdala reactivity, for example, is important, but it does not go far beyond a neural translation of the definition of a disorder characterized by emotional reactivity. Complicating matters, the pattern of data across studies may be complex because of the complex ways BPD patients try to regulate their affects. For example, the amygdala of BPD patients who dissociate may be relatively *less* reactive than that of non-BPD patients (Schmahl et al., 2004).

The majority of the research looking at the biological basis of impulsivity/impulsive aggression focuses on the role of reduced serotonergic responsivity (for reviews, see Skodol, Gunderson, Pfohl, et al., 2002; Soloff, Lynch, Kelly, Malone, & Mann, 2000). For example, some research associates lower levels of 5-hydroxytryptophan (e.g., Mann, 1998) with increased self-harming and suicidal behaviors. Using positron-emission tomography (PET), Leyton et al. (2001) identified an inverse relationship between alpha-methyl-L-tryptophan (converted to alpha-methyl-serotonin) and impulsivity as measured by errors on a go/no-go task. Other studies (De La Fuente et al., 1997; Soloff, Meltzer, Greer, Constantine, & Kelly, 2000) suggest that orbital prefrontal dysfunction may be associated with increased aggression via inhibition of limbic regions. Other neuropsychological studies implicate impaired functioning on laboratory tasks designed to evaluate planning and decision making abilities (Bazanis et al., 2002; Lenzenweger, Clarkin, Fertuck, & Kernberg, 2004), which could implicate prefrontal circuits more broadly.

Separation and Loss

A considerable body of research points to separation from or loss of parental figures during childhood as etiologically relevant to BPD. For example, a meta-analytic review found that 20% to 40% of BPD patients had experienced traumatic separations from one or both parents (Gunderson & Sabo, 1993). Childhood histories involving lengthy separations from, or the permanent loss of, one or both parents have been found to discriminate BPD patients from patients with schizophrenia, depression, and other PDs (Akiskal et al., 1985; Bradley, 1979; Frank & Paris, 1981; Goldberg, Mann, Wise, & Segall, 1985; Gunderson, Kerr, & Englund, 1980; Links, Steiner, Offord, & Eppel, 1988; Paris, Nowlis, & Brown, 1988; Soloff & Millward, 1983; Zanarini, Gunderson, Marino, Schwartz, & Frankenburg, 1989).

In evaluating the relationship of separation and loss to BPD, however, factors such as the child's age, nature and duration of the separation or loss, and availability of nurturant, enduring surrogate caregivers in the absence of the primary caregiver need to be taken into account. For example, a classic study of depression (see Brown & Harris, 1989, for details) found a constellation of symptoms resembling BPD to be highly prevalent among patients who had a peculiar kind of separation history (which they labeled "aberrant"), in which the mother appeared to have left the children for no "socially acceptable" reason (e.g., she abandoned her children for months because of her own instability). It is important to note when interpreting these findings that causal direction is not clear due to possible genetic confounds or gene-environment interactions.

Childhood Abuse

Early writing on BPD (Stern, 1938) focused on the etiologic role of childhood abuse, noting that "actual cruelty, neglect, and brutality by the parents of many years' duration are factors found in these patients. These factors operate more or less constantly over many years from earliest childhood. They are not single experiences" (p. 470). This early observation has been corroborated in the empirical literature, with numerous studies identifying a link between abuse, particularly childhood sexual abuse, and BPD (e.g., Ogata et al., 1990; Silk, Lohr, Ogata, & Westen, 1990; Westen, Ludolph, Misle, Ruffins, & Block, 1990; Zanarini, 1997). In Herman, Perry, and van der Kolk's (1989) sample of BPD patients, 81% had childhood histories that included abuse, both physical abuse (71%) and sexual abuse (67%). In a community-based longitudinal study of PDs, Johnson, Cohen, Brown, Smailes, and Bernstein (1999) found that experiences of childhood physical, sexual, and emotional abuse increased risk for development of virtually all of the DSM-IV PDs. However, when they adjusted for the effects of co-occurring PDs, only the Cluster B PDs remained significantly related to experiences of childhood maltreatment. Zelkowitz, Paris, Guzder, and Feldman (2001) found that people who had experienced childhood sexual abuse were four times more likely to develop BPD than those who had not. Not surprisingly, some studies did not find such a significant link between childhood abuse and BPD (see Fossati, Madeddu, & Maffei, 1999). The association between child abuse and BPD exists in the context of multiple, interactive genetic, environmental, and social factors, and the idea of one-to-one correspondence is an unfounded oversimplification (Bradley, Jenei, & Westen, 2005; Paris, 1997).

In addition to the presence/absence of abuse, several studies suggest that characteristics of abuse, including severity, age of onset, and number of types of abuse experienced, contribute to degree of impairment related to borderline pathology (McLean & Gallop, 2003; Silk, Lee, Hill, & Lohr, 1995; Yen et al., 2002; Zanarini et al., 2002). Studying BPD in adolescents, Ludolph et al. (1990) suggested that cumulative trauma, rather than a single traumatic event, appears to be more relevant to the development of BPD (see also Weaver & Clum, 1993). Thus, although not all patients with BPD have experienced childhood trauma, the current research indicates that traumatic experiences are a salient component of the developmental history of many individuals who develop BPD.

Family Environment

More generally, an unstable, nonnurturing family environment appears to contribute to the development of BPD. In adolescent patients, for example, the tendency to misunderstand people's actions and intentions (poor understanding of social causality) characteristic of BPD shows a strong association ($r = \sim.50$) with a simple metric of family instability, namely, the number of times the family moved (Westen, Ludolph, Block, Wixom, & Wiss, 1990). Much of the literature on traumatic precursors to PDs (and other psychiatric symptoms, such as depression) has not taken into account the impact of family environment, making it difficult to disentangle the impact of sexual or physical abuse from the overall family context within which abuse typically occurs, such as family chaos, disrupted attachments, multiple caregivers, parental neglect, alcoholism, and/or evidence of affective instability among family members (Dahl, 1995; Gunderson & Phillips, 1991; Ogata et al., 1990).

Studies of adverse childhood events have linked the number of such events to multiple adverse medical and psychiatric outcomes (Dong et al., 2004; Edwards, Holden, Anda, & Felitti, 2003). Research that has considered several of these variables together with regard to the etiology of PDs has often found that the context within which abuse occurs (e.g., problematic attachment relationships, emotional abuse, and neglect) is as strongly associated with BPD as the presence or absence of physical or sexual abuse (Johnson et al., 2001; Ludolph et al., 1990; Zanarini et al., 1989). For example, a recent study of the relationship between childhood abuse, family environment, and BPD found that family environment partially mediated the relationship between abuse and level of BPD symptoms (Bradley, Jenei, et al., 2005), although abuse showed a substantial unmediated relation to BPD. In other words, sexual trauma predicted BPD, but part of its impact reflected the effects of an unstable, nonnurturing family environment. The dearth of research on the relation between abuse and family environment is particularly problematic in the case of BPD, which is associated not only with the attribution of malevolence on others but also with fears of abandonment and aloneness that may be related to neglectful, absent, or unstable parenting (see Gunderson, 2001; Zanarini & Frankenburg, 1997).

One attempt to clarify this literature suggests that insecure attachment to parental figures, coupled with emotionally unstable or neglectful family environments, may account for the development of BPD, whereas physical or sexual abuse may account for symptom severity (Salzman, Salzman, & Wolfson, 1997). Other models suggest that sexual abuse may account for some of the severity of impulsive symptoms in BPD, such as self-mutilation, suicide attempts, substance abuse, promiscuity, running away, and assaultiveness (e.g., Westen, Ludolph, Misle, et al., 1990). Zanarini and Frankenburg (1997) reviewed research on the etiology of BPD and distinguished three types of trauma that they felt better explained the pathogenesis of BPD. Type I trauma includes "unfortunate but not entirely unavoidable or unexpectable experiences," including prolonged early separations, chronic insensitivity to the pre-borderline child's feelings and needs, and serious emotional discord in the family, perhaps leading to separation or divorce. Type II trauma includes experiences of verbal and emotional abuse, neglect of age-appropriate physical needs, and circumscribed episodes of parental psychiatric illness. Type III trauma includes experiences of clear physical and sexual abuse, chronic psychiatric illness in caretaker or caretakers (particularly Axis II psychopathology and substance abuse), and a generally chaotic and dysfunctional home environment (e.g., parents repeatedly engaging in shouting matches, children physically assaulting one another, constant disregard of family rules and invasions of other family members' boundaries). Zanarini and Frankenburg (1997) estimated that approximately half of borderline patients report a childhood characterized by type I and/or type II trauma, and the remaining half of borderline patients report a childhood characterized by all three types of trauma.

Attachment

Attachment theory (Bowlby, 1969, 1973) provides a framework for some of the most important recent theory and research on the etiology of BPD (see Agrawal, Gunderson, Holmes, & Lyons-Ruth, 2004, for a meta-analytic review). Research on attachment in BPD focuses on an infant's or young child's experience of unpredictable, frightening, and/or abusive caregiving that interrupts the formation of coherent internal working models of relationships. This presumably results in an inability to predict, understand, and flexibly respond to the actions of significant others (Lyons-Ruth & Jacobvitz, 1999; Main, Kaplan, & Cassidy, 1985). Attachment theorists describe a child's attachment status as "disorganized-disoriented" when the child is faced with an unsolvable dilemma: separation from a caregiver causes distress; this activates proximity seeking; the caregiver is unavailable, unpredictable, or frightening; and the infant or child is left without coherent strategies for making sense of or obtaining security from the caregiver. This disorganized-disoriented attachment pattern in infancy (similar to the characterization of "unresolved with respect to loss and trauma" in adult attachment) is marked in laboratory studies by incoherent and ineffective attempts to self-regulate following a separation from a caregiver. Instead, disorganized-disoriented infants demonstrate seemingly undirected or contradictory behavior, such as freezing, rocking, or head banging.

Research on disorganized attachment in children (beyond infancy) highlights perceptions of parental figures as unpredictable, unavailable, and frightening. In one series of studies, children with disorganized attachment were more likely to respond to pictures of distressed children separated from their parents with stories depicting violent harm to the child or others (Kaplan, 1987; Main et al., 1985). In other studies, parents are described as unavailable, frightening, or frightened (Solomon, George, & De Jong, 1995), and dolls representing the child engage in angry/violent and idiosyncratic/odd behavior (Cassidy, 1988). Interestingly, these findings parallel research on adolescent and adult patients with BPD using storytelling procedures such as the Thematic Apperception Test (TAT), which finds that BPD is associated with negative emotional tone of relationship descriptions and particularly by malevolence attributions (Westen, 1991b; Westen, Lohr, Silk, Gold, & Kerber, 1990; Westen, Ludolph, Block, et al., 1990).

Because "unresolved" is a qualifier rather than one of the three primary attachment patterns coded categorically from the Adult Attachment Interview

(AAI), the most common attachment pattern associated with BPD is preoccupied (analogous to anxious/ambivalent in infancy and childhood). A combination of unresolved and preoccupied attachment has been associated with BPD in adolescents as well as adults (Nakash-Eisikovits, Dutra, & Westen, 2002; Westen, Thomas, Nakash, & Bradley, 2006). In general, preoccupied attachment in combination with the unresolved qualifier resembles the interpersonal style of BPD patients, marked by rejection sensitivity, alternation between anxious preoccupation and anger with attachment figures, and incoherent strategies for attempting to make intimate contact with others.

Recent work integrating object relations and attachment theories connects insecure or disorganized attachment to BPD symptoms using the concept of mentalization (Fonagy, Target, Gergely, Allen, & Bateman, 2003). Mentalization refers to the ability to make sense of one's own and others' actions by reflecting on and understanding their mental states (including feelings, beliefs, wishes, and ideas). In healthy development, this capacity is developed in the context of attachment relationships with primary caregivers, during which infants and children develop internal working models of self, others, and relationships (Bowlby, 1988). According to Fonagy, an inability to make sense of one's own and others' mental (and particular emotional) states not only results from interactions with inexplicable caregivers but also renders anticipation of attachment figures' actions impossible, leading to difficulty in self-regulating emotion.

Difficulties with mentalization can also be seen in an implicit or explicit belief in a one-to-one correspondence between one's perceptions (of situations, others' feelings and motives, etc.) and reality, and hence in an inability to consider possible alternate interpretations. This often leads to instability of interpersonal relationships, as whatever emotion one feels in reaction to others (e.g., anger, happiness) is perceived as directly and unquestionably reflective of the other's feelings or intentions (e.g., intent to harm), whether correctly or incorrectly perceived. According to this model, deficits in mentalization also contribute to an unstable sense of self and a sense of emptiness.

Interaction of Biological and Psychosocial Risk Factors

Despite the relatively neat categorization of putative risk factors presented above, research dating back to Harlow's monkeys should lead to circumspection in making distinct attributions to nature or nurture in the etiology of BPD or any other psychiatric disorder. What begins as a biological vulnerability may lead to a cascade of environmental events, just as what may begin as an environmental effect may become "hard-wired." Data on the interplay of risk factors in the development of BPD do not exist at this point, primarily because BPD is not officially diagnosed until age 18 and comprehensive longitudinal studies of the development of personality disorders beginning in infancy have yet to be conducted. However, a number of studies in domains related to BPD (e.g., childhood sexual and physical abuse, attachment disorganization, impulsivity and depressed mood) have demonstrated that both psychological and biological influences play important roles (see Judd & McGlashan, 2003, for a review).

Two areas of research are particularly relevant to BPD. Caspi, Moffitt, and colleagues (Caspi et al., 2002; Caspi et al., 2003) have focused on gene-environment interactions in a large longitudinal sample in New Zealand. In a landmark study (2002), they found that a functional polymorphism in the promoter region of the serotonin transporter (5-HTT) gene moderated the influence of stressful life events in both childhood and adulthood on subsequent depression. Stressful events in adulthood, as well as abuse in childhood, predicted subsequent depressive symptoms and suicidality—two features that in combination often point to the presence of BPD—in individuals with the short allele of the 5-HTT promoter as compared to individuals homozygous for the long allele. In a second study (2003), they found that a functional polymorphism in a gene regulating monoamine oxidase (MAO) moderated the relationship between child abuse and antisocial behavior in adulthood.

Research on the neurobiology of early life stress also highlights the importance of the interaction of biological and environmental factors in the development of psychopathology. These studies suggest that early life stress modifies brain circuits involved in stress regulation, resulting in a type of "biological priming" that interacts with genetic vulnerabilities to increase the risk of later psychopathology (Heim, Meinlschmidt, & Nemeroff, 2003). Though none of the research to date directly addresses the development of BPD, the types of early life stress studied (notably early separation from mother in animal analogue studies and childhood sexual and physical abuse in human studies) as well as the domains of documented outcomes (e.g., depression and substance abuse) are germane to an understanding of the interaction of genetic and biological risk factors in BPD.

Prognosis and Natural Course of the Disorder

A small but growing body of research on the longitudinal course of BPD exists, and although the findings of these studies are not entirely consistent, several broad characterizations emerge. One is that patients tend to lose their BPD diagnosis over time. For example, the longitudinal McLean Adult Development Study found a remission rate of 35% at 2 years, 50% at 4 years, and 69% at 6 years (Zanarini, Frankenburg, Hennen, & Silk, 2003).

To what extent the instability in the borderline diagnosis (and other PD diagnoses) is an artifact of arbitrary cutoff points for categorical diagnosis, the mixed diagnostic criteria for BPD in the DSM (enduring personality characteristics interspersed with typically stress-dependent behaviors), or the limited test-retest reliability of structured interviews at intervals beyond 6 weeks is unclear. What *is* clear is that dimensional assessments of both BPD (number of criteria met) and traits associated with BPD (e.g., negative affectivity, neuroticism) show far more temporal stability than categorical diagnoses (Lenzenweger, Johnson, & Willett, 2004; Skodol et al., 2005).

Although longer-term follow-up studies have the disadvantage of less structured diagnostic procedures, they provide additional data suggesting a course of general improvement if BPD patients can survive their 20s and 30s. In one long-term follow-up study, Paris and Zweig-Frank (2001) found a high remission rate consistent with more recent studies using structured interviews, with only 25% of patients still meeting BPD criteria at 15 years and 7.8% meeting criteria at 27 years. McGlashan (1986) found that BPD patients discharged from an intensive inpatient program fared best two decades following discharge. These data, consistent with other data on externalizing disorders such as antisocial PD and substance abuse disorders, suggest that BPD tends to "burn out" with age. In long-term follow-up studies by McGlashan (1986) and by Stone (1987; 1992), patients with better outcomes tended to be higher in intelligence, more talented in the arts, more physically attractive, and/or described as more likable than those with poorer outcomes. The more chronically impaired patients were more likely to have sustained problems with alcohol abuse, histories of severe physical or sexual abuse, severe problems with impulsivity, comorbidity for antisocial PD, or schizotypal features.

BPD, however, is marked by internalizing symptoms and interpersonal difficulties as well as the more notable externalizing symptoms. Data suggest that although the impulsive and aggressive (both other- and self-directed) features tend to improve with time, core personality attributes such as negative affect, emotion dysregulation, and difficulties in intimate relationships tend to persist, whether or not the person continues to meet formal criteria for BPD. Depressive and anxious symptoms tend to remain high even among "recovered" BPD patients. Likewise, problems related to interpersonal relationships, including social isolation and fear of abandonment, tend to endure over time (McGlashan, 1986; Paris & Zweig-Frank, 2001; Zanarini et al., 2003). There is some suggestion that long-term interpersonal patterns among BPD patients tend to be bimodal, with some patients tending to become socially isolated (likely as a way of regulating the intensely distressing interpersonal patterns that tend to exacerbate BPD symptoms), whereas others become better able to maintain committed relationships. Some patients become symptomatic again during midlife in response to separation, divorce, or death of a spouse (McGlashan, 1986; Paris & Zweig-Frank, 2001; Stone, 1987, 1992).

One of the major risks for BPD patients seen in these and other studies is suicide. Long-term studies of patients with BPD suggest a suicide rate in the range of 3% to 10% (Black, Blum, Pfohl, & Hale, 2004). Following patients over a 27-year period, Paris and Zweig-Frank (2001) found a 10.3% rate of suicide (most of which occurred before age 40). Two of the most robust variables predicting greater risk of suicide in BPD patients include substance abuse and comorbid depression, although the latter is characteristic of most BPD patients (Black et al., 2004; Fyer et al., 1988; Isometsa et al., 1996).

Treatment Approaches

Patients with BPD are often considered difficult to treat. The first treatments for borderline patients, which began to emerge in the 1950s and 1960s, were modified forms of psychoanalytic psychotherapy, two of which have recently been tested in randomized controlled trials (RCTs). Cognitive-behavioral therapies for BPD began to emerge in the 1980s, when Linehan developed dialectical behavior therapy (DBT; Linehan, 1993). Integrative therapies have not been tested empirically but are widely practiced. We describe each treatment approach in turn.

Psychodynamic Psychotherapy

Because of centrality of the construct of personality (or character) to its conceptions of treatment, and because of the legacy of early theories on borderline states and personality organization, psychodynamic approaches constitute the largest body of theoretical work on the treatment of BPD. Psychodynamic approaches to BPD all share a grounding in developmental psychopathology, arguing that the only way to understand the disorder is through understanding the way development has gone awry in the way the patient experiences the self and others, regulates emotions, and regulates impulses (see Bradley & Westen, 2005). Although psychodynamic psychotherapy for BPD varies widely, two approaches have predominated in the clinical literature. The first is Kernberg's (1975) approach, which represents a confluence of multiple psychoanalytic schools of thought, particularly ego psychology (which focuses on adaptive functions) and object relations theory (which focuses on interpersonal relationships and the representation of self and others). The second, derived from the self-psychological approach of Kohut (1977), is based on work by Adler and Buie (Adler, 1981, 1989; Adler & Buie, 1979; Buie & Adler, 1982), which focuses on identity and self-soothing.

Similar to all psychodynamic approaches to the treatment of BPD, Kernberg's approach attends to the interpersonal dynamics of BPD patients (e.g., fear of abandonment) and uses the relationship with the therapist to address distorted ways of understanding interpersonal relations. More specifically, Kernberg's perspective focuses on the importance of aggression in borderline patients (often projected onto others) and a defensive style marked by "splitting" (a tendency to see the self and others as all good or all bad). Kernberg's treatment focuses on confronting aggression and manipulation, helping patients attain more balanced views of the self and others, and interpreting conflicts impeding the capacity to love and work.

The self-psychological approach of Adler, Buie, and others assumes that borderline patients' problems lie less in their conflicts than in psychological deficits, particularly in their capacity to self-soothe. Whereas Kernberg tends to see the aggression of borderline patients as primary, the self-psychological approach views borderline patients' rage as secondary to other feelings, such as the pain of abandonment. From this perspective, BPD is a developmental disorder derived from a failure to develop soothing images of primary caregivers that the person can call upon in times of distress. Thus the primary problem facing patients with BPD is the inability to self-soothe and the need to find others who can help them regulate their feelings as well as their self-esteem. This approach to treatment emphasizes empathic attunement with borderline patients and works to help them internalize soothing functions not developed in childhood.

Like most psychodynamic therapies, the ratio of theory to empirical outcome research is unfortunately high. However, two psychodynamic approaches to the treatment of BPD have recently been manualized (using principle-based manuals) and tested in RCTs. The first, based on Kernberg's work, is called transference-focused psychotherapy (TFP). The second, based on Fonagy's attachment research, is called mentalization-based treatment (MBT). Both share a primary focus on changing patients' mental representations of themselves and others.

Transference-Focused Psychotherapy

Transference-focused psychotherapy (Clarkin, Yeomans, & Kernberg, 1999; Yeomans, 2004) places primary emphasis on the poorly integrated representations that empirically are characteristic of patients with BPD (Westen, 1991b; Westen & Shedler, 1999a; Zittel & Westen, 2005). The treatment proceeds through a hierarchy of goals, moving from containment of suicidal and self-destructive behavior and establishment of a stable treatment frame to a focus on dominant relationship patterns. As the name implies, TFP focuses on clarification, confrontation, and interpretation within the context of the patient-therapist relationship. TFP focuses on present-oriented identification of the dominant relationship paradigm (e.g., idealizer-idealized, victim-victimizer) active in the patient-therapist relationship. This process includes observing and interpreting changes in this relational configuration (e.g., a switch in role from victim to victimizer or perpetrator) and increasing patient awareness of split representations of self and others.

The principle underlying TFP is that increased awareness and understanding of distortions and expectations the patient brings to relationships will lead to more coherent, integrated views of the self and others, which will in turn generate an increased ability to regulate emotions, particularly those emerging from interpersonal interactions. A preliminary study of TFP (Clarkin et al., 2001) evaluated 23 female patients in twice-weekly TFP over the course of 12 months. Examining pre-to-post change, the study found significantly reduced levels of suicide attempts, decreased severity of injury resulting from self-harming behavior, and fewer days and numbers of hospitalizations. A randomized controlled trial of TFP comparing it with supportive psychodynamic therapy (treatment as usual at Kernberg's site) and DBT has recently been completed (Clarkin, Levy, Lenzenweger, & Kernberg,

2004). Although all three treatments produced positive outcomes, of interest is that the hypothesized mediating variable (changes in the structure of
representations of self and others) appeared linked to change only in the TFP
condition.

Mentalization-Based Therapy

Mentalization-based therapy is a relatively recent effort to operationalize
an approach to treatment grounded in attachment theory (Fonagy, Target, &
Gergely, 2000). This approach focuses on developing increased mentalization
capacities in BPD patients. One of the aims of the treatment approach is to
help patients identify and understand emotions by clarifying and naming
them, understanding immediate precipitants, understanding the emotion in
the context of past and current relationships, learning to express the emotion appropriately, and learning to understand the response others are most
likely to have in reaction to the patient's emotional expression (Bateman &
Fonagy, 2003). The therapist maintains a "mentalizing stance" by focusing
on and discussing the here-and-now mental states of the therapist and patient.
Transference interpretations are kept simple and made with respect to relatively immediate or "experience near" circumstances (e.g., the patient's tendency to quit psychotherapy when she begins to feel too close to the therapist),
avoiding historical interpretations (e.g., how this is related to her early experiences with her mother).

A preliminary study of MBT (Bateman & Fonagy, 1999) compared a control group ($n = 19$) of patients receiving "general psychiatric services" with
patients ($n = 19$) participating in a psychoanalytically oriented partial hospitalization program based on an MBT approach. The maximum length of the
partial hospitalization program was 18 months. All patients were assessed at
3-month intervals over an 18-month period. Results indicated decreased self-
mutilation and suicide attempts; reduced length of inpatient hospitalization;
and decreases in self-reported anxiety, depression, and interpersonal problems. Data collected at 18-month follow-up (e.g., 36 months from start of
treatment) found that these treatment benefits were maintained (Bateman &
Fonagy, 2001). These promising but preliminary data led to an outpatient
adaptation of MBT with a more clearly operationalized treatment manual
(Bateman & Fonagy, 2004), with a treatment study currently under way.

Cognitive-Behavioral Therapy (CBT)

The first and best studied CBT approach to treatment of BPD is DBT,
a modular, manualized treatment program for patients with BPD that may be
implemented in inpatient or outpatient settings. DBT relies on a combination
of skills training, usually implemented in group format, in four areas: mind-
fulness, interpersonal effectiveness, distress tolerance, and emotion regulation.

In addition to skills training in a group format, DBT includes an individual therapy component with several distinctive features. These include a functional analysis of behavior (focusing particularly on self-harming and therapy inter-fering behaviors); a "validating" approach focused on depathologizing the patient's difficulties and emphasizing how impulsive and self-harming behav-iors such as parasuicidal behavior are understandable, albeit not effective, efforts to manage distress or emotion dysregulation; and 24-hour therapist availability for suicidality coupled with behavioral principles intended to mit-igate the need for such phone calls.

DBT is the only treatment for BPD that has been widely subjected to empirical scrutiny, and it has proven effective in decreasing suicide attempts, self-injurious behaviors (e.g., cutting, binge eating), and hospitalizations (Koons et al., 2001; Linehan, Armstrong, Suarez, Allmon, & Heard, 1991; Linehan, Heard, & Armstrong, 1993; Verheul et al., 2003). Other studies have found changes in a variety of domains, such as anger and dissociation (Linehan, Tutek, Heard, & Armstrong, 1994). A full review of studies on DBT is beyond the scope of this chapter (for reviews, see Robins & Chapman, 2004; Scheel, 2000; Westen, 2000). More recently, Young (Young, Klosko, & Weishaar, 2003) and Beck, Davis, and Freeman (2004) have developed more cognitive approaches to the treatment of PDs, including BPD. A recent study of long-term treatment using Young's schema-focused therapy produced promising results (Giesen-Bloo, et al., 2006).

Integrative Treatment

The three treatments described above represent only the most broadly known and best-evaluated approaches. A number of other psychodynamic, cognitive-behavioral, and integrative approaches to the treatment of BPD also exist but are beyond the constraints of this chapter (see Aviram, Hellerstein, Gerson, & Stanley, 2004; Blum, Pfohl, St. John, Monahan, & Black, 2002; Brown, Newman, Charlesworth, Crits-Christoph, & Beck, 2004; Ryle, 2004; Westen, 1991a, 2000). Some common elements, however, cut across most of these treatments for BPD, and make considerable sense in light of the nature of borderline psychopathology.

The first is the importance of establishing a clear framework for the treat-ment that spells out expectations and boundaries for both the therapist and the patient. A second is frequency and length of treatment, with each approach including some form of biweekly contact over the course of at least twelve months. Third, all of the treatment approaches for BPD attend closely to the dynamics of the relationship between the therapist and the patient and make discussion of this relationship a central aspect of therapy. Fourth, although the construct is framed differently, emotion and impulse dysregu-lation is at the center of virtually all approaches.

Fifth and finally, treatments tend to proceed through a series of stages, similar to those proposed in a stage-based approach to the treatment of the near-neighbor construct of "complex posttraumatic stress disorder" (e.g., Brown, Scheflin, & Hammond, 1998; Herman, 1992). The first stage, linked to keeping the patient alive and in treatment, focuses on stabilization of behavior and reduction of emotion dysregulation (e.g., getting impulsive self-harmful behaviors under control). The second stage focuses on understanding of past experiences with a focus on how prior life experiences are manifest in current patterns (as opposed to exploration of the past as an archaeological dig, as in more classic psychoanalytic approaches). The third stage addresses reorganization of both internal (representational and affect-regulatory) and external (behavioral) processes related to interpersonal relationships. Although these principles remain untested, current funding priorities in the United States and Britain, where most of the treatment research on BPD has been conducted, do not encourage the testing of treatments of a duration (i.e., years) that virtually all experts on BPD, from Kernberg to Linehan, indicate are necessary for adequate, effective treatment of the disorder. In practice, however, we suspect that effective treatment of BPD likely requires flexibility and integration across treatment approaches, particularly given the mélange of personality problems and Axis I symptoms with which BPD patients typically present.

Future Directions for the Study of BPD

Research on BPD has expanded exponentially over the last 25 years. Here we briefly describe three domains we believe to be central to progress in research on BPD: identification of improved diagnostic criteria for BPD, approaches to BPD diagnosis, and exploration of potential subtypes of BPD.

How Can We Improve the Diagnostic Criteria for BPD?

Despite consensus on the problems with the current BPD diagnostic criteria, no such consensus exists on the best remedy. The least radical solution would be to continue with diagnostic business as usual by tinkering with the current diagnostic criteria to create a modestly improved criterion set (e.g., modifying the affective lability criterion to include both pervasive negative affect and affect dysregulation). This approach, however, has not solved the problems with the BPD diagnosis over the last 25 years, and it is unlikely that any set of 7 to 10 items will adequately capture this complex, multifaceted disorder while distinguishing it from near-neighbor disorders.

An alternative, more radical approach is a construct validation approach, which would take a large group of candidate criteria; collect data from a large, diverse sample without assuming any preexisting diagnostic groupings; and use statistical aggregation techniques to identify and validate emergent traits or configurations of traits. Practically speaking, it is unlikely that the field will allow for elimination of the current BPD diagnosis (presuming this would be the result of full-scale construct validation). Although some resistance to wholesale reworking of the BPD diagnosis no doubt results from inertia and the comfort with the familiar (not to mention the time and money spent developing assessments for the current diagnosis), some rests on the fact that BPD is a clinically useful construct backed by a large body of research. Data of this sort collected with the use of self-report instruments have allowed researchers to construct a BPD prototype from the traits represented in the five-factor model (Trull, Widiger, Lynam, & Costa, 2003), and similar data have identified both a trait and a personality constellation heavily marked by borderline features, called emotion dysregulation or emotionally dysregulated PD, in both adolescents and adults (Shedler & Westen, 2004; Westen, Dutra, & Shedler, 2005; Westen & Shedler, 1999b; Westen, Shedler, Durrett, Glass, & Martens, 2003).

A compromise between business as usual and radical overhaul would be a hybrid, or "construct validation lite," approach. This procedure would involve selecting a group of patients with a moderate to high degree of match to the current BPD diagnosis and then identifying their most salient personality characteristics from an item pool that includes but is not limited to DSM-IV criteria. Using a broad range of both patients and candidate criteria would allow for a more comprehensive description of personality features of BPD without "throwing the baby out with the bathwater."

How Should We Diagnose BPD?

Regardless of the criteria ultimately used to diagnose BPD, a second question regarding diagnosis remains, namely, how diagnostic criteria should be applied to individual cases. As noted by Sokal (1974), taxonomy (developing a classification) and diagnosis (identifying cases) are independent aspects of the classification process. Researchers have proposed several alternatives to the current DSM procedure of making categorical (yes/no) decisions on each diagnostic criterion, counting the number of criteria met, and applying arbitrary cutoffs. The least radical is simply to use the same procedure except to dimensionalize it, using number of symptoms met as a dimensional diagnosis, perhaps supplemented by categorical diagnosis for clinical communication. A second, less conservative method is a prototype matching approach (see Westen & Bradley, 2005; Westen & Shedler, 2000; Westen et al., 2006), in which clinicians rate the resemblance between the patient and a diagnostic prototype (e.g., in the form of a paragraph descriptive of a prototypical patient with the disorder). A recently completed study (unpublished data) finds that clinicians can make dimensional diagnoses using prototype matching with a simple five-point scale (1 = description does not apply; 2 = patient has *some features* of this disorder; 3 = patient has *significant features* of this disorder; 4 = patient *has* this disorder, diagnosis applies; 5 = patient *exemplifies* this disorder, prototypical case) with high reliability. Other research finds that this prototype matching approach decreases diagnostic comorbidity when compared with dimensional diagnoses made by counting symptoms, with slight improvements, rather than decrements, in construct validity (Westen et al., 2006). Finally, the most radical approach would be to eliminate the BPD diagnosis and replace it with a four- or five-factor trait diagnosis, and to "reconstruct" the BPD diagnosis if necessary using four or five factor prototypes as described by Widiger and his colleagues (Trull et al., 2003). To what extent one of these approaches is more empirically valid and clinically useful than the others will require head-to-head comparisons, in which multiple approaches are all tested in the same data set. Unfortunately, to date, research has typically tested each approach in isolation or in comparison with only the current DSM-IV approach.

Do Subtypes of BPD Exist?

The heterogeneity in the clinical presentations that can yield a BPD diagnosis raises the question of whether the diagnosis may include meaningful subtypes or subgroups. Grinker, Werble, and Drye (1968), who undertook the first empirical study of borderline pathology, conducted the first research identifying subtypes of BPD. Using a sample of 51 psychiatric inpatients, they identified four groups of BPD patients: a more psychotic group (which later influenced the schizotypal diagnosis in DSM-III), a more neurotic group, a "core" borderline group, and an "as-if" (identity-changing) group. Theorizing about subgroups of borderline patients rests primarily on clinical observation (e.g., Oldham, 2001; Stone, 1994). However, recent research using the SWAP-200 and SWAP-II has consistently produced two- and three-cluster solutions in DSM-IV–defined adults and adolescents with BPD (Bradley, Zittel, et al., 2005; Conklin, Bradley, & Westen, 2006; Conklin & Westen, 2005; Westen & Shedler, 1999b; Zittel & Westen, 2002). The first two subtypes have been replicated across all samples. The first is an internalizing dysregulated subtype marked by severe dysphoria and desperate efforts to manage it (e.g., through cutting or suicide attempts). The second is an externalizing dysregulated subgroup marked by a tendency to be rageful rather than depressed and to try to self-regulate by blaming or attacking others instead of oneself. The third is a histrionic-impulsive subtype marked by a tendency to experience both intense positive and intense negative emotions and attempts to regulate both positive and negative affect through impulsive and sensation-seeking behavior. Across both adolescent and adult samples, these subtypes have demonstrated meaningful differences with respect to external correlates indicative of construct validity, such as adaptive functioning and etiology. Moreover, although the DSM criteria may capture many aspects of the externalizing dysregulated subtype, the intense pain manifest in the internalizing subtype is not captured by the diagnostic criteria.

Conclusion

Borderline personality disorder is a complex disorder—or, more likely, spectrum of pathology—whose phenomenology, etiology, prognosis, and treatment researchers have made great strides in understanding since its official introduction into the psychiatric nomenclature in 1980 in DSM-III. Nevertheless, the diagnosis itself is clearly in need of revision to minimize artifactual comorbidity with the majority of the other nine PDs in DSM-IV and to maximize both its construct validity and clinical utility.

References

Adler, G. (1981). The borderline-narcissistic personality disorder continuum. *American Journal of Psychiatry, 138,* 46–50.

Adler, G. (1989). Uses and limitations of Kohut's self psychology in the treatment of borderline patients. *Journal of the American Psychoanalytic Association, 37,* 761–785.

Adler, G., & Buie, D. (1979). Aloneness and borderline psychopathology: The possible relevance of child development issues. *International Journal of Psychoanalysis, 60,* 83–96.

Agrawal, H. R., Gunderson, J. G., Holmes, B. M., & Lyons-Ruth, K. (2004). Attachment studies with borderline patients: A review. *Harvard Review of Psychiatry, 12,* 94–104.

Akiskal, H. S. (1996). The prevalent clinical spectrum of bipolar disorders: Beyond DSM-IV. *Journal of Clinical Psychopharmacology, 16,* 4S–14S.

Akiskal, H. S. (2004). Demystifying borderline personality: Critique of the concept and unorthodox reflections on its natural kinship with the bipolar spectrum. *Acta Psychiatrica Scandinavica, 110,* 401–407.

Akiskal, H. S., Chen, S. E., Davis, G. C., Puzantian, V. R., Kashgarian, M., & Bolinger, J. M. (1985). Borderline: An adjective in search of a noun. *Journal of Clinical Psychiatry, 46,* 41–48.

American Psychiatric Association. (1980). *Diagnostic and statistical manual of mental disorders* (3rd ed.). Washington, DC: Author.

American Psychiatric Association. (1994). *Diagnostic and statistical manual of mental disorders* (4th ed.). Washington, DC: Author.

American Psychiatric Association. (2000). *Diagnostic and statistical manual of mental disorders* (4th ed., text revision). Washington, DC: Author.

Aviram, R. B., Hellerstein, D. J., Gerson, J., & Stanley, B. (2004). Adapting supportive psychotherapy for individuals with borderline personality disorder who self-injure or attempt suicide. *Journal of Psychiatric Practice, 10,* 145–155.

Barasch, J., Kroll, J., Carey, K., & Sines, L. (1983). Discriminating borderline personality disorder from other personality disorders: Cluster and analysis of the Diagnostic Interview for Borderline. *Archives of General Psychiatry, 40,* 1297–1302.

Bateman, A., & Fonagy, P. (1999). The effectiveness of partial hospitalization in the treatment of borderline personality disorder: A randomized controlled trial. *American Journal of Psychiatry, 156,* 1563–1569.

Bateman, A., & Fonagy, P. (2001). Treatment of borderline personality disorder with psychoanalytically oriented partial hospitalization: An 18-month follow-up. *American Journal of Psychiatry, 158,* 36–41.

Bateman, A., & Fonagy, P. (2003). The development of an attachment-based treatment program for borderline personality disorder. *Bulletin of the Menninger Clinic, 67,* 187–211.

Bateman, A., & Fonagy, P. (2004). Mentalization-based treatment of BPD. *Journal of Personality Disorders, 18,* 36–51.

Bazanis, E., Rogers, R. D., Dowson, J. H., Taylor, P., Meux, C., Staley, C., et al. (2002). Neurocognitive deficits in decision-making and planning of patients with DSM-III-R borderline personality disorder. *Psychological Medicine, 32,* 1395–1405.

Beck, A. T., Davis, D. D., & Freeman, A. (2004). *Cognitive therapy of personality disorders* (2nd ed.). New York: Guilford Press.

Becker, D. F., Grilo, C. M., Edell, W. S., & McGlashan, T. H. (2000). Comorbidity of borderline personality disorder with other personality disorders in hospitalized adolescents and adults. *American Journal of Psychiatry, 157,* 2011–2016.

Black, D. W., Blum, N., Pfohl, B., & Hale, N. (2004). Suicidal behavior in borderline personality disorder: Prevalence, risk factors, prediction, and prevention. *Journal of Personality Disorders, 18*(3), 226–239.

Blum, N., Pfohl, B., St. John, D., Monahan, P., & Black, D. W. (2002). A cognitive-behavioral systems-based group treatment for outpatients with borderline personality disorder: A preliminary report. *Comprehensive Psychiatry, 43,* 301–310.

Bowlby, J. (1969). *Attachment* (Vol. 1). New York: Basic Books.

Bowlby, J. (1973). *Separation* (Vol. 2). London: Hogarth Press.

Bowlby, J. (1988). *A secure base: Parent-child attachment and healthy human development.* New York: Basic Books.

Bradley, R., Jenei, J., & Westen, D. (2005). Etiology of borderline personality disorder: Disentangling the contributions of intercorrelated antecedents. *Journal of Nervous and Mental Disease, 193,* 24–31.

Bradley, R., & Westen, D. (2005). The psychodynamics of borderline personality disorder: A view from developmental psychopathology. *Development and Psychopathology, 17*(4), 927–957.

Bradley, R., Zittel, C., & Westen, D. (2005). Borderline personality disorder in adolescence: Phenomenology and subtypes. *Journal of Child Psychology and Psychiatry, 46,* 1006–1019.

Bradley, S. J. (1979). The relationship of early maternal separation to borderline personality in children and adolescents: A pilot study. *American Journal of Psychiatry, 136,* 424–426.

Brown, D., Scheflin, A. W., & Hammond, D. C. (1998). *Memory, trauma treatment, and the law.* New York: W.W. Norton.

Brown, G. K., Newman, C. F., Charlesworth, S. E., Crits-Christoph, P., & Beck, A. T. (2004). An open clinical trial of cognitive therapy for borderline personality disorder. *Journal of Personality Disorders, 18,* 257–271.

Brown, G. W., & Harris, T. O. (1989). *Life events and illness.* New York: Guilford Press.

Buie, D. H., & Adler, G. (1982). Definitive treatment of the borderline personality. *International Journal of Psychoanalytic Psychotherapy, 9,* 51–87.

Caspi, A., McClay, J., Moffitt, T., Mill, J., Martin, J., Craig, I. W., et al. (2002). Role of genotype in the cycle of violence in maltreated children. *Science, 297,* 851–854.

Caspi, A., Sugden, K., Moffitt, T. E., Taylor, A., Craig, I. W., Harrington, H., et al. (2003). Influence of life stress on depression: Moderation by a polymorphism in the 5-HTT gene. *Science, 301,* 386–389.

Cassidy, J. (1988). Child-mother attachment and the self in six-year-olds. *Child Development, 59,* 121–134.

Clark, L. A., & Harrison, J. A. (2001). Assessment instruments. In W. J. Livesley (Ed.), *Handbook of personality disorders: Theory, research, and treatment*. New York: Guilford Press.

Clark, L. A., Livesley, W. J., & Morey, L. (1997). Personality disorder assessment: The challenge of construct validity. *Journal of Personality Disorders, 11*, 205–231.

Clarkin, J. F., Foelsch, P. A., Levy, K. N., Hull, J. W., Delaney, J. C., & Kernberg, O. F. (2001). The development of a psychodynamic treatment for patients with borderline personality disorder: A preliminary study of behavioral change. *Journal of Personality Disorders, 15*, 487–495.

Clarkin, J. F., Levy, K. N., Lenzenweger, M. F., & Kernberg, O. F. (2004). The Personality Disorders Institute/Borderline Personality Disorder Research Foundation randomized control trial for borderline personality disorder: Rationale, methods, and patient characteristics. *Journal of Personality Disorders, 18*, 52–72.

Clarkin, J. F., Widiger, T. A., Frances, A., Hurt, S. W., & Gilmore, M. (1983). Prototypic typology and the borderline personality disorder. *Journal of Abnormal Psychology, 92*, 263–275.

Clarkin, J. F., Yeomans, F. E., & Kernberg, O. F. (1999). *Psychotherapy for borderline personality*. New York: Wiley.

Clifton, A., Turkheimer, E., & Oltmanns, T. F. (2003). *Self and peer perspectives on pathological personality traits and interpersonal problems*. Unpublished manuscript, University of Virginia, Charlottesville.

Coccaro, E. F., Bergeman, C., & McClearn, G. E. (1993). Heritability of irritable impulsiveness: A study of twins reared together and apart. *Psychiatry Research, 48*(3), 229–242.

Conklin, C. Z., & Westen, D. (2005). Borderline personality disorder as seen in clinical practice: Implications for DSM-V. *American Journal of Psychiatry, 162*, 867–875.

Conklin, C. Z., Bradley, R., & Westen, D. (2006). Affect regulation in borderline personality disorder. *Journal of Nervous and Mental Disease, 194*(2), 69–77.

Cowdry, R. (1992). *Psychobiology and psychopharmacology of borderline personality disorder*. Madison, CT: International Universities Press.

Dahl, A. (1995). Borderline disorders: The validity of the diagnostic concept. *Psychiatric Development, 3*, 109–152.

De La Fuente, J. M., Goldman, S., Stanus, E., Vizuete, C., Morlan, I., Bobes, J., et al. (1997). Brain glucose metabolism in borderline personality disorder. *Journal of Psychiatric Research, 31*, 531–541.

Donegan, N. H., Sanislow, C. A., Blumberg, H. P., Fulbright, R. K., Lacadie, C., Skudlarski, P., et al. (2003). Amygdala hyperreactivity in borderline personality disorder: Implications for emotional dysregulation. *Biological Psychiatry, 54*(11), 1284–1293.

Dong, M., Anda, R. F., Felitti, V. J., Dube, S. R., Williamson, D. F., Thompson, T. J., et al. (2004). The interrelatedness of multiple forms of childhood abuse, neglect, and household dysfunction. *Child Abuse & Neglect, 28*, 771–784.

Driessen, M., Herrmann, J., Stahl, K., Zwaan, M., Meier, S., Hill, A., et al. (2000). Magnetic resonance imaging volumes of the hippocampus and the amygdala in women with borderline personality disorder and early traumatization. *Archives of General Psychiatry, 57*, 1115–1122.

Edwards, V. J., Holden, G. W., Anda, R. F., & Felitti, V. J. (2003). Experiencing multiple forms of childhood maltreatment and adult mental health: Results from the Adverse Childhood Experiences (ACE) study. *American Journal of Psychiatry, 160*, 1453–1460.

Ellison, J., Barsky, A., & Blum, N. R. (1989). Frequent repeaters to an emergency service. *Hospital & Community Psychiatry, 40*, 958–960.

Fiedler, E., Oltmanns, T., & Turkheimer, E. (2004). Traits associated with personality disorders and adjustment to military life: Predictive validity of self and peer reports. *Military Medicine, 169*, 32–40.

First, M. B., Spitzer, R. L., Gibbon, M., & Williams, J. B. W. (1997). *Structured clinical interview for DSM-IV personality disorders (SCID-II)*. Washington, DC: American Psychiatric Press.

Fonagy, P., Target, M., & Gergely, G. (2000). Attachment and borderline personality disorder. *Psychiatric Clinics of North America, 23*, 103–122.

Fonagy, P., Target, M., Gergely, G., Allen, J. G., & Bateman, A. (2003). The developmental roots of borderline personality disorder in early attachment relationships: A theory and some evidence. *Psychoanalytic Inquiry, 23*, 412–459.

Forman, E. M., Berk, M. S., Henriques, G. R., Brown, G. K., & Beck, A. T. (2004). History of multiple suicide attempts as a behavioral marker of severe psychopathology. *American Journal of Psychiatry, 161*, 437–443.

Fossati, A., Madeddu, F., & Maffei, C. (1999). Borderline personality disorder and childhood sexual abuse: A meta-analytic study. *Journal of Personality Disorders, 13*(3), 268–280.

Frank, H., & Paris, J. (1981). Recollections of family experience in borderline patients. *Archives of General Psychiatry, 38*, 1031–1034.

Fyer, M., Frances, A., Sullivan, T., Hurt, S., & Clarkin, J. (1988). Comorbidity of borderline personality disorder. *Archives of General Psychiatry, 45*, 348–352.

Giesen-Bloo, J., van Dyck, R., Spinhoven, P., van Tilburg, W., Dirksen, C., van Asselt, T., et al. (2006). Outpatient psychotherapy for borderline personality disorder: Randomized trial of schema-focused therapy vs. transference-focused psychotherapy. *Archives of General Psychiatry, 63*, 649–658.

Goldberg, R. L., Mann, L. S., Wise, T. N., & Segall, E. A. (1985). Parental qualities as perceived by borderline personality disorders. *Hillside Journal of Clinical Psychiatry, 7*, 134–140.

Goodman, M., & Yehuda, R. (2002). The relationship between psychological trauma and borderline personality disorder. *Psychiatric Annals, 32*(6), 337–345.

Grilo, C. M., Shea, M. T., Sanislow, C. A., Skodol, A. E., Gunderson, J. G., Stout, R. L., et al. (2004). Two-year stability and change of schizotypal, borderline, avoidant, and obsessive-compulsive personality disorders. *Journal of Consulting and Clinical Psychology, 72*(5), 767–775.

Grinker, R. R., Werble, B., & Drye, R. (1968). *The borderline syndrome: A behavioral study of ego functions*. New York: Basic Books.

Gross, R., Olfson, M., Gameroff, M., Shea, S., Feder, A., Fuentes, M., et al. (2002). Borderline personality disorder in primary care. *Archives of Internal Medicine, 162*, 53–60.

Gunderson, J. G. (2001). *Borderline personality disorder: A clinical guide*. Washington, DC: American Psychiatric Publishing.

Gunderson, J. G., Kerr, J., & Englund, D. W. (1980). The families of borderlines: A comparative study. *Archives of General Psychiatry, 37*, 27–33.

Gunderson, J. G., & Kolb, J. E. (1978). Discriminating features of borderline patients. *American Journal of Psychiatry, 135,* 792–796.

Gunderson, J. G., Kolb, J. E., & Austin, V. (1981). The diagnostic interview for borderline patients. *American Journal of Psychiatry, 138,* 896–903.

Gunderson, J. G., & Phillips, K. A. (1991). A current view of the interface between borderline personality disorder and depression. *American Journal of Psychiatry, 148*(8), 967–975.

Gunderson, J. G., & Sabo, A. N. (1993). "Borderline personality disorder and PTSD": Reply. *American Journal of Psychiatry, 150*(12), 1906–1907.

Gunderson, J. G., & Singer, M. T. (1975). Defining borderline patients: An overview. *American Journal of Psychiatry, 132,* 1–10.

Gunderson, J. G., Zanarini, M. C., & Kisiel, C. (1991). Borderline personality disorder: A review of data on DSM-III-R descriptions. *Journal of Personality Disorders, 5,* 340–352.

Gunderson, J. G., Zanarini, M. C., & Kisiel, C. (1995). Borderline personality disorder. In W. J. Livesley (Ed.), *The DSM-IV personality disorders* (pp. 141–157). New York: Guilford Press.

Heim, C., Meinlschmidt, G., & Nemeroff, C. B. (2003). Neurobiology of early-life stress. *Psychiatric Annals, 33,* 18–26.

Herman, J. L. (1992). Complex PTSD: A syndrome in survivors of prolonged and repeated trauma. *Journal of Traumatic Stress, 5,* 341–377.

Herman, J. L., Perry, J., & van der Kolk, B. A. (1989). Childhood trauma in borderline personality disorder. *American Journal of Psychiatry, 146*(4), 490–495.

Herpertz, S. C., Dietrich, T. M., Wenning, B., Krings, T., Erberich, S. G., Willmes, K., et al. (2001). Evidence of abnormal amygdala functioning in borderline personality disorder: A functional MRI study. *Biological Psychiatry, 50*(4), 292–298.

Isometsa, E. T., Henriksson, M. M., Heikkinen, M. E., Aro, H. M., Marttunen, M. J., Kuoppasalmi, K. I., et al. (1996). Suicide among subjects with personality disorders. *American Journal of Psychiatry, 153*(5), 667–673.

Johnson, J. G., Cohen, P., Brown, J., Smailes, E., & Bernstein, D. P. (1999). Childhood maltreatment increases risk for personality disorders during early adulthood. *Archives of General Psychiatry, 56*(7), 600–606.

Johnson, J. G., Cohen, P., Smailes, E., Skodol, A. E., Brown, J., & Oldham, J. M. (2001). Childhood verbal abuse and risk for personality disorders during adolescence and early adulthood. *Comprehensive Psychiatry, 42,* 16–23.

Judd, P. H., & McGlashan, T. (2003). *A developmental model of borderline personality disorder: Understanding variations in course and outcome.* Arlington, VA: American Psychiatric Publishing.

Kaplan, C. J. (1987). *Children's responses to the loss of a parent: The interaction between the family and the intrapsychic mourning process.* Unpublished manuscript, University of Massachusetts, Amherst.

Kernberg, O. (1967). Borderline personality organization. *Journal of the American Psychoanalytic Association, 15,* 641–685.

Kernberg, O. (1975). *Borderline conditions and pathological narcissism.* Northvale, NJ: Jason Aronson.

Klein, D. N. (2003). Patients' versus informants' reports of personality disorders in predicting 7½-year outcome in outpatients with depressive disorders. *Psychological Assessment, 15,* 216–222.

Klonsky, E. D., Oltmanns, T. F., & Turkheimer, E. (2002). Informant-reports of personality disorder: Relation to self-reports and future research directions. *Clinical Psychology: Science and Practice, 9,* 300–311.

Knight, R. P. (1953). Borderline states. *Bulletin of the Menninger Clinic, 17,* 1–12.

Knight, R. P. (1954). *Psychoanalytic psychiatry and psychology.* In clinical and theoretical papers from the Austen Riggs Center, Vol.1.

Kohut, H. (1977). *The restoration of the self.* Madison, CT: International Universities Press.

Koons, C. R., Robins, C. J., Tweed, J., Lynch, T. R., Gonzalez, A. M., Morse, J. Q., et al. (2001). Efficacy of dialectical behavior therapy in women veterans with borderline personality disorder. *Behavior Therapy, 32*(2), 371–390.

Lenzenweger, M. F., Clarkin, J. F., Fertuck, E. A., & Kernberg, O. F. (2004). Executive neurocognitive functioning and neurobehavioral systems indicators in borderline personality disorder: A preliminary study. *Journal of Personality Disorders, 18*(5), 421–438.

Lenzenweger, M. F., Johnson, M. D., & Willett, J. B. (2004). Individual growth curve analysis illuminates stability and change in personality disorder features: The longitudinal study of personality disorders. *Archives of General Psychiatry, 61*(10), 1015–1024.

Leyton, M., Okazawa, H., Diksic, M., Paris, J., Rosa, P., Mzengeza, S., et al. (2001). Brain regional alpha-[11C]methyl-L-tryptophan trapping in impulsive subjects with borderline personality disorder. *American Journal of Psychiatry, 158*(5), 775–782.

Linehan, M. M. (1993). *Skills-training manual for treatment of borderline personality disorder.* New York: Guilford Press.

Linehan, M. M., Armstrong, H. E., Suarez, A., Allmon, D., & Heard, H. L. (1991). Cognitive-behavioral treatment of chronically parasuicidal borderline patients. *Archives of General Psychiatry, 48,* 1060–1064.

Linehan, M. M., Heard, H. L., & Armstrong, H. E. (1993). Naturalistic follow-up of a behavioral treatment for chronically parasuicidal borderline patients. *Archives of General Psychiatry, 50,* 971–974.

Linehan, M. M., Tutek, D., Heard, H., & Armstrong, H. (1994). Interpersonal outcome of cognitive-behavioral treatment for chronically suicidal borderline patients. *American Journal of Psychiatry, 151*(12), 1771–1776.

Links, P. S., Steiner, M., Offord, D. R., & Eppel, A. B. (1988). Characteristics of borderline personality disorder: A Canadian study. *Canadian Journal of Psychiatry, 33,* 336–340.

Ludolph, P., Westen, D., Misle, B., Jackson, A., Wixom, J., & Weiss, F. C. (1990). The borderline diagnosis in adolescents: Symptoms and developmental history. *American Journal of Psychiatry, 147,* 470–476.

Lynam, D. R., & Widiger, T. A. (2001). Using the five-factor model to represent the DSM-IV personality disorders: An expert consensus approach. *Journal of Abnormal Psychology, 110*(3), 401–412.

Lyons-Ruth, K., & Jacobvitz, D. (1999). Attachment disorganization: Unresolved loss, relational violence, and lapses in behavioral and attentional strategies. In J. Cassidy & P. R. Shaver (Eds.), *Handbook of attachment: Theory, research and clinical applications* (pp. 550–554). New York: Guilford Press.

Main, M., Kaplan, N., & Cassidy, J. (1985). Security in infancy, childhood, and adulthood: A move to the level of representation. *Monographs of the Society for Research in Child Development, 50*(1–2), 66–104.

Mann, J. (1998). The role of in vivo neurotransmitter system imaging studies in understanding major depression. *Biological Psychiatry, 44*(11), 1077–1078.

McGlashan, T. H. (1986). The Chestnut Lodge follow-up study: III. Long-term outcome of borderline personalities. *Archives of General Psychiatry, 43,* 20–30.

McLean, L. M., & Gallop, R. (2003). Implications of childhood sexual abuse for adult borderline personality disorder and complex posttraumatic stress disorder. *American Journal of Psychiatry, 160,* 369–371.

Meehl, P. E. (1995). Bootstraps taxometrics: Solving the classification problem in psychopathology. *American Psychologist, 50*(4), 266–275.

Mellsop, G., Varghese, F., Joshua, S., & Hicks, A. (1982). The reliability and Axis II of DSM-III. *American Journal of Psychiatry, 139,* 1366–1367.

Nakash-Eisikovits, O., Dutra, L., & Westen, D. (2002). Relationship between attachment patterns and personality pathology in adolescents. *Journal of the American Academy of Child & Adolescent Psychiatry, 41,* 1111–1123.

Nigg, J. T., & Goldsmith, H. (1994). Genetics of personality disorders: Perspectives from personality and psychopathology research. *Psychological Bulletin, 115*(3), 346–380.

Nigg, J. T., Lohr, N. E., Westen, D., Gold, L. J., & Silk, K. R. (1992). Malevolent object representations in borderline personality disorder and major depression. *Journal of Abnormal Psychology, 101,* 61–67.

Ogata, S. N., Silk, K. R., Goodrich, S., Lohr, N. E., Westen, D., & Hill, E. M. (1990). Childhood sexual and physical abuse in adult patients with borderline personality disorder. *American Journal of Psychiatry, 147,* 1008–1013.

Oldham, J. M. (2001). Integrated treatment planning for borderline personality disorder. In J. Kay (Ed.), *Integrated treatment of psychiatric disorders* (Vol. 20, pp. 51–77). Washington, DC: American Psychiatric Publishing.

Oldham, J. M., Skodol, A. E., Kellman, H. D., Hyler, S., Rosnick, L., & Davies, M. (1992). Diagnosis of DSM-III-R personality disorders by two semistructured interviews: Patterns of comorbidity. *American Journal of Psychiatry, 149,* 213–220.

Oltmanns, T. F., Melley, A. H., & Turkheimer, E. (2002). Impaired social functioning and symptoms of personality disorders assessed by peer and self-report in a nonclinical population. *Journal of Personality Disorders, 16*(5), 437–452.

Paris, J. (1997). Childhood trauma as an etiological factor in the personality disorders. *Journal of Personality Disorders, 11*(1), 34–49.

Paris, J. (2003). *Personality disorders over time: Precursors, course, and outcome.* Washington, DC: American Psychiatric Publishing.

Paris, J., Nowlis, D., & Brown, R. (1988). Developmental factors in the outcome of borderline personality disorder. *Comprehensive Psychiatry, 29,* 147–150.

Paris, J., & Zweig-Frank, H. (2001). The 27-year follow-up of patients with borderline personality disorder. *Comprehensive Psychiatry, 42*(6), 482–487.

Pfohl, B., Blum, N., Zimmerman, M., & Stangl, D. (1989). *Structured interview for DSM-III-R personality—revised (SIDP-R).* Iowa City University of Iowa.

Pfohl, B., Coryell, W., Zimmerman, M., & Stangl, D. (1986). DSM-III personality disorders: Diagnostic overlap and internal consistency of the individual DSM-III criteria. *Comprehensive Psychiatry, 27,* 21–34.

Pilkonis, P. A., Heape, C. L., Proietti, J. M., Clark, S. W., McDavid, J. D., & Pitts, T. E. (1995). The reliability and validity of two structured diagnostic interviews for personality disorders. *Archives of General Psychiatry, 52,* 1025–1033.

Pilkonis, P. A., Heape, C. L., Ruddy, J., & Serrao, P. (1991). Validity in the diagnosis of personality disorders: The use of the LEAD standard. *Psychological Assessment, 31,* 46–54.

Plomin, R., Chipuer, H. M., & Loehlin, J. C. (1990). Behavioral genetics and personality. In L. A. Pervin (Ed.), *Handbook of personality: Theory and research* (pp. 225–243). New York: Guilford Press.

Reich, J., Boerstler, H., Yates, W., & Nduaguba, M. (1989). Utilization of medical resources in persons with DSM-III personality disorders in a community sample. *International Journal of Psychiatry in Medicine, 19*(1), 1–9.

Robins, C. J., & Chapman, A. L. (2004). Dialectical behavior therapy: Current status, recent developments, and future directions. *Journal of Personality Disorders, 18*(1), 73–89.

Rothschild, L., Cleland, C., Haslam, N., & Zimmerman, M. (2003). A taxometric study of borderline personality disorder. *Journal of Abnormal Psychology, 112*(4), 657–666.

Ryle, A. (2004). The contribution of cognitive analytic therapy to the treatment of borderline personality disorder. *Journal of Personality Disorders, 18,* 3–35.

Salzman, J. P., Salzman, C., & Wolfson, A. N. (1997). Relationship of childhood abuse and maternal attachment to the development of borderline personality disorder. In M. C. Zanarini (Ed.), *Role of sexual abuse in the etiology of borderline personality disorder* (pp. 71–91). Washington, DC: American Psychiatric Association.

Samuels, J., Eaton, W. W., Bienvenu, J., Clayton, P., Brown, H., Costa, P. T., Jr., et al. (2002). Prevalence and correlates of personality disorders in a community sample. *British Journal of Psychiatry 180,* 536–542.

Satorius, N., Kaelber, C., Cooper, J. E., Roper, M. T., Rae, D. S., Gulbinat, W., et al. (1993). Progress toward achieving a common language in psychiatry. *Archives of General Psychiatry, 50,* 115–124.

Scheel, K. R. (2000). The empirical basis of dialectical behavior therapy: Summary, critique, and implications. *Clinical Psychology: Science and Practice, 7*(1), 68–86.

Schmahl, C. G., Elzinga, B. M., Ebner, U. W., Simms, T., Sanislow, C., Vermetten, E., et al. (2004). Psychophysiological reactivity to traumatic and abandonment scripts in borderline personality and posttraumatic stress disorders: A preliminary report. *Psychiatry Research, 126*(1), 33–42.

Schmahl, C. G., Vermetten, E., Elzinga, B. M., & Bremner, J. (2003). Magnetic resonance imaging of hippocampal and amygdala volume in women with childhood abuse and borderline personality disorder. *Psychiatry Research: Neuroimaging, 122*(3), 193–198.

Shedler, J., & Westen, D. (2004). Dimensions of personality pathology: An alternative to the five-factor model. *American Journal of Psychiatry, 161,* 1743–1754.

Siever, L., & Davis, K. (1991). A psychobiological perspective on the personality disorders. *American Journal of Psychiatry, 148*(12), 1647–1658.

Silk, K. R., Lee, S., Hill, E. M., & Lohr, N. E. (1995). Borderline personality disorder symptoms and severity of sexual abuse. *American Journal of Psychiatry, 152,* 1059–1064.

Silk, K. R., Lohr, N. E., Ogata, S. N., & Westen, D. (1990). Borderline inpatients with affective disorder: Preliminary follow-up data. *Journal of Personality Disorders, 4*(2), 213–224.

Skodol, A. E., Gunderson, J. G., McGlashan, T. H., Dyck, I. R., Stout, R. L., Bender, D. S., et al. (2002). Functional impairment in patients with schizotypal, borderline, avoidant, or obsessive-compulsive personality disorder. *American Journal of Psychiatry, 159,* 276–283.

Skodol, A. E., Gunderson, J. G., Pfohl, B., Widiger, T. A., Livesley, W. J., & Siever, L. (2002). The borderline diagnosis: I. Psychopathology, comorbidity, and personality structures. *Biological Psychiatry, 51,* 936–950.

Skodol, A. E., Gunderson, J. G., Shea, M., McGlashan, T. H., Morey, L. C., Sanislow, C. A., et al. (2005). The Collaborative Longitudinal Personality Disorders Study (CLPS): Overview and implications. *Journal of Personality Disorders, 19*(5), 487–504.

Skodol, A. E., Oldham, J. M., Rosnick, L., Kellman, D., & Hyler, S. (1991). Diagnosis of DSM-III-R personality disorders: A comparison of two structured interviews. *International Journal of Methods in Psychiatric Research, 1,* 13–26.

Sokal, R. R. (1974). Classification: Purposes, principles, progress, prospects. *Science, 185*(4157), 1115–1123.

Soloff, P. H., Lynch, K. G., Kelly, T. M., Malone, K. M., & Mann, J. J. (2000). Characteristics of suicide attempts of patients with major depressive episode and borderline personality disorder: A comparative study. *American Journal of Psychiatry, 157,* 601–608.

Soloff, P. H., Meltzer, C. C., Greer, P. J., Constantine, D., & Kelly, T. M. (2000). A fenfluramine-activated FDG-PET study of borderline personality disorder. *Biological Psychiatry, 47*(6), 540–547.

Soloff, P. H., & Millward, J. W. (1983). Developmental histories of borderline patients. *Comprehensive Psychiatry, 24,* 574–588.

Solomon, J., George, C., & De Jong, A. (1995). Children classified as controlling at age six: Evidence of disorganized representational strategies and aggression at home and at school. *Development and Psychopathology, 7,* 447–463.

Spitzer, R. L., Endicott, J., & Gibbon, M. (1979). Crossing the border into borderline personality and borderline schizophrenia. *Archives of General Psychiatry, 36,* 17–24.

Stern, A. (1938). Psychoanalytic investigation and therapy in the borderline group of neuroses. *Psychoanalytic Quarterly,* 467–489.

Stone, M. H. (1987). Psychotherapy of borderline patients in light of long-term follow-up. *Bulletin of the Menninger Clinic, 51,* 231–247.

Stone, M. H. (1992). Borderline personality disorder: Course of illness. In J. F. Clarkin, E. Marziali, & H. Munroe-Blum (Eds.), *Borderline personality disorder: Clinical and empirical perspectives.* New York: Guilford Press.

Stone, M. H. (1993). Long-term outcome in personality disorders. *British Journal of Psychiatry, 162,* 299–313.

Stone, M. H. (1994). Characterologic subtypes of the borderline personality disorder: With a note on prognostic factors. *Psychiatric Clinics of North America, 17,* 773–784.

Stuart, S., Pfohl, B., Battaglia, M., Bellodi, L., Grove, W., & Cadoret, R. (1998). The co-occurrence of DSM-III-R personality disorders. *Journal of Personality Disorders, 12,* 302–315.

Thomas, C., Turkheimer, E., & Oltmanns, T. F. (2003). Factorial structure of pathological personality as evaluated by peers. *Journal of Abnormal Psychology, 112,* 81–91.

Torgersen, S. (1980). The oral, obsessive, and hysterical personality syndromes: A study of hereditary and environmental factors by means of the twin method. *Archives of General Psychiatry, 37*(11), 1272–1277.

Torgersen, S., Kringlen, E., & Cramer, V. (2001). The prevalence of personality disorders in a community sample. *Archives of General Psychiatry, 58,* 590–596.

Torgersen, S., Lygren, S., Oien, P. A., Skre, I., Onstad, S., Edvardsen, J., et al. (2000). A twin study of personality disorders. *Comprehensive Psychiatry, 41*(6), 416–425.

Trull, T. J. (2001). Structural relations between borderline personality disorder features and putative etiological correlates. *Journal of Abnormal Psychology, 110*(3), 471–481.

Trull, T. J., Widiger, T. A., Lynam, D. R., & Costa, P. T., Jr. (2003). Borderline personality disorder from the perspective of general personality functioning. *Journal of Abnormal Psychology 112*(2), 193–202.

Tyrer, P. J. (1996). Establishing the severity of personality disorder. *American Journal of Psychiatry, 153*(12), 1593–1597.

Verheul, R., van den Bosch, L. M. C., Koeter, M. W. J., De Ridder, M. A. J., Stinjnen, T., & van den Brink, W. (2003). Dialectical behaviour therapy for women with borderline personality disorder: 12-month, randomised clinical trial in the Netherlands. *British Journal of Psychiatry, 182,* 135–140.

Weaver, T. L., & Clum, G. A. (1993). Early family environments and traumatic experiences associated with borderline personality disorder. *Journal of Consulting and Clinical Psychology, 61*(6), 1068–1075.

Westen, D. (1991a). Cognitive-behavioral interventions in the psychoanalytic psychotherapy of borderline personality disorders. *Clinical Psychology Review, 11,* 211–230.

Westen, D. (1991b). Social cognition and object relations. *Psychological Bulletin, 109,* 429–455.

Westen, D. (1997). Divergences between clinical and research methods for assessing personality disorders: Implications for research and the evolution of Axis II. *American Journal of Psychiatry, 154,* 895–903.

Westen, D. (2000). Integrative psychotherapy: Integrating psychodynamic and cognitive-behavioral theory and technique. In C. R. Snyder & R. Ingram (Eds.), *Handbook of psychological change: Psychotherapy processes and practices for the 21st century* (pp. 217–242). New York: Wiley.

Westen, D., & Bradley, R. (2005). Prototype diagnosis of personality. In S. Strack (Ed.), *Handbook of personology and psychopathology* (pp. 238–256). New York: Wiley.

Westen, D., Bradley, R., & Shedler, J. (2005). Refining the borderline construct: Diagnostic criteria and trait structure. *Unpublished manuscript, Emory University, Atlanta, GA.*

Westen, D., Dutra, L., & Shedler, J. (2005). Assessing adolescent personality pathology: Quantifying clinical judgment. *British Journal of Psychiatry, 186,* 227–238.

Westen, D., Lohr, N., Silk, K. R., Gold, L., & Kerber, K. (1990). Object relations and social cognition in borderlines, major depressives, and normals: A thematic apperception test analysis. *Psychological Assessment, 2,* 355–364.

Westen, D., Ludolph, P., Block, M. J., Wixom, J., & Wiss, F. C. (1990). Developmental history and object relations in psychiatrically disturbed adolescent girls. *American Journal of Psychiatry, 147,* 1061–1068.

Westen, D., Ludolph, P., Misle, B., Ruffins, S., & Block, J. (1990). Physical and sexual abuse in adolescent girls with borderline personality disorder. *American Journal of Orthopsychiatry, 60,* 55–66.

Westen, D., & Muderrisoglu, S. (2003). Reliability and validity of personality disorder assessment using a systematic clinical interview: Evaluating an alternative to structured interviews. *Journal of Personality Disorders, 17,* 350–368.

Westen, D., & Muderrisoglu, S. (2006). Clinical assessment of pathological personality traits. *American Journal of Psychiatry, 163,* 1285–1287.

Westen, D., Muderrisoglu, S., Fowler, C., Shedler, J., & Koren, D. (1997). Affect regulation and affective experience: Individual differences, group differences, and measurement using a Q-sort procedure. *Journal of Consulting and Clinical Psychology, 65,* 429–439.

Westen, D., & Shedler, J. (1999a). Revising and assessing Axis II: 1. Developing a clinically and empirically valid assessment method. *American Journal of Psychiatry, 156,* 258–272.

Westen, D., & Shedler, J. (1999b). Revising and assessing Axis II: 2. Toward an empirically based and clinically useful classification of personality disorders. *American Journal of Psychiatry, 156,* 273–285.

Westen, D., & Shedler, J. (2000). A prototype matching approach to diagnosing personality disorders toward DSM-V. *Journal of Personality Disorders, 14,* 109–126.

Westen, D., Shedler, J., & Bradley, R. (2006). A prototype approach to personality diagnosis. *American Journal of Psychiatry, 163,* 838–848.

Westen, D., Shedler, J., Durrett, C., Glass, S., & Martens, A. (2003). Personality diagnosis in adolescence: DSM-IV Axis II diagnoses and an empirically derived alternative. *American Journal of Psychiatry, 160,* 952–966.

Westen, D., Thomas, C., Nakash, O., & Bradley, R. (2006). Clinical assessment of attachment patterns and personality disorder in adolescents and adults. *Journal of Consulting and Clinical Psychology, 74,* 1065–1085.

White, C. N., Gunderson, J. G., Zanarini, M. C., & Hudson, J. I. (2003). Family studies of borderline personality disorder: A review. *Harvard Review of Psychiatry, 11*(1), 8–19.

Widiger, T. A. (1995). Deletion of self-defeating and sadistic personality disorders. In W. J. Livesley (Ed.), *The DSM-IV personality disorders: Diagnosis and treatment of mental disorders* (pp. 359–373). New York: Guilford Press.

Yen, S., Shea, M. T., Battle, C. L., Johnson, D. M., Zlotnick, C., Dolan-Sewell, R., et al. (2002). Traumatic exposure and posttraumatic stress disorder in borderline, schizotypal, avoidant, and obsessive-compulsive personality disorders: Findings from the collaborative longitudinal personality disorders study. *Journal of Nervous and Mental Disease, 190,* 510–518.

Yeomans, F. E. (2004). Transference-focused psychotherapy in borderline personality disorder. *Psychiatric Annals, 34,* 449–454.

Young, J. E., Klosko, J. S., & Weishaar, M. (2003). *Schema therapy: A practitioner's guide.* New York: Guilford Press.

Zanarini, M. C. (1997). *Role of sexual abuse in the etiology of borderline personality disorder.* Washington, DC: American Psychiatric Publishing.

Zanarini, M. C., & Frankenburg, F. R. (1997). Pathways to the development of borderline personality disorder. *Journal of Personality Disorders, 11*(1), 93–104.

Zanarini, M. C., Frankenburg, F. R., DeLuca, C. J., Hennen, J., Khera, G. S., & Gunderson, J. G. (1998). The pain of being borderline: Dysphoric states specific to borderline personality disorder. *Harvard Review of Psychiatry, 6,* 201–207.

Zanarini, M. C., Frankenburg, F. R., Hennen, J., & Silk, K. R. (2003). The longitudinal course of borderline psychopathology: 6-year prospective follow-up of the phenomenology of borderline personality disorder. *American Journal of Psychiatry, 160*(2), 274–283.

Zanarini, M. C., Frankenburg, F. R., Hennen, J., & Silk, K. R. (2004). Mental health service utilization by borderline personality disorder patients and Axis II comparison subjects followed prospectively for 6 years. *Journal of Clinical Psychiatry, 65*(1), 28–36.

Zanarini, M. C., Frankenburg, F. R., Vujanovic, A. A., Hennen, J., Reich, D. B., & Silk, K. R. (2004). Axis II comorbidity of borderline personality disorder: Description of 6-year course and prediction to time-to-remission. *Acta Psychiatrica Scandinavica, 110*(6), 416–420.

Zanarini, M. C., Frankenburg, F. R., Yong, L., Raviola, G., Reich, D. B., Hennen, J., et al. (2004). Borderline psychopathology in the first-degree relatives of borderline and Axis II comparison probands. *Journal of Personality Disorders, 18,* 449–447.

Zanarini, M. C., Gunderson, J. G., Marino, M. F., Schwartz, E. O., & Frankenburg, F. R. (1989). Childhood experiences of borderline patients. *Comprehensive Psychiatry, 30,* 18–25.

Zanarini, M. C., Yong, L., Frankenburg, F. R., Hennen, J., Reich, D., Marino, M. F., et al. (2002). Severity of reported childhood sexual abuse and its relationship to severity of borderline psychopathology and psychosocial impairment among borderline inpatients. *Journal of Nervous and Mental Disease, 190*(6), 381–387.

Zelkowitz, P., Paris, J., Guzder, J., & Feldman, R. (2001). Diathesis and stressors in borderline pathology of childhood: The role of neuropsychological risk and trauma. *Journal of the American Academy of Child & Adolescent Psychiatry, 40*(1), 100–105.

Zimmerman, M., & Mattia, J. I. (1999). Axis I diagnostic comorbidity and borderline personality disorder. *Comprehensive Psychiatry, 40*(4), 245–252.

Zittel, C., & Westen, D. (1998). Conceptual issues and research findings on borderline personality disorder: What every clinician should know. *In Session, 4,* 5–20.

Zittel, C., & Westen, D. (2002). *Subtyping borderline personality disorder.* Presentation given at New Directions in Borderline Personality Disorder II, a conference jointly sponsored by the National Institutes of Mental Health and the Borderline Personality Disorder Research Foundation, New York.

8

Histrionic Personality Disorder

Pavel S. Blagov

Emory University

Katherine A. Fowler

Emory University

Scott O. Lilienfeld

Emory University

Histrionic personality disorder (HPD) is familiar to clinicians who attend to personality pathology and to literature devotees who ponder the nature of superficially dramatic, manipulative, and insatiably attention-seeking characters such as Blanche DuBois in Tennessee Williams's play *A Streetcar Named Desire*. Millon, Grossman, Millon, Meagher, and Ramnath (2004) provided the following description of HPD across nine clinical domains: behavioral acts are dramatic, interpersonal conduct is attention seeking, cognitive style is flighty, self-image is gregarious, representations of others are shallow, regulatory mechanisms rely on dissociation, the psychic structure is disjointed, and the mood and temperament are fickle. Despite its familiar feel, HPD remains enshrouded in a degree of historical confusion and conceptual uncertainty that researchers have not yet resolved. In this chapter, we track some of the theoretical and empirical efforts in clarifying the nature of HPD, summarize the available literature on treatment recommendations for the disorder, and propose directions for future research.

Current Definition

The current edition of the *Diagnostic and Statistical Manual of Mental Disorders* (DSM-IV-TR; American Psychiatric Association [APA], 2000) defines HPD primarily as a pervasive pattern of excessive emotionality and attention seeking that begins in early adulthood and presents across situations. Individuals may receive the diagnosis (code 301.50) if they meet five or more of eight criteria (APA, 2000, p. 714):

(1) is uncomfortable in situations in which he or she is not the center of attention

(2) interaction with others is often characterized by inappropriate sexually seductive or provocative behavior

(3) displays rapidly shifting and shallow expression of emotions

(4) consistently uses physical appearance to draw attention to self

(5) has a style of speech that is excessively impressionistic and lacking in detail

(6) shows self-dramatization, theatricality, and exaggerated expression of emotion

(7) is suggestible, i.e., easily influenced by others or circumstances

(8) considers relationships to be more intimate than they actually are

Thus a person with HPD may behave theatrically, dress provocatively, make up stories, engage in flattery and flirtation, complain of dramatic ills, throw a tantrum, or make a suicidal gesture all to draw attention to the self. The individual may fail to focus attention on the self, in which case the associated features of manipulativeness, inappropriate seductiveness, and dependency may become apparent. These features, along with a cognitive/emotional style characterized by shallow investment, excitement seeking, and shifting interests may thwart the person's relationships, thus depriving him or her from much-sought attention and leading to distress and depression. The DSM-IV estimates a 2% to 3% prevalence in the general population and a 10% to 15% prevalence in mental health settings (see Blashfield & Davis, 1993, for a higher estimate of 24%). HPD prevalence appears to be equal in men and women (Nestadt, Romanoski, Chalel, & Marchant, 1990) in nonclinical settings, even though in clinical ones more women received the diagnosis than did men. Means of attention seeking and dramatic expressiveness may vary across culture, gender, and age. Because of its hypothesized pervasive nature and resistance to change, the disorder is coded on Axis II (Cluster B).

Historical Roots

Hysteria

HPD shares a divergent history with the Axis I somatoform conditions called conversion disorder (a sensory or motor deficit due to psychological causes that mimics a neurological disorder, code 300.11) and somatization disorder (recurring and clinically significant somatic complaints other than pain not fully explained by a general medical condition, code 300.81). Historically, they are all linked to the ancient concept of *hysteria*, or "wandering womb." Such authors as Hippocrates and Plato attributed conversion symptoms and emotional outbursts in women to a displaced uterus caused by sexual discontent, reflecting Greek society's derogatory view of women as irrational creatures of lust. Similarly, Christian asceticism during the Middle Ages and the Reformation blamed women's mental illness on involvement in witchery due to sexual hunger and moral weakness in resisting Satanic temptation. During the Enlightenment and through the 19th century, medicine struggled to divorce itself from theological doctrines of possession. Explanations of hysteria shifted to a constitutional weakness of women's nervous system caused by their biological sex. Thus, whether physical or spiritual, and despite the fact that hysteria was diagnosed with increasing frequency in men, the construct tended to reflect the predominant sociocultural stereotype of women as inherently vulnerable, inferior, and emotionally uncontrolled. The extent to which the current criteria for HPD reflect gender bias remains the subject of a controversy today (see below).

Conversion Hysteria and Hysterical Personality

The term *hysteria* has been used to denote a variety of conditions ranging from extreme reactions to stress to isolated conversion symptoms, somatization, immaturity, a personality disorder (PD), or a personality trait (Easser & Lesser, 1965; Lazare, 1971; Pfohl, 1991). The differentiation between conversion hysteria and hysterical personality began with psychoanalytic literature on character as well as with the writings of Kraepelin, Schneider, and Kretschmer (see Bornstein, 1999). Freud's famed case work in this area (e.g., Freud & Breuer, 1895/2000) dealt primarily with conversion hysteria (e.g., the neurologically inexplicable loss of sensation in part of the body), which he explained as a neurotic compromise among sexual urges and internalized societal prohibitions. Psychoanalytic authors sought the origins of hysteria in the psychosexual development of the child (e.g., Abraham, 1927/1948; Fenichel, 1945; Marmor, 1953) and speculated about the importance of character (or personality) to the formation of symptoms. Reich (1933, 1949) drew attention to hysteria as a set of personality characteristics and differentiated conversion hysteria as a transient functional disorder from hysterical character (see Baumbacher & Amini, 1980–1981; Shapiro, 1965). The early analytic conceptualizations of both kinds of hysteria carried notions of women's deficiency due to penis envy and feelings of castration. In this way, they paralleled the antiwoman sentiment seen throughout the history of hysteria (Chodoff, 1982). Current psychoanalytic thought regarding histrionic personality has evolved considerably, and will be discussed in the section on psychotherapy.

The concept of hysterical personality was well developed by the middle of the 20th century (Alam & Merskey, 1992) and strongly resembled the current definition of HPD. DSM-I (APA, 1952) featured a symptom-based (neurotic) category, "hysteria" (conversion), and a personality-based category, "emotionally unstable personality." DSM-II (APA, 1968) distinguished between hysterical neurosis (conversion reaction and dissociative reaction) and hysterical (parenthetically, histrionic) personality. DSM-I and DSM-II received much criticism for their poor psychometric properties (Nathan, 1998). Nevertheless, they contributed to clarifying the distinction between conversion symptoms and hysterical personality, a concept that later found support in early empirical studies (e.g., Luisada, Peele, & Pittard, 1974).

Somatization and Briquet's Syndrome

Hysterical personality underwent further differentiation as findings emerged that, despite some overlap between hysterical personality and somatization, the two were not the same (Pollak, 1981). For example, in a survey of 91 psychiatric residents and faculty, Slavney (1978) found that all considered self-dramatization, followed by attention seeking, emotional instability, and seductiveness, to be the most diagnostically important and reliably recognized features of hysterical personality. These participants ranked conversion symptoms among the least important and reliable symptoms. The notion that hysterical personality features covaried with somatization symptoms persisted for some time in the diagnostic entity of Briquet's syndrome. Difficulties in distinguishing patients with isolated somatization features from patients with the more severe and pervasive Briquet's syndrome (e.g., Cloninger, Martin, Guze, & Clayton, 1986; Liskow, Clayton, Woodruff, Guze, & Cloninger, 1977) contributed to abandonment of the notions of hysteria and Briquet's syndrome and to the emergence of somatization disorder in DSM-III (APA, 1980).

HPD may not be as strongly associated with somatization disorder (SD) as might be expected from their shared historical roots. Estimates of HPD prevalence in individuals with SD have varied from 7.4% to 81.8% across samples (Rost, Akins, Brown, & Smith, 1992). The heterogeneity in these estimates is probably attributable to differences in both criteria used to operationalize SD and the characteristics of each sample. Using a structured interview (the Structured Clinical Interview for DSM-III-R Personality Disorders [SCID-II; Spitzer, Williams, & Gibbon, 1987]) with 94 patients with SD recruited from primary practices in Arkansas, Rost and her colleagues found prevalence rates of 12.8% for full-criteria HPD and 10.6% for subthreshold HPD (compared with an HPD prevalence of less than 5% in the general medical population). However, 61% of the patients had a co-occurring PD, the most prevalent PDs being avoidant, paranoid, self-defeating, and obsessive-compulsive. The authors speculated that these latter disorders may predispose patients to SD due to an overall discomfort with feelings, inability to view oneself as deserving of good health, or concerns over becoming sick. These PDs may go undocumented in patients with SD because they often do not prompt clinicians in general medical settings to consider a consultation with a mental health professional. On the other hand, patients with histrionic, antisocial, and borderline PDs, due to their interpersonally disruptive outbursts, are more likely to be referred for a psychiatric evaluation, and hence these disorders' co-occurrence with SD relative to that of other PDs may have been overestimated in older studies.

Histrionic Personality in DSM-III and DSM-III-R

In DSM-III (APA, 1980), the term "hysterical personality" was changed to "histrionic personality" to emphasize the histrionic (derived from the Latin word *histrio*, or actor) behavior pattern and to reduce the confusion caused by the historical links of the term hysteria to conversion symptoms (Chodoff, 1974; Spitzer, Williams, & Skodol, 1980). Some DSM-III criteria dropped out of the DSM-III-R (APA, 1987; i.e., craving for activity and excitement; irrational, angry outbursts or tantrums; and proneness to manipulative suicidal attempts) as a way of reducing the diagnostic overlap with other conditions, particularly borderline PD. Criteria 2 (inappropriate seductiveness) and 8 (impressionistic speech) in the DSM-III-R, in contrast, had been absent in the DSM-III and represent a return to the historical roots of the disorder.

Livesley and Schroeder (1991) examined the factorial structure of dimensional self-report ratings of PD symptoms in a sample of 274 heterogeneous volunteers and 133 patients with a primary diagnosis of PD and no major DSM-III-R Axis I diagnosis. Participants rated themselves on a five-point scale along symptoms of antisocial, borderline, histrionic, and narcissistic PDs as defined by the consensual judgment of a sample of psychiatrists familiar with the literature. The solution for HPD yielded four factors, two that appeared to overlap with other disorders (an exploitativeness factor similar to one seen in BPD, and a dependency factor similar to the DSM-III-R construct of dependent PD) and two that appeared specific to HPD: one representing the hysterical cognitive style and one related to dramatization.

According to Pfohl (1991), all criteria but 1 (constant demands for reassurance and praise) and 7 (self-centeredness and low frustration tolerance) for HPD in the DSM-III-R had good sensitivity coefficients and contributed to the overall internal consistency of the diagnosis.

External Validity of HPD

Pollak (1981) and Pfohl (1991) summarized research findings on HPD and concluded that sufficient evidence had accrued for the disorder's external validity. One concern, however, is that many of the older findings may be based on operationalizations of HPD that are not fully consistent with the current definition. Furthermore, many of the findings have not been sufficiently replicated. Unlike other PDs such as antisocial and borderline, we know little about the relation of HPD, particularly in the general population, to some of the most theoretically and clinically relevant external criteria. For example, we know little about its links to relationship satisfaction and stability, employment history, general health, and life satisfaction. Below we summarize some of the more recent findings that modestly build upon the reviews by Pollak (1981) and Pfohl (1991).

Projective Testing and Defense Style

Blais, Hilsenroth, and Fowler (1998) correlated DSM-IV symptom counts for HPD, as well as borderline, antisocial, and narcissistic PDs, with Rorschach variables in an archival study of 79 records of PD patients. Consistent with previous literature, only HPD symptoms correlated with the $FC + CF + C$ and T indices from the Exner system ($r_s = .35$ and $.30$, $p < .01$) with controlling for the number of responses (F denotes "form" responses, C denotes "color" responses, and T denotes "texture" responses). The $FC + CF + C$ variable measures the number of responses based primarily on color features of the blots and has been hypothesized to reflect emotionality, whereas T reflects the use of texture by the respondent and may be indicative of loneliness and interpersonal neediness. $FC + CF + C$ tended to correlate with ratings of the DSM-IV symptoms of seductiveness, shallow emotion, impressionistic speech, and focus on appearance, whereas T was linked to attention seeking, self-dramatization, misconstruing of the intimacy of relationships, and impressionistic speech. In addition, the attention seeking symptoms and scale 3 (Hysteria) of the Minnesota Multiphasic Personality Inventory–2 (MMPI-2) were linked to Lerner's denial (DEN) index for the Rorschach.

In Cramer's (1999) study of 91 adults of age 23 (45 men and 46 women), ratings of denial and projection based on the Thematic Apperception Test (TAT) correlated with the extent to which participants' California Q-Set profiles matched expert prototypes of borderline, psychopathic, narcissistic, and histrionic pathology. When defenses were coded as mature versus immature, immature denial and identification predicted histrionic features, with immature identification predicting histrionic pathology but not features of the other three disorders. The findings contradicted the proposition that histrionic features would be linked to maturity more so than would those of other PDs. Instead, like other kinds of personality dysfunction, histrionic personality exhibited a continuum of severity such that the more histrionic the person, the more immature his or her defense style. The nonclinical nature of the sample limits further interpretation. Nevertheless, it should be noted that the evidence linking C responses to emotionality is at best equivocal (Frank, 1990).

Neurocognitive Findings

The literature on neurocognitive and other biological markers of HPD is limited. Shapiro (1965) proposed that a global cognitive-perceptual style predisposes people to a hysterical personality, and Millon (1981) suggested that hysterical individuals lack cognitive-perceptual integration. Tests of derivative hypotheses have generally not found links between measures of histrionicity and perceptual variables (see Cale & Lilienfeld, 2002; Maynard & Meyer, 1996; Yovel, Revelle, & Mineka, 2005). In comparison with people with obsessive-compulsive tendencies, participants with histrionic personalities appear to be less rigid in their cognitive style but not necessarily inattentive to detail or distractible (Sacco & Olczak, 1996).

Biological Findings

Svanborg, Evenden-Matilla, Gustavsson, Uvnas-Moberg, and Asberg (2000) recruited 99 participants who were either beginning or undergoing nonpharmacological treatment for mood ($n = 37$) or anxiety ($n = 29$) disorders. The participants completed personality self-report questionnaires and a modified SCID-II screening questionnaire (Ekselius, Lindstrom, von Knorring, Bodlund, & Kullgren, 1994; Spitzer et al., 1987). There were no significant associations between symptom and personality measures and plasma levels of insulin or glucagon. Low fasting plasma glucose levels were associated with low Global Assessment of Functioning (GAF) scores, high scores on an impulsivity questionnaire, and a high number of self-assessed histrionic and narcissistic traits in men. In women, the relationship between glucose level and histrionic traits was also significant but positive. In light of previous research linking diminished glucose levels to cognitive impairment (Taylor & Rachman, 1988), social-emotional distress (Messer, Morris, & Gross, 1990), and antisocial behavior (Virkkunen, 1986), Svanborg and his colleagues (2000) suggested that the relationship between histrionicity and low glucose in men may indicate that the traits are maladaptive for men. The reverse relationship in women may suggest that for them such traits are linked to better adaptation. The conclusions remain speculative and call for attempts to replicate these studies.

Discriminant Validity, Co-occurrence, and Comorbidity

When a PD such as HPD is diagnosed with other DSM disorders in the same individuals, it may be difficult to judge whether the issue at stake is poor discriminant validity of the diagnostic criteria (e.g., diagnostic overlap), true comorbidity, or co-occurrence (Lilienfeld, Waldman, & Israel, 1994). This is especially true of HPD, due to the limited amount of research literature and variability and inconsistency in the use of assessment methods and diagnostic criteria.

Borderline and Narcissistic Personality Disorders

In the 1980s, researchers observed substantial overlap between borderline PD and other PDs (e.g., Widiger & Rogers, 1989). In a review of studies conducted from 1983 to 1990, Grueneich (1992) found that HPD was the PD most frequently associated with borderline personality disorder (BPD), with a median reliability of .44 for four studies using DSM-III criteria. Grueneich noted that the association between HPD and BPD appeared to be lower in studies using DSM-III-R criteria, probably due to the removal of two overlapping items: angry outbursts and manipulative suicidal gestures. In studies of emotional regulation and identity disturbance, Westen (see Westen & Heim, 2003; Wilkinson-Ryan & Westen, 2000) reported a subtype of BPD with salient histrionic features. Thus, the links between HPD and BPD are likely to be revisited in the future. Criterion discrimination between HPD and narcissistic personality disorder (NPD) is still poor in the DSM-IV (Blais & Norman, 1997).

Dependent Personality Disorder (DPD)

The notion that dependency characterizes HPD disappeared from the DSM under pressure to improve discriminant validity and to reduce the overlap between HPD and DPD. Nevertheless, the psychodynamic notion that underlying dependency motivates attention seeking in HPD has not been ruled out. In a sample of 491 psychology students, Bornstein (1998) found that those who met criteria for HPD and DPD on the Personality Diagnostic Questionnaire—Revised (PDQ-R; Hyler, Skodol, Kellman, Oldham, & Rosnick, 1990) had comparable scores on an implicit dependency index derived from the Rorschach. Furthermore, students with HPD and DPD scored higher on this measure than did students with other PDs or no PDs. The dependency scores on a self-report inventory did not differ among students with HPD, students with other PDs, and students with no PDs, whereas students with DPD scored higher than the other three groups on this explicit measure.

Bipolar Disorder

Even though a small body of literature reveals overlap between HPD and mania, the finding is limited to structured interviews that rely heavily on retrospective self-report (Strakowski, McElroy, Keck, & West, 1994) and may reflect method bias. Histrionic personality and hypomanic states may share impulsivity and extraversion. Indeed, Schotte, De Doncker, Maes, Cluydts, and Cosyns (1993) observed that high scores on scale 9 (*Ma*) and low scores on scale 0 (*Si*) of the MMPI were most indicative of DSM-III-R HPD in an inpatient Dutch sample (assessed using the SCID-II). Furthermore, the ability of scales 9 and 0 as well as Morey's HST Scale (Morey, Waugh, & Blashfield, 1985) to predict HPD could be derived from their assessment of introversion-extraversion. In addition, bipolar spectrum disorders and HPD share features of mood lability and emotional dysregulation, as Perugi et al. (1998) observed in a study of atypical depression. Within their sample of individuals with mood disorder and comorbid DSM-IV HPD, none met criteria for unipolar depression, whereas most met some criteria for bipolar II or cyclothymic disorder. Similarly, Westen and Shedler's (1999) empirical prototype for HPD contains items describing emotional dysregulation (i.e., "unable to soothe or comfort self when distressed," "emotions tend to spiral out of control," "emotions tend to change rapidly and unpredictably," and "tends to become irrational when strong emotions are stirred up"). The possibility that HPD and mania share an underlying cause or that HPD may predispose individuals to bipolar disorder requires further study.

Depression and Anxiety

HPD has been thought to make sufferers vulnerable to depression, anxiety, and parasuicidality due to its interference with obtainment of the relationships and attention such individuals so strongly desire. In a study of the relationship between PD symptomatology and Axis I disorders in an ethnically heterogeneous community sample of adolescent girls (Daley et al., 1999), 20.31% of the patients, (n = 63) met cutoffs for HPD on the Personality Diagnostic Questionnaire (PDQ; Hyler, Reider, Spitzer, & Williams, 1982) for DSM-III or the PDQ-R (Hyler et al., 1990) for DSM-III-R. Overall PD scores predicted concurrent depression scores as well as depression scores at follow-up 2 years later. Cluster B PD symptoms added to predictive power. HPD's relative contribution was unclear, but HPD was deemed present in 59% of the patients with a Cluster B disorder, who, in turn, comprised 34.38% of the sample. Thus, HPD may have been a factor in the development of depression (see also Crawford, Cohen, & Brook, 2001b) in light of the fact that the DSM-III and DSM-III-R criteria for HPD overlapped with those for BPD, which may be a better predictor of future Axis I symptoms than HPD. Using the SCID for the DSM-III-R, Ampollini and his colleagues (1999) selected 42 outpatients with panic disorder, 18 with major depression, 29 with both, and 48 healthy controls. Evaluations with the revised version of the Structured Interview for DSM-III-R Personality Disorders (SIDP-R; Pfohl, Blum, Zimmerman, & Stangl, 1989) by clinicians blind to Axis I diagnosis revealed that patients with panic disorder and patients with both panic disorder and major depression had significantly higher rates of HPD compared to controls or to patients with major depression alone. These and other studies support the notion that HPD may be comorbid with depressive and anxiety disorders.

Etiology

Little is known about the etiology of HPD. The clinically intuitive belief that HPD may develop in children whose strong needs for attention were met inconsistently by their parents is prevalent (Kraus & Reynolds, 2001), but it has not received rigorous tests. Coid (1999) examined the histories of 260 adults in forensic settings for specific risk factors related to DSM-III Axis II pathology and was unable to establish associations between HPD and developmental adversity or temperamental factors. Below we summarize some of the positive findings.

Genetics

Research on genetic contributions specific to HPD is insufficient. According to Maier, Franke, and Hawellek (1998), evidence for genetic contributions to personality pathology has accrued overall, but the findings vary across different disorders. Cluster B disorders, in particular, have not emerged as highly heritable. Research on the genetics of neurochemical mechanisms governing the dopaminergic and serotonergic systems of the brain has sparked interest, but it requires further study and replication. Torgersen and his colleagues (2000) interviewed 221 adult twin pairs (92 monozygotic [MZ] and 129 dizygotic [DZ]) about their lifetime histories of mental disorders. Using data collected with the SCID-II (Spitzer et al., 1987), they compared the prevalence of HPD among MZ and DZ probands and their co-twins. HPD yielded a substantial heritability coefficient of .67 in an AE model (which includes additive genetic factors and excludes shared environment) and a .52 effect for shared environment in a CE model (which includes shared environment and excludes genetic factors). Thus even though the study's authors emphasized the genetic factors, their findings suggest that both genetic and environmental factors are influential in the development of HPD. The study was limited by the primarily Norwegian sample and the fact that MZ status may be confounded in the classic behavior genetics model (e.g., by evocative genotype-environment correlations). For example, the higher concordance of HPD in MZ twins may be due to their more similar treatment by adults and peers in childhood and adolescence based on their similar appearance.

Developmental Considerations

Clinicians have long theorized about the contribution of developmental events and family environment to the development of HPD, but the links remain speculative. In this section we review four studies that point to possible developmental trajectories and developmental contributors to HPD.

Cohen and his colleagues (1994) compared 473 persons 55 years old or younger to 289 older individuals in a community sample, and they found that the two cohorts differed significantly on the prevalence of two DSM-III PDs: antisocial and histrionic. HPD prevalence was 4.3% in the younger and 2.2% in the older sample, consistent with the common view that PDs are observed less frequently in older populations because of either lesser prevalence or lesser severity. Possible explanations include cohort effects, age bias in diagnostic criteria, early mortality due to risky or impulsive behavior or suicide, social-emotional development due to learning, cortical maturation, and age-related neurochemical changes leading to decreased impulsivity or emotionality.

Baker, Capron, and Azorlosa (1996) screened undergraduates to find women who scored high on only the histrionic or the dependent scale of the Millon Clinical Multiaxial Inventory (MCMI; Millon, 1982) and also met DSM-III-R criteria for HPD or DPD but no other PD (as assessed by the SCID-II). Thus, 15 young women with "clean" HPD, 15 with DPD, and 15 controls completed a Family Environment Scale with 10 dimensions. The groups were similar on family cohesion, expansiveness, conflict, active-recreational orientation, moral-religious emphasis, and organization. The HPD group was higher than the DPD group and similar to controls on independence and achievement orientation. Participants with HPD rated the intellectual-cultural orientation of their families higher than did those with DPD or the controls. Both women with HPD and those with DPD rated their families higher in control than did controls. The study may be limited by the nonclinical nature of the sample and by the retrospective nature of the measures. In particular, people with HPD may recollect their family environments in ways consistent with their personality traits or interpersonal goals.

Crawford, Cohen, and Brook (2001a) assessed a large mixed-gender sample before age 10 and at ages 13, 15, and 20 using symptom scales for HPD, NPD, and BPD derived from items on the PDQ (Hyler et al., 1982), SCID-II (Spitzer et al., 1987), and other instruments. Overall, Cluster B pathology proved stable over time, yielding stability estimates of .63 in boys and .69 in girls over 8 years old. Specific disorder categories were less stable, with the likelihood of receiving a histrionic or narcissistic diagnosis declining between ages 13 and 18. Overall, Cluster B symptoms were strongly linked to internalizing symptoms in girls and to externalizing symptoms in both boys and girls, but the authors did not provide a breakdown of specific PDs. Subsequent analyses of the same data (Crawford et al., 2001b) indicated that in girls, internalizing symptoms at ages 10 to 14 predicted Cluster B symptoms in midadolescence, whereas externalizing symptoms at ages 12 to 17 predicted Cluster B pathology in young adulthood.

Cultural Factors

DSM-IV-TR cautions that cultural factors may affect specific manifestations of HPD symptoms, but it has been criticized for its lack of specificity regarding the nature of such factors and their specific impact on the diagnosis of most PDs and HPD in particular (Alarcon, 1996). For example, several authors hypothesize that HPD may be diagnosed less frequently in Asian and other cultures that discourage overt sexualization and more frequently in Hispanic and Latin American cultures that sanction overt sexuality (Johnson, 1993; Padilla, 1995; Trull & Widiger, 2003). However, there has been no systematic study of cultural differences in the presentation of HPD or of cultural factors in its etiology. Such factors have been examined in relation to the other two descendants of hysteria (conversion and somatization). In a transcultural psychiatric study of "hysterical structure" with a sample of 30 African and 30 Belgian patients matched for age, sex, and socioeconomic status, Pierloot and Ngoma (1988) found that the African patients tended to experience somatic symptoms resembling organic ones (e.g., headaches), while the Belgian patients were more likely to experience psychic symptoms (e.g., apathy). Additionally, while African patients were more likely to attribute their problems to supernatural forces, Belgian patients were more likely to cite internal causes. While this study examined differences in cultural manifestations of "hysterical structure" (a construct comprising mixed features of HPD and somatization disorder), its findings can be considered a preliminary indication that further examination of cultural differences in HPD is needed.

Conceptual and Diagnostic Issues

Seductiveness and Sexualization

DSM-II described the hysterical or histrionic personality as "often seductive" for the purpose of self-dramatization (with or without awareness), whereas DSM-III omitted the seductiveness criterion due to critiques citing gender bias. Seductiveness reappeared in DSM-III-R and DSM-IV, phrased as an objective criterion with an emphasis on sexualized and seductive behavior under inappropriate circumstances. Such items as "tends to be overly sexually seductive or provocative, whether consciously or unconsciously," "fantasizes about finding ideal, perfect love," and "tends to choose sexual or romantic partners who seem inappropriate" were highly descriptive of the HPD prototype derived empirically by Westen and Shedler (1999).

Despite its centrality to the description of the disorder, the nature of seductiveness in HPD has received little rigorous empirical attention. Psychoanalytic writers observed that the coquetry of people with hysterical personalities easily turns into disparagement (e.g., Reich, 1949). These authors suggested that hysterical individuals may deal with their anxiety surrounding close relationships by "acting it out" in the form of pseudohypersexuality (Fenichel, 1945) while avoiding true intimacy and remaining sexually unsatisfied. Modern psychodynamic thinkers similarly view sexualization as a counterphobic defense (McWilliams, 1994). This hypothesis has not received rigorous empirical tests and seems difficult to falsify, as doing so would require the development of a valid measure of sexual avoidance.

Comparing 33 women with HPD with 33 randomly selected women with similar demographics (all participants were drawn from a marital therapy program), Apt and Hurlbert (1994) found meaningful differences on self-report measures of sexual attitudes. Women with HPD reported greater sexual self-esteem, but also greater levels of sexual boredom, erotophobia, orgasmic dysfunction, lower sexual desire, and more frequent extramarital affairs. Apt and Hurlbert proposed that "sexual narcissism" characterizes patients with HPD, whose preoccupation with receiving attention and being attractive leads them to believe that they are also great lovers. Because they engage in sexuality as a means of ego gratification but do not experience intimacy or reciprocate, their sexual experiences are unsatisfying.

In hierarchical cluster analyses by Turner (1994), seductiveness loaded with self-centeredness and excessive concern with attractiveness, lending support to the notion of sexuality serving a narcissistic function. Excessive need for attention, however, loaded on a separate cluster. Finally, Reise and Wright (1996) did not find a relationship between histrionic features on the California Q-Set and uncommitted sexual relations in 195 undergraduates, although the tendency toward uncommitted sex correlated significantly with narcissism and psychopathy prototypes in men. Together, these findings suggest that sexualization in HPD may be a facet of self-centeredness or a means of regulating self-esteem.

Histrionic Personality and Gender

The extent to which gender influences or biases the diagnosis of HPD remains debated. Bias may influence clinical decisions more easily when clinicians make global decisions without considering individual diagnostic criteria separately. Ford and Widiger (1989) obtained 381 psychologists' ratings (24% women) of a case history of a person with HPD, antisocial personality disorder (APD), or balanced features. The sex of the person was either male, female, or unspecified. Clinicians rated a number of Axis I and II disorders on a seven-point scale, with ratings of 5–7 indicating presence of the disorder. For balanced histories, clinicians made the HPD and APD diagnoses with approximately equal frequency across conditions of patient gender. When the history was consistent with APD, clinicians tended to diagnose it much less frequently in a woman (15%) than they did in a man (42%) or a person with unspecified gender (48%), but they tended to diagnose HPD (46%) in women. When the history was that of HPD, they diagnosed it at very high rates in women (76%), lower rates for unspecified gender (64%), and the lowest rates in men (44%). The HPD history of a man elicited relatively high ratings of APD compared with the other gender conditions, although this difference was not statistically significant. Clinicians' ratings of individual diagnostic criteria, however, did not differ by sex. One possible alternative to a "sex bias" interpretation of these findings is that clinicians may have correctly taken into account the base rates of APD (higher among men) and HPD (which may be higher among women in clinical settings) when making overall diagnoses.

Other studies have yielded inconclusive results concerning sex bias in HPD diagnosis. Belitsky et al. (1996) asked 96 psychiatric residents (45 women) to rate Ford and Widiger's (1989) case histories described above.

Participants who received the APD history were more likely to diagnose APD correctly if the patient was a man and to underdiagnose it when the patient was a woman. The sex of the patient did not influence HPD diagnosis in this study, although it may have influenced ratings of prognosis (HPD received a more favorable prognosis if the sex of the patient was female, but female sex of the patient also led to more favorable prognosis overall).

Bias may be present not only in clinician's judgments but also in the extent to which HPD criteria reflect feminine versus masculine gender roles. Sprock (2000) compiled lists of HPD behavioral examples for the DSM-III-R and DSM-IV criteria by asking 120 undergraduates (60 women) to read the criteria and provide examples for each. Counterbalancing for student gender, one third of the undergraduates received instructions to write behaviors that would typify men with HPD, one third wrote about women, and one third received gender-unspecified instructions. Sprock then sent subsets of behaviors to 157 clinicians (58 psychiatrists and 97 psychologists) and asked them to rate the extent to which the behaviors were representative of either the diagnostic criteria or their own overall conceptualization of HPD. Masculine behaviors received significantly lower representativeness ratings when compared with feminine or gender-unspecified behaviors in both the HPD criteria condition and the overall conceptualization of HPD. Following this, bias concerns may be addressed by writing diagnostic criteria thought to capture masculine manifestations of HPD (e.g., bragging or hypermasculinity), or as suggested by some (e.g., Sprock, 2000), criteria that have been found empirically to represent HPD equally well in men and women (e.g., dramatic exaggeration in speech or jealousy at inattention). Some researchers have voiced concerns, however, that such an approach may lower the validity of the construct (Widiger, 1998).

Antisocial Personality Disorder and Psychopathy

The description of histrionic personality, especially in men (e.g., Luisada et al., 1974), shares a resemblance with APD. Warner (1978) demonstrated that various mental health professionals are likely to label a patient description as hysterical personality if the patient's sex was said to be female, but to diagnose APD and hysterical personality at nearly equal rates if the sex was said to be male. Thus, Warner suggested that APD and hysterical personality could be gender-typed forms of the same condition. Indeed, APD and HPD appear to co-occur in individuals more often than would be expected if they each occurred by chance (Lilienfeld, VanValkenburg, Larntz, & Akiskal, 1986), and histrionic men report high rates of antisocial acts (Luisada et al., 1974). APD overlaps moderately with the construct of psychopathy (Cleckley, 1941/1982), as do certain features of HPD, such as shallow expression of emotion, seductiveness, manipulativeness, and dishonesty. Hart and Hare (1989) reported a significant correlation between HPD and scores on an interview-based psychopathy measure.

Standage, Bilsbury, Jain, and Smith (1984) predicted that histrionic women, like psychopathic individuals, may have low perspective taking abilities. They compared 20 female inpatients meeting DSM-III criteria for histrionic personality with 20 depressed female inpatients matched for age, expressive vocabulary, and depression scores. The groups did not differ significantly on a paper-and-pencil measure of perspective taking, but the histrionic women scored significantly lower on the Socialization scale of the California Psychological Inventory and higher on the Psychoticism and Lie scales of the Eysenck Personality Questionnaire. Thus the histrionic inpatients scored high on measures that may be expected to relate to psychopathy and APD, either due to overlap between these constructs and HPD or due to co-occurrence of APD and HPD features in the sample. Additionally, the histrionic women in Standage et al.'s (1984) study had greater rates of features often associated with APD, such as attempted suicide, drug and alcohol abuse, unemployment, and first-degree relatives with a criminal history, than did depressed controls.

In a group of 180 undergraduates (90 women; 64% Caucasian), Hamburger, Lilienfeld, and Hogben (1996) tested the hypotheses that psychopathy underlies both APD and HPD and that the relationship of APD and HPD with psychopathy is moderated by both biological sex and gender roles. Scores on the Psychopathic Personality Inventory (PPI; Lilienfeld, 1990) predicted scores on measures of both APD ($r = .48$ and $.59$) and HPD ($r = .16$ and $.49$) with an alpha of less than $.05$. Furthermore, the relationship between PPI scores and APD scores was stronger among men than it was among women, whereas the relationship between PPI and HPD scores was stronger among women. The classification of participants as masculine, feminine, androgynous, or undifferentiated, however, did not emerge as a moderator of the relationship between psychopathy and APD or HPD.

Cale and Lilienfeld (2002) examined the hypothesis that APD and HPD could be behavioral manifestations of psychopathy moderated by biological sex in a nonclinical sample of 75 actors (36 women). The authors sampled actors because they deemed it likely to find high levels and a wide range of HPD symptoms such as emotionality, attention seeking, and dramatization. Correlational analyses of self-report and peer ratings revealed that psychopathy was more strongly associated with HPD in women and with APD in men.

Thus, even though the association between HPD, APD, and psychopathy has been replicated, the extent to which HPD and APD are gender-typed manifestations of the same latent construct or simply co-occur remains unclear and calls for further study.

Theoretical Conceptualizations

Psychodynamic and cognitive conceptualizations of HPD have been the most influential in the clinical field and have had the greatest impact on treatment. Therefore, we address these conceptualizations in the section on psychotherapy below. The dynamic and cognitive theories have met with increasing competition from neurobehavioral, trait, and attachment conceptualizations among researchers.

Neurobehavioral Model

According to Depue and Lenzenweger's (2001) neurobehavioral dimensional model, PDs are combinations of extremes on orthogonal traits of emotion, affiliation, and control. The ratio of agentic extraversion (or positive emotionality, mediated by the neurotransmitter dopamine in the ventral tegmental area) and neuroticism (or negative emotionality/anxiety, mediated by the central amygdala and the neurotransmitter norepinephrine) comprises one emotional dimension. Harm avoidance (fear, mediated by the stria terminalis and norepinephrine) comprises a second emotional dimension, whereas impulsivity (nonaffective constraint, mediated by serotonin) and affiliation (mediated by oxytocin and other gonadal steroids) are the nonaffective traits. In this model, HPD is characterized by a high ratio of agentic extraversion to neuroticism, low nonaffective constraint, and moderate to high affiliation. Theoretically, the high dopamine and low serotonin in these individuals predispose them to gregariousness and emotional lability. In a related evolutionary neurochemical model, Klein (1999) hypothesized that a noradrenergic primate regulatory mechanism responsive to social cues of interest or rejection may become dysregulated in some individuals.

Trait Models

Trait theorists conceptualize PDs as constellations of maladaptive or extreme variants of otherwise normative personality dispositions (Widiger & Bornstein, 2001). According to Widiger and Frances (1994), the five-factor model (FFM) may be useful in describing and diagnosing PDs. As part of a larger study, Lynam and Widiger (2001) asked 19 experts on HPD to think of and rate a prototypical person with HPD on a scale of 1 to 5 along items used to measure dimensions of the FFM. Ratings for the five broad domains, neuroticism (N), extraversion (E), openness (O), agreeableness (A), and conscientiousness (C), were neither high nor low, suggesting that clinicians thought that patients with HPD tended to be average or unremarkable on these dimensions. Ratings comprising the facets within each domain were more informative. On average, clinicians rated HPD as low on self-consciousness and high on impulsiveness (within the N domain); high on gregariousness, activity, excitement seeking, and positive emotions (within E); high on fantasy, feelings, and actions (within O), and low on self-discipline and deliberation (within C). In contrast, Brieger, Sommer, Bloink, and Marneros (2000) reported that, in a sample of 229 former patients and controls, high N, high E, and low C predicted dimensional scores on a histrionic personality dimension based on the criteria of the tenth revision of the International Classification of Disorders

(ICD-10; World Health Organization, 1993). Given such heterogeneous findings, application of the FFM in conceptualizing and diagnosing HPD may be premature.

Attachment Model

From an attachment perspective (Bartholomew, Kwong, & Hart, 2001), HPD is consistent with what is referred to as a preoccupied attachment style. Such individuals are theorized to hold a positive mental model of others (predisposing them to approach others) and a negative model of the self (predisposing them to feel vulnerable, especially to rejection). People with this attachment style are thought to have strong relational needs and actively seek relationships, but may be so hypervigilant that they respond to the slightest interpersonal stress or disappointment with increased attachment behaviors, which can overwhelm and scare away potential partners. Attachment theorists see the emotionality and need for attention in individuals with HPD as evidence for attachment anxiety, whereas they see the extraversion and perhaps sexualization as evidence of intense relational needs.

Assessment and Differential Diagnosis

No specialized instrument exists for the screening and assessment of HPD. However, two commonly used broad PD measures include HPD scales. The general psychometric properties of these instruments as well as those of their HPD scales are outlined below.

The Structured Clinical Interview for DSM-IV Personality Disorders (SCID-II; First, Gibbon, Spitzer, Williams, & Benjamin, 1997) has one item per criterion for each of the PD diagnoses, to be rated during the interview on a scale from 1 ("absent or false") to 3 ("threshold or true"). Most research on the SCID-II was conducted using its previous version, the DSM-III-R SCID-II (e.g., Dreessen & Arntz, 1998; Renneberg, Chambless, Dowdall, Fauerbach, & Gracely, 1992; Spitzer, Williams, Gibbon, & First, 1990), and indicates acceptable levels of interrater reliability and internal consistency. At least one paper (Maffei et al., 1997) reports adequate levels of interrater reliability (kappa = .92; intraclass correlation [ICC] = .95) and internal consistency (Armor's theta = .87) for HPD using the DSM-IV version of the SCID-II.

The Personality Diagnostic Questionnaire 4+ (PDQ-4+; Hyler & Rieder, 1994) is a self-report measure that (as the SCID-II) assesses DSM-IV criteria for the 10 primary PDs and the two designated for further study. Correlations among all PDQ-4+ and SCID-II scales were low to moderate, but significant ($r = .19–.42$), and PDQ-4+ scales exhibited mediocre internal consistencies. Only two scales (antisocial and dependent) showed strong powers of discrimination.

A larger concern in evaluating HPD is its differentiation from other disorders, and common comorbid conditions.

Treatments for HPD

With the exception of Linehan's (1993) study of dialectical behavior therapy for BPD, the literature offers little rigorous research on the treatment of Axis II disorders. What follows is a description of the extant research, which varies greatly in scope and quality.

General Characteristics of Treatment

A panel of three experts nominated and elected by the psychiatric community in Australia (Quality Assurance Project, 1991) concluded that long-term psychotherapy would be beneficial to HPD patients and also likely be cost-effective by minimizing adverse economic outcomes of the disorder. Nevertheless, it should be noted that they were not citing research evidence specific to HPD to buttress this assumption. They conceptualized DSM-III-R HPD as a variant of BPD and asserted that the dramatizing and sexualizing behavior of HPD patients is a way of asserting a false sense of identity to counteract the feelings of emptiness and lack of identity underlying borderline pathology. The limited empirical record (primarily single- and multiple-case reports) suggested that three or more years of relatively intense (e.g., twice-weekly) therapy may be needed for good outcomes in one half to two thirds of patients. This panel recommended outpatient individual, group, or combined therapy with hospitalization and medication only during crisis.

While acknowledging that brief therapy for HPD may not be optimal, Dorfman (2000) recommended increasing its effectiveness in the context of managed care by taking an integrative stance and maintaining a specific focus on short-term goals (dealing with acute distress) and long-term changes in interpersonal behavior. He related the case of a 49-year old woman who at the start of treatment communicated in vague and self-dramatizing ways, experienced herself as a victim and others as unsympathetic, suffered from turbulent abusive relationships, and complained of feelings of anxiety, depression, emptiness, and inadequacy. The sessions focused initially on creating a working alliance, then on helping the client label beliefs about dependency and abandonment in order to help her understand their impact on her relationships, and finally on replacement of dramatic manipulations with alternative interpersonal behavior. Dorfman conducted 13 biweekly sessions with this patient and gave her the option of boosters. Several months after termination, she reported only occasional dysphoria, avoided abusive relationships, and maintained some insight into her need for attention, but she continued to be emotionally reactive under stress and overly concerned with her appearance. The efficacy and cost-effectiveness of such brief treatments remain largely unexplored using formal methods.

Other researchers have investigated the influence of HPD on treatment characteristics such as termination. Hilsenroth, Holdwick, Castlebury, and Blais (1998) reviewed literature suggesting that PDs are common in psychiatric patients and adversely affect the outcome of treatment for Axis I disorders, and sought in particular to examine the links between Cluster B PDs and psychotherapy termination. In 90 patients with different PDs, the number of DSM-IV criteria for HPD met did not correlate significantly with the number of psychotherapy sessions. In a stepwise regression, HPD criterion 8, "considers relationships to be more intimate than they really are," predicted the number of therapy sessions independent of other significant predictors, such as the BPD criterion "frantic efforts to avoid real or imagined abandonment" and the NPD criterion "requires excessive admiration." Unfortunately, stepwise regression tends to capitalize on chance findings, and these findings may be difficult to replicate. Their generalizability may also be limited by the atypical nature of the sample, which included patients meeting criteria for only one PD, which is not usually the case in the community. Other researchers (Tyrer, Mitchard, Methuen, & Ranger, 2003) have found patients with HPD not particularly likely to either seek or reject therapy.

Expressive Psychodynamic Therapy

From a psychodynamic perspective, HPD is a hysterical character style (McWilliams, 1994; Shapiro, 1965) presenting at the borderline level of dysfunction (Kernberg, 1970, 1975). The hysterical style is characterized by diffuse, global, and impressionistic cognition that makes motivated inattention easy and self-understanding difficult. It can present at a neurotic, borderline, or psychotic level of severity (see also Pollak, 1981; Zisook, DeVaul, & Gammon, 1979), with borderline implying that the person has difficulty establishing a stable sense of self. Kernberg (2004) considers most histrionic patients to be in the high (meaning healthier) borderline range (see Kernberg, 2004, for the distinction between BPD and borderline personality organization.) Because patients' representations of the self and others are split into all-good and all-bad fragments, under conditions of stress and negative emotion the experience of self as all bad may lead to intense suffering and self-harm, whereas projective identification and the experience of others as evil may lead to rage. Yet the patient may depend on relationships with others to feel whole. Thus, manipulativeness and acting out may be self-defeating ways to maintain the attention of others. This psychodynamic conceptualization has a phenomenological appeal but remains wanting for empirical validation.

Psychodynamic therapists are likely to view such pathology as arrested development rather than conflict (Mitchell, 1988; Mitchell & Black, 1995; Quality Assurance Project, 1991). Therefore, they recommend modifications to the classical technique of therapist neutrality. Instead, they suggest more directive and expressive approaches (McWilliams, 1994, 2004) in which the therapist shows empathy, helps the client label and understand his or her dreaded feelings, promotes tolerance for anxiety and ambiguity, and helps establish a complex and realistic understanding of the self, others, and relationships. Because of these patients' fragile sense of identity and the dramatic shifts in how they feel about themselves and the therapist, firm boundaries and clear, consistent conditions of therapy are essential. For similar reasons, psychodynamic therapists often work with such patients face-to-face instead of using the couch, and they see them only once or twice a week. Research has not yet addressed the efficacy of the above recommendations.

The therapist attempts to promote healthy maturation by responding to elements of the patient's expression that are likely to be genuine and ignoring those that are impersonal or mendacious (Quality Assurance Project, 1991). Early in the treatment, the therapist focuses on building the alliance. Inevitably, the patient's unstable representations begin to create disruptions in the relationship due to idealization or devaluation, at which point the therapist points them out to the patient and links them to past and recent experiences. Patients learn to reflect on their feelings and interactions and realize that they can share negative aspects of the self with the therapist without falling apart or being abandoned, which is intended to help build self-esteem. The therapist gradually challenges the patient to link different aspects of his or her ways of experiencing the self and others to establish a sense of identity, continuity, and authenticity. Patients may use pseudoinsight, or superficial insights that are quickly forgotten and primarily aim to please and flatter the therapist, posing a challenge in later phases of treatment (Chodoff, 1978).

In a meta-analysis of controlled studies of psychodynamic ($n = 14$) and cognitive ($n = 11$) therapy outcome for PDs employing measures such as the Beck Depression Inventory, the Symptom Checklist–90 (SCL-90), the Health-Sickness Rating Scale, and the Global Adjustment Scale, Leichsenring and Leibing (2003) found large effect sizes for both kinds of therapy on self-report as well as observer ratings of outcome. More recently, Svartberg, Stiles, and Seltzer (2004) reported similar results. In addition, some evidence emerged for the long-term effectiveness of psychodynamic therapies (Leichsenring & Leibing, 2003). Nevertheless, the effectiveness of psychodynamic therapies has not yet been demonstrated in controlled studies for HPD per se. Similarly, the question of whether these therapies work by means of their hypothesized mechanisms needs to be addressed empirically.

Cognitive Therapy

Cognitive therapists conceptualize PDs as attributable to dysfunctional schemas that develop out of people's tendencies to cope in certain ways with interpersonal challenges (Beck & Freeman, 1990). A person who develops HPD may have had strong dependency and rejection sensitivity tendencies as a child and may have received strong reinforcement from others for attention seeking behavior or the exaggerated display of gender-typed behaviors. The former tendencies may result in a core belief that "I am basically unattractive," and the reinforcement history may lead to a core belief that "I need others to admire me in order to be happy." The individual compensates by believing "I am lovable, entertaining, and interesting," "I am entitled to admiration," and "People are there to admire me" (Beck & Freeman, 1990, p. 50). Thus, according to this framework, persons with HPD view themselves as deserving of unfaltering attention and view others positively as long as they provide it. Their overt cheerfulness conceals underlying anxiety and rejection sensitivity. People with HPD deal pragmatically with the belief that they are unattractive by seeking minute-to-minute interaction and attention in an attempt to counter this fear. They quickly act on their frustration if a person contradicts their compensatory beliefs by ignoring them. Thus, the person with HPD operates on conditional beliefs such as "Unless I captivate others, I am nothing," "If I can't entertain people, they will abandon me," and "If people don't respond, they are rotten." An associated belief is "I can go by my feelings," which gives one the freedom to express immediate feelings of affection or aggression toward others in exaggerated ways, regardless of their appropriateness. Thus, the histrionic approach to life is based on global, impressionistic, and fleeting cognitions that are at odds with the problem solving and focused set that cognitive therapy teaches.

Work in the cognitive approach begins by gradually helping the patient identify feelings and thoughts and then challenging irrational thoughts, first in relation to specific symptoms and gradually at a more global level. Patients with HPD may find homework assignments boring, which is why Beck and Freeman (1990) suggest that therapists encourage patients to use vivid imagination when working on homework (e.g., by phrasing their rational thoughts in dramatic ways). It may be helpful to clarify to patients that treatment will not eradicate the strong emotions they value but will make them more constructive. Emotional outbursts can be dealt with by clarifying the goal (e.g., to receive positive attention), listing the pros and cons of an outburst in relation to the goal, and coming up with alternative ways of reaching it. Such interventions may help stabilize the patient's relationships, but ultimately the therapy must help patients address their sense of identity and core beliefs. Patients may gradually write down things that describe themselves as a way of building a stable identity, and they may engage in small behavioral experiments to challenge their belief that they depend on others' care and attention. A rational argument has been made that this work could last for up to 3 years. However, the specific formulations and treatment recommendations of cognitive therapy for HPD, like those of psychodynamic therapy, have not been investigated extensively.

Cognitive therapy for PDs has been described in several volumes (e.g., Beck & Freeman, 1990; Beck, Freeman, & Davis, 2004; Young, 1999), but its empirical support still comes primarily from case studies (e.g., Bernstein, 2002; Morrison, 2000) and a small number of clinical trials (Leichsenring & Leibing, 2003; Svartberg et al., 2004), in which its effectiveness was comparable with that of psychodynamic therapy. The field is still wanting for empirical evaluations of the effectiveness of cognitive therapy specifically for HPD.

Other Therapies

A few other proposed therapies for HPD are worth mentioning, although they will not be discussed at length for brevity's sake. Horowitz (1997) described a rationally derived cognitive/psychodynamic approach that starts with a configurational assessment of symptoms, states of mind, defense styles, person schemas, and the level of severity. This approach involves three primary phases, one focusing on attainment of emotional and behavioral stabilization, one focusing on improving communication, and one focusing on modifying defenses. Horowitz did not specify treatment duration, but his framework implies that it would depend upon the level of severity. A related cognitive/analytic approach proposed by Ryle (1997) has received limited research support in Europe for the treatment of BPD (Garyfallos et al., 2002; Kerr, 1999).

The application of functional analytic therapy with histrionic patients as described by Callaghan, Summers, and Weidman (2003) may appeal to proponents of both interpersonal and behavioral approaches. They apply functional analysis principles within the therapeutic relationship by extinguishing or punishing interpersonally problematic behaviors and reinforcing desirable behaviors idiosyncratic for the patient. For example, therapists may share with clients the way their behavior made them feel, acting under the assumption that the client enacts the same maladaptive behaviors that occur outside of therapy and that their modification through feedback in therapy will generalize to other relationships. Although descriptive case studies implementing this approach with histrionic patients have been cited (e.g., Callaghan et al., 2003), sufficient empirical support for its effectiveness is still lacking.

While no clinical trials of pharmacotherapy for HPD currently exist, Kool, Dekker, Duijsens, De Jonghe, and Puite (2003) report some potentially relevant findings regarding pharmacotherapy for personality pathology in general. They compared two groups, one receiving pharmacotherapy only for depression (a selective serotonin reuptake inhibitor, a tricyclic antidepressant, or a reversible monoamine oxidase inhibitor for 6 months; $n = 25$), and one receiving pharmacotherapy and brief psychodynamic therapy ($n = 47$). Using a self-report inventory to measure personality pathology before treatment and 40 weeks later, they found that overall personality pathology (including histrionicity) decreased in the combined treatment group regardless of their improvement on depression, while only those patients who improved on depression in the pharmacotherapy group scored lower on personality pathology. The authors reported that patients with Cluster B pathology showed the least reduction in PD scores, but the role of HPD in this was unclear, as was the proportion of patients who had HPD. Other authors (e.g., Grossman, 2004) have suggested that, given the emotional regulation difficulties of patients with HPD, medications such as selective serotonin reuptake inhibitors, mood stabilizers, and anticonvulsants deserve research consideration.

Questions for Future Research

Many research questions remain pertaining to the conceptualization, etiology, and treatment of HPD. We will highlight four that we consider most significant as we move toward DSM-V:

1. **What are the real-world outcomes of HPD?** As noted earlier in this chapter, little is known about the clinical predictive power of HPD for outcomes such as relationship satisfaction and stability, employment history, general health, and life satisfaction. Furthermore, empirical studies should examine the degree to which factors such as Axis I comorbidity and severity of HPD presentation affect the degree to which negative life outcomes are experienced. Relatedly, some researchers (e.g., Svanborg et al., 2000) have cited preliminary biological evidence that histrionic features may be adaptive for some individuals. The conditions under which features of HPD can serve an adaptive function are another interesting direction for further research.

2. **Can endophenotypic markers of HPD help elucidate its degree of differentiation from allied conditions?** Continued overlap between HPD and other Axis II conditions such as BPD, NPD, and DPD calls for an examination of the degree to which these disorders can be differentiated as well as their incremental validity over and above each other in predicting clinically relevant outcomes. Endophenotypic markers, as assessed by laboratory measures, are an as of yet relatively unexplored but potentially interesting avenue for doing so.

3. **What is the current status of cultural differences in the presentation and course of HPD?** Not only is there a lack of empirical literature regarding the nature of cultural differences in HPD, but theoretical writings pertaining to this topic are likely outdated by now. For example, changes in the cultural and economic conditions in different global regions may have changed hypothesized prevalence rates of HPD. Furthermore, the degree to which HPD is more or less prevalent or may have distinctive features within cultural enclaves in nonnative countries (e.g., the U.S.) is also an unexplored question.

4. **What is the best course of treatment for HPD?** While the proposed treatments for HPD reviewed in this chapter are appealing from a phenomenological standpoint, it is clear that more rigorous treatment outcome research must examine these and other proposed therapies. Additionally, it is important to compare proposed treatments with one another on well-operationalized outcome variables in order to examine the possible differences in efficacy. When selecting targeted outcomes, in keeping with suggestions regarding personality considerations in treatment planning (see Harkness & Lilienfeld, 1997), clinicians and researchers should consider selecting some reflective of "characteristic adaptations" (behaviors arising from maladaptive traits) in addition to reduction of trait levels themselves. Such an approach is implied in therapies utilizing functional analytic (Callaghan et al., 2003) and interpersonal components (Dorfman, 2000) and awaits large-scale empirical validation.

References

Abraham, K. (1927/1948). *Manifestations of the female castration complex* (D. Bryan & A. Strachey, Trans.). London: Hogarth.

Alam, C. N., & Merskey, C. (1992). The development of the hysterical personality. *History of Psychiatry, 3*(2), 135–165.

Alarcon, R. D. (1996). Personality disorders and culture in DSM-IV: A critique. *Journal of Personality Disorders, 10*(3), 260–270.

American Psychiatric Association. (1952). *Diagnostic and statistical manual of mental disorders*. Washington, DC: Author.

American Psychiatric Association. (1968). *Diagnostic and statistical manual of mental disorders* (2nd ed.). Washington, DC: Author.

American Psychiatric Association. (1980). *Diagnostic and statistical manual of mental disorders* (3rd ed.). Washington, DC: Author.

American Psychiatric Association. (1987). *Diagnostic and statistical manual of mental disorders* (3rd ed., revised). Washington, DC: Author.

American Psychiatric Association. (2000). *Diagnostic and statistical manual of mental disorders* (4th ed., text revision). Washington, DC: Author.

Ampollini, P., Merchesi, C., Signifredi, R., Ghinaglia, E., Scardovi, F., Codeluppi, S., et al. (1999). Temperament and personality features in patients with major depression, panic disorder and mixed conditions. *Journal of Affective Disorders, 52,* 203–207.

Apt, C., & Hurlbert, D. F. (1994). The sexual attitudes, behavior, and relationships of women with histrionic personality disorder. *Journal of Sex & Marital Therapy, 20*(2), 125–133.

Baker, J. D., Capron, E. W., & Azorlosa, J. (1996). Family environment characteristics of persons with histrionic and dependent personality disorders. *Journal of Personality Disorders, 10*(1), 82–87.

Bartholomew, K., Kwong, M. J., & Hart, S. D. (2001). Attachment. In W. J. Livesley (Ed.), *Handbook of personality disorders: Theory, research, and treatment* (pp. 196–230). New York: Guilford Press.

Baumbacher, G., & Amini, F. (1980–1981). The hysterical personality disorder: A proposed classification of a diagnostic dilemma. *International Journal of Psychoanalytic Psychotherapy, 8,* 501–532.

Beck, A. T., & Freeman, A. (1990). *Cognitive therapy of the personality disorders.* New York: Guilford.

Beck, A. T., Freeman, A., & Davis, D. D. (2004). *Cognitive therapy of personality disorders* (2nd ed.). New York: Guilford Press.

Belitsky, C. A., Toner, B. B., Ali, A., Yu, B., Osborne, S. L., & deRooy, E. (1996). Sex-role attitudes and clinical appraisal in psychiatry residents. *Canadian Journal of Psychiatry, 41,* 503–508.

Bernstein, D. P. (2002). Cognitive therapy of personality disorders in patients with histories of emotional abuse or neglect. *Psychiatric Annals, 32*(10), 618–628.

Blais, M. A., Hilsenroth, M. H., & Fowler, J. C. (1998). Rorschach correlates of the DSM-IV histrionic personality disorder. *Journal of Personality Assessment, 70*(2), 355–364.

Blais, M. A., & Norman, D. K. (1997). A psychometric evaluation of the DSM-IV personality disorder criteria. *Journal of Personality Disorders, 11,* 168–176.

Blashfield, R. K., & Davis, R. T. (1993). Dependent and histrionic personality disorders. In P. B. Sutker & H. E. Adams (Eds.), *Comprehensive handbook of psychopathology* (pp. 395–409). New York: Plenum.

Bornstein, R. F. (1998). Implicit and self-attributed dependency needs in dependent and histrionic personality disorders. *Journal of Personality Assessment, 71*(1), 1–14.

Bornstein, R. F. (1999). Dependent and histrionic personality disorders. In T. Millon, P. H. Blaney, & R. D. Davis (Eds.), *Oxford textbook of psychopathology* (pp. 535–554). New York: Oxford University Press.

Brieger, P., Sommer, S., Bloink, R., & Marneros, A. (2000). The relationship between five-factor personality measurements and ICD-10 personality disorder dimensions: Results from a sample of 229 subjects. *Journal of Personality Disorders, 14*(3), 282–290.

Cale, E. M., & Lilienfeld, S. O. (2002). Histrionic personality disorder and antisocial personality disorder: Sex-differentiated manifestations of psychopathy. *Journal of Personality Disorders, 16*(1), 52–72.

Callaghan, G. M., Summers, C. J., & Weidman, M. (2003). The treatment of histrionic and narcissistic personality disorder behaviors: A single-subject demonstration of clinical improvement using functional analytic psychotherapy. *Journal of Contemporary Psychotherapy, 33*(4), 321–339.

Chodoff, P. (1974). The diagnosis of hysteria: An overview. *American Journal of Psychiatry, 131,* 1073–1078.

Chodoff, P. (1978). Psychotherapy of the hysterical personality disorder. *Journal of the American Academy of Psychoanalysis, 6*(4), 497–510.

Chodoff, P. (1982). Hysteria and women. *American Journal of Psychiatry, 139*(5), 545–551.

Cleckley, H. (1941/1982). *The mask of sanity.* St. Louis, MO: Mosby.

Cloninger, R., Martin, R. L., Guze, S., & Clayton, P. (1986). A prospective follow-up and family study of somatization in men and women. *American Journal of Psychiatry, 143,* 873–878.

Cohen, B. J., Nestadt, G., Samuels, J. F., Romanoski, A. J., McHugh, P. R., & Rabins, P. V. (1994). Personality disorder in later life: A community study. *British Journal of Psychiatry, 165,* 493–499.

Coid, J. W. (1999). Aetiological risk factors for personality disorders. *British Journal of Psychiatry, 174,* 530–538.

Cramer, P. (1999). Personality, personality disorders, and defense mechanisms. *Journal of Personality, 67*(3), 535–554.

Crawford, T. N., Cohen, P., & Brook, J. S. (2001a). Dramatic-erratic personality disorder symptoms: I. Continuity from early adolescence into adulthood. *Journal of Personality Disorders, 15*(4), 319–335.

Crawford, T. N., Cohen, P., & Brook, J. S. (2001b). Dramatic-erratic personality disorder symptoms: II. Developmental pathways from early adolescence to adulthood. *Journal of Personality Disorders, 15*(4), 336–350.

Daley, S. E., Hammen, C., Burge, D., Davila, J., Paley, B., Lindberg, N., et al. (1999). Depression and Axis II symptomatology in an adolescent community sample: Concurrent and longitudinal associations. *Journal of Personality Disorders, 13*(1), 47–59.

Depue, R. A., & Lenzenweger, M. F. (2001). A neurobehavioral dimensional model. In W. J. Livesley (Ed.), *Handbook of personality disorders: Theory, research, and treatment* (pp. 136–176). New York: Guilford Press.

Dorfman, W. I. (2000). Histrionic personality disorder. In M. Hersen & M. Biaggio (Eds.), *Effective brief therapies: A clinician's guide* (pp. 355–370). San Diego, CA: Academic Press.

Dreessen, L., & Arntz, A. (1998). Short-interval test-retest interrater reliability of the Structured Clinical Interview for DSM-III-R Personality Disorders (SCID-II) in outpatients. *Journal of Personality Disorders, 12*(2), 138–148.

Easser, B., & Lesser, S. (1965). Hysterical character and psychoanalysis. *Psychoanalytic Quarterly, 34,* 390–405.

Ekselius, L., Lindstrom, E., von Knorring, L., Bodlund, O., & Kullgren, G. (1994). SCID-II interviews and the SCID Screen questionnaire as diagnostic tools for personality disorders in DSM-III-R. *Acta Psychiatrica Scandinavica, 90,* 120–123.

Fenichel, O. (1945). *The psychoanalytic theory of neurosis.* New York: W. W. Norton.

First, M. B., Gibbon, M., Spitzer, R. L., Williams, J. B. W., & Benjamin, L. S. (1997). *User's guide for the Structured Clinical Interview for DSM-IV Axis II Personality Disorders (SCID-II).* Washington, DC: American Psychiatric Press.

First, M. B., Spitzer, R. L., Gibbon, M., & Williams, J. B. (1995). *Structured clinical interview for DSM-IV Axis I disorders.* New York: New York State Psychiatric Institute.

Ford, M. R., & Widiger, T. A. (1989). Sex bias in the diagnosis of histrionic and antisocial personality disorders. *Journal of Consulting and Clinical Psychology, 57*(2), 301–305.

Frank, G. (1990). Research on the clinical usefulness of the Rorschach: I. The diagnosis of schizophrenia. *Perceptual and Motor Skills, 71*(2), 573–578.

Freud, S., & Breuer, J. (1895/2000). Studies on hysteria. In J. Strachey (Ed.), *The standard edition of the complete psychological works of Sigmund Freud* (Vol. 2). London: Hogarth.

Garyfallos, G., Adamopoulous, A., Karastergious, A., Voikli, M., Zlatanos, D., & Tsifida, S. (2002). Evaluation of cognitive-analytic therapy (CAT) outcome: A 4–8 year follow up. *European Journal of Psychiatry, 16*(4), 197–209.

Grossman, R. (2004). Pharmacotherapy of personality disorders. In J. J. Magnavita (Ed.), *Handbook of personality disorders: Theory and practice* (pp. 331–355). Hoboken, NJ: Wiley.

Grueneich, R. (1992). The borderline personality disorder diagnoses: Reliability, diagnostic efficiency, and covariation with other personality disorder diagnoses. *Journal of Personality Disorders, 6*(3), 197–212.

Hamburger, M. E., Lilienfeld, S. O., & Hogben, M. (1996). Psychopathy, gender, and gender roles: Implications for antisocial and histrionic personality disorders. *Journal of Personality Disorders, 10*(1), 41–55.

Harkness, A. R, & Lilienfeld, S. O. (1997). Individual differences science for treatment planning: Personality traits. *Psychological Assessment, 9*(4), 349–360.

Hart, S. D., & Hare, R. D. (1989). Discriminant validity of the Psychopathy Checklist in a forensic psychiatric population. *Psychological Assessment, 1,* 211–218.

Hilsenroth, M. H., Holdwick, D. J. J., Castlebury, F. D., & Blais, M. A. (1998). The effects of DSM-IV Cluster B Personality Disorder symptoms on the termination and continuation of psychotherapy. *Psychotherapy, 35*(2), 163–176.

Horowitz, M. (1997). Psychotherapy for histrionic personality disorder. *Journal of Psychotherapy Practice and Research, 6*(2), 93–104.

Hyler, S. E., & Rieder, R. O. (1996). *Personality diagnostic questionnaire* (4th revision). New York: New York State Psychiatric Institute.

Hyler, S., Reider, R., Spitzer, R. L., & Williams, J. B. (1982). *The personality diagnostic questionnaire (PDQ).* New York: New York State Psychiatric Institute.

Hyler, S., Skodol, A. E., Kellman, H. D., Oldham, J. M., & Rosnick, L. (1990). Validity of the Personality Diagnostic Questionnaire—Revised: Comparison with two structured interviews. *American Journal of Psychiatry, 147,* 1043–1048.

Johnson, F. F. (1993). *Dependency and Japanese socialization.* New York: New York University Press.

Kernberg, O. (1970). A psychoanalytic classification of character pathology. *Journal of the American Psychoanalytic Association, 18,* 51–85.

Kernberg, O. (1975). *Borderline conditions and pathological narcissism.* Northvale, NJ: Jason Aronson.

Kernberg, O. (2004). Borderline personality disorder and borderline personality organization: Psychopathology and psychotherapy. In J. J. Magnavita (Ed.), *Handbook of personality disorders: Theory and practice* (pp. 92–119). Hoboken, NJ: Wiley.

Kerr, I. B. (1999). Cognitive-analytic therapy for borderline personality disorder in the context of a community mental health team: Individual and organizational psychodynamic implications. *British Journal of Psychiatry, 15*(4), 425–438.

Klein, D. F. (1999). Harmful dysfunction, disorder, disease, illness, and evolution. *Journal of Abnormal Psychology, 108,* 421–429.

Kool, S., Dekker, J., Duijsens, I. J., De Jonghe, F., & Puite, B. (2003). Changes in personality pathology after pharmacotherapy and combined therapy for depressed patients. *Journal of Personality Disorders, 17*(1), 60–72.

Kraus, G., & Reynolds, D. J. (2001). The "A-B-C's" of the Cluster B's: Identifying, understanding, and treating Cluster B personality disorders. *Clinical Psychology Review, 21*(3), 345–373.

Lazare, A. (1971). The hysterical character in psychoanalytic theory. *Archives of General Psychiatry, 25,* 131–137.

Leichsenring, F., & Leibing, E. (2003). The effectiveness of psychodynamic therapy and cognitive behavior therapy in the treatment of personality disorders: A meta-analysis. *American Journal of Psychiatry, 160,* 1223–1232.

Lilienfeld, S. O. (1990). *Development and preliminary validation of a self-report measure of psychopathic personality.* Unpublished doctoral dissertation, University of Minnesota, Minneapolis.

Lilienfeld, S. O., VanValkenburg, C., Larntz, K., & Akiskal, H. S. (1986). The relationship of histrionic personality disorder to antisocial personality and somatization disorder. *American Journal of Psychiatry, 143*(6), 718–722.

Lilienfeld, S. O., Waldman, I., & Israel, A. C. (1994). A critical examination of the use of the term and concept of comorbidity in psychopathology research. *Clinical Psychology: Science and Practice, 1,* 71–83.

Linehan, M. (1993). *Cognitive behavioral therapy for borderline personality disorders.* New York: Guilford.

Liskow, B. L., Clayton, P., Woodruff, R., Guze, S., & Cloninger, R. (1977). Briquet's syndrome, hysterical personality, and the MMPI. *American Journal of Psychiatry, 134*(10), 1137–1139.

Livesley, W. J., & Schroeder, M. L. (1991). Dimensions of Personality Disorder: The DSM-III-R Cluster B diagnoses. *Journal of Nervous and Mental Disease, 179*(6), 320–328.

Luisada, P. V., Peele, R., & Pittard, E. A. (1974). The hysterical personality in men. *American Journal of Psychiatry, 131*(5), 518–522.

Lynam, D. R., & Widiger, T. A. (2001). Using the five-factor model to represent the DSM-IV personality disorders: An expert consensus approach. *Journal of Abnormal Psychology, 110*(3), 401–412.

Maffei, C., Fossati, A., Agostoni, I., Barraco, A., Bagnato, M., Deborah, D., et al. (1997). Interrater reliability and internal consistency of the Structured Clinical Interview for DSM-IV Axis II Personality Disorders (SCID-II), version 2.0. *Journal of Personality Disorders, 11*(3), 279–284.

Maier, W., Franke, P., & Hawellek, B. (1998). Special feature: Family genetic research strategies for personality disorders. *Journal of Personality Disorders, 12*(3), 262–276.

Marmor, J. (1953). Orality in the hysterical personality. *Journal of the American Psychoanalytic Association, 1,* 656–671.

Maynard, R. E., & Meyer, G. E. (1996). Visual information processing with obsessive-compulsive and hysterical personalities. *Personality and Individual Differences, 20*(3), 389–399.

McWilliams, N. (1994). *Psychoanalytic diagnosis: Understanding personality structure in the clinical process.* New York: Guilford Press.

McWilliams, N. (2004). *Psychoanalytic psychotherapy: A practitioner's guide.* New York: Guilford Press.

Messer, S. C., Morris, T. L., & Gross, A. M. (1990). Hypoglycemia and psychopathology: A methodological review. *Clinical Psychology Review, 10,* 631–648.

Millon, T. (1981). *Disorders of personality, DSM-III, Axis II.* New York: Wiley.

Millon, T. (1982). *Millon clinical multiaxial inventory manual* (2nd ed.). Minneapolis, MN: National Computer Systems.

Millon, T., Grossman, S., Millon, C., Meagher, S., & Ramnath, R. (2004). *Personality disorders in modern life* (2nd ed.). Hoboken, NJ: Wiley.

Mitchell, S. A. (1988). *Relational concepts in psychoanalysis: An integration.* Cambridge, MA: Harvard University Press.

Mitchell, S. A., & Black, M. J. (1995). *Freud and beyond: A history of modern psychoanalytic thought.* New York: Basic Books.

Morey, L. C., Waugh, M. H., & Blashfield, R. K. (1985). MMPI scales for DSM-III personality disorders: Their derivation and correlates. *Journal of Personality Assessment, 49*(3), 245–251.

Morrison, N. (2000). Schema-focused cognitive therapy for complex long-standing problems: A single case study. *Behavioural and Cognitive Psychotherapy, 28*(3), 269–283.

Nathan, P. (1998). The DSM-IV and its antecedents: Enhancing syndromal diagnosis. In J. Barron (Ed.), *Making diagnosis meaningful: Enhancing evaluation and treatment of psychological disorders* (pp. 3–27). Washington, DC: American Psychological Association.

Nestadt, G., Romanoski, A. J., Chalel, R., & Marchant, A. (1990). An epidemiological study of histrionic personality disorder. *Psychological Medicine, 20,* 413–422.

Padilla, A. M. (1995). *Hispanic psychology: Critical issues in theory and research.* Newbury Park, CA: Sage.

Perugi, G., Akiskal, H. S., Lattanzi, L., Cecconi, D., Mastrocinque, C., Patronelli, A., et al. (1998). The high prevalence of "soft" bipolar (II) features in atypical depression. *Comprehensive Psychiatry, 39*(2), 63–71.

Pfohl, B. (1991). Histrionic personality disorder: A review of available data and recommendations for DSM-IV. *Journal of Personality Disorders, 5*(2), 150–166.

Pfohl, B., Blum, N., Zimmerman, M., & Stangl, D. (1989). *Structured interview for personality disorders, revised version.* Iowa City: University of Iowa.

Pierloot, R. A., & Ngoma, M. (1988). Hysterical manifestations in Africa and Europe: A comparative study. *British Journal of Psychiatry, 152,* 112–115.

Pollak, J. M. (1981). Hysterical personality: An appraisal in light of empirical research. *Genetic Psychology Monographs, 104*(71–105).

Quality Assurance Project. (1991). Treatment outlines for borderline, narcissistic, and histrionic personality disorders. *Australian and New Zealand Journal of Psychiatry, 25,* 392–403.

Reich, W. (1933). *Charakteranalyse* [Character analysis]. Leipzig, Germany: Verlag.

Reich, W. (1949). *Character analysis.* New York: Farrar, Straus, & Giroux.

Reise, S. P., & Wright, T. M. (1996). Personality traits, Cluster B personality disorders, and sociosexuality. *Journal of Research in Personality, 30,* 128–136.

Renneberg, B., Chambless, D. L., Dowdall, D. J., Fauerbach, J. A., & Gracely, E. J. (1992). The Structured Clinical Interview for DSM-III-R, Axis II and the Millon Clinical Multiaxial Inventory: A concurrent validity study of personality disorders among anxious outpatients. *Journal of Personality Disorders, 6*(2), 117–124.

Rost, K. M., Akins, R. N., Brown, F. W., & Smith, G. R. (1992). The comorbidity of DSM-III-R personality disorders in somatization disorder. *General Hospital Psychiatry, 14*(5), 322–326.

Ryle, A. (1997). *Cognitive analytic therapy and borderline personality disorder.* Chichester, UK: Wiley.

Sacco, J., & Olczak, P. V. (1996). Personality and cognition: Obsessivity, hystericism, and some correlates. *Journal of Social Behavior and Personality, 11*(1), 165–176.

Schotte, C., De Doncker, D., Maes, M., Cluydts, R., & Cosyns, P. (1993). MMPI assessment of the DSM-III-R histrionic personality disorder. *Journal of Personality Assessment, 60*(3), 500–510.

Shapiro, D. (1965). *Neurotic styles.* New York: Basic Books.

Slavney, P. R. (1978). The diagnosis of hysterical personality disorder: A study of attitudes. *Comprehensive Psychiatry, 19*(6), 501–507.

Spitzer, R. L., Williams, J. B., & Gibbon, M. (1987). *Structured clinical interview for DSM-III-R personality disorders (SCID-II).* New York: New York State Psychiatric Institute.

Spitzer, R. L, Williams, J. B. W., Gibbon, M., & First, M. B. (1990). *Structured clinical interview for DSM-III-R Axis II disorders (SCID-II).* Washington, DC: American Psychiatric Press.

Spitzer, R. L., Williams, J. B., & Skodol, A. E. (1980). DSM-III: The major achievements and an overview. *American Journal of Psychiatry, 137*(2), 151–164.

Sprock, J. (2000). Gender-typed behavioral examples of histrionic personality disorder. *Journal of Psychopathology and Behavioral Assessment, 22*(2), 107–121.

Standage, K., Bilsbury, C., Jain, S., & Smith, D. (1984). An investigation of role-taking in histrionic personalities. *Canadian Journal of Psychiatry, 29,* 407–411.

Strakowski, S. M., McElroy, S. L., Keck, P. W., & West, S. A. (1994). The co-occurrence of mania with medical and other psychiatric disorders. *International Journal of Psychiatry in Medicine, 24*(4), 305–328.

Svanborg, P., Evenden-Mattila, M., Gustavsson, P. J., Uvnas-Moberg, K., & Asberg, M. (2000). Association between plasma glucose and DSM-III-R Cluster B personality traits in psychiatric outpatients. *Neuropsychobiology, 41,* 79–87.

Svartberg, M., Stiles, T. C., & Seltzer, M. H. (2004). Randomized, controlled trial of the effectiveness of short-term dynamic psychotherapy and cognitive therapy for Cluster C personality disorders. *American Journal of Psychiatry, 161*(5), 810–817.

Taylor, L. A., & Rachman, S. J. (1988). The effects of blood sugar level changes on cognitive function, affective state, and somatic symptoms. *Journal of Behavioral Medicine, 11,* 279–291.

Torgersen, S., Lygren, S., Oien, P. A., Skre, I., Onstad, S., Edvardsen, J., et al. (2000). A twin study of personality disorders. *Comprehensive Psychiatry, 41*(6), 416–425.

Trull, T. J., & Widiger, T. A. (2003). Personality disorders. In G. Stricker, T. A. Widiger, & I. B. Wiener (Eds.), *Handbook of psychology: Clinical psychology* (Vol. 8, pp. 149–172). New York: Wiley.

Turner, R. M. (1994). Borderline, narcissistic, and histrionic personality disorders. In M. Hersen & R. T. Ammerman (Eds.), *Handbook for prescriptive treatments for adults* (pp. 393–420). New York: Pergamon Press.

Tyrer, P., Mitchard, S., Methuen, C., & Ranger, M. (2003). Treatment rejecting and treatment seeking personality disorders: Type R and type S. *Journal of Personality Disorders, 17*(3), 263–268.

Virkkunen, M. (1986). Reactive hypoglycemic tendency among habitually violent offenders. *Nutrition, 44,* 94–103.

Warner, R. (1978). The diagnosis of antisocial and hysterical personality disorder. *Journal of Nervous and Mental Disease, 166*(12), 839–845.

Westen, D., & Heim, A. K. (2003). Disturbances of self and identity in personality disorders. In M. R. Leary & J. P. Tangney (Eds.), *Handbook of self and identity* (pp. 643–664). New York: Guilford Press.

Westen, D., & Shedler, J. (1999). Revising and assessing Axis II: II. Toward an empirically based and clinically useful classification of personality disorders. *American Journal of Psychiatry, 156,* 273–285.

Widiger, T. A. (1998). Invited essay: Sex biases in the diagnosis of personality disorders: An example of sex bias. *Journal of Personality Disorders, 12*(2), 95–118.

Widiger, T. A., & Bornstein, R. F. (2001). Histrionic, narcissistic, and dependent personality disorders. In P. B. Sutker & H. E. Adams (Eds.), *Comprehensive handbook of psychopathology* (pp. 509–531). New York: Plenum.

Widiger, T. A., & Frances, A. J. (1994). Toward a dimensional model for the personality disorders. In P. T. Costa, Jr., & T. A. Widiger (Eds.), *Personality disorders and the five-factor model of personality* (pp. 19–39). Washington, DC: American Psychological Association.

Widiger, T. A., & Rogers, J. H. (1989). Prevalence and comorbidity of personality disorders. *Psychiatric Annals, 19,* 132–136.

Wilkinson-Ryan, T., & Westen, D. (2000). Identity disturbance in borderline personality disorder: An empirical investigation. *American Journal of Psychiatry, 157,* 528–541.

World Health Organization. (1993). *The ICD-10 classification of mental and behavioural disorders: Diagnostic criteria for research.* Geneva, Switzerland: Author.

Young, J. E. (1999). *Cognitive therapy for personality disorders: A schema-focused approach* (3rd ed.). Sarasota, FL: Professional Resource Press.

Yovel, I., Revelle, W., & Mineka, S. (2005). Who sees the trees before the forest? The obsessive-compulsive style of visual attention. *Psychological Science, 16*(2), 123–129.

Zisook, S., DeVaul, R. A., & Gammon, E. (1979). The hysterical facade. *American Journal of Psychoanalysis, 39*(2), 113–122.

9

Narcissistic Personality Disorder

Kenneth N. Levy
Pennsylvania State University

Joseph S. Reynoso
City University of New York

Rachel H. Wasserman
Pennsylvania State University

John F. Clarkin
Joan and Sanford I. Weill Medical College

Introduction

Clinical theorists across various orientations describe individuals diagnosed with narcissistic personality disorder as those characterized by a pervasive pattern of grandiosity, a sense of privilege or entitlement, an expectation of preferential treatment, an exaggerated sense of self-importance, and arrogant or haughty behaviors or attitudes (Westen & Shedler, 1999). Despite common

Authors' notes: The authors would like to thank Janine Schiavi for her helpful comments regarding an earlier draft of the paper. We would also like to thank Alec Baker, Courtney Fatemi-Badi, Whitney Francis, Lindsay L. Hill, Stephane Machado, Shelia Sherazi, Camille Vaughn, and especially Jennifer Hernandez, Denise Liu, and Jill McLeod for their clerical assistance. Correspondence concerning this manuscript should be addressed to Dr. Kenneth Levy, Department of Psychology, Pennsylvania State University, University Park, Pennsylvania 16802. E-mail: klevy@psu.edu

clinical usage, the concept of narcissistic personality disorder is highly controversial and of uncertain validity (Frances, 1980; Maier, Lichtermann, Klingler,
Heun, & Hallmayer, 1992; Siever & Klar, 1986; Vaillant & Perry, 1985). The
vast majority of the literature on narcissistic personality disorder has been theoretical and clinical rather than empirical. The research that does exist, with a
few important exceptions, has not been carried out programmatically. In this
chapter, we will summarize and integrate the best available scientific evidence
bearing on the etiology, assessment, diagnosis, course, and treatment of the
disorder. We will begin with a brief history of the concept of narcissistic personality disorder, then review and evaluate a number of conceptualizations,
and conclude with recommendations for further research on unresolved conceptual and methodological issues as we look toward DSM-V.

Brief History of the Concept

The term *narcissism* is derived from the Greek myth of Narcissus, who, mis-
taking his own image for another, fell in love with that image and died when
it failed to love him back.[1] The legend of Narcissus, originally written as
Homeric hymns in the seventh or eighth century BCE (Hamilton, 1942) and
popularized in Ovid's *Metamorphoses* (8/1958), has arisen from a relatively
obscure beginning to become one of the prototypical myths of our times,
with the coining of such terms as "culture of narcissism" and "me genera-
tion" (Lasch, 1979; Wolfe, 1976).

Pioneering English psychologist and sex researcher Havelock Ellis (1898)
first invoked this myth in a case study of a man who engaged in excessive masturbation to illustrate a psychological state whereby an individual becomes the
object of his own sexual desire. Following Ellis, Freud first used the term "narcissistic" in a footnote in his 1905 paper (Freud, 1905/1957) entitled *Three
Essays on Sexuality* in discussing the choice of sexual partners that have qualities similar to oneself. Thus, one of the earliest psychiatric meanings of narcissism had to do with sexual behavior (see Pulver, 1970, and van der Waals,
1965, for reviews). In 1911, Otto Rank wrote the first paper exclusively on
narcissism, linking it to vanity and self-admiration. In 1914, Freud published
On Narcissism: An Introduction (Freud, 1914/1957), in which he noted the
dynamic characteristic in narcissism of consistently keeping out of awareness
any information or feelings that would diminish one's sense of self. In this
paper he also discussed, from a developmental perspective, the movement from
the normal but relatively exclusive focus on the self to mature relatedness. In
all of these early papers, narcissism was described as a dimensional psychological state in much the same way that contemporary trait theorists describe
pathological manifestations of normal traits (although Rank and Freud viewed
narcissism as dynamic—that is, they saw grandiosity as a defense against feeling insignificant). In all these writings, narcissism was conceptualized as a
process or state rather than a personality type or disorder.[2]

The concept of a narcissistic personality or character was first articulated by Waelder in 1925. Waelder described individuals with narcissistic personality as condescending, feeling superior to others, preoccupied with themselves and with admiration, and exhibiting a marked lack of empathy, often most apparent in their sexuality, which is based on purely physical pleasure rather than combined with emotional intimacy. Although Freud had not discussed narcissism as a personality type in his 1914 paper, in 1931, following Waelder, he described the narcissistic character type. In 1939, Karen Horney distinguished healthy self-esteem from pathological narcissism and suggested that the term *narcissism* be restricted to unrealistic self-inflation. Following this work, Jones (1955) described pathological narcissistic traits, Abraham (1924/1949) drew a link between envy and narcissism, and Reich (1960) suggested that narcissism is a pathological form of self-esteem regulation in which self-inflation and aggression are used to protect one's self-concept.

In 1961, Nemiah explicitly described narcissism not only as a personality type but as a disorder when he coined the term "narcissistic character disorder." In 1967, Kernberg, as part of his articulation of borderline personality organization, presented a clinical description of what he called "narcissistic personality structure." In a later paper, Kernberg (1970) further articulated explicit descriptions of clinical characteristics and the bases for the diagnosis on readily observable behavior, distinguishing between normal and pathological narcissism. Kernberg's (1967) initial paper was followed by a paper by Kohut (1968), who introduced the term "narcissistic personality disorder." Kernberg's (1967) and Kohut's (1968) writings on narcissism were, in part, a reaction to increased clinical interest in treating these patients. Their papers in turn stimulated increased clinical interest in the concept. However, these clinical trends also paralleled trends in critical social theory (Adorno, 1967, 1968; Blatt, 1983; Horkheimer, 1936; Horkheimer & Adorno, 1944/1998; Lasch, 1979; Marcuse, 1955; Nelson, 1977; Stern, 1980; Westen, 1985; Wolfe, 1976).

Although Kohut and Kernberg disagreed on the etiology of narcissistic personality disorder, they agreed on much of its expression, particularly for those patients in the healthier range. Both of these authors have been influential in shaping the concept of narcissistic personality disorder, not only among psychoanalysts but also among contemporary personality researchers and theorists (Baumeister, Bushman, & Campbell, 2000; Campbell, 1999; Dickinson & Pincus, 2003; Emmons, 1981, 1984, 1987, 1989; John & Robins, 1994; Raskin & Hall, 1979; Raskin, Novacek, & Hogan, 1991a, 1991b; Raskin & Terry, 1988; Robins & John, 1997a, 1997b; Rose, 2002; Wink, 1991, 1992a, 1992b).

Narcissistic personality disorder (NPD) was first introduced into the official diagnostic system in the third edition of the *Diagnostic and Statistical Manual of Mental Disorders* (DSM-III; American Psychiatric Association [APA], 1980), owing to clinicians' widespread use of the concept and the identification of narcissism as a personality factor in a number of psychological studies (Ashby, Lee, & Duke, 1979; Block, 1971; Cattel, Horn, Sweney, & Radcliffe, 1964; Exner, 1969, 1973; Eysenck & Eysenck, 1975; Harder, 1979; Leary, 1957; Murray, 1938; Pepper & Strong, 1958; Raskin & Hall, 1979; Serkownek, 1975; see Frances, 1980). Nevertheless, the DSM-III definition of and criteria for NPD were developed by consensus of a committee of psychiatrists and psychologists from a summary of the pre-1978 literature, without the benefit of empirical evaluation by clinical study groups. The criteria represented amalgamations of the theoretical and clinical work of Kernberg (1966, 1970, 1975a), Kohut (1968, 1971), and Millon (1969), with "expert" input (see Frances, 1980, for description). DSM-III-R (APA, 1987) followed the criteria for DSM-III rather closely. However, the criteria were changed from mixed polythetic and monothetic criteria to entirely polythetic criteria. The interpersonal criterion, which had originally included four parts (entitlement, interpersonal exploitativeness, alternation between extremes of overidealization and devaluation of self and others, and lack of empathy), was reduced to three parts through the elimination of the part regarding alternation between extremes of overidealization and devaluation of self and others. The criterion that included both grandiosity and uniqueness was split into two separate criteria, and a criterion about preoccupation with feelings of envy was added. Recently, Westen and Shedler (1999) surveyed a large group of experienced psychiatrists and psychologists of varying clinical orientations regarding the personality characteristics of patients with varying personality disorders, including narcissistic personality disorder. Using factor-analytic procedures to derive an empirical profile, they found that the Axis II work groups captured most of the important features of narcissistic personality disorder as seen in clinical practice. However, they noted that narcissistic patients as described by clinicians appear to be more controlling, more likely to get into power struggles, and more competitive than DSM-IV suggests. (Of course, these findings may have resulted from a referral bias, and thus DSM would be accurate.)

Prevalence

The prevalence of narcissistic personality disorder in the general population is estimated to be between less than 1% and 5.3%, with an estimated median rate of 0.8% and a mode of 0.0% (Black, Noyes, Pfohl, Goldstein, & Blum, 1993; Bodlund, Ekselius, & Lindström, 1993; Drake, Adler, & Vaillant, 1988; Ekselius, Tillfors, Furmark, & Fredrikson, 2001; Klein et al., 1995; Maier et al., 1992; Moldin, Rice, Erlenmeyer-Kimling, & Squires-Wheeler, 1994; Reich, Yates, & Nduaguba, 1989; Samuels, Nestadt, Romanoski, Folstein, & McHugh, 1994; Torgersen, Kringlen, & Cramer, 2001; Zimmerman & Coryell, 1990). In clinical populations, the estimated prevalence has ranged from 1.3% to 17%, with prevalence rates being reported as higher in samples of personality-disordered patients (Andreoli, Gressot, Aapro, Tricot, & Gognalons, 1989; Clarkin, Levy, Lenzenweger, & Kernberg, 2004; Crosby & Hall, 1992; Dahl, 1986; Frances, Clarkin, Gilmore, Hurt, & Brown, 1984; Grilo et al., 1998; Hilsenroth, Holdwick, Castlebury, & Blais, 1998; Loranger et al., 1991; Loranger et al., 1994; McGlashan et al., 2000; Skodol, Buckley, & Charles, 1983; Zanarini, Frankenburg, Chauncey, & Gunderson, 1987).

In a survey of a community sample in Baltimore, Maryland, approximately 0.1% of the sample met criteria for NPD (Samuels et al., 1994). The use of NPD as the primary clinical diagnosis is probably relatively unusual in outpatient clinic settings compared to inpatient settings. For instance, Fabrega, Ulrich, Pilkonis, and Mezzich (1992) found that less than a 0.3% of 18,179 individuals screened while seeking outpatient psychiatric evaluation over a 6-year period were assigned a diagnosis of NPD. Only 10 individuals were given a primary diagnosis of NPD. In contrast, Grilo et al. (1998), in a consecutively admitted inpatient sample, found that 4% of adolescents and 6% of adults were diagnosed with NPD using structured interviews. Clarkin et al. (2004) found that 17% of patients reliably diagnosed with borderline personality disorder were also diagnosed with NPD using a structured interview (the International Personality Disorder Examination [Loranger, 1999]). In a study of military personnel, Crosby and his colleagues (Bourgeois, Crosby, Drexler, & Hall, 1993; Crosby & Hall, 1992) found that 20% (60 of 300) of active-duty outpatients had significant narcissistic features and that 4% met criteria for narcissistic personality disorder. NPD was the most common personality disorder in this sample, representing 39% of patients with any personality disorder, and narcissistic traits were the most prevalent personality traits among those referred for psychiatric evaluation by superior officers. Fava, Grandi, Zielezny, Rafanelli, and Canestrari (1996) found that NPD was significantly more common in patients with early-onset depression than in those with late-onset depression.

However, given the extensive literature within psychoanalytic and psychotherapeutic journals, the prevalence of NPD may be higher in outpatient private practice settings than in hospital outpatient departments. For example, Westen (1997) found that 76% of 1,901 clinicians (838 psychodynamic, 300 cognitive-behavioral, and 639 eclectic) randomly selected from the American Psychiatric Association and American Psychological Association reported treating patients with NPD. Doidge et al. (2002) surveyed 510 psychoanalytically oriented clinicians, who reported on over 1,700 patients in the United States, Australia, and Ontario, Canada. Psychoanalysts across the three countries reported that about 20% of their patients suffered from NPD, making it the top-ranked disorder overall in the U.S. and Ontario and the second-ranked disorder overall in Australia. Westen and Arkowitz-Westen (1998) surveyed 238 experienced clinicians

(36.4% psychiatrists, 63.6% psychologists; 44.8% psychodynamic, 16.1% cognitive-behavioral, and 34.3% eclectic) about patients in their practices. Using a diagnostic Q-sort procedure, these clinicians evaluated 714 patients, of whom 8.5% were reported to have NPD. Psychodynamic clinicians reported that 11.2% of their patients had narcissistic personality disorder, whereas eclectic clinicians reported that 5.7% of their patients had NPD and cognitive-behavioral clinicians reported that 3.9% of their patients had NPD. This difference in rates among clinicians of different orientations may reflect greater sensitivity to the disorder by psychodynamic clinicians, an overdiagnosis of or selective attention to the disorder by psychodynamic clinicians, or different conceptualizations of the disorder. Alternatively, it may reflect relatively accurate base rates in different types of clinical practices. Interestingly, DiGiuseppe, Robin, Szeszko, and Primavera (1995) reported that 107 of 742 patients (14.4%) presenting over an 18-month period met the cutoff for NPD on the Millon Clinical Multiaxial Inventory—II (MCMI-II; Millon, 1987) in a private nonprofit cognitive-behavioral outpatient clinic in Manhattan.

In sum, the prevalence of NPD appears to vary according to clinical setting and type of practice. The ambiguity in defining and interpreting the criteria may lead some clinicians to be reluctant to use the diagnosis, whereas other clinicians, who find the clinical formulations of Kernberg, Kohut, and others useful, may make more frequent use of the diagnosis. In addition, the diagnosis is more likely to be used in private practices and small clinics than in larger psychiatric hospital clinics and inpatient units. Finally, there may be geographic differences in the rates of NPD.

Diagnosis

The diagnosis of NPD has been the focus of controversy since its introduction in the DSM-III. One of the major issues in this controversy has been whether NPD is a distinct diagnostic entity. Studies have generally confirmed the validity of some of the overt characteristics of NPD as defined in DSM-IV, such as grandiosity, grandiose fantasy, desire for uniqueness, need for admiring attention, and arrogant, haughty behavior (Morey & Jones, 1998; Ronningstam & Gunderson, 1990; Westen, 1990a). In addition to the DSM criteria set for NPD, a number of other diagnostic schemes have been developed. Gunderson and his colleagues developed the Diagnostic Interview for Narcissism (DIN; Gunderson, Ronningstam, & Bodkin, 1990), a semistructured interview that evaluates 33 characteristics of pathological narcissism. Using the DIN, Ronningstam and Gunderson (1991) found that the following characteristics could discriminate narcissistic patients from other psychiatric patients: boastful and pretentious behavior, self-centered and self-referential behavior, and the belief that other people envy them because of their special talents or unique abilities. There are a number of psychoanalytic conceptions of NPD, although those of Akhtar

and Thomson (1982) and Kernberg (1983) are probably the most systematically described.

Beck and Freeman (1990) have proposed a cognitive model for diagnosing and assessing personality disorders based on the assumption that each
personality disorder can be classified by the unique cognitive content of
cognitive distortions and maladaptive core and conditional beliefs. The cognitive contents are inferred on the basis of the patients' behaviors and traits.
According to Beck and Freeman (1990), the narcissistic individual's core
beliefs include "Since I am special, I deserve special dispensations, privi-
leges, and prerogatives"; "I am superior to others and they should acknowledge this"; and "I'm above the rule" (pp. 50–51). Nelson-Gray, Huprich,
Kissling, and Ketchum (2004) examined the relationship between specific
dysfunctional thought patterns (or beliefs) and personality disorder.
Although specific dysfunctional thought patterns were generally related to
corresponding personality disorders, most thought patterns lacked specificity. For example, in addition to narcissistic thought pattern scores, histrionic, avoidant, dependent, paranoid, and obsessive-compulsive thought
pattern scores were also significantly related to NPD scores (histrionic
thought pattern scores being the most highly correlated). Beck, Butler,
Brown, Dahlsgaard, and Beck (2001) also reported on the relationship of
dysfunctional beliefs to personality disorders. They found that narcissistic
dysfunctional beliefs were higher in patients diagnosed with NPD compared
to those diagnosed with avoidant, dependent, obsessive-compulsive, and
paranoid personality disorders. However, they did not examine whether
narcissistic dysfunctional thought patterns were higher in patients with NPD
compared to histrionic, antisocial, and borderline patients, which would
have provided a more stringent test of specificity. Narcissistic dysfunctional
thought patterns were highly correlated with histrionic and antisocial dysfunctional thought patterns. Young (1994) developed a schema-focused
approach to the treatment of personality disorder by hypothesizing that
personality disorders are the result of one of 18 early maladaptive schemas.
Young (1998) suggested that those with NPD are characterized by three
core maladaptive schemas (entitlement, emotional deprivation, and defectiveness) and a number of secondary schemas (e.g., approval seeking, sub-
jugation, mistrust, avoidance) that are clustered into separate aspects of the
self (special self, vulnerable child, and self-soother), which all alternate in
reaction to changes and events in the environment. Although Young (1994)
developed a measure to assess which schemas are present or active, he was
not specific regarding the association between a particular schema and its
corresponding personality disorder, nor has there been any research examining the validity of this model.

A number of authors have recently described assessment and diagnosis
of personality disorders from a radical behavioral framework (Koerner,
Kohlenberg, & Parker, 1996; Nelson-Gray & Farmer, 1999; Turkat, 1990;
Turkat & Maisto, 1985; Turner, 1994; van Velzen & Emmelkamp, 1996).

Koerner et al. (1996) describe a functional analytic assessment procedure in which, in addition to patient reports of their behavior toward others, the therapist's private reactions and feelings are central to diagnosis. They note that if a therapist feels demeaned and belittled, the patient may have features of NPD. It is interesting to note that the approach advocated by these authors is very similar to traditional psychoanalytic approaches in which clinicians are encouraged to improve their diagnostic accuracy by focusing on their own countertransference responses to patients (Gunther, 1976; Kernberg, 1975a; Wolf, 1979).[3]

Assessment

There have been several attempts to construct measures to assess narcissism. The earliest measure was a self-report questionnaire developed by Henry Murray: the Thematic Apperception Test (TAT; Murray, 1943). Broadly speaking, clinicians and researchers can draw from six information sources when assessing personality disorders: self-report inventories, rating scales and checklists, clinical interviews and ratings, projective techniques, informants, and physiological measurements (neurotransmitter or hormone levels; Millon & Davis, 2000). Only the first three methods will be discussed here, as little data exist on the last three sources.

The self-report instruments for personality disorders most widely used in assessing NPD are the Millon Clinical Multiaxial Inventory (MCMI-III; Millon, Davis, & Millon, 1997), the Personality Diagnostic Questionnaire—Revised (PDQ-R; Hyler, Kellman, Oldham, & Skodol, 1992), the Personality Assessment Inventory (PAI; Morey, 1992), and the Dimensional Assessment of Personality Pathology—Basic Questionnaire (Livesley, Reiffer, Sheldon, & West, 1987). Other personality disorder measures with narcissism scales include the Schedule of Nonadaptive and Adaptive Personality (SNAP; Clark, 1989), the OMNI Personality Inventory (OMNI; Loranger, 2000), the Personality Inventory Questionnaire (PIQ-II; Widiger, 1987), the Wisconsin Personality Disorders Inventory–IV (WIPSI-IV; Klein et al., 1993), and the Minnesota Multiphasic Personality Inventory 2—Personality Disorder Scales (MMPI 2-PD; Morey, Waugh, & Blashfield, 1985). There have been a number of self-report scales developed specifically to assess narcissism. Some have been based on DSM-III criteria. These include the Narcissistic Personality Inventory (NPI; Raskin & Hall, 1979) and the Narcissistic Personality Disorders Scale (NPDS; Ashby et al., 1979). A number of scales have been developed based on MMPI items (Ashby et al., 1979; Morey et al., 1985; Pepper & Strong, 1958; Raskin & Novacek, 1989; Serkownek, 1975; Wink & Gough, 1990). Raskin and Novacek's scale consists of 42 items selected from the MMPI item pool, using the NPI as an empirical criterion. Two scales, Serkownek's (1975) Narcissism-Hypersensitivity Scale and Pepper and Strong's (1958) Ego-Sensitivity Scale, were based on factor analyses of MMPI items. Wink and

Gough also developed scales from the California Psychological Inventory (CPI; Gough, 1957, 1987). The most widely investigated narcissism scale is probably the NPI.

There have been a number of self-report scales developed from theoretical perspectives other than that of the DSM. Murray's (1938) narcissism scale assesses the dual dynamics of self-absorption and vulnerability.[4] The O'Brien Multiphasic Narcissism Inventory (O'Brien, 1987) is based on Alice Miller's (1981) conception of narcissism, which includes a healthy authentic experience of seeing how the world relates to oneself and a more dependent, controlling, self-serving way of relating. Robbins and his colleagues developed the Superiority and Goal Instability Scales based on Kohut's (1971) theory (Robbins, 1989, Robbins & Patton, 1985, Robbins & Schwitzer, 1988). Millon's narcissism scale from the MCMI is based on his own social learning theory. Phares and Erskine (1984) have developed a 28-item scale designed to measure the construct of "selfism" within a social-learning framework. The Bell Object Relations and Reality Testing Inventory (BOR-RTI; Bell, Billington, & Becker, 1986) includes an egocentrism scale. Other narcissism measures include the Margolis-Thomas Measure of Narcissism (MTMN; Mullins & Kopelman, 1988), the narcissistic-competitive items of the Interpersonal Checklist (ICL; LaForge & Suczek, 1955), and the Dynamic Personality Inventory (DPI; Grygier & Grygier, 1976).

Some theorists have recently suggested that the five-factor model of personality may be relevant to conceptualizing personality disorders. Although this model is controversial (see Davis & Millon, 1993, and Westen, 1996, for critiques), review of a number of studies (Ball, Kranzler, Poling, Rounsaville, & Tennen, 1997; Blais, 1997; Bradlee & Emmons, 1992; Cloninger & Svrakic, 1994; Coolidge, Aksamit, & Becker, 1994; Costa & McCrae, 1990; Duggan et al., 2003; Duijsens & Diekstra, 1996; Dyce & O'Connor, 1998; Hendin & Cheek, 1997; Hyer, Matheson, Ofman, & Retzlaff, 1994; Lehne, 1994; Soldz, Budman, Demby, & Merry, 1993; Trull, 1992; Yeung, Lyons, Waternaux, Faraone, & Tsuang, 1993; see Saulsman & Page, 2004, for a review) suggests that there is a strong positive correlation between NPD and extraversion, a strong negative correlation between NPD and agreeableness, and a moderate negative correlation between NPD and conscientiousness. Findings regarding NPD's relationship with neuroticism and openness to experience are inconsistent. Some researchers have found that NPD is positively related to neuroticism, whereas others have found a negative relationship (Bradlee & Emmons, 1992; Buss & Chiodo, 1991). The inconsistent findings regarding NPD's relationship to neuroticism may be related to the distinction between overt and covert narcissism (with covert narcissism being positively related to neuroticism and overt narcissism being negatively related to neuroticism). The overall picture of the narcissistic individual in the five-factor model is that of one who is extraverted yet disagreeable, and low in anxiety. This profile can be distinguished from antisocial and histrionic patterns, but not from a passive-aggressive one (Trull, 1992).[5]

Research examining the facets underlying the five factors could provide a sharper picture of the disorder and better validity data. For instance, it is likely that within the overarching extraversion factor, the facet of dominance is related to narcissism but the facet of warmth is not. If this is so, NPD can be discriminated from histrionic personality disorder. Likewise, research examining more differentiated aspects of NPD may help to better character-ize the disorder (see Bradlee & Emmons, 1992). For example, in examining the relationship between the NPI subscales and the five-factor model's neu-roticism, extraversion, and openness measure (NEO-PI; Costa & McCrae, 1985), Bradlee and Emmons (1992) found that the authority subscale of the NPI was positively related to the conscientiousness factor on the NEO-PI and that the superiority subscale of the NPI was positively related to the openness to experience factor on the NEO-PI. Loranger (2000), using factor analysis, found that exhibitionism, assertiveness, and ambition loaded positively on the narcissism scale and that modesty and sincerity loaded negatively.[6]

Shedler and Westen (2004) examined the comprehensiveness of the five-factor model compared to an expanded criteria set. Using the items restricted to the five-factor model, they could replicate the factor structure on a clinical sample. However, they found that the expanded criteria set provided a conceptually richer factor solution that did not resemble the five-factor model but instead resulted in 12 factors: psychological health, psychopathy, hostility, narcissism, emotion dysregulation, dysphoria, schizoid orientation, obsessionality, thought disorder, histrionic sexualiza-tion, dissociation, and sexual conflict. They concluded that although the five-factor model is useful for layperson descriptions of normal-range per-sonality features, it omits important clinical constructs and does not cap-ture the complexity of personality pathology.

Overall, self-report measures appear best suited either to assessing NPD at the dimensional level, particularly examining multidimensional aspects of narcissism, or as a screening measure for identifying individuals who might be likely to have a personality disorder. However, they are much less useful for identifying a specific disorder, such as NPD, due to problems with overendorsement of items, especially among distressed individuals, and the potential for underendorsement of items by defensive individuals.

There are also a number of observer-rated measures. Wink (1992a) devel-oped a California Q-Set narcissism prototype. Patton, Connor, and Scott (1982) developed 10 observer-rated scales to measure Kohut's (1971) formu-lations of narcissism based on self-psychology, although this measure is not well researched.

There are a number of structured interviews for DSM personality disor-ders that assess NPD, including the Structured Interview for DSM-IV Personality (SIDP-IV; Pfohl, Blum, & Zimmerman, 1997), Structured Clinical Interview for DSM-IV Personality Disorders (SCID-II; First, Spitzer, Gibbon, & Williams, 1995), International Personality Disorder Examination (IPDE; Loranger, 1999), Personality Disorder Interview—IV (PDI-IV; Widiger, 1995), Diagnostic Interview for Personality Disorders

(DIPD; Zanarini, Frankenburg, Chauncey, & Gunderson, 1987; Zanarini et al., 2000), and Personality Assessment Schedule (PAS; Tyrer et al., 1988).

Two additional instruments with unique properties are the Personality Assessment Form (PAF; Shea, Glass, Pilkonis, Watkins, & Docherty, 1987) and the Shedler-Westen Assessment Procedure (SWAP; Westen & Shedler, 1999). The PAF presents a brief paragraph that describes important features of each personality disorder, and the individual's similarity to the description is rated by an evaluator using a six-point scale. The PAF is not a structured interview in that it does not provide systematic assessment or questions for evaluation. The SWAP is a 200-item Q-set of personality-descriptive statements designed to quantify clinical judgment. Clinicians are directed to arrange the 200 items (presented on separate index cards) into eight categories with a fixed distribution, ranging from those that are not descriptive of the patient to those that are highly descriptive of the patient. One important finding with use of the SWAP is a reduction of comorbidity with other personality disorders, especially Cluster B personality disorders. This reduction in comorbidity appears important, because lack of discreteness of Axis II disorders has been a frequent criticism of the construct validity of these disorders. Gunderson's DIN (discussed above) appears to be the only interview measure designed to exclusively assess NPD.

In terms of projective measures, Exner (1969) discussed the pair response as an indicator of narcissism and later developed the Egocentricity Index (EGOI) as an index of excessive self-concern. Harder (1979) constructed a projective narcissism scale for use with the Early Memory Test, the TAT, or the Rorschach. The validity of the EGOI scale as a measure of narcissism is equivocal at best (Exner, 1995; Hilsenroth, Fowler, Padawer, & Handler, 1997; Nezworski & Wood, 1995), and the Harder scale has not been used widely by other investigators. A number of studies have examined Rorschach variables as they relate to the diagnosis of narcissism (Berg, Packer, & Nunno, 1993; Farris, 1988; Gacono, Meloy, & Berg, 1992; Hilsenroth, Hibbard, Nash, & Handler, 1993; Hilsenroth et al., 1997). Findings from these studies are difficult to interpret; however, consistent with the writings of Kernberg and Kohut, narcissistic patients generally look healthier psychologically on various outcome measures than patients with borderline personality disorder.

In sum, both self-report and interview measures have satisfactory reliability; however, at present the evidence for the concurrent validity of these methods to the diagnosis of NPD is only limited. In addition, there is only poor to moderate agreement across personality disorder diagnostic measures and methods (Perry, 1992). Generally, self-report measures result in much higher frequencies of NPD diagnosis than do clinicians or structured interviews. Structured interviews may underdiagnose NPD because of the face validity of the questions and the tendency of individuals with the disorder to deny pathology. Therefore, interviews that allow for the use of clinical judgment may have more validity for NPD diagnosis. Likewise, observation of behavior may be needed and more useful than self-report.

Some interviews specifically utilize behavioral observation. For further discussion of the psychometrics of these measures, see Hilsenroth, Handler, and Blais (1996).

Subtypes

The definition of NPD articulated in the DSM-III and its successors, DSM-III-R, DSM-IV (APA, 1994), and DSM-IV-TR (APA, 2000), has been criticized for failing to capture the intended clinical phenomena (Cooper & Ronningstam, 1992; Gabbard, 1989; Gunderson, Ronningstam, & Smith, 1991). These authors have noted that the DSM criteria, following the conceptual approaches of Kernberg and Millon, have emphasized a more overt form of narcissism. More recently, Cooper (1981), Akhtar and Thomson (1982), Gabbard (1989), and Wink (1991) have suggested that there are two subtypes of NPD: an overt form, also referred to as grandiose, oblivious, willful, exhibitionist, thick skinned, or phallic; and a covert form, also referred to as vulnerable, hypersensitive, closet, or thin skinned (Bateman, 1998; Britton, 2000; Gabbard, 1989; Masterson, 1981; Rosenfeld, 1987). The overt type is characterized by grandiosity, attention seeking, entitlement, arrogance, and little observable anxiety. These individuals can be socially charming despite being oblivious of others' needs, interpersonally exploitative, and envious. In contrast, the covert narcissist is hypersensitive to others' evaluations, inhibited, manifestly distressed, and outwardly modest. Gabbard (1989) describes these individuals as shy and "quietly grandiose," with an "extreme sensitivity to slight" which "leads to an assiduous avoidance of the spotlight" (p. 527). Both types are extraordinarily self-absorbed and harbor unrealistic, grandiose expectations of themselves. This overt-covert distinction has been empirically supported in at least six studies using factor analyses and correlational methods (Dickinson & Pincus, 2003; Hendin & Cheek, 1997; Hibbard & Bunce, 1995; Rathvon & Holmstrom, 1996; Rose, 2002; Wink, 1992b). Rather than distinguishing between overt and covert types as discrete forms of narcissism, Kernberg (1992) notes that the overt and covert expressions of narcissism may be different clinical manifestations of the disorder, with some traits being overt and others being covert. Kernberg contends that narcissistic individuals hold contradictory views of the self, which vacillate between the clinical expression of overt and covert symptoms. Thus the overtly narcissistic individual most frequently presents with grandiosity, exhibitionism, and entitlement. Nevertheless, in the face of failure or loss, these individuals will become depressed, depleted, and feel painfully inferior. The covertly narcissistic individual will often present as shy, timid, and inhibited, but, upon closer contact, reveal exhibitionistic and grandiose fantasies.

Using cluster analysis, DiGiuseppe et al. (1995) found three clusters of narcissistic patients in an outpatient setting. They named these clusters

(1) the true narcissist, (2) the compensating narcissist, and (3) the detached narcissist. Patients in all three clusters exhibited self-centeredness and entitlement. However, patients in the true and detached groups reported experiencing little emotional distress. In contrast, patients in the compensating group reported high levels of emotional vulnerability. The true and detached groups were similar except that the detached group was characterized by extreme interpersonal avoidance.

Other distinctions in the expression of NPD have been noted. Bursten (1973) proposed four types of narcissistic personalities: craving individuals, who are clinging, demanding, and needy; paranoid individuals, who are critical and suspicious; manipulative individuals, who derive satisfaction from conscious and deliberate deception of others; and phallic narcissists, who are aggressive, exhibitionistic, reckless, and daring. These distinctions seem overly broad and may include other disorders but generally correspond to the overt-covert distinction (e.g., paranoid and phallic correspond to the grandiose type and craving corresponds to the vulnerable type). In addition, these distinctions lack the complexity and sophistication of the dynamics noted by Kernberg and others. When discussing narcissism in the context of interpersonal relations, Kohut and Wolf (1978) distinguished among "merger-hungry" individuals, who must continually attach and define themselves through others; "contact shunning" individuals, who avoid social contact due to fear that their behaviors will not be admired or accepted; and "mirror-hungry" individuals, who tend to display themselves in front of others. Millon (1998) conceptualized NPD as a prototype and distinguished among several variations, or subtypes, in which the basic personality style may manifest itself. These subtypes represent configurations of a dominant basic personality style (e.g., NPD) and traits of other basic personality styles. For example, in addition to meeting criteria for NPD, his amorous subtype would show elevations in histrionic traits, his unprincipled subtype would show elevations in antisocial traits, and his compensatory subtype would show elevations in avoidant and/or passive-aggressive traits. To date, little research has been performed to establish the reliability or validity of Millon's distinctions.

Kernberg (1975a) classified narcissism along a dimension of severity from normal to pathological and distinguished among three levels of pathological narcissism based on the degree of differentiation and integration of representation. These three levels correspond to high, middle, and low functioning groups. At the highest level are those patients whose talents are adequate to achieve the levels of admiration necessary to gratify their grandiose needs. These patients may function successfully for a lifetime, but they are susceptible to breakdowns with advancing age as their grandiose desires go unfulfilled. At the middle level are patients with NPD proper, who present with a grandiose sense of self and little interest in true intimacy. At the lowest level are the continuum of patients who have comorbid borderline personality, whose sense of self is generally more diffuse and less stable and thus more frequently vacillates between pathological grandiosity and suicidality. These individuals' lives are generally more chaotic. Finally, Kernberg distinguished a type of NPD that he called "malignant narcissism." These patients are characterized by the typical NPD; however, they also display antisocial behavior, tend toward paranoid features, and take pleasure in their aggression and sadism toward others. Kernberg (1992) posited that these patients are at high risk for suicide, despite the absence of depression. He suggested that suicidality for these patients represents sadistic control over others, a dismissal of a denigrated world, or a display of mastery over death. Despite the richness of Kernberg's descriptions, we could find no direct research on malignant narcissism. It will be important to differentiate malignant narcissism from NPD proper (as well as from antisocial, paranoid, and borderline personality disorders) and to show that patients meeting Kernberg's criteria for malignant narcissism are at risk for the kinds of difficulties Kernberg described.

Comorbidity

A number of authors have suggested the importance of understanding the co-occurrence or comorbidity of theoretically discrete disorders (Blatt & Levy, 1998; Caron & Rutter, 1991; Carson, 1991; Clarkin & Kendell, 1992; Westen & Shedler, 1999). NPD has had problematically high overlap with other Axis II disorders, most notably antisocial, histrionic, borderline, and passive-aggressive personality disorders (Becker, Edell, Grilo, & McGlashan, 2000; Gunderson, Ronningstam, & Smith, 1991; Morey, 1988; Oldham et al., 1992; Stuart et al., 1998; Widiger et al., 1991; Zanarini et al., 1998), with rates often exceeding 50%. Most patients (80%) meeting criteria for NPD also meet criteria for borderline personality disorder (Pfohl, Coryell, Zimmerman, & Stangl, 1986). Of course, the comorbidity between NPD and borderline personality disorder is not surprising, given that Kernberg's original clinical formulations of NPD, from which many of the DSM-III criteria were adopted, were based on a selected clinical sample of patients with a primary diagnosis of borderline personality disorder (Kernberg, 1967, 1970, 1975a). However, the co-occurrence or comorbidity of NPD with other disorders, although not unique to NPD, is a major problem in justifying and maintaining its validity as a distinct clinical entity (McGlashan & Heinssen, 1989; Morey & Jones, 1998; Ronningstam & Gunderson, 1989).

Comorbidity can be examined within samples of patients diagnosed with NPD or by examining the rates of NPD among individuals with other disorders. Using the former approach, Ronningstam and Gunderson (1989), in two samples of NPD patients—38 inpatients and outpatients and 34 consecutively admitted outpatients—reported that 42% and 50% of the patients, respectively, had comorbid depressive mood disorder, 24% and 50% had comorbid substance abuse disorder, and 5% and 11% had comorbid bipolar disorder.

Ronningstam (1996) reviewed the available literature on concomitant NPD and Axis I disorders and found that between 12% and 38% of patients with substance use disorder and between 4% and 47% of those with bipolar disorder were diagnosed with NPD. Thus a lot of variation exists in the comorbidity between NPD and other disorders. The reasons are unclear, but one interpretation that can be distilled from these findings is that no single Axis I disorder is most often associated with NPD. A number of studies have examined the comorbidity of NPD with bipolar disorder (Bieling et al., 2003; Brieger, Ehrt, & Marneros, 2003; Carpenter, Clarkin, Glick, & Wilner, 1995; Corruble, Ginestet, & Guelfi, 1996; George, Miklowitz, Richards, Simoneau, & Taylor, 2003; Kutcher, Marton, & Korenblum, 1990; O'Connell, Mayo, & Sciutto, 1991; Pica et al., 1990; Pesslow, Sanfilipo, & Fieve, 1995; Stormberg, Ronningstam, Gunderson, & Tohen, 1998; Turley, Bates, Edwards, & Jackson, 1992). Generally, these studies found higher than average prevalence rates for NPD. These prevalence rates were much higher when the patients were actively hypomanic or manic compared to when they were euthymic, suggesting that mania should be considered in the differential diagnosis of NPD or that the criteria for NPD and mania need to be more clearly differentiated.

With regard to Axis II disorders, McGlashan and his colleagues (McGlashan et al., 2000), in conducting the Collaborative Longitudinal Personality Disorder Study, found that 8% of borderline personality disorder patients had comorbid NPD. This percentage did not differ from the percentage of patients with comorbid schizotypal personality disorder or the percentage of those with obsessive-compulsive personality disorder but was significantly higher than the percentage of patients with comorbid avoidant personality disorder.

Gender and Age Differences

Gender

The DSM-IV states that NPD is more common in men than in women. The analysis of gender differences in narcissism is complicated by the fact that the DSM's definition of NPD is based on clinical descriptions of case studies of male patients (Kernberg, 1975a; Kohut, 1971, 1977).[7] Consequently, several theorists have raised questions regarding whether narcissism as defined by the DSM can be generalized to women (e.g., Akhtar & Thomson, 1982; Philipson, 1985). A number of authors (Haaken, 1983; Harder & Lewis, 1987; Harder & Zalma, 1990; Hárnik, 1924; O'Leary & Wright, 1986; Philipson, 1985; Reich, 1953, 1960; Richman & Flaherty, 1988, 1990) have suggested that the distinction between covert and overt narcissism may exist along gender lines, with the grandiose type being stereotypically male and the hypersensitive type being stereotypically female. However, the empirical support for this contention remains equivocal.

Although a number of studies have found greater prevalence rates for NPD in men (Alnaes & Torgerson, 1988; Golomb, Fava, Abraham & Rosenbaum, 1995; Grilo et al., 1996; Ronningstam & Gunderson, 1991; Stone, 1989), these findings are inconsistent with many studies failing to find gender differences in the rates of NPD (Black, Noyes, Pfohl, Goldstein, & Blum, 1993; Grilo et al., 1996; Kass, Spitzer, & Williams, 1983; Plakun, 1989; Reich, 1987; Torgersen, Kringlen, & Cramer, 2001; Zimmerman & Coryell, 1989). Torgersen et al. (2001) found no differences between men and women in the prevalence of NPD, and Grilo et al. (1996), in an adult sample, found no gender differences in NPD. Ekselius, Bodlund, Knorring, Lindstrom, and Kullgren (1996) and Richman and Flaherty (1990) found no differences between men and women in narcissism at the categorical diagnostic level; however, both groups of researchers found gender differences at the criteria level. Richman and Flaherty (1990) found that men scored significantly higher on five of the six traits, whereas women scored significantly higher only on the criterion of becoming upset over slights. Ekselius et al. (1996) found gender differences on five criteria: (1) self-importance; (2) fantasies of unlimited power, success, beauty; (3) believes self to be special or only understood by special people; (4) lacks empathy; and (5) envious of others or believes others are envious of them. However, women scored higher on three of the four criteria, the exception being criterion 3 (believes self to be special or only understood by special people).

The findings regarding gender differences in dimensional scores on narcissism are also inconsistent (Auerbach, 1984; Emmons, 1984, 1987; Jackson, Ervin, & Hodge, 1992; Raskin et al., 1991a; Rhodewalt & Morf, 1995, 1998; Weirzbicki & Goldade, 1993). One somewhat consistent finding is that men score higher on average than women on dimensional measures of narcissism (Carroll, 1987; Farwell & Wohlwend-Lloyd, 1998; Gabriel, Critelli, & Ee, 1994; Narayan, 1990; Stangl, Pfohl, Zimmerman, Bowers, & Corenthal, 1985; Tschanz, Morf, & Turner, 1998; Watson, Grisham, Trotter, & Biderman, 1984). In a sample of predominantly Mormon men and women, Tschanz et al. (1998) found that although men and women showed highly similar patterns of narcissism, the NPI exploitativeness-entitlement factor was not as well integrated into the profile of narcissism for women. Some studies have found that women score higher on dimensional measures than men (Hynan, 2004; McCann et al., 2001). When gender differences were found, these tended to be small and of questionable meaningfulness (e.g., Buss & Chiodo, 1991; Carroll, 1987; McCann & Biaggio, 1989). In addition, it is unclear if and how gender moderates the relationship between narcissism and behavior, or other important variables, in systematic ways. In sum, the empirical support for gender differences remains ambiguous.

Age

The presence of narcissistic disturbances has been demonstrated in both children (Abrams, 1993; Bardenstein, 1994; Weise & Tuber, 2004) and adolescents (Bernstein et al., 1993; Grilo et al., 1998; Kernberg, Hajal, & Normandin, 1998; Westen, Shedler, Durrett, Glass, & Martens, 2003). In a consecutively admitted inpatient sample of adolescents, Grilo et al. (1998) found that 4% of the inpatients were reliably diagnosed with NPD using structured interviews. Bernstein et al. (1993), in a longitudinal study, found that the rates of NPD decreased from ages 11–14 to ages 18–21. NPD has been found in the elderly (Abrams, Alexopoulos, & Young, 1987; Abrams, Rosendahl, Card, & Alexopoulous, 1994; Ames and Molinari, 1994; Berezin, 1977; Kernberg, 1977).

Etiology

The empirical data on the etiology of NPD are extremely limited. The theoretical causes of narcissism are mainly derived from the psychodynamic object relations theories of Kernberg (1975a), Kohut (1971, 1977), and Masterson (1990). Most of the work by psychoanalytic theorists in this area has been based on inferences drawn in the clinical setting from patients' recollections of childhood family dynamics and/or analysis of how patients relate to therapists during session. More recently, Fonagy, Gergely, Jurist, and Target (2002) and Schore (1994) have discussed the development of narcissism from a psychoanalytic perspective, using a combination of object relations theory and more explicit integration of empirical findings from developmental psychology.

From an attachment theory perspective, Bowlby (1973, 1979) conceptualized narcissism as the result of an insecure attachment style between child and caretaker, which affects the child's emerging self-concept and developing view of the social world. Bowlby postulated that insecure attachment lies at the center of disordered personality traits and linked the overt expression of felt insecurity to specific characterological or personality disorders. Bowlby (1979) believed that attachment difficulties increase the vulnerability to psychopathology and that different types of insecure attachment patterns are linked to specific types of difficulties that may arise later in development. For instance, Bowlby (1973) connected anxious ambivalent attachment to "a tendency to make excessive demands on others and to be anxious and clingy when they are not met, such as is present in dependent and hysterical personalities" and avoidant attachment to "a blockage in the capacity to make deep relationships, such as is present in affectionless and psychopathic personalities" (p. 14). Avoidant attachment, Bowlby (1973) postulated, results from constantly being rebuffed in one's appeals for comfort or protection, and such individuals "may later be diagnosed as narcissistic" (p. 124).

In Kernberg's (1966, 1975a, 1975b, 1984, 1992) view, narcissism develops as a consequence of parental rejection, devaluation, and an emotionally invalidating environment in which parents are inconsistent in their investment in their children or often interact with their children to satisfy their own needs. For example, at times a parent may be cold, dismissive, and neglectful of a child, and then at other times, when it suits the parent's needs, be attentive and even intrusive. This parental devaluation hypothesis states that because of cold and rejecting parents, the child defensively withdraws and forms a pathologically grandiose self-representation. This self-representation, which combines aspects of the real child, the fantasized aspects of what the child wants to be, and the fantasized aspects of an ideal, loving parent, serves as an internal refuge from the experience of the early environment as harsh and depriving. The negative self-representation of the child is disavowed and not integrated into the grandiose representation, which is the seat of agency from which the narcissist operates. This split-off unacceptable self-representation can be seen in the emptiness, chronic hunger for admiration and excitement, and shame that also characterize the narcissist's experience (Akhtar & Thomson, 1982).

What Kernberg (1975a) sees as defensive and compensatory in the establishment of the narcissist's grandiose self-representation, Kohut (1971) views as a normal development process gone awry. Kohut sees pathological narcissism as resulting from failure to idealize the parents because of rejection or indifference. For Kohut, childhood grandiosity is normal and can be understood as a process by which the child attempts to identify with and become like his idealized parental figures. The child hopes to be admired by taking on attributes of perceived competence and power that he or she admires in others. In normal development, this early grandiose self eventually contributes to an integrated, vibrant sense of self, complete with realistic ambitions and goals. However, if this grandiose self is not properly modulated, what follows is the failure of the grandiose self to be integrated into the person's whole personality. According to Kohut, as an adult, a person with narcissism rigidly relates to others in "archaic" ways that befit a person in the early stages of proper self-development. Others are taken as extensions of the self (Kohut's term is "selfobject") and are relied upon to regulate one's self-esteem and anxieties regarding a stable identity. Because narcissists are unable to sufficiently manage the normal fluctuations of daily life and its affective correlates, other people are unwittingly relegated to roles of providing internal regulation for them (by way of unconditional support admiration and total empathic attunement), the same way a parent would provide internal regulation for a young child.

In contrast to Kernberg and Kohut, Millon (1981) articulated an evolution-based social learning theory of narcissism. Millon sees narcissism developing not as a response to parental devaluation but rather as a consequence of parental overvaluation. According to Millon, as a child, the narcissistic individual is treated as a special person, given much attention, and led by parents to believe he or she is lovable and perfect. Millon (1981) contends that such unrealistic overvaluation will lead to self-illusions that "cannot be sustained in the outer world" (p. 165). According to Millon, firstborn and only children are more vulnerable to narcissism because they tend to receive an abundance of attention and special treatment. However, the evidence is mixed regarding birth order, and there is no evidence that only-child status is related to narcissism. Two studies found that narcissism was related to firstborn status (Curtis & Cowell, 1993; Joubert, 1989); however, two studies found that narcissism was not related to birth order (Eyring & Sobelman, 1996; Narayan, 1990). Watson and Biderman (1989) also did not find any relationship between only-child status and narcissism. It is likely that the constructs of firstborn status and only-child status are not sensitive enough to account for the multiplicity of reasons that a parent may identify and treat a child as special or as threatening.

Also from a psychoanalytic perspective but attempting to bridge theory and empirical research is the promising work of Peter Fonagy (Fonagy et al., 2002). In drawing from scientific research to propose etiologic theories of NPD that conform to the most modern understanding of child development, Fonagy's work escapes some of the heavy criticism inspired by the developmental inconsistencies implicit in Kernberg's and Kohut's models (Auerbach, 1993; Westen, 1985). Fonagy and his colleagues (Fonagy et al., 2002) rest their theory of affect regulation and mentalization on a social biofeedback model of development that grew out of infant observational research (Gergely & Watson, 1996). In this model, the infant's psychological self is built through a pattern of contingency detection linked to parental affect mirroring. This process of affect mirroring provides the cognitive-affective scaffolding that leads to the infant's burgeoning representational capabilities. Fonagy and his colleagues posit that the pathological form of this process could make one vulnerable to the development of narcissistic pathology. In short, when parental affect mirroring is noncontingent in that the infant's emotion is acknowledged but misperceived by the caregiver, the baby will feel related to in ways that can only be experienced as foreign. In other words, in the early development of a subjective sense of self, the baby looks toward the primary caregiver to see his or her emotional state mirrored, elaborated, and fully established, but in the case of incongruent parental mirroring, he or she instead finds a noncontingent "alien self" reflected. According to this theory, the narcissist is one whose core sense of agency and experience is only partially integrated into his or her total personality, since it remains obscured by the ongoing experience of the false self. Because of the lack of integration of these two competing self-representations, the narcissist lacks the range of representational capabilities to regulate his or her affect and hold on to a stable self-representation, which is independent of others' perceptions of him or her.

Alan Schore (1994, 2003) focuses on the connection between neurophysiological development and parent-infant interactional processes in relation to the etiology of pathological narcissism. He describes the normal psychophysiological function of shame, which begins to serve an important role after the first year of life and continues to serve as a modulator for states of high arousal and affect. With respect to narcissistic pathology, Schore posits that the initial difficulties in the caregiver-infant dyad occur during the 16- to 24-month period. It is during this period, he suggests, that consistent improper parental modulating of infant affect, particularly during the infant's heightened affect states (which he sees as a form of grandiose hyperarousal), leaves the child without the ability to tolerate negative, shame-related affect resulting from normal narcissistic injury. Instead of being able to use shame to help regulate the self, the narcissist strives to evade the feeling of shame, which he or she experiences as intolerable and overwhelming. In many cases, Schore points out, misattunement takes the form of the mother hyperstimulating the child into dyscontrol, or failing to help the child recover from states of hypoarousal which she may have herself induced. As in Fonagy's model, what the narcissist lacked in childhood was the proper establishment of certain autoregulatory processes, mainly achieved within the infant-caregiver dyad during the first few years of life.

It is important to note that the theories of Kernberg, Kohut, Fonagy, Bowlby, and other psychodynamic theorists (e.g., Winnicott, 1960/1965) are probabilistic and not deterministic. That is, these theorists do not suggest that narcissistic personality develops in early childhood. Rather, each of these theories proposes that the potential for the disorder begins with early disruptions in the relationship with caregivers, but that these initial disruptions are elaborated over time due to the consistency of the caregiver's problematic behavior over the course of the child's development and the consistency created by the child's resulting expectations and behavior toward others. Fonagy's noncontingent parent is likely to continue to interact noncontingently with his or her child throughout the child's development, and the child is likely to experience ongoing difficulties in both integrating representations of the core and false selves and developing self-regulatory capacities. Likewise, Kernberg's cold and rejecting but intrusive parent is likely to continue to be cold, rejecting, and intrusive throughout the child's development, and the child is likely to continue to withdraw from the parent and increasingly attend to and depend on his or her defensively grandiose self-representation. Thus at each nodal point in development, the child experiences narcissism-inducing environments, and his or her range of behaviors and expectations is consistent with such environments. This idea that early vulnerabilities are maintained, reinforced, and possibly elaborated with subsequent experience is consistent with a number of current developmental theories of personality formation (Bowlby, 1979; Caspi, 2000; Cicchetti & Toth, 1998; Sroufe, Egeland, Carlson, & Collins, 2005) and the integrative work of Paul Wachtel (1977, 1994). Wachtel (1977, 1994) hypothesized that personality patterns, though heavily influenced by early experiences, are in large part sustained and perpetuated through current day-to-day interactions with others. He suggested that narcissistic individuals enlist others as "accomplices" in recapitulating experiences from the past and thus self-verifying beliefs about both oneself and others (Wachtel, 1987).

In a retrospective study of early parenting styles among college undergraduates, Watson, Little, and Biderman (1992) found that the Exploitativeness/ Entitlement subscale of the NPI was negatively correlated with mature authoritative parenting style and positively correlated with parental permissiveness. In Paul Wink's (1992b) longitudinal study of narcissism among a sample of Mills College women, he found that his group of "hypersensitive" (or covert) narcissists described their parental relationships as generally lacking warmth and claimed feelings of insecurity toward their mothers. His "willful" (or overt) narcissists reported an attitude of dislike toward their mothers with concurrent pride in their fathers.

Wink's (1992b) findings seem to confirm and even expand some of Block's (1971) observations of his female "dominating narcissists" group. Block followed this group from junior high school through adulthood and found that the familial context common among these women was characterized by parental discord; a dominant, self-indulgent, and extraverted father; and a neurotic, somewhat dysphoric, vulnerable mother. Block suggests that the extremely aggressive, condescending, self-indulgent, undercontrolled dominant narcissist seen in his adult sample was the product of identification with one's detached but impressive father.

Genetic hypotheses related to the development of narcissism have not been articulated. NPD has not been assessed in any family or adoption studies, although there are some initial twin study data relevant to its etiology. Livesley, Jang, Jackson, and Vernon (1993), using the Dimensional Assessment of Personality Pathology (DAPP), reported the heritability of narcissism to be 53%. The heritability of the specific traits of need for adulation, attention seeking, grandiosity, and need for approval ranged from 37% for grandiosity to 50% for need for approval. Torgersen and his colleagues (2000) examined heritability in 92 monozygotic (MZ) and 129 dizygotic (DZ) twin pairs using the SCID-II. They found 45% concordance in MZ twins and 9% in DZ twins using a broad definition of NPD (three or more criteria met). Heritability was 79%; however, this estimate was determined using broad definition diagnoses, best-fitting models did not include shared environmental effects, and interviewers assessed both twins and were not blind to zygosity status. All three of these limitations are known to inflate the estimates of genetic effects.

Two other studies examined the genetic effects of narcissism (Coolidge, Thede, & Jang, 2001, 2004). In these studies, parents were asked to assess their children's personality disorder features using the Coolidge Personality and Neuropsychological Inventory for Children (CPNI; Coolidge, 1998; Coolidge et al., 1990, 1992; Coolidge, Thede, Stewart, & Segal, 2002). In the 2001 study, 112 twin pairs (70 MZ and 42 DZ) were assessed; findings revealed a 66% concordance in MZ twins and a 34% concordance in DZ twins. In addition, these findings yielded a 66% heritability index. The generalizability of these findings is limited by three methodological shortcomings: (1) the effects of environment on development were not estimated, (2) the sample was not recruited representatively, and (3) personality disorder traits were rated by parents. Parents are of course not blind to zygosity, and there is evidence that they tend to overestimate trait concordance in MZ twins (Hoffman, 1991). In their 2004 study, Coolidge and his colleagues attempted to reduce the influence of preconceived ideas about twin similarity by having parents complete questionnaires on different days. A wholly environmental model specifying shared and nonshared environmental influences provided the most satisfactory fit to the narcissistic personality disorder scale; no heritable influence was detected for narcissistic personality disorder.

Paris (1993) suggested that the etiology of personality disorders is unlikely to be underpinned by simple, linear, monocausal processes; complex interactive processes among variables are likely to be involved in the etiology of personality disorders. A primary difficulty is the absence of a clear definitive phenotype, which is required for the establishment of inheritance. Lack of diagnostic clarity (e.g., misdiagnosis, overlap) inevitably leads to spurious estimates of inheritance (Jang & Vernon, 2001). Given the contradictory findings and limitations of the study designs, it is safe to say that at present the heritability of narcissistic personality disorder is uncertain.

Last, no studies have been conducted to directly identify biological markers for narcissistic personality disorder, although a number of studies have examined biological markers in near neighbor disorders, such as borderline personality disorder and antisocial personality disorder, and some studies have examined markers in vague groups that might have included narcissistic patients (e.g., patients with Cluster B personality disorders or those high in impulsive aggression). However, it is difficult to know if there is a specific effect for NPD.

Course and Long-Term Outcome

Data on the long-term course and outcome of NPD are sparse. There is little systematic follow-up information on this group. Plakun (1989) compared the long-term (approximately 14-year) outcome of 17 inpatients with NPD with that of 33 inpatients with borderline personality disorder and showed that the outcome of the latter was superior. NPD patients were more likely to have been readmitted and had poorer overall functioning and sexual satisfaction. McGlashan and Heinssen (1989) found that, over time, individuals with NPD show decreases in destructive interpersonal behaviors. However, both McGlashan and Heinssen (1989) and Stone (1989) found no differences over time in global functioning between narcissistic and borderline patients (provided there was no antisocial comorbidity). Ronningstam, Gunderson, and Lyons (1995) examined change in narcissism over a 3-year period in 20 treated patients diagnosed with NPD. They found that the majority of their patients (60%) who initially had NPD showed significant improvement in their levels of pathological narcissism at 3-year follow-up. Although grandiosity had differentiated narcissistic patients from borderline patients in an earlier study (Ronningstam & Gunderson, 1991), it did not predict stability of the disorder over time. Patients who continued to show high levels of narcissistic pathology were significantly more narcissistic in their interpersonal relationships and lacked a commitment to anyone.

Ronningstam and her colleagues (1995) found some evidence that three events might have effected change in the narcissistic pathology: (1) corrective achievements, (2) corrective disillusionments, and (3) corrective relationships. In a 30-month follow-up of depressed outpatients, Ferro, Klein, and Schwartz (1998) also found low stability for NPD, particularly compared to other personality disorders. In fact, narcissistic personality at baseline was more highly correlated with eight other disorders than with itself at follow-up. In contrast, Grilo, Becker, Edell, and McGlashan (2001) found that narcissism assessed dimensionally was stable over a 2-year period. These findings may be highly sample dependent, which makes them difficult to interpret and may limit their generalizability. Some of the studies involved inpatient samples, whereas others involved outpatients. For some patients, NPD was the primary or only disorder; for other patients, NPD was a comorbid disorder (with depression or borderline personality disorder). Only the Grilo et al. (2001) study utilized consecutively admitted patients. The use of nonconsecutive samples complicates the interpretation of the data, because the study groups may be skewed in some undefined way. For example, patients agreeing to participate may be more engaged with their therapists or may be more distressed, both of which factors have been related to better outcome (Clarkin & Levy, 2003). Second, some studies examined treated patients, which is likely to have influenced the outcome.

The most extensive work on the course of narcissism has been carried out in nonclinical samples in the context of examining normal development (Block, 1971; Wink, 1992a, 1992b). In *Lives Through Time,* Block (1971) reported that between ages 18 and 30, women classified as "dominant narcissists" increased in socialization and consideration of others. However, they continued to be egotistically dominating and exploitative. Over a 20-year period, Wink (1992b) examined the relationship between narcissism and midlife development in a sample of Mills College women who graduated between 1958 and 1960. Using the California Q-Set, Wink identified three patterns of narcissism—hypersensitive, willful, and autonomous (or healthy)—that showed quite distinct patterns of personality change during the transition from college to midlife. In their early 40s, hypersensitive narcissists showed a course of steady decline relative to how they had been functioning in their early 20s. Willful narcissists showed little change at age 43 relative to age 21, after showing some growth in their late 20s. Autonomous, or healthy, narcissists, following conflict in their late 20s, experienced a surge of personality development by their early 40s, as indicated by satisfying intimate interpersonal relationships and career satisfaction and successes.

Treatment Research

Recommendations for psychotherapeutic management of patients suffering from NPD are based primarily on clinical experience and theoretical formulations. These clinical case studies illustrate that some patients with NPD can be treated successfully while others fail to respond to treatment. These patients are believed to be difficult to treat because they are unable to admit weaknesses, appreciate the effect their behavior has on others, or incorporate feedback from others. However, no randomized controlled treatment studies on NPD exist (Groopman & Cooper, 2001; Oldham, 1988). There are a number of psychotherapy studies of patients with a specific personality disorder, a subset of personality disorders, personality disorders in general, or Axis I disorders that have included patients with NPD. However, these controlled studies are difficult to interpret because they focused on mixed personality disorders without specifying narcissistic cohorts. One exception is a naturalistic study by Teusch, Böhme, Finke, and Gastpar (2001), which examined the effects of client-centered psychotherapy (CCT) on personality disorders, alone and in combination with psychopharmacological treatment. They examined the effect of diagnostic subgroup of personality disorder on outcome. For NPD, they found that CCT, as compared to CCT plus medication,[8] led to greater reductions in depression. The authors speculated that the CCT-only group might have experienced more autonomy and self-efficacy. Given the difficulty in medicating personality-disordered patients, it is also possible that the prescribed medication regimens had a negative effect. Callaghan, Summers, and Weidman (2003) presented single-subject data on a patient with histrionic and NPD behaviors who was treated with functional analytic psychotherapy (Kohlenberg & Tsai, 1991). They reported significant changes in NPD behaviors during the psychotherapy sessions. Using lag sequential analysis, they linked therapist responses to in-session patient behavior. However, the researchers did not assess any external outcomes, and thus these in-session changes were not linked to any external measures of improvement. In terms of the course of psychotherapy, Hilsenroth, Fowler, & Padawer (1998), in a study of early termination in a university-based community clinic, found that NPD patients had the largest percentage of dropout (64%). In addition, the criterion "requires excessive admiration" was one of four DSM-IV criteria that significantly predicted dropout. The follow-up studies of Plakun, McGlashan, Ronningstam, and Stone and their respective colleagues (Plakun, 1989; McGlashan & Heinssen, 1989; Ronningstam et al., 1995; Stone, 1989) were all carried out on treated samples and therefore bear some limited implications for treatment. Generally, these studies show improvement over time in the treated samples. In Ronningstam et al.'s (1995) prospective follow-up study, retrospectively obtained information about treatment experiences suggested that treatment utilization was not differentially distributed among the patients who improved and those who did not. However, the authors acknowledged that the treatment reports were not sufficiently detailed or structured to enable one to draw valid conclusions. Pharmacological treatment of NPD without Axis I comorbidity has not been sufficiently studied. Abramson (1983) presented a series of case reports in which he prescribed the benzodiazepine lorazepam in adjunct to standard individual psychotherapy in the treatment of patients exhibiting what Kohut (1973) referred to as "narcissistic rage." In all three cases, lorazepam resulted in relief from tensions associated with feeling slighted and angry, with minimal adverse effects. However, although each case was characterized by extremely angry outbursts and rage in response to feelings of being insulted or slighted, it is not clear from the case reports that any of the patients met criteria for NPD. In addition, there are a number of important limitations of case report methodology (Raulin & Lilienfeld, 1999). Given the absence of controlled trials, lack of data in general, and the limitations of the studies carried out thus far, clinical practice guidelines for the disorder are yet to be formulated.

Narcissistic Personality Disorder and Suicidality

Some have suggested that suicidality in patients with NPD is high because their self-esteem is fragile (Perry, 1990). However, there is little research on suicidality and NPD. Kernberg (1992) posited that these patients are at high risk for suicide despite the absence of depression. Stone (1989) found that patients with comorbid borderline personality disorder and NPD were at higher risk for suicide than borderline patients without NPD. Apter and his colleagues (Apter, King, & Kron, 1993) conducted a postmortem study examining the diagnoses of a group of young men who had committed suicide. They found that over 20% of the young men had been diagnosed with NPD. Although the seminal Stone study is historically important and many findings from it have been confirmed by later research, the lack of blind, structured, and reliable interviews permits only tentative conclusions.

Narcissism and Culture

Although the concept of narcissism and the diagnosis of NPD have been conceptualized in a cultural and sociopolitical context, to date there has been little research on the relationship between culture and narcissism. Lasch (1979) called narcissism the "hallmark" of American culture in which "prevailing social conditions . . . tend to bring out narcissistic traits that are present, in varying degrees, in everyone" (p. 50). He posited that the modernization of Western society, with its focus on rugged individualism, mobility, breakdown of extended family systems, and increased consumerism, has contributed to the development of a pervasive narcissistic personality style.

Rivas (2001) suggested that the exclusion of NPD from the International Classification of Diseases (ICD) may provide some indication of the significantly lower prevalence of NPD in cultures outside the United States. He further suggested that this may be "evidence of its cultural entrenchment" (p. 30). However, just as some cultural styles may be mistaken for narcissistic personality traits, it is just as likely that some cultures may tolerate narcissistic traits and therefore minimize the disorder. It is certain that the paucity of research studies sufficiently examining any existing cultural differences in the expression, etiology, or prevalence of the disorder renders it difficult to conclude anything about the generalizability of pathological narcissism outside the United States.

In contrast, some have argued that a number of culturally determined interpersonal styles can be misconstrued as narcissistic (Alarcon & Foulks, 1995; Martinez, 1993; Smith, 1990) and that narcissism may be manifested differently in other cultures (Warren & Capponi, 1996). Roland (1991) suggested that Western-centric norms are not reflected in Japanese culture and that narcissism would appear more covert in Japan as opposed to the exhibitionistic form prevalent in America. However, Sato, Sakado, and Sato (1993) found that 18.8% of 96 nonbipolar outpatients with major depression in a Japanese clinic met criteria for DSM-III-R NPD (the overtly exhibitionistic American type). In fact, NPD was the third most common disorder overall, and the most common disorder among younger adult patients (under age 32). In contrast, Smith (1990) found fewer narcissistic traits among Asian-American women compared to Caucasian-American women (using the NPI [Raskin & Terry, 1988]). Recently, Foster, Campbell, and Twenge (2003) employed the Internet in a worldwide study of narcissism using the NPI. They found that self-identified White and Asian participants reported less narcissism than did either Black or Hispanic participants. Respondents from the United States produced the highest levels of narcissism compared to (in descending order) Europe, Canada, Asia, and the Middle East. Consistent with the findings of Foster et al. (2003), Choca, Shanley, Peterson, and Van Denburg (1990) examined the MCMI scores of African-American and Caucasian men hospitalized at a VA hospital and found that African-Americans scored higher on the narcissism scale than the Caucasians. The relative paucity of systematic research on culture highlights the need for increased and more sophisticated work in this area.

Further Research and Recommendations for DSM-V

Although research on NPD has generally been insufficient, there has been significant progress in the empirical research describing NPD. These data are based largely on systematic assessments of patient groups using structured clinical interviews to assess all Axis II disorders. The existing data suggest that NPD occurs frequently enough that DSM-V should continue to include it in some fashion. Nevertheless, there are a number of limitations in the existing data that should be addressed by DSM-V. First, most research on NPD has not examined the concordance between DSM-IV criteria and the essential features of the disorder as seen in clinical practice. Recent research by Westen and his colleagues (Westen & Shedler, 1999) has begun looking at this process; if it is replicated, this research will suggest that DSM-V broaden the criteria set to include controlling behaviors, tendency to engage in power struggles, and competitiveness. A second issue concerns the fact that patients who meet criteria for NPD rarely do not meet criteria for another Axis II disorder. Future research will need to discriminate NPD from other Axis II disorders or may suggest that there is an NPD variant of these disorders. Again, research by Westen and Shedler (1999) has shown that broadening the NPD criteria set significantly reduces the overlap with other Axis II disorders. In addition to these two issues, there is a desperate need for validation studies to determine if a NPD diagnosis predicts etiology, course, and/or treatment response. Ultimately, the value of the diagnosis will rest on whether or not it is useful for predicting adult outcomes and treatment response.

Conclusions

The concept of narcissistic character, disorder, and/or organization was first articulated in 1925 by Waelder and further expanded by Nemiah, Kernberg, Kohut, and Millon. NPD was introduced into the official diagnostic system in 1980 (APA), and its criteria are based heavily upon the writings of Kernberg, Kohut, and Millon.

Although there is general agreement on the trait and behavior descriptions of narcissism—focusing on the feelings of exaggerated self-importance, privilege, grandiosity, and expectation of special treatment—there is little consensus on the etiology, prevalence, assessment, and dynamics of the disorder. Despite the official recognition of the disorder in 1980, there has been disappointingly little empirical study of its course, treatment, and outcome. Data on the naturalistic course and outcome of the disorder are sparse, with information typically based upon small or selected samples of patients followed for relatively short periods of time. In general, these studies suggest that patients with NPD improve over time. One study suggests there may be meaningful subgroups of these patients with differential status over time.

There are no randomized, controlled treatment studies of patients with NPD. Consistent with clinical experience, the limited data available suggest that patients with significant narcissistic traits are prone to early dropout but show some improvement in response to treatment. Given the clinical interests and documented impairment of patients with the disorder, more research on its treatment and prevention is sorely needed.

Notes

1. Narcissus is a flower whose name derives is derived from the Greek word *narke* (where we get *narcotic*) by virtue of its power to alleviate pain and suffering.

2. In the course of his writings, Freud used the term "narcissism" to describe (1) a stage of normal infant development, (2) a normal aspect of self-interest and self-esteem, (3) a way of conducting interpersonal relationships, especially by choosing a partner based on his or her similarity to the self (overinvestment of self) rather than his or her real aspects, and (4) a way of relating to the environment characterized by a relative lack of interpersonal relations. These multiple uses of the term have resulted in significant confusion about the concept, which persists even today.

3. Kernberg discussed countertransference as one of the three main channels a therapist uses to understand a patient's experience. Additionally, Kohlenberg and Tsai (1994) discussed the similarities between a functional analytic approach and a psychoanalytic approach.

4. Murray (1938), building on earlier theorists, such as Freud, developed a measure that assessed both the grandiose self-centered aspect of narcissism and the tendency of these individuals to present this way to mask a fragile, vulnerable, hypersensitive self.

5. Passive-aggressive personality disorder is no longer included in DSM-IV, but studies of the comorbidity of DSM-III-R NPD have found it most often comorbid with passive-aggressive personality disorder (Oldham et al., 1992).

6. Hendin and Cheek (1997) found that the NPI correlated positively with extraversion and openness to experience and that hypersensitivity correlated negatively with extraversion, agreeableness, and openness to experience but positively with neuroticism. Exploitativeness-entitlement correlated negatively with agreeableness and positively with neuroticism.

7. Of the 29 cases presented as exemplary of narcissistic personality disorder in the three major works on narcissism (Kernberg's [1975a] *Borderline Conditions and Pathological Narcissism* and Kohut's [1971, 1977] *Analysis of the Self* and *Restoration of the Self*), only five of the cases are of women.

8. Thirty-seven of the 46 patients in this condition received antidepressants and a benzodiazepine, and nine patients received low-dose neuroleptics along with either benzodiazepines or beta blockers.

References

Abraham, K. (1924/1949). A short study of the development of the libido, viewed in the light of mental disorders. History of the development of the libido. In *Selected papers on psycho-analysis* (pp. 418–479). London: Hogarth Press.

Abrams, D. M. (1993). Pathological narcissism in an eight-year-old boy: An example of Bellak's TAT and CAT diagnostic system. *Psychoanalytic Psychology, 10,* 573–591.

Abrams, R. C., Alexopoulos, G. S., & Young, R. C. (1987). Geriatric depression and DSM-III-R personality disorder criteria. *Journal of the American Geriatrics Society, 35,* 383–386.

Abrams, R. C., Rosendahl, E., Card C., & Alexopoulous, G. S. (1994). Personality disorder correlates of late and early onset depression. *Journal of American Geriatrics Society, 42,* 727–731.

Abramson, R. (1983). Lorazepam for narcissistic rage. *Journal of Operational Psychiatry, 14,* 52–55.

Adorno, T. (1967). Sociology and psychology. *New Left Review, 46,* 67–80.

Adorno, T. (1968). Sociology and psychology. *New Left Review, 47,* 79–95.

Akhtar, S., & Thomson, J. A. (1982). Overview: Narcissistic personality disorder. *American Journal of Psychiatry, 139,* 12–20.

Alarcon, R. D., & Foulks, E. F. (1995). Personality disorders and culture: Contemporary clinical views (Part A). *Cultural Diversity and Mental Health, 1*(1), 3–17.

Alnaes, R., & Torgerson, S. (1988). DSM-III symptom disorders (Axis I) and personality disorders (Axis II) in an outpatient population. *Acta Psychiatrica Scandinavica, 78,* 485–492.

American Psychiatric Association. (1980). *Diagnostic and statistical manual of mental disorders* (3rd ed.). Washington, DC: Author.

American Psychiatric Association. (1987). *Diagnostic and statistical manual of mental disorders* (3rd ed., revised). Washington, DC: Author.

American Psychiatric Association. (1994). *Diagnostic and statistical manual of mental disorders* (4th ed.). Washington, DC: Author.

American Psychiatric Association. (2000). *Diagnostic and statistical manual of mental disorders* (4th ed., text revision). Washington, DC: Author.

Ames, A., & Molinari, V. (1994). Prevalence of personality disorders in community-living elderly. *Journal of Geriatric Psychiatry and Neurology, 7,* 189–194.

Andreoli, A., Gressot, G., Aapro, N., Tricot, L., & Gognalons, M. Y. (1989). Personality disorder as a predictor of outcome. *Journal of Personality Disorders, 3,* 307–320.

Apter, A., King, R. A., & Kron, S. (1993). Death without warning? A clinical postmortem study of suicide in 43 Israeli adolescent males. *Archives of General Psychiatry, 50,* 138–142.

Ashby, H. U., Lee, R. R., & Duke, E. H. (1979). *A narcissistic personality disorder MMPI scale.* Paper presented at the 87th Annual Convention of the American Psychological Association, New York.

Auerbach, J. S. (1984). Validation of two scales for narcissistic personality disorder. *Journal of Personality Assessment, 48,* 649–653.

Auerbach, J. S. (1993). The origins of narcissism and narcissistic personality disorder: A theoretical and empirical reformulation. In J. M. Masling & R. F. Bornstein (Eds.), *Empirical studies of psychoanalytic theories: Vol. 4. Psychoanalytic perspectives on psychopathology* (pp. 43–110). Washington, DC: American Psychological Association.

Ball, S. A., Kranzler, H. R., Poling, J. C., Rounsaville, B. J., & Tennen, H. (1997). Personality, temperament, and character dimensions and the DSM-IV personality disorders in substance abusers. *Journal of Abnormal Psychology, 106,* 545–553.

Bardenstein, K. (1994). *Narcissistic character disorder in children: Rorschach features.* Presented at the annual meeting of The Society for Personality Assessment, Chicago.

Bateman, A. W. (1998). Thick- and thin-skinned organizations and enactment in borderline and narcissistic disorders. *International Journal of Psychoanalysis, 79,* 13–25.

Baumeister, R. F., Bushman, B. J., & Campbell, W. K. (2000). Self-esteem, narcissism, and aggression: Does violence result from low self-esteem or from threatened egotism? *Current Directions in Psychological Science, 9,* 26–29.

Beck, A. T., Butler, A. C., Brown, G. K., Dahlsgaard, K. K., & Beck, J. S. (2001). Dysfunctional beliefs discriminate personality disorders. *Behavior Research and Therapy, 39,* 1213–1225.

Beck, A. T., & Freeman, A. M. (1990). *Cognitive therapy of personality disorders.* New York: Guilford Press.

Becker, D. F., Edell, W. S., Grilo, C. M., & McGlashan, T. H. (2000). Comorbidity of borderline personality disorder with other personality disorders in hospitalized adolescents and adults. *American Journal of Psychiatry, 157,* 2011–2016.

Bell, M., Billington, R., & Becker, B. (1986). A scale of the assessment of object relations: Reliability, validity, and factorial invariance. *Journal of Clinical Psychology, 42,* 733–741.

Berezin, M. A. (1977). Normal psychology of the aging process, revisited: II. The fate of narcissism in old age: Clinical case reports. *Journal of Geriatric Psychiatry, 10,* 9–26.

Berg, J., Packer, A., & Nunno, V. (1993). A Rorschach analysis: Parallel disturbance in thought and in self/object representation. *Journal of Personality Assessment, 61,* 311–323.

Bernstein, D. P., Cohen, P., Velez, C. N., Schwab-Stone, M., Siever, L. J., & Shinsato, L. (1993). Prevalence and stability of the DSM-III-R personality disorders in a community-based survey of adolescents. *American Journal of Psychiatry, 150,* 1237–1243.

Bieling, P. J., MacQueen, G. M., Marriott, M. J., Robb, J. C., Begin, H., Joffe, R. T., et al. (2003). Longitudinal outcome in patients with bipolar disorder assessed by life charting is influenced by DSM-IV personality disorder symptoms. *Bipolar Disorders, 5,* 14–21.

Black, D. W., Noyes, R., Pfohl, B., Goldstein, R. B., & Blum, N. (1993). Personality disorder in obsessive-compulsive volunteers, well comparison subjects, and their first-degree relatives. *American Journal of Psychiatry, 150,* 1226–1232.

Blais, M. A. (1997). Clinician ratings of the five-factor model of personality and the DSM-IV personality disorders. *Journal of Nervous and Mental Disease, 185,* 388–393.

Blatt, S. J. (1983). *Narcissism and egocentrism as concepts in individual and cultural development. Psychoanalysis & Contemporary Thought, 6,* 291–303.

Blatt, S. J., & Levy, K. N. (1998). A psychodynamic approach to the diagnosis of psychopathology. In J. W. Barron (Ed.), *Making diagnosis meaningful: Enhancing evaluation and treatment of psychological disorders* (pp. 73–109). Washington, DC: American Psychological Association.

Block, J. (1971). *Lives through time.* Berkeley, CA: Bancroft Books.

Bodlund, O., Ekselius, L., & Lindström, E. (1993). Personality traits and disorders among psychiatric outpatients and normal subjects on the basis of the SCID screen questionnaire. *Nordic Journal of Psychiatry, 47,* 425–433.

Bourgeois, J. J., Crosby, R. M., Drexler, K. G., & Hall, M. J. (1993). An examination of narcissistic personality traits as seen in a military population. *Military Medicine, 158,* 170–174.

Bowlby, J. (1973). *Separation: Anxiety and anger.* New York: Basic Books.

Bowlby, J. (1979). *The making and breaking of affectional bonds.* London: Tavistock.

Bradlee, P. M., & Emmons, R. A. (1992). Locating narcissism within the interpersonal circumplex and the five-factor model. *Personality and Individual Differences, 13,* 821–830.

Brieger, P., Ehrt, U., & Marneros, A. (2003). Frequency of comorbid personality disorders in bipolar and unipolar affective disorders. *Comprehensive Psychiatry, 44,* 28–34.

Britton, R. (2000). Hyper-subjectivity and hyper-objectivity in narcissistic disorders. *Fort Da: The Journal of the Northern California Society for Psychoanalytic Psychology, 6,* 18–23.

Bursten, B. (1973). Some narcissistic personality types. *International Journal of Psychoanalysis, 54,* 287–300.

Buss, D. M., & Chiodo, L. M. (1991). Narcissistic acts in everyday life. *Journal of Personality, 59,* 179–215.

Callaghan, G. M., Summers, C. J., & Weidman, M. (2003). The treatment of histrionic and narcissistic personality disorder behaviors: A single-subject demonstration of clinical improvement using functional analytic psychotherapy. *Journal of Contemporary Psychotherapy, 33,* 321–339.

Campbell, K. W. (1999). Narcissism and romantic attraction. *Journal of Personality and Social Psychology, 77,* 1254–1270.

Caron, C., & Rutter, M. (1991). Comorbidity in child psychopathology: Concepts, issues and research strategies. *Journal of Child Psychology and Psychiatry and Allied Disciplines, 32,* 1063–1080.

Carpenter, D., Clarkin, J. F., Glick, I. D., & Wilner, P. J. (1995). Personality pathology among married adults with bipolar disorder. *Journal of Affective Disorders, 34,* 269–274.

Carroll, L. (1987). A study of narcissism, affiliation, intimacy, and power motives among students in business administration. *Psychological Reports, 61(2),* 355–358.

Carson, R. C. (1991). Dilemmas in the pathway of the DSM-IV. *Journal of Abnormal Psychology, 100,* 302–307.

Caspi, A. (2000). The child is father of the man: Personality continuities from childhood to adulthood. *Journal of Personality and Social Psychology, 78,* 158–172.

Cattell, R. B., Horn, J. L., Sweney, A. B., & Radcliffe, J. A. (1964). *Handbook for the Motivation Analysis Test (MAT).* Champaign, IL: Institute for Personality and Ability Testing.

Choca, J. P., Shanley, L. A., Peterson, C. A., & Van Denburg, E. (1990). Racial bias and the MCMI. *Journal of Personality Assessment, 54,* 479–490.

Cicchetti, D., & Toth, S. L. (1998). The development of depression in children and adolescents. *American Psychologist, 53,* 221–241.

Clark, L. A. (1989). Depressive and anxiety disorders: Descriptive psychopathology and differential diagnosis. In P. C. Kendall & D. Watson (Eds.), *Anxiety and depression: Distinctive and overlapping features (pp. 83–129).* New York: Academic Press.

Clarkin, J. F., & Kendall, P. C. (1992). Comorbidity and treatment planning. *Journal of Clinical and Consulting Psychology, 60,* 904–908.

Clarkin, J. F., & Levy, K. N. (2003). A psychodynamic treatment for severe personality disorders: Issues in treatment development. *Psychoanalytic Inquiry, 23,* 248–267.

Clarkin, J. F., Levy, K. N., Lenzenweger, M. F., & Kernberg, O. F. (2004). The Personality Disorders Institute/Borderline Personality Disorder Research Foundation randomized control trial for borderline personality disorder: Rationale, methods, and patient characteristics. *Journal of Personality Disorders, 18,* 52–72.

Cloninger, C. R., & Svrakic, D. M. (1994). Differentiating normal and deviant personality by the seven-factor personality model. In M. Lorr & S. Strack (Eds.),

Differentiating normal and abnormal personality (pp. 40–64). New York: Springer.

Coolidge, F. L. (1998). *Coolidge personality and neuropsychological inventory for children: CPNI.* Colorado Springs, CO: Author.

Coolidge, F. L., Aksamit, C. R., & Becker, L. A. (1994). Prediction of recidivism in juvenile offenders. *Indian Journal of Psychology, 2,* 1–6.

Coolidge, F. L., Philbrick, P. B., Wooley, M. J., Bunting, E. K., Hyman, J. N., & Stager, M. A. (1990). The KCATI: Development of an inventory for the assessment of personality disorders in children. *Journal of Personality and Clinical Studies, 6,* 225–232.

Coolidge, F. L., Reilman, B. J., Becker, L. A., Cass, V. J., Coolidge, R. L., & Stocker, R. (1992). Emotional problems and neuropsychological symptoms in juvenile non-violent offenders. *Journal of Personality and Clinical Studies, 8*(1), 7–13.

Coolidge, F. L., Thede, L. L., & Jang, K. E. (2001). Heritability of personality disorders in childhood: A preliminary investigation. *Journal of Personality Disorders, 15,* 33–40.

Coolidge, F. L., Thede, L. L., & Jang, K. E. (2004). Are personality disorders psychological manifestations of executive function deficits? *Behavior Genetics, 34,* 75–84.

Coolidge, F. L., Thede, L. L., Stewart, S. E., & Segal, D. L. (2002). The Coolidge Personality and Neuropsychological Inventory for Children (CPNI): Preliminary psychometric characteristics. *Behavioral Modification, 26,* 550–566.

Cooper, A. (1981). Narcissism. In S. Arieti, H. Keith, & H. Brodie (Eds.), *American handbook of psychiatry* (Vol. 4, pp. 297–316). New York: Basic Books.

Cooper, A., & Ronningstam, E. (1992). Narcissistic personality disorder. In A. Tasman & M. B. Riba (Eds.), *American Psychiatric Press review of psychiatry* (Vol. 11). Washington, DC: American Psychiatric Press.

Corruble, E., Ginestet, D., & Guelfi, J. D. (1996). Comorbidity of personality disorders and unipolar major depression: A review. *Journal of Affective Disorders, 37,* 157–170.

Costa, P. T., Jr., & McCrae, R. R. (1985). The NEO Personality Inventory manual. Odessa, FL: Psychological Assessment Resources.

Costa, P. T., Jr., & McCrae, R. R. (1990). Personality disorders and the five-factor model of personality. *Journal of Personality Disorders, 4,* 362–371.

Crosby, R. M., & Hall, M. J. (1992). Psychiatric evaluation of self-referred and non-self-referred active duty military members. *Military Medicine, 157,* 224–229.

Curtis, J. M., & Cowell, D. R. (1993). Relation to birth order and scores on measures of pathological narcissism. *Psychological Reports, 72,* 311–315.

Dahl, A. A. (1986). Some aspects of the DSM-III personality disorders illustrated by a consecutive sample of hospitalized patients. *Acta Psychiatrica Scandinavica, 73,* 61–67.

Davis, R. D., & Millon, T. (1993). The five-factor model for personality disorders: Apt or misguided? *Psychological Inquiry, 4,* 104–109.

Dickinson, K. A., & Pincus, A. L. (2003). Interpersonal analysis of grandiose and vulnerable narcissism. *Journal of Personality Disorders, 17,* 188–207.

DiGiuseppe, R., Robin, M., Szeszko, P. R., & Primavera, L. (1995). Cluster analyses of narcissistic personality disorders on the MCMI-II. *Journal of Personality Disorders, 9,* 304–317.

Doidge, N., Simon, B., Brauer, L., Grant, D. C., First, M., Brunshaw, J., et al. (2002). Psychoanalytic patients in the U.S., Canada, and Australia: I. DSM-III-R, previous treatment, medications, and length of treatment. *Journal of the American Psychoanalytic Association, 50,* 575–614.

Drake, R. E., Adler, D. A., & Vaillant, G. E. (1988). Antecedents of personality disorders in a community sample of men. *Journal of Personality Disorders, 2,* 60–68.

Drake, R. E., & Vaillant, G. E. (1988). Introduction: Longitudinal views of personality disorder. *Journal of Personality Disorders, 2,* 44–48.

Duggan, C., Milton, J., Egan, V., McCarthy, L., Palmer, B., & Lee, A. (2003). Theories of general personality and mental disorder. *British Journal of Psychiatry, 182,* 19–23.

Duijsens, I. J., & Diekstra, R. F. W. (1996). DSM-III-R and ICD-10 personality disorders and their relationship with the Big Five dimensions of personality. *Personality and Individual Differences, 21,* 119–133.

Dyce, J. A., & O'Connor, B. P. (1998). Personality disorders and the five-factor model: A test of facet-level predictions. *Journal of Personality Disorders, 12,* 31–45.

Ekselius, L., Bodlund, O., Knorring, L. von, Lindstrom, E., & Kullgren, G. (1996). Sex differences in DSM-III-R, Axis II: Personality disorders. *Personality and Individual Differences, 20*(4), 457–461.

Ekselius, L., Tillfors, M., Furmark, T., & Fredrikson, M. (2001). Personality disorders in the general population: DSM-IV and ICD-10 defined prevalence as related to sociodemographic pro file. *Personality and Individual Differences, 30,* 311–320.

Ellis, H. (1898). Auto-eroticism: A psychological study. *Alienist and Neurologist, 19,* 260–299.

Emmons, R. A. (1981). Relationship between narcissism and sensation seeking. *Psychological Reports, 48,* 247–250.

Emmons, R. A. (1984). Factor analysis and construct validity of the narcissistic personality inventory. *Journal of Personality Assessment, 48,* 291–300.

Emmons, R. A. (1987). Narcissism: Theory and measurement. *Journal of Personality and Social Psychology, 52,* 11–17.

Emmons, R. A. (1989). The personal striving approach to personality. In L. A. Pervin (Ed.), *Goal concepts in personality and social psychology* (pp. 87–126). Hillsdale, NJ: Erlbaum.

Exner, J. (1969). Rorschach responses as an index of narcissism. *Journal of Personality Assessment, 33,* 324–330.

Exner, J. (1973). The self-focus sentence completion: A study of egocentricity. *Journal of Personality Assessment, 37,* 437–455.

Exner, J. (1995). Comment on "Narcissism in the comprehensive system for the Rorschach." *Clinical Psychology: Science and Practice, 2,* 200–206.

Eyring, W. E., III, & Sobelman, S. (1996). Narcissism and birth order. *Psychological Reports, 78,* 403–406.

Eysenck, H. J., & Eysenck, S. B. G. (1975). *Eysenck Personality Questionnaire manual.* San Diego, CA: Educational Testing Service.

Fabrega, H., Ulrich, R., Pilkonis, P., & Mezzich, J. (1992). Pure personality disorders in an intake psychiatric setting. *Journal of Personality Disorders, 6,* 153–161.

Farris, M. (1988). Differential diagnosis of borderline and narcissistic personality disorders. In H. Lerner & P. Lerner (Eds.), *Primitive mental states and the Rorschach* (pp. 299–338). New York: International Universities Press.

Farwell, L., & Wohlwend-Lloyd, R. (1998). Narcissistic processes: Optimistic expectations, favorable self-evaluations, and self-enhancing attributions. *Journal of Personality, 66,* 65–83.

Fava, G. A., Grandi, S., Zielezny, M., Rafanelli, C. & Canestrari, R. (1996). Four-year outcome for cognitive behavioral treatment of residual symptoms in major depression. *American Journal of Psychiatry, 153,* 945–947.

Ferro, T., Klein, D. N., & Schwartz, J. E. (1998). 30-month stability of personality disorder diagnosis in depressed outpatients. *American Journal of Psychiatry, 155,* 653–659.

First, M. B., Spitzer, R. L., Gibbon, M., & Williams, J. B. W. (1995). *Structured clinical interview for DSM-IV.* New York: New York State Psychiatric Institute.

Fonagy, P., Gergely, G., Jurist, E. L., & Target, M. (2002). *Affect regulation, mentalization and the development of the self.* New York: Other Press.

Foster, J. D., Campbell, W. K., & Twenge, J. M. (2003). Individual differences in narcissism: Inflated self-views across the lifespan and around the world. *Journal of Research in Personality, 37,* 469–486.

Frances, A. J. (1980). The DSM-III personality disorder section: A commentary. *American Journal of Psychiatry, 147,* 1439–1448.

Frances, A., Clarkin, J. F., Gilmore, M., Hurt, S. W., & Brown, R. (1984). Reliability of criteria for borderline personality disorder: A comparison of DSM-III and the diagnostic interview for borderline patients. *American Journal of Psychiatry, 141,* 1080–1084.

Freud, S. (1905/1957). Three essays on sexuality. In J. Strachey (Ed. and Trans.), *The standard edition of the complete psychological works of Sigmund Freud* (Vol. 7, pp. 125–245). London: Hogarth Press.

Freud, S. (1914/1957). On narcissism: An introduction. In J. Strachey (Ed. and Trans.), *The standard edition of the complete psychological works of Sigmund Freud* (Vol. 14, pp. 73–102). London: Hogarth Press.

Freud, S. (1931/1950). Libidinal types. In J. Strachey (Ed. and Trans.), *The standard edition of the complete psychological works of Sigmund Freud* (Vol. 21, pp. 217–220). London: Hogarth Press.

Gabbard, G. (1989). Two subtypes of narcissistic personality disorder. *Bulletin of the Menninger Clinic, 53,* 527–532.

Gabriel, M. T., Critelli, J. W., & Ee, J. S. (1994). Narcissistic illusions in self-evaluations of intelligence and attractiveness. *Journal of Personality, 62,* 143–155.

Gacono, C., Meloy, J., & Berg, J. (1992). Object relations, defensive operations, and affective states in narcissistic, borderline, and antisocial personality disorder. *Journal of Personality Assessment, 59,* 32–49.

George, E. L., Miklowitz, D. J., Richards, J. A., Simoneau, T. L., & Taylor, D. O. (2003). The comorbidity of bipolar disorders and Axis II personality disorders: Prevalence and clinical correlates. *Bipolar Disorders, 5,* 115–122.

Gergely, G., & Watson, J. S. (1996). The social biofeedback theory of parental affect mirroring. *International Journal of Psychoanalysis, 77,* 1181–1212.

Golomb, M., Fava, M., Abraham, M., & Rosenbaum, J. F. (1995). Gender differences in personality disorders. *American Journal of Psychiatry, 152,* 579–582.

Gough, H. G. (1957). *Manual for the California Psychological Inventory.* Palo Alto, CA: Consulting Psychologists Press.

Gough, H. G. (1987). *The California Psychological Inventory administrator's guide.* Palo Alto, CA: Consulting Psychologists Press.

Grilo, C. M., Becker, D. F., Edell, W. S., & McGlashan, T. H. (2001). Stability and change of DSM-III-R personality disorder dimensions in adolescents followed up 2 years after psychiatric hospitalization. *Comprehensive Psychiatry, 42,* 364–368.

Grilo, C. M., Becker, D. F., Fehon, D. C., Walker, M. L., Edell, W. S., & McGlashan, T. H. (1996). Gender differences in personality disorders in psychiatrically hospitalized adolescents. *American Journal of Psychiatry, 153,* 1089–1091.

Grilo, C. M., McGlashan, T. H., Quinlan, D. M., Walker, M. L., Greenfeld, D., & Edell, W. S. (1998). Frequency of personality disorders in two age cohorts of psychiatric inpatients. *American Journal of Psychiatry, 155,* 140–142.

Groopman, L. C., & Cooper, A. M. (2001). Narcissistic personality disorder. In G. O. Gabbard (Ed.), *Treatments of psychiatric disorders* (3rd ed., pp. 2309–2326). Washington, DC: American Psychiatric Press.

Grygier, J. G., & Grygier, P. (1976). *Dynamic personality inventory.* Montreal, Quebec, Canada: Institute of Psychological Research.

Gunderson, J. G., Ronningstam, E., & Bodkin, A. (1990). The diagnostic interview for narcissistic patients. *Archives of General Psychiatry, 47*(7), 676–680.

Gunderson, J. G., Ronningstam, E., & Smith, L. E. (1991). Narcissistic personality disorder: A review of data on DSM-III-R descriptions. *Journal of Personality Disorders, 5,* 167–177.

Gunther, M. S. (1976). The endangered self: A contribution to the understanding of narcissistic determinants of countertransference. *Annual of Psychoanalysis, 4,* 201–224.

Haaken, J. (1983). Sex differences and narcissistic disorders. *American Journal of Psychoanalysis, 43,* 315–324.

Hamilton, E. (1942). *Mythology.* Boston: Little, Brown.

Harder, D. W. (1979). The assessment of ambitious-narcissistic character style with three projective tests: The Early Memories, TAT, and Rorschach. *Journal of Personality Assessment, 43,* 23–32.

Harder, D. W., & Lewis, S. J. (1987). The assessment of shame and guilt. In J. N. Butcher & C. D. Spielberger (Eds.), *Advances in personality assessment* (Vol. 6., pp. 89–114). Hillsdale, NJ: Erlbaum.

Harder, D. W., & Zalma, A. (1990). Two promising shame and guilt scales: A construct validity comparison. *Journal of Personality Assessment, 55,* 729–745.

Hárnik, J. (1924). The various developments undergone by narcissism in men and in women. *International Journal of Psychoanalysis, 5,* 66–83.

Hendin, H. M., & Cheek, J. M. (1997). Assessing hypersensitive narcissism: A reexamination of Murray's narcissism scale. *Journal of Research in Personality, 31,* 588–599.

Hibbard, S., & Bunce, S. C. (1995, August). *Two paradoxes of narcissism.* Paper presented at the annual meeting of the American Psychological Association, New York.

Hilsenroth, M. J., Fowler, J. C., & Padawer, J. R. (1998). The Rorschach Schizophrenia Index (SCZI): An examination of reliability, validity, and diagnostic efficiency. *Journal of Personality Assessment, 70,* 514–534.

Hilsenroth, M. J., Fowler, J. C., Padawer, J. R., & Handler, L. (1997). Narcissism in the Rorschach revisited: Some reflections on empirical data. *Psychological Assessment, 9,* 113–121.

Hilsenroth, M., Handler, L., & Blais, M. (1996). Assessment of narcissistic personality disorder: A multimethod review. *Clinical Psychology Review, 16,* 655–683.

Hilsenroth, M., Hibbard, S., Nash, M., & Handler, L. (1993). A Rorschach study of narcissism, defense, and aggression in borderline, narcissistic and Cluster C personality disorders. *Journal of Personality Assessment, 60,* 346–361.

Hilsenroth, M., Holdwick, D., Castlebury, F., & Blais, M. (1998). The effects of DSM-IV Cluster B personality disorder symptoms on the termination and continuation of psychotherapy. *Psychotherapy, 35,* 163–176.

Hoffman, L. (1991). The influence of the family environment on personality: Accounting for sibling differences. *Psychological Bulletin, 110,* 187–203.

Horkheimer, M. (1936). Studien über Autorität und Familie [Studies of authority and family]. *Schriften des Instituts für Sozialforschung, 5,* 947.

Horkheimer, M., & Adorno, T. W. (1944/1998). *The dialectic of enlightenment* (J. Cumming, Trans.). New York: Continuum.

Horney, K. (1939). *New ways in psychoanalysis.* New York: Horton.

Hyer, L., Matheson, S., Ofman, P., & Retzlaff, P. D. (1994). MCMI-II high-point codes: Severe personality disorder and clinical syndrome extensions. *Journal of Clinical Psychology, 50,* 228–234.

Hyler, S. E., Kellman, H. D., Oldham, J. M., & Skodol, A. E. (1992). Validity of the Personality Diagnostic Questionnaire—Revised: A replication in an outpatient sample. *Comprehensive Psychiatry, 33,* 73–77.

Hynan, D. J. (2004). Unsupported gender differences on some personality disorder scales of the Millon Clinical Multiaxial Inventory—III. *Professional Psychology: Research and Practice, 35,* 105–110.

Jackson, L. A., Ervin, K. S., & Hodge, C. N. (1992). Narcissism and body image. *Journal of Research in Personality, 26,* 357–370.

Jang, K. L., & Livesley, W. J. (1999). Why do measures of normal and disordered personality correlate? A study of genetic comorbidity. *Journal of Personality Disorders, 13,* 10–17.

Jang, K. L., & Vernon, P. A. (2001). Genetics. In W. J. Livesley (Ed.), *Handbook of personality disorder: Theory, research, and treatment* (pp. 177–195). New York: Guilford Press.

John, O. P., & Robins, R. W. (1994). Accuracy and bias in self-perception: Individual differences in self-enhancement and the role of narcissism. *Journal of Personality and Social Psychology, 66,* 206–219.

Jones, E. (1955). *The life and work of Sigmund Freud* (Vol. 2.). New York: Basic Books.

Joubert, C. E. (1989). Birth order and narcissism. *Psychological Reports, 64,* 721–722.

Kass, F., Spitzer, R. L., & Williams, J. B. (1983). An empirical study of the issue of sex bias in the diagnostic criteria of DSM-III Axis II personality disorders. *American Psychologist, 38,* 799–801.

Kernberg, O. (1966). Structural derivatives of object relationships. *International Journal of Psychoanalysis, 47,* 236–253.

Kernberg, O. F. (1967). Borderline personality organization. *Journal of the American Psychoanalytic Association, 15,* 641–685.

Kernberg, O. (1970). Factors in the psychoanalytic treatment of narcissistic personalities. *Journal of the American Psychoanalytic Association, 18,* 51–85.

Kernberg, O. (1975a). *Borderline conditions and pathological narcissism.* New York: Jason Aronson.

Kernberg, O. (1975b). Further contributions to the treatment of narcissistic personalities: A reply to the discussion by Paul H. Ornstein. *International Journal of Psychoanalysis, 56,* 245–247.

Kernberg, O. F. (1977). The structural diagnosis of borderline personality organization. In P. Hartocollis (Ed.), *Borderline personality disorders: The concept, the syndrome, the patient*. New York: International Universities Press.

Kernberg, O. F. (1983). Objects relations theory and character analysis. *Journal of the American Psychoanalytic Association, 31*, 247–271.

Kernberg, O. (1984). *The treatment of severe character disorders*. New Haven, CT: Yale University Press.

Kernberg, O. (1992). *Aggression in personality disorders and its perversions*. New Haven, CT: Yale University Press.

Kernberg, P. F., Hajal, F., & Normandin, L. (1998). Narcissistic personality disorder in adolescent inpatients: A retrospective record review study of descriptive characteristics. In E. F. Ronningstam (Ed.), *Disorders of narcissism: Diagnostic, clinical, and empirical implications* (pp. 437–456). Washington, DC: American Psychiatric Association.

Klein, D. N., Riso, L. P., Donaldson, S. K., Schwartz, J. E., Anderson, R. L., Ouimette, P. C., et al. (1995). Family study of early-onset dysthymia: Mood and personality disorders in relatives of outpatients with dysthymia and episodic major depression and normal controls. *Archives of General Psychiatry, 52*, 487–496.

Klein, M. H., Benjamin, L. S., Rosenfeld, R., Treece, C., Husted, J., & Greist, J. H. (1993). The Wisconsin Personality Disorders Inventory: I. Development, reliability, and validity. *Journal of Personality Disorders, Suppl.*, 18–33.

Koerner, K., Kohlenberg, J. R., & Parker, C. R. (1996). Diagnosis of personality disorder: A radical behavioral alternative. *Journal of Consulting and Clinical Psychology, 64*, 1169–1176.

Kohlenberg, R., & Tsai, M. (1991). *Functional analytic psychotherapy: Creating intense and curative therapeutic relationships*. New York: Plenum.

Kohlenberg, R. J., & Tsai, M. (1994). Functional analytic psychotherapy: A behavioral approach to treatment and integration. *Journal of Psychotherapy Integration, 4*, 175–201.

Kohut, H. (1968). The psychoanalytic treatment of narcissistic personality disorders: Outline of a systematic approach. *Psychoanalytic Study of the Child, 23*, 86–113.

Kohut, H. (1971). *The analysis of the self*. New York: International Universities Press.

Kohut, H. (1973). Reflections on narcissism and narcissistic anger. *Psyche: Zeitschrift für Psychoanalyse und ihre Anwendungen, 27*, 513–554.

Kohut, H. (1977). *The restoration of the self*. New York: International Universities Press.

Kohut, H., & Wolf, E. S. (1978). The disorders of the self and their treatment: An outline. *International Journal of Psychoanalysis, 59*, 413–425.

Kutcher, S. P., Marton, P., & Korenblum, M. (1990). Adolescent bipolar illness and personality disorder. *Journal of the American Academy of Child & Adolescent Psychiatry, 29*, 355–358.

LaForge, R., & Suczek, R. F. (1955). The interpersonal dimension of personality: III. An interpersonal check list. *Journal of Personality, 24*, 94–112.

Lasch, C. (1979). *The culture of narcissism: American life in an age of diminishing expectations*. New York: Warner Books.

Leary, T. (1957). *Interpersonal diagnosis of personality*. New York: Ronald Press.

Lehne, G. K. (1994). The NEO–PI and the MCMI in the forensic evaluation of sex offenders. In P. T. Costa, Jr., & T. A. Widiger (Eds.), *Personality disorders and the five-factor model of personality* (pp. 175–188). Washington, DC: American Psychological Association.

Livesley, W. J., Jang, K. L., Jackson, D. N., & Vernon, P. A. (1993). Genetic and environmental contributions to dimensions of personality disorder. *American Journal of Psychiatry, 150,* 1826–1831.

Livesley, W. J., Reiffer, L. I., Sheldon, A. E. R., & West, M. (1987). Prototypicality ratings of DSM-III criteria for personality disorders. *Journal of Nervous and Mental Disease, 175,* 395–401.

Loranger, A. W. (1999). *International personality disorder examination: DSM-IV and ICD-10 interviews.* Odessa, FL: Psychological Assessment Resources.

Loranger, A. W. (2000). Personality disorders: General considerations. In M. G. Gelder, J. J. Lopez-lbor, & N. Andreasen (Eds.), *The New Oxford textbook of psychiatry* (Vol. 1, pp. 923–926). New York: Oxford University Press.

Loranger, A. W., Lenzenweger, M. F., Gartner, A. F., Susman, V. L., Herzig, J., Zammit, G. K., et al. (1991). Trait-state artifacts and the diagnosis of personality disorders. *Archives of General Psychiatry, 48,* 720–728.

Loranger, A. W., Sartorius, N., Andreoli, A., Berger, P., Buchheim, P., Channabasavanna, S. M., et al. (1994). The international personality disorder examination: The World Health Organization/Alcohol, Drug Abuse, and Mental Health Administration international pilot study of personality disorders. *Archives of General Psychiatry, 51,* 215–224.

Maier, W., Lichtermann, D., Klingler, T., Heun, R., & Hallmayer, J. (1992). Prevalences of personality disorders (DSM-III-R) in the community. *Journal of Personality Disorders, 6,* 187–196.

Marcuse, H. (1955). *Eros and civilization.* New York: Vintage Books.

Martinez, C. (1993). Psychiatric care of Mexican-Americans. In A. C. Gaw (Ed.), *Culture, ethnicity, and mental illness* (pp. 431–466). Washington, DC: American Psychiatric Press.

Masterson, J. F. (1981). *The narcissistic and borderline disorders.* New York: Brunner/ Mazel.

Masterson, J. F. (1990). Psychotherapy of borderline and narcissistic disorders: Establishing a therapeutic alliance (A developmental, self, and object relations approach). *Journal of Personality Disorders, 4,* 182–191.

McCann, J. T., & Biaggio, M. K. (1989). Narcissistic personality features and self-reported anger. *Psychological Reports, 64,* 55–58.

McCann, J. T., Flens, J. R., Campagna, V., Collman, P., Lazzaro, T., & Connor, E. (2001). The MCMI–III in child custody evaluations: A normative study. *Journal of Forensic Psychology Practice, 1,* 27–44.

McGlashan, T. H., Grilo, C. M., Skodol, A. E., Gunderson, J. G., Shea, M. T., Morey, L. C., et al. (2000). The Collaborative Longitudinal Personality Disorders Study: Baseline Axis I/II and II/II diagnostic co-occurrence. *Acta Psychiatrica Scandinavica, 102,* 256–264.

McGlashan, T. H., & Heinssen, R. K. (1989). Narcissistic, antisocial, and non-comorbid subgroups of borderline disorder: Are they distinct entities by long-term clinical profiles? *Psychiatric Clinics of North America, 12,* 621–641.

Miller, A. (1981). *The drama of the gifted child.* New York: Basic Books.

Millon, T. (1969). *Modern psychopathology.* Prospect Heights, IL: Waveland.

Millon, T. (1981). *Disorders of personality: DSM III, Axis II.* New York: Wiley.

Millon, T. (1987). *Millon Clinical Multiaxial Inventory—II manual.* Minneapolis, MN: National Computer Systems.

Millon, T. (1998). DSM narcissistic personality disorder: Historical reflections and future directions. In E. F. Ronningstam (Ed.), *Disorders of narcissism: Diagnostic, clinical, and empirical implications* (pp. 75–101). Washington, DC: American Psychiatric Association.

Millon, T., & Davis, R. (2000). *Personality disorders in modern life.* New York: Wiley.

Millon, T., Davis, R., & Millon, C. (1997). *The Millon Clinical Multiaxial Inventory-III manual.* Minneapolis, MN: National Computer Systems.

Moldin, S. O., Rice, J. P., Erlenmeyer-Kimling, L., & Squires-Wheeler, S. (1994). Latent structure of DSM-III-R, Axis II psychopathology in a normal sample. *Journal of Abnormal Psychology, 103,* 259–266.

Morey, L. C. (1988). Personality disorders in DSM-III and DSM-III-R: Convergence, coverage, and internal consistency. *American Journal of Psychiatry, 145,* 573–577.

Morey, L. C. (1992). *Personality assessment inventory: Spanish translation.* Odessa, FL: Psychological Assessment Resources.

Morey, L. C., & Jones, J. K. (1998). Empirical studies of the construct validity of narcissistic personality disorder. In E. F. Ronningstam (Ed.), *Disorders of narcissism: Diagnostic, clinical, and empirical implications* (pp. 351–373). Washington, DC: American Psychiatric Association.

Morey, L. C., Waugh, M. H., & Blashfield, R. K. (1985). MMPI scales for the DSM-III personality disorders: Their derivation and correlates. *Journal of Personality Assessment, 49,* 245–251.

Mullins, L. S., & Kopelman, R. E. (1988). Toward an assessment of the construct validity of four measures of narcissism. *Journal of Personality Assessment, 52,* 610–625.

Murray, H. A. (1938). *Explorations in personality: A clinical and experimental study of fifty men of college age.* Oxford, UK: Oxford University Press.

Murray, H. A. (1943). *Thematic Apperception Test manual.* Cambridge, MA: Harvard University Press.

Narayan, C. (1990). Birth order and narcissism. *Psychological Reports, 67,* 1184–1186.

Nelson, K. (1977). The syntagmatic-paradigmatic shift revisited: A review of research and theory. *Psychological Bulletin, 84,* 93–116.

Nelson-Gray, R. O, & Farmer, R. F. (1999). Behavioral assessment of personality disorders. *Behaviour Research and Therapy, 37,* 347–368.

Nelson-Gray, R. O., Huprich, S. K., Kissling, G. E., & Ketchum, K. R. (2004). A preliminary examination of Beck's cognitive theory of personality disorders in undergraduate analogues. *Personality and Individual Differences, 36,* 219–233.

Nemiah, J. C. (1961). *Foundations of psychopathology.* Oxford, UK: Oxford University Press.

Nezworski, T., & Wood, J. (1995). Narcissism in the comprehensive system for the Rorschach. *Clinical Psychology: Science and Practice, 2,* 179–199.

O'Brien, M. L. (1987). Examining the dimensionality of pathological narcissism: Factor analysis and construct validity of the O'Brien Multiphasic Narcissism Inventory. *Psychological Reports, 61,* 499–510.

O'Connell, R. A., Mayo, J. A., & Sciutto, M. S. (1991). PDQ-R personality disorders in bipolar patients. *Journal of Affective Disorders, 23,* 217–221.

Oldham, J. (1988). Brief treatment of narcissistic personality disorder. *Journal of Personality Disorders, 2,* 88–90.

Oldham, J. M., Skodol, A. E., Kellman, H. D., Hyler, S. E., Rosnick, L., & Davies, M. (1992). Diagnosis of DSM-III-R personality disorders by two structured interviews: Patterns of comorbidity. *American Journal of Psychiatry, 149,* 213–220.

O'Leary, J., & Wright, F. (1986). Shame and gender issues in pathological narcissism. *Psychoanalytic Psychology, 3,* 327–339.

Ovid. (8/1958). *The metamorphoses* (H. Gregory, Trans.). New York: Viking Press.

Paris, J. C. (1993). *Borderline personality disorder: Etiology and treatment.* Washington, DC: American Psychiatric Press.

Patton, M., Connor, G., & Scott, K. (1982). Kohut's psychology of the self: Theory and measures of counseling outcome. *Journal of Counseling Psychology, 29,* 268–282.

Pepper, L. J., & Strong, P. N. (1958). *Judgmental subscales for the MF scale of the MMPL.* Unpublished manuscript.

Perry, J. C. (1990). Personality disorders and suicide and self-destructive behavior. In D. Jacobs & H. Brown (Eds.), *Suicide: Understanding and responding.* Madison, CT: International Universities Press.

Perry, J. C. (1992). Problems and considerations in the valid assessment of personality disorders. *American Journal of Psychiatry, 149,* 1645–1653.

Pesslow, E. D., Sanfilipo, M. P., & Fieve, R. R. (1995). Relationship between hypomania and personality disorders before and after successful treatment. *American Journal of Psychiatry, 152,* 232–238.

Pfohl, B., Blum, N., & Zimmerman, M. (1997). *Structured interview for DSM personality.* Washington, DC: American Psychiatric Press.

Pfohl, B., Coryell, W., Zimmerman, M., & Stangl, D. (1986). DSM-III personality disorders: Diagnostic overlap and internal consistency of individual DSM-III criteria. *Comprehensive Psychiatry, 27,* 21–34.

Phares, E. J., & Erskine, N. (1984). The measurement of selfism. *Educational and Psychological Measurement, 44,* 597–608.

Philipson, I. (1985). Gender and narcissism. *Psychology of Women Quarterly, 9,* 213–228.

Pica, S., Edwards, J., Jackson, H. J., Bell, R. C., Bates, G. W., & Rudd, R. P. (1990). Personality disorders in recent-onset bipolar disorder. *Comprehensive Psychiatry, 31,* 499–510.

Plakun, E. M. (1989). Narcissistic personality disorder: A validity study and comparison to borderline personality disorder. *Psychiatric Clinics of North America, 12*(3), 603–620.

Pulver, S. (1970). Narcissism: The term and the concept. *Journal of the American Psychoanalytic Association, 18,* 319–341.

Rank, O. (1911). Ein beitrag zum narcissmus [A contribution to narcissism]. *Jahrbuch fur Psychoanalytische und Psychopathologische Forschungen, 3,* 410–423.

Raskin, R., & Hall, C. S. (1979). A narcissistic personality inventory. *Psychological Reports, 40,* 590.

Raskin, R., & Novacek, J. (1989). An MMPI description of the narcissistic personality. *Journal of Personality Assessment, 53,* 66–80.

Raskin, R., Novacek, J., & Hogan, R. (1991a). Narcissism, self-esteem, and defensive self-enhancement. *Journal of Personality, 59,* 20–38.

Raskin, R., Novacek, J., & Hogan, R. (1991b). Narcissistic self-esteem management. *Journal of Personality and Social Psychology, 60,* 911–918.

Raskin, R., & Terry, H. (1988). A principal-components analysis of the Narcissistic Personality Inventory and further evidence for its construct validity. *Journal of Personality and Social Psychology, 54,* 890–902.

Rathvon, N., & Holmstrom, R. W. (1996). An MMPI–2 portrait of narcissism. *Journal of Personality Assessment, 66,* 1–19.

Raulin, S. and Lilienfeld, S. (1999). Research strategies for studying psychopathology. In T. Millon, P. H. Blaney, & R. D. Davis (Eds.), *Oxford textbook of psychopathology* (Vol. 4, pp. 49–78). New York: Oxford University Press.

Reich, A. (1953). Narcissistic object choice in women. *Journal of the American Psychoanalytic Association, 1,* 22–44.

Reich, A. (1960). Pathologic forms of self-esteem regulation. *Psychoanalytic Study of the Child, 18,* 218–238.

Reich, J. (1987). Sex distribution of DSM-III personality disorders in psychiatric outpatients. *American Journal of Psychiatry, 144,* 485–488.

Reich, J., Yates, W., & Nduaguba, M. (1989). Prevalence of DSM-III personality disorders in the community. *Social Psychiatry and Psychiatric Epidemiology, 24,* 12–16.

Rhodewalt, F., & Morf, C. C. (1995). Self and interpersonal correlates of the Narcissistic Personality Inventory. *Journal of Research in Personality, 29,* 1–23.

Rhodewalt, F., & Morf, C. C. (1998). On self-aggrandizement and anger: A temporal analysis of narcissism and affective reactions to success and failure. *Journal of Personality and Social Psychology, 74,* 672–685.

Richman, J. A., & Flaherty, J. A. (1988). "Tragic man" and "tragic woman:" Gender differences in narcissistic styles. *Psychiatry, 51,* 368–377.

Richman, J. A., & Flaherty, J. A. (1990). Gender differences in narcissistic styles. In E. Plakun (Ed.), *New perspectives on narcissism* (pp. 73–100). Washington, DC: American Psychiatric Association.

Rivas, L. A. (2001). Controversial issues in the diagnosis of narcissistic personality disorder: A review of the literature. *Journal of Mental Health Counseling, 23,* 22–35.

Robbins, S. B. (1989). Validity of the Superiority and Goal Instability Scales as measures of defects in the self. *Journal of Personality Assessment, 53,* 122–132.

Robbins, S. B., & Patton, M. J. (1985). Self-psychology and career development: Construction of the Superiority and Goal Instability Scales. *Journal of Counseling Psychology, 32,* 221–231.

Robbins, S. B., & Schwitzer, A. M. (1988). Validity of the Superiority and Goal Instability Scales as predictors of women's adjustment to college life. *Measurement and Evaluation in Counseling and Development, 21,* 117–123.

Robins, R. W., & John, O. P. (1997a). The quest for self-insight: Theory and research on the accuracy of self-perceptions. In R. Hogan, J. Johnson, & S. R. Briggs (Eds.), *Handbook of personality psychology* (pp. 649–679). San Diego, CA: Academic Press.

Robins, R. W., & John, O. P. (1997b). Effects of visual perspective and narcissism on self-perception: Is seeing believing? *Psychological Science, 8,* 37–42.

Roland, A. (1991). *In search of self in India and Japan: Toward a cross-cultural psychology.* Princeton, NJ: Princeton University Press.

Ronningstam, E. (1996). Pathological narcissism and narcissistic personality disorder in Axis I disorders. *Harvard Review of Psychiatry, 3,* 326–340.

Ronningstam, E., & Gunderson, J. (1989). Descriptive studies on narcissistic personality disorder. *Psychiatric Clinics of North America, 12,* 585–601.

Ronningstam, E., & Gunderson, J. G. (1990). Identifying criteria for narcissistic personality disorder. *American Journal of Psychiatry, 147,* 918–922.

Ronningstam, E., & Gunderson, J. (1991). Differentiating borderline personality disorder from narcissistic personality disorder. *Journal of Personality Disorders, 5,* 225–232.

Ronningstam, E., Gunderson, J. G., & Lyons, M. (1995). Changes in pathological narcissism. *American Journal of Psychiatry, 152,* 253–257.

Rose, P. (2002). The happy and unhappy faces of narcissism. *Personality and Individual Differences, 33,* 379–392.

Rosenfeld, H. A. (1987). *Impasse and interpretation: Therapeutic and anti-therapeutic factors in the psychoanalytic treatment of psychotic, borderline, and neurotic patients.* London: Tavistock and the Institute of Psycho-Analysis.

Samuels, J. F., Nestadt, G., Romanoski, A. J., Folstein, M. F., & McHugh, P. R. (1994). DSM-III personality disorders in the community. *American Journal of Psychiatry, 151,* 1055–1062.

Sato T., Sakado, K., & Sato, S. (1993). DSM-III-R personality disorders in outpatients with non-bipolar depression: The frequency in a sample of Japanese and the relationship to the 4-month outcome under adequate antidepressant therapy. *European Archives of Psychiatry and Clinical Neuroscience, 242,* 273–278.

Saulsman, L. M., & Page, A. C. (2004). The five-factor model and personality disorder empirical literature: A meta-analytic review. *Clinical Psychology Review, 23,* 1055–1085.

Schore, A. N. (1994). *Affect regulation and the origin of the self: The neurobiology of emotional development.* Hillsdale, NJ: Erlbaum.

Schore, A. (2003). *Affect regulation and disorders of the self.* New York: W. W. Norton.

Serkownek, K. (1975). *Subscales for scale 5 and O of the MMPI.* Unpublished manuscript.

Shea, M. T., Glass, D., Pilkonis, P. A., Watkins, J., & Docherty, J. P. (1987). Frequency and implications of personality disorders in a sample of depressed outpatients. *Journal of Personality Disorders, 1,* 27–42.

Shedler, J., & Westen, D. (2004). Refining personality disorder diagnosis: Integrating science and practice. *American Journal of Psychiatry, 161,* 1350–1365.

Siever, L., & Klar, H. (1986). A review of DSM-III criteria for the personality disorders. In A. Frances & R. Hales (Eds.), *American Psychiatric Association annual review* (Vol. 5, pp. 299–301). Washington, DC: American Psychiatric Association.

Skodol, A. E., Buckley, P., & Charles, E. (1983). Is there a characteristic pattern in the treatment history of clinic outpatients with borderline personality? *Journal of Nervous and Mental Disease, 171,* 405–410.

Smith, B. M. (1990). The measurement of narcissism in Asian, Caucasian, and Hispanic American women. *Psychological Reports, 67*(3, Pt. 1), 779–785.

Soldz, S., Budman, S., Demby, A., & Merry, J. (1993). Representation of personality disorders in circumplex and five-factor space: Explorations with a clinical sample. *Psychological Assessment, 5,* 41–52.

Sroufe, L. A., Egeland, B., Carlson, E., & Collins, W. A. (2005). *The development of the person: The Minnesota Study of Risk and Adaptation from Birth to Adulthood.* New York: Guilford Press.

Stangl, D., Pfohl, B., Zimmerman, M., Bowers, W., & Corenthal, C. (1985). A structured interview for the DSM-III personality disorders: A preliminary report. *Archives of General Psychiatry, 42,* 591–596.

Stern, P. N. (1980). Grounded theory methodology: Its uses and processes. *Image, 12,* 20–23.

Stone, M. H. (1989). Long-term follow-up of narcissistic/borderline patients. *Psychiatric Clinics of North America, 12,* 621–641.

Stormberg, D., Ronningstam, E., Gunderson, J., & Tohen, M. (1998). Pathological narcissism in bipolar disorder patients. *Journal of Personality Disorders, 12,* 179–185.

Stuart, S., Pfohl, B., Battaglia, M., Bellodi, L., Grove, W., & Cadoret, R. (1998). The coocurrence of DSM-III-R personality disorders. *Journal of Personality Disorders, 12*(4), 302–315.

Teusch, L., Böhme, H., Finke, J., & Gastpar, M. (2001). Effects of client-centered psychotherapy for personality disorders alone and in combination with psychopharmacological treatment: An empirical follow-up study. *Psychotherapy and Psychosomatics, 70,* 328–336.

Torgersen, S., Kringlen, E., & Cramer, V. (2001). The prevalence of personality disorders in a community sample. *Archives of General Psychiatry, 58,* 590–596.

Torgersen, S., Lygren, S., Oien, A., Skre, I., Onstad, S., Edvardson, J., et al. (2000). A twin study of personality disorders. *Comprehensive Psychiatry, 41,* 416–425.

Trull, T. J. (1992). DSM-III-R personality disorders and the five-factor model of personality: An empirical comparison. *Journal of Abnormal Psychology, 101,* 553–560.

Tschanz, B. T., Morf, C. C., & Turner, C. M. (1998). Gender differences in the structure of narcissism: A multi-sample analysis of the Narcissistic Personality Inventory. *Sex Roles, 38,* 863–870.

Turkat, I. D. (1990). *The personality disorders: A psychological approach to clinical management.* Elmsford, NY: Pergamon Press.

Turkat, I. D., & Maisto, S. A. (1985). Personality disorders: Applications of the experimental method to the formulation and modification of personality disorders. In D. H. Barlow (Ed.), *Clinical handbook of psychological disorders: A step-by-step treatment manual* (pp. 503–570). New York: Guilford Press.

Turley, B., Bates, G. W., Edwards, J., & Jackson, H. J. (1992). MCMI-II diagnosis in recent-onset bipolar disorders. *Journal of Clinical Psychology, 48,* 320–329.

Turner, R. M. (1994). Borderline, narcissistic, and histrionic personality disorders. In M. Hersen & R. T. Ammerman (Eds.), *Handbook for prescriptive treatments for adults* (pp. 393–420). New York: Plenum.

Tyrer, P., Seivewright, N., Murphy, S., Ferguson, B., Kingdon, D., Barczak, P., et al. (1988). The Nottingham study of neurotic disorder: Comparison of drug and psychological treatments. *Lancet, 8605,* 235–240.

Vaillant, G. E., & Perry, J. C. (1985). Personality disorders. In H. I. Kaplan & B. J. Sadock (Eds.), *Comprehensive textbook of psychiatry/IV* (4th ed., Vol. 1, pp. 958–986). Baltimore: Williams & Wilkins.

van Velzen, C. J. M., & Emmelkamp, P. M. G. (1996). The assessment of personality disorder: Implications for cognitive and behavior therapy. *Behaviour Research and Therapy, 34,* 655–668.

van der Waals, H. G. (1965). Problems of narcissism. *Bulletin of the Menninger Clinic, 29,* 293–311.

Wachtel, P. L. (1977). *Psychoanalysis and behaviour therapy: Toward an integration.* New York: Basic Books.

Wachtel, P. (1987). *Action and insight.* New York: Guilford Press.

Wachtel, P. L. (1994). Cyclical processes in personality and psychopathology. *Journal of Abnormal Psychology, 103,* 51–54.

Waelder, R. (1925). The psychoses: Their mechanisms and accessibility to influence. *International Journal of Psychoanalysis, 6,* 259–281.

Warren, M. P., & Capponi, A. (1996). The role of culture in the development of narcissistic personality disorders in America, Japan, and Denmark. *Journal of Applied Social Sciences, 20,* 77–82.

Watson, P. J., & Biderman, M. D. (1989). Failure of only-child status to predict narcissism. *Perceptual and Motor Skills, 69,* 1346.

Watson, P. J., Grisham, S. O., Trotter, M. V., & Biderman, M. D. (1984). Narcissism and empathy: Validity evidence for the narcissistic personality inventory. *Journal of Personality Assessment, 48,* 301–305.

Watson, P. J., Little, T., & Biderman, M. D. (1992). Narcissism and parenting styles. *Psychoanalytic Psychology, 9*(2), 231–244.

Weirzbicki, M., & Goldade, P. (1993). Sex-typing of the Millon Clinical Multiaxial Inventory. *Psychological Reports, 72,* 1115–1121.

Weise, K., & Tuber, S. (2004). The self and object representations of narcissistically disturbed children: An empirical investigation. *Psychoanalytic Psychology, 21,* 244–258.

Westen, D. (1985). *Self and society: Narcissism, collectivism, and the development of morals.* New York: Cambridge University Press.

Westen, D. (1990a). The relations among narcissism, egocentrism, self-concept, and self-esteem. *Psychoanalysis & Contemporary Thought, 13,* 185–241.

Westen, D. (1990b). Toward a revised theory of borderline object relations: Implications of empirical research. *International Journal of Psychoanalysis, 71,* 661–693.

Westen, D. (1996). A model and a method for uncovering the nomothetic from the idiographic: An alternative to the five-factor model? *Journal of Research in Personality, 30,* 400–413.

Westen, D. (1997). Divergences between clinical and research methods for assessing personality disorders: Implications for research and the evolution of Axis II. *American Journal of Psychiatry, 154,* 895–903.

Westen, D., & Arkowitz-Westen, L. (1998). Limitations of Axis II in diagnosing personality pathology in clinical practice. *American Journal of Psychiatry, 155,* 1767–1771.

Westen, D., & Shedler, J. (1999). Revising and assessing Axis II: I. Developing a clinically meaningful and empirically valid assessment method. *American Journal of Psychiatry, 156,* 258–272.

Westen, D., Shedler, J., Durrett, C., Glass, S., & Martens, A. (2003). Personality diagnosis in adolescence: DSM-IV Axis II diagnoses and an empirically derived alternative. *American Journal of Psychiatry, 160,* 952–966.

Widiger, T. A. (1987). *Personality interview questions—revised.* Unpublished manuscript, University of Kentucky, Lexington.

Widiger, T. A. (1995). Deletion of the self-defeating and sadistic personality disorder diagnoses. In W. J. Livesley (Ed.), *The DSM-IV personality disorders* (pp. 359–373). New York: Guilford Press.

Widiger, T. A., Frances, A., Harris, M., Jacobsberg, I., Fyer, M., & Manning, D. (1991). Comorbidity among Axis II disorders. In J. Oldham (Ed.), *Personality disorders: New perspectives on diagnostic validity* (pp. 163–194). Washington, DC: American Psychiatric Press.

Wink, P. (1991). Two faces of narcissism. *Journal of Personality and Social Psychology, 61,* 590–597.

Wink, P. (1992a). Three narcissism scales for the California Q-Set. *Journal of Personality Assessment, 58,* 51–66.

Wink, P. (1992b). Three types of narcissism in women from college to mid-life. *Journal of Personality, 60,* 7–30.

Wink, P., & Gough, H. G. (1990). New narcissism scales for the California Psychological Inventory and MMPI. *Journal of Personality Assessment, 54,* 446–463.

Winnicott, D. W. (1960/1965). Ego distortions in terms of true and false self. In D. W. Winnicott, *The maturational processes and the facilitating environment* (pp. 140–152). New York: International Universities Press.

Wolf, E. S. (1979). Transferences and countertransferences in the analysis of disorders of the self. *Contemporary Psychoanalysis, 15,* 577–594.

Wolfe, T. (1976, August 23). The "me" decade and the third great awakening. *New York Magazine,* 26–40.

Yeung, A. S., Lyons, M. J., Waternaux, C. M., Faraone, S. V., & Tsuang, M. T. (1993). A family study of self-reported personality traits and DSM-III-R personality disorders. *Psychiatry Research, 48,* 243–255.

Young, J. E. (1994). *Cognitive therapy for personality disorders: A schema-focused approach* (Rev. ed.). Sarasota, FL: Professional Resource Press.

Young, J. E. (1998). *The Young schema questionnaire: Short form.* Retrieved November 10, 1999, from http://.home.sprynet.com/sprynet/schema/ysqs1.htm

Zanarini, M. C., Frankenburg, F. R., Chauncey, D. L., & Gunderson, J. G. (1987). The Diagnostic Interview for PDs: Interrater and test-retest reliability. *Comprehensive Psychiatry, 28,* 467–480.

Zanarini, M. C., Frankenburg, F. R., Dubo, E. D., Sickel, A. E., Trikha, A., Levin, A., et al. (1998). Axis I comorbidity of borderline personality disorder. *American Journal of Psychiatry, 155,* 1733–1739.

Zimmerman, M., & Coryell, W. (1989). DSM-III personality disorder diagnoses in a nonpatient sample. *Archives of General Psychiatry, 46,* 682–689.

Zimmerman, M., & Coryell, W. H. (1990). DSM-III personality disorder dimensions. *Journal of Nervous and Mental Disease, 178,* 686–692.

10

Avoidant Personality Disorder

James D. Herbert

Drexel University

Homo sapiens is a highly gregarious species. It would be difficult to overstate the importance of interpersonal relationships to our psychological functioning. Serious disruption of relationships with others can lead to a cascade of psychological and even medical problems. Avoidant personality disorder (APD) is a condition characterized by just such disruption in interpersonal functioning. According to the fourth edition of the *Diagnostic and Statistical Manual of Mental Disorders* (DSM-IV; American Psychiatric Association, 1994), the cardinal features of APD include social inhibition, feelings of inadequacy, and fear of negative evaluation. These concerns lead individuals with APD to avoid a wide range of social situations, especially those involving close interactions with others. Pervasive social anxiety and avoidance result in a circumscribed social world, with relatively few contacts outside of a small number of trusted confidants.

Like all personality disorders, APD begins in childhood or adolescence and is believed to follow a chronic, unremitting course without intervention. As discussed later, there is growing evidence that APD represents a severe variant of the generalized subtype social anxiety disorder. APD is thought to be among the most common of the personality disorders. In a large community sample, Torgersen, Kringlen, and Cramer (2001) found a prevalence rate of 5.0%; Ekselius, Tillfors, Furmark, and Fredrikson (2001) found a similar rate of 6.6% in a community sample. APD is also common in clinical samples. For example, Stuart et al. (1998) reported that 25% of a large sample of patients met criteria for APD.

Given its high prevalence and the ubiquity of social concerns in normal psychological functioning, it is not surprising that questions have been raised regarding whether APD represents a distinct diagnostic entity. Before reviewing the literature on the etiology and treatment of APD, I will examine the diagnostic status of the disorder.

Does APD Represent a Distinct Disorder?

A considerable body of research has examined the extent to which the symptoms of APD comprise a distinct diagnostic entity. Shyness, social inhibition and anxiety, interpersonal reticence, and social avoidance are common features of normal personality functioning as well as of many clinical conditions. In fact, the absence of some degree of social anxiety is itself often considered problematic (Frances, First, & Pincus, 1995). It is therefore not surprising that questions have been raised about the degree to which APD is distinguishable from other clinical conditions on the one hand and normal personality functioning on the other. One way in which this question has been addressed is by examining the overlap of APD with other clinical conditions.[1] Research reveals high diagnostic co-occurrence between APD and various anxiety disorders, including panic disorder, obsessive-compulsive disorder, generalized anxiety disorder, and of course social anxiety disorder, as discussed later; co-occurrence is likewise quite high with other Axis I disorders, including mood disorders, somatoform disorders, eating disorders, and body dysmorphic disorder (see Alden et al., 2002, for a review). APD also shows substantial overlap with certain Axis II personality disorders, particularly schizoid and dependent personality disorders (e.g., Stuart et al., 1998).

Although high degrees of diagnostic co-occurrence may raise questions about distinctiveness, the fact that two disorders frequently co-occur does not ipso facto preclude their representing distinct conditions. Many examples of highly co-occurring yet distinct disorders can be found in medicine (e.g., diabetes and coronary heart disease). To represent a distinct disorder, a set of symptoms must be shown not only to covary across individuals, but also to be distinct from more "basic" conditions. A disease in turn requires the recognition of a distinct pathogenic process, etiology, or both (Kazdin, 1983). In fact, despite high rates of diagnostic co-occurrence, an argument could be made that APD is distinct from most of the other conditions just described. Consider, for example, schizoid personality disorder (SPD). Although both disorders are associated with social withdrawal, the avoidant individual desperately desires social contact but fears rejection, whereas the schizoid is ambivalent at best toward others, preferring to live as a loner; this distinction was first made by Millon (1969). In fact, research demonstrates that the differential diagnosis of APD and SPD is rarely problematic (Trull, Widiger, & Frances, 1987). Similarly, although APD shares some features in common with depression, panic disorder, and generalized anxiety disorder, it is both conceptually and empirically distinct from each of these conditions. However, there is one condition from which it is less clear that APD is actually distinct.

APD and Social Anxiety Disorder

One of the most vexing problems with APD is its overlap with social anxiety disorder (SAD), also known as social phobia.[2] In fact, more research has addressed the distinction of these putatively separate disorders than any other issue relating to APD.

The two disorders evolved from unique historical traditions. Over the various incarnations of the DSM, however, their descriptions have converged, to the point that there is now considerable overlap in their diagnostic criteria. In fact, despite minor differences in wording, comparison of the diagnostic criteria reveals substantive overlap. Not surprisingly, as discussed later, research has demonstrated high diagnostic co-occurrence between the two disorders.

A number of studies have attempted to establish meaningful distinctions between the two conditions (e.g., Herbert, Hope, & Bellack, 1992; Holt, Heimberg, & Hope, 1992; Turner, Beidel, & Townsley, 1992). The consistent finding has been that whereas patients diagnosed with APD demonstrate more severe symptoms than those with generalized SAD and without APD, they do not differ qualitatively on theoretically important variables that would support the notion of distinct disorders. Moreover, psychotherapy trials reveal that although patients with APD begin and end treatment with more severe symptoms than those with SAD, the rate of improvement is comparable (Chambless, Tran, & Glass, 1997; Feske, Perry, Chambless, Renneberg, & Goldstein, 1996; Hope, Herbert, & White, 1995; Mersch, Jansen, & Arntz, 1995; Turner, Beidel, Cooley, Woody, & Messer, 1994). The most parsimonious conclusion is that APD and generalized SAD reflect the same spectrum of psychopathology (i.e., pathological social anxiety and avoidance) rather than distinct disorders.

Most scholars of anxiety disorders have in fact endorsed this conclusion (e.g., Craske, 1999; Heimberg & Becker, 2002; Herbert & Dalrymple, 2005; Hoffman, Heinrichs, & Moscovitch, 2004; McNeil, 2001; Turner et al., 1992). The implication, of course, is that the two diagnoses should somehow be combined in future revisions of the DSM. Heimberg (1996), Liebowitz et al. (1998), and Reich (2001) argued that APD should be subsumed within generalized SAD. These authors suggested, among other things, that clinicians may be more likely to employ pharmacotherapy or an empirically supported psychotherapy, such as cognitive-behavioral therapy, for an anxiety disorder than they would for a personality disorder. Personality disorder scholars, however, have been more reluctant to concede that the two disorders are largely the same and offer a number of arguments in favor of retaining APD as a distinct diagnosis from SAD, or even folding the generalized subtype of SAD into APD.

Five arguments have been advanced in favor of this perspective. First, the high degree of overlap of the disorders may be more apparent than real, and may represent an artifact of sampling characteristics. Second, the psychopathology described by APD fits better with the characteristics of a personality disorder than it does with an Axis I syndrome. Third and closely related, APD is thought to be more temporally stable than one would expect an Axis I disorder to be. Fourth, subsuming APD within generalized SAD would simply shift existing diagnostic problems to Axis I rather than solve them. Fifth and finally, eliminating APD would discourage basic personality research into the disorder. I discuss each of these arguments, along with counterarguments, next.

Overlap Between APD and Generalized SAD. Several studies reveal high rates of APD among patients diagnosed with generalized SAD. However, Arntz (1999) pointed out that the majority of these studies examined the presence of APD in samples of persons with social phobia. He argued that a true assessment of the overlap of APD and SAD also requires examination of the rates of SAD in samples diagnosed with APD, as well as consideration of the rates of each disorder in reference to other disorders. That is, it is possible that APD is as common in another anxiety disorder as it is in SAD. Using the Structured Clinical Interview for DSM-III-R Personality Disorders (Spitzer, Williams, & Gibbon, 1987), Jansen, Arntz, Merckelbach, and Mersch (1994) found that the rates of APD did not differ between a group of social phobics and panic disorder patients, although the former did have more avoidant traits. In an unpublished master's thesis, Tacken (1998) administered structured clinical interviews assessing both Axis I and Axis II disorders to a sample of 515 patients. Consistent with other studies, approximately half of the patients diagnosed with generalized SAD also met criteria for APD. If APD in fact represents a severe variant of SAD, one would expect all patients with APD to also meet criteria for SAD. However, among the 109 patients with APD, only 56 (51%) had generalized SAD, 12 (11%) had nongeneralized SAD, and 41 (38%) did not meet criteria for SAD at all. Arntz argued that these two studies support the distinctiveness of APD and SAD. However, neither of these studies definitively refutes the possibility that APD and generalized SAD reflect the same underlying spectrum of psychopathology. Much appears to ride on how one interprets the specific criteria that define each disorder, and the APD criteria in particular leave considerable room for interpretation. The criteria for each disorder are of course different; hence, one would not expect 100% overlap between them. The important question is whether the differences are meaningful or rather simply reflect different aspects of the same behavioral, cognitive, and affective themes. In addition, in keeping with the hierarchical organization in the DSM in which a separate diagnosis of a "lesser" disorder is not made if the symptoms can be attributed to a more severe disorder, it is possible that Tacken (1998) did not make a diagnosis of SAD if APD was also present in some cases, even if the criteria for both disorders were technically met.

Distinctive Features of Personality Disorders. Widiger (2003) argued that personality disorders are distinguished by three key features: early onset, chronic course, and ego-syntonic features (i.e., features that are viewed as consistent with one's identity) that reflect "problems with everyday functioning" (p. 103). It should be noted that ego-syntonicity implies only that the characteristics are accepted as part of one's identity. For many personality disorders, including APD, the individual may nevertheless view these features as undesirable or problematic. In contrast, Axis I disorders are thought to have variable onsets, episodic courses, and ego-dystonic symptoms that represent extreme departures from normality. Because the psychopathology described by APD has an onset in childhood or adolescence, tends to be chronic and unremitting without treatment, and is characterized by interpersonal symptoms disrupting routine functioning, it is held to be more consistent with the notion of personality disorder. Of course, generalized SAD also shares each of these factors. Moreover, it is not clear that the characteristics suggested by Widiger reliably distinguish Axis I and Axis II disorders in general. Schizophrenia, for example, would appear to meet each of these criteria, as would early-onset dysthymia, both of which are coded on Axis I. Although one might argue that the more extreme depressive symptoms of dysthymia and the psychotic symptoms of schizophrenia are not ego-syntonic and go beyond "problems with everyday functioning," could not the same be said for the extreme affective lability and parasuicidal behavior of borderline personality disorder?

Temporal Stability. A closely related argument is that personality disorders in general, and APD in particular, are more stable than the major psychiatric syndromes. A recent study by Shea and Yen (2003), however, raises serious questions about this common belief. These authors compared the temporal stability of personality disorders (including APD), mood disorders, and anxiety disorders by examining the results of three naturalistic longitudinal studies. Contrary to expectations, they found that the anxiety disorders had the lowest remission rates of all three classes of disorders, with SAD having the lowest rate of any disorder. In a subsequent prospective, longitudinal study, Shea et al. (2004) found high associations across time in the course of APD and SAD. Thus, it does not appear that APD can be distinguished from generalized SAD on the basis of temporal stability.

Shifting Problems to Axis I. Widiger (2003) also argued that subsuming APD within generalized SAD on Axis I would simply shift the various diagnostic difficulties associated with APD to a different location within the DSM nomenclature rather than resolve them. In particular, the difficulties in defining the boundary between normal and abnormal functioning that characterize the personality disorders would not be resolved by moving APD to Axis I. It is of course true that combining generalized SAD and APD into a single diagnosis would not resolve boundary issues between normalcy and pathology, but it would resolve at least one diagnostic dilemma: the difficulty of distinguishing between two supposedly distinct disorders that appear to reflect the same underlying phenomenon.

The Risk of Deemphasizing Personality Research. Finally, personality disorder researchers worry that eliminating APD would signal a shift away from the study and clinical consideration of personality factors. This is a legitimate concern. The way in which a disorder is classified in the DSM system tends to impact how it is conceptualized and the nature of research efforts and clinical interventions directed toward it. For example, the classification of posttraumatic stress disorder as an anxiety disorder may have restricted the consideration of symptoms not related to anxiety and processes related to the aftermath of trauma (Herbert & Sageman, 2004), leading some to suggest moving it to a new category of "stress related disorders" (Resick, 2004). Research on basic personality features in APD has been fruitful. For example, within the context of the five-factor model of personality (Costa & McCrae, 1990), a number of studies have found APD to be characterized by high levels of neuroticism and low levels of extraversion (see Alden et al., 2002, for a review). It is understandable that scholars would be concerned about a shift in emphasis away from the study of such personality factors. This is no reason, however, to maintain an artificial distinction between disorders. To the extent that personality research is relevant, it can make contributions to the understanding and treatment of this spectrum of psychopathology, whatever it is called (see Bienvenu & Stein, 2003, for a recent example of this kind of integration).

Given the dubious distinction between APD and generalized SAD, the discussion of etiology, assessment, and treatment that follows will draw from the literatures on both disorders. I will note the diagnostic status of the specific samples in the studies discussed.

Etiology

Although the etiology of APD and SAD remains unknown, research has implicated a range of factors in the development and maintenance of social anxiety and avoidance (Dalrymple, Herbert, & Gaudiano, 2005). These include such biological factors as genetic and childhood temperament as well as more traditional "psychological" factors, such as childhood experiences, cognitive biases, and social skills deficits.

Genetic Factors

Several studies support the heritability of APD and generalized SAD. First-degree relatives of probands with APD demonstrate higher rates of both APD and generalized SAD (Johnson et al., 1995; Tillfors, Furmark, Ekselius, & Fredrikson, 2001). Likewise, first-degree relatives of those with generalized SAD show elevated rates of both generalized SAD and APD, but not non-generalized SAD (Stein et al., 1998). Of course, these studies confound shared genetics with shared environments, limiting their interpretability. In one of the few twin studies of SAD, Kendler, Karkowski, and Prescott (1999) esti-mated the heritability of SAD to be approximately 50%, although this study is limited by the use of DSM-III criteria, a female-only sample, and the failure to distinguish generalized from nongeneralized SAD. In a twin study of a gen-eral community sample, Stein, Jang, and Livesley (2002) found that genetic influences accounted for 42% of the variance in fear of negative evaluation, a core cognitive feature associated with both APD and generalized SAD. These same genetic factors were associated with personality characteristics linked to APD, including submissiveness, anxiousness, and social avoidance.

However, other studies suggest that what may be inherited is anxiety proneness or even a broader dimension of negative affectivity (which is a major component of anxiety and depression). For example, in a twin study of female adolescents, Nelson et al. (2000) found evidence for shared genetic vulnerability between SAD and both major depressive disorder and alcohol dependence. The literature suggests that the considerable genetic contribu-tions to both APD and generalized SAD are not unique to either disorder, reflecting instead a more general vulnerability to negative affectivity, although there may be a smaller genetic role in social anxiety per se (Rapee & Spence, 2004). Furthermore, Ollendick and Hirshfeld-Becker (2002) suggested that genetic vulnerabilities probably manifest themselves differently at different developmental periods, although the specific patterns are not yet known.

Temperament

Kagan and his colleagues (1984, 1988) identified a temperamental style in young children known as behavioral inhibition (BI), which they described as a tendency to react to unfamiliar persons or situations with fear, restraint, withdrawal, or all three. Theorists hypothesized that BI might be associated with the subsequent development of SAD. In fact, several researchers have found that children with high BI are at higher risk for the later development of elevated levels of social anxiety and SAD (e.g., Biederman et al., 2001;

Mick & Telch, 1998). In addition, high BI children have been shown to have parents with elevated rates of SAD (Rosenbaum et al., 1991). There are three points worth noting about this literature. First, BI is at best only moderately stable, even within childhood (see Rapee & Spence, 2004, for a review). Second, many behaviorally inhibited children do not develop clinical levels of social anxiety or avoidance. Third, consistent with the findings on genetic factors discussed earlier, childhood BI appears to convey a risk for a range of adult psychopathology, including panic disorder, depression, violence, and alcohol abuse, rather than social anxiety or avoidance per se (Caspi, Moffitt, Newman, & Silva, 1996; Rosenbaum, et al., 2000).

Childhood Experiences

Theories of APD tend to emphasize pathological parenting experiences (Beck & Freeman, 1990; Millon, 1981; Pretzer & Beck, 1996). Likewise, anxiety theorists have highlighted parenting styles emphasizing excessive concern over social evaluation, overprotectiveness, and high degrees of criticism in the development of SAD (e.g., Chorpita & Barlow, 1998). In support of these hypotheses, several studies have found that patients with APD or SAD retrospectively report characteristic parental experiences as children. Stravynski, Elie, and Franche (1989) found that patients with APD (per DSM-III criteria) perceived their parents as shaming, guilt engendering, and less tolerant than matched nonclinical controls perceived their parents to be. Meyer and Carver (2000) reported that APD symptoms in a sample of students were correlated with negative childhood narratives generated through a semistructured writing exercise. Among the most negative narratives, a common theme was parental arguments and conflicts. Arbel and Stravynski (1991), however, did not find that APD patients recalled more parental threats or separation relative to matched controls, although they perceived their parents as less affectionate.

Several retrospective studies have found that adults with SAD report their parents as having been less warm, more concerned with social evaluation, and having used shame as a discipline style (Arrindell et al., 1989; Bruch & Heimberg, 1994; Lieb et al., 2000; Parker, 1979; Rapee & Melville, 1997). Although this line of research is suggestive, an obvious weakness is the reliance on retrospective self-report. It is quite possible that observed differences in reports of persons with APD or SAD relative to controls are a result of memory biases associated with current psychological state. This interpretation is bolstered by the research on cognitive biases in SAD discussed later. Another weakness is that most studies failed to include a clinical comparison group, so that the specificity of any findings to APD/SAD has not been established. Battle et al. (2004) found that not only patients with APD but also those with other personality disorders (e.g., borderline, schizotypal, and obsessive-compulsive) reported elevated rates of parental abuse and neglect.

McGinn, Cukor, and Sanderson (in press) found that retrospective ratings of parents as abusive and neglectful were associated with depression but not anxiety. Finally, the confound of shared environments and genetics is an additional limitation. It is possible that retrospective reports of things such as high concern over social evaluation, even if they are accurate, reflect shared genetic effects rather than any direct impact of parenting style. Just as estimates of heritability derived from family studies are limited by shared environmental effects, so too are studies of parenting effects limited by shared genetics.

A few researchers have attempted to address the limitations associated with retrospective self-report by directly examining parent-child interactions. In general, this research suggests that parents of children with anxiety disorders tend to be controlling and overinvolved (e.g., Hirshfeld, Biederman, Brody, Faraone, & Rosenbaum, 1997; Siqueland, Kendall, & Steinberg, 1996). Barrett, Rapee, Dadds, and Ryan (1996) also found that parents of children with anxiety disorders tended to encourage an avoidant coping style to a hypothetical threat situation. Hudson and Rapee (2001) found that mothers of anxious children demonstrated more intrusive involvement and more criticism of their children during a stressful task relative to nonclinical controls. However, the mothers of anxious children did not differ from the mothers of oppositional defiant children, who demonstrated similar behaviors. Moreover, only 21% of the anxious child group had avoidant disorder/SAD; the others included children with separation anxiety disorder, overanxious disorder/generalized anxiety disorder, and specific phobia. Although the observational research is suggestive of a link between overinvolved and critical parenting and SAD, the specificity of this link is dubious. Most studies have not included comparison groups, and those that have (e.g., Hudson & Rapee, 2001) do not find unique effects even for anxiety disorders, much less for APD/SAD. In addition, even if specific effects were observed, the causal direction would remain unclear. For example, overinvolved parenting might contribute to childhood anxiety and avoidance, but it could just as well reflect a reaction to an anxious and avoidant child, a phenomenon known as reactive gene-environment correlation (Plomin, 1994; Plomin, Owen, & McGuffin, 1994).

Cognitive Factors

Relatively little research has examined cognitive biases in APD, although a large literature exists with respect to SAD. This literature indicates that SAD is associated with several biases in information processing, including attentional, memory, and interpretation biases (see Clark, 2001, and Hirsch & Clark, 2004, for reviews). These biases are also evident in socially anxious youth (Ollendick & Hirshfeld-Becker, 2002). Persons with SAD tend to overestimate the likelihood of and cost associated with hypothetical negative social outcomes (Foa, Franklin, Perry, & Herbert, 1996). They tend to interpret ambiguous social situations negatively (Amir, Foa, & Coles, 1998; Stopa & Clark, 2000). They underestimate their performance in social interactions (Rapee & Lim, 1992; Stopa & Clark, 1993). Alden, Mellings, and Laposa (2004) found that relative to nonanxious controls, patients with SAD reacted to positively framed feedback following a conversational task with an increase in anticipatory anxiety related to a second conversation. The positive feedback may have increased the patients' perceptions of performance expectations, which they did not feel confident in meeting.

One of the most consistent cognitive findings is that patients with SAD show enhanced self-focused attention and corresponding decreased processing of external cues in social situations (e.g., Hope, Heimberg, & Klein, 1990; Mellings & Alden, 2000). The research on memory biases has been less consistent. Several studies have found that persons with SAD demonstrate a negative explicit memory bias, particularly related to their perceptions of how they are perceived by others, but only under conditions in which social threat is anticipated. Most studies, however, have failed to find evidence of biases in implicit memory (see Hirsch & Clark, 2004, for a review).

These information processing biases may explain one of the central paradoxes of APD and SAD: anxiety is not extinguished despite the fact that behavioral avoidance is rarely complete. That is, most individuals continue to engage to some degree in social interactions, yet habituation typically does not occur. Cognitive theorists suggest that such biases preclude the cognitive processing necessary for anxiety reduction. Similarly, experiential avoidance—the tendency to avoid aversive thoughts, feelings, images, memories, and so on— may contribute to the maintenance of the disorder despite the apparent absence of behavioral avoidance (Herbert & Cardaciotto, in press).

Social Skills Deficits

Given that persons with APD frequently avoid a range of social situations, it is not surprising that they fail to develop normal social skills. Turner and Beidel (1989) suggested that the presence of social skills deficits could distinguish APD from generalized SAD. Herbert and his colleagues (1992), however, found no differences between patients with APD and SAD relative to those with only SAD on behavioral measures of social skills, results that add to the evidence that APD and generalized SAD reflect the same spectrum of psychopathology.

A number of researchers have found that the social performance of persons with generalized SAD is rated as poorer relative to the performance of both clinical and nonclinical controls, and many of these samples included persons who also met criteria for APD (Baker & Edelmann, 2002; Fydrich, Chambless, Perry, Buergener, & Beazley, 1998; Hopko, McNeil, Zvolensky, & Eifert, 2001; Norton & Hope, 2001; Stopa & Clark, 1993). Several authors have noted, however, that these performance impairments do not necessarily reflect social skills deficits but may instead result from the disruptive effects of anxiety or the use of safety behaviors (Clark & Wells, 1995; Heimberg & Becker, 2002; Herbert, 1995; Kashdan & Herbert, 2001). Just as there is considerable variability across individuals in the degree of social impairments, it is likely that the nature of the impairments also differs, with a subset reflecting true skills deficits.

In summary, although both biological and psychosocial factors have been found to be associated with APD and SAD, these associations are generally not unique to this spectrum of psychopathology. Further research is needed to clarify the specific factors that lead to social anxiety and avoidance.

Assessment

Before formal assessment of APD, SAD, or both can begin, the individual must first come to the attention of a mental health professional. There is evidence that most persons suffering from these disorders are not recognized by professionals and do not seek professional help (Herbert, Crittenden, & Dalrymple, 2004). This is probably due to two reasons. First, because APD and SAD represent extremes of normal functioning, patients, their families, and even health care professionals often fail to recognize that the problem merits professional attention. Second, the very nature of the problem frequently contributes to reluctance to seek help. Once it is identified, however, both clinical interviews and self-report measures are useful assessment tools. Although such projective tests as the Rorschach inkblot test have traditionally been used in the assessment of personality pathology, their scientific status is highly dubious. Their use is therefore not recommended (Wood, Nezworski, Lilienfeld, & Garb, 2003).

The Clinical Interview

The most commonly used assessment tool for APD or SAD is the clinical interview, which varies widely in format, ranging from highly structured protocols to unstructured interviews. Structured clinical interviews are most commonly employed in research settings, as their standardization reduces interviewer bias and increases interrater reliability, whereas unstructured formats tend to be preferred in front-line clinical settings. Regardless of format, the typical goals of the clinical interview for APD include establishment of rapport, psychodiagnosis, and assessment of symptom patterns, phobic stimuli, and impairment in functioning.

The most commonly used structured interview for personality disorders (including APD) is the Structured Clinical Interview for DSM-IV Axis II Personality Disorders (SCID-II; First, Gibbon, Spitzer, Williams, & Benjamin, 1997). The SCID-II is known for being relatively user-friendly, and has been shown to have adequate psychometric properties (Maffei et al., 1997). Another structured interview commonly used to assess personality disorders is the Structured Interview for DSM-IV Personality (SIDP-IV; Pfohl, Blum, &

Zimmerman, 1997; Stangl, Pfohl, Zimmerman, Bowers, & Corenthal, 1985). The SIDP-IV is a semistructured interview designed as a "nonpejorative" measure of personality disorder symptoms. Interrater reliability has been shown to be quite high, with kappa of up to .94 (Bockian, Lee, & Fidanque, 2003). The International Personality Disorder Examination (IPDE; Loranger, Susman, Oldham, & Russakoff, 1987) is a popular instrument in research contexts, although it is rather long and cumbersome to administer, making it less popular in clinical settings. The IPDE has been shown to have good interrater reliability, with intraclass correlations ranging from .84 to .92 (Lenzenweger, 1999), as well as adequate temporal stability (Loranger et al., 1994). Another popular instrument, the Personality Disorder Interview—IV (Widiger, Mangine, Corbitt, Ellis, & Thomas, 1995), has not been subjected to psychometric evaluation, and the manual includes no normative data. Trull (1995) developed the Iowa Personality Disorder Screen (IPDS), a brief, 11-item screening interview; initial psychometric data are promising (Trull & Amdur, 2001). Considering the overlap between the criteria used to define APD and SAD, it is worth noting that the single item tapping symptoms of APD on the IPDS is "excessive social anxiety."

Self-Report Instruments

In addition to measures of personality traits, such as the revised NEO Personality Inventory (NEO-PI-R) or NEO Five-Factor Inventory (NEO-FFI; Costa & McCrae, 1992), several self-report measures of personality disorders have been developed. These vary in the degree to which the items adhere closely to the DSM-IV criteria for the various personality disorders. Among the more commonly used measures are the Millon Clinical Multiaxial Inventory—III (MCMI-III; Millon, Millon, & Davis, 1994), a 175-item questionnaire measuring both Axis I and Axis II conditions corresponding to the DSM-IV, and the Wisconsin Personality Disorders Inventory—IV (Klein & Benjamin, 1996), a 204-item self-report inventory based on an interpersonal model of personality functioning.

A serious problem with the assessment of personality disorders in general is the relatively low level of agreement among various measures putatively tapping the same constructs (Perry, 1992). Even among structured interviews such as the SCID-II and the IPDE, kappas for various personality disorders tend to be under .50 (Clark, Livesley, & Morey, 1997). Agreement is even lower between interview measures and self-report measures. For example, median correlations range from .26 to .38 between the SCID-II and MCMI-II (Kennedy et al., 1995; Marlowe et al., 1997). These relatively low correlations reflect some personality disorder scholars' concerns that patients may not be able or willing to accurately describe personality disorder features, rendering self-rating instruments of limited value for diagnostic purposes (Westen, 1997). Of course, low correlations alone do not necessarily indicate that any particular procedure is either inaccurate or not useful. For example, self-report instruments may tend to assess different aspects of personality disorders (e.g., self-perceptions, mood states) from those that interviews assess. In addition, interviews permit probing for multiple behavioral examples of a symptom or trait, which may lead to more informed global conclusions than those obtained from self-report measures.

Two approaches have been employed to increase diagnostic accuracy. The LEAD procedure (longitudinal expert evaluation using all available data; Spitzer, 1983) consists of a consensus diagnosis by a team of clinicians using data collected over the course of assessment and treatment. However, the concordance between LEAD diagnoses and those generated by structured interviews for the personality disorders has been disappointingly low. A second approach involves a Q-sort procedure developed by Westen and Shedler (2000). The Shedler-Westen Assessment Procedure–200 (SWAP-200) involves the clinician's sorting of 200 descriptive cards into one of seven categories according to how well each describes the patient, based on data gathered during a semistructured interview. Westen and Muderrisoglu (2003) found good interrater reliability between the SWAP-200 and semistructured clinical interview (median $r > .80$). However, Davidson, Obonsawin, Seils, and Patience (2003) found poor agreement between clinicians and their patients on the SWAP-200, raising questions about the instrument's validity. It is worth noting, however, that the highest agreement (although still only modest) was for the APD prototype.

In general, the psychometric data on instruments designed to assess Axis I disorders are more encouraging. It should be noted, however, that few studies have directly compared instruments targeting APD with those targeting SAD, and those that have done so did not distinguish the specific and generalized subtypes of SAD (e.g., Shea & Yen, 2003). Given the high diagnostic overlap between APD and generalized SAD, one would expect instruments assessing each construct to overlap significantly. Examination of the specific items within measures of APD and SAD supports this conclusion. Nevertheless, most measures of APD are subscales of larger instruments that cover the full range of personality disorders rather than focus exclusively on APD per se. In contrast, there exist several measures of SAD in and of itself, and even general measures of anxiety disorders tend to devote more items to assessing symptoms of SAD than corresponding measures of personality disorders devote to APD.

The most commonly employed structured interviews for SAD are the Anxiety Disorders Interview Schedule for DSM-IV (ADIS-IV; Brown, DiNardo, & Barlow, 1994) and the Structured Clinical Interview for Axis I DSM-IV Disorders (SCID-IV; First, Spitzer, Gibbon, & Williams, 1994). Commonly employed self-report measures include the Social Phobia and Anxiety Inventory (Turner, Beidel, Dancu, & Stanley, 1989) and the Social Phobia Scale (Mattick & Clark, 1998; see Herbert, Rheingold, & Brandsma, 2000, for a review of the assessment of SAD).

Treatment

Relatively few studies have examined the treatment of individuals specifically selected for APD (Alden et al., 2002). However, a substantial literature exists on the treatment of generalized SAD, and many of the samples include individuals who also met diagnostic criteria for APD. As noted earlier, studies that have compared treatment outcome among patients with generalized SAD with versus without APD have generally found that the former group begins and ends treatment more impaired than the latter group does, but the groups do not differ in their rate of improvement (Brown, Heimberg, & Juster, 1995; Hoffman, Newman, Becker, Taylor, & Roth, 1995; Hope et al., 1995). We will therefore supplement our review of the treatment of APD per se with a review of the treatment of generalized SAD.

Pharmacotherapy

A variety of psychopharmacological agents have been used for both APD and SAD, including the beta adrenergic antagonists, various benzodiazepine anxiolytics, the monoamine oxidase inhibitors (MAOIs), and various selective serotonin reuptake inhibitors (SSRIs; Trestman, Woo-Ming, deVegvar, & Siever, 2001). For nongeneralized (i.e., "specific") SAD, beta blockers or benzodiazepines are generally considered the first-line drug therapies, and they can be used on an as-needed basis. For patients with APD or generalized SAD, SSRIs are recommended, with MAOIs as alternatives for those who do not respond to SSRIs (Blanco, Schneier, & Liebowitz, 2001). For example, in a double-blind, placebo-controlled trial, Fahlén (1995) found that the reversible and selective MAOI-A brofaromine reduced not only symptoms of social anxiety but also avoidant personality traits in a sample of patients with SAD. In fact, the percentage of patients who met diagnostic criteria for APD dropped from 60% ($n = 15$) at pretreatment to 20% ($n = 5$) following 12 weeks of drug therapy. Although pharmacotherapy is generally effective during acute treatment, a serious limitation is the high rate of relapse following medication discontinuation. As discussed later, attempts to address relapse have focused on combining drug therapy and psychotherapy.

Psychotherapy

Although several authors have provided clinical descriptions of the traditional psychodynamic treatment of APD (e.g., Harper, 2004), such interventions have only rarely been subjected to systematic research, and they have been only for so-called time-limited versions of psychodynamic treatments. Barber, Morse, Krakauer, Chittams, and Crits-Christoph (1997) found significant reductions in avoidant symptoms in patients with APD following

52 sessions of time-limited supportive-expressive psychotherapy. Conclusions that can be drawn from this study are limited, however, by the absence of any control or comparison condition. Svartberg, Stiles, and Seltzer (2004) found comparable and positive results for 40-session programs of short-term dynamic psychotherapy and of cognitive therapy for patients with Cluster C personality disorders, 62% of whom had APD. Although the magnitude of these results suggested clinically meaningful effects, the study relied solely on self-rating instruments to assess treatment outcome. Moreover, measures commonly used in cognitive-behavioral therapy (CBT) trials were not used, precluding comparison of effect sizes with those from other studies.

In contrast to the paucity of research on psychodynamic psychotherapy, several studies have evaluated various forms of CBT for APD. In keeping with the common belief that APD is associated with social skills deficits, most of these studies included social skills training as a core treatment component. Alden (1989) found positive effects of systematic, graduated exposure for patients with APD; the addition of social skills training did not augment the effects of exposure alone. Stravynski, Lesage, Marcouiller, and Elie (1989) found social skills training (SST) plus group discussion, administered sequentially, to be effective for APD. In a small, uncontrolled trial for APD, Renneberg, Goldstein, Phillips, and Chambless (1990) found positive effects of a brief but intensive group treatment program consisting of systematic desensitization and SST.

The most extensively researched psychotherapy for SAD (with or without APD) is the cognitive-behavioral group therapy (CBGT) program developed by Heimberg and Becker (2002). CBGT is a time-limited, group-based program consisting of cognitive restructuring conducted in the context of simulated exposure exercises. The program is based on cognitive models of SAD and aims to modify dysfunctional cognitive processes believed to maintain social anxiety and avoidance. A number of studies from various research groups have documented the considerable effectiveness of CBGT (Chambless et al., 1997; Heimberg et al., 1998; Hope et al., 1995; Woody & Adessky, 2002). CBGT has been shown to be more effective than psychoeducation (Heimberg et al., 1990). Several studies have recently found that individual versions of the CBGT protocol appear to be at least as effective as the standard group format while offering the advantage of greater convenience in scheduling of treatment sessions (Herbert, Rheingold, Gaudiano, & Myers, 2004; Zaider et al., 2003).

A similar CBT program was recently developed by Clark and his colleagues (Clark et al., 2003; Stangier, Heidenreich, Peitz, Lauterbach, & Clark, 2003). Like Heimberg and Becker's CBGT, the Clark program focuses on cognitive change as the key target of intervention. Clark places relatively less emphasis on disputational methods of cognitive restructuring, however, utilizing instead video feedback of simulated social encounters to provide evidence against dysfunctional beliefs. Emphasis is also placed on fostering an external focus to disrupt the self-focused attention that characterizes SAD.

Neither the Heimberg and Becker nor the Clark protocol explicitly addresses deficits in social skills. As discussed earlier, there appears to be considerable heterogeneity among individuals with APD and generalized SAD with respect to social skills, suggesting that some patients may benefit from interventions that incorporate explicit SST. Several studies have found SST to be effective for SAD (e.g., Mersch, Emmelkamp, Bogels, & van der Sleen, 1989; Wlazlo, Schroeder-Hartwig, Hand, Kaiser, & Münchau, 1990). Turner and his colleagues (1994; Turner, Beidel, & Cooley-Quille, 1995) integrated SST with exposure, achieving promising results. Herbert and his colleagues (Herbert, Gaudiano, et al., 2005) recently found that a CBGT program that included social skills training was more effective for a sample of patients with generalized SAD, 75% of whom met criteria for APD, relative to standard CBGT without social skills training.

Combined Treatment

Researchers have recently investigated the possibility that a combination of pharmacotherapy and psychotherapy may be more beneficial than either monotherapy alone. Kool, Dekker, Duijsens, de Jonghe, and Puite (2003) found greater reduction in APD symptoms in depressed patients treated with a combination of antidepressants and short-term psychodynamic supportive psychotherapy relative to those treated with antidepressants only. The relevance of these findings to APD per se is difficult to gauge, however, as patients were selected for the presence of major depressive disorder, and it is not clear how many met diagnostic criteria for APD. Two large-scale studies, both of which are not yet published, have compared CBT combined with antidepressants in the treatment of SAD. Davidson et al. (2004) found no benefit of combined SSRI (fluoxetine) and CBT relative to either monotherapy alone; Heimberg and colleagues (Heimberg, 2002) found similar results with combined CBT and an MAOI (phenelzine). Haug et al. (2003) found that patients who received combined exposure therapy plus an SSRI (sertraline) actually fared significantly worse over a 28-week follow-up period than those who received exposure alone. The reasons for this surprising effect are unclear but could be related to patients taking medications making external attributions for their improvements, or to medications interfering with exposure-mediated habituation.

New Directions in Treatment

Despite the promising results of current intervention technologies, there remains significant room for improvement. Treatment does not produce improvement in all patients, and even among treatment responders, most remain at least somewhat symptomatic (see Herbert, Gaudiano, et al., 2005, for a discussion). These findings suggest the need for further treatment innovations. One obvious possibility is combined psychotherapy plus medication. As just discussed, however, the results of trials of combination interventions have proved disappointing.

An open trial of interpersonal psychotherapy recently yielded promising results and warrants further study (Lipsitz, Markowitz, Cherry, & Fyer, 1999). Herbert and Dalrymple (2004) adapted a novel form of CBT known as acceptance and commitment therapy (Hayes, Strosahl, & Wilson, 1999), which encourages overcoming avoidance of distressing thoughts and feelings while promoting behavior change, for generalized SAD. Preliminary results from an open trial are promising (Dalrymple & Herbert, 2004).

Recent efforts have begun to focus on the dissemination of treatments to front-line clinical settings. For example, the recent shift in emphasis away from group-based CBT and toward individual therapy described earlier speaks to the need for treatment programs that are easily transportable to clinical settings. In terms of efficiency, Herbert, Rheingold, and Goldstein (2002) found surprising efficacy of a brief, 6-week version of CBT.

Conclusion and Future Directions

Since its initial appearance in the DSM-III more than two decades ago, we have learned a great deal about the nature, etiology, assessment, and treatment of APD. Nevertheless, many questions remain, and current interventions leave considerable room for improvement.

Perhaps the most pressing issue is resolution of the diagnostic dilemma regarding the generalized subtype of SAD. There is compelling evidence that APD and generalized SAD are drawn from the same fundamental spectrum of psychopathology. The coexistence of the two diagnostic labels for the same underlying phenomenon contributes to diagnostic confusion among clinicians and hampers communication among researchers (Farmer, 2000). It therefore makes little sense to continue the status quo in future generations of the DSM. This conclusion of course raises the question of which label should prevail, a question on which personality scholars and anxiety theorists predictably differ. Generalized SAD and APD appear to be virtually identical. However, both conditions differ on many dimensions, including heritability and treatment response, from such "nongeneralized" SAD as public speaking phobia, which has alternatively been labeled "discrete," "specific," or "circumscribed" SAD. One solution would be to distinguish formally specific SAD from APD/generalized SAD. Consistent with the original DSM-III conceptualization, the former could be termed "social phobia," which would be limited to anxiety and avoidance of a single social situation. APD and generalized SAD could then become "social anxiety and avoidance disorder," a term that captures both the subjective distress provoked by social situations and the resulting tendency to engage in experiential and behavioral avoidance. Whether this or another diagnostic scheme is implemented, the issue should be resolved with the publication of the DSM-V. It is worth noting that this issue bears implications for the broader relationship between other spectrums of psychopathology that appear to cut across current Axis I and Axis II disorders (e.g., schizophrenia and schizotypal personality disorder; obsessive-compulsive disorder and obsessive-compulsive personality disorder).

Personality scholars understandably worry that eliminating APD as a distinct diagnosis could result in a loss of focus on personality factors in social anxiety and avoidance. However, this need not be the case. To the extent that personality factors are relevant, they can make contributions to psychopathology regardless of where it is located and named in a nosological scheme. For example, Hoffman et al. (2004) proposed an interesting dimensional approach to the classification of disorders of social anxiety and avoidance that is based in part on the work of personality theorists. Such work highlights the importance of investigating basic processes that may underlie various forms of psychopathology that cut across diagnostic categories and that are linked to normal psychological functioning (Harvey, Watkins, Mansell, & Shafran, 2004).

Finally, although impressive advances have been made in the treatment of APD and SAD over the past two decades, much more remains to be done. Some of the especially promising possibilities include the incorporation of technologies such as video feedback, treatments focused on interpersonal relationships, and interventions targeting experiential avoidance of distressing cognitions and affect as alternatives to the disputational strategies associated with traditional CBT. One thing is clear: the next two decades promise to be every bit as exciting as the preceding two in the quest to understand, assess, and treat problems of social anxiety and avoidance.

Notes

1. In keeping with the recommendations of Lilienfeld, Waldman, and Israel (1994), I use such terms as "overlap" and "diagnostic co-occurrence" rather than the more familiar "comorbidity" to describe the relationship of APD with other disorders. These terms avoid unnecessary connotations about the underlying structure of the diagnostic categories.

2. Although "social anxiety disorder" and "social phobia" are often used interchangeably, there is a growing preference for the former term, which many believe better reflects the pervasiveness of social anxiety and avoidance among most individuals with the condition (Liebowitz, Heimberg, Fresco, Travers, & Stein, 2000).

References

Alden, L. (1989). Short-term structured treatment for avoidant personality disorder. *Journal of Consulting and Clinical Psychology, 57*, 756–764.

Alden, L. E., Laposa, J. M., Taylor, C. T., & Ryder, A. G. (2002). Avoidant personality disorder: Current status and future directions. *Journal of Personality Disorders, 16*, 1–29.

Alden, L. E., Mellings, T. M. B., & Laposa, J. M. (2004). Framing social information and generalized social phobia. *Behaviour Research and Therapy, 42,* 588–600.

American Psychiatric Association. (1994). *Diagnostic and statistical manual of mental disorders* (4th ed.). Washington, DC: Author.

Amir, N., Foa, E. B., & Coles, M. E. (1998). Negative interpretation bias in social phobia. *Behaviour Research and Therapy, 36,* 945–957.

Arbel, N., & Stravynski, A. (1991). A retrospective study of separation in the development of adult avoidant personality disorder. *Acta Psychiatrica Scandinavica, 83,* 174–178.

Arntz, A. (1999). Do personality disorders exist? On the validity of the concept and its cognitive-behavioral formulation and treatment. *Behaviour Research and Therapy, 37,* S97–S134.

Arrindell, W. A., Kwee, M. G. T., Methorst, G. J., van der Ende, J., Pol, E., & Moritz, B. J. M. (1989). Perceived parental rearing styles of agoraphobic and socially phobic in-patients. *British Journal of Psychiatry, 155,* 526–535.

Baker, S. R., & Edelmann, R. J. (2002). Is social phobia related to lack of social skills? Duration of skill-related behaviours and ratings of behavioural adequacy. *British Journal of Clinical Psychology, 41,* 243–257.

Barber, J. P., Morse, J. Q., Krakauer, I. D., Chittams, J., & Crits-Christoph, K. (1997). Change in obsessive-compulsive and avoidant personality disorders following time-limited supportive-expressive therapy. *Psychotherapy, 34,* 133–143.

Barrett, P. M., Rapee, R. M., Dadds, M. R., & Ryan, S. (1996). Family enhancement of cognitive style in anxious and aggressive children. *Journal of Abnormal Child Psychology, 24,* 187–203.

Battle, C. L., Shea, M. T., Johnson, D. M., Yen, S., Zlotnick, C., Zanarini, M. C., et al. (2004). Childhood maltreatment associated with adult personality disorders: Findings from the collaborative longitudinal personality disorders study. *Journal of Personality Disorders, 18,* 193–211.

Beck, A. T., & Freeman, A. (1990). *Cognitive therapy of personality disorders.* New York: Guilford Press.

Biederman, J., Hirshfeld-Becker, D. R., Rosenbaum, J. F., Herot, C., Friedman, D., Snidman, N., et al. (2001). Further evidence of association between behavioral inhibition and social anxiety in children. *American Journal of Psychiatry, 158,* 1673–1679.

Bienvenu, O. J., & Stein, M. B. (2003). Personality and anxiety disorders: A review. *Journal of Personality Disorders, 17,* 139–151.

Blanco, C., Schneier, F. R., & Liebowitz, M. R. (2001). Psychopharmacology. In S. G. Hofmann & P. M. DiBartolo (Eds.), *From social anxiety to social phobia: Multiple perspectives* (pp. 335–353). Boston: Allyn & Bacon.

Bockian, N. R., Lee, A., & Fidanque, C. S. (2003). Personality disorders and spinal cord injury: A pilot study. *Journal of Clinical Psychology in Medical Settings, 10,* 307–313.

Brown, E. J., Heimberg, R. G., & Juster, H. R. (1995). Social phobia subtype and avoidant personality disorder: Effect of severity of social phobia, impairment, and outcome of cognitive-behavioral treatment. *Behavior Therapy, 26,* 467–486.

Brown, T. A., DiNardo, P. A., & Barlow, D. H. (1994). *Anxiety disorders interview schedule for DSM-IV (ADIS-IV).* Albany, NY: Graywind.

Bruch, M. A., & Heimberg, R. G. (1994). Differences in perceptions of parental and personal characteristics between generalized and nongeneralized social phobics. *Journal of Anxiety Disorders, 8,* 155–168.

Caspi, A., Moffitt, T. E., Newman, D. L., & Silva, P. A. (1996). Behavioral observations at age 3 years predict adult psychiatric disorders: Longitudinal evidence from a birth cohort. *Archives of General Psychiatry, 53,* 1033–1039.

Chambless, D. L., Tran, G. Q., & Glass, C. R. (1997). Predictors of response to cognitive-behavioral group therapy for social phobia. *Journal of Anxiety Disorders, 11,* 211–240.

Chorpita, B. F., & Barlow, D. H. (1998). The development of anxiety: The role of control in the early environment. *Psychological Bulletin, 124,* 3–21.

Clark, D. M. (2001). A cognitive perspective on social phobia. In W. R. Crozier & L. E. Alden (Eds.), *International handbook of social anxiety: Concepts, research and interventions relating to the self and shyness* (pp. 405–430). New York: John Wiley.

Clark, D. M., Ehlers, A., McManus, F., Hackmann, A., Fennell, M., Campbell, H., et al. (2003). Cognitive therapy vs. fluoxetine in generalized social phobia: A randomized placebo controlled trial. *Journal of Consulting and Clinical Psychology, 71,* 1058–1067.

Clark, D. M., & Wells, A. (1995). A cognitive model of social phobia. In R. G. Heimberg, M. R. Liebowitz, D. A. Hope, & F. R. Schneier (Eds.), *Social phobia: Diagnosis, assessment and treatment* (pp. 69–93). New York: Guilford Press.

Clark, L. A., Livesley, W. J., & Morey, L. (1997). Personality disorder assessment: The challenge of construct validity. *Journal of Personality Disorders, 11,* 205–231.

Costa, P. T., Jr., & McCrae, R. R. (1990). Personality disorders and the five-factor model of personality. *Journal of Personality Disorders, 4,* 362–371.

Costa, P. T., Jr., & McCrae, R. R. (1992). *Revised NEO Personality Inventory (NEO-PI-R) and NEO Five-Factor Inventory (NEO-FFI) professional manual.* Odessa, FL: Psychological Assessment Resources.

Craske, M. G. (1999). *Anxiety disorders: Psychological approaches to theory and treatment.* Boulder, CO: Westview.

Dalrymple, K. L., & Herbert, J. D. (2004, November). *Acceptance and commitment therapy for generalized social anxiety disorder: Initial findings from a pilot study.* Paper presented at the meeting of the Association for Advancement of Behavior Therapy, New Orleans, LA.

Dalrymple, K. L., Herbert, J. D., & Gaudiano, B. A. (2005). *Onset of illness and developmental factors in social anxiety disorder: Findings from a retrospective interview.* Manuscript submitted for publication.

Davidson, J. R. T., Foa, E. B., Huppert, J. D., Keefe, F. J., Franklin, M. E., Compton, J. S., et al. (2004). Fluoxetine, comprehensive cognitive behavioral therapy, and placebo in generalized social phobia. *Archives of General Psychiatry, 61,* 1005–1013.

Davidson, K. M., Obonsawin, M. C., Seils, M., & Patience, L. (2003). Patient and clinician agreement on personality using the SWAP-200. *Journal of Personality Disorders, 17,* 208–218.

Ekselius, L., Tillfors, M., Furmark, T., & Fredrikson, M. (2001). Personality disorders in the general population: DSM-IV and ICD-10 defined prevalence as related to sociodemographic profile. *Personality and Individual Differences, 30,* 311–320.

Fahlén, T. (1995). Personality traits in social phobia: II. Changes during drug treatment. *Journal of Clinical Psychiatry, 56,* 569–573.

Farmer, R. F. (2000). Issues in the assessment and conceptualization of personality disorders. *Clinical Psychology Review, 20,* 823–851.

Feske, U., Perry, K. J., Chambless, D. L., Renneberg, B., & Goldstein, A. J. (1996). Avoidant personality disorder as a predictor for treatment outcome among generalized social phobics. *Journal of Personality Disorders, 10,* 174–184.

First, M. B., Gibbon, M., Spitzer, R. L., Williams, J. B. W., & Benjamin, L. (1997). *User's guide for the Structured Clinical Interview for DSM-IV Axis II Personality Disorders (SCID-II).* Washington, DC: American Psychiatric Association.

First, M. B., Spitzer, R. L., Gibbon, M., & Williams, J. B. W. (1994). *Structured clinical interview for Axis I DSM-IV disorders: Patient edition.* New York: Biometrics Research Department.

Foa, E., Franklin, M., Perry, K., & Herbert, J. D. (1996). Cognitive biases in generalized social phobia. *Journal of Abnormal Psychology, 105,* 433–439.

Frances, A. J., First, M. B., & Pincus, H. A. (1995). *DSM-IV guidebook.* Washington, DC: American Psychiatric Press.

Fydrich, T., Chambless, D. L., Perry, K. J., Buergener, F., & Beazley, M. B. (1998). Behavioral assessment of social performance: A rating system for social phobia. *Behaviour Research and Therapy, 36,* 995–1010.

Harper, R. G. (2004). *Personality-guided therapy in behavioral medicine.* Washington, DC: American Psychological Association.

Harvey, A. G., Watkins, E., Mansell, W., & Shafran, R. (2004). *Cognitive behavioural processes across psychological disorders: A transdiagnostic approach to research and treatment.* Oxford, UK: Oxford University Press.

Haug, T. T., Blomhoff, S., Hellstrøm, K., Holme, I., Humble, M., Madsbu, H. P., et al. (2003). Exposure therapy and sertraline in social phobia: 1-year follow-up of a randomized controlled trial. *British Journal of Psychiatry, 182,* 312–318.

Hayes, S. C., Strosahl, K. D., & Wilson, K. G. (1999). *Acceptance and commitment therapy: An experiential approach to behavior change.* New York: Guilford Press.

Heimberg, R. G. (1996). Social phobia, avoidant personality disorder and the multiaxial conceptualization of interpersonal anxiety. In P. M. Salkovskis (Ed.), *Trends in cognitive and behavioural therapies* (pp. 43–61). New York: Wiley.

Heimberg, R. G. (2002, November). *The understanding and treatment of social anxiety: What a long strange trip it's been (and will be).* Paper presented at the Association for Advancement of Behavior Therapy, Reno, NV.

Heimberg, R. G., & Becker, R. E. (2002). *Cognitive-behavioral group therapy for social phobia: Basic mechanisms and clinical strategies.* New York: Guilford Press.

Heimberg, R. G., Dodge, C. S., Hope, D. A., Kennedy, C. R., Zollo, L. J., & Becker, R. E. (1990). Cognitive behavioral group treatment for social phobia: Comparison with a credible placebo control. *Cognitive Therapy and Research, 14,* 1–23.

Heimberg, R. G., Liebowitz, M. R., Hope, D. A., Schneier, F. R., Hold, C. S., Welkowitz, L., et al. (1998). Cognitive-behavioral group therapy versus phenelzine in social phobia: 12-week outcome. *Archives of General Psychiatry, 55,* 1133–1141.

Herbert, J. D. (1995). An overview of the current status of social phobia. *Applied and Preventive Psychology, 4,* 39–51.

Herbert, J. D., & Cardaciotto, L. (in press). Social anxiety disorder. In S. Orsillo & L. Roemer (Eds.), *Acceptance and mindfulness-based approaches to anxiety: Conceptualization and treatment.* New York: Kluwer Academic Publishers.

Herbert, J. D., Crittenden, K., & Dalrymple, K. L. (2004). Knowledge of social anxiety disorder relative to attention deficit hyperactivity disorder among educational professionals. *Journal of Clinical Child and Adolescent Psychology, 33,* 366–372.

Herbert, J. D., & Dalrymple, K. L. (2004). *Acceptance and commitment therapy for social anxiety disorder: A treatment manual.* Unpublished manuscript, Drexel University, Philadelphia, PA.

Herbert, J. D., & Dalrymple, K. (2005). Social anxiety disorder. In A. Freeman, S. H. Felgoise, A. M. Nezu, C. M. Nezu, & M. A. Reinecke (Eds.), *Encyclopedia of cognitive behavior therapy* (pp. 368–372). New York: Springer.

Herbert, J. D., Gaudiano, B. A., Rheingold, A., Harwell, V., Dalrymple, K., & Nolan, E. M. (2005). Social skills training augments the effectiveness of cognitive behavior group therapy for social anxiety disorder. *Behavior Therapy, 36,* 125–138.

Herbert, J. D., Hope, D., & Bellack, A. (1992). Validity of the distinction between generalized social phobia and avoidant personality disorder. *Journal of Abnormal Psychology, 101,* 332–339.

Herbert, J. D., Rheingold, A., & Brandsma, L. (2000). Assessment of social anxiety. In S. G. Hofmann & P. M. DiBartolo (Eds.), *From social anxiety to social phobia: Multiple perspectives* (pp. 20–45). Needham Heights, MA: Allyn & Bacon.

Herbert, J. D., Rheingold, A., Gaudiano, B. A., & Myers, V. H. (2004). Standard versus extended cognitive behavior therapy for social anxiety disorder: A randomized-controlled trial. *Behavioural and Cognitive Psychotherapy, 32,* 1–17.

Herbert, J. D., Rheingold, A. A., & Goldstein, S. G. (2002). Brief cognitive behavioral group therapy for social anxiety disorder. *Cognitive and Behavioral Practice, 9,* 1–8.

Herbert, J. D., & Sageman, M. (2004). First do no harm: Emerging guidelines for the treatment of posttraumatic reactions. In G. Rosen (Ed.), *Posttraumatic stress disorder: Issues and controversies.* West Sussex, UK: Wiley.

Hirsch, C. R., & Clark, D. M. (2004). Information-processing bias in social phobia. *Clinical Psychology Review, 24,* 799–825.

Hirshfeld, D. R., Biederman, J., Brody, L., Faraone, S. V., & Rosenbaum, J. F. (1997). Associations between expressed emotion and child behavioral inhibition and psychopathology: A pilot study. *Journal of the American Academy of Child & Adolescent Psychiatry, 36,* 205–213.

Hoffman, S. G., Heinrichs, N., & Moscovitch, D. A. (2004). The nature and expression of social phobia: Toward a new classification. *Clinical Psychology Review, 24,* 769–797.

Hoffman, S. G., Newman, M. G., Becker, E., Taylor, C. B., & Roth, W. T. (1995). Social phobia with and without avoidant personality disorder: Preliminary behavior therapy outcome findings. *Journal of Anxiety Disorders, 9,* 427–438.

Holt, C. S., Heimberg, R. G., & Hope, D. A. (1992). Avoidant personality disorder and the generalized subtype of social phobia. *Journal of Abnormal Psychology, 101,* 318–325.

Hope, D. A., Heimberg, R. G., & Klein, J. F. (1990). Social anxiety and the recall of interpersonal information. *Journal of Cognitive Psychotherapy, 4,* 185–195.

Hope, D. A., Herbert, J. D., & White, C. (1995). Diagnostic subtype, avoidant personality disorder, and efficacy of cognitive-behavioral group therapy for social phobia. *Cognitive Therapy and Research, 19,* 339–417.

Hopko, D. R., McNeil, D. W., Zvolensky, M. J., & Eifert, G. H. (2001). The relation between anxiety and skill in performance-based anxiety disorders: A behavioral formulation of social phobia. *Behavior Therapy, 32,* 185–207.

Hudson, J. L., & Rapee, R. M. (2001). Parent-child interactions and anxiety disorders: An observational study. *Behaviour Research and Therapy, 39,* 1411–1427.

Jansen, M. A., Arntz, A., Merckelbach, H., & Mersch, P. P. A. (1994). Personality disorders and features in social phobia and panic disorder. *Journal of Abnormal Psychology, 103,* 391–395.

Johnson, B. A., Brent, D. A., Connolly, J., Bridge, J., Matta, J., Constantine, D., et al. (1995). Familial aggregation of adolescent personality disorders. *Journal of the American Academy of Child & Adolescent Psychiatry, 34,* 798–804.

Kagan, J., Reznick, J. S., Clarke, C., Snidman, N., & Garcia-Coll, C. (1984). Behavioral inhibition to the unfamiliar. *Child Development, 55,* 2212–2225.

Kagan, J., Reznick, J. S., & Snidman, N. (1988). Biological bases of childhood shyness. *Science, 240,* 167–171.

Kashdan, T. B., & Herbert, J. D. (2001). Social anxiety disorder in childhood and adolescence: Current status and future directions. *Clinical Child and Family Psychology Review, 4,* 37–61.

Kazdin, A. E. (1983). Psychiatric diagnosis, dimensions of dysfunction, and child behavior therapy. *Behavior Therapy, 14,* 73–99.

Kendler, K. S., Karkowski, L. M., & Prescott, C. A. (1999). Fears and phobias: Reliability and heritability. *Psychological Medicine, 29,* 539–553.

Kennedy, S. H., Katz, R., Rockert, W., Mendolwitz, S., Raleveski, E., & Clewes, J. (1995). Assessment of personality disorders in anorexia nervosa and bulimia nervosa: A comparison of self-report and structured interview methods. *Journal of Nervous and Mental Disease, 183,* 358–364.

Klein, M. H., & Benjamin, L. S. (1996). *The Wisconsin personality disorders inventory—IV.* Madison: University of Wisconsin.

Kool, S., Dekker, J., Duijsens, I. J., de Jonghe, F., & Puite, B. (2003). Changes in personality pathology after pharmacotherapy and combined therapy for depressed patients. *Journal of Personality Disorders, 17,* 60–72.

Lenzenweger, M. F. (1999). Stability and change in personality disorder features: The longitudinal study of personality disorders. *Archives of General Psychiatry, 56,* 1009–1015.

Lieb, R., Wittchen, H. U., Hoefler, M., Fuetsch, M., Stein, M. B., & Merikangas, K. R. (2000). Parental psychopathology, parenting styles, and the risk of social phobia in offspring: A prospective-longitudinal community study. *Archives of General Psychiatry, 57,* 859–866.

Liebowitz, M. R., Barlow, D. H., Ballenger, J. C., Davidson, J., Foa, E. B., Fyer, A. J., et al. (1998). DSM-IV anxiety disorders: Final overview. In T. A. Widiger, A. J. Frances, H. A. Pincus, R. Ross, M. B. First, W. Davis, & M. Kline (Eds.), *DSM-IV sourcebook* (Vol. 4, pp. 1047–1076). Washington, DC: American Psychiatric Association.

Liebowitz, M. R., Heimberg, R. G., Fresco, D. M., Travers, J., & Stein, M. B. (2000). Social phobia or social anxiety disorder: What's in a name? *Archives of General Psychiatry, 57,* 191–192.

Lilienfeld, S. O., Waldman, I. D., & Israel, A. C. (1994). A critical examination of the use of the term and concept of comorbidity in psychopathology research. *Clinical Psychology: Science and Practice, 1,* 71–83.

Lipsitz, J. D., Markowitz, J. D., Cherry, S., & Fyer, A. J. (1999). Open trial of interpersonal psychotherapy for the treatment of social phobia. *American Journal of Psychiatry, 156,* 1814–1816.

Loranger, A. W., Sartorius, N., Andreoli, A., Berger, P., Buchheim, S. M., Channabasavanna, B., et al. (1994). The International Personality Disorder Examination: The World Health Organization/Alcohol, Drug Abuse, and Mental Health Administration international pilot study of personality disorders. *Archives of General Psychiatry, 51*, 215–224.

Loranger, A. W., Susman, V. L., Oldham, J. M., & Russakoff, L. M. (1987). Personality Disorder Examination: A preliminary report. *Journal of Personality Disorders, 1,* 1–13.

Maffei, C., Fossati, A., Agostoni, I., Barraco, A., Bagnato, M., Donati, D., et al. (1997). Interrater reliability and internal consistency of the Structured Clinical Interview for DSM-IV Axis II Personality Disorders (SCID-II), Version 2.0. *Journal of Personality Disorders, 11,* 279–284.

Marlowe, D. B., Husband, S. D., Bonieskie, L. M., Kirby, K. C., & Platt, J. J. (1997). Structured interview versus self-report test vantages for the assessment personality pathology in cocaine dependence. *Journal of Personality Disorders, 11,* 177–190.

Mattick, R. P., & Clark, J. C. (1998). Development and validation of measures of social phobia scrutiny fear and social interaction anxiety. *Behavioural Research and Therapy, 36,* 455–470.

McGinn, L. K., Cukor, D., & Sanderson, W. C. (in press). The relationship between parenting style, cognitive style and anxiety and depression: Does increased early adversity influence symptom severity through the mediating role of cognitive style? *Cognitive Therapy and Research.*

McNeil, D. W. (2001). Terminology and evolution of constructs in social anxiety and social phobia. In S. G. Hofmann & P. M. DiBartolo (Eds.), *From social anxiety to social phobia: Multiple perspectives* (pp. 8–19). Needham Heights, MA: Allyn & Bacon.

Mellings, T. M. B., & Alden, L. E. (2000). Cognitive processes in social anxiety: The effects of self-focus, rumination and anticipatory processing. *Behaviour Research and Therapy, 38,* 243–257.

Mersch, P. P. A., Emmelkamp, P. M. G., Bogels, S. M., & van der Sleen, J. (1989). Social phobia: Individual response patterns and the effects of behavioral and cognitive interventions. *Behaviour Research and Therapy, 27,* 421–434.

Mersch, P. P. A., Jansen, M. A., & Arntz, A. (1995). Social phobia and personality disorder: Severity of complaint and treatment effectiveness. *Journal of Personality Disorders, 9,* 143–159.

Meyer, B., & Carver, C. S. (2000). Negative childhood accounts, sensitivity, and pessimism: A study of avoidant personality disorder features in college students. *Journal of Personality Disorders, 14,* 233–248.

Mick, M. A., & Telch, M. J. (1998). Social anxiety and history of behavioral inhibition in young adults. *Journal of Anxiety Disorders, 12,* 1–20.

Millon, T. (1969). *Modern psychopathology: A biosocial approach to maladaptive learning and functioning.* Philadelphia: Saunders.

Millon, T. (1981). *Disorders of personality.* New York: Wiley.

Millon, T., Millon, C., & Davis, R. (1994). *MCMI-III manual.* Minneapolis, MN: National Computer Systems.

Nelson, E. C., Grant, J. D., Bucholz, K. K., Glowinski, A., Madden, P. A. F., Reich, W., et al. (2000). Social phobia in a population-based female adolescent twin sample: Co-morbidity and associated suicide-related symptoms. *Psychological Medicine, 30,* 797–804.

Norton, P. J., & Hope, D. A. (2001). Kernels of truth or distorted perceptions: Self and observer ratings of social anxiety and performance. *Behavior Therapy, 32,* 765–786.

Ollendick, T. H., & Hirshfeld-Becker, D. R. (2002). The developmental psychopathology of social anxiety disorder. *Biological Psychiatry, 51,* 44–58.

Parker, G. (1979). Reported parental characteristics of agoraphobics and social phobics. *British Journal of Psychiatry, 135,* 555–560.

Perry, J. C. (1992). Problems and considerations in the valid assessment of personality disorders. *American Journal of Psychiatry, 149,* 1645–1653.

Pfohl, B., Blum, N., & Zimmerman, M. (1997). *Structured interview for DSM-IV personality.* Washington, DC: American Psychiatric Association.

Plomin, R. (1994). *Genetics and experience: The interplay between nature and nurture.* Thousand Oaks, CA: Sage.

Plomin, R., Owen, M. J., & McGuffin, P. (1994). The genetic basis of complex human behaviors. *Science, 264,* 1733–1739.

Pretzer, J. L., & Beck, A. T. (1996). A cognitive theory of personality disorders. In J. F. Clarkin & M. F. Lenzenweger (Eds.), *Major theories of personality disorders* (pp. 36–105). New York: Guilford Press.

Rapee, R. M., & Lim, L. (1992). Discrepancy between self and observer ratings of performance in social phobics. *Journal of Abnormal Psychology, 101,* 728–731.

Rapee, R. M., & Melville, L. F. (1997). Retrospective recall of family factors in social phobia and panic disorder. *Depression and Anxiety, 5,* 7–11.

Rapee, R. M., & Spence, S. H. (2004). The etiology of social phobia: Empirical evidence and an initial model. *Clinical Psychology Review, 24,* 737–767.

Reich, J. (2001). The relationship of social phobia to avoidant personality disorder. In S. G. Hofmann & P. M. DiBartolo (Eds.), *From social anxiety to social phobia: Multiple perspectives* (pp. 148–161). Needham Heights, MA: Allyn & Bacon.

Renneberg, B., Goldstein, A. J., Phillips, D., & Chambless, D. L. (1990). Intensive behavioral group treatment of avoidant personality disorder. *Behavior Therapy, 21,* 363–377.

Resick, P. A. (2004, November). *Beyond cognitive processing: A reconceptualization of posttrauma pathology.* Paper presented at the meeting of the Association for Advancement of Behavior Therapy, New Orleans, LA.

Rosenbaum, J. F., Biederman, J., Hirshfeld, D. R., Bolduc, E. A, Faraone, S. V., Kagan, J., et al. (1991). Further evidence of an association between behavioral inhibition and anxiety disorders: Results from a family study of children from a non-clinical sample. *Journal of Psychiatric Research, 25,* 49–65.

Rosenbaum, J. F., Biederman, J., Hirshfeld-Becker, D. R., Kagan, J., Snidman, N., Friedman, D., et al. (2000). A controlled study of behavioral inhibition in children of parents with panic disorder and depression. *American Journal of Psychiatry, 157,* 2002–2010.

Shea, M. T., Stout, R. L., Yen, S., Pagano, M. E., Skodol, A. E., Morey, L. C., et al. (2004). Associations in the course of personality disorders and Axis I disorders over time. *Journal of Abnormal Psychology, 113,* 499–508.

Shea, M. T., & Yen, S. (2003). Stability as a distinction between Axis I and Axis II disorders. *Journal of Personality Disorders, 17,* 373–386.

Siqueland, L., Kendall, P. C., & Steinberg, L. (1996). Anxiety in children: Perceived family environments and observed family interaction. *Journal of Clinical Child Psychology, 25,* 225–237.

Spitzer, R. L. (1983). Psychiatric diagnosis: Are clinicians still necessary? *Comprehensive Psychiatry, 24,* 399–411.

Spitzer, R. L., Williams, J. B. W., & Gibbon, M. (1987). *Structured clinical interview for DSM-III-R personality disorders (SCID-II)*. New York: New York State Psychiatric Institute.

Stangl, D., Pfohl, B., Zimmerman, M., Bowers, W., & Corenthal, C. (1985). A structured interview for the DSM-III personality disorders: A preliminary report. *Archives of General Psychiatry, 42*, 591–596.

Stein, M. B., Chartier, M. J., Hazen, A. L., Kozak, M. V., Tancer, M. E., Lander, S., et al. (1998). A direct interview family study of generalized social phobia. *American Journal of Psychiatry, 155*, 90–97.

Stein, M. B., Jang, K. L., & Livesley, W. J. (2002). Heritability of social-anxiety related concerns and personality characteristics: A twin study. *Journal of Nervous and Mental Disease, 190*, 219–224.

Stangier, U., Heidenreich, T., Peitz, M., Lauterbach, W., & Clark, D. M. (2003). Cognitive therapy for social phobia: Individual versus group treatment. *Behaviour Research and Therapy, 41*, 991–1007.

Stopa, L., & Clark, D. M. (1993). Cognitive processes in social phobia. *Behaviour Research and Therapy, 31*, 255–267.

Stopa, L., & Clark, D. M. (2000). Social phobia and interpretation of social events. *Behaviour Research and Therapy, 38*, 273–283.

Stravynski, A., Elie, R., & Franche, R. L. (1989). Perceptions of early parenting by patients diagnosed with avoidant personality disorder: A test of the overprotection hypothesis. *Acta Psychiatrica Scandinavica, 80*, 415–420.

Stravynski, A., Lesage, A., Marcouiller, M., & Elie, R. (1989). A test of the therapeutic mechanism in social skills training with avoidant personality disorder. *Journal of Nervous and Mental Disease, 177*, 739–744.

Stuart, S., Pfohl, B., Battaglia, M., Bellodi, L., Grove, W., & Cadoret, R. (1998). The co-occurrence of DSM-III-R personality disorders. *Journal of Personality Disorders, 12*, 302–315.

Svartberg, M., Stiles, T. C., & Seltzer, M. H. (2004). Randomized, controlled trial of the effectiveness of short-term dynamic psychotherapy and cognitive therapy for Cluster C personality disorders. *American Journal of Psychiatry, 161*, 810–817.

Tacken, K. H. M. (1998). *De samenhang tussen social fobie en ontwijkende persoonlijkheidsstoornis* [The association between social phobia and avoidant personality disorder]. Unpublished master's thesis, University of Maastricht, the Netherlands.

Tillfors, M., Furmark, T., Ekselius, L., & Fredrikson, M. (2001). Social phobia and avoidant personality disorder as related to parental history of social anxiety: A general population study. *Behaviour Research and Therapy, 39*, 289–298.

Torgersen, S., Kringlen, E., & Cramer, V. (2001). The prevalence of personality disorders in a community sample. *Archives of General Psychiatry, 58*, 590–596.

Trestman, R. L., Woo-Ming, A. M., deVegvar, M., & Siever, L. J. (2001). Treatment of personality disorders. In A. F. Schatzberg & C. B. Nemeroff (Eds.), *Essentials of clinical psychopharmacology*. Washington, DC: American Psychiatric Publishing.

Trull, T. J. (1995). Borderline personality disorder features in nonclinical young adults: 1. Identification and validation. *Psychological Assessment, 7*, 33–41.

Trull, T. J., & Amdur, M. (2001). Diagnostic efficiency of the Iowa Personality Disorder Screen items in a nonclinical sample. *Journal of Personality Disorders, 15*, 351–357.

Trull, T. J., Widiger, T. A., & Frances, A. (1987). Covariation of criteria sets for avoidant, schizoid, and dependent personality disorders. *American Journal of Psychiatry, 144,* 767–771.

Turner, S. M., & Beidel, D. C. (1989). Social phobia: Clinical syndrome, diagnosis, and comorbidity. *Clinical Psychology Review, 9,* 3–18.

Turner, S. M., Beidel, D. C., & Cooley-Quille, M. R. (1995). Two-year follow-up of social phobics treated with social effectiveness therapy. *Behaviour Research and Therapy, 33,* 553–555.

Turner, S. M., Beidel, D. C., Cooley, M. R., Woody, S. R., & Messer, S. C. (1994). A multicomponent behavioral treatment for social phobia: Social effectiveness therapy. *Behaviour Research and Therapy, 32,* 381–390.

Turner, S. M., Beidel, D. C., Dancu, C. V., & Stanley, M. A. (1989). An empirically derived inventory to measure social fears and anxiety: The Social Phobia and Anxiety Inventory. *Psychological Assessment, 1,* 35–40.

Turner, S. M., Beidel, D. C., & Townsley, R. M. (1992). Social phobia: A comparison of specific and generalized subtypes and avoidant personality disorder. *Journal of Abnormal Psychology, 101,* 326–331.

Westen, D. (1997). Divergences between Axis II instruments and clinical diagnostic procedures: Implications for research and the evolution of Axis II. *American Journal of Psychiatry, 154,* 895–903.

Westen, D., & Muderrisoglu, S. (2003). Assessing personality disorders using a systematic clinical interview: Evaluation of an alternative to structured interviews. *Journal of Personality Disorders, 17,* 351–369.

Westen, D., & Shedler, J. (2000). A prototype matching approach to personality disorders: Toward DSM-V. *Journal of Personality Disorders, 14,* 109–126.

Widiger, T. A. (2003). Personality disorder and Axis I psychopathology: The problematic boundary of Axis I and Axis II. *Journal of Personality Disorders, 17,* 90–108.

Widiger, T. A., Mangine, S., Corbitt, E. M., Ellis, C. G., & Thomas, G. V. (1995). *Personality Disorder Interview–IV: A semistructured interview for the assessment of personality disorders.* Odessa, FL: Psychological Assessment Resources.

Wlazlo, Z., Schroeder-Hartwig, K., Hand, I., Kaiser, G., & Münchau, N. (1990). Exposure in vivo vs. social skills training for social phobia: Long-term outcome and differential effects. *Behaviour Research and Therapy, 28,* 181–193.

Wood, J. M., Nezworski, M. T., Lilienfeld, S. O., & Garb, H. N. (2003). *What's wrong with the Rorschach? Science confronts the controversial inkblot test.* San Francisco: Jossey-Bass.

Woody, S. R., & Adessky, R. S. (2002). Therapeutic alliance, group cohesion, and homework compliance during cognitive-behavioral group treatment for social phobia. *Behavior Therapy, 33,* 5–27.

Zaider, T., Heimberg, R. G., Roth, D. A., Hope, D. A., & Turk, C. L. (2003, November). Individual CBT for social anxiety disorder: Preliminary findings. In D. A. Roth (Chair), *Cognitive behavior therapy for social phobia: Recent findings and future directions.* Symposium conducted at the meeting of the Association for Advancement of Behavior Therapy, Boston.

11

Dependent
Personality Disorder

Robert F. Bornstein

Adelphi University

Although Kraepelin (1913), Schneider (1923), and other early diagnosticians discussed at length the clinical implications of exaggerated dependency needs, dependent personality traits received only passing mention in the first edition of the *Diagnostic and Statistical Manual of Mental Disorders* (DSM-I; American Psychiatric Association [APA], 1952). The DSM-I precursor of dependent personality disorder (DPD) was actually a subtype of the passive-aggressive personality, the "passive-aggressive personality, passive-dependent type" (APA, 1952, p. 37). Problematic dependency received even less attention in the DSM-II (APA, 1968), and it was not until publication of the DSM-III (APA, 1980) that DPD became a full-fledged diagnostic category. The DSM-III description of DPD included three broad, overlapping symptoms: (1) passivity in interpersonal relationships, (2) willingness to subordinate one's needs to those of others, and (3) lack of self-confidence.

The DSM-III-R (APA, 1987) criteria for DPD were far more detailed than those of the DSM-III, and these criteria have changed little in recent revisions of the manual.[1] In both the DSM-IV (APA, 1994) and DSM-IV-TR (APA, 2000), DPD is defined as "a pervasive and excessive need to be taken care of that leads to submissive and clinging behavior and fears of separation" (APA, 1994, p. 668). The person must show five of the following eight

Author's notes: Preparation of this chapter was supported by National Institute of Mental Health grant MH63723–01A1. Correspondence regarding this manuscript should be sent to Robert F. Bornstein, Ph.D., Derner Institute of Advanced Psychological Studies, 212 Blodgett Hall, Adelphi University, Garden City, New York 11530. Voice mail: 516–877–4736. Fax: 516–877–4754. E-mail: Bornstein@adelphi.edu

symptoms to receive a DPD diagnosis: (1) difficulty making everyday decisions without excessive advice and reassurance, (2) need for others to assume responsibility for most major areas of life, (3) difficulty expressing disagreement, (4) difficulty initiating projects or doing things on one's own, (5) going to excessive lengths to obtain nurturance and support, (6) feelings of being uncomfortable and helpless when alone, (7) urgent seeking of another source of support when an important relationship ends, and (8) unrealistic preoccupation with fears of being left to care for oneself.

Since the early 1950s, there have been more than 600 published studies of the etiology and dynamics of dependent personality traits (Bornstein, 2005), and during the past two decades clinicians and researchers have become particularly interested in understanding the antecedents, correlates, and consequences of DPD. Personality and social researchers have focused on the interpersonal and health implications of excessive dependency, whereas clinical researchers have emphasized the links between DPD and other psychological disorders, and the relation between dependent personality traits and treatment outcome.

This chapter reviews empirical and clinical evidence related to DPD. I begin by discussing theoretical conceptualizations of DPD and examine research on the etiology of the disorder. Next, I outline issues related to assessment and diagnosis and explore data bearing on the treatment implications of DPD. Finally I discuss unresolved questions and future directions in DPD research.

Theoretical Conceptualizations of DPD

Like many diagnostic categories, the DSM-I description of DPD was strongly influenced by psychodynamic theory (see Bornstein, 1993, for a discussion). Recognizing the value of a diagnostic system that is broad, inclusive, and not bound to any particular theoretical framework, the authors of more recent versions of the DSM have tried to make each syndrome's description as atheoretical as possible. For the most part, this effort has been successful, although many DSM-IV diagnoses continue to reflect the influence of specific theoretical frameworks (Widiger & Clark, 2000). It is likely that this theoretical influence will continue to some degree in the DSM-V.

In the following sections I discuss four theoretical frameworks that have been particularly influential in the conceptualization of DPD.

Psychodynamic Models

Although the most widely discussed psychoanalytic perspective on dependency is Freud's well-known "oral fixation" model (Freud, 1905/1953), research does not support the hypothesis that variations in infantile feeding and weaning behaviors play a role in the development of dependent personality traits (Bornstein, 1996). Many psychodynamic researchers (e.g., Luborsky & Crits-Christoph, 1990) now conceptualize problematic dependency as resulting from unconscious conflicts, which take two general forms: (1) conflicts between two competing urges (e.g., a wish to be cared for versus an urge to compete) and (2) impulse-defense conflicts (e.g., when an urge to be cared for conflicts with societal expectations regarding acceptable adult behavior). Other psychodynamic researchers (e.g., Blatt, 1991) have developed models that are aligned closely with object relations theory, and trace the development of problematic dependency to a mental representation of the self as weak and ineffectual.

Cognitive Models

Cognitive models of DPD focus on the ways in which a person's characteristic manner of thinking and processing information helps foster and maintain dependent behavior. As Freeman and Leaf (1989) noted, dependency-related automatic thoughts (i.e., reflexive self-statements that reflect the person's perceived lack of competence) are central in this process. These automatic thoughts are accompanied by negative self-statements—self-deprecating internal monologues wherein dependent persons reaffirm various reasons (real and imagined) for their perceived lack of competence and skill (Overholser, 1987). Automatic thoughts and negative self-statements combine to create a persistent attributional bias that reinforces the person's sense of vulnerability and weakness. A vicious cycle ensues wherein each new challenge triggers a set of cognitive responses that exacerbate the dependent person's feelings of helplessness; as the person's sense of helplessness increases, each new challenge seems even more insurmountable (Young, 1994).

Behavioral and Social Learning Models

The basic premise of the behavioral perspective on DPD is that people exhibit dependent behaviors because those behaviors are rewarded, were rewarded, or are perceived by the individual as being likely to bring rewards. As Ainsworth (1969, p. 970) noted, within this framework dependency is regarded as "a class of behaviors, learned in the context of the infant's dependency relationship with his mother. . . . although the first dependency relationship is a specific one, dependency is viewed as generalizing to subsequent interpersonal relationships." To the extent that help- and support-seeking are rewarded by primary caregivers, the developing child will be more likely to exhibit these responses in other social interactions (Sroufe, Fox, & Pancake, 1983).

A natural outgrowth of this behavioral view is the premise that—regardless of how they are acquired initially—dependent behaviors are shaped in social settings. Studies confirm that intermittent reinforcement of dependent behavior propagates problematic dependency in adults as well as children (Sroufe et al., 1983; Turkat & Carlson, 1984). Some researchers further suggest that vicarious reinforcement (i.e., observation of dependency-derived rewards in others) and modeling also play a role in the dynamics of dependency (e.g., White, 1986).

Trait Models

Numerous trait models of DPD have emerged over the years, and although these models differ in the details, they share a common goal of identifying the core traits that comprise a dependent personality orientation (see Millon, 1996). Costa and McCrae's (1985, 1992) five-factor model (FFM) has been the most influential trait model of dependency in recent years (see Costa & Widiger, 1994). The FFM classifies personality traits along five broad dimensions—neuroticism, extraversion, openness, agreeableness, and conscientiousness—and recent research confirms that high levels of trait dependency and DPD are associated with elevated levels of neuroticism and low levels of openness (Bornstein & Cecero, 2000).[2]

Other influential trait models of DPD include Benjamin's (1996) structural analysis of social behavior (SASB) model and Pincus and Gurtman's (1995) three-vector subtype model. Both models have received strong empirical support (see Gurtman, 1992; Pincus & Wilson, 2001), although Benjamin's SASB framework has been evaluated in a broad array of clinical and community samples whereas support for Pincus and Gurtman's three-vector model has come primarily from studies of college students.

The Etiology of DPD

Researchers have long speculated that DPD might be traceable in part to genetic factors, and recent findings support these speculations. When Torgersen et al. (2000) contrasted DPD prevalence rates in 92 monozygotic and 129 dizygotic twin pairs, they found substantially greater diagnostic concordance in monozygotic twins, and concluded that approximately 30% of the variance in adult DPD symptoms reflected genetic influences. Similar findings emerged in studies that assessed the heritability of trait dependency rather than DPD (e.g., O'Neill & Kendler, 1998). As is true of many investigations in this area, however, methodological and measurement limitations (e.g., unquantified gene-environment covariation) do not allow strong inferences to be drawn regarding causal links between genetic precursors and subsequent dependent behavior. Although no studies have determined precisely what inherited factors may be associated with increased likelihood of DPD later in life, certain temperament variables (e.g., withdrawal, soothability) warrant further investigation.

Beyond genetics, two other processes have been implicated in the etiology of DPD.

Parenting

Research suggests that overprotective parenting and authoritarian parenting, alone or in combination, are associated with increased likelihood that a child will show problematic dependency and DPD later in life (Head, Baker & Williamson, 1991; Vaillant, 1980). Although these parenting styles differ in many ways, both send a similar message to the child. Overprotective parenting teaches children that they are vulnerable and weak and cannot survive without the protection of powerful caregivers. Authoritarian parenting teaches children that the way to get by in life is to look outward (rather than inward) for guidance and direction, and accede to others' expectations and demands. Thus both parenting styles contribute to the development of a representation of the self as weak and ineffectual, and may increase dependent attitudes and behaviors (see Bornstein, 1993, for a discussion of this issue).

Culture

Because collectivist cultures (e.g., China, India) tend to emphasize group cohesion and interpersonal ties more strongly than individual achievement, persons raised in these cultures typically show higher levels of self-reported dependency than do persons raised in individualistic cultures such as America and Great Britain (Cross, Bacon & Morris, 2000). Ironically, because dependent, other-centered behavior is normative in many collectivist cultures, DPD symptoms often go unnoticed by clinicians, who are more likely to label independent behavior as dysfunctional (Bornstein, 2005). Studies only uncover increases in problematic dependency when DPD prevalence rates are assessed in samples of clinical or community populations who differ with respect to cultural background; these cross-cultural differences remain even when participants are matched on an array of demographic and diagnostic variables (e.g., age, socioeconomic status, number and type of co-occurring diagnoses; see Johnson, 1993; Neki, 1976).[3]

DPD Assessment and Diagnosis

In diagnosing DPD, clinicians should be aware of two issues. First, because dependency is typically seen as a sign of weakness and immaturity, many adults—especially men—are reluctant to acknowledge dependent thoughts and feelings even if they experience them (Bornstein, 1995). Second, increases in depression are associated with temporary increases in self-reported dependency, and even modest changes in mood states may have some impact on dependency levels in clinical and community participants (Hirschfeld, Klerman, Clayton, & Keller, 1983).

With these caveats in mind, two general strategies have been used by clinicians to diagnose DPD. Each strategy has certain advantages and certain disadvantages as well.

Diagnostic Interviews

As is true for the majority of Axis II personality disorders (PDs), inter-diagnostician reliability for DPD is modest at best, with kappa coefficients typically in the .25 to .35 range (e.g., Blais, Benedict, & Norman, 1996). Considerable effort has gone into increasing the reliability of diagnostic interviews for Axis II disorders, and recent revisions in the DSM have been implemented in part to increase clinicians' ability to distinguish ostensibly similar syndromes (Bornstein, 1998). In recent years three diagnostic interviews have been used most often to quantify DPD symptoms and diagnoses: the Structured Clinical Interview for DSM Personality Disorders (SCID-II; Spitzer, Williams, Gibbon, & First, 1990); the International Personality Disorder Examination (IPDE; Loranger, 1995); and the Structured Interview for DSM Personality—Revised (SIDP-R; Pfohl, Blum, Zimmerman, & Stangl, 1989). A review of the psychometric properties of diagnostic interviews for DPD is provided by Bornstein (2005).

Questionnaire Measures

Some clinicians and clinical researchers use questionnaire measures of DPD in lieu of diagnostic interviews. These measures have two noteworthy advantages: (1) they are easy to administer and score and (2) they circumvent diagnostic limitations that stem from interviewer unreliability. Two self-report instruments have been used most frequently to diagnose DPD in recent years: the Millon Clinical Multiaxial Inventory–III (MCMI-III; Millon, Millon, & Davis, 1994) and the Personality Diagnostic Questionnaire–4+ (PDQ-4+; Davison, Morven, & Taylor, 2001). Other widely used questionnaire dependency measures include the Interpersonal Dependency Inventory (IDI; Hirschfeld et al., 1977) and the Depressive Experiences Questionnaire (DEQ; Blatt, D'Afflitti, & Quinlan, 1976). A review of the construct validity of self-report measures of dependency and DPD is provided by Bornstein (1999).

Integrating Data in DPD Diagnosis

Given the time and expense involved in administering a structured diagnostic interview, some clinicians have recommended that questionnaires be used as a screening tool to identify a patient's most likely diagnoses, with follow-up interviews focusing primarily on these syndromes (see Widiger &

Coker, 2002). Given the large number of well-validated measures of trait dependency (Bornstein, 1999) and the documented impact of dependency on treatment process and outcome (e.g., Hoffart & Martinson, 1993; Poldrugo & Forti, 1988), administration of one or more trait dependency tests may also be warranted, especially for patients whose history or current behavior suggests problematic dependency. Detailed discussion of strategies for integrating different sources of dependency test data is provided by Bornstein (2002).

Epidemiology and Comorbidity

Problematic dependency is widespread in community as well as clinical populations and is associated with an array of psychological disorders. As detailed below, studies of DPD epidemiology and comorbidity offer only mixed support for the guidelines put forth in the DSM-IV (APA, 1994) and DSM-IV-TR (APA, 2000).

Epidemiology

Although the DSM-IV-TR indicates that DPD is "among the most frequently reported Personality Disorders encountered in mental health settings" (APA, 2000, p. 723), extant data suggest that this statement should be qualified. It is clear that DPD is diagnosed frequently in psychiatric inpatients: studies typically report DPD prevalence rates between 15% and 25% in hospital and rehabilitation settings (e.g., Oldham et al., 1995). The base rate of DPD in outpatients is not particularly high, however. In most studies it ranges from 0% to 10% (Klein, 2003; Poldrugo & Forti, 1988), considerably lower than the prevalence rates of several other PDs (e.g., borderline, histrionic, narcissistic, avoidant, obsessive-compulsive).

Bornstein's (1997) meta-analysis of epidemiological studies indicated that gender—like setting—moderates DPD prevalence rates. When data were collapsed across setting and diagnostic method, the overall base rate of DPD was 11% in women and 8% in men. Although this difference may seem modest, it is statistically significant ($?^2$ [1, $N = 5,965$] = 13.53, $p = .0005$) and suggests that the base rate of DPD is 40% higher in women than men. Virtually identical patterns have been obtained in more recent investigations of this issue (e.g., Melley, Oltmanns, & Turkheimer, 2002).

Although the existence of gender differences in DPD prevalence rates is well established, the factors that underlie these differences remain elusive. Two decades ago Kaplan (1983) argued that the DPD diagnostic criteria were biased against women in that they tapped normative female gender role–related behavior in addition to more problematic aspects of dependency (however, see Williams & Spitzer, 1983, for a critique of this position). As Bornstein (1997) noted, research suggests that three factors, alone or in combination, may account for these DPD gender differences: (1) criterion bias (i.e., gender role confounds in the DPD symptom criteria as suggested by Kaplan, 1983), (2) self-report bias (i.e., men's reluctance to acknowledge dependent attitudes and behaviors), and (3) diagnostician bias (i.e., the possibility that clinicians overperceive dependency in women due to gender role–based expectancies). Additional data are needed to ascertain the degree to which each of these factors may be responsible for gender differences in DPD prevalence rates.

Comorbidity

The DSM-IV-TR (APA, 2000) indicates that three Axis I diagnostic classes—mood disorders, anxiety disorders, and adjustment disorder—show substantial comorbidity with DPD. Evidence supports the continued inclusion of these three categories as conditions comorbid with DPD in future versions of the DSM (Nietzel & Harris, 1990; Piper et al., 2001; Sans & Avia, 1994), but studies also suggest that three other Axis I diagnostic classes co-occur with DPD at higher than expected rates: substance use disorders (Nace, Davis & Gaspari, 1991), eating disorders (Bornstein, 2001), and somatization disorder (Hayward & King, 1990).

The DSM-IV-TR (APA, 2000) lists three Axis II PDs—borderline, histrionic, and avoidant—as comorbid with DPD. Studies indicate that DPD actually shows significant comorbidity and covariation with the majority of Axis II syndromes, including many that bear little obvious relation, either behaviorally or dynamically, to DPD. For example, Barber and Morse (1994) found that DPD showed significant comorbidity with paranoid, schizotypal, antisocial, borderline, histrionic, narcissistic, and obsessive-compulsive PDs in a mixed-sex sample of psychiatric outpatients. Sinha and Watson (2001) and Wise (1996) obtained similar results when they assessed the covariation of Axis II symptom levels in samples of college students and psychiatric inpatients.[4]

These problematic comorbidity findings are not unique to DPD, and they raise questions regarding the discriminant validity of Axis II diagnoses in general (Bornstein, 1998; Westen & Shedler, 1999). Some researchers (e.g., Westen & Shedler, 1999) argue that these patterns reflect fundamental flaws in the categories used to classify Axis II psychopathology and suggest that these categories be reformulated. Others (e.g., Bornstein, 1998) argue that these patterns reflect naturally occurring covariation in various dimensions of personality pathology and suggest that a dimensional approach to PD symptom evaluation may be more useful than the current model.

Treatment Considerations

Over the years there has been a great deal of speculation regarding treatment of problematic dependency. Clinicians have provided recommendations for intervention strategies based on cognitive (Overholser & Fine, 1994), psychodynamic (Coen, 1992), behavioral (Turkat, 1990), and experiential (Schneider & May, 1995) models (see Bornstein, 2005, 2007, for reviews). Given this extensive clinical literature, there has been surprisingly little research assessing changes in DPD symptom levels during the course of psychotherapy. However, there have been a number of studies examining the impact of DPD symptoms on treatment process and outcome.

The Impact of Psychotherapy on DPD Symptoms

Only two studies assessed the impact of psychotherapy on DPD symptoms, and these investigations produced conflicting results. Rathus, Sanderson, Miller, and Wetzler (1995) found a significant decrease in MCMI-II dependency scores (Millon, 1987) from before treatment to after treatment in a sample of 18 agoraphobic outpatients receiving 12 weeks of cognitive-behavioral therapy, although the absence of a no-treatment control group limits the conclusions that can be drawn from these data. In contrast to the findings of Rathus et al., Black, Monahan, Wesner, Gabel, and Bowers (1996) reported no significant change in PDQ-derived dependency scores (Hyler, Rieder, Williams, Spitzer, Hendler & Lyons, 1988) from before treatment to after treatment in 44 outpatients with panic disorder receiving 8 weeks of cognitive therapy.[5]

Additional studies are needed to determine which therapeutic modalities are most effective in treatment of problematic dependency. Given the complex, multifaceted nature of dependency, it is likely that integrative treatment models will yield more positive outcomes than strategies derived from a single theoretical framework (Bornstein, 2005, 2007). As research in this area moves forward, it may be possible to determine which treatment strategies are most useful for various subsets of dependent patients who differ with respect to comorbid psychopathology and underlying personality structure.

The Impact of DPD Symptoms on Therapeutic Outcome

Somewhat more consistent results were obtained in studies assessing the moderating effects of DPD symptoms on treatment outcome than in studies assessing the impact of treatment of DPD symptoms. For example, Hoffart and Martinson (1993) found that high MCMI-II (Millon, 1987) dependency scores were associated with more positive outcome in a sample of 77 depressed inpatients receiving intensive multimodal treatment. Rathus et al. (1995) found that SCID-II (Spitzer et al., 1990) DPD diagnoses were associated with a trend toward more positive outcome in 18 agoraphobic outpatients undergoing 12 weeks of cognitive-behavioral therapy. Poldrugo and Forti (1988) found that DPD diagnoses were associated with increased abstinence in 404 alcoholic outpatients receiving yearlong group therapy following intensive inpatient treatment. The only study reporting no relation between DPD and psychotherapy outcome was conducted by Chambless, Renneberg, Goldstein, and Gracely (1992), who found that SCID-II DPD diagnoses did not predict treatment outcome in 51 agoraphobic outpatients receiving intensive 2-week behavioral group therapy plus individual multimodal treatment.

No studies have documented the pathways through which dependency-related traits influence treatment process and outcome, but research suggests that dependent patients exhibit behaviors that both facilitate and undermine treatment. For example, dependent psychotherapy patients are cooperative and conscientious, but they also report more "pseudoemergencies" than nondependent patients and make more requests for after-hours contact (Emery & Lesher, 1982). Dependent patients do not delay as long as nondependent patients when psychological symptoms appear, but they also have difficulty terminating treatment after their symptoms remit (Greenberg & Bornstein, 1989). Dependency may also affect psychotherapy by altering therapist behavior: studies confirm that some therapists become anxious when dependent patients form a strong attachment early in therapy, whereas others infantilize and exploit dependent patients, perceiving them as childlike, fragile, and immature (Abramson, Cloud, Keese, & Keese, 1994; Ryder & Parry-Jones, 1982).

Unresolved Questions and Future Directions

Although clinicians' understanding of DPD has come a long way since the DSM-I description of "passive dependency" (APA, 1952), much remains to be learned regarding the dynamics of dependent personality traits. Three areas in particular require continued attention from clinicians and clinical researchers.

Assessing and Revising DPD Symptoms

When Bornstein (1997) evaluated empirical evidence bearing on the eight DSM-IV DPD symptoms (APA, 1994), he found that four of these symptoms were supported by the results of laboratory, clinical, and field data: difficulty making everyday decisions without excessive advice and reassurance from others (symptom 1), going to excessive lengths to obtain nurturance and support from others (symptom 5), feelings of being uncomfortable and helpless when alone because of exaggerated fears of being unable to care for oneself (symptom 6), and unrealistic preoccupation with fears of being left to take care of oneself (symptom 8). Two symptoms had never been tested empirically: the need for others to assume responsibility for most major areas of life (symptom 2) and the urgent seeking of another relationship as a source of care and support when an important relationship ends (symptom 7). Two symptoms had been contradicted repeatedly: difficulty expressing disagreement with others because of fear of loss of support or approval (symptom 3) and difficulty initiating projects or doing things on one's own (symptom 4).[6]

Bornstein (1997) proposed an alternative set of DPD symptom criteria for future versions of the diagnostic manual and summarized extant data supporting the validity of each symptom as an index of problematic dependency. The central changes in these alternative DPD symptom criteria included (1) explicit reference to the role that cognitive factors play in the etiology and dynamics of DPD in the DPD essential criterion, (2) removal of DSM-IV DPD symptoms 3 and 4, and (3) replacement of these symptoms with two empirically validated symptoms: "uses a variety of self-presentation strategies (e.g., ingratiation, supplication, exemplification, self-promotion) to obtain and maintain nurturant, supportive relationships" and "focuses his or her efforts on strengthening a relationship with the person most likely to be able to offer help and support over the long term" (p. 182; see also Bornstein, 2005, for a detailed discussion of these proposed criteria and a review of supporting evidence).

Without question, changes are needed in the DPD symptom criteria in future versions of the diagnostic manual. Just as important, however, a different approach to DPD symptom validation is required. For many years, DPD symptom criteria—like those of most other PDs—have been evaluated primarily with respect to internal consistency (i.e., symptom covariation) and their relationship to other Axis II syndromes (i.e., distinctiveness). Although these validation strategies are useful, increased attention to behavioral evidence is needed: researchers must assess the degree to which the behaviors characterizing each DPD symptom are actually exhibited by dependent persons in various contexts and settings (Bornstein, 2003).

Alternative Conceptual Frameworks

Many clinicians have argued that a dimensional approach to PD diagnosis would be more useful than the current threshold model: In contrast to many Axis I syndromes, PD-related traits exist on a continuum, and it is difficult to specify a point at which these traits warrant diagnosis and treatment (see Widiger & Clark, 2000, for a discussion). A dimensional approach may be particularly applicable to DPD, because dependent traits are common in clinical and community samples and are expressed in myriad ways, some maladaptive and others adaptive (Pincus & Gurtman, 1995). Thus a DPD intensity rating may approximate the true distribution of dependency and DPD in the general population more closely than the current dichotomous (present-absent) classification (cf. Meehl, 1992).

Several frameworks have been described for conceptualizing DPD using a continuum rather than a threshold approach. Most prominent among these is the five-factor model (Costa & McCrae, 1985, 1992), and evidence suggests that DPD is associated with predictable patterns of scores on the FFM domains (Costa & Widiger, 1994). Other researchers (e.g., Bornstein & Languirand, 2003) have argued for a two-dimensional rating system, with dependent traits and behaviors rated in terms of intensity and adaptiveness.

Evidence confirms that even relatively intense dependency strivings can be problematic in certain situations (e.g., when insecurity undermines relationship stability), but adaptive in others (e.g., when help seeking enhances performance at work). Moreover, certain persons express dependent strivings in a flexible, modulated manner that enables them to obtain needed help and support, whereas others express dependency in ways that undermine their help- and support-seeking efforts (see Bornstein et al., 2003).

The Temporal and Situational Stability of DPD

As is true of most Axis II syndromes, there are few data evaluating age-related changes in DPD through middle and late adulthood. Studies suggest a populationwide increase in dependent behavior in later adulthood, although this is primarily a consequence of the increase in functional (i.e., physical) dependency that occurs in old age (Baltes, 1996). Longitudinal research on DPD indicates considerable stability in dependency levels throughout adulthood: those individuals who show high rates of DPD symptoms relative to their peers during early adulthood continue to show comparatively high levels of DPD symptoms later in life (Abrams & Horowitz, 1996).

Findings regarding situational variability contrast markedly with those documenting temporal stability. Contrary to the assertions of the DSM-IV-TR (APA, 2000) and most theoretical models of dependency (e.g., Blatt, 1991; Turkat, 1990), research indicates that dependent strivings are expressed in very different ways in different contexts and settings. As Bornstein (1992, 1993) noted, even though the dependent person's core beliefs and motives remain stable over time and across situations, his or her behavior changes dramatically in response to perceived opportunities and risks. When the dependent person believes that passive behavior will strengthen ties to potential nurturers and caregivers, passivity ensues; when the dependent person believes that active behavior is needed to strengthen these ties, assertive—even aggressive—behavior ensues (see Pincus & Wilson, 2001).

Thus, future conceptualizations of DPD must not only focus more closely on behavioral validation of DPD symptoms but should also specify the situational contingencies that moderate dependent behavior. Only when information regarding the internal dynamics of dependency is combined with information regarding the contextual factors that influence the outward expression of dependent strivings and motives can DPD be understood more completely, predicted more accurately, and treated more effectively.

Notes

1. The only substantive change in DPD symptoms from DSM-III-R (APA, 1987) to DSM-IV (APA, 1994) was the elimination of one symptom, "feels devastated or helpless when close relationships end" (APA, 1987, p. 354), because a sizable proportion of patients with borderline personality disorder also showed this symptom.

2. Although DPD is associated with only modest elevations in FFM agreeableness scores, the absence of a stronger DPD-agreeableness link may reflect the heterogeneity of interpersonal styles associated with dependency: some dependent individuals are indeed compliant and agreeable, but others are quite assertive—even aggressive—when an important relationship is threatened (Bornstein, Riggs, Hill, & Calabrese, 1996; Thompson & Zuroff, 1998).

3. Research also indicates that gender role socialization helps determine self-reported dependency, with women and men who score high on measures of femininity reporting high levels of trait dependency and DPD, and women and men who score high on measures of masculinity reporting lower levels of dependency (Bornstein, Bowers, & Bonner, 1996).

4. DPD–antisocial PD comorbidity—though counterintuitive—may reflect two processes. First, some dependent persons can become quite manipulative when an important relationship is threatened (Bornstein et al., 1996; Pincus & Wilson, 2001). Second, the compliance and yielding behavior associated with DPD can lead some dependent people to be susceptible to negative social influence and engage in self-defeating or hurtful behavior when induced to do so by a figure of authority (see Bornstein, 1993, for a discussion of this influence process as a factor in the dependency–tobacco use relationship).

5. Several investigations have assessed the impact of psychotropic medications on DPD symptom levels, but these studies produced inconclusive results. Some researchers reported significant decreases in DPD symptoms following antidepressant treatment (e.g., Zaretsky et al., 1997); others found no change (e.g., Rector, Bagby, Segal, Joffe, & Levitt, 2000).

6. Studies yielding results inconsistent with these symptoms include those conducted by Bornstein et al. (1996), Pincus and Wilson (2001), and Thompson and Zuroff (1998).

References

Abrams, R. C., & Horowitz, S. V. (1996). Personality disorders after age 50: A meta-analysis. *Journal of Personality Disorders, 10,* 271–281.

Abramson, P. R., Cloud, M. Y., Keese, N., & Keese, R. (1994). How much is too much? Dependency in a psychotherapeutic relationship. *American Journal of Psychotherapy, 48,* 294–301.

Ainsworth, M. D. S. (1969). Object relations, dependency, and attachment: A theoretical review of the infant-mother relationship. *Child Development, 40,* 969–1025.

American Psychiatric Association. (1952). *Diagnostic and statistical manual of mental disorders.* Washington, DC: Author.

American Psychiatric Association. (1968). *Diagnostic and statistical manual of mental disorders* (2nd ed.). Washington, DC: Author.

American Psychiatric Association. (1980). *Diagnostic and statistical manual of mental disorders* (3rd ed.). Washington, DC: Author.

American Psychiatric Association. (1987). *Diagnostic and statistical manual of mental disorders* (3rd ed., revised). Washington, DC: Author.

American Psychiatric Association. (1994). *Diagnostic and statistical manual of mental disorders* (4th ed.). Washington, DC: Author.

American Psychiatric Association. (2000). *Diagnostic and statistical manual of mental disorders* (4th ed., text revision). Washington, DC: Author.

Baltes, M. M. (1996). *The many faces of dependency in old age.* Cambridge, UK: Cambridge University Press.

Barber, J. P., & Morse, J. Q. (1994). Validation of the Wisconsin Personality Disorders Inventory with the SCID-II and PDE. *Journal of Personality Disorders, 8,* 307–319.

Benjamin, L. S. (1996). *Interpersonal diagnosis and treatment of personality disorders.* New York: Guilford Press.

Black, D. W., Monahan, P., Wesner, R., Gabel, J., & Bowers, W. (1996). The effect of fluvoxamine, cognitive therapy, and placebo on abnormal personality traits in 44 patients with panic disorder. *Journal of Personality Disorders, 10,* 185–194.

Blais, M. A., Benedict, K. B., & Norman, D. K. (1996). The perceived clarity of the Axis II criteria sets. *Journal of Personality Disorders, 10,* 16–22.

Blatt, S. J. (1991). A cognitive morphology of psychopathology. *Journal of Nervous and Mental Disease, 179,* 449–458.

Blatt, S. J., D'Afflitti, J. P., & Quinlan, D. M. (1976). Experiences of depression in normal young adults. *Journal of Abnormal Psychology, 85,* 383–389.

Bornstein, R. F. (1992). The dependent personality: Developmental, social, and clinical perspectives. *Psychological Bulletin, 112,* 3–23.

Bornstein, R. F. (1993). *The dependent personality.* New York: Guilford Press.

Bornstein, R. F. (1995). Sex differences in objective and projective dependency tests: A meta-analytic review. *Assessment, 2,* 319–331.

Bornstein, R. F. (1996). Beyond orality: Toward an object relations/interactionist reconceptualization of the etiology and dynamics of dependency. *Psychoanalytic Psychology, 13,* 177–203.

Bornstein, R. F. (1997). Dependent personality disorder in the DSM-IV and beyond. *Clinical Psychology: Science and Practice, 4,* 175–187.

Bornstein, R. F. (1998). Reconceptualizing personality disorder in the DSM-V: The discriminant validity challenge. *Clinical Psychology: Science and Practice, 5,* 333–343.

Bornstein, R. F. (1999). Criterion validity of objective and projective dependency tests: A meta-analytic assessment of behavioral prediction. *Psychological Assessment, 11,* 48–57.

Bornstein, R. F. (2001). A meta-analysis of the dependency–eating disorders relationship: Strength, specificity, and temporal stability. *Journal of Psychopathology and Behavioral Assessment, 23,* 151–162.

Bornstein, R. F. (2002). A process dissociation approach to objective-projective test score interrelationships. *Journal of Personality Assessment, 78,* 47–68.

Bornstein, R. F. (2003). Behaviorally referenced experimentation and symptom validation: A paradigm for 21st century personality disorder research. *Journal of Personality Disorders, 17,* 1–18.

Bornstein, R. F. (2005). *The dependent patient: A practitioner's guide.* Washington, DC: American Psychological Association.

Bornstein, R. F. (2007). Dependent personality disorder: Effective time-limited therapy. *Current Psychiatry, 6,* 37–45.

Bornstein, R. F., Bowers, K. S., & Bonner, S. (1996). Relationships of objective and projective dependency scores to sex role orientation in college student participants. *Journal of Personality Assessment, 66,* 555–568.

Bornstein, R. F., & Cecero, J. J. (2000). Deconstructing dependency in a five-factor world: A meta-analytic review. *Journal of Personality Assessment, 74,* 324–343.

Bornstein, R. F., & Languirand, M. A. (2003). *Healthy dependency.* New York: Newmarket Press.

Bornstein, R. F., Languirand, M. A., Geiselman, K. J., Creighton, J. A., West, M. A., Gallagher, H. A., et al. (2003). Construct validity of the Relationship Profile Test: A self-report measure of dependency-detachment. *Journal of Personality Assessment, 80,* 64–74.

Bornstein, R. F., Riggs, J. M., Hill, E. L., & Calabrese, C. (1996). Activity, passivity, self-denigration, and self-promotion: Toward an interactionist model of interpersonal dependency. *Journal of Personality, 64,* 637–673.

Chambless, D. L., Renneberg, B., Goldstein, A., & Gracely, E. J. (1992). MCMI-diagnosed personality disorders among agoraphobic outpatients. *Journal of Anxiety Disorders, 6,* 193–211.

Coen, S. J. (1992). *The misuse of persons: Analyzing pathological dependency.* Hillsdale, NJ: Analytic Press.

Costa, P. T., Jr., & McCrae, R. R. (1985). *The NEO Personality Inventory manual.* Odessa, FL: Psychological Assessment Resources.

Costa, P. T., Jr., & McCrae, R. R. (1992). *Revised NEO Personality Inventory (NEO-PI-R) and NEO Five-Factor Inventory (NEO-FFI) professional manual.* Odessa, FL: Psychological Assessment Resources.

Costa, P. T., Jr., & Widiger, T. A. (Eds.). (1994). *Personality disorders and the five-factor model of personality.* Washington, DC: American Psychological Association.

Cross, S. E., Bacon, P. L., & Morris, M. L. (2000). The relational-interdependent self-construal and relationships. *Journal of Personality and Social Psychology, 78,* 791–808.

Davison, S., Morven, L., & Taylor, P. J. (2001). Examination of the screening properties of the Personality Diagnostic Questionnaire 4+ (PDQ-4+) in a prison population. *Journal of Personality Disorders, 15,* 180–194.

Emery, G., & Lesher, E. (1982). Treatment of depression in older adults: Personality considerations. *Psychotherapy, 19,* 500–505.

Freeman, A., & Leaf, R. C. (1989). Cognitive therapy applied to personality disorders. In A. Freeman, K. M. Simon, L. E. Beutler, & H. Arkowitz (Eds.), *Comprehensive handbook of cognitive therapy* (pp. 403–434). New York: Plenum.

Freud, S. (1905/1953). Three essays on the theory of sexuality. In *Standard edition of the complete psychological works of Sigmund Freud* (Vol. 7, pp. 125–248). London: Hogarth.

Greenberg, R. P., & Bornstein, R. F. (1989). Length of psychiatric hospitalization and oral dependency. *Journal of Personality Disorders, 3,* 199–204.

Gurtman, M. B. (1992). Construct validity of interpersonal personality measures: The interpersonal circumplex as a nomological net. *Journal of Personality and Social Psychology, 63,* 105–118.

Hayward, C., & King, R. (1990). Somatization and personality disorder traits in nonclinical volunteers. *Journal of Personality Disorders, 4,* 402–406.

Head, S. B., Baker, J. D., & Williamson, D. A. (1991). Family environment characteristics and dependent personality disorder. *Journal of Personality Disorders, 5,* 256–263.

Hirschfeld, R. M. A., Klerman, G. L., Clayton, P. J., & Keller, M. B. (1983). Personality and depression: Empirical findings. *Archives of General Psychiatry, 40,* 993–998.

Hirschfeld, R. M. A., Klerman, G. L., Gough, H. G., Barrett, J., Korchin, S. J., & Chodoff, P. (1977). A measure of interpersonal dependency. *Journal of Personality Assessment, 41,* 610–618.

Hoffart, A., & Martinsen, E. W. (1993). The effect of personality disorders and anxious-depressive comorbidity on outcome in patients with unipolar depression and with panic disorder and agoraphobia. *Journal of Personality Disorders, 7,* 304–311.

Hyler, S. E., Rieder, R. O., Williams, J. B. W., Spitzer, R. L., Hendler, J., & Lyons, M. (1988). The Personality Diagnostic Questionnaire: Development and preliminary results. *Journal of Personality Disorders, 2,* 229–237.

Johnson, F. A. (1993). *Dependency and Japanese socialization.* New York: New York University Press.

Kaplan, M. (1983). A woman's view of DSM-III. *American Psychologist, 38,* 786–792.

Klein, D. N. (2003). Patients' versus informants' reports of personality disorders in predicting 7-year outcome in outpatients with depressive disorders. *Psychological Assessment, 15,* 216–222.

Kraepelin, E. (1913). *Psychiatrie: Ein lehrbuch* [Psychiatry: A textbook]. Leipzig, Germany: Barth.

Loranger, A. W. (1995). *International Personality Disorder Examination (IPDE) manual.* Unpublished manuscript, Cornell University Medical College.

Luborsky, L., & Crits-Christoph, P. (1990). *Understanding transference: The core conflictual relationship theme method.* New York: Basic Books.

Meehl, P. E. (1992). Factors and taxa, traits and types: Differences of degree and differences in kind. *Journal of Personality, 60,* 117–174.

Melley, A. H., Oltmanns, T. F., & Turkheimer, E. (2002). The Schedule for Nonadaptive and Adaptive Personality (SNAP): Temporal stability and predictive validity of the diagnostic scales. *Assessment, 9,* 181–187.

Millon, T. (1987). *Millon Clinical Multiaxial Inventory–II manual.* Minneapolis, MN: National Computer Systems.

Millon, T. (1996). *Disorders of personality: DSM-IV and beyond.* New York: Wiley.

Millon, T., Millon, C., & Davis, R. (1994). *Millon clinical multiaxial inventory–III.* Minneapolis, MN: National Computer Systems.

Nace, E. P., Davis, C. W., & Gaspari, J. P. (1991). Axis II comorbidity in substance abusers. *American Journal of Psychiatry, 148,* 118–120.

Neki, J. S. (1976). An examination of the cultural relativism of dependence as a dynamic of social and therapeutic relationships: I. Socio-developmental. *British Journal of Medical Psychology, 49,* 1–10.

Nietzel, M. T., & Harris, M. J. (1990). Relationship of dependency and achievement/autonomy to depression. *Clinical Psychology Review, 10,* 279–297.

Oldham, J. M., Skodol, A. E., Kellman, H. D., Hyler, S. E., Doidge, N., Rosnick, L., et al. (1995). Comorbidity of Axis I and Axis II disorders. *American Journal of Psychiatry, 152,* 571–578.

O'Neill, F. A., & Kendler, K. S. (1998). Longitudinal study of interpersonal dependency in female twins. *British Journal of Psychiatry, 172,* 154–158.

Overholser, J. C. (1987). Facilitating autonomy in passive-dependent persons: An integrative model. *Journal of Contemporary Psychotherapy, 17,* 250–269.

Overholser, J. C., & Fine, M. A. (1994). Cognitive-behavioral treatment of excessive interpersonal dependency: A four-stage psychotherapy model. *Journal of Cognitive Psychotherapy, 8,* 55–70.

Pfohl, B., Blum, N., Zimmerman, M., & Stangl, D. (1989). *Structured interview for DSM-III-R personality (SIDP-R)*. Iowa City: University of Iowa.

Pincus, A. L., & Gurtman, M. B. (1995). The three faces of interpersonal dependency: Structural analysis of self-report dependency measures. *Journal of Personality and Social Psychology, 69,* 744–758.

Pincus, A. L., & Wilson, K. R. (2001). Interpersonal variability in dependent personality. *Journal of Personality, 69,* 223–251.

Piper, W. E., Ogrodniczuk, J. S., Joyce, A. S., McCallum, M., Weideman, R., & Azim, H. F. (2001). Ambivalence and other relationship predictors of grief in psychiatric outpatients. *Journal of Nervous and Mental Disease, 189,* 781–787.

Poldrugo, F., & Forti, B. (1988). Personality disorders and alcoholism treatment outcome. *Drug and Alcohol Dependence, 21,* 171–176.

Rathus, J. H., Sanderson, W. C., Miller, A. L., & Wetzler, S. (1995). Impact of personality functioning on cognitive behavioral treatment of panic disorder. *Journal of Personality Disorders, 9,* 160–168.

Rector, N. A., Bagby, R. M., Segal, Z. V., Joffe, R. T., & Levitt, A. (2000). Self-criticism and dependency in depressed patients treated with cognitive therapy or pharmacotherapy. *Cognitive Therapy and Research, 24,* 571–584.

Ryder, R. D., & Parry-Jones, W. L. (1982). Fear of dependence and its value in working with adolescents. *Journal of Adolescence, 5,* 71–81.

Sans, J., & Avia, D. (1994). Cognitive specificity in social anxiety and depression: Self-statements, self-focused attention, and dysfunctional attitudes. *Journal of Social and Clinical Psychology, 13,* 105–137.

Schneider, K. (1923). *Die psychopathischen persönlichkeiten* [The psychopathic personalities]. Vienna: Deuticke.

Schneider, K. J., & May, R. (1995). *The psychology of existence: An integrative, clinical perspective*. New York: McGraw-Hill.

Sinha, B. K., & Watson, D. C. (2001). Personality disorder in university students: A multitrait-multimethod matrix study. *Journal of Personality Disorders, 15,* 235–244.

Spitzer, R. L., Williams, J. B. W., Gibbon, M., & First, M. B. (1990). *Structured clinical interview for DSM-III-R personality disorders (SCID-II)*. Washington, DC: American Psychiatric Press.

Sroufe, L. A., Fox, N. E., & Pancake, V. R. (1983). Attachment and dependency in developmental perspective. *Child Development, 54,* 1615–1627.

Thompson, R., & Zuroff, D. C. (1998). Dependent and self-critical mothers' responses to adolescent autonomy and competence. *Personality and Individual Differences, 24,* 311–324.

Torgersen, S., Lygren, S., Oien, P. A., Skre, I., Onstad, S., Edvardsen, J., et al. (2000). A twin study of personality disorders. *Comprehensive Psychiatry, 41,* 416–425.

Turkat, I. D. (1990). *The personality disorders: A psychological approach to clinical management*. New York: Pergamon Press.

Turkat, I. D., & Carlson, C. R. (1984). Data-based versus symptomatic formulation of treatment: The case of a dependent personality. *Journal of Behavior Therapy and Experimental Psychiatry, 15,* 153–160.

Vaillant, G. E. (1980). Natural history of male psychological health: VIII. Antecedents of alcoholism and orality. *American Journal of Psychiatry, 137,* 181–186.

Westen, D., & Shedler, J. (1999). Revising and assessing Axis II: 1. Developing a clinically and empirically valid assessment method. *American Journal of Psychiatry, 156,* 258–272.

White, H. (1986). Damsels in distress: Dependency themes in fiction for children and adolescents. *Adolescence, 21,* 251–256.

Widiger, T. A., & Clark, L. A. (2000). Toward DSM-V and the classification of psychopathology. *Psychological Bulletin, 126,* 946–963.

Widiger, T. A., & Coker, L. A. (2002). Assessing personality disorders. In J. N. Butcher (Ed.), *Clinical personality assessment* (2nd ed., pp. 407–434). London: Oxford University Press.

Williams, J. B., & Spitzer, R. L. (1983). The issue of sex bias in DSM-III: A critique of "A woman's view of the DSM-III" by Marcie Kaplan. *American Psychologist, 38,* 793–798.

Wise, E. A. (1996). Comparative validity of MMPI-2 and MCMI-II personality disorder classifications. *Journal of Personality Assessment, 66,* 569–582.

Young, J. E. (1994). *Cognitive therapy for personality disorders: A schema-focused approach.* Sarasota, FL: Professional Resources Press.

Zaretsky, A. E., Fava, M., Davidson, K. G., Pava, J. A., Matthews, J., & Rosenbaum, J. F. (1997). Are dependency and self-criticism risk factors for major depressive disorder? *Canadian Journal of Psychiatry, 42,* 291–297.

12 Obsessive-Compulsive Personality Disorder

Jennifer Bartz
Mount Sinai School of Medicine

Alicia Kaplan
Mount Sinai School of Medicine

Eric Hollander
Mount Sinai School of Medicine

Obsessive-compulsive personality disorder (OCPD), as Phillips and Gunderson (1994) noted, has a long history in clinical psychology and psychiatry and is one of the few personality disorders (PDs) to be included in every edition of the *Diagnostic and Statistical Manual of Mental Disorders* (DSM; American Psychiatric Association [APA], 1952, 1968, 1980, 1987, 1994, 2000). OCPD is one of the Cluster C PDs, which are characterized by fear and anxiety. DSM-IV-TR defines OCPD as "a pervasive pattern of preoccupation with orderliness, perfectionism, and mental and interpersonal control, at the expense of flexibility, openness, and efficiency, beginning by early adulthood and present in a variety of contexts . . ." (APA, 2000, p. 729). Diagnostic criteria include four or more of the following characteristics: (1) preoccupation

Authors' notes: Preparation of this chapter was supported by grants from the National Institute of Mental Health, the National Institute on Neurological Disorders and Stroke, the National Institute on Drug Abuse, and the Food and Drug Administration and investigator-initiated research grants from Solvay, Wyeth, Pfizer, and Ortho-McNeil. Correspondence regarding this manuscript should be addressed to Jennifer Bartz, Compulsive and Impulsive Disorders Program, Mount Sinai School of Medicine, One Gustave L. Levy Place, Box 1230, New York, New York 10029. Phone: 212–241–6051. E-mail: jennifer.bartz@mssm.edu

with details, rules, lists, order, organization, or schedules to the extent that the major point of the activity is lost; (2) perfectionism that interferes with task completion; (3) excessive devotion to work and productivity to the exclusion of leisure activities and friendships; (4) overconscientiousness, scrupulousness, and inflexibility about matters of morality, ethics, or values; (5) inability to discard worn-out or worthless objects even when they have no sentimental value; (6) reluctance to delegate tasks or to work with others unless they submit exactly the individual's way of doing things; (7) a miserly spending style toward both self and others; and (8) rigidity and stubbornness.

In DSM-III-R (APA, 1987), such features as "indecisiveness" and "restricted expression of affection" were also included as criteria; these are now described as associated features of the disorder due to poor discriminate properties (Pfohl & Blum, 1995). The ninth revision of the International Classification of Diseases (ICD) refers to this disorder as "anankastic personality" (World Health Organization, 1977). Historically, OCPD has been referred to as "anal character" (psychoanalytic tradition), "compulsive personality" (DSM-I; APA, 1952), "obsessive-compulsive personality" (DSM-II; APA, 1968), "compulsive personality disorder" (DSM-III; APA, 1980), and "obsessive-compulsive personality disorder" (DSM-III-R; APA, 1987). Notwithstanding the numerous name changes, the descriptions of this disorder that have emerged over the years have been relatively consistent, as Pollak (1979) noted in his seminal review.

A central question in the literature on OCPD concerns the nature of its relationship to the similarly named Axis I disorder, obsessive-compulsive disorder (OCD). OCD is characterized by obsessions and/or compulsions that are found to be intrusive, excessive, and unmanageable and that lead to impaired functioning (APA, 2000). The classic distinction between these two disorders is that obsessions and compulsions in OCD are thought to be ego-dystonic (i.e., perceived as originating from outside the self or unacceptable to the self), whereas OCPD character traits are thought to be ego-syntonic (i.e., perceived as originating from within the self and consistent with and acceptable to the self; Pollak, 1987; Stein & Hollander, 1993). These boundaries, however, are not always firmly held, because OCD patients can have fluctuating insight into their symptomatology; indeed, the specifier "with poor insight" was added to the DSM-IV criteria for OCD due to reports of individuals with OCD who believe their obsessions are reasonable (Foa & Kozak, 1995). Similarly, OCPD patients often seek treatment for their maladaptive symptoms (e.g., impaired social relationships), suggesting they have some insight into their condition. Although many theories have been put forth about the relationship between these two disorders, little evidence to date supports a unique relationship, and these two disorders are generally regarded as separate and distinct (Stein & Hollander, 1993). That said, OCPD may be conceptualized as an obsessive-compulsive–related disorder, as we will discuss.

In this chapter we review the history of OCPD, addressing its major theoretical conceptualizations and etiology. We also discuss assessment and diagnostic tools as well as epidemiology and comorbidity with other Axis II and Axis I disorders, highlighting the relationship between OCPD and both OCD and eating disorders. We then turn to a discussion of treatment options, outlining and critiquing approaches from individual psychotherapy, including psychodynamic, interpersonal, cognitive, and behavioral therapies, group therapy, and pharmacological therapy. We conclude with a discussion of unresolved questions and possible directions for future research.

Major Theoretical Conceptualizations

Psychoanalytic Models

In the early 1900s, Freud wrote about OCPD, which he referred to as the "anal retentive" or "anal character" type because of its putative origins in bowel training and the sublimation of anal erotic impulses (which were thought to be particularly strong in these individuals; Freud, 1906–1908/1959). He noted the regular combination of three character traits—namely, orderliness, parsimony, and obstinacy—that were associated with the anal character. According to Freud, orderliness is reflected in concerns with bodily cleanliness and overconscientiousness, parsimony is displayed in the tendency to be frugal and stingy, and obstinacy is evidenced in the tendency to be negativistic and defiant. Interestingly, Freud linked obstinacy to feelings of rage; although rage is not a criterion for OCPD, other theorists have noted the association between OCPD and rage, anger, hostility, and/or aggression (Millon, 1996; Rado, 1974; Reich, 1949; Stein et al., 1996; Villemarette-Pittman, Stanford, Greve, Houston, & Mathias, 2004).

Abraham (1927) further extended the theory of the anal character, in particular highlighting the exaggerated pleasure these individuals take in indexing, ordering, arranging things symmetrically, and compiling lists; indeed, he noted, their pleasure in planning so far surpasses their pleasure in executing that often the activity itself will be left undone. Abraham also noted their perseverance, but emphasized the unproductive nature of this trait as well as the tendency to postpone every action. With respect to order and cleanliness, Abraham laid emphasis on their ambivalence. That is, these individuals may appear to be tidy and well organized, but this appearance only masks disarray. As Abraham writes, "On the writing table, for instance, every object will have its special place . . . In the drawers, however, complete disorder reigns . . ." (p. 389). Abraham also noted the great deal of pleasure these individuals take in their possessions and their inability to discard worn-out or worthless objects. With respect to interpersonal relationships, Abraham observed the compulsive individual's unaccommodating attitude, insistence on controlling interactions with others, and tendency to be highly critical. Finally, Abraham called attention to the "stamp" of the anal character—that is, his (or her) morose expression and surly attitude (p. 391).

Reich (1949) also contributed to the discussion of OCPD, at this point referred to as the "compulsive" character. Echoing Abraham, Reich emphasized these individuals' "pedantic concern for orderliness" (p. 193) and also drew attention to their tendency toward "circumstantial, ruminative thinking" (p. 194), indecision, doubt, distrust, flat affective reactions, and indifferent attitude toward others. Rado (1974) was the next major theorist to write about OCPD. As Millon (1996) noted, Rado's formulation brings out its contradictory nature. Rado noted that these individuals are highly sensitive but tend to be critical, mean, and vengeful toward others; they avoid overt conflict but nevertheless bear grudges. According to Rado, these divergent impulses are rooted in their "stronger-than-average" craving for autonomous self-realization and their still stronger desire to be loved and cared for (p. 200), which sets the stage for an obedience-defiance conflict and a great deal of rage. Indeed, Rado believed that "repressed defiant rage" was at the heart of this character type (p. 207).

Finally, Millon (1996) described the compulsive personality as comprising the polar opposite qualities of the dependent (other-oriented) and antisocial (self-oriented) personalities. Consistent with earlier theorists, Millon described OCPD as an unresolved struggle between obedience and defiance. Whereas most people feel comfortable turning to themselves *and* close others for rewards and protection, OCPD individuals are conflicted in this regard: on the outside they are conforming and submissive, but on the inside they "churn with defiance" (p. 506). Millon posited that these conflicting impulses lead to a vicious cycle in which the more they submit, the angrier and more rebellious they feel, and the angrier and more rebellious they feel, the more they feel the need to submit to control these dangerous impulses.

Cognitive Models

Shapiro (1965) was one of the first theorists to emphasize the importance of thinking style in OCPD, delineating three problematic areas in particular. First, Shapiro observed these individuals' intellectual rigidity, which is marked by a "special limitation of attention" (p. 27). As he describes, the obsessive-compulsive thinking style tends to be intensely focused, detail oriented, and limited in mobility, flexibility, and range, which precludes the experience of spontaneity. Second, Shapiro noted their intense activity as well as their distorted sense of autonomy. These individuals are intensely effortful, but their effort is undermined by their lack of conviction. Shapiro argued that for obsessive-compulsive individuals, the object of their will is not something external to achieve but the will itself: they feel they must continually exert pressure on themselves, and that any form of relaxation is unsafe because they may lose control. Finally, Shapiro observed their loss of reality, which, he hypothesized, resulted from their vacillation between a state of doubt and dogma. Interestingly, Shapiro noted, both of these states are the consequence of their rigid thinking style. Doubt arises because their narrow focus makes them susceptible to insignificant details. As Shapiro writes, "What may be, for the normal person, an insignificant detail in relation to the whole will often be, for the obsessive-compulsive person, sufficient reason to radically change the whole" (p. 52). Dogma, Shapiro argued, is used to compensate and overcome doubt and is fueled by their restricted thinking style, which allows them to avoid new information and feel easily satisfied with their beliefs.

Beck, Freeman, Davis, and colleagues (2004) have also described a number of cognitive distortions and maladaptive schemas associated with OCPD. In particular, dichotomous thinking—that is, the tendency to see things as black and white, and all or nothing—may fuel their rigidity, perfectionism, and tendency to procrastinate. Magnification and catastrophizing likely contribute to their tendency to overestimate the consequences of imperfection, mistakes, and errors. Moralistic thinking dominated by "shoulds" and "musts" likely leads to a heightened sense of responsibility and contributes to the tendency to override desires and preferences. Finally, maladaptive schemas about perfection ("Mistakes are intolerable") and control ("I must be careful and thorough") are also implicated in OCPD (Beck et al., 2004).

Interpersonal Models

Benjamin (1996) proposed a model for OCPD that attempts to locate these individuals' quest for order, fear of mistakes, excessive self-discipline and self-criticism, and tendency to rigidly follow rules in their early childhood experiences with cold and controlling parental figures. Specifically, Benjamin (1996) theorized that OCPD individuals were raised by caregivers who held exceedingly high expectations of them, emphasized following the rules and performing correctly, and readily punished them for failures but rarely rewarded them for successes. In an effort to cope, Benjamin argued, the child takes on the caregiver's values and beliefs through a process of introjection and identification. Along similar lines, Turkat and Maisto (1985) conjectured about the atmosphere in which these individuals were raised, arguing that individuals with OCPD likely failed to learn empathy and emotional interaction skills because their families emphasized productivity and rule following over emotional expressivity and interpersonal relationships.

Although early environmental experiences may play a role in the development of OCPD, it is important to keep in mind potential genetic confounds. Parents may directly pass on to their children genes that contribute to specific personality profiles (e.g., cold and controlling); moreover, early environments are complicated by the fact that they are influenced by the parents' own genes (Scarr & McCartney, 1983). Basically, parents create an environment for their children due to their own genetic propensities, and because parents also pass on these genes to their children, the children are going to be particularly responsive to these environments.

Etiology

Environment

According to the early Freudians, as Pollak (1979) noted, the anal character arises from difficulties between children and their caregivers during the anal stage of development (second to third year). It is theorized that inherent in bowel training is a conflict between the child's desire to be autonomous and the caretaker's desire to ensure that the child conforms to societal and cultural standards. If problems arise during this period (e.g., if the caretaker is too demanding, or if training comes too early or late), anal fixations can take form, sowing seeds for the development of the anal character (Pollak, 1979). As outlined, many theorists following Freud wrote about the anal character, but they did not all share Freud's etiologic assumptions (Pollak, 1979). Some theorized that perfectionism, orderliness, and an attempt to maintain control, rather than bowel training per se, may be strategies individuals use to defend against the insecurity resulting from the excessive parental control that often occurs during the bowel training period (but is not exclusive to it; Carr, 1974; Pollak, 1979). In his review, Pollak found little support for the association between bowel training styles and the development of obsessive-compulsive character traits. That said, he noted some empirical investigations as well as some clinical observations supporting a relationship between anal character traits in children and the existence of similar traits in their parents. Indeed, a second environmental theory argues that OCPD results from imitation and modeling of caregivers who are themselves rigid, controlling, and obsessive (Carr, 1974). As noted earlier, however, the role of early environment in the development of OCPD is complicated by potential genetic factors.

Biology

It has long been theorized that biology may play a role in the development of OCPD (even Freud referred to constitutional factors in his discussion of the anal character). In their review of genes and PDs, Nigg and Goldsmith (1994) noted that while evidence concerning the heritability of OCPD is mixed, some research suggests that trait obsessiveness in the normal range is moderately heritable. One study of 419 pairs of nonpatient twins reared together found an estimated heritability of obsessionality of 46% for males and 62% for females (a combined additive gene influence was estimated to be 44% for the entire sample). However, another study found only modest to nonexistent evidence for the heritability of this personality trait. Nigg and Goldsmith went on to cite evidence supporting the existence of a genetic component in OCD and concluded that, given the genetic data for normal personality traits and severe OCD, future research should address whether

OCPD and neighboring phenomena (e.g., OCD, tics, Tourette's syndrome, neuroticism, conscientiousness) reflect one or more etiologic dimensions.

Obsessive-Compulsive Spectrum

The theory of an obsessive-compulsive (OC) spectrum of disorders (Hollander, 1993) may be a useful framework for exploring the question raised by Nigg and Goldsmith (1994) and may also be helpful in identifying biological contributions to OCPD. The notion of a spectrum of obsessive-compulsive–related disorders was proposed in response to findings that a number of disorders (e.g., OCD, body dysmorphic disorder, certain eating disorders, autism spectrum disorders) share obsessive-compulsive features and evidence similarities in patient characteristics, course, comorbidity, neurobiology, and treatment response (Allen, King, & Hollander, 2003; Stein, 2000; Stein & Hollander, 1993). The fact that such diverse disorders have similarities on these different levels suggests that they may be related, hence the notion of a spectrum of obsessive-compulsive–related disorders.

OCPD may be a good candidate for the obsessive-compulsive spectrum. From a phenomenological perspective, OCPD is associated with rigid routines and obsessional symptoms and features. From a neurobiological perspective, OCPD, like OCD, is characterized by low risk taking and high harm avoidance (Cloninger, 1987). Because serotonin mediates harm avoidance, serotonergic dysfunction may play a role in OCPD. Indeed, OCD is known to involve serotonin dysfunction, and selective serotonin reuptake inhibitors are the first line in pharmacotherapy for OCD, although success has been limited (Kaplan & Hollander, 2003). OCPD, however, may differ from OCD but share features with some obsessive-compulsive–related disorders, which have an overlap with impulsivity. Stein et al. (1996) noted that OCPD is associated with both compulsive and impulsive traits and symptoms. Thus, OCPD may involve serotonergic dysfunction with both compulsive and impulsive symptomatology. Consistent with this hypothesis, Stein et al. (1996) found that compulsive personality disordered patients scored higher on impulsive aggression (as assessed by the Assaultiveness and Irritability subscales of the Buss-Durkee Hostility Inventory [Buss & Durkee, 1957]) than noncompulsive patients and exhibited significantly more blunted prolactin responses (a measure of net serotonin functioning), indicating deficits in central serotonin, which is associated with impulsive and aggressive behavior. Stein et al. suggested that these individuals may be more accurately characterized by impaired harm *assessment* rather then harm avoidance per se. That is, although OCPD individuals are especially alert to potential risks and negative consequences, their attentional and inhibitory deficits make behavioral regulation more difficult. Stein et al. cautioned, however, that their findings were based on individuals with comorbid OCPD/OCD diagnoses and may not necessarily apply to those with an OCPD-only diagnosis.

The association between OCPD and hoarding also supports categorizing OCPD as an obsessive-compulsive–related disorder. Hoarding is currently a diagnostic criterion of OCPD and is a symptom frequently associated with OCD; however, hoarding is associated with other disorders (e.g., schizophrenia, dementia, anorexia nervosa, autism) as well, and questions have recently been raised about the classification of hoarding (Fontenelle, Mendlowicz, Soares, & Versiani, 2004; Stein, Seedat, & Potocnik, 1999). Kaplan and Hollander (2004) suggested that a distinct neuroanatomic circuitry may be involved in hoarding. A recent positron-emission tomography (PET) study found that OCD hoarders displayed lower glucose metabolism in the dorsal anterior cingulate gyrus than OCD nonhoarders; compulsive hoarders also had lower glucose metabolism in the posterior cingulate gyrus and cuneus, whereas OCD nonhoarders had higher glucose metabolism in the bilateral thalamus and caudate (Saxena et al., 2004). Saxena et al. argued that obsessive-compulsive hoarding may be a distinct neurobiological subgroup or OCD variant. Fontenelle et al. also cited evidence suggesting that hoarding may be associated with a distinct set of neurobiological features: OCD hoarders are more likely to have family histories of hoarding, they display a unique set of cognitive deficits involving spatial encoding strategies, and hoarding symptoms in OCD are associated with poorer response to both behavioral and pharmacological treatments. Stein et al. (1999) have argued that hoarding may best be characterized as an obsessive-compulsive–related disorder rather than a symptom of OCD and OCPD. With respect to OCPD, clinical evidence suggests that hoarding is more common in OCPD and attention deficit hyperactivity disorder than in OCD, and that OCPD runs in the families of hoarders.

Adaptation to Axis I Disorders

Finally, some have argued that OCPD develops as an adaptation to some Axis I disorders. For example, one hypothesis holds that OCPD develops in some OCD patients as an adaptation to the illness (Swedo, Leonard, & Rapoport, 1990; Swedo, Rapoport, Leonard, Lenane, & Cheslow, 1989). As Swedo et al. (1989) explained, a child who initially feels compelled to write the number 7 perfectly may become slow, careful, and rigid in an effort to "get it right the first time" and "beat the compulsion" (p. 339). Baer and Jenike (1998) cited some support for this hypothesis. For example, one study compared adults who were hospitalized for OCD in childhood to controls with no psychiatric history and found that although these two groups did not differ in PD diagnosis, the adults who still had OCD were more likely to have OCPD than those who no longer had OCD (Thomsen & Mikkelsen, 1993).

Villemarette-Pittman et al. (2004) noted the long-standing association in the psychiatric and clinical literature between aggressive behavior and obsessive-compulsive personality traits and proposed a compensatory theory of OCPD in which compulsive behaviors develop in response to poor impulse control in a subgroup of individuals with impulsive aggression. As these researchers explain,

> It is possible that some members of the larger impulsive aggressive population have developed a more structured lifestyle in an attempt to maintain control over their behavior. Unfortunately, the intensity of their loss of control sometimes warrants an equally intense need for control. This need may manifest itself as an adoption of rigid routines and increased attention to details, behaviors that begin as a way to cope with problems with self-regulation but become a lifestyle dedicated to structure and inflexibility. (p. 15)

To test this hypothesis, Villemarette-Pittman et al. identified a group of clinic- and self-referred impulsive aggressive individuals and evaluated them for PD. OCPD was the most common diagnosis (52%) in the self-referred group and the second most common diagnosis (24%) in the clinic-referred group. Importantly, these researchers noted that when they looked at the life histories, impulsive aggressive behaviors had an earlier onset than OCPD symptoms, lending support to their hypothesis that compulsive behaviors developed in response to impulsive aggression. This theory is intriguing and consistent with Stein et al.'s (1996) findings of increased impulsive aggression in OCPD.

Assessment and Diagnosis

As Villemarette-Pittman et al. (2004) observed, it is important to keep in mind two caveats when diagnosing OCPD. First, OCPD traits are fairly common in the general population; thus, clinicians should not be assessing whether or not OCPD traits are present, but they should be attentive to the severity of these traits and whether or not they cause significant functional impairment and/or subjective distress. Second, care should be taken not to confuse a diagnosis of OCPD with a diagnosis of OCD.

Semistructured interviews for OCPD include the Structured Interview for DSM-IV Personality (SIDP-IV; a revision of the SIDP and SIDP-R interviews modified to generate DSM-IV PD diagnoses; Pfohl, Blum, & Zimmerman, 1997), the Personality Disorders Examination (PDE; Loranger, Susman, Oldham, & Russakoff, 1987), the Personality Disorder Interview–IV (PDI-IV; a revision of the PDI modified to generate DSM-IV PD diagnoses; Widiger, Mangine, Corbitt, Ellis, & Thomas, 1995), the Diagnostic Interview for DSM-IV Personality Disorders (DIPD-IV; a revision of the DIPD modified to generate DSM-IV PD diagnoses; Zanarini, Frankenburg, Sickel, & Yong, 1996), the Structured Clinical Interview for DSM-III-R Personality Disorders (SCID-II; First, Spitzer, Gibbon, & Williams, 1995), and the revised DSM-IV version of the SCID-II, the SCID-II 2.0 (First, Spitzer, Gibbon, Williams, & Benjamin, 1994).

As Zanarini et al. (2000) report, most of the original interviews have attained adequate levels of reliability, especially when administered by their developer. With respect to OCPD, the DIPD, PDE, PDI, and SIDP yielded interrater kappa values of .92, .88, .67, and .36, respectively. In their study investigating the reliability of the DIPD-IV, Zanarini et al. (2000) report good interrater kappa and test-retest kappa for obsessive-compulsive personality (.71 and .74, respectively). Moreover, the dimensional rating reliabilities were substantially higher than those found for the categorical diagnosis of OCPD (Pearson $r = .85$ and test-retest Pearson $r = .82$). Maffei et al. (1997) investigated the interrater reliability of the SCID-II 2.0 in a large mixed psychiatric sample and found interrater kappas for OCPD to be in the moderate to excellent range (.83 for the categorical assessment and .93 for the dimensional assessment).

There are also self-report measures that can be used to assess OCPD. The Millon Clinical Multiaxial Inventory—III (MCMI-III; Millon, 1994) is a 175-item measure purporting to assess Axis I and Axis II diagnoses from the DSM-IV. The Personality Diagnostic Questionnaire—IV (PDQ-IV; Hyler & Rieder, 1996) is a 100-item measure designed to yield personality diagnoses consistent with DSM-IV diagnostic criteria for Axis II disorders. These measures are useful for screening, but a full structured interview is generally recommended for diagnosis. There are also self-report measures that can be used to assess personality *features* related to such Axis II disorders as OCPD. These include the Multidimensional Personality Questionnaire (MPQ; Tellegen, 1982), revised NEO Personality Inventory (NEO-PI-R; Costa & McCrae, 1992), Schedule for Nonadaptive and Adaptive Personality (SNAP; Clark, 1993) and Dimensional Assessment of Personality Pathology (DAPP; Livesley & Jackson, in press; Livesley, Jackson, & Schroeder, 1989). Finally, projective measures such as the Rorschach and the Thematic Apperception Test (TAT) have also been noted in the assessment of OCPD (Millon, 1996; Beck et al., 2004). However, to our knowledge, there is no controlled research indicating that the TAT can be used to validly detect OCPD traits, and there is, at best, weak support for the validity of Exner's Obsessive Style Index and other Rorschach indices of obsessional thinking and behavior (see Wood, Lilienfeld, Garb, & Nezworski, 2000).

Epidemiology

According to DSM-IV-TR (APA, 2000), the prevalence of OCPD is about 1% in community samples and about 3% to 10% in clinical samples. Nestadt et al. (1991) evaluated individuals participating in the Epidemiological Catchment Area survey conducted in the Baltimore area for compulsive PD (using DSM-III criteria) and estimated a prevalence rate of 1.7% in the general population; those most likely to receive a diagnosis were white, married, employed males. Samuels et al. (2002) investigated the prevalence of OCPD in a community sample from the Baltimore Epidemiological Catchment Area follow-up survey. Using DSM-IV criteria, this study found an OCPD prevalence rate of 1.2% (0.9% when using weighted results, which are thought to better represent the general population).

As is the case with many other PDs, the prevalence rate of OCPD is generally higher in clinical populations. Zimmerman, Rothschild, and Chelminski (2005) summarized 11 studies investigating the prevalence of DSM PDs in clinical epidemiological studies from 1985 to 2000 and reported OCPD prevalence rates ranging from 0.5% to 34.6%. Base rate differences and differences in assessment tools may have contributed to the variability in the prevalence rates. In their own study, which was strengthened by sampling patients presenting to a community-based outpatient clinic rather than a specialty research clinic and by the use of valid and reliable assessment procedures (SCID and SIDP-IV), Zimmerman et al. found that 8.7% of all patients met diagnostic criteria for OCPD. Finally, the prevalence of OCPD has also been found to be a function of changes in clinical criteria. Baer et al. (1990) found that the incidence of OCPD was increased in a sample of OCD patients when DSM-III-R criteria were used instead of DSM-III criteria. One likely reason for this increase is changes in the number of criteria required for diagnosis. As Jenike (1998) noted, DSM-III-R requires only five of nine criteria to be met for diagnosis, whereas DSM-III requires four of five criteria to be met.

Comorbidity

Axis II Disorders

Pfohl and Blum (1995) reviewed the literature regarding the co-occurrence of OCPD and other Axis II disorders and found that paranoid, avoidant, and borderline PDs had the highest comorbidity rates (> 50%) with OCPD, although these findings were not consistent across the five studies evaluated. These authors note that although the association between OCDP and paranoid and avoidant PDs seems reasonable, given their relatively congruent profiles, the association between borderline PD, which is associated with interpersonal impulsivity, and OCPD, which is associated with interpersonal constriction and risk aversion, is more surprising. Pfohl and Blum speculate that the association between OCPD and borderline PD may be more a function of similar behaviors masking different underlying motivations. They also point out that differences in the manner in which diagnostic criteria were assessed across studies may have been a factor. In addition, base rate differences in these PDs across settings may have contributed to inconsistent comorbidity rates. More recent investigations of Axis II comorbidity in patients with OCPD have found elevated odds ratios for paranoid, schizoid, and narcissistic PDs but not borderline PD (Zimmerman et al., 2005).

Axis I Disorders

According to DSM-IV-TR (APA, 2000), individuals with anxiety disorders, including social phobia and specific phobia, have an increased likelihood of meeting criteria for OCPD. Research has found OCPD to be associated with ulcerative colitis (Rabavilas, Christodoulou, Lappas, Perissaki, & Stefanis, 1980), hypochondriacal states (Kenyon, 1976), depressive disorders (Hardy et al., 1995; Insel, 1984), anxiety disorders (Kasen et al., 2001), and self-mutilation (Gardner & Gardner, 1975). In addition, two Axis I disorders—OCD and eating disorders, anorexia nervosa in particular—have received special attention regarding their relationship to OCPD.

OCD

The relationship between OCPD and OCD has been the subject of much debate (see Pollak, 1987, for a review). As Pollak noted, according to the psychoanalytic perspective, both disorders are rooted in the management of anal-sadistic impulses. Other theorists have argued that OCD and OCPD fall on a continuum of severity (OCPD being a less severe version of OCD), and that OCPD is a predisposing factor for OCD. This hypothesis, however, has not generally been supported (Pollak, 1987; Villemarette-Pittman et al., 2004). For example, one study found evidence of OCD symptoms *prior* to 10 years of age in compulsive personality patients (Baer et al., 1990). Pollak reviewed the evidence on the co-occurrence of OCD and OCPD and concluded that there was no necessary relationship between these two disorders despite occasional findings. Insel (1982) similarly concluded that the two disorders were quantitatively and qualitatively distinct. Nevertheless, a relationship between these two disorders continues to be explored and debated.

The OCD-OCPD debate is fueled in part by the fact that studies looking at the prevalence of OCPD in patients with OCD vary widely. Two recent reviews report comorbidity rates ranging from 2% to 60% (Diaferia et al., 1997) and from 3% to 36% (Albert, Maina, Forner, & Bogetto, 2004). In their review, Pfohl and Blum (1995) noted that OCD is more frequently comorbid with avoidant and dependent PDs than with OCPD. Similarly, Black and Noyes (1997) noted that even though many people with OCD display OCPD traits, and even though PDs—especially those from Cluster C—frequently co-occur with OCD, few patients meet criteria for OCPD (see also Baer & Jenike, 1992). More recently, however, Denys, Tenney, van Megen, de Geus, and Westenberg (2004) investigated the prevalence of Axis I and Axis II disorders in a large cohort ($N = 420$) of OCD patients and found OCPD to be the most prevalent personality disorder, with 9% meeting criteria for OCPD—five times the prevalence rate found in the community sample comparison group. Tenney, Schotte, Denys, van Megen, and Westenberg (2003) also investigated the prevalence of DSM-IV PDs in a sample of severely disordered OCD patients and found that OCPD had the highest prevalence rates; this finding held regardless of whether the diagnosis was made by clinical interview (10.8%), semistructured interview with the SCID-II (24.6%), or self-reports (29.2%). (It is noteworthy, however, that although OCPD was the most prevalent PD regardless of assessment type, there was little correspondence among the different methods used to diagnose OCPD.) These studies, however, are limited because they did not have psychiatric comparison groups; thus the findings may have been due simply to the increased prevalence of PDs in patients with Axis I diagnoses compared to the general population.

Other studies have added psychiatric comparison groups, but results are still mixed. Diaferia et al. (1997) investigated the prevalence of OCPD in patients with OCD, major depressive disorder, and panic disorder and found OCPD to be significantly more frequent in OCD patients than in the other two patient groups. By contrast, Albert et al. (2004) investigated the prevalence of OCPD in individuals with OCD and panic disorder and found that although OCPD was more prevalent in patients with OCD than in the general population, it was equally prevalent in panic disorder patients. Similarly, Wu, Clark, and Watson (2006) investigated the relationship between OCPD and OCD from a categorical and dimensional perspective and did not find support for a specific OCD-OCPD association: 15% of patients with OCD met criteria for OCPD, but this percentage did not differ from the prevalence rate found in the general outpatient group; moreover, more OCD patients met criteria for avoidant PD then for OCPD.

Overall, there is no conclusive support for a straightforward OCD-OCPD link at this point; however, the phenomenological similarities between these two disorders, as well as the fact that many OCD individuals have obsessional traits, suggests that these two disorders may have a more complicated relationship. Two recent studies may shed light on this issue. Samuels et al. (2000) evaluated personality characteristics of OCD probands and their first-degree relatives and control probands (identified in a community sample and individually matched to case probands) and their first-degree relatives. This study found that case probands were more likely to have a PD, particularly avoidant PD or OCPD (32%), and also scored significantly higher on neuroticism (mean = 64.0). In addition, OCPD was twice as common in the first-degree relatives of OCD probands; case relatives also scored significantly higher on neuroticism (mean = 52.1). Samuels et al. concluded that neuroticism and OCPD may share a common familial etiology with OCD. These researchers cautioned, however, that the nature of the relationship between these phenotypes requires further examination. As Samuels et al. speculate, OCPD, OCD, and neuroticism may reflect the same underlying vulnerability (e.g., differing only in severity or in that they require different factors for differentiation into specific clinical phenomena), or they may be distinct entities, one reflecting a direct expression and the others emerging as a result of additional genetic and/or environmental factors.

Finally, the heterogeneous nature of OCD (as well as that of OCPD; see Wu et al., 2006) may also be an important factor to consider when thinking about the OCD-OCPD relationship. Nestadt et al. (2003) employed latent class analysis to distinguish OCD subgroups in a sample of OCD case and control probands and their first-degree relatives. Results revealed a four-class structure: the first three classes were thought to differ only in severity, whereas the fourth class was considered qualitatively distinct. OCPD was found to be significantly associated with this first class, suggesting that the link between OCPD and OCD may exist for a subset of individuals with OCD. Future research, however, is needed to address this issue more directly.

Eating Disorders

Given that such traits as perfectionism, a preoccupation with order and symmetry, excessive persistence and compliance, and a high need for control are characteristic of both OCPD and eating disorders (EDs)—in particular anorexia nervosa (AN)—some researchers have asked whether a "special relationship" exists between EDs, OCPD, and OCD (Serpell, Livingstone, Neiderman, & Lask, 2002). Research investigating the co-occurrence of EDs and PDs in general has yielded widely divergent findings, with estimates ranging from 27% to 93% (Grilo et al., 2003), and studies investigating the comorbidity between OCPD and EDs have similarly yielded estimates ranging from 3.3% to 60% (Serpell et al., 2002). Some studies have found increased rates of Cluster C PDs in patients with AN (Herzog, Keller, Lavori, Kenny, & Sacks, 1992; Piran, Lerner, Garfinkel, Kennedy, & Brouillette, 1988; Skodol et al., 1993; Wonderlich, Swift, Slotnick, & Goodman, 1990); in these studies, avoidant PD was the most common diagnosis. However, Wonderlich et al. found evidence of increased OCPD in patients with restricting AN, Herzog et al. found a concurrent diagnosis of OCPD in 10% of patients with restricting AN, and Gartner, Marcus, Halmi, and Loranger (1989) found that 25.7% of patients with anorexia and/or bulimia had an OCPD diagnosis. As noted, though, not all have found evidence of an association between AN and OCPD (Grilo et al., 2003). Other research suggests that OCPD and/or OCPD traits may persist after recovery from AN. Matsunaga et al. (2000) found that 15% of individuals who had recovered from AN at least 1 year earlier met criteria for OCPD. Moreover, a prospective long-term outcome study of teenage-onset AN found that although the majority of AN cases were free from an ED 10 years after onset, more than one third of the AN cases were characterized by OCD, OCPD, and/or autism spectrum disorders (Nilsson, Gillberg, Gillberg, & Rastam, 1999).

Other research suggests that OCPD traits may predispose people to develop an ED, especially AN. Anderluh and colleagues (Anderluh, Tchanturia, Rabe-Hesketh, & Treasure, 2003) found that development of an ED was predicted by retrospective reports of childhood obsessive-compulsive personality traits, and that the odds of developing an ED increased as a function of the number of obsessive traits held in childhood. It was hypothesized that such childhood obsessive-compulsive traits as perfectionism may be risk factors for the development of AN. Similarly, Halmi and colleagues (2005) conducted a study assessing perfectionism, OCPD, and OCD in a sample of 607 individuals with EDs. Results revealed that eating-disordered individuals with OCPD, either alone or in combination with OCD, had the highest perfectionism scores. These authors concluded that the combination of perfectionism—especially concerns about mistakes and doubts about competency—and OCPD may be an important behavioral feature associated with eating disorder vulnerability. Coming to a similar conclusion, Lilienfeld, Wonderlich, Riso, Crosby, and Mitchell (2006) reviewed the literature from prospective, quasiprospective, retrospective, and family studies and argued that perfectionism and obsessive-compulsive personality traits are likely a predisposing factor for the development of EDs. Family studies (although limited) point to the possibility of a shared familial transmission of AN and OCPD: Lilienfeld et al. (1998) found increased rates of OCPD among relatives of those diagnosed with AN (but not those diagnosed with bulimia nervosa), independent of whether probands had OCPD. Along with Anderluh et al.'s and Halmi et al.'s findings, this research provides support for the notion that obsessive-compulsive personality traits may be factors in the development of both AN and OCPD.

Treatment

Before turning to a discussion of specific treatment options, we note a few challenges to which therapists should be alert when treating OCPD. Like individuals with other PDs, those with OCPD often seek treatment at the request of others, such as spouses, family members, and employers, and do not see themselves as having a problem. Along similar lines, Millon (1996) noted that these individuals also seek treatment because of such physical ailments as anxiety attacks, immobilization, extreme fatigue, or sexual dysfunction, and are often unaware of any underlying psychological condition. Thus the therapist's first challenge is to make these patients aware of their psychological problem. Second, as Salzman (1980) noted, therapists need to be wary of such defensive strategies as rationalization, isolation, undoing (i.e., attempts to "undo" an unpleasant outcome by mentally replaying or ritualistically reenacting it), and reaction formation (i.e., attempts to control unacceptable feelings or impulses by engaging in behavioral patterns that are directly opposed to them) that are characteristic of OCPD (Salzman, 1980). Third, OCPD individuals tend to intellectualize their problems and avoid discussing their emotions. As a result, therapists need to steer clear of getting drawn into academic discussions that are unproductive from a therapeutic perspective (Salzman, 1980; Sperry, 2003). Finally, as Benjamin (1996) has pointed out, individuals with OCPD often try to be the perfect patient (e.g., doing homework assignments perfectly). Given that the drive for perfection is a core feature of this disorder, therapists should discourage this tendency.

Individual Psychotherapy

Psychodynamic and Interpersonal Therapies. Overall, insight-oriented, dynamic therapies, including psychoanalysis, have been recommended as the treatment of choice for OCPD (Baer & Jenike, 1990; Jenike, 1998; Salzman, 1980; Sperry, 2003; Stein & Hollander, 1993). As Salzman (1980) noted, this kind of therapy has three main goals: (1) expose OCPD individuals to their fears concerning insecurity and uncertainty and encourage risk taking, (2) help them address issues related to perfectionism and develop more realistic expectations of themselves and others, and (3) help them recognize and experience their feelings (rather than avoid them) and teach them that such things as anger, dependency, and lust are basic human characteristics. In addition, several theorists have noted important modifications—primarily concerning the therapist's activity level—that should be made when adopting this approach (for summaries, see Jenike, 1998; Salzman, 1980; Sperry, 2003).

Although psychodynamic therapy has been discussed as the treatment of choice for OCPD, there are relatively few well-controlled studies establishing the efficacy of this approach—indeed, as Barber, Morse, Krakauer, Chittams, and Crits-Christoph (1997) noted, there has been very little research investigating any form of treatment for OCPD. One of the best treatment studies to date was conducted by Winston et al. (1994). This study investigated the effects of short-term dynamic psychotherapy and brief adaptational psychotherapy—both of which involve an active and confrontational approach—on a group of personality-disordered patients (including those with compulsive PD). Participants were randomly assigned to one of the two treatment conditions or to a waiting list control group. Following approximately 40 weeks of treatment, the two treatment groups showed significant improvement on target complaints, the Symptom Checklist–90–R (Derogatis, 1983) and the Social Adjustment Scale–SR (Weissman & Bothwell, 1976) compared to the waiting list control group. Moreover, target complaint ratings were not significantly different from those at the termination of therapy when participants were followed up 1.5 years later.

Barber et al. (1997) investigated the effects of time-limited supportive-expressive (SE) dynamic therapy in an open trial with individuals diagnosed with obsessive-compulsive or avoidant PD. This study found that 85% of OCPD individuals were free from their PD and had improved on measures of depression, anxiety, general functioning, and interpersonal problems following 52 sessions of SE therapy, compared to only 61.5% of those with avoidant PD. One of the strengths of this study is that it assessed changes in PD; however, a major limitation of this study is the lack of a control group. Consequently, it is impossible to rule out such factors as placebo effect, effort justification, demand characteristics, and spontaneous improvement due to maturation, making it difficult to draw any firm conclusions about SE therapy as an effective form of treatment for OCPD. That said, the results suggest that SE is more effective for those with OCPD than for those with avoidant PD.

Barber and Muenz (1996) investigated the effects of interpersonal psychotherapy (IPT) and cognitive therapy (CT) in treating obsessive and avoidant personality. This study used the National Institute of Mental Health's Treatment of Depression Collaborative Research Program data set, in which individuals with major depressive disorder were randomly assigned to an IPT, CT, imipramine plus clinical treatment, or placebo plus clinical management control condition. Barber and Muenz (1996) selected those who had scores of 4 or higher on the Personality Assessment Form (PAF; Shea et al., 1990) for avoidant or obsessive PD and who had received either IPT or CT. IPT was found to be more effective in reducing depression (as assessed by self-report and clinical ratings) in depressed patients with obsessional personality, whereas CT was more effective for those with avoidant personality. Although these findings are encouraging, this study focused on depressed individuals with a PD and assessed changes in depression rather than changes in PD. Moreover, obsessive and avoidant personality traits were assessed using a single item rather than a full structured clinical interview.

Cognitive-Behavioral Therapy. Given that a rigid, rule-based, detail-oriented, indecisive cognitive style is a core feature of OCPD, in theory, cognitive therapy (CT) should be useful in treating this PD. According to Beck et al. (2004), the goal of cognitive therapy in OCPD would be to modify maladaptive schemas (i.e., knowledge structures that serve as frameworks for solving problems, guiding action, and interpreting information) and automatic (i.e., spontaneous or involuntary) thoughts related to control and perfection. In addition, Millon (1996) noted that behavioral therapy may be promising in addressing phobic avoidance and ritualized behavior. Specifically, flooding, desensitization, response prevention, satiation training (Salzman, 1980), and thought stopping have been recommended for the treatment of OCPD (Millon, 1996).

Research on the effectiveness of cognitive therapy is mixed. Beck et al. (2004) refer to clinical evidence supporting cognitive therapy in treating OCPD; however, to date empirical evidence is inconclusive. Barber and Muenz's (1996) study found IPT to be superior to CT in treating depressed individuals meeting PAF criteria for obsessive PD. However, Hardy and colleagues (1995) found some support for cognitive behavioral therapy (CBT) in treating Cluster C PDs, including OCPD. This study compared the effects of CBT and psychodynamic interpersonal (PI) psychotherapy in a sample of depressed patients with Cluster C PDs and those without any PD (NPD group). At the outset, the PD group had higher levels of symptom severity than the NPD group. Group differences in symptom severity were maintained at posttreatment and at 1-year follow-up for those who received PI therapy but were eliminated for those who received CBT, suggesting that PI psychotherapy is less effective if a Cluster C PD is present, whereas CBT is similarly effective regardless of PD diagnosis. However, this study lacked a control group and consequently is subject to the limitations outlined earlier. Moreover, the sample was small (only 27 participants received a PD diagnosis), and PD was not assessed at posttreatment; thus it is unclear whether CBT had a direct effect on PD. It is also noteworthy that the form of interpersonal psychotherapy used in this study was not identical to that used in the Barber and Muenz study. Although PI and IPT are similarly named and both based in psychodynamic theory, PI uses traditional psychodynamic methods involving the therapeutic relationship to effect change, whereas IPT focuses on alleviating symptoms of depression by examining the patient's current life and interpersonal relationships.

Social Skills Training. Finally, OCPD individuals may benefit from social skills training, given their interpersonal problems (Turkat & Maisto, 1985; Sperry, 2003). Turkat and Maisto (1985) argue that teaching social skills, especially emotion-related social skills (e.g., empathy; acceptance of other's emotions; ability to identify, be comfortable with, and appropriately express emotions) may be helpful for dealing with the interpersonal problems associated with OCPD as well as with the depression that often arises in response to interpersonal issues. To date there is no empirical evidence looking at social skills training in OCPD; however, there is some tentative evidence to suggest that social skills training is helpful in treating the social deficits found in Asperger's syndrome (Barnhill, Cook, Tebbenkamp, & Myles, 2002; Strain & Hoyson, 2000).

Group Therapy

Opinions about the effectiveness of group therapy are mixed, and again, well-controlled studies are lacking. Some have noted that group therapy can be an effective way to address issues related to control and the interpersonal problems characteristic of OCPD. For example, Wells, Glickauf-Hughes, and Buzzell (1990) recommended group therapy due to the unique opportunities afforded by group situations that are not available in the context of individual therapy. As these authors explain, group situations require OCPD individuals to share power and relinquish control; moreover, OCPD individuals may be more receptive to feedback from peers than from a therapist, who may be perceived as an authority figure; and, finally, group situations can provide OCPD individuals with a unique opportunity to witness and learn from their peers' experiences in therapy (e.g., they can see that mistakes are not always fatal and that taking risks can lead to positive results; Wells et al., 1990). However, others have noted that individuals with OCPD may resist group therapy or be particularly disruptive (Millon, 1996; Phillips & Gunderson, 1994).

Pharmacotherapy

Although there are no specific medications for the treatment of OCPD, antidepressant, antiobsessional (e.g., clomipramine), and anticonvulsant medications may be helpful. Currently, selective serotonin reuptake inhibitors (SSRIs) are the mainstay of treatment for OCD, and Stein and Hollander

(1993) report anecdotal evidence of the efficacy of serotonergic agents in patients with OCPD. SSRIs may allow OCPD patients to be less rigid, and, by decreasing their anxiety, less likely to procrastinate. With respect to empirical support for pharmacotherapy, most of the studies conducted thus far have focused on PDs in general, or on individuals with OCD and concomitant PDs. Ricciardi et al. (1992) conducted a study investigating pharmacological and/or behavioral therapy for OCD patients with concomitant PDs (including OCPD) and found that after 4 months of treatment, nine of the 10 patients who responded to treatment no longer met criteria for a PD. Another study, however, found that OCD patients with comorbid OCPD had poorer response to proserotonergic pharmacological treatment (clomipramine or fluvoxamine) than OCD patients without comorbid OCPD (Cavedini, Erzegovesi, Ronchi, & Bellodi, 1997). Yet another study did not find this negative treatment outcome for Axis II disorders in patients with OCD (Baer, Jenike, Black, et al., 1992). Finally, Greve and Adams (2002) reported anecdotal evidence for the anticonvulsant carbamazepine in the treatment of OCPD; these researchers hypothesized that the mood-stabilizing properties of anticonvulsants should be particularly effective in treating the irritability and hostility associated with OCPD.

Combining pharmacotherapy with psychotherapy may also be useful (Jenike, 1998; Sperry, 2003), because alleviating depression and anxiety should make OCPD patients more cooperative and open to therapy (Jenike, 1998). Kool, Dekker, Duijsens, de Jonghe, and Puite (2003) investigated the effects of pharmacotherapy alone or in conjunction with short psychodynamic supportive psychotherapy (SPSP) on changes in personality pathology (including OCPD) in an outpatient sample of depressed individuals with or without a PD. This study found a significant reduction in personality pathology for those who received combined therapy regardless of whether they had recovered from depression, whereas in the pharmacotherapy alone condition, personality pathology decrease was limited to those who had recovered from depression. Although this study did not focus specifically on OCPD (25% of the PD sample received an OCPD diagnosis), patients with Cluster C PDs benefited the most from the combined treatment. The findings from this study as well as those from the Barber et al. (1997) study are encouraging, as they suggest that it is possible to affect PDs. That said, given the limitations of pre-post designs, these results need to be replicated in a study with a control group.

Unresolved Questions and Future Directions

When Pollak authored his review on the obsessive-compulsive personality in 1979, numerous studies had been conducted to establish support for etiologic assumptions, clinical observations, and descriptions regarding this PD. Since Pollak's review, research on OCPD has waned considerably. As Villemarette-Pittman et al. (2004) noted, only 40 articles on OCPD were published between 1996 and 2001. Others have also remarked on the surprisingly little empirical attention OCPD has received in the past two decades (Grilo, 2004). In this section, we discuss unresolved questions and some possible directions for future research. As noted, controlled outcome studies for the treatment of OCPD are sorely needed. In particular, social skills training, cognitive therapy, and pharmacotherapy used alone or in combination may be promising, and studies are needed to establish treatment parameters and identify subpopulations that may benefit from these approaches. In addition, we believe two other areas deserve attention.

The Relationship Between OCPD and Other Similar Disorders

The nature of the relationship between OCPD and OCD has been the subject of much debate over the years. We have suggested that OCPD may best be conceptualized as an obsessive-compulsive–related disorder. Thus the relationship of OCPD to OCD would be similar to that of any other obsessive-compulsive–related disorders: OCPD is not required in the developmental trajectory of OCD, but it is likely that OCPD and OCD share a distal phenotype. Some have also suggested a special relationship between OCPD, OCD, and EDs, and, as Gillberg and Rastam (1992) have noted, there are intriguing similarities among OCPD, EDs, and autism spectrum disorders, particularly Asperger's syndrome. Like OCPD, Asperger's is associated with narrow, restricted interests; inflexible adherence to routines and/or rituals; insistence that people do things a specific way; and severe social deficits (APA, 2000). OCPD and autism spectrum disorders, Asperger's in particular, are also more common in males than in females.

The OC spectrum may provide a fruitful framework for exploring the relationship among these disorders and may help us understand how patients who present with one disorder, such as anorexia nervosa, subsequently develop one or more related disorders. Like EDs and autism spectrum disorders, OCPD is associated with perfectionism, control issues, and significant social impairments (Gillberg & Rastam, 1992). Autism spectrum disorders and certain EDs are theorized to be OC spectrum disorders: EDs reflect obsessions and compulsions related to the body and eating, and autism spectrum disorders are frequently marked by compulsive, stereotypical behavior. Moreover, in contrast to the obsessions and compulsions associated with OCD, which are typically ego-dystonic, the obsessions and compulsions associated with EDs, autism spectrum disorders, and OCPD are typically ego-syntonic. As noted, researchers are beginning to look at the presence of childhood compulsive personality traits in eating-disordered patients (Anderluh et al., 2003). Along similar lines, future research should explore the history of individuals with OCPD. Did these individuals exhibit narrow, restricted interests, evidence social deficits, and/or engage in self-stimulatory behaviors in childhood?

Alternative Conceptual Frameworks

It has recently been suggested that borderline PD may best be conceptualized as an emotion dysregulation disorder and that it be moved out of the Axis II Cluster B category and included in the Axis I bipolar spectrum disorders category. This view is supported by the fact that mood stabilizers such as divalproex sodium are helpful in the treatment of borderline PD (Hollander et al., 2003). Similarly, it could be argued that OCPD should be moved to Axis I and categorized as an obsessive-compulsive–related disorder (Hollander & Allen, 2006). Evidence supporting this would include overlapping symptomatology, cognitive profile, comorbidity, treatment response, brain circuitry, and family studies and genetic data. As we have argued, there is considerable overlap between OCPD and other OC spectrum disorders (in particular, certain EDs and possibly autism spectrum disorders), especially in terms of symptomatology and cognitive profile. Moreover, Nigg and Goldsmith (1994) noted the overlap between OCPD and such "neighboring phenomena" (p. 370) as tics and Tourette's syndrome, both of which are thought to be OC spectrum disorders. Preliminary evidence suggests that, like other OC spectrum disorders, OCPD may respond to SSRIs.

Endophenotype-based research strategies may be particularly useful in understanding the relationship between OCPD and other OC spectrum disorders. Endophenotypes—which can be neurophysiological, biochemical, endocrinological, neuroanatomical, cognitive, or neuropsychological—have become an important focus in the study of psychiatric disorders because they are hypothesized to be indicators of the genetic underpinnings of disorders and therefore can be used to guide and inform genetic research and aid in disease classification and diagnosis (Gottesman & Gould, 2003). Inherent in the notion of an OC spectrum of disorders is that although these disorders have different phenotypes, they likely share endophenotypes. One research strategy would be to identify potential common endophenotypes and determine whether individuals with different OC spectrum disorders and/or their nonaffected family members display the endophenotype at a higher rate than the general population. These studies would be helpful in identifying OCPD traits that share a common familial etiology with other OC spectrum disorders, which can then be used to direct the focus of genetic research. Ultimately, these markers can help us better understand the etiology of OCPD and identify individuals who will benefit from specific treatments.

References

Abraham, K. (1927). Contributions to the theory of the anal character (D. Bryan & A. Strachey, Trans.). In E. Jones (Ed.), *Selected papers of Karl Abraham* (pp. 370–392). London: Hogarth Press.

Albert, U., Maina, G., Forner, F., & Bogetto, F. (2004). DSM-IV obsessive-compulsive personality disorder: Prevalence in patients with anxiety disorders and in healthy comparison subjects. *Comprehensive Psychiatry, 45,* 325–332.

Allen, A., King, A., & Hollander, E. (2003). Obsessive-compulsive spectrum disorders. *Dialogues in Clinical Neuroscience, 5,* 259–271.

American Psychiatric Association. (1952). *Diagnostic and statistical manual of mental disorders.* Washington, DC: Author.

American Psychiatric Association. (1968). *Diagnostic and statistical manual of mental disorders* (2nd ed.). Washington, DC: Author.

American Psychiatric Association. (1980). *Diagnostic and statistical manual of mental disorders* (3rd ed.). Washington, DC: Author.

American Psychiatric Association. (1987). *Diagnostic and statistical manual of mental Disorders* (3rd ed., revised). Washington, DC: Author.

American Psychiatric Association. (1994). *Diagnostic and statistical manual of mental disorders* (4th ed.). Washington, DC: Author.

American Psychiatric Association. (2000). *Diagnostic and statistical manual of mental Disorders* (4th ed., text revision). Washington, DC: Author.

Anderluh, M. B., Tchanturia, K., Rabe-Hesketh, S., & Treasure, J. (2003). Childhood obsessive compulsive personality traits in adult women with eating disorders: Defining a broader eating disorder phenotype. *American Journal of Psychiatry, 160,* 242–247.

Baer, L., & Jenike, M. A. (1992). Personality disorders in major depressive disorder. *Psychiatric Clinics of North America, 15,* 803–812.

Baer, L., & Jenike, M. A. (1998). Personality disorders in obsessive-compulsive disorder. In M. A. Jenike, L. Baer, & W. E. Minichiello (Eds.), *Obsessive-compulsive disorders: Practical management* (3rd ed., pp. 65–83). New York: Mosby.

Baer, L., Jenike, M. A., Black, D. W., Treece, C., Rosenfeld, R., & Greist, J. (1992). Effect of Axis II diagnoses on treatment outcome with clomipramine in 55 patients with obsessive-compulsive disorder. *Archives of General Psychiatry, 49,* 862–866.

Baer, L., Jenike, M. A., Ricciardi, J. N., Holland, A. D., Seymour, R. J., Minichiello, W. E., et al. (1990). Standardized assessment of personality disorders in obsessive-compulsive disorder. *Archives of General Psychiatry, 47,* 826–830.

Barber, J. P., Morse, J. Q., Krakauer, I. D., Chittams, J., & Crits-Christoph, K. (1997). Change in obsessive-compulsive and avoidant personality disorders following time-limited supportive expressive therapy. *Psychotherapy, 34,* 133–143.

Barber, J. P., & Muenz, L. R. (1996). The role of avoidance and obsessiveness in matching patients to cognitive and interpersonal psychotherapy: Empirical findings from the treatment for depression collaborative research program. *Journal of Consulting and Clinical Psychology, 64,* 951–958.

Barnhill, G. P., Cook, K. T., Tebbenkamp, K., & Myles, B. S. (2002). The effectiveness of social skills intervention targeting nonverbal communication for adolescents with Asperger's syndrome and related pervasive developmental delays. *Focus on Autism and Other Developmental Disorders, 17,* 112–118.

Beck, A. T., Freeman, A., Davis, D. D., & Associates (2004). *Cognitive therapy of personality disorders* (2nd ed.). New York: Guilford Press.

Benjamin, L. S. (1996). *Interpersonal diagnosis and treatment of personality disorders* (2nd ed.). New York: Guilford Press.

Black, D. W., & Noyes, R. (1997). Obsessive-compulsive disorder and Axis II. *International Review of Psychiatry, 9,* 111–118.

Buss, A. H., & Durkee, A. (1957). An inventory for assessing difference kinds of hostility. *Journal of Consulting Psychology, 21,* 343–348.

Carr, A. T. (1974). Compulsive neurosis: A review of the literature. *Psychological Bulletin, 81,* 311–318.

Cavedini, P., Erzegovesi, S., Ronchi, P., & Bellodi, L. (1997). Predictive value of obsessive-compulsive personality disorder in antiobsessional pharmacological treatment. *European Neuropsychopharmacology, 7,* 45–49.

Clark, L. A. (1993). *Schedule for Nonadaptive and Adaptive Personality (SNAP): Manual for administration, scoring, and interpretation.* Minneapolis: University of Minnesota Press.

Cloninger, C. R. (1987). A systematic method for clinical descriptions and classification of personality variants: A proposal. *Archives of General Psychiatry, 44,* 573–588.

Costa, P. T., Jr., & McCrae, R. R. (1992). *The NEO-PI-R: The Revised NEO Personality Inventory manual.* Odessa, FL: Psychological Assessment Resources.

Denys, D., Tenney, N., van Megen, H. J., de Geus, F., & Westenberg, H. G. (2004). Axis I and II comorbidity in a large sample of patients with obsessive-compulsive disorder. *Journal of Affective Disorders, 80,* 155–162.

Derogatis, L. R. (1983). *SCL-90-R: Administration, scoring, and procedures manual: II.* Towson, MD: Clinical Psychometric Research.

Diaferia, G., Bianchi, I., Bianchi, M. L., Cavedini, P., Erzegovesi, S., & Bellodi, L. (1997). Relationship between obsessive-compulsive personality disorder and obsessive-compulsive disorder. *Comprehensive Psychiatry, 38,* 38–42.

First, M. B., Spitzer, R. L., Gibbon, M., Williams, J. B. W., & Benjamin, L. (1994). *Structured clinical interview for DSM-IV Axis II personality disorders (SCID-II): Version 2.0.* New York: New York State Psychiatric Institute.

First, M. B., Spitzer, R. L., Gibbon, M., & Williams, J. B. W. (1995). The Structured Clinical Interview for DSM-III-R Personality Disorders (SCID-II): I. Description. *Journal of Personality Disorders, 9,* 83–91.

Freud, S. (1906–1908/1959). Character and anal eroticism. In J. Strachey (Ed. & Trans.), *The standard edition of the complete psychological works of Sigmund Freud* (Vol. 9, pp. 169–175). London: Hogarth Press.

Foa, E. B., & Kozak, M. J. (1995). DSM-IV field trial: Obsessive-compulsive disorder. *American Journal of Psychiatry, 152,* 90–96.

Fontenelle, L. F., Mendlowicz, M. V., Soares, I. D., & Versiani, M. (2004). Patients with obsessive-compulsive disorder and hoarding symptoms: A distinctive clinical subtype? *Comprehensive Psychiatry, 45,* 375–383.

Gardner, A. R., & Gardner, A. J. (1975). Self-mutilation, obsessionality and narcissism. *British Journal of Psychiatry, 127,* 127–132.

Gartner, A. F., Marcus, R. N., Halmi, K., & Loranger, A. W. (1989). DSM-III-R personality disorders in patients with eating disorders. *American Journal of Psychiatry, 146,* 1585–1591.

Gillberg, C., & Rastam, M. (1992). Do some cases of anorexia reflect underlying autistic-like conditions? *Behavioral Neurology, 5,* 27–32.

Gottesman, I. I., & Gould, T. D. (2003). The endophenotype concept in psychiatry: Etymology and strategic intentions. *American Journal of Psychiatry, 160,* 636–645.

Greve, K. W., & Adams, D. (2002). Treatment of features of obsessive-compulsive personality disorder using carbamazepine. *Psychiatry and Clinical Neurosciences, 56,* 207–208.

Grilo, C. M. (2004). Factor structure of DSM-IV criteria for obsessive compulsive personality disorder in patients with binge eating disorder. *Acta Psychiatrica Scandinavica, 109,* 64–68.

Grilo, C. M., Sanislow, C. A., Skodol, A. E., Gunderson, J. G., Stout, R. L., Shea, M. T., et al. (2003). Do eating disorders co-occur with personality disorders? Comparison groups matter. *International Journal of Eating Disorders, 33,* 155–164.

Halmi, K. A., Tozzi, F., Thornton, L. M., Crow, S., Fichter, M. M., Kaplan, A. S., et al. (2005). The relation among perfectionism, obsessive-compulsive personality disorder and obsessive-compulsive disorder in individuals with eating disorders. *International Journal of Eating Disorders, 38,* 371–374.

Hardy, G. E., Barkham, M., Shapiro, D. A., Stiles, W. B., Rees, A., & Reynolds, S. (1995). Impact of Cluster C personality disorders on outcomes of contrasting brief psychotherapies for depression. *Journal of Consulting and Clinical Psychology, 63,* 997–1004.

Herzog, D. B., Keller, M. B., Lavori, P. W., Kenny, G. M., & Sacks, N. R. (1992). The prevalence of personality disorders in 210 women with eating disorders. *Journal of Clinical Psychiatry, 53,* 147–152.

Hollander, E. (1993). *Obsessive-compulsive related disorders.* Washington, DC: American Psychiatric Press.

Hollander, E., & Allen, A. (2006). Is compulsive buying a real disorder, and is it really compulsive? *American Journal of Psychiatry, 163,* 1670–1672.

Hollander, E., Tracy, K. A., Swann, A. C., Coccaro, E. F., McElroy, S. L., Wozniak, P., et al. (2003). Divalproex in the treatment of impulsive aggression: Efficacy in Cluster B personality disorders. *Neuropsychopharmacology, 28,* 1186–1197.

Hyler, S. E., & Rieder, R. O. (1996). *Personality diagnostic questionnaire* (4th revision). New York: New York State Psychiatric Institute.

Insel, T. R. (1982). Obsessive compulsive disorder: Five clinical questions and a suggested approach. *Comprehensive Psychiatry, 23,* 241–251.

Insel, T. R. (1984). *Obsessive-compulsive disorder.* Washington, DC: American Psychiatric Press.

Jenike, M. A. (1998). Psychotherapy of obsessive-compulsive personality disorder. In M. A. Jenike, L. Baer, & W. E. Minichiello (Eds.), *Obsessive-compulsive disorders: Practical management* (3rd ed., pp. 611–624). New York: Mosby.

Kaplan, A., & Hollander, E. (2003). A review of pharmacologic treatments for obsessive-compulsive disorder. *Psychiatric Services, 54,* 1111–1118.

Kaplan, A., & Hollander, E. (2004). Comorbidity in compulsive hoarding: A case report. *CNS Spectrums, 9,* 71–73.

Kasen, S., Cohen, P., Skodol, A. E., Johnson, J. G., Smailes, E., & Brook, J. S. (2001). Childhood depression and adult personality disorder: Alternative pathways of continuity. *Archives of General Psychiatry, 58,* 231–236.

Kenyon, F. E. (1976). Hypochondrical states. *British Journal of Psychiatry, 129,* 1–14.

Kool, S., Dekker, J., Duijsens, I. J., de Jonghe, F., & Puite, B. (2003). Changes in personality pathology after pharmacotherapy and combined therapy for depressed patients. *Journal of Personality Disorders, 17,* 60–72.

Lilienfeld, L. R., Kaye, W. H., Greeno, C. G., Merikangas, K. R., Plotnicov, K., Pollice, C., et al. (1998). A controlled family study of anorexia nervosa and bulimia nervosa: Psychiatric disorders in first-degree relatives and effects of proband comorbidity. *Archives of General Psychiatry, 55,* 603–610.

Lilienfeld, L. R., Wonderlich, S., Riso, L. P., Crosby, R., & Mitchell, J. (2006). Eating disorders and personality: A methodological and empirical review. *Clinical Psychology Review, 26,* 299–320.

Livesley, W. J., & Jackson, D. N. (in press). *Manual for the Dimensional Assessment of Personality Pathology—Basic Questionnaire*. London: Research Psychologists' Press.

Livesley, W. J., Jackson, D. N., & Schroeder, M. L. (1989). A study of the factorial structure of personality pathology, *Journal of Personality Disorders, 3,* 298–306.

Loranger, A. W., Susman, V. L., Oldham, J. M., & Russakoff, L. M. (1987). The Personality Disorders Examination: A preliminary report. *Journal of Personality Disorders, 1,* 1–13.

Maffei, C., Fossati, A., Agostoni, I., Barraco, A., Bagnato, M., Deborah, D., et al. (1997). Interrater reliability and internal consistency of the Structured Clinical Interview for DSM-IV Axis II Personality Disorders (SCID-II), Version 2.0. *Journal of Personality Disorders, 11,* 279–84.

Matsunaga, H., Kaye, W. H., McConaha, C., Plotnicov, K., Pollice, C., & Rao, R. (2000). Personality disorders among subjects recovered from eating disorders. *International Journal of Eating Disorders, 27,* 353–357.

Millon, T. (1994). *Millon Clinical Multiaxial Inventory–III: Manual and scoring booklet*. Minneapolis, MN: National Computer Systems.

Millon, T. (1996). Compulsive personality disorders: The conforming pattern. In T. Million & R. D. Davis (Eds.), *Disorders of personality: DSM-IV and beyond* (2nd ed., pp. 505–539). New York: Wiley.

Nestadt, G., Addington, A., Samuels, J., Liang, K.Y., Bienvenu, O. J., Riddle, M., et al. (2003). The identification of OCD-related subgroups based on comorbidity. *Biological Psychiatry, 53,* 914–920.

Nestadt, G., Romanoski, A. J., Brown, C. H., Chahal, R., Merchant, A., Folstein, M. F., et al. (1991). DSM-III compulsive personality disorder: An epidemiological survey. *Psychological Medicine, 21,* 461–471.

Nigg, J. T., & Goldsmith, H. H. (1994). Genetics of personality disorders: Perspectives from personality and psychopathology research. *Psychological Bulletin, 115,* 346–380.

Nilsson, E. W., Gillberg, C., Gillberg, I. C., & Rastam, M. (1999). Ten-year follow-up of adolescent-onset anorexia nervosa: Personality disorders. *Journal of the American Academy of Child & Adolescent Psychiatry, 38,* 1389–1395.

Pfohl, B., & Blum, N. (1995). Obsessive-compulsive personality disorder. In W. J. Livesley (Ed.), *The DSM-IV personality disorders*. New York: Guilford Press.

Pfohl, B., Blum, N., & Zimmerman, M. (1989). *Structured interview for DSM-IV personality*. Washington DC: American Psychiatric Press.

Phillips, K. A., & Gunderson, J. G. (1994). Personality disorders. In R. E. Hales, S. C. Yudofsky, & J. A. Talbott (Eds.), *The American Psychiatric Press textbook of psychiatry* (2nd ed., pp. 701–728). Washington, DC: American Psychiatric Press.

Piran, N., Lerner, P., Garfinkel, P. E., Kennedy, S. H., & Brouillette, C. (1988). Personality disorders in anorexic patients. *International Journal of Eating Disorders, 7,* 589–599.

Pollak, J. M. (1979). Obsessive-compulsive personality: A review. *Psychological Bulletin, 86,* 225–241.

Pollak, J. M. (1987). Relationship of obsessive-compulsive personality to obsessive-compulsive disorder: A review of the literature. *The Journal of Psychology, 121,* 137–148.

Rabavilas, A. D., Christodoulou, G. N., Lappas, J., Perissaki, C., & Stefanis, C. (1980). Relation of obsessional traits to anxiety in patients with ulcerative colitis. *Psychotherapy and Psychosomatics, 33,* 155–159.

Rado, S. (1974). Obsessive behavior. In S. Arieti & E. B. Brody (Eds.), *American handbook of psychiatry* (2nd ed., Vol. 3, pp. 195–208). New York: Basic Books.

Reich, W. (1949). *Character analysis* (T. P. Wolfe, Trans.). New York: Orgone Institute Press.

Ricciardi, J. N., Baer, L., Jenike, M. A., Fischer, S. C., Sholtz, D., & Buttolph, M. L. (1992). Changes in DSM-III-R diagnoses following treatment of obsessive-compulsive disorder. *American Journal of Psychiatry, 149,* 829–831.

Salzman, L. (1980). Psychotherapy with the obsessive personality. In T. B. Karasu & L. Bellak (Eds.), *Specialized techniques in individual psychotherapy* (pp. 184–198). New York: Brunner/Mazel.

Samuels, J., Eaton, W. W., Bienvenu, O. J., Brown, C. H., Costa, P. T., Jr., & Nestadt, G. (2002). Prevalence and correlates of personality disorders in a community sample. *British Journal of Psychiatry, 180,* 536–542.

Samuels, J., Nestadt, G., Bienvenu, O. J., Costa, P. T., Jr., Riddle, M. A., Liang, K., et al. (2000). Personality disorders and normal personality dimensions in obsessive-compulsive disorder. *British Journal of Psychiatry, 177,* 457–462.

Saxena, S., Brody, A. L, Maidment, K. M., Smith, E. C., Zohrabi, N., Katz, E., et al. (2004). Cerebral glucose metabolism in obsessive-compulsive hoarding. *American Journal of Psychiatry, 161,* 1038–1048.

Scarr, S., & McCartney, K. (1983). How people make their own environments: A theory of genotype↔environment effects. *Child Development, 54,* 424–435.

Serpell, L., Livingstone, A., Neiderman, M., & Lask, B. (2002). Anorexia nervosa: Obsessive-compulsive disorder, obsessive-compulsive personality disorder, or neither? *Clinical Psychology Review, 22,* 647–669.

Shapiro, D. (1965). *Neurotic styles.* New York: Basic Books.

Shea, M. T., Pilkonis, P. A., Beckham, E., Collins, J. F., Elkin, I., Sotsky, S. M., et al. (1990). Personality disorders and treatment outcome in the NIMH Treatment of Depression Collaborative Research Program. *American Journal of Psychiatry, 147,* 711–718.

Skodol, A. E., Oldham, J. M., Hyler, S. E., Kellman, H. D., Doidge, N., & Davies, M. (1993). Comorbidity of DSM-III-R eating disorders and personality disorders. *International Journal of Eating Disorders, 14,* 403–416.

Sperry, L. (2003). *Handbook of diagnosis and treatment of DSM-IV-TR personality disorders* (2nd ed.). New York: Brunner-Routledge.

Stein, D. J. (2000). Neurobiology of the obsessive-compulsive spectrum disorders. *Biological Psychiatry, 47,* 296–304.

Stein, D. J., & Hollander, E. (1993). The spectrum of obsessive-compulsive related disorders. In E. Hollander (Ed.), *Obsessive-compulsive related disorders* (pp. 241–262). Washington, DC: American Psychiatric Press.

Stein, D. J., Seedat, S., & Potocnik, F. (1999). Hoarding: A review. *Israel Journal of Psychiatry & Related Sciences, 36,* 35–46.

Stein, D. J., Trestman, R. L., Mitropoulou, V., Coccaro, E. F., Hollander, E., & Siever, L. J. (1996). Impulsivity and serotonergic function in compulsive personality disorder. *Journal of Neuropsychiatry and Clinical Neurosciences, 8,* 393–398.

Strain, P. S., & Hoyson, M. (2000). The need for longitudinal, intensive social skill intervention: LEAP follow-up outcomes for children with autism. *Topics in Early Childhood Special Education, 20,* 116–122.

Swedo, S. E., Leonard, H. L., & Rapoport, J. L. (1990). Childhood-onset obsessive-compulsive disorder. In M. A. Jenike, L. Baer, & W. E. Minichiello (Eds.),

Obsessive-compulsive disorders: Theory and management (2nd ed., pp. 28–38). Chicago: Mosby.

Swedo, S. E., Rapoport, J. L., Leonard, H., Lenane, M., & Cheslow, D. (1989). Obsessive-compulsive disorder in children and adolescents: Clinical phenomenology of 70 consecutive cases. *Archives of General Psychiatry, 46,* 335–341.

Tellegen, A. (1982). *Brief manual for the Differential Personality Questionnaire.* Unpublished manuscript, University of Minnesota, Minneapolis.

Tenney, N. H., Schotte, C. K., Denys, D. A., van Megen, H. J., & Westenberg, H. G. (2003). Assessment of DSM-IV personality disorders in obsessive-compulsive disorder: Comparison of clinical diagnosis, self-report questionnaire, and semistructured interview. *Journal of Personality Disorders, 17,* 550–561.

Thomsen, P. H., & Mikkelsen, H. U. (1993). Development of personality disorders in children and adolescents with obsessive-compulsive disorder. A 6- to 22-year follow-up study. *Acta Psychiatrica Scandinavica, 87,* 456–462.

Turkat, I. D., & Maisto, S. A. (1985). Personality disorders: Application of the experimental method to the formulation and modification of personality disorders. In D. H. Barlow (Ed.), *Clinical handbook of psychological disorders: A step-by-step treatment manual* (pp. 502–570). New York: Guilford Press.

Villemarette-Pittman, N. R., Stanford, M. S., Greve, K. W., Houston, R. J., & Mathias, C. W. (2004). Obsessive-compulsive personality disorder and behavioral disinhibition. *The Journal of Psychology, 138,* 5–22.

Weissman, M. M., & Bothwell, S. (1976). Assessment of social adjustment by patient self-report: I. *Archives of General Psychiatry, 33,* 1111–1115.

Wells, M. C., Glickauf-Hughes, C., & Buzzell, V. (1990). Treating obsessive-compulsive personalities in psychodynamic/interpersonal group therapy. *Psychotherapy, 27,* 366–379.

Widiger, T. A., Mangine, S., Corbitt, E. M., Ellis, C. G., & Thomas, G. V. (1995). *Personality Disorder Interview–IV: A semistructured interview for the assessment of personality disorders.* Odessa, FL: Psychological Assessment Resources.

Winston, A., Laikin, M., Pollack, J., Samstag, L. W., McCullough, L., & Muran, J. C. (1994). Short-term psychotherapy of personality disorders. *American Journal of Psychiatry, 151,* 190–194.

Wonderlich, S. A., Swift, W. J., Slotnick, H. B., & Goodman, S. (1990). DSM-III-R personality disorders in eating disorder subtypes. *International Journal of Eating Disorders, 9,* 607–616.

Wood, J. M., Lilienfeld, S. O., Garb, H. N., & Nezworski, M. T. The Rorschach test in clinical diagnosis: A critical review, with a backward look at Garfield (1947). *Journal of Clinical Psychology, 56,* 395–430.

World Health Organization. (1977). *International classification of diseases* (9th revision). Geneva, Switzerland: Author.

Wu, K. D., Clark, L. A., & Watson, D. (2006). Relations between obsessive-compulsive disorder and personality: Beyond Axis I–Axis II comorbidity. *Journal of Anxiety Disorders, 20,* 695–717.

Zanarini, M. C., Frankenburg, F. R., Sickel, A. E., & Yong, L. (1996). *The diagnostic interview for DSM-IV personality disorders.* Belmont, MA: McLean Hospital.

Zanarini, M. C., Skodol, A. E., Bender, D., Dolan, R., Sanislow, C., Schaefer, E., et al. (2000). The Collaborative Longitudinal Personality Disorders Study: Reliability of Axis I and II diagnoses. *Journal of Personality Disorders, 14,* 291–299.

Zimmerman, M., Rothschild, L., & Chelminski, I. (2005). The prevalence of DSM-IV personality disorders in psychiatric outpatients. *American Journal of Psychiatry, 162,* 1911–1918.

13

Passive-Aggressive, Depressive, and Sadistic Personality Disorders

Leslie C. Morey
Texas A&M University

Christopher J. Hopwood
Texas A&M University

Daniel N. Klein
State University of New York at Stony Brook

T he problem of diagnostic coverage remains a matter of significant the-oretical and empirical debate as the mental health field approaches the fifth edition of the *Diagnostic and Statistical Manual of Mental Disorders* (DSM-V). The extensive use of the diagnosis "personality disorder not other-wise specified" (PDNOS) highlights the problem. Verheul and Widiger (2004) investigated the use of PDNOS. They found that, when structured interviews were used, PDNOS was the third most common personality disor-der (PD) diagnosis (after borderline and avoidant), and when unstructured interviews were used, it was the most common. They estimated the prevalence of PDNOS in clinical samples to be 8% to 13% and in PD samples to be 21% to 49%. One reason for the widespread prevalence of PDNOS is that indi-viduals may meet a variety of symptoms from various Axis II diagnoses but not enough symptoms from any single disorder to achieve diagnosis

(American Psychiatric Association [APA], 1994). This problem may be relieved by the use of noncategorical diagnoses (e.g., dimensions or prototypes) that do not require a specific number of symptoms for clinical significance.

Another reason for the high prevalence of PDNOS may be that individuals meet diagnostic criteria for PDs not included in the manual (APA, 1994). This chapter discusses three PDs that have previously been considered potential Axis II diagnoses and for which diagnostic criteria have been systematically constructed: passive-aggressive (PAPD), depressive (DPD), and sadistic (SPD). PAPD and DPD are listed in the Appendix of DSM-IV-TR (APA, 2000). Although SPD is not currently listed in the Appendix, it was mentioned in the Appendix of DSM-III, and its inclusion in Axis II remains a matter of debate.

Passive-Aggressive Personality Disorder

History and Etiology

PAPD was introduced into the psychiatric nomenclature by the American military to describe individuals who expressed opposition to authority in an indirect manner (Millon & Radanov, 1995). However, the syndrome appeared earlier in psychoanalytic discussions of the oral sadistic character, which results from a fixation at the oral biting stage (Millon & Radanov, 1995). Several contemporary theories have posited specific hypotheses about the etiology of and effective treatment strategies for PAPD.

A variety of etiologic models have been offered. Benjamin (1993) viewed PAPD as the result of a dramatic change in interpersonal development. In her view, the disorder is a result of parents who nurtured normally during infancy and then replaced their affection with unreasonable demands and harsh punishment later in the child's development. As a result, individuals diagnosed with PAPD are proposed to be power sensitive: they may see authority figures as unfair, neglecting, demanding, and cruel. PAPD individuals thereby learn to use an initial strategy of compliance and a secondary strategy of covert defiance. Pretzer and Beck (1996) viewed PAPD as resulting from a view of self as self-sufficient and vulnerable to control combined with a view of others as intrusive, demanding, interfering, controlling, and dominating. The primary dysfunctional beliefs of PAPD individuals, according to this cognitive theory, involve fear of interference by others, the idea that control by others is intolerable, and the necessity of doing things without others' help. Another potential cognitive (though not necessarily causal) mechanism of PAPD was offered by Lilienfeld and Penna (2001), who found that individuals diagnosed with PAPD appear to be particularly anxiety sensitive, or to harbor beliefs that anxiety beliefs have adverse consequences. The main strategies employed by PAPD individuals include passive resistance, surface submissiveness, and evasion of rules.

Millon (Millon & Davis, 1996; Millon & Radanov, 1995) eschewed the term "passive-aggressive" in favor of "negativistic PD" to reflect the widening of diagnostic/syndromal coverage consistent with his view. His view is that, whereas the term *passive-aggressive* denotes a discrete interpersonal strategy, *negativistic personality* connotes a personality style. Millon's polarity model posits that an individual's adaptive strategies (i.e., personality) can be efficiently described by three polarities: activity versus passivity in procuring reinforcement, motivation to enhance pleasure versus decrease pain, and self versus others as determinants of behavior. In his polarity model, negativistic PD reflects weakness on the pleasure seeking dimension, strength on the activity dimension, and conflict on the self/other dimension. According to Millon's formulation, negativistic individuals cannot decide whether they want to behave in order to increase personal or other satisfaction, and therefore engage in what appear to others as unpredictable, self-defeating behaviors.

PAPD was a part of the first, second, and third editions of the DSM (APA, 1952, 1968, 1980) but was moved to the Appendix in the fourth edition (APA, 1994). One reason for its removal from Axis II was a lack of clarity about the coverage of the syndrome. Passive-aggressive behavior itself refers to a single symptom, namely, passive resistance to a direct command or request. Some have agreed with Millon that this symptom is best understood in the context of syndromal correlates. In contrast, Wetzler and Morey (1999) noted that by most empirical criteria, the diagnostic validity of PAPD was similar to that of most other personality disorders that were retained in DSM-IV. However, researchers remain concerned about the overlap of the diagnosis with other PDs, the psychometric characteristics of measures of PAPD, and a paucity of data on the proposed syndrome.

Diagnosis: Prevalence, Reliability, and Clinical Utility

Prevalence estimates have not been consistent, partly due to variability in measurement methods. Nevertheless, studies have generally indicated that PAPD is no less prevalent than several PDs that remain on Axis II (e.g., Widiger & Rogers, 1989). Black, Goldstein, and Mason (1992) obtained a 10.5% prevalence rate for DSM-III PAPD in a community sample, making it the most prevalent personality disorder by a comfortable margin. Zimmerman and Coryell (1989) also found PAPD to be the most common PD diagnosis in a nonpatient sample. However, other community studies have reported prevalence rates of less than 1% (Lenzenweger, Loranger, Korfine, & Neff, 1997; Samuels, Nestadt, Romanoski, Folstein, & McHugh, 1994). Passive-aggressive features may be particularly common in younger individuals. For example, Grilo et al. (1998) assessed DSM-III-R PDs in a sample of 255 adolescent and young adult inpatients. Overall, 64% of adolescents and 66% of adults were diagnosed with a PD, and PAPD was diagnosed for 20% of adolescents and 9% of adults, a significant age difference. Burket and Myers

(1995) found that PAPD was the most prevalent PD (56%) in a small sample of adolescents diagnosed with conduct disorder using a structured interview to assess PDs. There is also empirical support for the validity of the concept in this age group. For example, Johnson et al. (2000) collected data from 717 adolescents and prospectively assessed violent behavior. After controlling for parental psychopathology and socioeconomic status, age, sex, and other psychopathology, PAPD was one of only three personality disorders (the others being paranoid and narcissistic) associated with risk for violent acts and criminal behavior during adolescence and early adulthood. These authors also noted the similarity of several factors associated with both PDs and violent behavior, including emotion dysregulation, deficiencies in social cognition, frustration, and anger, although their data could not establish the role of these factors in the relation they found and they did not speak to the specific relation of these factors with PAPD.

A number of studies of the gender distribution of passive-aggressive PD have yielded equivocal results. The genesis of the concept lies in the largely male military population, and it has typically been assumed that the majority of passive-aggressive patients are men (Rosenberg, 1987). However, empirical results have been mixed, with gender distribution estimates ranging from 3:1 male (Spitzer, Williams, Kass, & Davies, 1989) to 3:1 female (Maier, Lichtermann, Klinger, Heun, & Hallmayer, 1992).

Prior to the introduction of revisions to the concept in DSM-IV, a number of diagnostic instruments provided for the assessment of PAPD. In general, the reliability estimates were satisfactory and comparable with, if not better than, those for other personality disorders. For example, Zanarini, Frankenburg, Chauncey, and Gunderson (1987) obtained a kappa of .95 for PAPD diagnoses from the Diagnostic Interview for Personality Disorders (DIDP; Zanarini et al., 1987). Using this same instrument in a different sample, this group identified an interrater reliability of .90 and a test-retest reliability of .80 for the PAPD criteria over a 7- to 10-day interval (Zanarini & Frankenberg, 2001). Interrater reliability estimates from the Structured Clinical Interview for DSM-IV Axis II Personality Disorders: Version 2.0 (SCID-II 2.0; First, Spitzer, Gibbon, & Williams, 1994) tend to be more variable, with estimates ranging from .50 (Brooks, Baltazar, McDowell, & Munjack, 1991) and .66 (Arntz, Van Beijsterveldt, Hoekstra, & Hofman, 1992) up to .92 (Fossati et al., 2000). In addition to these interviews, a variety of self-report methods have been developed for the assessment of PAPD, the most widely used being the Personality Diagnostic Questionnaire (PDQ; Hyler, 1994), the Minnesota Multiphasic Personality Inventory (MMPI; Morey, Waugh, & Blashfield, 1985), and the Millon Clinical Multiaxial Inventory (MCMI; e.g., Millon, 1987). The PDQ scale for PAPD tends to have relatively lower internal consistency (Cronbach's alpha estimates ranging from .49 to .66; Trull, Goodwin, Schopp, & Hillenbrand, 1993; Hyler et al., 1989; Wilberg, Dammen, & Friis, 2000) than the other two instruments, which is not surprising, given its relative brevity. For example, internal consistency estimates for the MMPI PAPD scale range from .64 to .74 (Morey et al., 1985; Trull et al., 1993), and for the MCMI, alphas as high as .83 have been reported (Sinha & Watson, 2001). With respect to test-retest reliability, the MMPI PAPD scale appears to be somewhat more stable than its counterparts, with values of .73 to .76 (Hurt, Clarkin, & Morey, 1990; Trull et al., 1993) comparing favorably with values in the .61 to .67 range for the PDQ (Trull et al., 1993) and MCMI (Overholser, 1990). Interestingly, among the different self-report instruments, the PAPD scales tend to demonstrate greater convergence than do those for any other PD (Sinha & Watson, 2001).

There is relatively little research providing a direct comparison of the PAPD diagnosis with its DSM-IV counterpart, negativistic PD. Sprock and Hunsucker (1998) asked Ph.D. psychologists from a variety of theoretical orientations to describe a patient they had seen who was a good example of PAPD in terms of PAPD (DSM-III-R) and negativistic PD (DSM-IV) criteria. Participants rated the typicality of the symptoms from DSM-III-R and DSM-IV Axes I and II. An intraclass correlation of .62 among clinicians was observed across all PAPD/negativistic PD ratings, signifying reasonable agreement among clinicians regarding which symptoms were most proto-typical. The mean prototypicality rating was higher for the symptoms taken from DSM-III-R than for the negativistic symptoms taken from DSM-IV.

External Correlates

PAPD has demonstrated important correlational patterns with various clin-ically relevant constructs, including suicidality, authority conflicts, criminal behavior, and other PDs. Joiner and Rudd (2002) assessed Axis I and II psy-chopathology with the MCMI (Millon, 1983) in 250 individuals referred for severe suicidality in a military setting. Passive-aggressive symptoms displayed unique (i.e., effects of other PDs partialed out) associations with eight out of 11 Axis I scales, more than did any other PD. In addition, PAPD was the only PD to be uniquely associated with hopelessness, as assessed by the Beck Hopelessness Scale (Beck, Weissman, Lester, & Trexler, 1974), and with sui-cidality, as assessed by the Suicidal Probability Scale (Cull & Gill, 1989).

In keeping with the origins of the diagnosis, Vereycken, Vertommen, and Corveleyn (2002) used the MCMI (Millon, 1983) to assess PDs in a sample of 108 military patients referred by clinicians due to authority conflicts. They observed a PAPD prevalence of 42%, and it was the only PD significantly related to the chronicity of authority conflicts. In addition, overlap of PAPD with other PDs (41%) was not significantly different from the overlap between other diagnoses (48%). However, the authors expressed concern about how findings might relate to the specific conceptualization offered by Millon and presumably measured by the MCMI. Specifically, Millon viewed PAPD as a personality style characterized by active ambivalence in procuring reinforcement, as PAPD individuals are thought to vacillate between taking autonomy and accepting authority. Thus, results may not generalize to narrower conceptions of the disorder, such as that of the DSM.

Although PAPD is not unique within Axis II in that it tends to covary with other PDs, some studies have suggested that the covariance patterns are not systematic. In other words, PAPD does not appear to fit neatly into a cluster, although it was considered a Cluster C disorder in DSM-III-R. This pattern has been taken to indicate that PAPD is best considered a situational response in the context of other or nonspecific personality pathology rather than a distinct disorder (Baerg, 1995; Widiger et al., 1990). However, there are a number of studies indicating that PAPD may be more "aggressive" than it is "passive." For example, Vereycken et al. (2002) found that PAPD individuals displayed considerable externalizing behaviors in relation to authority figures, while Morey (1988) found that the PAPD criteria grouped most closely with the more externalizing disorders, such as antisocial and narcissistic, rather than the Cluster C "anxious/fearful" disorders. Similarly, Fossati et al. (2000) reported a strong and specific relationship between DSM-IV conceptions of PAPD and narcissistic PD in their sample, and they suggested that PAPD may be more appropriately thought of as a subtype of narcissistic PD.

Future Directions

The demonstration of conceptual and empirical relations between PAPD and oppositional defiance suggests a developmental process and may offer a clue to the etiology of PAPD (Millon & Davis, 1996). Interpersonal and cognitive mechanisms have been offered as additional areas worthy of investigation. Measures of PAPD demonstrate psychometric strengths and weaknesses comparable with those of other PDs and are commonly considered clinically useful (Wetzler & Morey, 1999). However, research suggesting empirical validity and clinical utility of the diagnosis will probably be necessary for inclusion of the disorder in Axis II to occur. Major areas of suggested future work include:

• *Diagnostic Coverage.* Although passive-aggressive behavior itself is typically thought of as a single symptom, it has been argued that PAPD represents a syndrome with a variety of manifestations. This view, supported in particular by Millon (e.g., Millon & Davis, 1996, is controversial. This conceptual ambiguity was probably instrumental in the exclusion of the disorder from DSM-IV. Additional research on the validity of PAPD as a syndrome and on the relation between syndromal and symptomatic conceptions of PAPD is clearly needed for the construction of a PAPD criteria set amenable to DSM-V. For example, Sprock and Hunsucker (1998) suggested that negativistic PD, as proposed by Millon, may be better suited to a female prototype, which tends to be more diagnostically heterogeneous, whereas PAPD is more suited to a male prototype.

- *External Correlates.* Every candidate disorder benefits from evidence that it predicts phenomena that are clinically important. Disorders in the Appendices of the DSM presumably suffer from decreased scientific attention, and PAPD has not been an exception. However, some of the research reviewed in this chapter has demonstrated the reliability and external validity of PAPD in both its symptomatic and syndromal forms. Similar work may justify the inclusion of PAPD in future versions of the DSM. The relation between PAPD and other PDs is also an important area of future research, particularly the extent to which PAPD fills a gap in the current diagnostic coverage of personality disorders. Given the problem of Axis II diagnostic overlap, the discriminant validity of PAPD must be closely examined before it can be considered a separable clinical disorder.

- *Treatment Response.* All PDs currently suffer from a limited understanding of treatment responsiveness. Specific treatment strategies for PAPD have been suggested, but these treatments remain largely untested. For example, Benjamin (1993) suggested that PAPD requires a nondirective approach in which the therapist expects provocation and is able to relate it to generalized interpersonal patterns. She stated that "the NEG [PAPD] will not look at his or her patterns until the agenda—suffering to prove the therapist abusive or incompetent—has been at least temporarily set aside" (p. 289). When this interpersonal issue is resolved, directive techniques such as assertiveness training can perhaps be implemented to initiate the generalization and habituation of effective interpersonal behaviors. Alternatively, Pretzer and Beck (1996) proposed a therapeutic approach derived from cognitive theories that involves addressing the potential for core relationship issues by framing the treatment collaboratively and directly addressing the dysfunctional beliefs that they believe to be central to PAPD (whether interpersonal or related to internal experience). Empirical evaluation of these treatment strategies (and development of new approaches) would be of benefit to clinicians treating PAPD, and it might also clarify some of the diagnostic issues already discussed.

Sadistic Personality Disorder

History and Etiology

Krafft-Ebing (1898) first used the term "sadism" to describe the desire to inflict pain upon a sexual object. Psychodynamic drive theories have hypothesized sadism to be a natural element of the male's sex drive (Freud, 1915/1957), whereas relational theories have tended to view it as a defense against object loss (e.g., Avery, 1977). The most common contemporary view of sadism, supported by some empirical evidence, is that there is a descriptive (and presumably etiologic) difference between generalized sadistic behavior and sexual sadism (Fiester & Gay, 1995), in that sexual sadism is pleasure derived from others' suffering that is restricted to sexual behavior. In keeping with this broader concept, Kernberg (1984) posited the concept of malignant narcissism to describe patients who, during a treatment aimed at the destruction of a grandiose self-structure, engage in treatment-threatening behaviors, and this concept appears to share features with SPD. Little has been done to test these formulations empirically, and very little has been done by theorists of other approaches to delineate an etiologic formulation for the disorder.

In DSM-III-R, SPD represented a pervasive pattern of cruel, demeaning, and aggressive behavior indicated by an individual's meeting four of eight possible symptoms: cruelty or violence for the purpose of establishing relational dominance, humiliation of others, harsh treatment of someone under the individual's control, amusement with the suffering of others, deception for the purpose of harming others, use of intimidation to coerce others, restriction of the autonomy of relational partners, and fascination with violent themes. In addition, these symptoms had to occur across more than one relationship and not for the sole purpose of sexual arousal.

Diagnosis: Prevalence, Reliability, and Clinical Utility

Sadistic personality disorder, representing a pattern of sadistic behavior across multiple domains, grew out of the literature preceding the advent of DSM-III-R (APA, 1987) and was included in its Appendix. SPD was subsequently excluded from Appendix B in DSM-IV (APA, 1994) due to a lack of empirical evidence supporting the diagnosis. Nevertheless, its status as a valid diagnosis continues to be a matter of empirical, ethical, and theoretical discussion (e.g., Kaminer & Stein, 2001).

Supporters of the construct have often come from forensic settings, where related behaviors would be expected to be more common. These authors feel that SPD is a concept that adds useful diagnostic information to antisocial personality disorder (Fiester & Gay, 1995). The disorder indeed appears to be more common in such settings; for example, a 13.2% prevalence estimate was obtained in a general forensic setting (Timmerman & Emmelkamp, 2001), and a 27.2% estimate was reported in a sample of sex offenders (Berger, Berner, Bolterauer, Gutierrez, & Berger, 1999). Gay (1989) diagnosed 12 of 235 adults (5.1%) accused of child abuse and referred by the court for custody evaluations with SPD according to DSM-III criteria. Spitzer, Fiester, Gay, and Pfohl (1991) reported that 2.5% of all cases seen by forensic psychiatrists over the course of a year met the diagnosis. By comparison, Reich (1993) reported an 8.1% prevalence of SPD in outpatient sample.

The gender distribution of SPD was described in DSM-III-R as "far more common" in men. The disorder appears to have perhaps the most asymmetrical gender distribution of any personality disorder, with some studies reporting prevalence in males in the sample to be as high as 98% (Spitzer et al., 1991) or even 100% (Frieman & Widiger, 1989). Sprock, Blashfield, and Smith (1990) asked 49 undergraduates unfamiliar with the DSM-III-R to rank Axis II criteria (including those for self-defeating and sadistic PDs) along a gender dimension. SPD was seen as the most prototypically male, followed by antisocial and schizoid PDs, and all SPD criteria were considered more prototypically male than female by both men and women raters. Fiester and Gay (1995) note that such data raise concerns regarding sex bias and invalid labeling, although this issue has not been addressed empirically.

Reliability data for the diagnosis are relatively sparse. Fiester and Gay (1995) cited an unpublished report by Frieman and Widiger (1989), who found an interrater reliability estimate of .85 for SPD. A more recent study by Zanarini and Frankenberg (2001), using the DIPD structured interview, reported an interrater reliability of 0.86 for the SPD criteria but a test-retest estimate of only 0.42 over a 7- to 10-day interval. Internal consistency of the DSM-III-R criteria appeared to be satisfactory; moderate to high sensitivity (.65–.94) and specificity (.93–.99) estimates in the prediction of the diagnosis were found across SPD criteria by Spitzer et al. (1991), although Fuller, Blashfield, Miller, and Hester (1992) obtained somewhat lower values. Cacciola, Rutherford, Alterman, McKay, and Mulvaney (1998) obtained a kappa of .47 in a sample of opiate-dependent patients, which was higher than that of any PD with the exception of antisocial personality disorder (APD), and demonstrated 95.73% exact agreement in the diagnosis over a 2-year interval.

The discriminant validity of SPD, particularly with respect to other personality disorders, has been a consistent concern. SPD was found to overlap significantly with avoidant, borderline, antisocial, and paranoid PDs in a clinical sample (Berger, 1991). In Reich's (1993) outpatient sample, at least half of the SPD sample were also diagnosed with paranoid PD, antisocial PD, or both. In their study of sex offenders, Berger et al. (1999) reported substantial comorbidity with antisocial and borderline personality diagnoses, noting that in only four of 19 cases was SPD the only diagnosis received. These authors concluded that their results did not support viewing SPD as a discrete disorder, but rather supported consideration of it as a subtype of ASPD. In contrast, in the Gay (1989) study of child abusers, of the 12 diagnosed with SPD, 10 did not meet criteria for any other PD and only one met criteria for antisocial PD.

With respect to clinical utility, Spitzer et al. (1991) reported that 76% of forensic psychiatrists found the SPD diagnosis useful because it denotes features not found in APD alone. Also, clinicians appear to be proficient at matching the SPD diagnosis to a prototypical case history (Blashfield & Breen, 1989). However, critics of the diagnosis have raised various legal and ethical concerns. For example, some have argued that the diagnosis might be used by lawbreakers as an insanity defense to mitigate penalties, and a survey conducted by Spitzer et al. (1991) indicated that a majority of forensic mental health professionals believe this would be a concern if the diagnosis were included in Axis II. However, the same study indicated that only 1%

were familiar with a case of legal misuse of SPD. It has also been suggested that proponents of self-defeating PD promoted SPD, a predominantly male disorder (Fiester & Gay, 1995; Sprock, Blashfield, & Smith, 1990), to neutralize criticism that their proposed disorder unfairly targeted women (see Widger, 1995). Others have expressed concern that the term could become a stigmatizing label. Most of these concerns do not appear to be shared by a majority of forensic psychologists (Spitzer et al., 1991).

External Correlates

Relatively little is known about clinical correlates of SPD beyond Axis I comorbidity. Reich's (1993) sample of SPD outpatients were commonly comorbid for major depressive disorder, alcohol use disorders, panic disorder, and posttraumatic stress disorder. Berger et al. (1999) found that SPD patients had an alcohol or substance use disorder in 31.6% of cases, and that SPD patients were more likely than non-SPD patients to meet diagnostic criteria for Axis I sexual sadism and to report sadistic fantasies during intercourse or masturbation.

Holt, Meloy, and Strack (1999) used the Psychopathy Checklist—Revised (Hare, 1991) to classify 41 prison inmates as psychopathic or nonpsychopathic and as violent or sexually violent. They measured sadistic personality and behavior with the Millon Clinical Multiaxial Inventory–II (MCMI-II; Millon, 1987), the Personality Disorder Examination (PDE, Loranger, Susman, Oldham, & Russakof, 1988), and the sexual sadism criteria from DSM-IV. PDE and MCMI-II ratings of sadistic traits were higher in the psychopathic samples than they were in the nonpsychopathic samples, but the construct did not differentiate between violent and sexually violent groups. These findings support the relation between SPD and psychopathy and highlight the distinction between sadistic personality and sadism as a paraphilia.

SPD is thought to be associated with a history of early abuse. Gay (1989) found that, in a sample of SPD individuals, 75% reported a history of physical abuse, 42% a history of emotional abuse, 16% a history of sexual abuse, and 8% a history of neglect. Forensic mental health professionals reported similar rates for their patients (Spitzer et al., 1991). Reich (1993) used logistic regression analyses to differentiate SPD from antisocial, Axis I, and nonclinical controls based on Axis II pathology in the family history. He found that SPD individuals were significantly more likely than those from any other group to have family members diagnosed with a PD from Cluster C and also significantly more likely than those with antisocial PD to have a family member diagnosed with a PD from Cluster A. These findings indicate that environmental factors play an important role in the development of a sadistic personality, and they suggest an increased probability that SPD individuals suffered abuse and neglect during development, as would be anticipated if their caregivers had PDs.

Future Directions

One presumable advantage of including a diagnostic label in the DSM is that it would catalyze research on the construct. This did not appear to happen with SPD during the tenure of DSM-III-R, and its exclusion from DSM-IV further dampened research interest. As a result, the status of the validity of SPD remains unclear. Based on limited evidence, it appears that SPD can be reliably diagnosed and is as prevalent as some other PDs, particularly in forensic samples (Fiester & Gay, 1995). However, several issues remain unresolved.

• *Relation to APD.* Data in which SPD criteria are shown to be diagnostically distinct from antisocial PD criteria or in which SPD is shown to predict external correlates above and beyond the other PDs, particularly APD, is necessary before SPD is likely to be reconsidered for inclusion in the DSM. Considering SPD a subtype of APD, based on a recognition that SPD shares important characteristics with antisocial PD but that the diagnoses are, at times, usefully distinguished (Benjamin, 1993; Fiester & Gay, 1995; Kernberg, 1984), may maintain the distinction between the constructs without requiring an additional diagnosis.

• *Legal, Moral, and Ethical issues.* The debate regarding the diagnosis represents an interface of scientific, mental health, and legal domains. As such, a dialogue between representatives of these professions will be necessary in the future delineation of the disorder as well as its role and application in society. Sociologic studies (e.g., Spitzer et al., 1991) have the potential to accurately inform the field about the relative prevalence and utility of various assumptions within and across disciplines, and they can usefully supplement data regarding the reliability and validity of the diagnosis.

• *Psychometric Data.* Despite our suggestion of the importance of untestable ethical and moral issues, we are largely in agreement with Widiger (1995): "What the authors of DSM-V will need to reach a fully informed decision will be objective and dispassionate research that is focused directly on the key issues, such as the clinical utility and validity of a diagnosis . . . of SPD to perpetrators of abuse" (p. 369). Until more data demonstrating the clinical importance of SPD emerge from the literature, it is unlikely that SPD will be formally included in Axis II.

Depressive Personality Disorder

History and Etiology

DSM-I and DSM-II included a category for cyclothymic (or affective) personality, which could assume hypomanic, depressive, or alternating forms. In DSM-III and DSM-III-R, the construct of depressive personality disorder was subsumed under the rubric of dysthymic disorder. However, as discussed later, there are conceptual and empirical differences between dysthymic disorder and DPD (Klein, 1990; Phillips, Gunderson, Hirschfeld, & Smith, 1990). Hence, DSM-IV included DPD in the Appendix as a separate condition requiring further study.

Until the 1960s, most of the interest in DPD was limited to the German phenomenological literature (e.g., Kraepelin, 1921; Schneider, 1958). Kraepelin described individuals with "depressive temperament" as gloomy, lacking self-confidence, self-reproachful, ruminative, introverted, and lacking in vitality and initiative. He believed that the depressive temperament was heritable and one of the "fundamental states" underlying the major mood disorders. Schneider described DPD in similar terms but rejected the idea of a biogenetic link between DPD and the major mood disorders.

In the 1960s through the 1980s, a number of psychoanalytic investigators made important contributions to the literature on DPD (e.g., Bemporad, 1976; Laughlin, 1967). For example, Kernberg (1988) proposed the construct of "depressive-masochistic character disorder," which is characterized by an excessively punitive superego, difficulty expressing aggression, and overdependence on others. Many of these authors emphasized the role of disturbances in early relationships in the development of DPD.

Diagnosis: Prevalence, Reliability, and Clinical Utility

In addition to the DSM-IV, there are two other sets of diagnostic criteria for DPD. Akiskal (1983) developed criteria based on Schneider's (1958) descriptive work, and Gunderson, Phillips, Triebwasser, and Hirschfeld (1994) developed criteria that encompassed the work of both the phenomenological and psychoanalytic literatures. The three criteria sets overlap substantially but vary somewhat in content and breadth. Hirschfeld and Holzer (1994) found that DSM-IV's criteria were the most inclusive, Gunderson et al.'s criteria were intermediate, and Akiskal's criteria were the narrowest.

The DSM-IV criteria for DPD have good internal consistency (McDermut, Zimmerman, & Chelminski, 2003). The interrater reliability of DPD diagnoses, assessed with both paired rater and independent rater designs, is adequate to good (Gunderson et al., 1994; Klein, 1990; Klein & Miller, 1993; Markowitz et al., in press; McDermut et al., 2003; Zanarini et al., 2000).

A number of measures are available to assess DPD. Several semistructured diagnostic interviews that assess the full range of Axis II disorders include the DSM-IV criteria for DPD (First et al., 1994; Pfohl, Blum, & Zimmerman, 1997; Zanarini et al., 2000). Gunderson et al. (1994) developed a comprehensive semistructured interview, the Diagnostic Interview for Depressive Personality (DIDP), to assess most of the traits associated with DPD in the descriptive and psychoanalytic literatures. This interview consists of 30 traits in four general areas: depressive/negativistic, introverted/tense, unassertive/passive, and masochistic. Finally, Huprich, Margrett, Barthelemy, and Fine (1996) developed a 41-item self-report measure: the Depressive Personality Disorder Inventory (DPDI). Several studies have provided support for the internal consistency and convergent and discriminant validity of the DPDI in clinical and nonclinical samples (Huprich et al., 1996; Huprich, Sanford, & Smith, 2002). As is the case for other personality disorders, there is only a modest correspondence among different measures of DPD (Huprich, 2004).

No data on the prevalence of DPD in the general population are available. Several studies have reported that the prevalence of DPD in outpatient samples ranges from 22% to 26% (Klein, 1990; McDermut et al., 2003). There do not appear to be consistent differences between persons with and without DPD regarding sex, race, education, or socioeconomic status (Hirschfeld & Holzer, 1994; Klein, 1990; Klein & Miller, 1993; Markowitz et al., in press; McDermut, Zimmerman, & Chelminski, 2003; Phillips et al., 1998). The lack of consistent sex differences is noteworthy in light of the higher rates of major depressive and dysthymic disorder in women.

Data on the clinical utility of DPD are limited. However, in a survey of clinicians, Westen (1997) found that 35% reported currently treating one or more patients with characterological forms of depression that did not meet criteria for any existing (i.e., non-Appendix) Axis I or II disorder. Moreover, 77% of clinicians reported currently treating one or more patients with DPD; the only Axis II condition with a higher frequency was borderline personality disorder.

External Correlates

Relationship to Axis I Mood and Axis II Disorders. There has been a great deal of controversy regarding the overlap between DPD and the mood disorders, particularly dysthymic disorder (Ryder, Bagby, & Schuller, 2002). The two conditions have a common heritage and a number of common clinical features and are presumed to have a stable, chronic course. However, they also differ in important respects. The DSM-IV criteria for dysthymic disorder require persistent depressed mood, and several vegetative symptoms are included in the list of associated symptoms. In contrast, DPD is defined in terms of personality traits or dispositions, often of a cognitive nature.

A number of researchers have examined the relationship between DPD and mood disorders using a variety of subject populations and criteria for DPD (Hirschfeld & Holzer, 1994; Klein, 1990; Klein & Miller, 1993; Klein & Shih, 1998; Markowitz et al., in press; McDermut et al., 2003; Phillips et al., 1998). Most found a significant association between DPD and dysthymia. However, the magnitude of the associations is quite modest, with fewer than half of individuals with DPD meeting criteria for dysthymic disorder and less than half of individuals with dysthymic disorder meeting criteria for DPD. Several studies have also documented significant associations between DPD and a number of Axis II disorders (Klein & Shih, 1998; Markowitz et al., in press; McDermut et al., 2003; Phillips et al., 1998). The two most commonly co-occurring personality disorders in subjects with DPD are avoidant and borderline personality. However, the magnitude of the associations between DPD and the existing Axis II disorders is modest, and DPD does not appear to be redundant with any of the other personality disorders.

Personality Dimensions. Several studies have also examined the relationship between DPD and dimensions of normal personality. They provide information on the convergent validity of DPD and may be useful in elaborating the meaning of the construct. These studies indicate that persons with DPD have significantly higher levels of neuroticism/negative affectivity and significantly lower levels of extraversion/positive affectivity than controls, but do not differ on measures of constraint versus impulsivity (Klein, 1990; Klein & Shih, 1998; Lyoo, Gunderson, & Phillips, 1998; Markowitz et al., in press).

Family History. One of the oldest controversies regarding DPD is whether it is a genetically influenced temperamental variant of the major mood disorders (Kraepelin, 1921) or the extreme end of a dimension of normal personality that is unrelated to the major mood disorders (Schneider, 1958). There are no genetically informative (i.e., twin or adoption) studies of DPD. However, there have been four family history studies in which probands with and without DPD were interviewed regarding lifetime Axis I disorders in their first-degree relatives (Cassano, Akiskal, Perugi, Musetti, & Savino, 1992; Klein, 1990; Klein & Miller, 1993; McDermut et al., 2003), and two family studies in which the offspring or first-degree relatives of patients with mood disorders and controls were assessed for DPD (Klein, 1999; Klein, Clark, Dansky, & Margolis, 1988).

The family history studies have consistently found an increased rate of mood disorders in the relatives of probands with DPD. Importantly, several of these studies have reported that the rate of mood disorders in relatives was elevated even in the subgroup of DPD probands with no lifetime history of mood disorder, indicating that the findings were not attributable to comorbid mood disorders in the probands (Klein & Miller, 1993; McDermut et al., 2003). The two family studies both reported that the relatives of patients with mood disorders had higher rates of DPD than the relatives of controls. Interestingly, both studies found that the rate of DPD was particularly elevated in relatives of patients with *chronic* depressive disorders. Taken together, these data are consistent with the idea that there is a spectrum of mood disorders ranging from DPD to dysthymic disorder and at least some forms of major depressive disorder, all of which share a common familial liability (Akiskal, 1989, but see McDermut et al., 2003, for a discussion of evidence that is inconsistent with a simple spectrum model).

Early Adversity. Psychoanalytic perspectives on DPD have emphasized the role of object loss and the early environment. Unfortunately, data on this topic are limited. Huprich (2001) reported that college students with threshold or subthreshold DPD reported greater early object loss in responding to the Thematic Apperception Test (TAT; Murray, 1943) than did students without DPD but with depressive or dysthymic features, and that DPD was associated with interpersonal loss measured via self-report to a greater extent than depressive or dysthymic diagnoses (Huprich, 2001).

Stability and Course. A key assumption regarding the construct of depressive personality is that it is relatively stable over time. Two prospective studies have addressed this issue. In a 2-year follow-up of a large sample of persons with personality disorders and/or major depressive disorder, Markowitz et al. (in press) found that kappa for the association between baseline and follow-up diagnoses (i.e., stability) of DPD was .29 (.47 after correcting for imperfect interrater reliability). The intraclass correlation between DPD dimensional scores at baseline and at follow-up was .41 (.57 after adjusting for unreliability). Laptook, Klein, and Dougherty (2005) assessed DPD at 30-month intervals for 10 years in a sample of outpatients with major depressive disorder, dysthymic disorder, or both. Kappas for the association between DPD diagnoses at baseline and at the 5- and 10-year assessments were .46 and .30, respectively (.64 and .42, respectively, after correcting for unreliability). The intraclass correlation for DPD dimensional scores across all five assessments was .57. These data indicate that DPD is only moderately stable over time. However, the level of stability in these studies is comparable to the stability of most other personality disorder diagnoses (McDavid & Pilkonis, 1996).

Kraepelin (1921) and contemporary theorists such as Akiskal (1989) have hypothesized that DPD is associated with an increased risk for developing mood disorders. Kwon et al. (2000) provided support for this view. In a 3-year longitudinal study of young women with DPD and no comorbid Axis I and II disorders and young women with no history of psychopathology, the DPD group exhibited a significantly greater risk of developing dysthymic disorder. Interestingly, DPD did not predict an increased rate of major depressive disorder, which is consistent with family study data suggesting that DPD is more closely related to chronic mood disorders than it is to episodic mood disorders (Klein, 1999; Klein et al., 1988).

Prognostic and Treatment Implications. We are unaware of any clinical trials of the treatment of DPD. However, DPD appears to have prognostic implications for treatment response and course in Axis I depressive disorders. In a 15-week clinical trial of treatment for major depressive disorder, Shahar, Blatt, Zuroff, and Pilkonis (2003) found that after controlling for other Axis II traits, DPD traits predicted a significantly lower level of improvement in depressive symptoms. Similarly, in a 2-year follow-up study of a large sample with major depressive disorder, Markowitz et al. (in press) reported that a baseline diagnosis of DPD was associated with a significantly lower rate of remission from the index major depressive episode. Finally, in a 10-year naturalistic follow-up of outpatients with dysthymic disorder, Laptook et al. (2005) found that a baseline diagnosis of DPD predicted a significantly slower rate of improvement in depressive symptoms.

Future Directions

• The data indicate that, as currently defined, DPD and dysthymic disorder are related but distinct constructs. Nonetheless, there continues to be controversy regarding whether they are sufficiently distinct categories to both be included in the DSM-V. To inform this decision, it will be important to explore whether it is possible to make minor revisions in the criteria for dysthymic disorder, such as allowing loss of interest or pleasure to substitute for depressed mood (as it does in major depressive disorder) or eliminating vegetative symptoms (as in the alternative criteria for dysthymic disorder in the DSM-IV Appendix), that would incorporate DPD without diminishing the validity of dysthymic disorder. If these efforts failed, it would strengthen the argument for including DPD as a separate diagnostic category.

• Another major consideration in determining the status of DPD in DSM-V is its clinical utility. There is some evidence that clinicians perceive a need for a DPD category and that it has prognostic implications, but further research on clinical utility is needed.

• Most research on DPD has focused on nosological issues. At this point, it is important to expand the focus to the epidemiology, etiology, and pathogenesis of DPD. A critical aspect of this work should include exploring how DPD is similar to and different from the Axis I mood disorders.

• Finally, there has been a conspicuous lack of research on the treatment of DPD. There is a need to develop treatments that are specifically targeted for DPD, adapt existing treatments for depression and personality disorders for use with DPD, and conduct clinical trials of psychosocial and pharmacological interventions.

References

Akiskal, H. S. (1983). Dysthymia: Psychopathology of proposed chronic depressive subtypes. *American Journal of Psychiatry, 140,* 11–20.

Akiskal, H. S. (1989). Validating affective personality types. In L. Robins & J. Barrett (Eds.), *The validity of psychiatric diagnosis* (pp. 217–227). New York: Raven Press.

American Psychiatric Association. (1952). *Diagnostic and statistical manual of mental disorders.* Washington, DC: Author.

American Psychiatric Association. (1968). *Diagnostic and statistical manual of mental disorders* (2nd ed.). Washington, DC: Author.

American Psychiatric Association. (1980). *Diagnostic and statistical manual of mental disorders* (3rd ed.). Washington, DC: Author.

American Psychiatric Association. (1987). *Diagnostic and statistical manual of mental disorders* (3rd ed., revised). Washington, DC: Author.

American Psychiatric Association. (1994). *Diagnostic and statistical manual of mental disorders* (4th ed.). Washington, DC: Author.

American Psychiatric Association. (2000). *Diagnostic and statistical manual of mental disorders* (4th ed., text revision). Washington, DC: Author.

Arntz, A., Van Beijsterveldt, B., Hoekstra, R., & Hofman, A. (1992). The interrater reliability of a Dutch version of the Structured Clinical Interview for DSM-III-R Personality Disorders. *Acta Psychiatrica Scandinavica, 85,* 394–400.

Avery, N. (1977). Sadomasochism: A defense against object loss. *Psychoanalytic Review, 64,* 101–109.

Baerg, E. (1995). Commentary on passive-aggressive (negativistic) personality disorder. In W. J. Livesley (Ed.), *The DSM-IV personality disorders* (pp. 326–328). New York: Guilford Press.

Beck, A. T., Weissman, A., Lester, D., & Trexler, L. (1974). The measurement of pessimism: The Hopelessness Scale. *Journal of Consulting and Clinical Psychology, 42,* 861–865.

Bemporad, J. (1976). Psychotherapy of the depressive character. *Journal of the American Academy of Psychoanalysis, 4,* 347–372.

Benjamin, L. S. (1993). *Interpersonal diagnosis and treatment of personality disorders.* New York: Guilford Press.

Berger, P. (1991). [Prevalence of personality disorders in a clinical sample]. Unpublished raw data.

Berger, P., Berner, W., Bolterauer, J., Gutierrez, K., & Berger, K. (1999). Sadistic personality disorder in sex offenders: Relationship to antisocial personality disorder and sexual sadism. *Journal of Personality Disorders, 13*(2), 175–186.

Black, D. W., Goldstein, R. B., & Mason, E. E. (1992). Prevalence of mental disorder in 88 morbidly obese bariatric clinic patients. *American Journal of Psychiatry, 149,* 227–234.

Blashfield, R. K., & Breen, M. J. (1989). Face validity of the DSM-III-R personality disorders. *American Journal of Psychiatry, 146,* 1575–1579.

Brooks, R. B., Baltazar, P. L., McDowell, D. E., & Munjack, D. J. (1991). Personality disorders co-occurring with panic disorder with agoraphobia. *Journal of Personality Disorders, 5,* 328–336.

Burket, R. C., & Myers, W. C. (1995). Axis I and personality comorbidity in adolescents with conduct disorder. *Bulletin of the American Academy of Psychiatry & the Law, 23*(1), 73–82.

Cacciola, J. S., Rutherford, M. J., Alterman, A. I., McKay, J. R., & Mulvaney, F. D. (1998). Long-term test-retest reliability of personality disorder diagnoses in opiate dependent patients. *Journal of Personality Disorders, 12*(4), 332–337.

Cassano, G. B., Akiskal, H. S., Perugi, G., Musetti, L., & Savino, M. (1992). The importance of measures of affective temperaments in genetic studies of mood disorders. *Journal of Psychiatric Research, 26,* 257–268.

Cull, J., & Gill, W. (1989). *The Suicide Probability Scale manual.* Los Angeles: Western Psychological Services.

Fiester, S. J., & Gay, M. (1995). Sadistic personality disorder. In W. J. Livesley (Ed.), *The DSM-IV personality disorders.* (pp. 329–340). New York: Guilford Press.

First, M. B., Spitzer, R. L., Gibbon, M., & Williams, J. B. W. (1994). *Structured clinical interview for DSM-IV Axis II personality disorders (SCID-II): Version 2.0.* New York: New York State Psychiatric Institute.

Fossati, A., Maffei, C., Bagnato, M., Donati, D., Donini, M., Fiorilli, M., et al. (2000). A psychometric study of DSM-IV passive-aggressive (negativistic) personality disorder criteria. *Journal of Personality Disorders, 14*(1), 72–83.

Freud, S. (1915/1957). Instincts and their vicissitudes. In J. W. Strachey (Ed. and Trans.), *The standard edition of the complete psychological works of Sigmund Freud* (Vol. 14). London: Hogarth Press.

Frieman, K., & Widiger, T. A. (1989). [Co-occurrence and diagnostic efficiency statistics]. Unpublished raw data.

Fuller, A. K., Blashfield, R. K., Miller, M., & Hester, T. (1992). Sadistic and self-defeating personality disorder criteria in a rural clinic sample. *Journal of Clinical Psychology, 48,* 827–831.

Gay, M. (1989). Personality disorders among child abusers. In R. L. Spitzer (Chair), *Psychiatric diagnosis, victimization, and women.* Symposium conducted at the 142nd annual meeting of the American Psychiatric Association, San Francisco, CA.

Grilo, C. M., McGlashan, M. D., Quinlan, D. M., Walker, M. L., Greenfeld, D., & Edell, W. S. (1998). Frequency of personality disorders in two age cohorts of psychiatric inpatients. *American Journal of Psychiatry, 155,* 140–142.

Gunderson, J. G., Phillips, K. A., Triebwasser, J. T., & Hirschfeld, R. M. A. (1994). The diagnostic interview for depressive personality. *American Journal of Psychiatry, 151,* 1300–1304.

Hare, R. (1991). *The Hare Psychopathy Checklist—Revised manual.* Toronto, Ontario, Canada: Multi-Health Systems.

Hirschfeld, R. M. A., & Holzer, C. E., III. (1994). Depressive personality disorder: Clinical implications. *Journal of Clinical Psychiatry, 55,* 10–17.

Holt, S. E., Meloy, J. R., & Strack, S. (1999). Sadism and psychopathy in violent and sexually violent offenders. *Journal of the American Academy of Psychiatry & the Law, 27*(1), 23–32.

Huprich, S. L. (2001). Object loss and object relations in depressive personality analogues. *Bulletin of the Menninger Clinic, 65,* 549–559.

Huprich, S. K. (2003). Depressive personality and its relationship to depressed mood, interpersonal loss, negative parental perceptions, and perfectionism. *Journal of Nervous and Mental Disease, 191,* 73–79.

Huprich, S. K. (2004). Convergent and discriminant validity of three measures of depressive personality disorder. *Journal of Personality Assessment, 82,* 321–328.

Huprich, S. K., Margrett, J., Barthelemy, K. J., & Fine, M. A. (1996). The Depressive Personality Disorder Inventory: An initial examination of its psychometric properties. *Journal of Clinical Psychology, 52,* 153–159.

Huprich, S. K., Sanford, K., & Smith, M. (2002). Psychometric evaluation of the Depressive Personality Disorder Inventory. *Journal of Personality Disorders, 16,* 255–269.

Hurt, S. W., Clarkin, J. F., & Morey, L. C. (1990). An examination of the stability of the MMPI personality disorder scales. *Journal of Personality Assessment, 54,* 16–23.

Hyler, S. E. (1994). *Personality disorder questionnaire–4+.* New York: New York State Psychiatric Institute.

Hyler, S. E., Rieder, R. O., Williams, J. B. W., Spitzer, R. L., Lyons, M., & Hendler, J. (1989). A comparison of clinical interview and self-report of DSM-III personality disorders in 552 patients. *Comprehensive Psychiatry, 30,* 170–178.

Johnson, J. G., Cohen, P., Smailes, E., Kasen, S., Oldham, J. M., Skodol, A. E., et al. (2000). Adolescent personality disorders associated with violence and criminal behavior during adolescence and early adulthood. *American Journal of Psychiatry, 157*(9), 1406–1412.

Joiner, T. E., & Rudd, M. D. (2002). The incremental validity of passive-aggressive personality symptoms rivals or exceeds that of other personality symptoms in suicidal outpatients. *Journal of Personality Assessment, 79*(1), 161–170.

Kaminer, D., & Stein, D. J. (2001). Sadistic personality disorder in perpetrators of human rights abuses: A South African case study. *Journal of Personality Disorders, 15*(6), 475–486.

Kernberg, O. (1984). *Severe personality disorders: Psychotherapeutic strategies.* New Haven, CT: Yale University Press.

Kernberg, O. F. (1988). Clinical dimensions of masochism. *Journal of the American Psychoanalytic Association, 36,* 1005–1029.

Klein, D. N. (1990). Depressive personality: Reliability, validity, and relation to dysthymia. *Journal of Abnormal Psychology, 99,* 412–421.

Klein, D. N. (1999). Depressive personality in the relatives of outpatients with dysthymic disorder and episodic major depressive disorder and normal controls. *Journal of Affective Disorders, 55,* 19–27.

Klein, D. N., Clark, D. C., Dansky, L., & Margolis, E. T. (1988). Dysthymia in the offspring of parents with primary unipolar affective disorder. *Journal of Abnormal Psychology, 97,* 265–274.

Klein, D. N., & Miller, G. A. (1993). Depressive personality in nonclinical subjects. *American Journal of Psychiatry, 150,* 1718–1724.

Klein, D. N., & Shih, J. (1998). Depressive personality: Thirty-month stability and relationships to DSM-III-R personality disorders and normal personality dimensions. *Journal of Abnormal Psychology, 107,* 319–327.

Kraepelin, E. (1921). *Manic depressive insanity and paranoia.* Edinburgh, UK: Livingstone.

Krafft-Ebing, R. von. (1898). *Psychopathia sexualis* (10th ed.). Stuttgart, Germany: Enke.

Kwon, J. S., Kim, Y-M., Chang, C-G., Park, B-J., Kim, L., Yoon, D. J., et al. (2000). Three-year follow-up of women with the sole diagnosis of depressive personality disorder: Subsequent development of dysthymia and major depression. *American Journal of Psychiatry, 157,* 1966–1972.

Laptook, R. S., Klein, D. N., & Dougherty, L. R. (2005). *Ten-year stability of depressive personality disorder in depressed outpatients.* Manuscript submitted for publication.

Laughlin, H.P. (1967). *The neuroses.* Washington, DC: Butterworths.

Lenzenweger, M. F., Loranger, A. W., Korfine, L., & Neff, C. (1997). Detecting personality disorders in a nonclinical population: Application of a 2-stage procedure for case identification. *Archives of General Psychiatry, 54,* 345–351.

Lilienfeld, S. O., & Penna, S. (2001). Anxiety sensitivity: Relations to psychopathy, DSM-IV personality disorder features, and personality traits. *Journal of Anxiety Disorders, 15,* 367–393.

Loranger, A. W., Susman, V. L., Oldham, J. M., & Russakof, M. (1988). *The Personality Disorder Examination (PDE) manual.* Yonkers, NY: DV Communications.

Lyoo, I. K., Gunderson, J. G., & Phillips, K. A. (1998). Personality dimensions associated with depressive personality disorder. *Journal of Personality Disorders, 12,* 46–55.

Maier, W., Lichtermann, D., Klingler, T., Heun, R., & Hallmayer, J. (1992). Prevalence of personality disorders (DSM-III-R) in the community. *Journal of Personality Disorders, 6,* 187–196.

Markowitz, J. C., Skodol, A. E., Petkova, E., Xie, H., Cheng, J., Hellerstein, D. J., et al. (in press). Longitudinal comparison of depressive personality disorder and dysthymic disorder. *Comprehensive Psychiatry*.

McDavid, J. D., & Pilkonis, P. A. (1996). The stability of personality disorder diagnoses. *Journal of Personality Disorders, 10,* 1–15.

McDermut, W., Zimmerman, M., & Chelminski, I. (2003). The construct validity of depressive personality disorder. *Journal of Abnormal Psychology, 112,* 49–60.

Millon, T. (1983). *Millon Clinical Multiaxial Inventory manual.* Minneapolis, MN: Interpretive Scoring Systems.

Millon, T. (1987). *Millon Clinical Multiaxial Inventory manual* (2nd ed.). Minneapolis, MN: National Computer Systems.

Millon, T., & Davis, R. (1996). *Disorders of personality: DSM-IV and beyond* (2nd ed.). New York: Wiley.

Millon, T., & Radanov, J. (1995). Passive-aggressive (negativistic) personality disorder. In W. J. Livesley (Ed.), *The DSM-IV personality disorders* (pp. 312–325). New York: Guilford Press.

Morey, L. C. (1988). The categorical representation of personality disorder: A cluster analysis of DSM-III-R personality features. *Journal of Abnormal Psychology, 97,* 314–321.

Morey, L. C., Waugh, M. H., & Blashfield, R. K. (1985). MMPI scales for DSM-III personality disorders: Their derivation and correlates. *Journal of Personality Assessment, 49,* 245–251.

Murray, H. A. (1943). *Thematic apperception test.* New York: Oxford University Press.

Overholser, J. C. (1990). Retest reliability of the Millon Clinical Multiaxial Inventory. *Journal of Personality Assessment, 55*(1), 202.

Pfohl, B., Blum, N., & Zimmerman, M. (1997). *Structured interview for DSM-IV personality (SIDP-IV).* Washington, DC: American Psychiatric Press.

Phillips, K. A., Gunderson, J. G., Hirschfeld, R. M. A., & Smith, L. E. (1990). A review of the depressive personality. *American Journal of Psychiatry, 147,* 830–837.

Phillips, K. A., Gunderson, J. G., Triebwasser, J., Kimball, C. R., Faedda, G., Lyoo, I. K., et al. (1998). Reliability and validity of depressive personality disorder. *American Journal of Psychiatry, 155,* 1044–1048.

Pretzer, J. L., & Beck, A. T. (1996). A cognitive theory of personality disorders. In. J. F. Clarkin and M. F. Lenzenweger (Eds.), *Major theories of personality disorder* (pp. 36–105). New York: Guilford Press.

Reich, J. (1993). Prevalence and characteristics of sadistic personality disorder in an outpatient veterans population. *Psychiatry Research, 48,* 267–276.

Rosenberg, M. S. (1987). Characteristics of the passive-aggressive personality disorder: Males. *Journal of Training Practical Professional Psychology, 1,* 29–42.

Ryder, A. G., Bagby, R. M., & Schuller, D. R. (2002). The overlap of depressive personality disorder and dysthymia: A categorical problem with a dimensional solution. *Harvard Review of Psychiatry, 10,* 337–352.

Samuels, J. F., Nestadt, G., Romanoski, A. J., Folstein, M. F., & McHugh, P. R. (1994). DSM-III personality disorders in the community. *American Journal of Psychiatry, 151,* 1055–1062.

Schneider, K. (1958). *Psychopathic personalities.* London: Cassell.

Shahar, G., Blatt, S. J., Zuroff, D. C., & Pilkonis, P. A. (2003). Role of perfectionism and personality disorder features in response to brief treatment for depression. *Journal of Consulting and Clinical Psychology, 71,* 629–633.

Sinha, B. K., & Watson, D. C. (2001). Personality disorder in university students: A multitrait-multimethod matrix study. *Journal of Personality Disorders, 15,* 235–244.

Spitzer, R. L., Fiester, S., Gay, M., & Pfohl, B. (1991). Is sadistic personality disorder a valid diagnosis? The results of a survey of forensic psychiatrists. *American Journal of Psychiatry, 148,* 875–879.

Spitzer, R. L., Williams, J. B., Kass, F., & Davies, M. (1989). National field trial of the DSM-III-R diagnostic criteria for self-defeating personality disorder. *American Journal of Psychiatry, 146,* 1561–1567.

Sprock, J., Blashfield, R. K., & Smith, R. (1990). Gender weighting of DSM-III-R personality disorder criteria. *American Journal of Psychiatry, 147,* 586–590.

Sprock, J., & Hunsucker, L. (1998). Symptoms of prototypic patients with passive-aggressive personality disorder: DSM-III-R versus DSM-IV negativistic. *Comprehensive Psychiatry, 39*(5), 287–295.

Timmerman, I. G. H., & Emmelkamp, P. M. G. (2001). The prevalence and comorbidity of Axis I and Axis II pathology in a group of forensic patients. *International Journal of Offender Therapy and Comparative Criminology, 45,* 198–213.

Trull, T. J., Goodwin, A. H., Schopp, L. H., & Hillenbrand, T. L. (1993). Psychometric properties of a cognitive measure of personality disorders. *Journal of Personality Assessment, 61,* 536–546.

Vereycken, J., Vertommen, H., & Corveleyn, J. (2002). Authority conflicts and personality disorders. *Journal of Personality Disorders, 16*(1), 41–51.

Verheul, R., & Widiger, T. A. (2004). A meta-analysis of the prevalence and usage of the personality disorder not otherwise specified (PDNOS) diagnosis. *Journal of Personality Disorders, 18*(4), 309–319.

Westen, D. (1997). Divergences between clinical and research methods for assessing personality disorders: Implications for research and the evolution of Axis II. *American Journal of Psychiatry, 154,* 895–903.

Wetzler, S., & Morey, L. C. (1999). Passive-aggressive personality disorder: The demise of a syndrome. *Psychiatry, 62,* 49–59.

Widiger, T. A. (1995). Deletion of self-defeating and sadistic personality disorders. In W. J. Livesley (Ed.), *The DSM-IV personality disorders* (pp. 359–373). New York: Guilford Press.

Widiger, T. A., Frances, A. J., Harris, M., Jacobsberg, L. B., Fyer, M., & Manning, D. (1990). Comorbidity among Axis II disorders. In J. M. Oldham (Ed.), *Personality disorders: New perspectives on diagnostic validity.* Washington, DC: American Psychiatric Press.

Widiger, T. A., & Rogers, J. H. (1989). Prevalence and comorbidity of personality disorders. *Psychiatric Annals, 19*(3), 132–136.

Wilberg, T., Dammen, T., & Friis, S. (2000). Comparing Personality Diagnostic Questionnaire–4+ with longitudinal, expert, all data (LEAD) standard diagnoses in a sample with a high prevalence of Axis I and Axis II disorders. *Comprehensive Psychiatry, 41,* 295–302.

Zanarini, M. C., & Frankenburg, F. R. (2001). Attainment and maintenance of reliability of Axis I and II disorders over the course of a longitudinal study. *Comprehensive Psychiatry, 42,* 369–374.

Zanarini, M. C., Frankenburg, F. R., Chauncey, D. L., & Gunderson, J. G. (1987). The Diagnostic Interview for PDs: Interrater and test-retest reliability. *Comprehensive Psychiatry, 28,* 467–480.

Zanarini, M. C., Skodol, A. E., Bender, D., Dolan, R., Sanislow, C., Schaefer, E., et al. (2000). The Collaborative Longitudinal Personality Disorders Study: Reliability of Axis I and II diagnoses. *Journal of Personality Disorders, 14,* 291–299.

Zimmerman, M., & Coryell, W. (1989). DSM-III personality disorder diagnoses in a nonpatient sample: Demographic correlates and comorbidity. *Archives of General Psychiatry, 46,* 682–689.

Index _____

About the Editors _____

William O'Donohue, Ph.D., is a licensed clinical psychologist and professor of psychology at the University of Nevada, Reno. Dr. O'Donohue has received over $1,500,000 in federal grant money from sources including the National Institute of Mental Health and the National Institute of Justice. In addition, he has edited more than 35 books, written more than 70 book chapters, and published more than 100 articles in scholarly journals. Dr. O'Donohue is currently directing a major treatment development/ outcome evaluation project involving integrated care.

Katherine A. Fowler, Ph.D., completed her doctoral degree in clinical psychology at Emory University in Atlanta, Georgia, in 2007. She will begin a postdoctoral research fellowship in clinical neuroscience at the National Institute of Mental Health in Bethesda, Maryland, upon graduation. Her research interests include conceptualization, biological and etiological foundations, and assessment of psychopathic personality, multivariate statistical modeling, and the influence of personality on violence and criminality. Her clinical interests include behavior therapy, personality assessment, and forensic evaluation.

Scott O. Lilienfeld, Ph.D., is associate professor of psychology at Emory University in Atlanta, Georgia. Dr. Lilienfeld is founder and editor of the new journal *Scientific Review of Mental Health Practice* and is past (2001–2002) president of the Society for a Science of Clinical Psychology, which is Section III within Division 12 (Society of Clinical Psychology) of the American Psychological Association (APA). He also served as the Division 12 program chair for the 2001 APA Convention. He is a member of eight journal editorial boards, including those of *Assessment, Psychological Assessment,* and *Clinical Psychology Review,* and he has served as an external reviewer for over 50 journals and several grant proposals. Dr. Lilienfeld has published over 160 articles, book chapters, and books in the areas of personality disorders (particularly psychopathic personality), personality assessment, anxiety disorders, psychiatric classification and diagnosis, and questionable practices in clinical psychology. In 1998, Dr. Lilienfeld received the David Shakow Award for Outstanding Early Career Contributions to Clinical Psychology from APA Division 12.

About the Contributors

Jennifer Bartz, Ph.D., received her doctorate in psychology from McGill University in 2004 and is currently a postdoctoral research fellow at the Mount Sinai School of Medicine in New York City, where her research focuses on the neurobiology of obsessive-compulsive spectrum disorders. Dr. Bartz's main research interests include personality factors related to the desire for structure and intolerance for uncertainty and how they influence people's understanding and experience of their social world as well as adult attachment and the role of insecure relational schemas in close relationship development.

David P. Bernstein, Ph.D., is associate professor in the Department of Medical, Clinical, and Experiment Psychology at Maastricht University, the Netherlands, where he also directs the Personality Disorders section of the Experimental Psychopathology Research Institute (EPP). He is former president of the Association for Research on Personality Disorders and a vice president of the International Society for the Study of Personality Disorders. His major areas of research and clinical interests are personality disorders, psychological trauma, and forensic issues. His current focus is on developing and testing the efficacy of treatments for severe personality disorders in forensic patients.

Pavel S. Blagov, M.A., is a doctoral candidate in clinical psychology at Emory University, where he obtained a master's degree in psychology. His research interests include personality pathology classification and emotional influences on reasoning. His current research focuses on subthreshold personality constellations, histrionic personality disorder in adults and adolescents, psychopathy, and motivated cognition in political and legal decision making. Previously, he has presented research on and written about the role of autobiographical memory processes in personality and psychotherapy.

Annie M. Bollini, Ph.D., received her doctorate in clinical psychology from Emory University, completed her postdoctoral training at Emory School of Medicine, and is a licensed clinical psychologist in Georgia. Her main research areas have included schizophrenia and spectrum disorders, cognitive functioning, and stress. Currently, she is a behavioral scientist at the Centers for Disease Control & Prevention in Atlanta, Georgia. She conducts research and develops and evaluates programs on HIV/AIDS prevention in international projects, mainly in African countries.

Robert F. Bornstein, Ph.D., received his doctorate in clinical psychology from the State University of New York at Buffalo and is professor of psychology at Adelphi University. Dr. Bornstein has published widely on personality dynamics, assessment, and treatment. He wrote *The Dependent Personality* (Guilford Press, 1993) and *The Dependent Patient: A Practitioner's Guide* (American Psychological Association, 2005). Dr. Bornstein's research has been funded by the National Institute of Mental Health and the National Science Foundation; he received the Society for Personality Assessment's 1995, 1999, and 2002 awards for Distinguished Contributions to the Personality Assessment Literature, and the American Psychological Foundation 2005 Theodore Millon Award for Excellence in Personality Research.

Rebekah Bradley, Ph.D., is an assistant professor in the Department of Psychiatry and Behavioral Sciences at Emory University in Atlanta, Georgia. She is also the director of the Trauma Recovery Program and the Atlanta Veterans Medical Center. Her current areas of research include the impact of traumatic experiences, particularly childhood abuse; the etiology and treatment of posttraumatic stress disorder; and the etiology, classification, and treatment of personality disorders, particularly borderline personality disorder. She received her master's degree in psychology from Wesleyan University and her doctorate in clinical community psychology from the University of South Carolina.

John F. Clarkin, Ph.D., is codirector of the Personality Disorder Institute at New York Presbyterian Hospital, Westchester Division, and clinical professor of psychology in Psychiatry at the Joan and Sanford I. Weill Medical College and Graduate School of Medical Sciences of Cornell University in New York City. He is the author and coauthor of several books on the treatment of severe personality disorders and has written over 100 articles and chapters focusing on the symptoms and treatment of personality-disordered patients. He is past president of the International Society for Psychotherapy Research.

Carolyn Zittel Conklin, Ph.D., is a staff psychologist in the Harvard Medical School psychiatry program. She was awarded the 2006 Scientific Paper Award from the American Psychoanalytic Association; her paper, "Countertransference Phenomena and Personality Pathology in Clinical Practices: An Empirical Investigation" (published in the *American Journal of Psychiatry*, 2005), was deemed the best published empirical paper on a psychoanalytic topic. Dr. Conklin is interested in the areas of adult ambulatory service, psychodynamic psychotherapy, and treatment of borderline personality disorder.

James D. Herbert, Ph.D., is a professor of psychology at Drexel University, where he serves as director of clinical training of the Ph.D. program in clinical psychology as well as associate dean of the College of Arts and Sciences. He received his doctorate from the University of North Carolina at Greensboro in 1989. He serves as the director of the Anxiety Treatment and Research Program at Drexel and has an active research program on the assessment and treatment of social anxiety disorder. He has published widely on the behavioral treatment of anxiety disorders as well as on quackery and pseudoscience in mental health.

Eric Hollander, M.D., is the principal investigator for a number of current federal grants, including a grant from the NIH Greater New York Autism Center of Excellence, the NIMH Research Training Grant in Psychopharmacology and Outcomes Research, and a grant from an FDA-funded multicenter treatment trial of pediatric body dysmorphic disorder. He is the principal investigator of the autism Clinical Trials Network and chair of the eight-center NIH STAART Autism Steering Committee. During his career, Dr. Hollander has published more than 450 scientific reports in the psychiatric field. He has edited 19 books, including *Autism Spectrum Disorder* (2003), the *American Psychiatric Publishing Textbook of Anxiety Disorders* (2002), and *The Clinical Manual of Impulse Control Disorders* (2006). Dr. Hollander also serves as a reviewer for eight medical journals.

Christopher J. Hopwood, M.S., is a doctoral candidate at Texas A&M University. He received a master's degree from Eastern Michigan University. His research interests include personality assessment, personality pathology, and interpersonal process.

Oren Kalus, M.D., is a Board Certified psychiatrist in private practice and on staff at a community mental health clinic in Kingston, N.Y. Dr. Kalus's interest in schizoid P.D. dates from his tenure as an assistant professor at Mount Sinai School of Medicine and a member of a research group headed by Dr. Larry Siever on personality disorders. Since leaving Mount Sinai in 1993 he has pursued a largely clinical career both providing direct care and lecturing and providing workshops to clinicians on cognitive neuroscience. Dr. Kalus's most recent area of interest entails the convergence between psychopathology and art. Dr. Kalus recently presented a poster on an aesthetic form of derealization in the artist Alberto Giacommeti at the 2006 Toward Science of Consciousness Conference in Tucson, Ariz.

Alicia Kaplan, M.D., is affiliated with the Department of Psychiatry, Mount Sinai School of Medicine. She has published on the classification and treatment of obsessive-compulsive disorder and related conditions.

Daniel N. Klein, Ph.D., received his doctorate in clinical psychology from the State University of New York at Buffalo. He is currently professor of psychology and psychiatry and behavioral science at Stony Brook University. Dr. Klein's research focuses on the mood and personality disorders and on the role of temperament and personality in psychopathology. He has been an associate editor of the *Journal of Abnormal Psychology*, is past president of the Society for Research in Psychopathology, and is president-elect of the Society for a Science of Clinical Psychology.

Kenneth N. Levy, Ph.D., is an assistant professor in the Department of Psychology at Pennsylvania State University and directs the Laboratory for Personality, Psychopathology, and Psychotherapy Research. Dr. Levy teaches graduate seminars in psychotherapy research and personality theory and supervises a clinical training practicum emphasizing contemporary psychodynamic psychotherapy for personality disorders. He is also an adjunct assistant professor of Psychology in Psychiatry at the Joan and Sanford I. Weill Medical College of Cornell University, where he is a faculty fellow at the Personality Disorders Institute (PDI). Dr. Levy has authored more than 50 articles and chapters in the areas of developmental psychopathology, attachment theory, personality disorders, and psychotherapy research.

Vijay A. Mittal, M.A., is a doctoral candidate affiliated with the Clinical Psychology Department at Emory University. He studies longitudinal development of adolescents at risk for psychotic disorders. More specifically, he focuses on investigating neural, endocrine, and behavioral markers associated with the schizophrenia prodrome and high risk for psychopathology. He is particularly interested in examining the potential of movement abnormalities to inform neural diathesis–stress conceptualizations of schizophrenia.

Leslie C. Morey, Ph.D., is department head and professor of psychology at Texas A&M University. He received his doctorate in clinical psychology from the University of Florida and has served on the faculties at Vanderbilt University, Harvard Medical School, the Yale University School of Medicine, and the University of Tulsa. He has served as associate editor of *Assessment* and *Journal of Personality Assessment* and as consulting editor for a number of journals, including *Journal of Personality Disorders* and *Psychological Bulletin*.

Christopher J. Patrick, Ph.D., is Starke R. Hathaway Distinguished Professor and director of clinical training in the Department of Psychology at the University of Minnesota. He graduated from the University of British Columbia in 1987, where he completed his dissertation entitled "The Validity of Lie Detection With Criminal Psychopaths." He has published extensively in the areas of psychopathy, antisocial behavior, and substance use/abuse; his other research interests include emotion, personality, psychophysiology, and cognitive neuroscience. He is the recipient of Distinguished Early Career Contribution awards from the American Psychological Association (1995) and the Society for Psychophysiological Research (1993). He is a consulting editor for *Psychological Assessment* and *Journal of Abnormal Psychology* as well as a former associate editor of *Psychophysiology*.

Joseph S. Reynoso, M.Phil., is an advanced doctoral candidate in clinical psychology at the City College of New York and the Graduate School and University Center of the City University of New York. He completed his internship in clinical psychology at Kings County Hospital Center in Brooklyn, New York, concentrating on adult inpatient and emergency psychiatry. Mr. Reynoso is currently a psychology fellow training at Columbia University's Counseling and Psychological Services. His professional interests include the measurement of romantic love, treatment of severe psychopathology, and psychoanalytic therapy with underserved populations. He has coauthored chapters and articles on attention deficit hyperactivity disorder assessment, personality disorders, and psychotherapy research.

Larry J. Siever, M.D., is professor of psychiatry and vice chair for VA Affairs at Mount Sinai School of Medicine in New York City. He also serves as executive director of the Mental Illness Research, Education and Clinical Center (MIRECC) and chief of the psychiatry program at the Bronx VA Medical Center in the Bronx, New York. Dr. Siever has published over 350 peer-reviewed articles. He earned his Bachelor of Arts degree from Harvard College in Cambridge, Massachusetts, and his doctorate from Stanford University School of Medicine in Stanford, California. He directs the Mood and Personality Disorders program at Mount Sinai, a federally funded research program that investigates the neurobiology of the schizophrenic spectrum personality disorders, such as schizotypal personality disorder, and impulsive/affectively unstable personality disorders, such as borderline personality disorder. He is a member of the American College of Neuropsychopharmacology (ACNP) and past president of the Society of Biologic Psychiatry, from which he received the A. E. Bennett Award for clinical research.

J. David Useda, Ph.D., attained a doctorate in clinical psychology at the University of Missouri-Columbia and a postdoctorate at the University of Rochester School of Medicine and Dentistry's Center for the Study and Prevention of Suicide. Dr. Useda has conducted research and published in his area of expertise: personality and its disorders. He remains an adjunct faculty member at the University of Rochester's Department of Psychiatry and is in private practice. Together, Dr. Useda and his wife are happily raising a son.

Elaine Walker, Ph.D., is a professor of psychology and neuroscience in the Department of Psychology at Emory University. She leads a research laboratory funded by the National Institute of Mental Health to study the development of adolescents at risk for mental illness. Her research focuses on child and adolescent development and brain changes associated with adolescence. She has published over 150 scientific articles and six books dealing with mental health and neuroscience.

Rachel H. Wasserman, B.A., is a doctoral student in clinical psychology at Pennsylvania State University. Her research and professional interests include mechanisms of change in the treatment of borderline personality disorder, longitudinal approaches to the assessment of outcome, the role of therapeutic alliance in the treatment of patients with severe psychopathology, and psychoanalytic psychotherapy. Ms. Wasserman has coauthored articles on expectancy effects, meditation, cortical plasticity, and mechanisms of change in psychotherapy.

Drew Westen, Ph.D., is a professor in the Department of Psychology and the Department of Psychiatry at Emory University. He received his doctorate in clinical psychology from the University of Michigan and subsequently taught at the University of Michigan, Harvard Medical School, and Boston University. Professor Westen is both a clinician and a researcher; he has written over 150 scientific papers and three books, and his work on the classification of personality pathology in adolescents and adults has been funded by the National Institute of Mental Health. He is currently completing a book on politics entitled *The Political Brain: The Role of Emotion in Deciding the Fate of the Nation.*

Thomas A. Widiger, Ph.D., is the T. Marshall Hahn Professor of Psychology at the University of Kentucky. He received his doctorate in clinical psychology in 1981 from Miami University in Ohio and completed his internship at Cornell University Medical College, Westchester Division. He has published over 200 articles and chapters in scientific, clinical, and academic journals and texts in the area of the diagnosis and classification of personality disorders. He currently serves as associate editor for the *Journal of Abnormal Psychology, Journal of Personality and Social Psychology, Journal of Personality Disorders,* and *Annual Review of Clinical Psychology,* as well as consulting editor for a few additional journals. He was the research coordinator for DSM-IV and served as cochair of the DSM-V Research Planning Conference for Personality Disorders.